The Sound and the Fury

An Authoritative Text
Backgrounds and Contexts
Criticism

Second Edition

A NORTON CRITICAL EDITION

William Faulkner
THE SOUND
AND THE FURY

AN AUTHORITATIVE TEXT

BACKGROUNDS AND CONTEXTS

CRITICISM

Second Edition

Edited by

DAVID MINTER

RICE UNIVERSITY

W·W·NORTON & COMPANY *New York · London*

Copyright © 1994, 1987, 1984, 1956, 1929 by W. W. Norton & Company, Inc.

Printed in the United States of America.

The text of this book is composed in Electra
with the display set in Bernhard Modern
Composition by Vail
Manufacturing by Maple-Vail
Book design by Antonina Krass

Library of Congress Cataloging-in-Publication Data

Faulkner, William, 1897–1962.
The sound and the fury : an authoritative text, backgrounds, and context
criticism / edited by David Minter. — 2nd ed.
p. cm. — (A Norton critical edition)
Includes bibliographical references (p.).
1. Faulkner, William, 1897–1962. Sound and the fury. I. Title.
PS3511.A86S7 1994
813'.52—dc20 93–5785

ISBN 0–393–96481–7

W. W. Norton & Company, Inc., 500 Fifth Avenue, New York, N.Y. 10110
www.wwnorton.com

W. W. Norton & Company Ltd., Castle House, 75/76 Wells Street,
London W1T 3QT

6 7 8 9 0

Contents

Preface to the Second Edition

The Sound and the Fury, William Faulkner's fourth novel, was published on October 7, 1929. Over the next several months, as the stock market lurched toward panic and then collapse, reviewers responded to its strange surface and structure with puzzlement, scorn, and praise. Writing for the *Nation*, Clifton Fadiman described Faulkner's themes and characters as too "trivial" to justify "the enormous and complex craftsmanship expended on them." Writing for *Hound and Horn*, Dudley Fitts criticized Faulkner for using "deliberate obscurity" and "considerable incoherence" to shroud "melodrama." On November 30, a month after Winfield Townley Scott had assured readers of the Providence *Sunday Journal* that they had nothing to worry about (it was a "tiresome" novel, he wrote, full of "sound and fury—signifying nothing"), Howard Rockey warned readers of the Philadelphia *Inquirer* that *The Sound and the Fury* might drive them "to apply for admission to the nearest insane asylum."

On balance, however, the reviews were favorable. Lyle Saxon, writing for the New York *Herald Tribune*, called *The Sound and the Fury* "a great book"; Basil Davenport, for the *Saturday Review*, described it as "original and impressive"; and Henry Nash Smith, for the *Southwest Review*, described it as disclosing "unguessed possibilities . . . of provincial life without loss of universality." One early reader, Evelyn Scott, whose long novel *The Wave* was also published in 1929, called it a "unique and distinguished" contribution "to the permanent literature of fiction"—and in the process anticipated the special role that artists (Conrad Aiken, Albert Camus, Jean-Paul Sartre, Ralph Ellison, Eudora Welty, Robert Penn Warren) would play in making Faulkner's greatness visible to us.

Unlike the reviews, sales of *The Sound and the Fury* spoke with a single voice. A first printing of nearly 1800 copies was supplemented by two smaller printings, triggered mainly by the brief notoriety of *Sanctuary* (1931), Faulkner's sixth novel. A total of just over 3300 copies satisfied American readers for fifteen years. By the time the novel was reprinted in 1946, it had been out of print for several years, as had other Faulkner books.

Over the last fifty years, a remarkable revival of interest has established Faulkner as a major literary figure and *The Sound and the Fury*, the most written about of all his novels, as a classic of modern literature. In this process of cultural assimilation, publishers as well as scholars have played a major role. Letters and interviews have been published, as have two versions of an "Introduction" that Faulkner wrote for *The Sound and the Fury* in 1933. We now have a veritable mountain of criticism on Faulkner's fiction. On *The Sound and the Fury* alone there is an abundance.

For this Norton Critical Edition, I have organized selected works under three rubrics. In "Backgrounds" I include the Appendix that Faulkner wrote in 1945 and sometimes referred to as a fifth telling of his story; his map of Yoknapatawpha County; selected letters written around the time of the composition and publication of *The Sound and the Fury*; a brief excerpt from a memoir by Faulkner's friend Ben Wasson, who played an important role in preparing the novel for publication; two versions of an "Introduction" to the novel that Faulkner wrote in 1933; and brief excerpts from several of his interviews. In "Cultural and Historical Contexts" I include provocative excerpts from four works that help to situate Faulkner's fiction in the history and culture of the American South and of the United States. And in "Criticism" I include a wide range of assessments of *The Sound and the Fury*, the first written in 1939, the last in 1992. Together these works reflect the remarkable changes that have taken place in our responses to the novel over the last several decades. In addition I include a selected Bibliography that covers critical discussions from 1929 to 1992.

For the inquisitive reader, to whom this edition of *The Sound and the Fury* is addressed, these varied materials should prove useful. Especially for new readers, however, the place to begin is with the novel itself, mindful that a part of its remarkable achievement lies in its success in teaching readers how to read it. In the process by which a work like *The Sound and the Fury* begins as a puzzling text and becomes an established classic, there is loss as well as gain, particularly if we assume that we have succeeded in domesticating its radical newness. What follows, therefore, before the "Backgrounds" and the historical and critical discussions, is the text of *The Sound and the Fury*, as established by Noel Polk in 1984 and revised slightly in 1987. This text follows Faulkner's original intent as closely as scrupulous scholarship can follow it, and it is presented here with annotation intended to supplement desk dictionaries. It is my hope that readers using this edition of *The Sound and the Fury*, especially new readers, will submit themselves to its strange force, remembering that works of literature enrich our lives by stretching our capacities for thought and feeling.

Finally, I want to acknowledge the assistance of the late Barry Wade and Carol Bemis of W. W. Norton; of Alan Clark, Marie Nitschke, Eric Nitschke, Lee Pederson, Jo Taylor, Floyd Watkins, and Sally Wolff of Emory University; of Matthew Santirocco of the University of Pennsyl-

vania; and of Caroline Minter and Louise Penner of Rice University. I
also owe a special debt to Calvin Brown's A *Glossary of Faulkner's South,*
which has been of great value in preparing the notes to the text.

My part in preparing the first edition of this work I dedicated to my
son, Christopher, as he began his college career. My part in preparing
this edition I dedicate to my daughter, Frances, as she nears the end of
hers.

Editor's Note[†]

This new edition of *The Sound and the Fury* is based upon a comparison of Faulkner's holograph manuscript, the carbon typescript (both documents in the Faulkner Collection of the Alderman Library at the University of Virginia), and the 1929 Cape & Smith first edition. Every effort has been made to produce a text which conforms to Faulkner's "final intentions" for the novel; unfortunately, the relationships among the extant manuscript and the printed materials and the little we know about the circumstances of editing, proofreading, and publication make it impossible to reconstruct in all cases exactly what those "final intentions" were. That is, there are numerous differences between the carbon typescript and the first edition; but since neither the setting copy (the typescript actually sent to the editor and compositor) nor any set of galleys has been preserved, there is no way to determine with certainty whether any single variant is the result of Faulkner's changes on typescript or galleys, of an editor's intervention at any point in the publishing process, or of a compositor's errors in setting type. In general, this edition reproduces the text of the carbon typescript unless there was compelling reason to accept any reading from the 1929 edition. Faulkner's holograph manuscript has been consulted regularly to help solve textual problems.

There is not enough space here to provide a complete textual apparatus for this novel. The tables appended are intended merely to record, for the interested reader, a highly selective sampling of some of the more significant variations among the present text, the carbon typescript, and the first edition. Table A records differences between the present text and the 1929 first edition; Table B, differences between this text and the carbon typescript. Both tables are keyed to page and line numbers of the present text. The reading to the left of the bracket is the reading of the new edition; in Table A, the reading to the right of the bracket is that of the 1929 text; in Table B, of the carbon typescript.

† By Noel Polk, who prepared the current text.

TABLE A

Differences between the present text and the 1929 Cape & Smith first edition:

6.25	Are you. Are you.] Are you.	68.16	the new text; each ¶ begins flush left.]
14.24	Open] "Open	68.41	home.] home in Mississippi.
14.25	Versh.] Versh."	69.10	healing] heading
14.25	Spread] "Spread	73.20	unitarial] Unitarian
14.25	floor. [floor."	91.14–	[No ¶ indentation here;
14.26	Now] "Now	100.9	each ¶ begins flush left.]
14.26	feet.] feet."	93.11	to the house [The new edition restores this line to the text; omitted in the first edition.]
15.26	stooped] stopped		
17.33	You] "You		
17.36	Quentin.] Quentin."		
17.37	Didn't] "Didn't		
17.38	on.] on."		
24.28	Didn't he didn't he] Didn't he	109.43	Harvard] Harvard like Quentin
47.1	said] said, Quentin,	109.43	ground] ground like Father
50.8	folded] wrapped	115.41	dope.] coca-cola.
50.31–	students. They'll think	119.32	Father's] Father's funeral
32	you go to Harvard.] students.	112.47–	your name. You'd be
52.40	"Maybe you want a tailor's goose," the clerk said. "They] The clerk said, "These	123.2	better off if you were down there] you
		146.18	shot] coca-cola
54.33–	*still. My bowels moved for thee.*] *still.*	156.32	both of them] Caddy and Quentin
57.17	*Jason*] *Jason a position in the bank.*	173.20	kin do dat] gwine preach today
62.12	and Versh] Versh said	174.4	shaling] shading
66.6–	[No ¶ indentations in		

TABLE B

Differences between the present text and the carbon typescript:

5.1	What] Versh, what		puffed his face. The candles went away.] He blew out the candles.
5.2	for, Versh."] for."		
6.32	Jason] Mr. Jason		
35.13–	him." She set the cake on the table.] him."	53.29	window.] window, thinking that if she had just been a boy she'd
14			
35.39	He leaned down and		

have invented windows
you could raise easily
instead of fine names
for the cars.

55.9– and through my coat
10 touched the letters I had
written.] and touched
the letters through my
coat

61.20– his black hand, in the
21 sun.] the sun, in his
dark hand.

61.30 boy."] boy. Whatever it
is, Marcus Lafayette   I
had forgotten about
that. He told me once

that his name used to
be Marcus something
else, but when they
moved away and he
went to school and
became an American,
he says, his name got
changed to Marcus
Lafayette, in honor of
France and America,
he said   Listenbee
will value it for the
giver's sake and sight
unseen, I thanks you."

62.12 and Versh] Versh

The Text of
THE SOUND
AND THE FURY

This new edition of *The Sound and the Fury* is the first corrected version of the book to appear in paperback since the book was originally published in 1929. The text is based on a comparison—under the direction of Noel Polk—of the first edition and Faulkner's original manuscript and carbon typescript.

—*Publisher's Note to the 1984 Random House edition*

April Seventh, 1928.

Through the fence, between the curling flower spaces, I could see them hitting. They were coming toward where the flag was and I went along the fence. Luster was hunting in the grass by the flower tree. They took the flag out, and they were hitting. Then they put the flag back and they went to the table, and he hit and the other hit. Then they went on, and I went along the fence. Luster came away from the flower tree and we went along the fence and they stopped and we stopped and I looked through the fence while Luster was hunting in the grass.

"Here, caddie." He hit. They went away across the pasture. I held to the fence and watched them going away.

"Listen at you, now." Luster said. "Aint you something, thirty three years old, going on that way. After I done went all the way to town to buy you that cake. Hush up that moaning. Aint you going to help me find that quarter so I can go to the show tonight."

They were hitting little, across the pasture. I went back along the fence to where the flag was. It flapped on the bright grass and the trees.

"Come on." Luster said. "We done looked there. They aint no more coming right now. Les go down to the branch and find that quarter before them niggers finds it."

It was red, flapping on the pasture. Then there was a bird slanting and tilting on it. Luster threw. The flag flapped on the bright grass and the trees. I held to the fence.

"Shut up that moaning." Luster said. "I cant make them come if they aint coming, can I. If you dont hush up, mammy aint going to have no birthday for you. If you dont hush, you know what I going to do. I going to eat that cake all up. Eat them candles, too. Eat all them thirty three candles. Come on, les go down to the branch. I got to find my quarter. Maybe we can find one of they balls. Here. Here they is. Way over yonder. See." He came to the fence and pointed his arm. "See them. They aint coming back here no more. Come on."

We went along the fence and came to the garden fence, where our shadows were. My shadow was higher than Luster's on the fence. We came to the broken place and went through it.

"Wait a minute." Luster said. "You snagged on that nail again. Cant you never crawl through here without snagging on that nail."

Caddy uncaught me and we crawled through. Uncle Maury said to not let anybody see us, so we better stoop over, Caddy said. Stoop over, Benjy. Like this, see. We stooped over and crossed the garden, where the flowers rasped and rattled against us. The ground was hard. We climbed the fence, where the pigs were grunting and snuffing. I expect they're sorry because one of them got killed today, Caddy said. The ground was hard, churned and knotted.

Keep your hands in your pockets, Caddy said. Or they'll get froze. You dont want your hands froze on Christmas, do you.

"It's too cold out there." Versh said. "You dont want to go out doors."

"What is it now." Mother said.

"He want to go out doors." Versh said.

"Let him go." Uncle Maury said.

"It's too cold." Mother said. "He'd better stay in. Benjamin. Stop that, now."

"It wont hurt him." Uncle Maury said.

"You, Benjamin." Mother said. "If you dont be good, you'll have to go to the kitchen."

"Mammy say keep him out the kitchen today." Versh said. "She say she got all that cooking to get done."

"Let him go, Caroline." Uncle Maury said. "You'll worry yourself sick over him."

"I know it." Mother said. "It's a judgment on me. I sometimes wonder."

"I know, I know." Uncle Maury said. "You must keep your strength up. I'll make you a toddy."

"It just upsets me that much more." Mother said. "Dont you know it does."

"You'll feel better." Uncle Maury said. "Wrap him up good, boy, and take him out for a while."

Uncle Maury went away. Versh went away.

"Please hush." Mother said. "We're trying to get you out as fast as we can. I dont want you to get sick."

Versh put my overshoes and overcoat on and we took my cap and went out. Uncle Maury was putting the bottle away in the sideboard in the diningroom.

"Keep him out about half an hour, boy." Uncle Maury said. "Keep him in the yard, now."

"Yes, sir." Versh said. "We dont never let him get off the place."

We went out doors. The sun was cold and bright.

"Where you heading for." Versh said. "You dont think you going to town, does you." We went through the rattling leaves. The gate was cold. "You better keep them hands in your pockets." Versh said. "You get them froze onto that gate, then what you do. Whyn't you wait for them in the house." He put my hands into my pockets. I could hear him rattling in the leaves. I could smell the cold. The gate was cold.

"Here some hickeynuts. Whooey. Git up that tree. Look here at this squirl, Benjy."

I couldn't feel the gate at all, but I could smell the bright cold.

"You better put them hands back in your pockets."

Caddy was walking. Then she was running, her booksatchel swinging and jouncing behind her.

"Hello, Benjy." Caddy said. She opened the gate and came in and stooped down. Caddy smelled like leaves. "Did you come to meet me." she said. "Did you come to meet Caddy. What did you let him get his hands so cold for, Versh."

"I told him to keep them in his pockets." Versh said. "Holding on to that ahun gate."

"Did you come to meet Caddy." she said, rubbing my hands. "What is it. What are you trying to tell Caddy." Caddy smelled like trees and like when she says we were asleep.

What are you moaning about, Luster said. You can watch them again when we get to the branch. Here. Here's you a jimson weed. He gave me the flower. We went through the fence, into the lot.

"What is it." Caddy said. "What are you trying to tell Caddy. Did they send him out, Versh."

"Couldn't keep him in." Versh said. "He kept on until they let him go and he come right straight down here, looking through the gate."

"What is it." Caddy said. "Did you think it would be Christmas when I came home from school. Is that what you thought. Christmas is the day after tomorrow. Santy Claus, Benjy. Santy Claus. Come on, let's run to the house and get warm." She took my hand and we ran through the bright rustling leaves. We ran up the steps and out of the bright cold, into the dark cold. Uncle Maury was putting the bottle back in the sideboard. He called Caddy. Caddy said,

"Take him in to the fire, Versh. Go with Versh." she said. "I'll come in a minute."

We went to the fire. Mother said,

"Is he cold, Versh."

"Nome." Versh said.

"Take his overcoat and overshoes off." Mother said. "How many times do I have to tell you not to bring him into the house with his overshoes on."

"Yessum." Versh said. "Hold still, now." He took my overshoes off and unbuttoned my coat. Caddy said,

"Wait, Versh. Cant he go out again, Mother. I want him to go with me."

"You'd better leave him here." Uncle Maury said. "He's been out enough today."

"I think you'd both better stay in." Mother said. "It's getting colder, Dilsey says."

"Oh, Mother." Caddy said.

"Nonsense." Uncle Maury said. "She's been in school all day. She needs the fresh air. Run along, Candace."

"Let him go, Mother." Caddy said. "Please. You know he'll cry."

"Then why did you mention it before him." Mother said. "Why did you come in here. To give him some excuse to worry me again. You've been out enough today. I think you'd better sit down here and play with him."

"Let them go, Caroline." Uncle Maury said. "A little cold wont hurt them. Remember, you've got to keep your strength up."

"I know." Mother said. "Nobody knows how I dread Christmas. Nobody knows. I am not one of those women who can stand things. I wish for Jason's and the children's sakes I was stronger."

"You must do the best you can and not let them worry you." Uncle Maury said. "Run along, you two. But dont stay out long, now. Your mother will worry."

"Yes, sir." Caddy said. "Come on, Benjy. We're going out doors again." She buttoned my coat and we went toward the door.

"Are you going to take that baby out without his overshoes." Mother said. "Do you want to make him sick, with the house full of company."

"I forgot." Caddy said. "I thought he had them on."

We went back. "You must think." Mother said.   *Hold still now* Versh said. He put my overshoes on. "Someday I'll be gone, and you'll have to think for him."   *Now stomp* Versh said. "Come here and kiss Mother, Benjamin."

Caddy took me to Mother's chair and Mother took my face in her hands and then she held me against her.

"My poor baby." she said. She let me go. "You and Versh take good care of him, honey."

"Yessum." Caddy said. We went out. Caddy said,

"You needn't go, Versh. I'll keep him for a while."

"All right." Versh said. "I aint going out in that cold for no fun." He went on and we stopped in the hall and Caddy knelt and put her arms around me and her cold bright face against mine. She smelled like trees.

"You're not a poor baby. Are you. Are you. You've got your Caddy. Haven't you got your Caddy."

Cant you shut up that moaning and slobbering, Luster said. Aint you shamed of yourself, making all this racket. We passed the carriage house, where the carriage was. It had a new wheel.

"Git in, now, and set still until your maw come." Dilsey said. She shoved me into the carriage. T. P. held the reins. "Clare I dont see how come Jason wont get a new surrey." Dilsey said. "This thing going to fall to pieces under you all some day. Look at them wheels."

Mother came out, pulling her veil down. She had some flowers.

"Where's Roskus." she said.

"Roskus cant lift his arms, today." Dilsey said. "T. P. can drive all right."

"I'm afraid to." Mother said. "It seems to me you all could furnish me with a driver for the carriage once a week. It's little enough I ask, Lord knows."

"You know just as well as me that Roskus got the rheumatism too bad to do more than he have to, Miss Cahline." Dilsey said. "You come on and get in, now. T. P. can drive you just as good as Roskus."

"I'm afraid to." Mother said. "With the baby."

Dilsey went up the steps. "You calling that thing a baby." she said. She took Mother's arm. "A man big as T. P. Come on, now, if you going."

"I'm afraid to." Mother said. They came down the steps and Dilsey helped Mother in. "Perhaps it'll be the best thing, for all of us." Mother said.

"Aint you shamed, talking that way." Dilsey said. "Dont you know it'll take more than a eighteen year old nigger to make Queenie run away. She older than him and Benjy put together. And dont you start no projecking with Queenie, you hear me. T. P. If you dont drive to suit Miss Cahline, I going to put Roskus on you. He aint too tied up to do that."

"Yessum." T. P. said.

"I just know something will happen." Mother said. "Stop, Benjamin."

"Give him a flower to hold." Dilsey said. "That what he wanting." She reached her hand in.

"No, no." Mother said. "You'll have them all scattered."

"You hold them." Dilsey said. "I'll get him one out." She gave me a flower and her hand went away.

"Go on now, fore Quentin see you and have to go too." Dilsey said.

"Where is she." Mother said.

"She down to the house playing with Luster." Dilsey said. "Go on, T. P. Drive that surrey like Roskus told you, now."

"Yessum." T. P. said. "Hum up, Queenie."

"Quentin." Mother said. "Dont let   "

"Course I is." Dilsey said.

The carriage jolted and crunched on the drive. "I'm afraid to go and leave Quentin." Mother said. "I'd better not go. T. P." We went through the gate, where it didn't jolt anymore. T. P. hit Queenie with the whip.

"You, T. P." Mother said.

"Got to get her going." T. P. said. "Keep her wake up till we get back to the barn."

"Turn around." Mother said. "I'm afraid to go and leave Quentin."

"Cant turn here." T. P. said. Then it was broader.

"Cant you turn here." Mother said.

"All right." T. P. said. We began to turn.

"You, T. P." Mother said, clutching me.

"I got to turn around some how." T. P. said. "Whoa, Queenie." We stopped.

"You'll turn us over." Mother said.

"What you want to do, then." T. P. said.

"I'm afraid for you to try to turn around." Mother said.

"Get up, Queenie." T. P. said. We went on.

"I just know Dilsey will let something happen to Quentin while I'm gone." Mother said. "We must hurry back."

"Hum up,[1] there." T. P. said. He hit Queenie with the whip.

"You, T. P." Mother said, clutching me. I could hear Queenie's feet and the bright shapes went smooth and steady on both sides, the shadows of them flowing across Queenie's back. They went on like the bright tops of wheels. Then those on one side stopped at the tall white post where the soldier was.[2] But on the other side they went on smooth and steady, but a little slower.

"What do you want." Jason said. He had his hands in his pockets and a pencil behind his ear.

"We're going to the cemetery." Mother said.

"All right." Jason said. "I dont aim to stop you, do I. Was that all you wanted with me, just to tell me that."

"I know you wont come." Mother said. "I'd feel safer if you would."

"Safe from what." Jason said. "Father and Quentin cant hurt you."

Mother put her handkerchief under her veil. "Stop it, Mother." Jason said. "Do you want to get that damn looney to bawling in the middle of the square. Drive on, T. P."

"Hum up, Queenie." T. P. said.

"It's a judgment on me." Mother said. "But I'll be gone too, soon."

"Here." Jason said.

"Whoa." T. P. said. Jason said,

"Uncle Maury's drawing on you for fifty. What do you want to do about it."

"Why ask me." Mother said. "I dont have any say so. I try not to worry you and Dilsey. I'll be gone soon, and then you   "

"Go on, T. P." Jason said.

"Hum up, Queenie." T. P. said. The shapes flowed on. The ones on the other side began again, bright and fast and smooth, like when Caddy says we are going to sleep.

Cry baby, Luster said. Aint you shamed. We went through the barn. The stalls were all open. You aint got no spotted pony to ride now, Luster said. The floor was dry and dusty. The roof was falling. The slanting holes were full of spinning yellow. What do you want to go that way, for. You want to get your head knocked off with one of them balls.

"Keep your hands in your pockets." Caddy said. "Or they'll be froze. You dont want your hands froze on Christmas, do you."

We went around the barn. The big cow and the little one were standing in the door, and we could hear Prince and Queenie and Fancy

---

1. Similar to the command "Get up."
2. The statue of the Confederate soldier on the town square.

stomping inside the barn. "If it wasn't so cold, we'd ride Fancy." Caddy
said. "But it's too cold to hold on today." Then we could see the branch,
where the smoke was blowing. "That's where they are killing the pig."
Caddy said. "We can come back by there and see them." We went down
the hill.

"You want to carry the letter." Caddy said. "You can carry it." She
took the letter out of her pocket and put it in mine. "It's a Christmas
present." Caddy said. "Uncle Maury is going to surprise Mrs Patterson
with it. We got to give it to her without letting anybody see it. Keep your
hands in your pockets good, now." We came to the branch.

"It's froze." Caddy said. "Look." She broke the top of the water and
held a piece of it against my face. "Ice. That means how cold it is." She
helped me across and we went up the hill. "We cant even tell Mother
and Father. You know what I think it is. I think it's a surprise for Mother
and Father and Mr Patterson both, because Mr Patterson sent you some
candy. Do you remember when Mr Patterson sent you some candy last
summer."

There was a fence. The vine was dry, and the wind rattled in it.

"Only I dont see why Uncle Maury didn't send Versh." Caddy said.
"Versh wont tell." Mrs Patterson was looking out the window. "You wait
here." Caddy said. "Wait right here, now. I'll be back in a minute. Give
me the letter." She took the letter out of my pocket. "Keep your hands
in your pockets." She climbed the fence with the letter in her hand and
went through the brown, rattling flowers. Mrs Patterson came to the
door and opened it and stood there.

*Mr Patterson was chopping in the green flowers. He stopped chopping
and looked at me. Mrs Patterson came across the garden, running. When
I saw her eyes I began to cry. You idiot, Mrs Patterson said, I told him
never to send you alone again. Give it to me. Quick. Mr Patterson came
fast, with the hoe. Mrs Patterson leaned across the fence, reaching her
hand. She was trying to climb the fence. Give it to me, she said, Give it
to me. Mr Patterson climbed the fence. He took the letter. Mrs Patterson's
dress was caught on the fence. I saw her eyes again and I ran down the
hill.*

"They aint nothing over yonder but houses." Luster said. "We going
down to the branch."

They were washing down at the branch. One of them was singing. I
could smell the clothes flapping, and the smoke blowing across the branch.

"You stay down here." Luster said. "You aint got no business up
yonder. Them folks hit you, sho."

"What he want to do."

"He dont know what he want to do." Luster said. "He think he want
to go up yonder where they knocking that ball. You sit down here and
play with your jimson weed. Look at them chillen playing in the branch,
if you got to look at something. How come you cant behave yourself like

folks." I sat down on the bank, where they were washing, and the smoke blowing blue.

"Is you all seen anything of a quarter down here." Luster said.

"What quarter."

"The one I had here this morning." Luster said. "I lost it somewhere. It fell through this here hole in my pocket. If I dont find it I cant go to the show tonight."

"Where'd you get a quarter, boy. Find it in white folks' pocket while they aint looking."

"Got it at the getting place." Luster said. "Plenty more where that one come from. Only I got to find that one. Is you all found it yet."

"I aint studying no quarter. I got my own business to tend to."

"Come on here." Luster said. "Help me look for it."

"He wouldn't know a quarter if he was to see it, would he."

"He can help look just the same." Luster said. "You all going to the show tonight."

"Dont talk to me about no show. Time I get done over this here tub I be too tired to lift my hand to do nothing."

"I bet you be there." Luster said. "I bet you was there last night. I bet you all be right there when that tent open."

"Be enough niggers there without me. Was last night."

"Nigger's money good as white folks, I reckon."

"White folks gives nigger money because know first white man comes along with a band going to get it all back, so nigger can go to work for some more."

"Aint nobody going make you go to that show."

"Aint yet. Aint thought of it, I reckon."

"What you got against white folks."

"Aint got nothing against them. I goes my way and lets white folks go theirs. I aint studying that show."

"Got a man in it can play a tune on a saw. Play it like a banjo."

"You go last night." Luster said. "I going tonight. If I can find where I lost that quarter."

"You going take him with you, I reckon."

"Me." Luster said. "You reckon I be found anywhere with him, time he start bellering."

"What does you do when he start bellering."

"I whips him." Luster said. He sat down and rolled up his overalls. They played in the branch.

"You all found any balls yet." Luster said.

"Aint you talking biggity. I bet you better not let your grandmammy hear you talking like that."

Luster got into the branch, where they were playing. He hunted in the water, along the bank.

"I had it when we was down here this morning." Luster said.

"Where bouts you lose it."

"Right out this here hole in my pocket." Luster said. They hunted in the branch. Then they all stood up quick and stopped, then they splashed and fought in the branch. Luster got it and they squatted in the water, looking up the hill through the bushes.

"Where is they." Luster said.

"Aint in sight yet."

Luster put it in his pocket. They came down the hill.

"Did a ball come down here."

"It ought to be in the water. Didn't any of you boys see it or hear it."

"Aint heard nothing come down here." Luster said. "Heard something hit that tree up yonder. Dont know which way it went."

They looked in the branch.

"Hell. Look along the branch. It came down here. I saw it."

They looked along the branch. Then they went back up the hill.

"Have you got that ball." the boy said.

"What I want with it." Luster said. "I aint seen no ball."

The boy got in the water. He went on. He turned and looked at Luster again. He went on down the branch.

The man said "Caddie" up the hill. The boy got out of the water and went up the hill.

"Now, just listen at you." Luster said. "Hush up."

"What he moaning about now."

"Lawd knows." Luster said. "He just starts like that. He been at it all morning. Cause it his birthday, I reckon."

"How old he."

"He thirty three." Luster said. "Thirty three this morning."

"You mean, he been three years old thirty years."

"I going by what mammy say." Luster said. "I dont know. We going to have thirty three candles on a cake, anyway. Little cake. Wont hardly hold them. Hush up. Come on back here." He came and caught my arm. "You old looney." he said. "You want me to whip you."

"I bet you will."

"I is done it. Hush, now." Luster said. "Aint I told you you cant go up there. They'll knock your head clean off with one of them balls. Come on, here." He pulled me back. "Sit down." I sat down and he took off my shoes and rolled up my trousers. "Now, git in that water and play and see can you stop that slobbering and moaning."

I hushed and got in the water *and Roskus came and said to come to supper and Caddy said,*

It's not supper time yet. I'm not going.

She was wet. We were playing in the branch and Caddy squatted down and got her dress wet and Versh said,

"Your mommer going to whip you for getting your dress wet."

"She's not going to do any such thing." Caddy said.

"How do you know." Quentin said.

"That's all right how I know." Caddy said. "How do you know."

"She said she was." Quentin said. "Besides, I'm older than you."

"I'm seven years old." Caddy said. "I guess I know."

"I'm older than that." Quentin said. "I go to school. Dont I, Versh."

"I'm going to school next year." Caddy said. "When it comes. Aint I, Versh."

"You know she whip you when you get your dress wet." Versh said.

"It's not wet." Caddy said. She stood up in the water and looked at her dress. "I'll take it off." she said. "Then it'll dry."

"I bet you wont." Quentin said.

"I bet I will." Caddy said.

"I bet you better not." Quentin said.

Caddy came to Versh and me and turned her back.

"Unbutton it, Versh." she said.

"Dont you do it, Versh." Quentin said.

"Taint none of my dress." Versh said.

"You unbutton it, Versh." Caddy said. "Or I'll tell Dilsey what you did yesterday." So Versh unbuttoned it.

"You just take your dress off." Quentin said. Caddy took her dress off and threw it on the bank. Then she didn't have on anything but her bodice and drawers, and Quentin slapped her and she slipped and fell down in the water. When she got up she began to splash water on Quentin, and Quentin splashed water on Caddy. Some of it splashed on Versh and me and Versh picked me up and put me on the bank. He said he was going to tell on Caddy and Quentin, and then Quentin and Caddy began to splash water at Versh. He got behind a bush.

"I'm going to tell mammy on you all." Versh said.

Quentin climbed up the bank and tried to catch Versh, but Versh ran away and Quentin couldn't. When Quentin came back Versh stopped and hollered that he was going to tell. Caddy told him that if he wouldn't tell, they'd let him come back. So Versh said he wouldn't, and they let him.

"Now I guess you're satisfied." Quentin said. "We'll both get whipped now."

"I dont care." Caddy said. "I'll run away."

"Yes you will." Quentin said.

"I'll run away and never come back." Caddy said. I began to cry. Caddy turned around and said "Hush" So I hushed. Then they played in the branch. Jason was playing too. He was by himself further down the branch. Versh came around the bush and lifted me down into the water again. Caddy was all wet and muddy behind, and I started to cry and she came and squatted in the water.

"Hush now." she said. "I'm not going to run away." So I hushed. Caddy smelled like trees in the rain.

What is the matter with you, Luster said. Cant you get done with that moaning and play in the branch like folks.

Whyn't you take him on home. Didn't they told you not to take him off the place.

He still think they own this pasture, Luster said. Cant nobody see down here from the house, noways.

We can. And folks dont like to look at a looney. Taint no luck in it.

Roskus came and said to come to supper and Caddy said it wasn't supper time yet.

"Yes tis." Roskus said. "Dilsey say for you all to come on to the house. Bring them on, Versh." He went up the hill, where the cow was lowing.

"Maybe we'll be dry by the time we get to the house." Quentin said.

"It was all your fault." Caddy said. "I hope we do get whipped." She put her dress on and Versh buttoned it.

"They wont know you got wet." Versh said. "It dont show on you. Less me and Jason tells."

"Are you going to tell, Jason." Caddy said.

"Tell on who." Jason said.

"He wont tell." Quentin said. "Will you, Jason."

"I bet he does tell." Caddy said. "He'll tell Damuddy."

"He cant tell her." Quentin said. "She's sick. If we walk slow it'll be too dark for them to see."

"I dont care whether they see or not." Caddy said. "I'm going to tell, myself. You carry him up the hill, Versh."

"Jason wont tell." Quentin said. "You remember that bow and arrow I made you, Jason."

"It's broke now." Jason said.

"Let him tell." Caddy said. "I dont give a cuss. Carry Maury up the hill, Versh." Versh squatted and I got on his back.

See you all at the show tonight, Luster said. Come on, here. We got to find that quarter.

"If we go slow, it'll be dark when we get there." Quentin said.

"I'm not going slow." Caddy said. We went up the hill, but Quentin didn't come. He was down at the branch when we got to where we could smell the pigs. They were grunting and snuffing in the trough in the corner. Jason came behind us, with his hands in his pockets. Roskus was milking the cow in the barn door.

The cows came jumping out of the barn.

"Go on." T. P. said. "Holler again. I going to holler myself. Whooey." Quentin kicked T. P. again. He kicked T. P. into the trough where the pigs ate and T. P. lay there. "Hot dog." T. P. said. "Didn't he get me then. You see that white man kick me that time. Whooey."

I wasn't crying, but I couldn't stop. I wasn't crying, but the ground wasn't still, and then I was crying. The ground kept sloping up and the cows ran up the hill. T. P. tried to get up. He fell down again and the

cows ran down the hill. Quentin held my arm and we went toward the
barn. Then the barn wasn't there and we had to wait until it came back.
I didn't see it come back. It came behind us and Quentin set me down
in the trough where the cows ate. I held on to it. It was going away too,
and I held to it. The cows ran down the hill again, across the door. I
couldn't stop. Quentin and T. P. came up the hill, fighting. T. P. was
falling down the hill and Quentin dragged him up the hill. Quentin hit
T. P. I couldn't stop.

"Stand up." Quentin said. "You stay right here. Dont you go away
until I get back."

"Me and Benjy going back to the wedding." T. P. said. "Whooey."

Quentin hit T. P. again. Then he began to thump T. P. against the
wall. T. P. was laughing. Every time Quentin thumped him against the
wall he tried to say Whooey, but he couldn't say it for laughing. I quit
crying, but I couldn't stop. T. P. fell on me and the barn door went
away. It went down the hill and T. P. was fighting by himself and he
fell down again. He was still laughing, and I couldn't stop, and I tried
to get up and I fell down, and I couldn't stop. Versh said,

"You sho done it now. I'll declare if you aint. Shut up that yelling."

T. P. was still laughing. He flopped on the door and laughed.
"Whooey." he said. "Me and Benjy going back to the wedding. Sassprill-
luh."[3] T. P. said.

"Hush." Versh said. "Where you get it."

"Out the cellar." T. P. said. "Whooey."

"Hush up." Versh said. "Where bouts in the cellar."

"Anywhere." T. P. said. He laughed some more. "Moren a hundred
bottles lef. Moren a million. Look out, nigger, I going to holler."

Quentin said, "Lift him up."

Versh lifted me up.

"Drink this, Benjy." Quentin said. The glass was hot. "Hush, now."
Quentin said. "Drink it."

"Sassprilluh." T. P. said. "Lemme drink it, Mr Quentin."

"You shut your mouth." Versh said. "Mr Quentin wear you out."

"Hold him, Versh." Quentin said.

They held me. It was hot on my chin and on my shirt. "Drink."
Quentin said. They held my head. It was hot inside me, and I began
again. I was crying now, and something was happening inside me and I
cried more, and they held me until it stopped happening. Then I hushed.
It was still going around, and then the shapes began. Open the crib,
Versh. They were going slow. Spread those empty sacks on the floor.
They were going faster, almost fast enough. Now. Pick up his feet. They

3. A variant of sarsaparilla, a sweet soft drink similar to root beer with the predominant flavor
from birch oil and sassafras. But the context suggests that they are drinking something alcoholic.

went on, smooth and bright. I could hear T. P. laughing. I went on
with them, up the bright hill.

At the top of the hill Versh put me down. "Come on here, Quentin."
he called, looking back down the hill. Quentin was still standing there
by the branch. He was chunking into the shadows where the branch
was.

"Let the old skizzard stay there." Caddy said. She took my hand and
we went on past the barn and through the gate. There was a frog on the
brick walk, squatting in the middle of it. Caddy stepped over it and
pulled me on.

"Come on, Maury." she said. It still squatted there until Jason poked
at it with his toe.

"He'll make a wart on you." Versh said. The frog hopped away.

"Come on, Maury." Caddy said.

"They got company tonight." Versh said.

"How do you know." Caddy said.

"With all them lights on." Versh said. "Light in every window."

"I reckon we can turn all the lights on without company, if we want
to." Caddy said.

"I bet it's company." Versh said. "You all better go in the back and
slip upstairs."

"I dont care." Caddy said. "I'll walk right in the parlor where they
are."

"I bet your pappy whip you if you do." Versh said.

"I dont care." Caddy said. "I'll walk right in the parlor. I'll walk right
in the dining room and eat supper."

"Where you sit." Versh said.

"I'd sit in Damuddy's chair." Caddy said. "She eats in bed."

"I'm hungry." Jason said. He passed us and ran on up the walk. He
had his hands in his pockets and he fell down. Versh went and picked
him up.

"If you keep them hands out your pockets, you could stay on your
feet." Versh said. "You cant never get them out in time to catch yourself, fat as you is."

Father was standing by the kitchen steps.

"Where's Quentin." he said.

"He coming up the walk." Versh said. Quentin was coming slow. His
shirt was a white blur.

"Oh." Father said. Light fell down the steps, on him.

"Caddy and Quentin threw water on each other." Jason said.

We waited.

"They did." Father said. Quentin came, and Father said, "You can
eat supper in the kitchen tonight." He stooped and took me up, and the
light came tumbling down the steps on me too, and I could look down

at Caddy and Jason and Quentin and Versh. Father turned toward the steps. "You must be quiet, though." he said.

"Why must we be quiet, Father." Caddy said. "Have we got company."

"Yes." Father said.

"I told you they was company." Versh said.

"You did not." Caddy said. "I was the one that said there was. I said I would   "

"Hush." Father said. They hushed and Father opened the door and we crossed the back porch and went in to the kitchen. Dilsey was there, and Father put me in the chair and closed the apron down and pushed it to the table, where supper was. It was steaming up.

"You mind Dilsey, now." Father said. "Dont let them make any more noise than they can help, Dilsey."

"Yes, sir." Dilsey said. Father went away.

"Remember to mind Dilsey, now." he said behind us. I leaned my face over where the supper was. It steamed up on my face.

"Let them mind me tonight, Father." Caddy said.

"I wont." Jason said. "I'm going to mind Dilsey."

"You'll have to, if Father says so." Caddy said. "Let them mind me, Father."

"I wont." Jason said. "I wont mind you."

"Hush." Father said. "You all mind Caddy, then. When they are done, bring them up the back stairs, Dilsey."

"Yes, sir." Dilsey said.

"There." Caddy said. "Now I guess you'll mind me."

"You all hush, now." Dilsey said. "You got to be quiet tonight."

"Why do we have to be quiet tonight." Caddy whispered.

"Never you mind." Dilsey said. "You'll know in the Lawd's own time." She brought my bowl. The steam from it came and tickled my face. "Come here, Versh." Dilsey said.

"When is the Lawd's own time, Dilsey." Caddy said.

"It's Sunday." Quentin said. "Dont you know anything."

"Shhhhhh." Dilsey said. "Didn't Mr Jason say for you all to be quiet. Eat your supper, now. Here, Versh. Git his spoon." Versh's hand came with the spoon, into the bowl. The spoon came up to my mouth. The steam tickled into my mouth. Then we quit eating and we looked at each other and we were quiet, and then we heard it again and I began to cry.

"What was that." Caddy said. She put her hand on my hand.

"That was Mother." Quentin said. The spoon came up and I ate, then I cried again.

"Hush." Caddy said. But I didn't hush and she came and put her arms around me. Dilsey went and closed both the doors and then we couldn't hear it.

"Hush, now." Caddy said. I hushed and ate. Quentin wasn't eating, but Jason was.

"That was Mother." Quentin said. He got up.

"You set right down." Dilsey said. "They got company in there, and you in them muddy clothes. You set down too, Caddy, and get done eating."

"She was crying." Quentin said.

"It was somebody singing." Caddy said. "Wasn't it, Dilsey."

"You all eat your supper, now, like Mr Jason said." Dilsey said. "You'll know in the Lawd's own time." Caddy went back to her chair.

"I told you it was a party." she said.

Versh said, "He done et all that."

"Bring his bowl here." Dilsey said. The bowl went away.

"Dilsey." Caddy said. "Quentin's not eating his supper. Hasn't he got to mind me."

"Eat your supper, Quentin." Dilsey said. "You all got to get done and get out of my kitchen."

"I dont want any more supper." Quentin said.

"You've got to eat if I say you have." Caddy said. "Hasn't he, Dilsey."

The bowl steamed up to my face, and Versh's hand dipped the spoon in it and the steam tickled into my mouth.

"I dont want any more." Quentin said. "How can they have a party when Damuddy's sick."

"They'll have it down stairs." Caddy said. "She can come to the landing and see it. That's what I'm going to do when I get my nightie on."

"Mother was crying." Quentin said. "Wasn't she crying, Dilsey."

"Dont you come pestering at me, boy." Dilsey said. "I got to get supper for all them folks soon as you all get done eating."

After a while even Jason was through eating, and he began to cry.

"Now you got to tune up." Dilsey said.

"He does it every night since Damuddy was sick and he cant sleep with her." Caddy said. "Cry baby."

"I'm going to tell on you." Jason said.

He was crying. "You've already told." Caddy said. "There's not anything else you can tell, now."

"You all needs to go to bed." Dilsey said. She came and lifted me down and wiped my face and hands with a warm cloth. "Versh, can you get them up the back stairs quiet. You, Jason, shut up that crying."

"It's too early to go to bed now." Caddy said. "We dont ever have to go to bed this early."

"You is tonight." Dilsey said. "Your paw say for you to come right on up stairs when you et supper. You heard him."

"He said to mind me." Caddy said.

"I'm not going to mind you." Jason said.

"You have to." Caddy said. "Come on, now. You have to do like I say."

"Make them be quiet, Versh." Dilsey said. "You all going to be quiet, aint you."

"What do we have to be so quiet for, tonight." Caddy said.

"Your mommer aint feeling well." Dilsey said. "You all go on with Versh, now."

"I told you Mother was crying." Quentin said. Versh took me up and opened the door onto the back porch. We went out and Versh closed the door black. I could smell Versh and feel him. You all be quiet, now. We're not going up stairs yet. Mr Jason said for you to come right up stairs. He said to mind me. I'm not going to mind you. But he said for all of us to. Didn't he, Quentin. I could feel Versh's head. I could hear us. Didn't he, Versh. Yes, that right. Then I say for us to go out doors a while. Come on. Versh opened the door and we went out.

We went down the steps.

"I expect we'd better go down to Versh's house, so we'll be quiet." Caddy said. Versh put me down and Caddy took my hand and we went down the brick walk.

"Come on." Caddy said. "That frog's gone. He's hopped way over to the garden, by now. Maybe we'll see another one." Roskus came with the milk buckets. He went on. Quentin wasn't coming with us. He was sitting on the kitchen steps. We went down to Versh's house. I liked to smell Versh's house. *There was a fire in it and T. P. squatting in his shirt tail in front of it, chunking it into a blaze.*

Then I got up and T. P. dressed me and we went to the kitchen and ate. Dilsey was singing and I began to cry and she stopped.

"Keep him away from the house, now." Dilsey said.

"We cant go that way." T. P. said.

We played in the branch.

"We cant go around yonder." T. P. said. "Dont you know mammy say we cant."

Dilsey was singing in the kitchen and I began to cry.

"Hush." T. P. said. "Come on. Les go down to the barn."

Roskus was milking at the barn. He was milking with one hand, and groaning. Some birds sat on the barn door and watched him. One of them came down and ate with the cows. I watched Roskus milk while T. P. was feeding Queenie and Prince. The calf was in the pig pen. It nuzzled at the wire, bawling.

"T. P." Roskus said. T. P. said Sir, in the barn. Fancy held her head over the door, because T. P. hadn't fed her yet. "Git done there." Roskus said. "You got to do this milking. I cant use my right hand no more."

T. P. came and milked.

"Whyn't you get the doctor." T. P. said.

"Doctor cant do no good." Roskus said. "Not on this place."

"What wrong with this place." T. P. said.

"Taint no luck on this place." Roskus said. "Turn that calf in if you done."

Taint no luck on this place, Roskus said. The fire rose and fell behind him and Versh, sliding on his and Versh's face. Dilsey finished putting me to bed. The bed smelled like T. P. I liked it.

"What you know about it." Dilsey said. "What trance you been in."

"Dont need no trance." Roskus said. "Aint the sign of it laying right there on that bed. Aint the sign of it been here for folks to see fifteen years now."

"Spose it is." Dilsey said. "It aint hurt none of you and yourn, is it. Versh working and Frony married off your hands and T. P. getting big enough to take your place when rheumatism finish getting you."

"They been two, now." Roskus said. "Going to be one more. I seen the sign, and you is too."

"I heard a squinch owl[4] that night." T. P. said. "Dan wouldn't come and get his supper, neither. Wouldn't come no closer than the barn. Begun howling right after dark. Versh heard him."

"Going to be more than one more." Dilsey said. "Show me the man what aint going to die, bless Jesus."

"Dying aint all." Roskus said.

"I knows what you thinking." Dilsey said. "And they aint going to be no luck in saying that name, lessen you going to set up with him while he cries."

"They aint no luck on this place." Roskus said. "I seen it at first but when they changed his name I knowed it."

"Hush your mouth." Dilsey said. She pulled the covers up. It smelled like T. P. "You all shut up now, till he get to sleep."

"I seen the sign." Roskus said.

"Sign T. P. got to do all your work for you." Dilsey said. *Take him and Quentin down to the house and let them play with Luster, where Frony can watch them, T. P., and go and help your paw.*

We finished eating. T. P. took Quentin up and we went down to T. P.'s house. Luster was playing in the dirt. T. P. put Quentin down and she played in the dirt too. Luster had some spools and he and Quentin fought and Quentin had the spools. Luster cried and Frony came and gave Luster a tin can to play with, and then I had the spools and Quentin fought me and I cried.

"Hush." Frony said. "Aint you shamed of yourself. Taking a baby's play pretty." She took the spools from me and gave them back to Quentin.

"Hush, now." Frony said. "Hush, I tell you."

4. Screech owl.

"Hush up." Frony said. "You needs whipping, that's what you needs."
She took Luster and Quentin up. "Come on here." she said. We went
to the barn. T. P. was milking the cow. Roskus was sitting on the box.

"What's the matter with him now." Roskus said.

"You have to keep him down here." Frony said. "He fighting these
babies again. Taking they play things. Stay here with T. P. now, and
see can you hush a while."

"Clean that udder good now." Roskus said. "You milked that young
cow dry last winter. If you milk this one dry, they aint going to be no
more milk."

Dilsey was singing.

"Not around yonder." T. P. said. "Dont you know mammy say you
cant go around there."

They were singing.

"Come on." T. P. said. "Les go play with Quentin and Luster. Come
on."

Quentin and Luster were playing in the dirt in front of T. P.'s house.
There was a fire in the house, rising and falling, with Roskus sitting
black against it.

"That's three, thank the Lawd." Roskus said. "I told you two years
ago. They aint no luck on this place."

"Whyn't you get out, then." Dilsey said. She was undressing me.
"Your bad luck talk got them Memphis notions into Versh. That ought
to satisfy you."

"If that all the bad luck Versh have." Roskus said.

Frony came in.

"You all done." Dilsey said.

"T. P. finishing up." Frony said. "Miss Cahline want you to put
Quentin to bed."

"I'm coming just as fast as I can." Dilsey said. "She ought to know by
this time I aint got no wings."

"That's what I tell you." Roskus said. "They aint no luck going be on
no place where one of they own chillen's name aint never spoke."

"Hush." Dilsey said. "Do you want to get him started."

"Raising a child not to know its own mammy's name." Roskus said.

"Dont you bother your head about her." Dilsey said. "I raised all of
them and I reckon I can raise one more. Hush, now. Let him get to
sleep if he will."

"Saying a name." Frony said. "He dont know nobody's name."

"You just say it and see if he dont." Dilsey said. "You say it to him
while he sleeping and I bet he hear you."

"He know lot more than folks thinks." Roskus said. "He knowed they
time was coming, like that pointer done. He could tell you when hisn
coming, if he could talk. Or yours. Or mine."

"You take Luster outen that bed, mammy." Frony said. "That boy conjure him."

"Hush your mouth." Dilsey said. "Aint you got no better sense than that. What you want to listen to Roskus for, anyway. Get in, Benjy."

Dilsey pushed me and I got in the bed, where Luster already was. He was asleep. Dilsey took a long piece of wood and laid it between Luster and me. "Stay on your side now." Dilsey said. "Luster little, and you dont want to hurt him."

You cant go yet, T. P. said. Wait.

We looked around the corner of the house and watched the carriages go away.

"Now." T. P. said. He took Quentin up and we ran down to the corner of the fence and watched them pass. "There he go." T. P. said. "See that one with the glass in it.[5] Look at him. He laying in there. See him."

Come on, Luster said, I going to take this here ball down home, where I wont lose it. Naw, sir, you cant have it. If them men sees you with it, they'll say you stole it. Hush up, now. You cant have it. What business you got with it. You cant play no ball.

Frony and T. P. were playing in the dirt by the door. T. P. had lightning bugs in a bottle.

"How did you all get back out." Frony said.

"We've got company." Caddy said. "Father said for us to mind me tonight. I expect you and T. P. will have to mind me too."

"I'm not going to mind you." Jason said. "Frony and T. P. dont have to either."

"They will if I say so." Caddy said. "Maybe I wont say for them to."

"T. P. dont mind nobody." Frony said. "Is they started the funeral yet."

"What's a funeral." Jason said.

"Didn't mammy tell you not to tell them." Versh said.

"Where they moans." Frony said. "They moaned two days on Sis Beulah Clay."

They moaned at Dilsey's house. Dilsey was moaning. When Dilsey moaned Luster said, Hush, and we hushed, and then I began to cry and Blue howled under the kitchen steps.[6] Then Dilsey stopped and we stopped.

"Oh." Caddy said. "That's niggers. White folks dont have funerals."

"Mammy said us not to tell them, Frony." Versh said.

"Tell them what." Caddy said.

Dilsey moaned, and when it got to the place I began to cry and Blue howled under the steps. Luster, Frony said in the window. Take them

---

5. The horse-drawn hearse with glass windows.
6. According to folk beliefs, dogs often howl after a death in the family.

*down to the barn. I cant get no cooking done with all that racket. That
hound too. Get them outen here.*

*I aint going down there, Luster said. I might meet pappy down there.
I seen him last night, waving his arms in the barn.*

"I like to know why not." Frony said. "White folks dies too. Your
grandmammy dead as any nigger can get, I reckon."

"Dogs are dead." Caddy said. "And when Nancy fell in the ditch and
Roskus shot her and the buzzards came and undressed her."

The bones rounded out of the ditch, where the dark vines were in the
black ditch, into the moonlight, like some of the shapes had stopped.
Then they all stopped and it was dark, and when I stopped to start again
I could hear Mother, and feet walking fast away, and I could smell it.
Then the room came, but my eyes went shut. I didn't stop. I could smell
it. T. P. unpinned the bed clothes.

"Hush." he said. "Shhhhhhhh."

But I could smell it. T. P. pulled me up and he put on my clothes
fast.

"Hush, Benjy." he said. "We going down to our house. You want to
go down to our house, where Frony is. Hush. Shhhhh."

He laced my shoes and put my cap on and we went out. There was a
light in the hall. Across the hall we could hear Mother.

"Shhhhhh, Benjy." T. P. said. "We'll be out in a minute."

A door opened and I could smell it more than ever, and a head came
out. It wasn't Father. Father was sick there.

"Can you take him out of the house."

"That's where we going." T. P. said. Dilsey came up the stairs.

"Hush." she said. "Hush. Take him down home, T. P. Frony fixing
him a bed. You all look after him, now. Hush, Benjy. Go on with
T. P."

She went where we could hear Mother.

"Better keep him there." It wasn't Father. He shut the door, but I
could still smell it.

We went down stairs. The stairs went down into the dark and T. P.
took my hand, and we went out the door, out of the dark. Dan was
sitting in the back yard, howling.

"He smell it." T. P. said. "Is that the way you found it out."

We went down the steps, where our shadows were.

"I forgot your coat." T. P. said. "You ought to had it. But I aint going
back."

Dan howled.

"Hush now." T. P. said. Our shadows moved, but Dan's shadow
didn't move except to howl when he did.

"I cant take you down home, bellering like you is." T. P. said. "You
was bad enough before you got that bullfrog voice. Come on."

We went along the brick walk, with our shadows. The pig pen smelled like pigs. The cow stood in the lot, chewing at us. Dan howled.

"You going to wake the whole town up." T. P. said. "Cant you hush."

We saw Fancy, eating by the branch. The moon shone on the water when we got there.

"Naw, sir." T. P. said. "This too close. We cant stop here. Come on. Now, just look at you. Got your whole leg wet. Come on, here." Dan howled.

The ditch came up out of the buzzing grass. The bones rounded out of the black vines.

"Now." T. P. said. "Beller your head off if you want to. You got the whole night and a twenty acre pasture to beller in."

T. P. lay down in the ditch and I sat down, watching the bones where the buzzards ate Nancy, flapping black and slow and heavy out of the ditch.

I had it when we was down here before, Luster said. I showed it to you. Didn't you see it. I took it out of my pocket right here and showed it to you.

"Do you think buzzards are going to undress Damuddy." Caddy said. "You're crazy."

"You're a skizzard." Jason said. He began to cry.

"You're a knobnot." Caddy said. Jason cried. His hands were in his pockets.

"Jason going to be rich man." Versh said. "He holding his money all the time."

Jason cried.

"Now you've got him started." Caddy said. "Hush up, Jason. How can buzzards get in where Damuddy is. Father wouldn't let them. Would you let a buzzard undress you. Hush up, now."

Jason hushed. "Frony said it was a funeral." he said.

"Well it's not." Caddy said. "It's a party. Frony dont know anything about it. He wants your lightning bugs, T. P. Let him hold it a while."

T. P. gave me the bottle of lightning bugs.

"I bet if we go around to the parlor window we can see something." Caddy said. "Then you'll believe me."

"I already knows." Frony said. "I dont need to see."

"You better hush your mouth, Frony." Versh said. "Mammy going whip you."

"What is it." Caddy said.

"I knows what I knows." Frony said.

"Come on." Caddy said. "Let's go around to the front."

We started to go.

"T. P. wants his lightning bugs." Frony said.

"Let him hold it a while longer, T. P." Caddy said. "We'll bring it back."

"You all never caught them." Frony said.

"If I say you and T. P. can come too, will you let him hold it." Caddy said.

"Aint nobody said me and T. P. got to mind you." Frony said.

"If I say you dont have to, will you let him hold it." Caddy said.

"All right." Frony said. "Let him hold it, T. P. We going to watch them moaning."

"They aint moaning." Caddy said. "I tell you it's a party. Are they moaning, Versh."

"We aint going to know what they doing, standing here." Versh said.

"Come on." Caddy said. "Frony and T. P. dont have to mind me. But the rest of us do. You better carry him, Versh. It's getting dark."

Versh took me up and we went on around the kitchen.

When we looked around the corner we could see the lights coming up the drive. T. P. went back to the cellar door and opened it.

You know what's down there, T. P. said. Soda water. I seen Mr Jason come up with both hands full of them. Wait here a minute.

T. P. went and looked in the kitchen door. Dilsey said, What are you peeping in here for. Where's Benjy.

He out here, T. P. said.

Go on and watch him, Dilsey said. Keep him out the house now.

Yessum, T. P. said. Is they started yet.

You go on and keep that boy out of sight, Dilsey said. I got all I can tend to.

A snake crawled out from under the house. Jason said he wasn't afraid of snakes and Caddy said he was but she wasn't and Versh said they both were and Caddy said to be quiet, like Father said.

You aint got to start bellering now, T. P. said. You want some this sassprilluh.

It tickled my nose and eyes.

If you aint going to drink it, let me get to it, T. P. said. All right, here tis. We better get another bottle while aint nobody bothering us. You be quiet, now.

We stopped under the tree by the parlor window. Versh set me down in the wet grass. It was cold. There were lights in all the windows.

"That's where Damuddy is." Caddy said. "She's sick every day now. When she gets well we're going to have a picnic."

"I knows what I knows." Frony said.

The trees were buzzing, and the grass.

"The one next to it is where we have the measles." Caddy said. "Where do you and T. P. have the measles, Frony."

"Has them just wherever we is, I reckon." Frony said.

"They haven't started yet." Caddy said.

They getting ready to start, T. P. said. You stand right here now while I get that box so we can see in the window. Here, les finish drinking this here sassprilluh. It make me feel just like a squinch owl inside.

We drank the sassprilluh and T. P. pushed the bottle through the lattice, under the house, and went away. I could hear them in the parlor and I clawed my hands against the wall. T. P. dragged the box. He fell down, and he began to laugh. He lay there, laughing into the grass. He got up and dragged the box under the window, trying not to laugh.

"I skeered I going to holler." T. P. said. "Git on the box and see is they started."

"They haven't started because the band hasn't come yet." Caddy said.

"They aint going to have no band." Frony said.

"How do you know." Caddy said.

"I knows what I knows." Frony said.

"You dont know anything." Caddy said. She went to the tree. "Push me up, Versh."

"Your paw told you to stay out that tree." Versh said.

"That was a long time ago." Caddy said. "I expect he's forgotten about it. Besides, he said to mind me tonight. Didn't he didn't he say to mind me tonight."

"I'm not going to mind you." Jason said. "Frony and T. P. are not going to either."

"Push me up, Versh." Caddy said.

"All right." Versh said. "You the one going to get whipped. I aint." He went and pushed Caddy up into the tree to the first limb. We watched the muddy bottom of her drawers. Then we couldn't see her. We could hear the tree thrashing.

"Mr Jason said if you break that tree he whip you." Versh said.

"I'm going to tell on her too." Jason said.

The tree quit thrashing. We looked up into the still branches.

"What you seeing." Frony whispered.

I saw them. Then I saw Caddy, with flowers in her hair, and a long veil like shining wind. Caddy Caddy

"Hush." T. P. said. "They going to hear you. Get down quick." He pulled me. Caddy. I clawed my hands against the wall Caddy. T. P. pulled me. "Hush." he said. "Hush. Come on here quick." He pulled me on. Caddy "Hush up, Benjy. You want them to hear you. Come on, les drink some more sassprilluh, then we can come back if you hush. We better get one more bottle or we both be hollering. We can say Dan drunk it. Mr Quentin always saying he so smart, we can say he sassprilluh dog, too."

The moonlight came down the cellar stairs. We drank some more sassprilluh.

"You know what I wish." T. P. said. "I wish a bear would walk in that cellar door. You know what I do. I walk right up to him and spit in he eye. Gimme that bottle to stop my mouth before I holler."

T. P. fell down. He began to laugh, and the cellar door and the moonlight jumped away and something hit me.

"Hush up." T. P. said, trying not to laugh. "Lawd, they'll all hear us. Get up." T. P. said. "Get up, Benjy, quick." He was thrashing about and laughing and I tried to get up. The cellar steps ran up the hill in the moonlight and T. P. fell up the hill, into the moonlight, and I ran against the fence and T. P. ran behind me saying "Hush up hush up." Then he fell into the flowers, laughing, and I ran into the box. But when I tried to climb onto it it jumped away and hit me on the back of the head and my throat made a sound. It made the sound again and I stopped trying to get up, and it made the sound again and I began to cry. But my throat kept on making the sound while T. P. was pulling me. It kept on making it and I couldn't tell if I was crying or not, and T. P. fell down on top of me, laughing, and it kept on making the sound and Quentin kicked T. P. and Caddy put her arms around me, and her shining veil, and I couldn't smell trees anymore and I began to cry.

Benjy, Caddy said, Benjy. *She put her arms around me again, but I went away.* "What is it, Benjy." she said. "Is it this hat." She took her hat off and came again, and I went away.

"Benjy." she said. "What is it, Benjy. What has Caddy done."

"He dont like that prissy dress." Jason said. "You think you're grown up, dont you. You think you're better than anybody else, dont you. Prissy."

"You shut your mouth." Caddy said. "You dirty little beast. Benjy."

"Just because you are fourteen, you think you're grown up, dont you." Jason said. "You think you're something. Dont you."

"Hush, Benjy." Caddy said. "You'll disturb Mother. Hush."

But I didn't hush, and when she went away I followed, and she stopped on the stairs and waited and I stopped too.

"What is it, Benjy." Caddy said. "Tell Caddy. She'll do it. Try."

"Candace." Mother said.

"Yessum." Caddy said.

"Why are you teasing him." Mother said. "Bring him here."

We went to Mother's room, where she was lying with the sickness on a cloth on her head.

"What is the matter now." Mother said. "Benjamin."

"Benjy." Caddy said. She came again, but I went away.

"You must have done something to him." Mother said. "Why wont you let him alone, so I can have some peace. Give him the box and please go on and let him alone."

Caddy got the box and set it on the floor and opened it. It was full of stars. When I was still, they were still. When I moved, they glinted and sparkled. I hushed.

Then I heard Caddy walking and I began again.

"Benjamin." Mother said. "Come here." I went to the door. "You, Benjamin." Mother said.

"What is it now." Father said. "Where are you going."

"Take him downstairs and get someone to watch him, Jason." Mother said. "You know I'm ill, yet you   "

Father shut the door behind us.

"T. P." he said.

"Sir." T. P. said downstairs.

"Benjy's coming down." Father said. "Go with T. P."

I went to the bathroom door. I could hear the water.

"Benjy." T. P. said downstairs.

I could hear the water. I listened to it.

"Benjy." T. P. said downstairs.

I listened to the water.

I couldn't hear the water, and Caddy opened the door.

"Why, Benjy." she said. She looked at me and I went and she put her arms around me. "Did you find Caddy again." she said. "Did you think Caddy had run away." Caddy smelled like trees.

We went to Caddy's room. She sat down at the mirror. She stopped her hands and looked at me.

"Why, Benjy. What is it." she said. "You mustn't cry. Caddy's not going away. See here." she said. She took up the bottle and took the stopper out and held it to my nose. "Sweet. Smell. Good."

I went away and I didn't hush, and she held the bottle in her hand, looking at me.

"Oh." she said. She put the bottle down and came and put her arms around me. "So that was it. And you were trying to tell Caddy and you couldn't tell her. You wanted to, but you couldn't, could you. Of course Caddy wont. Of course Caddy wont. Just wait till I dress."

Caddy dressed and took up the bottle again and we went down to the kitchen.

"Dilsey." Caddy said. "Benjy's got a present for you." She stooped down and put the bottle in my hand. "Hold it out to Dilsey, now." Caddy held my hand out and Dilsey took the bottle.

"Well I'll declare." Dilsey said. "If my baby aint give Dilsey a bottle of perfume. Just look here, Roskus."

Caddy smelled like trees. "We dont like perfume ourselves." Caddy said.

She smelled like trees.

"Come on, now." Dilsey said. "You too big to sleep with folks. You a big boy now. Thirteen years old. Big enough to sleep by yourself in Uncle Maury's room." Dilsey said.

Uncle Maury was sick. His eye was sick, and his mouth. Versh took his supper up to him on the tray.

"Maury says he's going to shoot the scoundrel." Father said. "I told him he'd better not mention it to Patterson before hand." He drank.

"Jason." Mother said.

"Shoot who, Father." Quentin said. "What's Uncle Maury going to shoot him for."

"Because he couldn't take a little joke." Father said.

"Jason." Mother said. "How can you. You'd sit right there and see Maury shot down in ambush, and laugh."

"Then Maury'd better stay out of ambush." Father said.

"Shoot who, Father." Quentin said. "Who's Uncle Maury going to shoot."

"Nobody." Father said. "I dont own a pistol."

Mother began to cry. "If you begrudge Maury your food, why aren't you man enough to say so to his face. To ridicule him before the children, behind his back."

"Of course I dont." Father said. "I admire Maury. He is invaluable to my own sense of racial superiority. I wouldn't swap Maury for a matched team. And do you know why, Quentin."

"No, sir." Quentin said.

"*Et ego in arcadia*[7] I have forgotten the latin for hay." Father said. "There, there." he said. "I was just joking." He drank and set the glass down and went and put his hand on Mother's shoulder.

"It's no joke." Mother said. "My people are every bit as well born as yours. Just because Maury's health is bad."

"Of course." Father said. "Bad health is the primary reason for all life. Created by disease, within putrefaction, into decay. Versh."

"Sir." Versh said behind my chair.

"Take the decanter and fill it."

"And tell Dilsey to come and take Benjamin up to bed." Mother said.

"You a big boy." Dilsey said. "Caddy tired sleeping with you. Hush now, so you can go to sleep." The room went away, but I didn't hush, and the room came back and Dilsey came and sat on the bed, looking at me.

"Aint you going to be a good boy and hush." Dilsey said. "You aint, is you. See can you wait a minute, then."

She went away. There wasn't anything in the door. Then Caddy was in it.

"Hush." Caddy said. "I'm coming."

I hushed and Dilsey turned back the spread and Caddy got in between the spread and the blanket. She didn't take off her bathrobe.

"Now." she said. "Here I am." Dilsey came with a blanket and spread it over her and tucked it around her.

---

7. Sometimes attributed to Bart. Schidone (1570–1615), who wrote the words *Et in Arcadia ego* ("I [Death] am even in Arcadia") on his picture of two young shepheds contemplating a skull they are holding. Also found on a picture by Guercino (1570–1666), this phrase is sometimes altered to *Et ego in Arcadia*, "I too have lived in Arcadia," which expresses the idea of a supreme happiness now lost.

"He be gone in a minute." Dilsey said. "I leave the light on in your room."

"All right." Caddy said. She snuggled her head beside mine on the pillow. "Goodnight, Dilsey."

"Goodnight, honey." Dilsey said. The room went black. *Caddy smelled like trees.*

We looked up into the tree where she was.

"What she seeing, Versh." Frony whispered.

"Shhhhhhh." Caddy said in the tree. Dilsey said,

"You come on here." She came around the corner of the house. "Whyn't you all go on up stairs, like your paw said, stead of slipping out behind my back. Where's Caddy and Quentin."

"I told her not to climb up that tree." Jason said. "I'm going to tell on her."

"Who in what tree." Dilsey said. She came and looked up into the tree. "Caddy." Dilsey said. The branches began to shake again.

"You, Satan." Dilsey said. "Come down from there."

"Hush." Caddy said, "Dont you know Father said to be quiet." Her legs came in sight and Dilsey reached up and lifted her out of the tree.

"Aint you got any better sense than to let them come around here." Dilsey said.

"I couldn't do nothing with her." Versh said.

"What you all doing here." Dilsey said. "Who told you to come up to the house."

"She did." Frony said. "She told us to come."

"Who told you you got to do what she say." Dilsey said. "Get on home, now." Frony and T. P. went on. We couldn't see them when they were still going away.

"Out here in the middle of the night." Dilsey said. She took me up and we went to the kitchen.

"Slipping out behind my back." Dilsey said. "When you knowed it's past your bedtime."

"Shhhh, Dilsey." Caddy said. "Dont talk so loud. We've got to be quiet."

"You hush your mouth and get quiet, then." Dilsey said. "Where's Quentin."

"Quentin's mad because we had to mind me tonight." Caddy said. "He's still got T. P.'s bottle of lightning bugs."

"I reckon T. P. can get along without it." Dilsey said. "You go and find Quentin, Versh. Roskus say he seen him going towards the barn." Versh went on. We couldn't see him.

"They're not doing anything in there." Caddy said. "Just sitting in chairs and looking."

"They dont need no help from you all to do that." Dilsey said. We went around the kitchen.

Where you want to go now, Luster said. You going back to watch them knocking ball again. We done looked for it over there. Here. Wait a minute. You wait right here while I go back and get that ball. I done thought of something.

The kitchen was dark. The trees were black on the sky. Dan came waddling out from under the steps and chewed my ankle. I went around the kitchen, where the moon was. Dan came scuffling along, into the moon.

"Benjy." T. P. said in the house.

The flower tree by the parlor window wasn't dark, but the thick trees were. The grass was buzzing in the moonlight where my shadow walked on the grass.

"You, Benjy." T. P. said in the house. "Where you hiding. You slipping off. I knows it."

Luster came back. Wait, he said. Here. Dont go over there. Miss Quentin and her beau in the swing yonder. You come on this way. Come back here, Benjy.

It was dark under the trees. Dan wouldn't come. He stayed in the moonlight. Then I could see the swing and I began to cry.

Come away from there, Benjy, Luster said. You know Miss Quentin going to get mad.

It was two now, and then one in the swing. Caddy came fast, white in the darkness.

"Benjy." she said. "How did you slip out. Where's Versh."

She put her arms around me and I hushed and held to her dress and tried to pull her away.

"Why, Benjy." she said. "What is it. T. P." she called.

The one in the swing got up and came, and I cried and pulled Caddy's dress.

"Benjy." Caddy said. "It's just Charlie. Dont you know Charlie."

"Where's his nigger." Charlie said. "What do they let him run around loose for."

"Hush, Benjy." Caddy said. "Go away, Charlie. He doesn't like you." Charlie went away and I hushed. I pulled at Caddy's dress.

"Why, Benjy." Caddy said. "Aren't you going to let me stay here and talk to Charlie a while."

"Call that nigger." Charlie said. He came back. I cried louder and pulled at Caddy's dress.

"Go away, Charlie." Caddy said. Charlie came and put his hands on Caddy and I cried more. I cried loud.

"No, no." Caddy said. "No. No."

"He cant talk." Charlie said. "Caddy."

"Are you crazy." Caddy said. She began to breathe fast. "He can see. Dont. Dont." Caddy fought. They both breathed fast. "Please. Please." Caddy whispered.

"Send him away." Charlie said.

"I will." Caddy said. "Let me go."

"Will you send him away." Charlie said.

"Yes." Caddy said. "Let me go." Charlie went away. "Hush." Caddy said. "He's gone." I hushed. I could hear her and feel her chest going.

"I'll have to take him to the house." she said. She took my hand. "I'm coming." she whispered.

"Wait." Charlie said. "Call the nigger."

"No." Caddy said. "I'll come back. Come on, Benjy."

"Caddy." Charlie whispered, loud. We went on. "You better come back. Are you coming back." Caddy and I were running. "Caddy." Charlie said. We ran out into the moonlight, toward the kitchen.

"Caddy." Charlie said.

Caddy and I ran. We ran up the kitchen steps, onto the porch, and Caddy knelt down in the dark and held me. I could hear her and feel her chest. "I wont." she said. "I wont anymore, ever. Benjy. Benjy." Then she was crying, and I cried, and we held each other. "Hush." she said. "Hush. I wont anymore." So I hushed and Caddy got up and we went into the kitchen and turned the light on and Caddy took the kitchen soap and washed her mouth at the sink, hard. Caddy smelled like trees.

I kept a telling you to stay away from there, Luster said. They sat up in the swing, quick. Quentin had her hands on her hair. He had a red tie.

You old crazy loon, Quentin said. I'm going to tell Dilsey about the way you let him follow everywhere I go. I'm going to make her whip you good.

"I couldn't stop him." Luster said. "Come on here, Benjy."

"Yes you could." Quentin said. "You didn't try. You were both snooping around after me. Did Grandmother send you all out here to spy on me." She jumped out of the swing. "If you dont take him right away this minute and keep him away, I'm going to make Jason whip you."

"I cant do nothing with him." Luster said. "You try it if you think you can."

"Shut your mouth." Quentin said. "Are you going to get him away."

"Ah, let him stay." he said. He had a red tie. The sun was red on it. "Look here, Jack." He struck a match and put it in his mouth. Then he took the match out of his mouth. It was still burning. "Want to try it." he said. I went over there. "Open your mouth." he said. I opened my mouth. Quentin hit the match with her hand and it went away.

"Goddam you." Quentin said. "Do you want to get him started. Dont you know he'll beller all day. I'm going to tell Dilsey on you." She went away running.

"Here, kid." he said. "Hey. Come on back. I aint going to fool with him."

Quentin ran on to the house. She went around the kitchen.

"You played hell then, Jack." he said. "Aint you."

"He cant tell what you saying." Luster said. "He deef and dumb."

"Is." he said. "How long's he been that way."

"Been that way thirty three years today." Luster said. "Born looney. Is you one of them show folks."

"Why." he said.

"I dont ricklick seeing you around here before." Luster said.

"Well, what about it." he said.

"Nothing." Luster said. "I going tonight."

He looked at me.

"You aint the one can play a tune on that saw, is you." Luster said.

"It'll cost you a quarter to find that out." he said. He looked at me. "Why dont they lock him up." he said. "What'd you bring him out here for."

"You aint talking to me." Luster said. "I cant do nothing with him. I just come over here looking for a quarter I lost so I can go to the show tonight. Look like now I aint going to get to go." Luster looked on the ground. "You aint got no extra quarter, is you." Luster said.

"No." he said. "I aint."

"I reckon I just have to find that other one, then." Luster said. He put his hand in his pocket. "You dont want to buy no golf ball neither, does you." Luster said.

"What kind of ball." he said.

"Golf ball." Luster said. "I dont want but a quarter."

"What for." he said. "What do I want with it."

"I didn't think you did." Luster said. "Come on here, mulehead." he said. "Come on here and watch them knocking that ball. Here. Here something you can play with along with that jimson weed." Luster picked it up and gave it to me. It was bright.

"Where'd you get that." he said. His tie was red in the sun, walking.

"Found it under this here bush." Luster said. "I thought for a minute it was that quarter I lost."

He came and took it.

"Hush." Luster said. "He going to give it back when he done looking at it."

"Agnes Mabel Becky."[8] he said. He looked toward the house.

"Hush." Luster said. "He fixing to give it back."

He gave it to me and I hushed.

"Who come to see her last night." he said.

"I dont know." Luster said. "They comes every night she can climb down that tree. I dont keep no track of them."

8. The most popular contraceptive early this century was a condom called the Merry Widow, which was sold in circular metal boxes, three to a box. The top label read "Three Merry Widows Agnes Mabel Becky."

"Damn if one of them didn't leave a track." he said. He looked at the house. Then he went and lay down in the swing. "Go away." he said. "Dont bother me."

"Come on here." Luster said. "You done played hell now. Time Miss Quentin get done telling on you."

We went to the fence and looked through the curling flower spaces. Luster hunted in the grass.

"I had it right here." he said. I saw the flag flapping, and the sun slanting on the broad grass.

"They'll be some along soon." Luster said. "There some now, but they going away. Come on and help me look for it."

We went along the fence.

"Hush." Luster said. "How can I make them come over here, if they aint coming. Wait. They'll be some in a minute. Look yonder. Here they come."

I went along the fence, to the gate, where the girls passed with their booksatchels. "You, Benjy." Luster said. "Come back here."

You cant do no good looking through the gate, T. P. said. Miss Caddy done gone long ways away. Done got married and left you. You cant do no good, holding to the gate and crying. She cant hear you.

What is it he wants, T. P. Mother said. Cant you play with him and keep him quiet.

He want to go down yonder and look through the gate, T. P. said.

Well, he cannot do it, Mother said. It's raining. You will just have to play with him and keep him quiet. You, Benjamin.

Aint nothing going to quiet him, T. P. said. He think if he down to the gate, Miss Caddy come back.

Nonsense, Mother said.

I could hear them talking. I went out the door and I couldn't hear them, and I went down to the gate, where the girls passed with their booksatchels. They looked at me, walking fast, with their heads turned. I tried to say, but they went on, and I went along the fence, trying to say, and they went faster. Then they were running and I came to the corner of the fence and I couldn't go any further, and I held to the fence, looking after them and trying to say.

"You, Benjy." T. P. said. "What you doing, slipping out. Dont you know Dilsey whip you."

"You cant do no good, moaning and slobbering through the fence." T. P. said. "You done skeered them chillen. Look at them, walking on the other side of the street."

How did he get out, Father said. Did you leave the gate unlatched when you came in, Jason.

Of course not, Jason said. Dont you know I've got better sense than to do that. Do you think I wanted anything like this to happen. This family is bad enough, God knows. I could have told you, all the time. I reckon you'll send him to Jackson, now. If Mr Burgess dont shoot him first.

Hush, Father said.

I could have told you, all the time, Jason said.

It was open when I touched it, and I held to it in the twilight. I wasn't crying, and I tried to stop, watching the girls coming along in the twilight. I wasn't crying.

"There he is."

They stopped.

"He cant get out. He wont hurt anybody, anyway. Come on."

"I'm scared to. I'm scared. I'm going to cross the street."

"He cant get out."

I wasn't crying.

"Dont be a fraid cat. Come on."

They came on in the twilight. I wasn't crying, and I held to the gate. They came slow.

"I'm scared."

"He wont hurt you. I pass here every day. He just runs along the fence."

They came on. I opened the gate and they stopped, turning. I was trying to say, and I caught her, trying to say, and she screamed and I was trying to say and trying and the bright shapes began to stop and I tried to get out. I tried to get it off of my face, but the bright shapes were going again. They were going up the hill to where it fell away and I tried to cry. But when I breathed in, I couldn't breathe out again to cry, and I tried to keep from falling off the hill and I fell off the hill into the bright, whirling shapes.

Here, looney, Luster said. Here come some. Hush your slobbering and moaning, now.

They came to the flag. He took it out and they hit, then he put the flag back.

"Mister." Luster said.

He looked around. "What." he said.

"Want to buy a golf ball." Luster said.

"Let's see it." he said. He came to the fence and Luster reached the ball through.

"Where'd you get it." he said.

"Found it." Luster said.

"I know that." he said. "Where. In somebody's golf bag."

"I found it laying over here in the yard." Luster said. "I'll take a quarter for it."

"What makes you think it's yours." he said.

"I found it." Luster said.

"Then find yourself another one." he said. He put it in his pocket and went away.

"I got to go to that show tonight." Luster said.

"That so." he said. He went to the table. "Fore caddie." he said. He hit.

"I'll declare." Luster said. "You fusses when you dont see them and you fusses when you does. Why cant you hush. Dont you reckon folks gets tired of listening to you all the time. Here. You dropped your jimson weed." He picked it up and gave it back to me. "You needs a new one. You bout wore that one out." We stood at the fence and watched them.

"That white man hard to get along with." Luster said. "You see him take my ball." They went on. We went on along the fence. We came to the garden and we couldn't go any further. I held to the fence and looked through the flower spaces. They went away.

"Now you aint got nothing to moan about." Luster said. "Hush up. I the one got something to moan over, you aint. Here. Whyn't you hold on to that weed. You be bellering about it next." He gave me the flower. "Where you heading now."

Our shadows were on the grass. They got to the trees before we did. Mine got there first. Then we got there, and then the shadows were gone. There was a flower in the bottle. I put the other flower in it.

"Aint you a grown man, now." Luster said. "Playing with two weeds in a bottle. You know what they going to do with you when Miss Cahline die. They going to send you to Jackson, where you belong. Mr Jason say so. Where you can hold the bars all day long with the rest of the looneys and slobber. How you like that."

Luster knocked the flowers over with his hand. "That's what they'll do to you at Jackson when you starts bellering."

I tried to pick up the flowers. Luster picked them up, and they went away. I began to cry.

"Beller." Luster said. "Beller. You want something to beller about. All right, then. Caddy." he whispered. "Caddy. Beller now. Caddy."

"Luster." Dilsey said from the kitchen.

The flowers came back.

"Hush." Luster said. "Here they is. Look. It's fixed back just like it was at first. Hush, now."

"You, Luster." Dilsey said.

"Yessum." Luster said. "We coming. You done played hell. Get up." He jerked my arm and I got up. We went out of the trees. Our shadows were gone.

"Hush." Luster said. "Look at all them folks watching you. Hush."

"You bring him on here." Dilsey said. She came down the steps. "What you done to him now." she said.

"Aint done nothing to him." Luster said. "He just started bellering."

"Yes you is." Dilsey said. "You done something to him. Where you been."

"Over yonder under them cedars." Luster said.

"Getting Quentin all riled up." Dilsey said. "Why cant you keep him away from her. Dont you know she dont like him where she at."

"Got as much time for him as I is." Luster said. "He aint none of my uncle."

"Dont you sass me, nigger boy." Dilsey said.

"I aint done nothing to him." Luster said. "He was playing there, and all of a sudden he started bellering."

"Is you been projecking with his graveyard." Dilsey said.

"I aint touched his graveyard." Luster said.

"Dont lie to me, boy." Dilsey said. We went up the steps and into the kitchen. Dilsey opened the firedoor and drew a chair up in front of it and I sat down. I hushed.

What you want to get her started for, Dilsey said. Whyn't you keep him out of there.

He was just looking at the fire, Caddy said. Mother was telling him his new name. We didn't mean to get her started.

I knows you didn't, Dilsey said. Him at one end of the house and her at the other. You let my things alone, now. Dont you touch nothing till I get back.

"Aint you shamed of yourself." Dilsey said. "Teasing him." She set the cake on the table.

"I aint been teasing him." Luster said. "He was playing with that bottle full of dogfennel and all of a sudden he started up bellering. You heard him."

"You aint done nothing to his flowers." Dilsey said.

"I aint touched his graveyard." Luster said. "What I want with his truck. I was just hunting for that quarter."

"You lost it, did you." Dilsey said. She lit the candles on the cake. Some of them were little ones. Some were big ones cut into little pieces. "I told you to go put it away. Now I reckon you want me to get you another one from Frony."

"I got to go to that show, Benjy or no Benjy." Luster said. "I aint going to follow him around day and night both."

"You going to do just what he want you to, nigger boy." Dilsey said. "You hear me."

"Aint I always done it." Luster said. "Dont I always does what he wants. Dont I, Benjy."

"Then you keep it up." Dilsey said. "Bringing him in here, bawling and getting her started too. You all go ahead and eat this cake, now, before Jason come. I dont want him jumping on me about a cake I bought with my own money. Me baking a cake here, with him counting every egg that comes into this kitchen. See can you let him alone now, less you dont want to go to that show tonight."

Dilsey went away.

"You cant blow out no candles." Luster said. "Watch me blow them out." He leaned down and puffed his face. The candles went away. I began to cry. "Hush." Luster said. "Here. Look at the fire whiles I cuts this cake."

I could hear the clock, and I could hear Caddy standing behind me, and I could hear the roof. It's still raining, Caddy said. I hate rain. I hate everything. And then her head came into my lap and she was crying, holding me, and I began to cry. Then I looked at the fire again and the bright, smooth shapes went again. I could hear the clock and the roof and Caddy.

I ate some cake. Luster's hand came and took another piece. I could hear him eating. I looked at the fire.

A long piece of wire came across my shoulder. It went to the door, and then the fire went away. I began to cry.

"What you howling for now." Luster said. "Look there." The fire was there. I hushed. "Cant you set and look at the fire and be quiet like mammy told you." Luster said. "You ought to be ashamed of yourself. Here. Here's you some more cake."

"What you done to him now." Dilsey said. "Cant you never let him alone."

"I was just trying to get him to hush up and not sturb Miss Cahline." Luster said. "Something got him started again."

"And I know what that something name." Dilsey said. "I'm going to get Versh to take a stick to you when he comes home. You just trying yourself. You been doing it all day. Did you take him down to the branch."

"Nome." Luster said. "We been right here in this yard all day, like you said."

His hand came for another piece of cake. Dilsey hit his hand. "Reach it again, and I chop it right off with this here butcher knife." Dilsey said. "I bet he aint had one piece of it."

"Yes he is." Luster said. "He already had twice as much as me. Ask him if he aint."

"Reach hit one more time." Dilsey said. "Just reach it."

That's right, Dilsey said. I reckon it'll be my time to cry next. Reckon Maury going to let me cry on him a while, too.

His name's Benjy now, Caddy said.

How come it is, Dilsey said. He aint wore out the name he was born with yet, is he.

Benjamin came out of the bible, Caddy said. It's a better name for him than Maury was.

How come it is, Dilsey said.

Mother says it is, Caddy said.

Huh, Dilsey said. Name aint going to help him. Hurt him, neither. Folks dont have no luck, changing names. My name been Dilsey since fore I could remember and it be Dilsey when they's long forgot me.

*How will they know it's Dilsey, when it's long forgot, Dilsey, Caddy
said.*

It'll be in the Book, honey, Dilsey said. Writ out.[9]

Can you read it, Caddy said.

*Wont have to, Dilsey said. They'll read it for me. All I got to do is say
Ise here.*

The long wire came across my shoulder, and the fire went away. I
began to cry.

Dilsey and Luster fought.

"I seen you." Dilsey said. "Oho, I seen you." She dragged Luster out
of the corner, shaking him. "Wasn't nothing bothering him, was they.
You just wait till your pappy come home. I wish I was young like I use
to be, I'd tear them years right off your head. I good mind to lock you
up in that cellar and not let you go to that show tonight, I sho is."

"Ow, mammy." Luster said. "Ow, mammy."

I put my hand out to where the fire had been.

"Catch him." Dilsey said. "Catch him back."

My hand jerked back and I put it in my mouth and Dilsey caught me.
I could still hear the clock between my voice. Dilsey reached back and
hit Luster on the head. My voice was going loud every time.

"Get that soda." Dilsey said. She took my hand out of my mouth. My
voice went louder then and my hand tried to go back to my mouth, but
Dilsey held it. My voice went loud. She sprinkled soda on my hand.

"Look in the pantry and tear a piece off of that rag hanging on the
nail." she said. "Hush, now. You dont want to make your maw sick
again, does you. Here, look at the fire. Dilsey make your hand stop
hurting in just a minute. Look at the fire." She opened the fire door. I
looked at the fire, but my hand didn't stop and I didn't stop. My hand
was trying to go to my mouth, but Dilsey held it.

She wrapped the cloth around it. Mother said,

"What is it now. Cant I even be sick in peace. Do I have to get up
out of bed to come down to him, with two grown negroes to take care of
him."

"He all right now." Dilsey said. "He going to quit. He just burnt his
hand a little."

"With two grown negroes, you must bring him into the house, bawling." Mother said. "You got him started on purpose, because you know
I'm sick." She came and stood by me. "Hush." she said. "Right this
minute. Did you give him this cake."

"I bought it." Dilsey said. "It never come out of Jason's pantry. I fixed
him some birthday."

"Do you want to poison him with that cheap store cake." Mother said.

"Is that what you are trying to do. Am I never to have one minute's peace."

"You go on back up stairs and lay down." Dilsey said. "It'll quit smarting him in a minute now, and he'll hush. Come on, now."

"And leave him down here for you all to do something else to." Mother said. "How can I lie there, with him bawling down here. Benjamin. Hush this minute."

"They aint nowhere else to take him." Dilsey said. "We aint got the room we use to have. He cant stay out in the yard, crying where all the neighbors can see him."

"I know, I know." Mother said. "It's all my fault. I'll be gone soon, and you and Jason will both get along better." She began to cry.

"You hush that, now." Dilsey said. "You'll get yourself down again. You come on back up stairs. Luster going to take him to the liberry and play with him till I get his supper done."

Dilsey and Mother went out.

"Hush up." Luster said. "You hush up. You want me to burn your other hand for you. You aint hurt. Hush up."

"Here." Dilsey said. "Stop crying, now." She gave me the slipper, and I hushed. "Take him to the liberry." she said. "And if I hear him again, I going to whip you myself."

We went to the library. Luster turned on the light. The windows went black, and the dark tall place on the wall came and I went and touched it. It was like a door, only it wasn't a door.

The fire came behind me and I went to the fire and sat on the floor, holding the slipper. The fire went higher. It went onto the cushion in Mother's chair.

"Hush up." Luster said. "Cant you never get done for a while. Here I done built you a fire, and you wont even look at it."

Your name is Benjy, Caddy said. Do you hear. Benjy. Benjy.

Dont tell him that, Mother said. Bring him here.

Caddy lifted me under the arms.

Get up, Mau—— I mean Benjy, she said.

Dont try to carry him, Mother said. Cant you lead him over here. Is that too much for you to think of.

I can carry him, Caddy said. "Let me carry him up, Dilsey."

"Go on, Minute." Dilsey said. "You aint big enough to tote a flea. You go on and be quiet, like Mr Jason said."

There was a light at the top of the stairs. Father was there, in his shirt sleeves. The way he looked said Hush. Caddy whispered,

"Is Mother sick."

Versh set me down and we went into Mother's room. There was a fire. It was rising and falling on the walls. There was another fire in the mirror. I could smell the sickness. It was on a cloth folded on Mother's head.

Her hair was on the pillow. The fire didn't reach it, but it shone on her hand, where her rings were jumping.

"Come and tell Mother goodnight." Caddy said. We went to the bed. The fire went out of the mirror. Father got up from the bed and lifted me up and Mother put her hand on my head.

"What time is it." Mother said. Her eyes were closed.

"Ten minutes to seven." Father said.

"It's too early for him to go to bed." Mother said. "He'll wake up at daybreak, and I simply cannot bear another day like today."

"There, there." Father said. He touched Mother's face.

"I know I'm nothing but a burden to you." Mother said. "But I'll be gone soon. Then you will be rid of my bothering."

"Hush." Father said. "I'll take him downstairs a while." He took me up. "Come on, old fellow. Let's go down stairs a while. We'll have to be quiet while Quentin is studying, now."

Caddy went and leaned her face over the bed and Mother's hand came into the firelight. Her rings jumped on Caddy's back.

Mother's sick, Father said. Dilsey will put you to bed. Where's Quentin.

Versh getting him, Dilsey said.

Father stood and watched us go past. We could hear Mother in her room. Caddy said "Hush." Jason was still climbing the stairs. He had his hands in his pockets.

"You all must be good tonight." Father said. "And be quiet, so you wont disturb Mother."

"We'll be quiet." Caddy said. "You must be quiet now, Jason." she said. We tiptoed.

We could hear the roof. I could see the fire in the mirror too. Caddy lifted me again.

"Come on, now." she said. "Then you can come back to the fire. Hush, now."

"Candace." Mother said.

"Hush, Benjy." Caddy said. "Mother wants you a minute. Like a good boy. Then you can come back. Benjy."

Caddy let me down, and I hushed.

"Let him stay here, Mother. When he's through looking at the fire, then you can tell him."

"Candace." Mother said. Caddy stooped and lifted me. We staggered. "Candace." Mother said.

"Hush." Caddy said. "You can still see it. Hush."

"Bring him here." Mother said. "He's too big for you to carry. You must stop trying. You'll injure your back. All of our women have prided themselves on their carriage. Do you want to look like a washerwoman."

"He's not too heavy." Caddy said. "I can carry him."

"Well, I dont want him carried, then." Mother said. "A five year old child. No, no. Not in my lap. Let him stand up."

"If you'll hold him, he'll stop." Caddy said. "Hush." she said. "You can go right back. Here. Here's your cushion. See."

"Dont, Candace." Mother said.

"Let him look at it and he'll be quiet." Caddy said. "Hold up just a minute while I slip it out. There, Benjy. Look."

I looked at it and hushed.

"You humor him too much." Mother said. "You and your father both. You dont realise that I am the one who has to pay for it. Damuddy spoiled Jason that way and it took him two years to outgrow it, and I am not strong enough to go through the same thing with Benjamin."

"You dont need to bother with him." Caddy said. "I like to take care of him. Dont I. Benjy."

"Candace." Mother said. "I told you not to call him that. It was bad enough when your father insisted on calling you by that silly nickname, and I will not have him called by one. Nicknames are vulgar. Only common people use them. Benjamin." she said.

"Look at me." Mother said.

"Benjamin." she said. She took my face in her hands and turned it to hers.

"Benjamin." she said. "Take that cushion away, Candace."

"He'll cry." Caddy said.

"Take that cushion away, like I told you." Mother said. "He must learn to mind."

The cushion went away.

"Hush, Benjy." Caddy said.

"You go over there and sit down." Mother said. "Benjamin." She held my face to hers.

"Stop that." she said. "Stop it."

But I didn't stop and Mother caught me in her arms and began to cry, and I cried. Then the cushion came back and Caddy held it above Mother's head. She drew Mother back in the chair and Mother lay crying against the red and yellow cushion.

"Hush, Mother." Caddy said. "You go up stairs and lay down, so you can be sick. I'll go get Dilsey." She led me to the fire and I looked at the bright, smooth shapes. I could hear the fire and the roof.

Father took me up. He smelled like rain.

"Well, Benjy." he said. "Have you been a good boy today."

Caddy and Jason were fighting in the mirror.

"You, Caddy." Father said.

They fought. Jason began to cry.

"Caddy." Father said. Jason was crying. He wasn't fighting anymore, but we could see Caddy fighting in the mirror and Father put me down and went into the mirror and fought too. He lifted Caddy up. She fought. Jason lay on the floor, crying. He had the scissors in his hand. Father held Caddy.

"He cut up all Benjy's dolls." Caddy said. "I'll slit his gizzle."

"Candace." Father said.

"I will." Caddy said. "I will." She fought. Father held her. She kicked at Jason. He rolled into the corner, out of the mirror. Father brought Caddy to the fire. They were all out of the mirror. Only the fire was in it. Like the fire was in a door.

"Stop that." Father said. "Do you want to make Mother sick in her room."

Caddy stopped. "He cut up all the dolls Mau——Benjy and I made." Caddy said. "He did it just for meanness."

"I didn't." Jason said. He was sitting up, crying. "I didn't know they were his. I just thought they were some old papers."

"You couldn't help but know." Caddy said. "You did it just   "

"Hush." Father said. "Jason." he said.

"I'll make you some more tomorrow." Caddy said. "We'll make a lot of them. Here, you can look at the cushion, too."

Jason came in.

I kept telling you to hush, Luster said.

What's the matter now, Jason said.

"He just trying hisself." Luster said. "That the way he been going on all day."

"Why dont you let him alone, then." Jason said. "If you cant keep him quiet, you'll have to take him out to the kitchen. The rest of us cant shut ourselves up in a room like Mother does."

"Mammy say keep him out the kitchen till she get supper." Luster said.

"Then play with him and keep him quiet." Jason said. "Do I have to work all day and then come home to a mad house." He opened the paper and read it.

You can look at the fire and the mirror and the cushion too, Caddy said. You wont have to wait until supper to look at the cushion, now. We could hear the roof. We could hear Jason too, crying loud beyond the wall.

Dilsey said, "You come, Jason. You letting him alone, is you."

"Yessum." Luster said.

"Where Quentin." Dilsey said. "Supper near bout ready."

"I dont know'm." Luster said. "I aint seen her."

Dilsey went away. "Quentin." she said in the hall. "Quentin. Supper ready."

We could hear the roof. Quentin smelled like rain, too.

What did Jason do, he said.

He cut up all Benjy's dolls, Caddy said.

Mother said to not call him Benjy, Quentin said. He sat on the rug by us. I wish it wouldn't rain, he said. You cant do anything.

You've been in a fight, Caddy said. Haven't you.

It wasn't much, Quentin said.

You can tell it, Caddy said. Father'll see it.

I dont care, Quentin said. I wish it wouldn't rain.

Quentin said, "Didn't Dilsey say supper was ready."

"Yessum." Luster said. Jason looked at Quentin. Then he read the paper again. Quentin came in. "She say it bout ready." Luster said. Quentin jumped down in Mother's chair. Luster said,

"Mr Jason."

"What." Jason said.

"Let me have two bits." Luster said.

"What for." Jason said.

"To go to the show tonight." Luster said.

"I thought Dilsey was going to get a quarter from Frony for you." Jason said.

"She did." Luster said. "I lost it. Me and Benjy hunted all day for that quarter. You can ask him."

"Then borrow one from him." Jason said. "I have to work for mine." He read the paper. Quentin looked at the fire. The fire was in her eyes and on her mouth. Her mouth was red.

"I tried to keep him away from there." Luster said.

"Shut your mouth." Quentin said. Jason looked at her.

"What did I tell you I was going to do if I saw you with that show fellow again." he said. Quentin looked at the fire. "Did you hear me." Jason said.

"I heard you." Quentin said. "Why dont you do it, then."

"Dont you worry." Jason said.

"I'm not." Quentin said. Jason read the paper again.

I could hear the roof. Father leaned forward and looked at Quentin. Hello, he said. Who won.

"Nobody." Quentin said. "They stopped us. Teachers."

"Who was it." Father said. "Will you tell."

"It was all right." Quentin said. "He was as big as me."

"That's good." Father said. "Can you tell what it was about."

"It wasn't anything." Quentin said. "He said he would put a frog in her desk and she wouldn't dare to whip him."

"Oh." Father said. "She. And then what."

"Yes, sir." Quentin said. "And then I kind of hit him."

We could hear the roof and the fire, and a snuffling outside the door.

"Where was he going to get a frog in November." Father said.

"I dont know, sir." Quentin said.

We could hear them.

"Jason." Father said. We could hear Jason.

"Jason." Father said. "Come in here and stop that."

We could hear the roof and the fire and Jason.

"Stop that, now." Father said. "Do you want me to whip you again." Father lifted Jason up into the chair by him. Jason snuffled. We could hear the fire and the roof. Jason snuffled a little louder.

"One more time." Father said. We could hear the fire and the roof.

Dilsey said, All right. You all can come on to supper.

Versh smelled like rain. He smelled like a dog, too. We could hear the fire and the roof.

We could hear Caddy walking fast. Father and Mother looked at the door. Caddy passed it, walking fast. She didn't look. She walked fast.

"Candace." Mother said. Caddy stopped walking.

"Yes, Mother." she said.

"Hush, Caroline." Father said.

"Come here." Mother said.

"Hush, Caroline." Father said. "Let her alone."

Caddy came to the door and stood there, looking at Father and Mother. Her eyes flew at me, and away. I began to cry. It went loud and I got up. Caddy came in and stood with her back to the wall, looking at me. I went toward her, crying, and she shrank against the wall and I saw her eyes and I cried louder and pulled at her dress. She put her hands out but I pulled at her dress. Her eyes ran.

Versh said, Your name Benjamin now. You know how come your name Benjamin now. They making a bluegum[1] out of you. Mammy say in old time your granpaw changed nigger's name, and he turn preacher, and when they look at him, he bluegum too. Didn't use to be bluegum, neither. And when family woman look him in the eye in the full of the moon, chile born bluegum. And one evening, when they was about a dozen them bluegum chillen running around the place, he never come home. Possum hunters found him in the woods, et clean. And you know who et him. Them bluegum chillen did.

We were in the hall. Caddy was still looking at me. Her hand was against her mouth and I saw her eyes and I cried. We went up the stairs. She stopped again, against the wall, looking at me and I cried and she went on and I came on, crying, and she shrank against the wall, looking at me. She opened the door to her room, but I pulled at her dress and we went to the bathroom and she stood against the door, looking at me. Then she put her arm across her face and I pushed at her, crying.

What are you doing to him, Jason said. Why cant you let him alone.

I aint touching him, Luster said. He been doing this way all day long. He needs whipping.

---

1. A person who has bluish gums and whose bite, according to superstition, is poisonous.

He needs to be sent to Jackson, Quentin said. How can anybody live in a house like this.

If you dont like it, young lady, you'd better get out, Jason said.

I'm going to, Quentin said. Dont you worry.

Versh said, "You move back some, so I can dry my legs off." He shoved me back a little. "Dont you start bellering, now. You can still see it. That's all you have to do. You aint had to be out in the rain like I is. You's born lucky and dont know it." He lay on his back before the fire.

"You know how come your name Benjamin now." Versh said. "Your mamma too proud for you. What mammy say."

"You be still there and let me dry my legs off." Versh said. "Or you know what I'll do. I'll skin your rinktum."

We could hear the fire and the roof and Versh.

Versh got up quick and jerked his legs back. Father said, "All right, Versh."

"I'll feed him tonight." Caddy said. "Sometimes he cries when Versh feeds him."

"Take this tray up." Dilsey said. "And hurry back and feed Benjy."

"Dont you want Caddy to feed you." Caddy said.

Has he got to keep that old dirty slipper on the table, Quentin said. Why dont you feed him in the kitchen. It's like eating with a pig.

If you dont like the way we eat, you'd better not come to the table, Jason said.

Steam came off of Roskus. He was sitting in front of the stove. The oven door was open and Roskus had his feet in it. Steam came off the bowl. Caddy put the spoon into my mouth easy. There was a black spot on the inside of the bowl.

Now, now, Dilsey said. He aint going to bother you no more.

It got down below the mark. Then the bowl was empty. It went away. "He's hungry tonight." Caddy said. The bowl came back. I couldn't see the spot. Then I could. "He's starved, tonight." Caddy said. "Look how much he's eaten."

Yes he will, Quentin said. You all send him out to spy on me. I hate this house. I'm going to run away.

Roskus said, "It going to rain all night."

You've been running a long time, not to've got any further off than mealtime, Jason said.

See if I dont, Quentin said.

"Then I dont know what I going to do." Dilsey said. "It caught me in the hip so bad now I cant scarcely move. Climbing them stairs all evening."

Oh, I wouldn't be surprised, Jason said. I wouldn't be surprised at anything you'd do.

Quentin threw her napkin on the table.

Hush your mouth, Jason, Dilsey said. She went and put her arm around Quentin. Sit down, honey, Dilsey said. He ought to be shamed of hisself, throwing what aint your fault up to you.

"She sulling again, is she." Roskus said.

"Hush your mouth." Dilsey said.

Quentin pushed Dilsey away. She looked at Jason. Her mouth was red. She picked up her glass of water and swung her arm back, looking at Jason. Dilsey caught her arm. They fought. The glass broke on the table, and the water ran into the table. Quentin was running.

"Mother's sick again." Caddy said.

"Sho she is." Dilsey said. "Weather like this make anybody sick. When you going to get done eating, boy."

Goddam you, Quentin said. Goddam you. We could hear her running on the stairs. We went to the library.

Caddy gave me the cushion, and I could look at the cushion and the mirror and the fire.

"We must be quiet while Quentin's studying." Father said. "What are you doing, Jason."

"Nothing." Jason said.

"Suppose you come over here to do it, then." Father said.

Jason came out of the corner.

"What are you chewing." Father said.

"Nothing." Jason said.

"He's chewing paper again." Caddy said.

"Come here, Jason." Father said.

Jason threw into the fire. It hissed, uncurled, turning black. Then it was gray. Then it was gone. Caddy and Father and Jason were in Mother's chair. Jason's eyes were puffed shut and his mouth moved, like tasting. Caddy's head was on Father's shoulder. Her hair was like fire, and little points of fire were in her eyes, and I went and Father lifted me into the chair too, and Caddy held me. She smelled like trees.

She smelled like trees. In the corner it was dark, but I could see the window. I squatted there, holding the slipper. I couldn't see it, but my hands saw it, and I could hear it getting night, and my hands saw the slipper but I couldn't see myself, but my hands could see the slipper, and I squatted there, hearing it getting dark.

Here you is, Luster said. Look what I got. He showed it to me. You know where I got it. Miss Quentin give it to me. I knowed they couldn't keep me out. What you doing, off in here. I thought you done slipped back out doors. Aint you done enough moaning and slobbering today, without hiding off in this here empty room, mumbling and taking on. Come on here to bed, so I can get up there before it starts. I cant fool with you all night tonight. Just let them horns toot the first toot and I done gone.

We didn't go to our room.

"This is where we have the measles." Caddy said. "Why do we have to sleep in here tonight."

"What you care where you sleep." Dilsey said. She shut the door and sat down and began to undress me. Jason began to cry. "Hush." Dilsey said.

"I want to sleep with Damuddy." Jason said.

"She's sick." Caddy said. "You can sleep with her when she gets well. Cant he, Dilsey."

"Hush, now." Dilsey said. Jason hushed.

"Our nighties are here, and everything." Caddy said. "It's like moving."

"And you better get into them." Dilsey said. "You be unbuttoning Jason."

Caddy unbuttoned Jason. He began to cry.

"You want to get whipped." Dilsey said. Jason hushed.

Quentin, Mother said in the hall.

What, Quentin said beyond the wall. We heard Mother lock the door. She looked in our door and came in and stooped over the bed and kissed me on the forehead.

When you get him to bed, go and ask Dilsey if she objects to my having a hot water bottle, Mother said. Tell her that if she does, I'll try to get along without it. Tell her I just want to know.

Yessum, Luster said. Come on. Get your pants off.

Quentin and Versh came in. Quentin had his face turned away. "What are you crying for." Caddy said.

"Hush." Dilsey said. "You all get undressed, now. You can go on home, Versh."

I got undressed and I looked at myself, and I began to cry. Hush, Luster said. Looking for them aint going to do no good. They're gone. You keep on like this, and we aint going have you no more birthday. He put my gown on. I hushed, and then Luster stopped, his head toward the window. Then he went to the window and looked out. He came back and took my arm. Here she come, he said. Be quiet, now. We went to the window and looked out. It came out of Quentin's window and climbed across into the tree. We watched the tree shaking. The shaking went down the tree, then it came out and we watched it go away across the grass. Then we couldn't see it. Come on, Luster said. There now. Hear them horns. You get in that bed while my foots behaves.

There were two beds. Quentin got in the other one. He turned his face to the wall. Dilsey put Jason in with him. Caddy took her dress off.

"Just look at your drawers." Dilsey said. "You better be glad your maw aint seen you."

"I already told on her." Jason said.

"I bound you would." Dilsey said.

"And see what you got by it." Caddy said. "Tattletale."

"What did I get by it." Jason said.

"Whyn't you get your nightie on." Dilsey said. She went and helped Caddy take off her bodice and drawers. "Just look at you." Dilsey said. She wadded the drawers and scrubbed Caddy behind with them. "It done soaked clean through onto you." she said. "But you wont get no bath this night. Here." She put Caddy's nightie on her and Caddy climbed into the bed and Dilsey went to the door and stood with her hand on the light. "You all be quiet now, you hear." she said.

"All right." Caddy said. "Mother's not coming in tonight." she said. "So we still have to mind me."

"Yes." Dilsey said. "Go to sleep, now."

"Mother's sick." Caddy said. "She and Damuddy are both sick."

"Hush." Dilsey said. "You go to sleep."

The room went black, except the door. Then the door went black. Caddy said, "Hush, Maury" putting her hand on me. So I stayed hushed. We could hear us. We could hear the dark.

It went away, and Father looked at us. He looked at Quentin and Jason, then he came and kissed Caddy and put his hand on my head.

"Is Mother very sick." Caddy said.

"No." Father said. "Are you going to take good care of Maury."

"Yes." Caddy said.

Father went to the door and looked at us again. Then the dark came back, and he stood black in the door, and then the door turned black again. Caddy held me and I could hear us all, and the darkness, and something I could smell. And then I could see the windows, where the trees were buzzing. Then the dark began to go in smooth, bright shapes, like it always does, even when Caddy says that I have been asleep.

June Second, 1910.

When the shadow of the sash appeared on the curtains it was between seven and eight oclock and then I was in time again, hearing the watch. It was Grandfather's and when Father gave it to me he said I give you the mausoleum of all hope and desire; it's rather excruciating-ly[1] apt that you will use it to gain the reducto absurdum[2] of all human experience which can fit your individual needs no better than it fitted his or his father's. I give it to you not that you may remember time, but that you might forget it now and then for a moment and not spend all your breath trying to conquer it. Because no battle is ever won he said. They are not even fought. The field only reveals to man his own folly and despair, and victory is an illusion of philosophers and fools.

1. Faulkner uses the unusual hyphen to suggest a particular pronunciation, stressing the "ly."
2. A corruption of the Latin phrase *reductio ad absurdum*.

It was propped against the collar box and I lay listening to it. Hearing it, that is. I dont suppose anybody ever deliberately listens to a watch or a clock. You dont have to. You can be oblivious to the sound for a long while, then in a second of ticking it can create in the mind unbroken the long diminishing parade of time you didn't hear. Like Father said down the long and lonely light-rays you might see Jesus walking, like. And the good Saint Francis that said Little Sister Death, that never had a sister.[3]

Through the wall I heard Shreve's bed-springs and then his slippers on the floor hishing. I got up and went to the dresser and slid my hand along it and touched the watch and turned it face-down and went back to bed. But the shadow of the sash was still there and I had learned to tell almost to the minute, so I'd have to turn my back to it, feeling the eyes animals used to have in the back of their heads when it was on top, itching. It's always the idle habits you acquire which you will regret. Father said that. That Christ was not crucified: he was worn away by a minute clicking of little wheels. That had no sister.

And so as soon as I knew I couldn't see it, I began to wonder what time it was. Father said that constant speculation regarding the position of mechanical hands on an arbitrary dial which is a symptom of mind-function. Excrement Father said like sweating. And I saying All right. Wonder. Go on and wonder.

If it had been cloudy I could have looked at the window, thinking what he said about idle habits. Thinking it would be nice for them down at New London[4] if the weather held up like this. Why shouldn't it? The month of brides, the voice that breathed[5] *She ran right out of the mirror, out of the banked scent. Roses. Roses. Mr and Mrs Jason Richmond Compson announce the marriage of.* Roses. Not virgins like dogwood, milkweed. I said I have committed incest, Father I said. Roses. Cunning and serene. If you attend Harvard one year, but dont see the boat-race, there should be a refund. Let Jason have it. Give Jason a year at Harvard.

Shreve stood in the door, putting his collar on, his glasses glinting rosily, as though he had washed them with his face. "You taking a cut this morning?"

"Is it that late?"

He looked at his watch. "Bell in two minutes."

"I didn't know it was that late." He was still looking at the watch, his mouth shaping. "I'll have to hustle. I cant stand another cut. The dean told me last week——" He put the watch back into his pocket. Then I quit talking.

3. As he was dying, Saint Francis of Assisi is reputed to have said, "Welcome my sister death."
4. Town in Connecticut where the annual Harvard-Yale boat-race is held.
5. Later Quentin completes this phrase, "The voice that breathed o'er Eden." See the first line of "Holy Matrimony," a poem by John Keble. See also Genesis 3.8.

"You'd better slip on your pants and run," he said. He went out.

I got up and moved about, listening to him through the wall. He entered the sitting-room, toward the door.

"Aren't you ready yet?"

"Not yet. Run along. I'll make it."

He went out. The door closed. His feet went down the corridor. Then I could hear the watch again. I quit moving around and went to the window and drew the curtains aside and watched them running for chapel, the same ones fighting the same heaving coat-sleeves, the same books and flapping collars flushing past like debris on a flood, and Spoade. Calling Shreve my husband. Ah let him alone, Shreve said, if he's got better sense than to chase after the little dirty sluts, whose business. In the South you are ashamed of being a virgin. Boys. Men. They lie about it. Because it means less to women, Father said. He said it was men invented virginity not women. Father said it's like death: only a state in which the others are left and I said, But to believe it doesn't matter and he said, That's what's so sad about anything: not only virginity and I said, Why couldn't it have been me and not her who is unvirgin and he said, That's why that's sad too; nothing is even worth the changing of it, and Shreve said if he's got better sense than to chase after the little dirty sluts and I said Did you ever have a sister? Did you? Did you?

Spoade was in the middle of them like a terrapin in a street full of scuttering dead leaves, his collar about his ears, moving at his customary unhurried walk. He was from South Carolina, a senior. It was his club's boast that he never ran for chapel and had never got there on time and had never been absent in four years and had never made either chapel or first lecture with a shirt on his back and socks on his feet. About ten oclock he'd come in Thompson's, get two cups of coffee, sit down and take his socks out of his pocket and remove his shoes and put them on while the coffee cooled. About noon you'd see him with a shirt and collar on, like anybody else. The others passed him running, but he never increased his pace at all. After a while the quad was empty.

A sparrow slanted across the sunlight, onto the window ledge, and cocked his head at me. His eye was round and bright. First he'd watch me with one eye, then flick! and it would be the other one, his throat pumping faster than any pulse. The hour began to strike. The sparrow quit swapping eyes and watched me steadily with the same one until the chimes ceased, as if he were listening too. Then he flicked off the ledge and was gone.

It was a while before the last stroke ceased vibrating. It stayed in the air, more felt than heard, for a long time. Like all the bells that ever rang still ringing in the long dying light-rays and Jesus and Saint Francis talking about his sister. Because if it were just to hell; if that were all of it. Finished. If things just finished themselves. Nobody else there but her and me. If we could just have done something so dreadful that they would have fled hell except us. *I have committed incest I said Father it was I it was not Dalton Ames*   And when he put Dalton Ames. Dalton Ames. Dalton Ames. When he put the pistol in my hand I didn't. That's why I didn't. He would be there and she would and I would. Dalton Ames. Dalton Ames. Dalton Ames. If we could have just done something so dreadful and Father said That's sad too people cannot do anything that dreadful they cannot do anything very dreadful at all they cannot even remember tomorrow what seemed dreadful today and I said, You can shirk all things and he said, Ah can you. And I will look down and see my murmuring bones and the deep water like wind, like a roof of wind, and after a long time they cannot distinguish even bones upon the lonely and inviolate sand. Until on the Day when He says Rise[6] only the flat-iron would come floating up. It's not when you realise that nothing can help you — religion, pride, anything — it's when you realise that you dont need any aid. Dalton Ames. Dalton Ames. Dalton Ames. If I could have been his mother lying with open body lifted laughing, holding his father with my hand refraining, seeing, watching him die before he lived. *One minute she was standing in the door*

I went to the dresser and took up the watch, with the face still down. I tapped the crystal on the corner of the dresser and caught the fragments of glass in my hand and put them into the ashtray and twisted the hands off and put them in the tray. The watch ticked on. I turned the face up, the blank dial with little wheels clicking and clicking behind it, not knowing any better. Jesus walking on Galilee and Washington not telling lies. Father brought back a watch-charm from the Saint Louis Fair[7] to Jason: a tiny opera glass into which you squinted with one eye and saw a skyscraper, a ferris wheel all spidery, Niagara Falls on a pinhead. There was a red smear on the dial. When I saw it my thumb began to smart. I put the watch down and went into Shreve's room and got the iodine and painted the cut. I cleaned the rest of the glass out of the rim with a towel.

I laid out two suits of underwear, with socks, shirts, collars and ties, and packed my trunk. I put in everything except my new suit and an old one and two pairs of shoes and two hats, and my books. I carried the books into the sitting-room and stacked them on the table, the ones I had brought from home and the ones   *Father said it used to be a gentleman was known by his books; nowadays he is known by the ones he has not returned*   and locked the trunk and addressed it. The quarter hour sounded. I stopped and listened to it until the chimes ceased.

I bathed and shaved. The water made my finger smart a little, so I painted it again. I put on my new suit and put my watch on and packed the other suit and the accessories and my razor and brushes in my hand

6. See Revelation 20.13.
7. Louisiana Purchase Exposition, 1904, held to celebrate the centennial of the Louisiana Purchase. This fair did much to popularize the automobile.

bag, and folded the trunk key into a sheet of paper and put it in an envelope and addressed it to Father, and wrote the two notes and sealed them.

The shadow hadn't quite cleared the stoop. I stopped inside the door, watching the shadow move. It moved almost perceptibly, creeping back inside the door, driving the shadow back into the door. *Only she was running already when I heard it. In the mirror she was running before I knew what it was. That quick her train caught up over her arm she ran out of the mirror like a cloud, her veil swirling in long glints her heels brittle and fast clutching her dress onto her shoulder with the other hand, running out of the mirror the smells roses roses the voice that breathed o'er Eden. Then she was across the porch I couldn't hear her heels then in the moonlight like a cloud, the floating shadow of the veil running across the grass, into the bellowing. She ran out of her dress, clutching her bridal, running into the bellowing where T. P. in the dew Whooey Sassprilluh Benjy under the box bellowing. Father had a V-shaped silver cuirass on his running chest*

Shreve said, 'Well, you didn't. . . . Is it a wedding or a wake?"

"I couldn't make it," I said.

"Not with all that primping. What's the matter? You think this was Sunday?'

"I reckon the police wont get me for wearing my new suit one time," I said.

"I was thinking about the Square students. They'll think you go to Harvard. Have you got too proud to attend classes too?"

"I'm going to eat first." The shadow on the stoop was gone. I stepped into sunlight, finding my shadow again. I walked down the steps just ahead of it. The half hour went. Then the chimes ceased and died away.

Deacon wasn't at the postoffice either. I stamped the two envelopes and mailed the one to Father and put Shreve's in my inside pocket, and then I remembered where I had last seen the Deacon. It was on Decoration Day, in a G.A.R.[8] uniform, in the middle of the parade. If you waited long enough on any corner you would see him in whatever parade came along. The one before was on Columbus' or Garibaldi's[9] or somebody's birthday. He was in the Street Sweepers' section,[1] in a stovepipe hat, carrying a two inch Italian flag, smoking a cigar among the brooms and scoops. But the last time was the G.A.R. one, because Shreve said:

"There now. Just look at what your grandpa did to that poor old nigger."

8. Grand Army of the Republic, a veterans organization formed at the end of the Civil War. *Decoration Day*: a day set apart for decorating the graves of soldiers who died in the Civil War; formal celebration began May 30, 1868, as Memorial Day.
9. Giuseppe Garibaldi (1807–1882) was a freedom fighter, general, and nationalist leader in Italy.
1. The section of the parade where street sweepers walked to sweep up after the horses.

"Yes," I said. "Now he can spend day after day marching in parades. If it hadn't been for my grandfather, he'd have to work like whitefolks."

I didn't see him anywhere. But I never knew even a working nigger that you could find when you wanted him, let alone one that lived off the fat of the land. A car came along. I went over to town and went to Parker's and had a good breakfast. While I was eating I heard a clock strike the hour. But then I suppose it takes at least one hour to lose time in, who has been longer than history getting into the mechanical progression of it.

When I finished breakfast I bought a cigar. The girl said a fifty cent one was the best, so I took one and lit it and went out to the street. I stood there and took a couple of puffs, then I held it in my hand and went on toward the corner. I passed a jeweller's window, but I looked away in time. At the corner two bootblacks caught me, one on either side, shrill and raucous, like blackbirds. I gave the cigar to one of them, and the other one a nickel. Then they let me alone. The one with the cigar was trying to sell it to the other for the nickel.

There was a clock, high up in the sun, and I thought about how, when you dont want to do a thing, your body will try to trick you into doing it, sort of unawares. I could feel the muscles in the back of my neck, and then I could hear my watch ticking away in my pocket and after a while I had all the other sounds shut away, leaving only the watch in my pocket. I turned back up the street, to the window. He was working at the table behind the window. He was going bald. There was a glass in his eye — a metal tube screwed into his face. I went in.

The place was full of ticking, like crickets in September grass, and I could hear a big clock on the wall above his head. He looked up, his eye big and blurred and rushing beyond the glass. I took mine out and handed it to him.

"I broke my watch."

He flipped it over in his hand. "I should say you have. You must have stepped on it."

"Yes, sir. I knocked it off the dresser and stepped on it in the dark. It's still running though."

He pried the back open and squinted into it. "Seems to be all right. I cant tell until I go over it, though. I'll go into it this afternoon."

"I'll bring it back later," I said. "Would you mind telling me if any of those watches in the window are right?"

He held my watch on his palm and looked up at me with his blurred rushing eye.

"I made a bet with a fellow," I said. "And I forgot my glasses this morning."

"Why, all right," he said. He laid the watch down and half rose on his stool and looked over the barrier. Then he glanced up at the wall. "It's twen——"

"Dont tell me," I said, "please sir. Just tell me if any of them are right."

He looked at me again. He sat back on the stool and pushed the glass up onto his forehead. It left a red circle around his eye and when it was gone his whole face looked naked. "What're you celebrating today?" he said. "That boat race aint until next week, is it?"

"No, sir. This is just a private celebration. Birthday. Are any of them right?"

"No. But they haven't been regulated and set yet. If you're thinking of buying one of them———"

"No, sir. I dont need a watch. We have a clock in our sitting room. I'll have this one fixed when I do." I reached my hand.

"Better leave it now."

"I'll bring it back later." He gave me the watch. I put it in my pocket. I couldn't hear it now, above all the others. "I'm much obliged to you. I hope I haven't taken up your time."

"That's all right. Bring it in when you are ready. And you better put off this celebration until after we win that boat race."

"Yes, sir. I reckon I had."

I went out, shutting the door upon the ticking. I looked back into the window. He was watching me across the barrier. There were about a dozen watches in the window, a dozen different hours and each with the same assertive and contradictory assurance that mine had, without any hands at all. Contradicting one another. I could hear mine, ticking away inside my pocket, even though nobody could see it, even though it could tell nothing if anyone could.

And so I told myself to take that one. Because Father said clocks slay time. He said time is dead as long as it is being clicked off by little wheels; only when the clock stops does time come to life. The hands were extended, slightly off the horizontal at a faint angle, like a gull tilting into the wind. Holding all I used to be sorry about like the new moon holding water,[2] niggers say. The jeweller was working again, bent over his bench, the tube tunnelled into his face. His hair was parted in the center. The part ran up into the bald spot, like a drained marsh in December.

I saw the hardware store from across the street. I didn't know you bought flat-irons by the pound.

"Maybe you want a tailor's goose,"[3] the clerk said. "They weigh ten pounds." Only they were bigger than I thought. So I got two six-pound little ones, because they would look like a pair of shoes wrapped up. They felt heavy enough together, but I thought again how Father had said about the reducto absurdum of human experience, thinking how

2. If the horns of the crescent moon are turned up so that they will "hold water," the weather will be dry; otherwise, it will pour out water, and there will be rain.
3. A tailor's pressing iron, which holds hot water.

the only opportunity I seemed to have for the application of Harvard. Maybe by next year; thinking maybe it takes two years in school to learn to do that properly.

But they felt heavy enough in the air. A car came. I got on. I didn't see the placard on the front. It was full, mostly prosperous looking people reading newspapers. The only vacant seat was beside a nigger. He wore a derby and shined shoes and he was holding a dead cigar stub. I used to think that a Southerner had to be always conscious of niggers. I thought that Northerners would expect him to. When I first came East I kept thinking You've got to remember to think of them as colored people not niggers, and if it hadn't happened that I wasn't thrown with many of them, I'd have wasted a lot of time and trouble before I learned that the best way to take all people, black or white, is to take them for what they think they are, then leave them alone. That was when I realised that a nigger is not a person so much as a form of behavior; a sort of obverse reflection of the white people he lives among. But I thought at first that I ought to miss having a lot of them around me because I thought that Northerners thought I did, but I didn't know that I really had missed Roskus and Dilsey and them until that morning in Virginia. The train was stopped when I waked and I raised the shade and looked out. The car was blocking a road crossing, where two white fences came down a hill and then sprayed outward and downward like part of the skeleton of a horn, and there was a nigger on a mule in the middle of the stiff ruts, waiting for the train to move. How long he had been there I didn't know, but he sat straddle of the mule, his head wrapped in a piece of blanket, as if they had been built there with the fence and the road, or with the hill, carved out of the hill itself, like a sign put there saying You are home again. He didn't have a saddle and his feet dangled almost to the ground. The mule looked like a rabbit. I raised the window.

"Hey, Uncle," I said. "Is this the way?"

"Suh?" He looked at me, then he loosened the blanket and lifted it away from his ear.

"Christmas gift!" I said.

"Sho comin, boss. You done caught me, aint you."

"I'll let you off this time."[4] I dragged my pants out of the little hammock and got a quarter out. "But look out next time. I'll be coming back through here two days after New Year, and look out then." I threw the quarter out the window. "Buy yourself some Santy Claus."

"Yes, suh," he said. He got down and picked up the quarter and rubbed it on his leg. "Thanky, young marster. Thanky." Then the train began to move. I leaned out the window, into the cold air, looking back.

---

4. On Christmas Day, or during the following week, custom held that the first person to say "Christmas gift" was entitled to a small gift of money or food.

He stood there beside the gaunt rabbit of a mule, the two of them shabby
and motionless and unimpatient. The train swung around the curve,
the engine puffing with short, heavy blasts, and they passed smoothly
from sight that way, with that quality about them of shabby and timeless
patience, of static serenity: that blending of childlike and ready incom-
petence and paradoxical reliability that tends and protects them it loves
out of all reason and robs them steadily and evades responsibility and
obligations by means too barefaced to be called subterfuge even and is
taken in theft or evasion with only that frank and spontaneous admiration for the victor which a gentleman feels for anyone who beats him in
a fair contest, and withal a fond and unflagging tolerance for whitefolks'
vagaries like that of a grandparent for unpredictable and troublesome
children, which I had forgotten. And all that day, while the train wound
through rushing gaps and along ledges where movement was only a
laboring sound of the exhaust and groaning wheels and the eternal
mountains stood fading into the thick sky, I thought of home, of the
bleak station and the mud and the niggers and country folks thronging
slowly about the square, with toy monkeys and wagons and candy in
sacks and roman candles sticking out, and my insides would move like
they used to do in school when the bell rang.

I wouldn't begin counting until the clock struck three. Then I would
begin, counting to sixty and folding down one finger and thinking of the
other fourteen fingers waiting to be folded down, or thirteen or twelve
or eight or seven, until all of a sudden I'd realise silence and the unwinking minds, and I'd say "Ma'am?" "Your name is Quentin, isn't it?" Miss
Laura would say. Then more silence and the cruel unwinking minds
and hands jerking into the silence. "Tell Quentin who discovered the
Mississippi River, Henry." "DeSoto." Then the minds would go away,
and after a while I'd be afraid I had gotten behind and I'd count fast and
fold down another finger, then I'd be afraid I was going too fast and I'd
slow up, then I'd get afraid and count fast again. So I never could come
out even with the bell, and the released surging of feet moving already,
feeling earth in the scuffed floor, and the day like a pane of glass struck
a light, sharp blow, and my insides would move, sitting still. *Moving
sitting still. My bowels moved for thee. One minute she was standing in
the door. Benjy. Bellowing. Benjamin the child of mine old age[5] bellowing. Caddy! Caddy!*

*I'm going to run away. He began to cry she went and touched him.
Hush. I'm not going to. Hush. He hushed. Dilsey.*

*He smell what you tell him when he want to. Dont have to listen nor
talk.*

*Can he smell that new name they give him? Can he smell bad luck?
What he want to worry about luck for? Luck cant do him no hurt.*

5. See Genesis 21.7.

What they change his name for then if aint trying to help his luck?

The car stopped, started, stopped again. Below the window I watched the crowns of people's heads passing beneath new straw hats not yet unbleached. There were women in the car now, with market baskets, and men in work-clothes were beginning to outnumber the shined shoes and collars.

The nigger touched my knee. "Pardon me," he said. I swung my legs out and let him pass. We were going beside a blank wall, the sound clattering back into the car, at the women with market baskets on their knees and a man in a stained hat with a pipe stuck in the band. I could smell water, and in a break in the wall I saw a glint of water and two masts, and a gull motionless in midair, like on an invisible wire between the masts, and I raised my hand and through my coat touched the letters I had written. When the car stopped I got off.

The bridge was open to let a schooner through. She was in tow, the tug nudging along under her quarter, trailing smoke, but the ship herself was like she was moving without visible means. A man naked to the waist was coiling down a line on the fo'c's'le head. His body was burned the color of leaf tobacco. Another man in a straw hat without any crown was at the wheel. The ship went through the bridge, moving under bare poles like a ghost in broad day, with three gulls hovering above the stern like toys on invisible wires.

When it closed I crossed to the other side and leaned on the rail above the boathouses. The float was empty and the doors were closed. Crew just pulled in the late afternoon now, resting up before. The shadow of the bridge, the tiers of railing, my shadow leaning flat upon the water, so easily had I tricked it that would not quit me. At least fifty feet it was, and if I only had something to blot it into the water, holding it until it was drowned, the shadow of the package like two shoes wrapped up lying on the water. Niggers say a drowned man's shadow was watching for him in the water all the time. It twinkled and glinted, like breathing, the float slow like breathing too, and debris half submerged, healing out to the sea and the caverns and the grottoes of the sea. The displacement of water is equal to the something of something.[6] Reducto absurdum of all human experience, and two six-pound flat-irons weigh more than one tailor's goose. What a sinful waste Dilsey would say. Benjy knew it when Damuddy died. He cried. *He smell hit. He smell hit.*

The tug came back downstream, the water shearing in long rolling cylinders, rocking the float at last with the echo of passage, the float lurching onto the rolling cylinder with a plopping sound and a long jarring noise as the door rolled back and two men emerged, carrying a

6. While bathing, Archimedes of Syracuse (287–212 B.C.) noticed that he displaced water equal in volume to his own body; he formulated the principle that when a body floats in a liquid, its weight is equal to the weight of liquid displaced, and that when it is immersed, its weight is diminished by that amount.

shell. They set it in the water and a moment later Bland came out, with the sculls. He wore flannels, a gray jacket and a stiff straw hat. Either he or his mother had read somewhere that Oxford students pulled in flannels and stiff hats, so early one March they bought Gerald a one pair shell and in his flannels and stiff hat he went on the river. The folks at the boathouse threatened to call a policeman, but he went anyway. His mother came down in a hired auto, in a fur suit like an arctic explorer's, and saw him off in a twenty-five mile wind and a steady drove of ice floes like dirty sheep. Ever since then I have believed that God is not only a gentleman and a sport; he is a Kentuckian too. When he sailed away she made a detour and came down to the river again and drove along parallel with him, the car in low gear. They said you couldn't have told they'd ever seen one another before, like a King and Queen, not even looking at one another, just moving side by side across Massachusetts on parallel courses like a couple of planets.

He got in and pulled away. He pulled pretty well now. He ought to. They said his mother tried to make him give rowing up and do something else the rest of his class couldn't or wouldn't do, but for once he was stubborn. If you could call it stubbornness, sitting in his attitudes of princely boredom, with his curly yellow hair and his violet eyes and his eyelashes and his New York clothes, while his mamma was telling us about Gerald's horses and Gerald's niggers and Gerald's women. Husbands and fathers in Kentucky must have been awful glad when she carried Gerald off to Cambridge. She had an apartment over in town, and Gerald had one there too, besides his rooms in college. She approved of Gerald associating with me because I at least revealed a blundering sense of noblesse oblige by getting myself born below Mason and Dixon, and a few others whose Geography met the requirements (minimum). Forgave, at least. Or condoned. But since she met Spoade coming out of chapel one He said she couldn't be a lady no lady would be out at that hour of the night she never had been able to forgive him for having five names, including that of a present English ducal house. I'm sure she solaced herself by being convinced that some misfit Maingault or Mortemar[7] had got mixed up with the lodge-keeper's daughter. Which was quite probable, whether she invented it or not. Spoade was the world's champion sitter-around, no holds barred and gouging discretionary.

The shell was a speck now, the oars catching the sun in spaced glints, as if the hull were winking itself along him along.[8] *Did you ever have a sister? No but they're all bitches. Did you ever have a sister? One minute she was. Bitches. Not bitch one minute she stood in the door* Dalton Ames. Dalton Ames. Dalton Shirts. I thought all the time they were

7. Names for European aristocracy.
8. Noel Polk describes his restoration of "along him" to "along" as an important way of accenting "the contrast between Quentin's obsession with drowning in the peaceful grottoes of the sea and the extroverted Gerald Bland's capacity to glide smoothly along the water's surface."

khaki, army issue khaki, until I saw they were of heavy Chinese silk or finest flannel because they made his face so brown his eyes so blue. Dalton Ames. It just missed gentility. Theatrical fixture. Just papier-mache, then touch. Oh. Asbestos. Not quite bronze. *But wont see him at the house.*

Caddy's a woman too remember. She must do things for women's reasons too.

Why wont you bring him to the house, Caddy? Why must you do like nigger women do in the pasture the ditches the dark woods hot hidden furious in the dark woods.

And after a while I had been hearing my watch for some time and I could feel the letters crackle through my coat, against the railing, and I leaned on the railing, watching my shadow, how I had tricked it. I moved along the rail, but my suit was dark too and I could wipe my hands, watching my shadow, how I had tricked it. I walked it into the shadow of the quai. Then I went east.

Harvard my Harvard boy Harvard harvard That pimple-faced infant she met at the field-meet with colored ribbons. Skulking along the fence trying to whistle her out like a puppy. Because they couldn't cajole him into the diningroom Mother believed he had some sort of spell he was going to cast on her when he got her alone. Yet any blackguard   *He was lying beside the box under the window bellowing*   that could drive up in a limousine with a flower in his buttonhole. *Harvard. Quentin this is Herbert. My Harvard boy. Herbert will be a big brother has already promised Jason*

Hearty, celluloid like a drummer.[9] Face full of teeth white but not smiling. *I've heard of him up there.* All teeth but not smiling. *You going to drive?*

Get in Quentin.

You going to drive.

It's her car aren't you proud of your little sister owns first auto in town Herbert his present. Louis has been giving her lessons every morning didn't you get my letter Mr and Mrs Jason Richmond Compson announce the marriage of their daughter Candace to Mr Sydney Herbert Head on the twenty-fifth of April one thousand nine hundred and ten at Jefferson Mississippi. At home after the first of August number Something Something Avenue South Bend Indiana. Shreve said Aren't you even going to open it? *Three days. Times. Mr and Mrs Jason Richmond Compson* Young Lochinvar[1] rode out of the west a little too soon, didn't he?

I'm from the south. You're funny, aren't you.

---

9. Traveling salesman.
1. See Sir Walter Scott, "Marmion," which was once used in many elementary school books. In the fifth canto, Lochinvar, the hero, rescues his fair Ellen, who is about to be married to a "laggard in love and a dastard in war." Lochinvar arrives at the bridal feast, claims the lady, swings her onto his horse, and rides off with her.

O yes I knew it was somewhere in the country.

You're funny, aren't you. You ought to join the circus.

I did. That's how I ruined my eyes watering the elephant's fleas. *Three times* These country girls. You cant ever tell about them, can you. Well, any way Byron never had his wish,[2] thank God. *But not hit a man in glasses* Aren't you even going to open it? *It lay on the table a candle burning at each corner upon the envelope tied in a soiled pink garter two artificial flowers. Not hit a man in glasses.*

Country people poor things they never saw an auto before lots of them honk the horn Candace so *She wouldn't look at me* they'll get out of the way *wouldn't look at me* your father wouldn't like it if you were to injure one of them I'll declare your father will simply have to get an auto now I'm almost sorry you brought it down Herbert I've enjoyed it so much of course there's the carriage but so often when I'd like to go out Mr Compson has the darkies doing something it would be worth my head to interrupt he insists that Roskus is at my call all the time but I know what that means I know how often people make promises just to satisfy their consciences are you going to treat my little baby girl that way Herbert but I know you wont Herbert has spoiled us all to death Quentin did I write you that he is going to take Jason into his bank when Jason finishes high school Jason will make a splendid banker he is the only one of my children with any practical sense you can thank me for that he takes after my people the others are all Compson *Jason furnished the flour. They made kites on the back porch and sold them for a nickel a piece, he and the Patterson boy. Jason was treasurer.*

There was no nigger in this car, and the hats unbleached as yet flowing past under the window. Going to Harvard. We have sold Benjy's *He lay on the ground under the window, bellowing. We have sold Benjy's pasture so that Quentin may go to Harvard* a brother to you. Your little brother.

You should have a car it's done you no end of good dont you think so Quentin I call him Quentin at once you see I have heard so much about him from Candace.

Why shouldn't you I want my boys to be more than friends yes Candace and Quentin more than friends *Father I have committed* what a pity you had no brother or sister *No sister no sister had no sister* Dont ask Quentin he and Mr Compson both feel a little insulted when I am strong enough to come down to the table I am going on nerve now I'll pay for it after it's all over and you have taken my little daughter away from me *My little sister had no.*[3] *If I could say Mother. Mother*

2. Contrary to Quentin's remark, most scholars now believe it probable that the relationship between Byron and his half-sister, Augusta Leigh, was consummated.
3. See Song of Solomon 8.8: "We have a little sister, and she hath no breasts: what shall we do for our sister in the day when she shall be spoken for?"

Unless I do what I am tempted to and take you instead I dont think Mr Compson could overtake the car.

Ah Herbert Candace do you hear that *She wouldn't look at me soft stubborn jaw-angle not back-looking* You needn't be jealous though it's just an old woman he's flattering a grown married daughter I cant believe it.

Nonsense you look like a girl you are lots younger than Candace color in your cheeks like a girl *A face reproachful tearful an odor of camphor and of tears a voice weeping steadily and softly beyond the twilit door the twilight-colored smell of honeysuckle. Bringing empty trunks down the attic stairs they sounded like coffins French Lick.[4] Found not death at the salt lick*

Hats not unbleached and not hats. In three years I can not wear a hat. I could not. Was. Will there be hats then since I was not and not Harvard then. Where the best of thought Father said clings like dead ivy vines upon old dead brick. Not Harvard then. Not to me, anyway. Again. Sadder than was. Again. Saddest of all. Again.

Spoade had a shirt on; then it must be. When I can see my shadow again if not careful that I tricked into the water shall tread again upon my impervious shadow.[5] But no sister. I wouldn't have done it. *I wont have my daughter spied on* I wouldn't have.

How can I control any of them when you have always taught them to have no respect for me and my wishes I know you look down on my people but is that any reason for teaching my children my own children I suffered for to have no respect Trampling my shadow's bones into the concrete with hard heels and then I was hearing the watch, and I touched the letters through my coat.

I will not have my daughter spied on by you or Quentin or anybody no matter what you think she has done

At least you agree there is reason for having her watched

I wouldn't have I wouldn't have. *I know you wouldn't I didn't mean to speak so sharply but women have no respect for each other for themselves*

But why did she The chimes began as I stepped on my shadow, but it was the quarter hour. The Deacon wasn't in sight anywhere. *think I would have could have*

She didn't mean that that's the way women do things it's because she loves Caddy

The street lamps would go down the hill then rise toward town I walked upon the belly of my shadow. I could extend my hand beyond it. *feeling Father behind me beyond the rasping darkness of summer and August the street lamps* Father and I protect women from one another

4. Resort town in southern Indiana.
5. In superstition, if you step on your own shadow, you will die.

from themselves our women *Women are like that they dont acquire knowledge of people we are for that they are just born with a practical fertility of suspicion that makes a crop every so often and usually right they have an affinity for evil for supplying whatever the evil lacks in itself for drawing it about them instinctively as you do bed-clothing in slumber fertilising the mind for it until the evil has served its purpose whether it ever existed or no* He was coming along between a couple of freshmen. He hadn't quite recovered from the parade, for he gave me a salute, a very superior-officerish kind.

"I want to see you a minute," I said, stopping.

"See me? All right. See you again, fellows," he said, stopping and turning back; "glad to have chatted with you." That was the Deacon, all over. Talk about your natural psychologists. They said he hadn't missed a train at the beginning of school in forty years, and that he could pick out a Southerner with one glance. He never missed, and once he had heard you speak, he could name your state. He had a regular uniform he met trains in, a sort of Uncle Tom's cabin outfit, patches and all.

"Yes, suh. Right dis way, young marster, hyer we is," taking your bags. "Hyer, boy, come hyer and git dese grips." Whereupon a moving mountain of luggage would edge up, revealing a white boy of about fifteen, and the Deacon would hang another bag on him somehow and drive him off. "Now, den, dont you drap hit. Yes, suh, young marster, jes give de old nigger yo room number, and hit'll be done got cold dar when you arrives."

From then on until he had you completely subjugated he was always in or out of your room, ubiquitous and garrulous, though his manner gradually moved northward as his raiment improved, until at last when he had bled you until you began to learn better he was calling you Quentin or whatever, and when you saw him next he'd be wearing a cast-off Brooks suit and a hat with a Princeton club I forget which band that someone had given him and which he was pleasantly and unshakably convinced was a part of Abe Lincoln's military sash. Someone spread the story years ago, when he first appeared around college from wherever he came from, that he was a graduate of the divinity school. And when he came to understand what it meant he was so taken with it that he began to retail the story himself, until at last he must have come to believe he really had. Anyway he related long pointless anecdotes of his undergraduate days, speaking familiarly of dead and departed professors by their first names, usually incorrect ones. But he had been guide mentor and friend to unnumbered crops of innocent and lonely freshmen, and I suppose that with all his petty chicanery and hypocrisy he stank no higher in heaven's nostrils than any other.

"Haven't seen you in three-four days," he said, staring at me from his still military aura. "You been sick?"

"No. I've been all right. Working, I reckon. I've seen you, though."

"Yes?"

"In the parade the other day."

"Oh, that. Yes, I was there. I dont care nothing about that sort of thing, you understand, but the boys likes to have me with them, the vet'runs does. Ladies wants all the old vet'runs to turn out, you know. So I has to oblige them."

"And on that Wop holiday too," I said. "You were obliging the W. C. T. U.[6] then, I reckon."

"That? I was doing that for my son-in-law. He aims to get a job on the city forces. Street cleaner. I tells him all he wants is a broom to sleep on. You saw me, did you?"

"Both times. Yes."

"I mean, in uniform. How'd I look?"

"You looked fine. You looked better than any of them. They ought to make you a general, Deacon."

He touched my arm, lightly, his hand that worn, gentle quality of niggers' hands. "Listen. This aint for outside talking. I dont mind telling you because you and me's the same folks, come long and short." He leaned a little to me, speaking rapidly, his eyes not looking at me. "I've got strings out, right now. Wait till next year. Just wait. Then see where I'm marching. I wont need to tell you how I'm fixing it; I say, just wait and see, my boy." He looked at me now and clapped me lightly on the shoulder and rocked back on his heels, nodding at me. "Yes, sir. I didn't turn Democrat three years ago for nothing. My son-in-law on the city; me—— Yes, sir. If just turning Democrat'll make that son of a bitch go to work. . . . And me: just you stand on that corner yonder a year from two days ago, and see."

"I hope so. You deserve it, Deacon. And while I think about it——" I took the letter from my pocket. "Take this around to my room tomorrow and give it to Shreve. He'll have something for you. But not till tomorrow, mind."

He took the letter and examined it. "It's sealed up."

"Yes. And it's written inside, Not good until tomorrow."

"H'm," he said. He looked at the envelope, his mouth pursed. "Something for me, you say?"

"Yes. A present I'm making you."

He was looking at me now, the envelope white in his black hand, in the sun. His eyes were soft and irisless and brown, and suddenly I saw Roskus watching me from behind all his whitefolks' claptrap of uniforms and politics and Harvard manner, diffident, secret, inarticulate and sad. "You aint playing a joke on the old nigger, is you?"

"You know I'm not. Did any Southerner ever play a joke on you?"

"You're right. They're fine folks. But you cant live with them."

6. Women's Christian Temperance Union. *Wop holiday*: Quentin's term for Columbus Day.

"Did you ever try?" I said. But Roskus was gone. Once more he was that self he had long since taught himself to wear in the world's eye, pompous, spurious, not quite gross.

"I'll confer to your wishes, my boy."

"Not until tomorrow, remember."

"Sure," he said; "understood, my boy. Well——"

"I hope——" I said. He looked down at me, benignant, profound. Suddenly I held out my hand and we shook, he gravely, from the pompous height of his municipal and military dream. "You're a good fellow, Deacon. I hope. . . . You've helped a lot of young fellows, here and there."

"I've tried to treat all folks right," he said. "I draw no petty social lines. A man to me is a man, wherever I find him."

"I hope you'll always find as many friends as you've made."

"Young fellows. I get along with them. They dont forget me, neither," he said, waving the envelope. He put it into his pocket and buttoned his coat. "Yes, sir," he said. "I've had good friends."

The chimes began again, the half hour. I stood in the belly of my shadow and listened to the strokes spaced and tranquil along the sunlight, among the thin, still little leaves. Spaced and peaceful and serene, with that quality of autumn always in bells even in the month of brides. *Lying on the ground under the window bellowing* He took one look at her and knew. Out of the mouths of babes.[7] *The street lamps* The chimes ceased. I went back to the postoffice, treading my shadow into pavement. *go down the hill then they rise toward town like lanterns hung one above another on a wall.* Father said because she loves Caddy she loves people through their shortcomings. Uncle Maury straddling his legs before the fire must remove one hand long enough to drink Christmas. Jason ran on, his hands in his pockets fell down and lay there like a trussed fowl until Versh set him up. *Whyn't you keep them hands outen your pockets when you running you could stand up then* Rolling his head in the cradle rolling it flat across the back. Caddy told Jason and Versh that the reason Uncle Maury didn't work was that he used to roll his head in the cradle when he was little.

Shreve was coming up the walk, shambling, fatly earnest, his glasses glinting beneth the running leaves like little pools.

"I gave Deacon a note for some things. I may not be in this afternoon, so dont you let him have anything until tomorrow, will you?

"All right." He looked at me. "Say, what're you doing today, anyhow? All dressed up and mooning around like the prologue to a suttee. Did you go to Psychology this morning?"

"I'm not doing anything. Not until tomorrow, now."

"What's that you got there?"

7. See Matthew 21.16 and Psalms 8.2.

"Nothing. Pair of shoes I had half-soled. Not until tomorrow, you hear?"

"Sure. All right. Oh, by the way, did you get a letter off the table this morning?"

"No."

"It's there. From Semiramis.[8] Chauffeur brought it before ten oclock."

"All right. I'll get it. Wonder what she wants now."

"Another band recital, I guess. Tumpty ta ta Gerald blah. 'A little louder on the drum, Quentin'. God, I'm glad I'm not a gentleman." He went on, nursing a book, a little shapeless, fatly intent. *The street lamps* do you think so because one of our forefathers was a governor and three were generals and Mother's werent

any live man is better than any dead man but no live or dead man is very much better than any other live or dead man *Done in Mother's mind though. Finished. Finished. Then we were all poisoned* you are confusing sin and morality women dont do that your mother is thinking of morality whether it be sin or not has not occurred to her

Jason I must go away you keep the others I'll take Jason and go where nobody knows us so he'll have a chance to grow up and forget all this the others dont love me they have never loved anything with that streak of Compson selfishness and false pride Jason was the only one my heart went out to without dread

nonsense Jason is all right I was thinking that as soon as you feel better you and Caddy might go up to French Lick

and leave Jason here with nobody but you and the darkies

she will forget him then all the talk will die away *found not death at the salt licks*

maybe I could find a husband for her *not death at the salt licks*

The car came up and stopped. The bells were still ringing the half hour. I got on and it went on again, blotting the half hour. No: the three quarters. Then it would be ten minutes anyway. To leave Harvard *your mother's dream for sold Benjy's pasture for*

what have I done to have been given children like these Benjamin was punishment enough and now for her to have no more regard for me her own mother I've suffered for her dreamed and planned and sacrificed I went down into the valley[9] yet never since she opened her eyes has she given me one unselfish thought at times I look at her I wonder if she can be my child except Jason he has never given me one moment's sorrow since I first held him in my arms I knew then that he was to be my joy and my salvation[1] I thought that Benjamin was punishment enough for any sins I have committed I thought he was my punishment for putting aside my pride and marrying a man who held himself above

8. A famous Assyrian princess.
9. See Psalms 23.4.
1. See Psalms 51.2.

me I dont complain I loved him above all of them because of it because my duty though Jason pulling at my heart all the while but I see now that I have not suffered enough I see now that I must pay for your sins as well as mine what have you done what sins have your high and mighty people visited upon me but you'll take up for them you always have found excuses for your own blood only Jason can do wrong because he is more Bascomb than Compson while your own daughter my little daughter my baby girl she is she is no better than that when I was a girl I was unfortunate I was only a Bascomb I was taught that there is no halfway ground that a woman is either a lady or not but I never dreamed when I held her in my arms that any daughter of mine could let herself dont you know I can look at her eyes and tell you may think she'd tell you but she doesn't tell things she is secretive you dont know her I know things she's done that I'd die before I'd have you know that's it go on criticise Jason accuse me of setting him to watch her as if it were a crime while your own daughter can I know you dont love him that you wish to believe faults against him you never have yes ridicule him as you always have Maury you cannot hurt me any more than your children already have and then I'll be gone and Jason with no one to love him shield him from this I look at him every day dreading to see this Compson blood beginning to show in him at last with his sister slipping out to see what do you call it then have you ever laid eyes on him will you even let me try to find out who he is it's not for myself I couldn't bear to see him it's for your sake to protect you but who can fight against bad blood you wont let me try we are to sit back with our hands folded while she not only drags your name in the dirt but corrupts the very air your children breathe Jason you must let me go away I cannot stand it let me have Jason and you keep the others they're not my flesh and blood like he is strangers nothing of mine and I am afraid of them I can take Jason and go where we are not known I'll go down on my knees and pray for the absolution of my sins that he may escape this curse try to forget that the others ever were

If that was the three quarters, not over ten minutes now. One car had just left, and people were already waiting for the next one. I asked, but he didn't know whether another one would leave before noon or not because you'd think that interurbans. So the first one was another trolley. I got on. You can feel noon. I wonder if even miners in the bowels of the earth. That's why whistles: because people that sweat, and if just far enough from sweat you wont hear whistles and in eight minutes you should be that far from sweat in Boston. Father said a man is the sum of his misfortunes. One day you'd think misfortune would get tired, but then time is your misfortune Father said. A gull on an invisible wire attached through space dragged. You carry the symbol of your frustration into eternity. Then the wings are bigger Father said only who can play a harp.

I could hear my watch whenever the car stopped, but not often they were already eating *Who would play a* Eating the business of eating inside of you space too space and time confused Stomach saying noon brain saying eat oclock All right I wonder what time it is what of it. People were getting out. The trolley didn't stop so often now, emptied by eating.

Then it was past. I got off and stood in my shadow and after a while a car came along and I got on and went back to the interurban station. There was a car ready to leave, and I found a seat next the window and it started and I watched it sort of frazzle out into slack tide flats, and then trees. Now and then I saw the river and I thought how nice it would be for them down at New London if the weather and Gerald's shell going solemnly up the glinting forenoon and I wondered what the old woman would be wanting now, sending me a note before ten oclock in the morning. What picture of Gerald I to be one of the *Dalton Ames oh asbestos Quentin has shot* background. Something with girls in it. Women do have *always his voice above the gabble voice that breathed* an affinity for evil, for believing that no woman is to be trusted, but that some men are too innocent to protect themselves. Plain girls. Remote cousins and family friends whom mere acquaintanceship invested with a sort of blood obligation noblesse oblige. And she sitting there telling us before their faces what a shame it was that Gerald should have all the family looks because a man didn't need it, was better off without it but without it a girl was simply lost. Telling us about Gerald's women in a *Quentin has shot Herbert he shot his voice through the floor of Caddy's room* tone of smug approbation. "When he was seventeen I said to him one day 'What a shame that you should have a mouth like that it should be on a girl's face' and can you imagine. *the curtains leaning in on the twilight upon the odor of the apple tree her head against the twilight her arms behind her head kimono-winged the voice that breathed o'er eden clothes upon the bed by the nose seen above the apple* what he said? just seventeen, mind. 'Mother' he said 'it often is'." And him sitting there in attitudes regal watching two or three of them through his eyelashes. They gushed like swallows swooping his eyelashes. Shreve said he always had *Are you going to look after Benjy and Father*

The less you say about Benjy and Father the better when have you ever considered them Caddy

Promise

You needn't worry about them you're getting out in good shape

Promise I'm sick you'll have to promise wondered who invented that joke but then he always had considered Mrs Bland a remarkably preserved woman he said she was grooming Gerald to seduce a duchess sometime. She called Shreve that fat Canadian youth twice she arranged a new room-mate for me without consulting me at all, once for me to move out, once for

He opened the door in the twilight. His face looked like a pumpkin pie.

"Well, I'll say a fond farewell. Cruel fate may part us, but I will never love another. Never."

"What are you talking about?"

"I'm talking about cruel fate in eight yards of apricot silk and more metal pound for pound than a galley slave and the sole owner and proprietor of the unchallenged peripatetic john of the late Confederacy." Then he told me how she had gone to the proctor to have him moved out and how the proctor had revealed enough low stubbornness to insist on consulting Shreve first. Then she suggested that he send for Shreve right off and do it, and he wouldn't do that, so after that she was hardly civil to Shreve. "I make it a point never to speak harshly of females," Shreve said, "but that woman has got more ways like a bitch than any lady in these sovereign states and dominions." and now Letter on the table by hand, command orchid scented colored If she knew I had passed almost beneath the window knowing it there without   My dear Madam I have not yet had an opportunity of receiving your communication but I beg in advance to be excused today or yesterday and tomorrow or when As I remember that the next one is to be how Gerald throws his nigger downstairs and how the nigger plead to be allowed to matriculate in the divinity school to be near marster marse gerald and How he ran all the way to the station beside the carriage with tears in his eyes when marse gerald rid away I will wait until the day for the one about the sawmill husband came to the kitchen door with a shotgun Gerald went down and bit the gun in two and handed it back and wiped his hands on a silk handkerchief threw the handkerchief in the stove I've only heard that one twice

shot him through the   I saw you come in here so I watched my chance and came along thought we might get acquainted have a cigar

Thanks I dont smoke

No things must have changed up there since my day mind if I light up

Help yourself

Thanks I've heard a lot I guess your mother wont mind if I put the match behind the screen will she a lot about you Candace talked about you all the time up there at the Licks   I got pretty jealous I says to myself who is this Quentin anyway I must see what this animal looks like because I was hit pretty hard see soon as I saw the little girl I dont mind telling you it never occurred to me it was her brother she kept talking about she couldn't have talked about you any more if you'd been the only man in the world husband wouldn't have been in it you wont change your mind and have a smoke

I dont smoke

In that case I wont insist even though it is a pretty fair weed cost me twenty-five bucks a hundred wholesale friend of in Havana yes I guess there are lots of changes up there I keep promising myself a visit but I never get around to it been hitting the ball now for ten years I cant get away from the bank during school fellow's habits change things that seem important to an undergraduate you know tell me about things up there

I'm not going to tell Father and Mother if that's what you are getting at Not going to tell not going to oh that that's what you are talking about is it you understand that I dont give a damn whether you tell or not understand that a thing like that unfortunate but no police crime I wasn't the first or the last I was just unlucky you might have been luckier

You lie

Keep your shirt on I'm not trying to make you tell anything you dont want to meant no offense of course a young fellow like you would consider a thing of that sort a lot more serious than you will in five years

I dont know but one way to consider cheating I dont think I'm likely to learn different at Harvard

We're better than a play you must have made the Dramat well you're right no need to tell them we'll let bygones be bygones eh no reason why you and I should let a little thing like that come between us I like you Quentin I like your appearance you dont look like these other hicks I'm glad we're going to hit it off like this I've promised your mother to do something for Jason but I would like to give you a hand too Jason would be just as well off here but there's no future in a hole like this for a young fellow like you

Thanks you'd better stick to Jason he'd suit you better than I would

I'm sorry about that business but a kid like I was then I never had a mother like yours to teach me the finer points it would just hurt her unnecessarily to know it yes you're right no need to that includes Candace of course

I said Mother and Father

Look here take a look at me how long do you think you'd last with me

I wont have to last long if you learned to fight up at school too try and see how long I would

You damned little what do you think you're getting at

Try and see

My God the cigar what would your mother say if she found a blister on her mantel just in time too look here Quentin we're about to do something we'll both regret I like you liked you as soon as I saw you I says he must be a damned good fellow whoever he is or Candace wouldn't be so keen on him listen I've been out in the world now for ten years things dont matter so much then you'll find that out let's you and I get together on this thing sons of old Harvard and all I guess I wouldn't know the place now best place for a young fellow in the world I'm going to send my sons there give them a better chance than I had wait dont go yet let's discuss this thing a young man gets these ideas and I'm all for them does

him good while he's in school forms his character good for tradition the
school but when he gets out into the world he'll have to get his the best
way he can because he'll find that everybody else is doing the same thing
and be damned to here let's shake hands and let bygones be bygones for
your mother's sake remember her health come on give me your hand
here look at it it's just out of convent look not a blemish not even been
creased yet see here

To hell with your money

No no come on I belong to the family now see I know how it is with a
young fellow he has lots of private affairs it's always pretty hard to get the
old man to stump up for I know haven't I been there and not so long
ago either but now I'm getting married and all specially up there come
on dont be a fool listen when we get a chance for a real talk I want to
tell you about a little widow over in town

I've heard that too keep your damned money

Call it a loan then just shut your eyes a minute and you'll be fifty

Keep your hands off of me you'd better get that cigar off the mantel

Tell and be damned then see what it gets you if you were not a damned
fool you'd have seen that I've got them too tight for any half-baked Gal-
ahad of a brother your mother's told me about your sort with your head
swelled up come in oh come in dear Quentin and I were just getting
acquainted talking about Harvard did you want me cant stay away from
the old man can she

Go out a minute Herbert I want to talk to Quentin

Come in come in let's all have a gabfest and get acquainted I was just
telling Quentin

Go on Herbert go out a while

Well all right then I suppose you and bubber do want to see one another
once more eh

You'd better take that cigar off the mantel

Right as usual my boy then I'll toddle along let them order you around
while they can Quentin after day after tomorrow it'll be pretty please to
the old man wont it dear give us a kiss honey

Oh stop that save that for day after tomorrow

I'll want interest then dont let Quentin do anything he cant finish oh by
the way did I tell Quentin the story about the man's parrot and what
happened to it a sad story remind me of that think of it yourself ta-ta see
you in the funnypaper

Well

Well

What are you up to now

Nothing

You're meddling in my business again didn't you get enough of that last
summer

Caddy you've got fever   *You're sick how are you sick*

I'm just sick. I cant ask.
Shot his voice through the
Not that blackguard Caddy

Now and then the river glinted beyond things in sort of swooping glints, across noon and after. Good after now, though we had passed where he was still pulling upstream majestical in the face of god gods. Better. Gods. God would be canaille too in Boston in Massachusetts. Or maybe just not a husband. The wet oars winking him along in bright winks and female palms. Adulant. Adulant if not a husband he'd ignore God. *That blackguard, Caddy*   The river glinted away beyond a swooping curve.

I'm sick you'll have to promise
Sick how are you sick
I'm just sick I cant ask anybody yet promise you will
If they need any looking after it's because of you how are you sick
Under the window we could hear the car leaving for the station, the 8:10 train. To bring back cousins. Heads. Increasing himself head by head but not barbers. Manicure girls. We had a blood horse once. In the stable yes, but under leather a cur. *Quentin has shot all of their voices through the floor of Caddy's room*

The car stopped. I got off, into the middle of my shadow. A road crossed the track. There was a wooden marquee with an old man eating something out of a paper bag, and then the car was out of hearing too. The road went into trees, where it would be shady, but June foliage in New England not much thicker than April at home. I could see a smoke stack. I turned my back to it, tramping my shadow into the dust. *There was something terrible in me sometimes at night I could see it grinning at me I could see it through them grinning at me through their faces it's gone now and I'm sick*

Caddy
Dont touch me just promise
If you're sick you cant
Yes I can after that it'll be all right it wont matter dont let them send him to Jackson promise
I promise Caddy Caddy
Dont touch me dont touch me
What does it look like Caddy
What
That that grins at you that thing through them
I could still see the smoke stack. That's where the water would be, healing out to the sea and the peaceful grottoes. Tumbling peacefully they would, and when He said Rise only the flat irons. When Versh and I hunted all day we wouldn't take any lunch, and at twelve oclock I'd get hungry. I'd stay hungry until about one, then all of a sudden I'd even forget that I wasn't hungry anymore. *The street lamps go down the hill*

*then heard the car go down the hill. The chair-arm flat cool smooth under
my forehead shaping the chair the apple tree leaning on my hair above
the eden clothes by the nose seen*   You've got fever I felt it yesterday it's
like being near a stove.

Dont touch me.

Caddy you cant do it if you are sick. That blackguard.

I've got to marry somebody. *Then they told me the bone would have
to be broken again*

At last I couldn't see the smoke stack. The road went beside a wall.
Trees leaned over the wall, sprayed with sunlight. The stone was cool.
Walking near it you could feel the coolness. Only our country was not
like this country. There was something about just walking through it. A
kind of still and violent fecundity that satisfied even bread-hunger like.
Flowing around you, not brooding and nursing every niggard stone.
Like it were put to makeshift for enough green to go around among the
trees and even the blue of distance not that rich chimaera. *told me the
bone would have to be broken again and inside me it began to say Ah Ah
Ah and I began to sweat. What do I care I know what a broken leg is all
it is it wont be anything I'll just have to stay in the house a little longer
that's all and my jaw-muscles getting numb and my mouth saying Wait
Wait just a minute through the sweat ah ah ah behind my teeth and
Father damn that horse damn that horse. Wait it's my fault. He came
along the fence every morning with a basket toward the kitchen dragging
a stick along the fence every morning I dragged myself to the window cast
and all and laid for him with a piece of coal Dilsey said you goin to ruin
yoself aint you got no mo sense than that not fo days since you bruck hit.
Wait I'll get used to it in a minute wait just a minute I'll get*

Even sound seemed to fail in this air, like the air was worn out with
carrying sounds so long. A dog's voice carries further than a train, in the
darkness anyway. And some people's. Niggers. Louis Hatcher never even
used his horn carrying it and that old lantern. I said, "Louis, when was
the last time you cleaned that lantern?"

"I cleant hit a little while back. You member when all dat flood-watter
wash dem folks away up yonder? I cleant hit dat ve'y day. Old woman
and me settin fo de fire dat night and she say 'Louis, whut you gwine do
ef dat flood git out dis fur?' and I say 'Dat's a fack. I reckon I had better
clean dat lantun up.' So I cleant hit dat night."

"That flood was way up in Pennsylvania," I said. "It couldn't ever
have got down this far."

"Dat's whut you says," Louis said. "Watter kin git des ez high en wet
in Jefferson ez hit kin in Pennsylvaney, I reckon. Hit's de folks dat says
de high watter cant git dis fur dat comes floatin out on de ridge-pole,
too."

"Did you and Martha get out that night?"

"We done jest dat. I cleant dat lantun and me and her sot de balance of de night on top o dat knoll back de graveyard. En ef I'd a knowed of aihy one higher, we'd a been on hit instead."

"And you haven't cleaned that lantern since then."

"Whut I want to clean hit when dey aint no need?"

"You mean, until another flood comes along?"

"Hit kep us outen dat un."

"Oh, come on, Uncle Louis," I said.

"Yes, suh. You do yo way en I do mine. Ef all I got to do to keep outen de high watter is to clean dis yere lantun, I wont quoil wid no man."

"Unc' Louis wouldn't ketch nothin wid a light he could see by," Versh said.

"I wuz huntin possums in dis country when dey was still drowndin nits in yo pappy's head wid coal oil, boy," Louis said. "Ketchin um, too."

"Dat's de troof," Versh said. "I reckon Unc' Louis done caught mo possums than aihy man in dis country."

"Yes, suh," Louis said. "I got plenty light fer possums to see, all right. I aint heard none o dem complainin. Hush, now. Dar he. Whooey. Hum awn, dawg." And we'd sit in the dry leaves that whispered a little with the slow respiration of our waiting and with the slow breathing of the earth and the windless October, the rank smell of the lantern fouling the brittle air, listening to the dogs and to the echo of Louis' voice dying away. He never raised it, yet on a still night we have heard it from our front porch. When he called the dogs in he sounded just like the horn he carried slung on his shoulder and never used, but clearer, mellower, as though his voice were a part of darkness and silence, coiling out of it, coiling   into   it   again.   WhoOoooo.   WhoOoooo.   Who-Ooooooooooooooooo. *Got to marry somebody*

Have there been very many Caddy

I dont know too many will you look after Benjy and Father

You dont know whose it is then does he know

Dont touch me will you look after Benjy and Father

I began to feel the water before I came to the bridge. The bridge was of gray stone, lichened, dappled with slow moisture where the fungus crept. Beneath it the water was clear and still in the shadow, whispering and clucking about the stone in fading swirls of spinning sky. *Caddy that*

I've got to marry somebody Versh told me about a man who mutilated himself. He went into the woods and did it with a razor, sitting in a ditch. A broken razor flinging them backward over his shoulder the same motion complete the jerked skein of blood backward not looping. But that's not it. It's not not having them. It's never to have had them then I could say O That That's Chinese I dont know Chinese. And Father said it's because you are a virgin: dont you see? Women are never vir-

gins. Purity is a negative state and therefore contrary to nature. It's nature
is hurting you not Caddy and I said That's just words and he said So is
virginity and I said you dont know. You cant know and he said Yes. On
the instant when we come to realise that tragedy is second-hand.

Where the shadow of the bridge fell I could see down for a long way,
but not as far as the bottom. When you leave a leaf in water a long time
after a while the tissue will be gone and the delicate fibers waving slow
as the motion of sleep. They dont touch one another, no matter how
knotted up they once were, no matter how close they lay once to the
bones. And maybe when He says Rise the eyes will come floating up
too, out of the deep quiet and the sleep, to look on glory. And after a
while the flat irons would come floating up. I hid them under the end
of the bridge and went back and leaned on the rail.

I could not see the bottom, but I could see a long way into the motion
of the water before the eye gave out, and then I saw a shadow hanging
like a fat arrow stemming into the current. Mayflies skimmed in and out
of the shadow of the bridge just above the surface. *If it could just be a
hell beyond that: the clean flame*[2] *the two of us more than dead. Then
you will have only me then only me then the two of us amid the pointing
and the horror beyond the clean flame* The arrow increased without motion,
then in a quick swirl the trout lipped a fly beneath the surface with that
sort of gigantic delicacy of an elephant picking up a peanut. The fading
vortex drifted away down stream and then I saw the arrow again, nose
into the current, wavering delicately to the motion of the water above
which the May flies slanted and poised. *Only you and me then amid the
pointing and the horror walled by the clean flame*

The trout hung, delicate and motionless among the wavering shadows. Three boys with fishing poles came onto the bridge and we leaned
on the rail and looked down at the trout. They knew the fish. He was a
neighborhood character.

"They've been trying to catch that trout for twenty-five years. There's
a store in Boston offers a twenty-five dollar fishing rod to anybody that
can catch him."

"Why dont you all catch him, then? Wouldn't you like to have a
twenty-five dollar fishing rod?"

"Yes," they said. They leaned on the rail, looking down at the trout.
"I sure would," one said.

"I wouldn't take the rod," the second said. "I'd take the money instead."

"Maybe they wouldn't do that," the first said. "I bet he'd make you
take the rod."

"Then I'd sell it."

"You couldn't get twenty-five dollars for it."

"I'd take what I could get, then. I can catch just as many fish with

2. See Luke 16.24–25.

this pole as I could with a twenty-five dollar one." Then they talked about what they would do with twenty-five dollars. They all talked at once, their voices insistent and contradictory and impatient, making of unreality a possibility, then a probability, then an incontrovertible fact, as people will when their desires become words.

"I'd buy a horse and wagon," the second said.

"Yes you would," the others said.

"I would. I know where I can buy one for twenty-five dollars. I know the man."

"Who is it?"

"That's all right who it is. I can buy it for twenty-five dollars."

"Yah," the others said. "He dont know any such thing. He's just talking."

"Do you think so?" the boy said. They continued to jeer at him, but he said nothing more. He leaned on the rail, looking down at the trout which he had already spent, and suddenly the acrimony, the conflict, was gone from their voices, as if to them too it was as though he had captured the fish and bought his horse and wagon, they too partaking of that adult trait of being convinced of anything by an assumption of silent superiority. I suppose that people, using themselves and each other so much by words, are at least consistent in attributing wisdom to a still tongue, and for a while I could feel the other two seeking swiftly for some means by which to cope with him, to rob him of his horse and wagon.

"You couldn't get twenty-five dollars for that pole," the first said. "I bet anything you couldn't."

"He hasn't caught that trout yet," the third said suddenly, then they both cried:

"Yah, what'd I tell you? What's the man's name? I dare you to tell. There aint any such man."

"Ah, shut up," the second said. "Look. Here he comes again." They leaned on the rail, motionless, identical, their poles slanting slenderly in the sunlight, also identical. The trout rose without haste, a shadow in faint wavering increase; again the little vortex faded slowly downstream. "Gee," the first one murmured.

"We dont try to catch him anymore," he said. "We just watch Boston folks that come out and try."

"Is he the only fish in this pool?"

"Yes. He ran all the others out. The best place to fish around here is down at the Eddy."

"No it aint," the second said. "It's better at Bigelow's Mill two to one." Then they argued for a while about which was the best fishing and then left off all of a sudden to watch the trout rise again and the broken swirl of water suck down a little of the sky. I asked how far it was to the nearest town. They told me.

"But the closest car line is that way," the second said, pointing back down the road. "Where are you going?"

"Nowhere. Just walking."

"You from the college?"

"Yes. Are there any factories in that town?"

"Factories?" They looked at me.

"No," the second said. "Not there." They looked at my clothes. "You looking for work?"

"How about Bigelow's Mill?" the third said. "That's a factory."

"Factory my eye. He means a sure enough factory."

"One with a whistle," I said. "I haven't heard any one oclock whistles yet."

"Oh," the second said. "There's a clock in the unitarial steeple. You can find out the time from that. Haven't you got a watch on that chain?"

"I broke it this morning." I showed them my watch. They examined it gravely.

"It's still running," the second said. "What does a watch like that cost?"

"It was a present," I said. "My father gave it to me when I graduated from high school."

"Are you a Canadian?" the third said. He had red hair.

"Canadian?"

"He dont talk like them," the second said. "I've heard them talk. He talks like they do in minstrel shows."

"Say," the third said. "Aint you afraid he'll hit you?"

"Hit me?"

"You said he talks like a colored man."

"Ah, dry up," the second said. "You can see the steeple when you get over that hill there."

I thanked them. "I hope you have good luck. Only dont catch that old fellow down there. He deserves to be let alone."

"Cant anybody catch that fish," the first said. They leaned on the rail, looking down into the water, the three poles like three slanting threads of yellow fire in the sun. I walked upon my shadow, tramping it into the dappled shade of trees again. The road curved, mounting away from the water. It crossed the hill, then descended winding, carrying the eye, the mind on ahead beneath a still green tunnel, and the square cupola above the trees and the round eye of the clock but far enough. I sat down at the roadside. The grass was ankle deep, myriad. The shadows on the road were as still as if they had been put there with a stencil, with slanting pencils of sunlight. But it was only a train, and after a while it died away beyond the trees, the long sound, and then I could hear my watch and the train dying away, as though it were running through another month or another summer somewhere, rushing away under the poised gull and all things rushing. Except Gerald. He would be sort of grand too, pulling in lonely state across the noon, rowing himself right out of noon, up the long bright air like an apotheosis, mounting into a drowsing infinity where only he and the gull, the one terrifically motionless, the other in a steady and measured pull and recover that partook of inertia itself, the world punily beneath their shadows on the sun. *Caddy that blackguard that blackguard Caddy*

Their voices came over the hill, and the three slender poles like balanced threads of running fire. They looked at me passing, not slowing.

"Well," I said. "I dont see him."

"We didn't try to catch him," the first said. "You cant catch that fish."

"There's the clock," the second said, pointing. "You can tell the time when you get a little closer."

"Yes," I said. "All right." I got up. "You all going to town?"

"We're going to the Eddy for chub," the first said.

"You cant catch anything at the Eddy," the second said.

"I guess you want to go to the mill, with a lot of fellows splashing and scaring all the fish away."

"You cant catch any fish at the Eddy."

"We wont catch none nowhere if we dont go on," the third said.

"I dont see why you keep on talking about the Eddy," the second said. "You cant catch anything there."

"You dont have to go," the first said. "You're not tied to me."

"Let's go to the mill and go swimming," the third said.

"I'm going to the Eddy and fish," the first said. "You can do as you please."

"Say, how long has it been since you heard of anybody catching a fish at the Eddy?" the second said to the third.

"Let's go to the mill and go swimming," the third said. The cupola sank slowly beyond the trees, with the round face of the clock far enough yet. We went on in the dappled shade. We came to an orchard, pink and white. It was full of bees; already we could hear them.

"Let's go to the mill and go swimming," the third said. A lane turned off beside the orchard. The third boy slowed and halted. The first went on, flecks of sunlight slipping along the pole across his shoulder and down the back of his shirt. "Come on," the third said. The second boy stopped too. *Why must you marry somebody Caddy*

Do you want me to say it do you think that if I say it it wont be

"Let's go up to the mill," he said. "Come on."

The first boy went on. His bare feet made no sound, falling softer than leaves in the thin dust. In the orchard the bees sounded like a wind getting up, a sound caught by a spell just under crescendo and sustained. The lane went along the wall, arched over, shattered with bloom, dissolving into trees. Sunlight slanted into it, sparse and eager. Yellow butterflies flickered along the shade like flecks of sun.

"What do you want to go to the Eddy for?" the second boy said. "You can fish at the mill if you want to."

"Ah, let him go," the third said. They looked after the first boy. Sunlight slid patchily across his walking shoulders, glinting along the pole like yellow ants.

"Kenny," the second said. *Say it to Father will you I will am my fathers Progenitive I invented him created I him Say it to him it will not be for he will say I was not and then you and I since philoprogenitive*

"Ah, come on," the third boy said. "They're already in." They looked after the first boy. "Yah," they said suddenly, "go on then, mamma's boy. If he goes swimming he'll get his head wet and then he'll get a licking." They turned into the lane and went on, the yellow butterfies slanting about them along the shade.

it is because there is nothing else I believe there is something else but there may not be and then I You will find that even injustice is scarcely worthy of what you believe yourself to be   He paid me no attention, his jaw set in profile, his face turned a little away beneath his broken hat.

"Why dont you go swimming with them?" I said. *that blackguard Caddy*

Were you trying to pick a fight with him were you

A liar and a scoundrel Caddy was dropped from his club for cheating at cards got sent to Coventry[3] *caught cheating at midterm exams and expelled*

Well what about it I'm not going to play cards with

"Do you like fishing better than swimming?" I said. The sound of the bees diminished, sustained yet, as though instead of sinking into silence, silence merely increased between us, as water rises. The road curved again and became a street between shady lawns with white houses. *Caddy that blackguard can you think of Benjy and Father and do it not of me*

What else can I think about what else have I thought about   The boy turned from the street. He climbed a picket fence without looking back and crossed the lawn to a tree and laid the pole down and climbed into the fork of the tree and sat there, his back to the road and the dappled sun motionless at last upon his white shirt. *else have I thought about I cant even cry I died last year I told you I had but I didn't know then what I meant I didn't know what I was saying* Some days in late August at home are like this, the air thin and eager like this, with something in it sad and nostalgic and familiar. Man the sum of his climatic experiences Father said. Man the sum of what have you. A problem in impure properties carried tediously to an unvarying nil: stalemate of dust and desire. *but now I know I'm dead I tell you*

---

3. To send one to "Coventry" is to take no notice of him, to make him feel that he is in disgrace by ignoring him. It is said that the citizens of Coventry once had so great a dislike of soldiers that a woman seen speaking to one was instantly ostracized; hence when a soldier was sent to Coventry, he was cut off from all social intercourse.

Then why must you listen we can go away you and Benjy and me where nobody knows us where The buggy was drawn by a white horse, his feet clopping in the thin dust; spidery wheels chattering thin and dry, moving uphill beneath a rippling shawl of leaves. Elm. No: ellum. Ellum.

On what on your school money the money they sold the pasture for so you could go to Harvard dont you see you've got to finish now if you dont finish he'll have nothing

Sold the pasture His white shirt was motionless in the fork, in the flickering shade. The wheels were spidery. Beneath the sag of the buggy the hooves neatly rapid like the motions of a lady doing embroidery, diminishing without progress like a figure on a treadmill being drawn rapidly offstage. The street turned again. I could see the white cupola, the round stupid assertion of the clock. *Sold the pasture*

Father will be dead in a year they say if he doesn't stop drinking and he wont stop he cant stop since I since last summer and then they'll send Benjy to Jackson I cant cry I cant even cry one minute she was standing in the door the next minute he was pulling at her dress and bellowing his voice hammered back and forth between the walls in waves and she shrinking against the wall getting smaller and smaller with her white face her eyes like thumbs dug into it until he pushed her out of the room his voice hammering back and forth as though its own momentum would not let it stop as though there were no place for it in silence bellowing

When you opened the door a bell tinkled, but just once, high and clear and small in the neat obscurity above the door, as though it were gauged and tempered to make that single clear small sound so as not to wear the bell out nor to require the expenditure of too much silence in restoring it when the door opened upon the recent warm scent of baking; a little dirty child with eyes like a toy bear's and two patent-leather pigtails.

"Hello, sister." Her face was like a cup of milk dashed with coffee in the sweet warm emptiness. "Anybody here?"

But she merely watched me until a door opened and the lady came. Above the counter where the ranks of crisp shapes behind the glass her neat gray face her hair tight and sparse from her neat gray skull, spectacles in neat gray rims riding approaching like something on a wire, like a cash box in a store. She looked like a librarian. Something among dusty shelves of ordered certitudes long divorced from reality, desiccating peacefully, as if a breath of that air which sees injustice done

"Two of these, please, ma'am."

From under the counter she produced a square cut from a newspaper and laid it on the counter and lifted the two buns out. The little girl watched them with still and unwinking eyes like two currants floating motionless in a cup of weak coffee Land of the kike home of the wop. Watching the bread, the neat gray hands, a broad gold band on the left forefinger, knuckled there by a blue knuckle.

"Do you do your own baking, ma'am?"

"Sir?" she said. Like that. Sir? Like on the stage. Sir? "Five cents. Was there anything else?"

"No, ma'am. Not for me. This lady wants something." She was not tall enough to see over the case, so she went to the end of the counter and looked at the little girl.

"Did you bring her in here?"

"No, ma'am. She was here when I came."

"You little wretch," she said. She came out around the counter, but she didn't touch the little girl. "Have you got anything in your pockets?"

"She hasn't got any pockets," I said. "She wasn't doing anything. She was just standing here, waiting for you."

"Why didn't the bell ring, then?" She glared at me. She just needed a bunch of switches, a blackboard behind her 2 x 2 e 5. "She'll hide it under her dress and a body'd never know it. You, child. How'd you get in here?"

The little girl said nothing. She looked at the woman, then she gave me a flying black glance and looked at the woman again. "Them foreigners," the woman said. "How'd she get in without the bell ringing?"

"She came in when I opened the door," I said. "It rang once for both of us. She couldn't reach anything from here, anyway. Besides, I dont think she would. Would you, sister?" The little girl looked at me, secretive, contemplative. "What do you want? bread?"

She extended her fist. It uncurled upon a nickel, moist and dirty, moist dirt ridged into her flesh. The coin was damp and warm. I could smell it, faintly metallic.

"Have you got a five cent loaf, please, ma'am?"

From beneath the counter she produced a square cut from a newspaper sheet and laid it on the counter and wrapped a loaf into it. I laid the coin and another one on the counter. "And another one of those buns, please, ma'am."

She took another bun from the case. "Give me that parcel," she said. I gave it to her and she unwrapped it and put the third bun in and wrapped it and took up the coins and found two coppers in her apron and gave them to me. I handed them to the little girl. Her fingers closed about them, damp and hot, like worms.

"You going to give her that bun?" the woman said.

"Yessum," I said. "I expect your cooking smells as good to her as it does to me."

I took up the two packages and gave the bread to the little girl, the woman all iron-gray behind the counter, watching us with cold certitude. "You wait a minute," she said. She went to the rear. The door opened again and closed. The little girl watched me, holding the bread against her dirty dress.

"What's your name?" I said. She quit looking at me, but she was still motionless. She didn't even seem to breathe. The woman returned. She had a funny looking thing in her hand. She carried it sort of like it might have been a dead pet rat.

"Here," she said. The child looked at her. "Take it," the woman said, jabbing it at the little girl. "It just looks peculiar. I calculate you wont know the difference when you eat it. Here. I cant stand here all day." The child took it, still watching her. The woman rubbed her hands on her apron. "I got to have that bell fixed," she said. She went to the door and jerked it open. The little bell tinkled once, faint and clear and invisible. We moved toward the door and the woman's peering back.

"Thank you for the cake," I said.

"Them foreigners," she said, staring up into the obscurity where the bell tinkled. "Take my advice and stay clear of them, young man."

"Yessum," I said. "Come on, sister." We went out. "Thank you, ma'am."

She swung the door to, then jerked it open again, making the bell give forth its single small note. "Foreigners," she said, peering up at the bell.

We went on. "Well," I said. "How about some ice cream?" She was eating the gnarled cake. "Do you like ice cream?" She gave me a black still look, chewing. "Come on."

We came to the drugstore and had some ice cream. She wouldn't put the loaf down. "Why not put it down so you can eat better?" I said, offering to take it. But she held to it, chewing the ice cream like it was taffy. The bitten cake lay on the table. She ate the ice cream steadily, then she fell to on the cake again, looking about at the showcases. I finished mine and we went out.

"Which way do you live?" I said.

A buggy, the one with the white horse it was. Only Doc Peabody is fat. Three hundred pounds. You ride with him on the uphill side, holding on. Children. Walking easier than holding uphill. *Seen the doctor yet   have you seen   Caddy*

I dont have to I cant ask now afterward it will be all right it wont matter

Because women so delicate so mysterious Father said. Delicate equilibrium of periodical filth between two moons balanced. Moons he said full and yellow as harvest moons her hips thighs. Outside outside of them always but. Yellow. Feet soles with walking like. Then know that some man that all those mysterious and imperious concealed. With all that inside of them shapes an outward suavity waiting for a touch to. Liquid putrefaction like drowned things floating like pale rubber flabbily filled getting the odor of honeysuckle all mixed up.

"You'd better take your bread on home, hadn't you?"

She looked at me. She chewed quietly and steadily; at regular intervals a small distension passed smoothly down her throat. I opened my package and gave her one of the buns. "Goodbye," I said.

I went on. Then I looked back. She was behind me. "Do you live down this way?" She said nothing. She walked beside me, under my elbow sort of, eating. We went on. It was quiet, hardly anyone about *getting the odor of honeysuckle all mixed She would have told me not to let me sit there on the steps hearing her door twilight slamming hearing Benjy still crying Supper she would have to come down then getting honeysuckle all mixed up in it*   We reached the corner.

"Well, I've got to go down this way," I said. "Goodbye." She stopped too. She swallowed the last of the cake, then she began on the bun, watching me across it. "Goodbye," I said. I turned into the street and went on, but I went to the next corner before I stopped.

"Which way do you live?" I said. "This way?" I pointed down the street. She just looked at me. "Do you live over that way? I bet you live close to the station, where the trains are. Dont you?" She just looked at me, serene and secret and chewing. The street was empty both ways, with quiet lawns and houses neat among the trees, but no one at all except back there. We turned and went back. Two men sat in chairs in front of a store.

"Do you all know this little girl? She sort of took up with me and I cant find where she lives."

They quit looking at me and looked at her.

"Must be one of them new Italian families," one said. He wore a rusty frock coat. "I've seen her before. What's your name, little girl?" She looked at them blackly for a while, her jaws moving steadily. She swallowed without ceasing to chew.

"Maybe she cant speak English," the other said.

"They sent her after bread," I said. "She must be able to speak something."

"What's your pa's name?" the first said. "Pete? Joe? name John huh?" She took another bite from the bun.

"What must I do with her?" I said. "She just follows me. I've got to get back to Boston."

"You from the college?"

"Yes, sir. And I've got to get on back."

"You might go up the street and turn her over to Anse. He'll be up at the livery stable. The marshal."

"I reckon that's what I'll have to do," I said. "I've got to do something with her. Much obliged. Come on, sister."

We went up the street, on the shady side, where the shadow of the broken façade blotted slowly across the road. We came to the livery stable. The marshal wasn't there. A man sitting in a chair tilted in the broad low door, where a dark cool breeze smelling of ammonia blew among the ranked stalls, said to look at the postoffice. He didn't know her either.

"Them furriners. I cant tell one from another. You might take her across the tracks where they live, and maybe somebody'll claim her."

We went to the postoffice. It was back down the street. The man in the frock coat was opening a newspaper.

"Anse just drove out of town," he said. "I guess you'd better go down past the station and walk past them houses by the river. Somebody there'll know her."

"I guess I'll have to," I said. "Come on, sister." She pushed the last piece of the bun into her mouth and swallowed it. "Want another?" I said. She looked at me, chewing, her eyes black and unwinking and friendly. I took the other two buns out and gave her one and bit into the other. I asked a man where the station was and he showed me. "Come on, sister."

We reached the station and crossed the tracks, where the river was. A bridge crossed it, and a street of jumbled frame houses followed the river, backed onto it. A shabby street, but with an air heterogeneous and vivid too. In the center of an untrimmed plot enclosed by a fence of gaping and broken pickets stood an ancient lopsided surrey and a weathered house from an upper window of which hung a garment of vivid pink.

"Does that look like your house?" I said. She looked at me over the bun. "This one?" I said, pointing. She just chewed, but it seemed to me that I discerned something affirmative, acquiescent even if it wasn't eager, in her air. "This one?" I said. "Come on, then." I entered the broken gate. I looked back at her. "Here?" I said. "This look like your house?"

She nodded her head rapidly, looking at me, gnawing into the damp halfmoon of the bread. We went on. A walk of broken random flags, speared by fresh coarse blades of grass, led to the broken stoop. There was no movement about the house at all, and the pink garment hanging in no wind from the upper window. There was a bell pull with a porcelain knob, attached to about six feet of wire when I stopped pulling and knocked. The little girl had the crust edgeways in her chewing mouth.

A woman opened the door. She looked at me, then she spoke rapidly to the little girl in Italian, with a rising inflexion, then a pause, interrogatory. She spoke to her again, the little girl looking at her across the end of the crust, pushing it into her mouth with a dirty hand.

"She says she lives here," I said. "I met her down town. Is this your bread?"

"No spika," the woman said. She spoke to the little girl again. The little girl just looked at her.

"No live here?" I said. I pointed to the girl, then at her, then at the door. The woman shook her head. She spoke rapidly. She came to the edge of the porch and pointed down the road, speaking.

I nodded violently too. "You come show?" I said. I took her arm, waving my other hand toward the road. She spoke swiftly, pointing.

"You come show," I said, trying to lead her down the steps.

"Si, si," she said, holding back, showing me whatever it was. I nodded again.

"Thanks. Thanks. Thanks." I went down the steps and walked toward the gate, not running, but pretty fast. I reached the gate and stopped and looked at her for a while. The crust was gone now, and she looked at me with her black, friendly stare. The woman stood on the stoop, watching us.

"Come on, then," I said. "We'll have to find the right one sooner or later."

She moved along just under my elbow. We went on. The houses all seemed empty. Not a soul in sight. A sort of breathlessness that empty houses have. Yet they couldn't all be empty. All the different rooms, if you could just slice the walls away all of a sudden. Madam, your daughter, if you please. No. Madam, for God's sake, your daughter. She moved along just under my elbow, her shiny tight pigtails, and then the last house played out and the road curved out of sight beyond a wall, following the river. The woman was emerging from the broken gate, with a shawl over her head and clutched under her chin. The road curved on, empty. I found a coin and gave it to the little girl. A quarter. "Goodbye, sister," I said. Then I ran.

I ran fast, not looking back. just before the road curved away I looked back. She stood in the road, a small figure clasping the loaf of bread to her filthy little dress, her eyes still and black and unwinking. I ran on.

A lane turned from the road. I entered it and after a while I slowed to a fast walk. The lane went between back premises — unpainted houses with more of those gay and startling colored garments on lines, a barn broken-backed, decaying quietly among rank orchard trees, unpruned and weed-choked, pink and white and murmurous with sunlight and with bees. I looked back. The entrance to the lane was empty. I slowed still more, my shadow pacing me, dragging its head through the weeds that hid the fence.

The lane went back to a barred gate, became defunctive in grass, a mere path scarred quietly into new grass. I climbed the gate into a wood-lot and crossed it and came to another wall and followed that one, my shadow behind me now. There were vines and creepers where at home would be honeysuckle. Coming and coming especially in the dusk when it rained, getting honeysuckle all mixed up in it as though it were not enough without that, not unbearable enough. *What did you let him for kiss kiss*

I didn't let him I made him watching me getting mad What do you think of that? Red print of my hand coming up through her face like turning a light on under your hand her eyes going bright

It's not for kissing I slapped you. Girl's elbows at fifteen Father said you swallow like you had a fishbone in your throat what's the matter with

*you and Caddy across the table not to look at me. It's for letting it be
some darn town squirt I slapped you you will will you now I guess you
say calf rope. My red hand coming up out of her face. What do you think
of that scouring her head into the. Grass sticks criss-crossed into the flesh
tingling scouring her head. Say calf rope say it*

I didn't kiss a dirty girl like Natalie anyway The wall went into shadow,
and then my shadow, I had tricked it again. I had forgot about the river
curving along the road. I climbed the wall. And then she watched me
jump down, holding the loaf against her dress.

I stood in the weeds and we looked at one another for a while.

"Why didn't you tell me you lived out this way, sister?" The loaf was
wearing slowly out of the paper; already it needed a new one. "Well,
come on then and show me the house." *not a dirty girl like Natalie. It
was raining we could hear it on the roof, sighing through the high sweet
emptiness of the barn.*

There? touching her

Not there

*There? not raining hard but we couldn't hear anything but the roof
and if it was my blood or her blood*

She pushed me down the ladder and ran off and left me Caddy did

Was it there it hurt you when Caddy did ran off was it there

Oh She walked just under my elbow, the top of her patent leather
head, the loaf fraying out of the newspaper.

"If you dont get home pretty soon you're going to wear that loaf out.
And then what'll your mamma say?" *I bet I can lift you up*

You cant I'm too heavy

*Did Caddy go away did she go to the house you cant see the barn from
our house did you ever try to see the barn from*

It was her fault she pushed me she ran away

I can lift you up see how I can

Oh her blood or my blood Oh   We went on in the thin dust, our feet
silent as rubber in the thin dust where pencils of sun slanted in the trees.
And I could feel water again running swift and peaceful in the secret
shade.

"You live a long way, dont you. You're mighty smart to go this far to
town by yourself." *It's like dancing sitting down did you ever dance sitting down? We could hear the rain, a rat in the crib, the empty barn
vacant with horses. How do you hold to dance do you hold like this*

Oh

I used to hold like this you thought I wasn't strong enough didn't you

Oh Oh Oh Oh

I hold to use like this I mean did you hear what I said I said

oh oh oh oh

The road went on, still and empty, the sun slanting more and more.
Her stiff little pigtails were bound at the tips with bits of crimson cloth.

A corner of the wrapping flapped a little as she walked, the nose of the loaf naked. I stopped.

"Look here. Do you live down this road? We haven't passed a house in a mile, almost."

She looked at me, black and secret and friendly.

"Where do you live, sister? Dont you live back there in town?"

There was a bird somewhere in the woods, beyond the broken and infrequent slanting of sunlight.

"Your papa's going to be worried about you. Dont you reckon you'll get a whipping for not coming straight home with that bread?"

The bird whistled again, invisible, a sound meaningless and profound, inflexionless, ceasing as though cut off with the blow of a knife, and again, and that sense of water swift and peaceful above secret places, felt, not seen not heard.

"Oh, hell, sister." About half the paper hung limp. "That's not doing any good now." I tore it off and dropped it beside the road. "Come on. We'll have to go back to town. We'll go back along the river."

We left the road. Among the moss little pale flowers grew, and the sense of water mute and unseen. *I hold to use like this I mean I use to hold She stood in the door looking at us her hands on her hips*

You pushed me it was your fault it hurt me too

We were dancing sitting down I bet Caddy cant dance sitting down

Stop that stop that

I was just brushing the trash off the back of your dress

You keep your nasty old hands off of me it was your fault you pushed me down I'm mad at you

I don't care she looked at us stay mad she went away We began to hear the shouts, the splashings; I saw a brown body gleam for an instant.

Stay mad. My shirt was getting wet and my hair. Across the roof hearing the roof loud now I could see Natalie going through the garden among the rain. Get wet I hope you catch pneumonia go on home Cowface. I jumped hard as I could into the hogwallow the mud yellowed up to my waist stinking I kept on plunging until I fell down and rolled over in it "Hear them in swimming, sister? I wouldn't mind doing that myself." If I had time. When I have time. I could hear my watch. *mud was warmer than the rain it smelled awful. She had her back turned I went around in front of her. You know what I was doing? She turned her back I went around in front of her the rain creeping into the mud flatting her bodice through her dress it smelled horrible. I was hugging her that's what I was doing. She turned her back I went around in front of her. I was hugging her I tell you.*

I dont give a damn what you were doing

You dont you dont I'll make you I'll make you give a damn. She hit my hands away I smeared mud on her with the other hand I couldn't feel

*the wet smacking of her hand I wiped mud from my legs smeared it on
her wet hard turning body hearing her fingers going into my face but I
couldn't feel it even when the rain began to taste sweet on my lips*

They saw us from the water first, heads and shoulders. They yelled
and one rose squatting and sprang among them. They looked like bea-
vers, the water lipping about their chins, yelling.

"Take that girl away! What did you want to bring a girl here for? Go
on away!"

"She wont hurt you. We just want to watch you for a while."

They squatted in the water. Their heads drew into a clump, watching
us, then they broke and rushed toward us, hurling water with their hands.
We moved quick.

"Look out, boys; she wont hurt you."

"Go on away, Harvard!" It was the second boy, the one that thought
the horse and wagon back there at the bridge. "Splash them, fellows!"

"Let's get out and throw them in," another said. "I aint afraid of any
girl."

"Splash them! Splash them!" They rushed toward us, hurling water.
We moved back. "Go on away!" they yelled. "Go on away!"

We went away. They huddled just under the bank, their slick heads
in a row against the bright water. We went on. "That's not for us, is it."
The sun slanted through to the moss here and there, leveller. "Poor kid,
you're just a girl." Little flowers grew among the moss, littler than I had
ever seen. "You're just a girl. Poor kid." There was a path, curving along
beside the water. Then the water was still again, dark and still and swift.
"Nothing but a girl. Poor sister." *We lay in the wet grass panting the
rain like cold shot on my back. Do you care now do you do you*

*My Lord we sure are in a mess get up. Where the rain touched my
forehead it began to smart my hand came red away streaking off pink in
the rain. Does it hurt*

Of course it does what do you reckon

*I tried to scratch your eyes out my Lord we sure do stink we better try
to wash it off in the branch*   "There's town again, sister. You'll have to
go home now. I've got to get back to school. Look how late it's getting.
You'll go home now, wont you?" But she just looked at me with her
black, secret, friendly gaze, the half-naked loaf clutched to her breast.
"It's wet. I thought we jumped back in time." I took my handkerchief
and tried to wipe the loaf, but the crust began to come off, so I stopped.
"We'll just have to let it dry itself. Hold it like this." She held it like
that. It looked kind of like rats had been eating it now.   *and the water
building and building up the squatting back the sloughed mud stinking
surfaceward pocking the pattering surface like grease on a hot stove. I told
you I'd make you*

I dont give a goddam what you do

Then we heard the running and we stopped and looked back and saw him coming up the path running, the level shadows flicking upon his legs.

"He's in a hurry. We'd——" then I saw another man, an oldish man running heavily, clutching a stick, and a boy naked from the waist up, clutching his pants as he ran.

"There's Julio," the little girl said, and then I saw his Italian face and his eyes as he sprang upon me. We went down. His hands were jabbing at my face and he was saying something and trying to bite me, I reckon, and then they hauled him off and held him heaving and thrashing and yelling and they held his arms and he tried to kick me until they dragged him back. The little girl was howling, holding the loaf in both arms. The half naked boy was darting and jumping up and down, clutching his trousers and someone pulled me up in time to see another stark naked figure come around the tranquil bend in the path running and change direction in midstride and leap into the woods, a couple of garments rigid as boards behind it. Julio still struggled. The man who had pulled me up said, "Whoa, now. We got you." He wore a vest but no coat. Upon it was a metal shield. In his other hand he clutched a knotted, polished stick.

"You're Anse, aren't you?" I said. "I was looking for you. What's the matter?"

"I warn you that anything you say will be used aganst you," he said. "You're under arrest."

"I killa heem," Julio said. He struggled. Two men held him. The little girl howled steadily, holding the bread. "You steala my seester," Julio said. "Let go, meesters."

"Steal his sister?" I said. "Why, I've been——"

"Shet up," Anse said. "You can tell that to Squire."

"Steal his sister?" I said. Julio broke from the men and sprang at me again, but the marshal met him and they struggled until the other two pinioned his arms again. Anse released him, panting.

"You durn furriner," he said. "I've a good mind to take you up too, for assault and battery." He turned to me again. "Will you come peaceable, or do I handcuff you?"

"I'll come peaceable," I said. "Anything, just so I can find someone ——do something with—— Stole his sister," I said. "Stole his——"

"I've warned you," Anse said. "He aims to charge you with meditated criminal assault. Here, you, make that gal shut up that noise."

"Oh," I said. Then I began to laugh. Two more boys with plastered heads and round eyes came out of the bushes, buttoning shirts that had already dampened onto their shoulders and arms, and I tried to stop the laughter, but I couldn't.

"Watch him, Anse, he's crazy, I believe."

"I'll h-have to qu-quit," I said. "It'll stop in a mu-minute. The other

time it said ah ah ah," I said, laughing. "Let me sit down a while." I sat
down, they watching me, and the little girl with her streaked face and
the gnawed looking loaf, and the water swift and peaceful below the
path. After a while the laughter ran out. But my throat wouldn't quit
trying to laugh, like retching after your stomach is empty.

"Whoa, now," Anse said. "Get a grip on yourself."

"Yes," I said, tightening my throat. There was another yellow butter-
fly, like one of the sunflecks had come loose. After a while I didn't have
to hold my throat so tight. I got up. "I'm ready. Which way?"

We followed the path, the two others watching Julio and the little girl
and the boys somewhere in the rear. The path went along the river to
the bridge. We crossed it and the tracks, people coming to the doors to
look at us and more boys materialising from somewhere until when we
turned into the main street we had quite a procession. Before the drug
store stood an auto, a big one, but I didn't recognise them until Mrs
Bland said,

"Why, Quentin! Quentin Compson!" Then I saw Gerald, and Spoade
in the back seat, sitting on the back of his neck. And Shreve. I didn't
know the two girls.

"Quentin Compson!" Mrs Bland said.

"Good afternoon," I said, raising my hat. "I'm under arrest. I'm sorry
I didn't get your note. Did Shreve tell you?"

"Under arrest?" Shreve said. "Excuse me," he said. He heaped himself up and climbed over their feet and got out. He had on a pair of my
flannel pants, like a glove. I didn't remember forgetting them. I didn't
remember how many chins Mrs Bland had, either. The prettiest girl was
with Gerald in front, too. They watched me through veils, with a kind
of delicate horror. "Who's under arrest?" Shreve said. "What's this, mister?"

"Gerald," Mrs Bland said. "Send these people away. You get in this
car, Quentin."

Gerald got out. Spoade hadn't moved.

"What's he done, Cap?" he said. "Robbed a hen house?"

"I warn you," Anse said. "Do you know the prisoner?"

"Know him," Shreve said. "Look here——"

"Then you can come along to the squire's. You're obstructing justice.
Come along." He shook my arm.

"Well, good afternoon," I said. "I'm glad to have seen you all. Sorry
I couldn't be with you."

"You, Gerald," Mrs Bland said.

"Look here, constable," Gerald said.

"I warn you you're interfering with an officer of the law," Anse said.
"If you've anything to say, you can come to the squire's and make cog-
nizance of the prisoner." We went on. Quite a procession now, Anse
and I leading. I could hear them telling them what it was, and Spoade

asking questions, and then Julio said something violently in Italian and I looked back and saw the little girl standing at the curb, looking at me with her friendly, inscrutable regard.

"Git on home," Julio shouted at her. "I beat hell outa you."

We went down the street and turned into a bit of lawn in which, set back from the street, stood a one storey building of brick trimmed with white. We went up the rock path to the door, where Anse halted everyone except us and made them remain outside. We entered, a bare room smelling of stale tobacco. There was a sheet iron stove in the center of a wooden frame filled with sand,[4] and a faded map on the wall and the dingy plat of a township. Behind a scarred littered table a man with a fierce roach of iron gray hair peered at us over steel spectacles.

"Got him, did ye, Anse?" he said.

"Got him, Squire."

He opened a huge dusty book and drew it to him and dipped a foul pen into an inkwell filled with what looked like coal dust.

"Look here, mister," Shreve said.

"The prisoner's name," the squire said. I told him. He wrote it slowly into the book, the pen scratching with excruciating deliberation.

"Look here, mister," Shreve said. "We know this fellow. We——"

"Order in the court," Anse said.

"Shut up, bud," Spoade said. "Let him do it his way. He's going to anyhow."

"Age," the squire said. I told him. He wrote that, his mouth moving as he wrote. "Occupation." I told him. "Harvard student, hey?" he said. He looked up at me, bowing his neck a little to see over the spectacles. His eyes were clear and cold, like a goat's. "What are you up to, coming out here kidnapping children?"

"They're crazy, Squire," Shreve said. "Whoever says this boy's kidnapping——"

Julio moved violently. "Crazy?" he said. "Dont I catcha heem, eh? Dont I see weetha my own eyes——"

"You're a liar," Shreve said. "You never——"

"Order, order," Anse said, raising his voice.

"You fellers shet up," the squire said. "If they dont stay quiet, turn'em out, Anse." They got quiet. The squire looked at Shreve, then at Spoade, then at Gerald. "You know this young man?" he said to Spoade.

"Yes, your honor," Spoade said. "He's just a country boy in school up there. He dont mean any harm. I think the marshal'll find it's a mistake. His father's a congregational minister."

"H'm," the squire said. "What was you doing, exactly?" I told him, he watching me with his cold, pale eyes. "How about it, Anse?"

"Might have been," Anse said. "Them durn furriners."

---

4. The sand provided protection from fire caused by stray coals.

"I American," Julio said. "I gotta da pape'."

"Where's the gal?"

"He sent her home," Anse said.

"Was she scared or anything?"

"Not till Julio there jumped on the prisoner. They were just walking along the river path, towards town. Some boys swimming told us which way they went."

"It's a mistake, Squire," Spoade said. "Children and dogs are always taking up with him like that. He cant help it."

"H'm," the squire said. He looked out of the window for a while. We watched him. I could hear Julio scratching himself. The squire looked back.

"Air you satisfied the gal aint took any hurt, you, there?"

"No hurt now," Julio said sullenly.

"You quit work to hunt for her?"

"Sure I quit. I run. I run like hell. Looka here, looka there, then man tella me he seen him giva her she eat. She go weetha."

"H'm," the squire said. "Well, son, I calculate you owe Julio something for taking him away from his work."

"Yes, sir," I said. "How much?"

"Dollar, I calculate."

I gave Julio a dollar.

"Well," Spoade said. "If that's all——I reckon he's discharged, your honor?"

The squire didn't look at him. "How far'd you run him, Anse?"

"Two miles, at least. It was about two hours before we caught him."

"H'm," the squire said. He mused a while. We watched him, his stiff crest, the spectacles riding low on his nose. The yellow shape of the window grew slowly across the floor, reached the wall, climbing. Dust motes whirled and slanted. "Six dollars."

"Six dollars?" Shreve said. "What's that for?"

"Six dollars," the squire said. He looked at Shreve a moment, then at me again.

"Look here," Shreve said.

"Shut up," Spoade said. "Give it to him, bud, and let's get out of here. The ladies are waiting for us. You got six dollars?"

"Yes," I said. I gave him six dollars.

"Case dismissed," he said.

"You get a receipt," Shreve said. "You get a signed receipt for that money."

The squire looked at Shreve mildly. "Case dismissed," he said without raising his voice.

"I'll be damned——" Shreve said.

"Come on here," Spoade said, taking his arm. "Good afternoon, Judge. Much obliged." As we passed out the door Julio's voice rose again, violent, then ceased. Spoade was looking at me, his brown eyes quizzical, a little cold. "Well, bud, I reckon you'll do your girl chasing in Boston after this."

"You damned fool," Shreve said. "What the hell do you mean anyway, straggling off here, fooling with these damn wops?"

"Come on," Spoade said. "They must be getting impatient."

Mrs Bland was talking to them. They were Miss Holmes and Miss Daingerfield and they quit listening to her and looked at me again with that delicate and curious horror, their veils turned back upon their little white noses and their eyes fleeing and mysterious beneath the veils.

"Quentin Compson," Mrs Bland said. "What would your mother say. A young man naturally gets into scrapes, but to be arrested on foot by a country policeman. What did they think he'd done, Gerald?"

"Nothing," Gerald said.

"Nonsense. What was it, you, Spoade?"

"He was trying to kidnap that little dirty girl, but they caught him in time," Spoade said.

"Nonsense," Mrs Bland said, but her voice sort of died away and she stared at me for a moment, and the girls drew their breaths in with a soft concerted sound. "Fiddlesticks," Mrs Bland said briskly. "If that isn't just like these ignorant lowclass Yankees. Get in, Quentin."

Shreve and I sat on two small collapsible seats. Gerald cranked the car and got in and we started.

"Now, Quentin, you tell me what all this foolishness is about," Mrs Bland said. I told them, Shreve hunched and furious on his little seat and Spoade sitting again on the back of his neck beside Miss Daingerfield.

"And the joke is, all the time Quentin had us all fooled," Spoade said. "All the time we thought he was the model youth that anybody could trust a daughter with, until the police showed him up at his nefarious work."

"Hush up, Spoade," Mrs Bland said. We drove down the street and crossed the bridge and passed the house where the pink garment hung in the window. "That's what you get for not reading my note. Why didn't you come and get it? Mr MacKenzie says he told you it was there."

"Yessum. I intended to, but I never went back to the room."

"You'd have let us sit there waiting I dont know how long, if it hadn't been for Mr MacKenzie. When he said you hadn't come back, that left an extra place, so we asked him to come. We're very glad to have you anyway, Mr MacKenzie." Shreve said nothing. His arms were folded and he glared straight ahead past Gerald's cap. It was a cap for motoring in England. Mrs Bland said so. We passed that house, and three others, and another yard where the little girl stood by the gate. She didn't have the bread now, and her face looked like it had been streaked with coaldust. I waved my hand, but she made no reply, only her head turned slowly as the car passed, following us with her unwinking gaze. Then we ran beside the wall, our shadows running along the wall, and after a while we passed a piece of torn newspaper lying beside the road and I began to laugh again. I could feel it in my throat and I looked off into the trees where the afternoon slanted, thinking of afternoon and of the bird and the boys in swimming. But still I couldn't stop it and then I knew that if I tried too hard to stop it I'd be crying and I thought about how I'd thought about I could not be a virgin, with so many of them walking along in the shadows and whispering with their soft girlvoices lingering in the shadowy places and the words coming out and perfume and eyes you could feel not see, but if it was that simple to do it wouldn't be anything and if it wasn't anything, what was I and then Mrs Bland said, "Quentin? Is he sick, Mr MacKenzie?" and then Shreve's fat hand touched my knee and Spoade began talking and I quit trying to stop it.

"If that hamper is in his way, Mr MacKenzie, move it over on your side. I brought a hamper of wine because I think young gentlemen should drink wine, although my father, Gerald's grandfather" *ever do that Have you ever done that In the gray darkness a little light her hands locked about*

"They do, when they can get it," Spoade said. "Hey, Shreve?" *her knees her face looking at the sky the smell of honeysuckle upon her face and throat*

"Beer, too," Shreve said. His hand touched my knee again. I moved my knee again. *like a thin wash of lilac colored paint talking about him bringing*

"You're not a gentleman," Spoade said. *him between us until the shape of her blurred not with dark*

"No. I'm Canadian," Shreve said. *talking about him the oar blades winking him along winking the Cap made for motoring in England and all time rushing beneath and they two blurred within the other forever more he had been in the army had killed men*

"I adore Canada," Miss Daingerfield said. "I think it's marvellous."

"Did you ever drink perfume?" Spoade said. *with one hand he could lift her to his shoulder and run with her running Running*

"No," Shreve said. *running the beast with two backs[5] and she blurred in the winking oars running the swine of Euboeleus running coupled within how many Caddy*

"Neither did I," Spoade said. *I dont know too many there was something terrible in me terrible in me Father I have committed Have you ever*

---

5. In *Othello*, Iago uses this expression to describe lovemaking. *Euboeleus:* When Persephone was carried off by Pluto, a swineherd called Eubuleus was herding his swine at the spot, and his herd was engulfed in the chasm down which Pluto vanished with Persephone. In an ancient Greek fertility rite, Eubuleus's fate was recalled by flinging pigs into the chasms of Demeter and Persephone. Women then fetched the decayed remains and, after a purity ritual, sowed the flesh with seeds in the ground to secure a good crop and ensure human fertility. Cakes of dough in the shape of serpents and phalli were cast into the caverns to symbolize fertility.

done that We didnt we didnt do that did we do that

"and Gerald's grandfather always picked his own mint before breakfast, while the dew was still on it. He wouldn't even let old Wilkie touch
it do you remember Gerald but always gathered it himself and made his
own julep. He was as crotchety about his julep as an old maid, measuring everything by a recipe in his head. There was only one man he ever
gave that recipe to; that was" *we did how can you not know it if youll
just wait Ill tell you how it was it was a crime we did a terrible crime it
cannot be hid you think it can but wait   Poor Quentin youve never done
that have you   and Ill tell you how it was Ill tell Father then itll have
to be because you love Father then well have to go away amid the pointing and the horror the clean flame Ill make you say we did Im stronger
than you Ill make you know we did you thought it was them but it was
me listen I fooled you all the time it was me you thought I was in the
house where that damn honeysuckle trying not to think the swing the
cedars the secret surges the breathing locked drinking the wild breath the
yes Yes Yes yes* "never be got to drink wine himself, but he always said
that a hamper what book did you read that in the one where Gerald's
rowing suit of wine was a necessary part of any gentlemen's picnic
basket" *did you love them Caddy did you love them When they touched
me I died*

one minute she was standing there the next he was yelling and pulling
at her dress they went into the hall and up the stairs yelling and shoving
at her up the stairs to the bathroom door and stopped her back against
the door and her arm across her face yelling and trying to shove her into
the bathroom when she came in to supper T. P. was feeding him he
started again just whimpering at first until she touched him then he
yelled she stood there her eyes like cornered rats then I was running in
the gray darkness it smelled of rain and all flower scents the damp warm
air released and crickets sawing away in the grass pacing me with a small
travelling island of silence Fancy watched me across the fence blotchy
like a quilt on a line I thought damn that nigger he forgot to feed her
again I ran down the hill in that vacuum of crickets like a breath travelling across a mirror she was lying in the water her head on the sand spit
the water flowing about her hips there was a little more light in the water
her skirt half saturated flopped along her flanks to the waters motion in
heavy ripples going nowhere renewed themselves of their own movement I stood on the bank I could smell the honeysuckle on the water
gap the air seemed to drizzle with honeysuckle and with the rasping of
crickets a substance you could feel on the flesh
is Benjy still crying
I dont know yes I dont know
poor Benjy
I sat down on the bank the grass was damp a little then I found my shoes
wet

get out of that water are you crazy

but she didnt move her face was a white blur framed out of the blur of the sand by her hair

get out now

she sat up then she rose her skirt flopped against her draining she climbed the bank her clothes flopping sat down

why dont you wring it out do you want to catch cold

yes

the water sucked and gurgled across the sand spit and on in the dark among the willows across the shallow the water rippled like a piece of cloth holding still a little light as water does

hes crossed all the oceans all around the world

then she talked about him clasping her wet knees her face tilted back in the gray light the smell of honeysuckle there was a light in mothers room and in Benjys where T. P. was putting him to bed

do you love him

her hand came out I didnt move it fumbled down my arm and she held my hand flat against her chest her heart thudding

no no

did he make you then he made you do it let him he was stronger than you and he tomorrow Ill kill him I swear I will father neednt know until afterward and then you and I nobody need ever know we can take my school money we can cancel my matriculation Caddy you hate him dont you dont you

she held my hand against her chest her heart thudding I turned and caught her arm

Caddy you hate him dont you

she moved my hand up against her throat her heart was hammering there

poor Quentin

her face looked at the sky it was low so low that all smells and sounds of night seemed to have been crowded down like under a slack tent especially the honeysuckle it had got into my breathing it was on her face and throat like paint her blood pounded against my hand I was leaning on my other arm it began to jerk and jump and I had to pant to get any air at all out of that thick gray honeysuckle

yes I hate him I would die for him Ive already died for him I die for him over and over again everytime this goes

when I lifted my hand I could still feel crisscrossed twigs and grass burning into the palm

poor Quentin

she leaned back on her arms her hands locked about her knees

youve never done that have you

what done what

that what I have what I did

yes yes lots of times with lots of girls
then I was crying her hand touched me again and I was crying against
her damp blouse then she lying on her back looking past my head into
the sky I could see a rim of white under her irises I opened my knife
do you remember the day damuddy died when you sat down in the water
in your drawers
yes
I held the point of the knife at her throat
it wont take but a second just a second then I can do mine I can do
mine then
all right can you do yours by yourself
yes the blades long enough Benjys in bed by now
yes
it wont take but a second Ill try not to hurt
all right
will you close your eyes
no like this youll have to push it harder
touch your hand to it
but she didnt move her eyes were wide open looking past my head at the
sky
Caddy do you remember how Dilsey fussed at you because your drawers
were muddy
dont cry
Im not crying Caddy
push it are you going to
do you want me to
yes push it
touch your hand to it
dont cry poor Quentin
but I couldnt stop she held my head against her damp hard breast I could
hear her heart going firm and slow now not hammering and the water
gurgling among the willows in the dark and waves of honeysuckle coming up the air my arm and shoulder were twisted under me
what is it what are you doing
her muscles gathered I sat up
its my knife I dropped it
she sat up
what time is it
I dont know
she rose to her feet I fumbled along the ground
Im going let it go
to the house
I could feel her standing there I could smell her damp clothes feeling
her there

its right here somewhere
let it go you can find it tomorrow come on
wait a minute Ill find it
are you afraid to
here it is it was right here all the time
was it come on
I got up and followed we went up the hill the crickets hushing before us
its funny how you can sit down and drop something and have to hunt
all around for it
the gray it was gray with dew slanting up into the gray sky then the trees
beyond
damn that honeysuckle I wish it would stop
you used to like it
we crossed the crest and went on toward the trees she walked into me
she gave over a little the ditch was a black scar on the gray grass she
walked into me again she looked at me and gave over we reached the
ditch
lets go this way
what for
lets see if you can still see Nancys bones I havent thought to look in a
long time have you
it was matted with vines and briers dark
they were right here you cant tell whether you see them or not can you
stop Quentin
come on
the ditch narrowed closed she turned toward the trees
stop Quentin
Caddy
I got in front of her again
Caddy
stop it
I held her
Im stronger than you
she was motionless hard unyielding but still
I wont fight stop youd better stop
Caddy dont Caddy
it wont do any good dont you know it wont let me go
the honeysuckle drizzled and drizzled I could hear the crickets watching
us in a circle she moved back went around me on toward the trees
you go on back to the house you neednt come
I went on
why dont you go on back to the house
damn that honeysuckle
we reached the fence she crawled through I crawled through when I rose

from stooping he was coming out of the trees into the gray toward us
coming toward us tall and flat and still even moving like he was still she
went to him
this is Quentin Im wet Im wet all over you dont have to if you dont want
to
their shadows one shadow her head rose it was above his on the sky
higher their two heads
you dont have to if you dont want to
then not two heads the darkness smelled of rain of damp grass and leaves
the gray light drizzling like rain the honeysuckle coming up in damp
waves I could see her face a blur against his shoulder he held her in one
arm like she was no bigger than a child he extended his hand
glad to know you
we shook hands then we stood there her shadow high against his shadow
one shadow
whatre you going to do Quentin
walk a while I think Ill go through the woods to the road and come back
through town
I turned away going
goodnight
Quentin
I stopped
what do you want
in the woods the tree frogs were going smelling rain in the air they
sounded like toy music boxes that were hard to turn and the honeysuckle
come here
what do you want
come here Quentin
I went back she touched my shoulder leaning down her shadow the blur
of her face leaning down from his high shadow I drew back
look out
you go on home
Im not sleepy Im going to take a walk
wait for me at the branch
Im going for a walk
Ill be there soon wait for me you wait
no Im going through the woods
I didnt look back the tree frogs didnt pay me any mind the gray light like
moss in the trees drizzling but still it wouldnt rain after a while I turned
went back to the edge of the woods as soon as I got there I began to smell
honeysuckle again I could see the lights on the courthouse clock and the
glare of town the square on the sky and the dark willows along the branch
and the light in mothers windows the light still on in Benjys room and I
stooped through the fence and went across the pasture running I ran in
the gray grass among the crickets the honeysuckle getting stronger and

stronger and the smell of water then I could see the water the color of
gray honeysuckle I lay down on the bank with my face close to the
ground so I couldnt smell the honeysuckle I couldnt smell it then and I
lay there feeling the earth going through my clothes listening to the
water and after a while I wasnt breathing so hard and I lay there thinking
that if I didnt move my face I wouldnt have to breathe hard and smell it
and then I wasnt thinking about anything at all she came along the bank
and stopped I didnt move
its late you go on home
what
you go on home its late
all right
her clothes rustled I didnt move they stopped rustling
are you going in like I told you
I didnt hear anything
Caddy
yes I will if you want me to I will
I sat up she was sitting on the ground her hands clasped about her knee
go on to the house like I told you
yes Ill do anything you want me to anything yes
she didnt even look at me I caught her shoulder and shook her hard
you shut up
I shook her
you shut up you shut up
yes
she lifted her face then I saw she wasnt even looking at me at all I could
see that white rim
get up
I pulled her she was limp I lifted her to her feet
go on now
was Benjy still crying when you left
go on
we crossed the branch the roof came in sight then the windows upstairs
hes asleep now
I had to stop and fasten the gate she went on in the gray light the smell
of rain and still it wouldnt rain and honeysuckle beginning to come from
the garden fence beginning she went into the shadow I could hear her
feet then
Caddy
I stopped at the steps I couldnt hear her feet
Caddy
I heard her feet then my hand touched her not warm not cool just still
her clothes a little damp still
do you love him now
not breathing except slow like far away breathing

Caddy do you love him now
I dont know
outside the gray light the shadows of things like dead things in stagnant
water
I wish you were dead
do you you coming in now
are you thinking about him now
I dont know
tell me what youre thinking about tell me
stop stop Quentin
you shut up you shut up you hear me you shut up are you going to shut
up
all right I will stop well make too much noise
Ill kill you do you hear
lets go out to the swing theyll hear you here
Im not crying do you say Im crying
no hush now well wake Benjy up
you go on into the house go on now
I am dont cry Im bad anyway you cant help it
theres a curse on us its not our fault is it our fault
hush come on and go to bed now
you cant make me theres a curse on us
finally I saw him he was just going into the barbershop he looked out I
went on and waited
Ive been looking for you two or three days
you wanted to see me
Im going to see you
he rolled the cigarette quickly with about two motions he struck the
match with his thumb
we cant talk here suppose I meet you somewhere
Ill come to your room are you at the hotel
no thats not so good you know that bridge over the creek in there back
of
yes all right
at one oclock right
yes
I turned away
Im obliged to you
look
I stopped looked back
she all right
he looked like he was made out of bronze his khaki shirt
she need me for anything now
Ill be there at one
she heard me tell T. P. to saddle Prince at one oclock she kept watching

me not eating much she came
too
what are you going to do
nothing cant I go for a ride if I want to
youre going to do something what is it
none of your business whore whore
T. P. had Prince at the side door
I wont want him Im going to walk
I went down the drive and out the gate I turned into the lane then I ran
before I reached the bridge I saw him leaning on the rail the horse was
hitched in the woods he looked over his shoulder then he turned his
back he didnt look up until I came onto the bridge and stopped he had
a piece of bark in his hands breaking pieces from it and dropping them
over the rail into the water
I came to tell you to leave town
he broke a piece of bark deliberately dropped it carefully into the water
watched it float away
I said you must leave town
he looked at me
did she send you to me
I say you must go not my father not anybody I say it
listen save this for a while I want to know if shes all right have they been
bothering her up there
thats something you dont need to trouble yourself about
then I heard myself saying Ill give you until sundown to leave town
he broke a piece of bark and dropped it into the water then he laid the
bark on the rail and rolled a cigarette with those two swift motions spun
the match over the rail
what will you do if I dont leave
Ill kill you dont think that just because I look like a kid to you
the smoke flowed in two jets from his nostrils across his face
how old are you
I began to shake my hands were on the rail I thought if I hid them hed
know why
Ill give you until tonight
listen buddy whats your name Benjys the natural isnt he
you are
Quentin
my mouth said it I didnt say it at all
Ill give you till sundown
Quentin
he raked the cigarette ash carefully off against the rail he did it slowly
and carefully like sharpening a pencil my hands had quit shaking
listen no good taking it so hard its not your fault kid it would have been
some other fellow

did you ever have a sister did you
no but theyre all bitches
I hit him my open hand beat the impulse to shut it to his face his hand
moved as fast as mine the cigarette went over the rail I swung with the
other hand he caught it too before the cigarette reached the water he
held both my wrists in the same hand his other hand flicked to his armpit
under his coat behind him the sun slanted and a bird singing somewhere
beyond the sun we looked at one another while the bird singing he
turned my hands loose
look here
he took the bark from the rail and dropped it into the water it bobbed up
the current took it floated away his hand lay on the rail holding the pistol
loosely we waited
you cant hit it now
no
it floated on it was quite still in the woods I heard the bird again and the
water afterward the pistol came up he didnt aim at all the bark disap-
peared then pieces of it floated up spreading he hit two more of them
pieces of bark no bigger than silver dollars
thats enough I guess
he swung the cylinder out and blew into the barrel a thin wisp of smoke
dissolved he reloaded the three chambers shut the cylinder he handed it
to me butt first
what for I wont try to beat that
youll need it from what you said Im giving you this one because youve
seen what itll do
to hell with your gun
I hit him I was still trying to hit him long after he was holding my wrists
but I still tried then it was like I was looking at him through a piece of
colored glass I could hear my blood and then I could see the sky again
and branches against it and the sun slanting through them and he holding me on my feet
did you hit me
I couldnt hear
what
yes how do you feel
all right let go
he let me go I leaned against the rail
do you feel all right
let me alone Im all right
can you make it home all right
go on let me alone
youd better not try to walk take my horse
no you go on

you can hang the reins on the pommel and turn him loose hell go back
to the stable
let me alone you go on and let me alone
I leaned on the rail looking at the water I heard him untie the horse and
ride off and after a while I couldnt hear anything but the water and then
the bird again I left the bridge and sat down with my back against a tree
and leaned my head against the tree and shut my eyes a patch of sun
came through and fell across my eyes and I moved a little further around
the tree I heard the bird again and the water and then everything sort of
rolled away and I didnt feel anything at all I felt almost good after all
those days and the nights with honeysuckle coming up out of the darkness into my room where I was trying to sleep even when after a while I
knew that he hadnt hit me that he had lied about that for her sake too
and that I had just passed out like a girl but even that didnt matter
anymore and I sat there against the tree with little flecks of sunlight
brushing across my face like yellow leaves on a twig listening to the water
and not thinking about anything at all even when I heard the horse
coming fast I sat there with my eyes closed and heard its feet bunch
scuttering the hissing sand and feet running and her hard running hands
fool fool are you hurt
I opened my eyes her hands running on my face
I didnt know which way until I heard the pistol I didnt know where I
didnt think he and you running off slipping
I didnt think he would have
she held my face between her hands bumping my head against the tree
stop stop that
I caught her wrists
quit that quit it
I knew he wouldnt I knew he wouldnt
she tried to bump my head against the tree
I told him never to speak to me again I told him
she tried to break her wrists free
let me go
stop it Im stronger than you stop it now
let me go Ive got to catch him and ask his let me go Quentin please let
me go let me go
all at once she quit her wrists went lax
yes I can tell him I can make him believe anytime I can make him
Caddy
she hadnt hitched Prince he was liable to strike out for home if the
notion took him
anytime he will believe me
do you love him Caddy
do I what

she looked at me then everything emptied out of her eyes and they looked
like the eyes in statues blank and unseeing and serene
put your hand against my throat
she took my hand and held it flat against her throat
now say his name
Dalton Ames
I felt the first surge of blood there it surged in strong accelerating beats
say it again
her face looked off into the trees where the sun slanted and where the
bird
say it again
Dalton Ames
her blood surged steadily beating and beating against my hand

It kept on running for a long time, but my face felt cold and sort of
dead, and my eye, and the cut place on my finger was smarting again. I
could hear Shreve working the pump, then he came back with the basin
and a round blob of twilight wobbling in it, with a yellow edge like a
fading balloon, then my reflection. I tried to see my face in it.

"Has it stopped?" Shreve said. "Give me the rag." He tried to take it
from my hand.

"Look out," I said. "I can do it. Yes, it's about stopped now." I dipped
the rag again, breaking the balloon. The rag stained the water. "I wish I
had a clean one."

"You need a piece of beefsteak for that eye," Shreve said. "Damn if
you wont have a shiner tomorrow. The son of a bitch," he said.

"Did I hurt him any?" I wrung out the handkerchief and tried to clean
the blood off of my vest.

"You cant get that off," Shreve said. "You'll have to send it to the
cleaner's. Come on, hold it on your eye, why dont you."

"I can get some of it off," I said. But I wasn't doing much good.
"What sort of shape is my collar in?"

"I dont know," Shreve said. "Hold it against your eye. Here."

"Look out," I said. "I can do it. Did I hurt him any?"

"You may have hit him. I may have looked away just then or blinked
or something. He boxed the hell out of you. He boxed you all over the
place. What did you want to fight him with your fists for? You goddam
fool. How do you feel?"

"I feel fine," I said. "I wonder if I can get something to clean my
vest."

"Oh, forget your damn clothes. Does your eye hurt?"

"I feel fine," I said. Everything was sort of violet and still, the sky
green paling into gold beyond the gable of the house and a plume of
smoke rising from the chimney without any wind. I heard the pump
again. A man was filling a pail, watching us across his pumping shoul-

der. A woman crossed the door, but she didn't look out. I could hear a cow lowing somewhere.

"Come on," Shreve said. "Let your clothes alone and put that rag on your eye. I'll send your suit out first thing tomorrow."

"All right. I'm sorry I didn't bleed on him a little, at least."

"Son of a bitch," Shreve said. Spoade came out of the house, talking to the woman I reckon, and crossed the yard. He looked at me with his cold, quizzical eyes.

"Well, bud," he said, looking at me, "I'll be damned if you dont go to a lot of trouble to have your fun. Kidnapping, then fighting. What do you do on your holidays? burn houses?"

"I'm all right," I said. "What did Mrs Bland say?"

"She's giving Gerald hell for bloodying you up. She'll give you hell for letting him, when she sees you. She dont object to the fighting, it's the blood that annoys her. I think you lost caste with her a little by not holding your blood better. How do you feel?"

"Sure," Shreve said. "If you cant be a Bland, the next best thing is to commit adultery with one or get drunk and fight him, as the case may be."

"Quite right," Spoade said. "But I didn't know Quentin was drunk."

"He wasn't," Shreve said. "Do you have to be drunk to want to hit that son of a bitch?"

"Well, I think I'd have to be pretty drunk to try it, after seeing how Quentin came out. Where'd he learn to box?"

"He's been going to Mike's every day, over in town," I said.

"He has?" Spoade said. "Did you know that when you hit him?"

"I dont know," I said. "I guess so. Yes."

"Wet it again," Shreve said. "Want some fresh water?"

"This is all right," I said. I dipped the cloth again and held it to my eye. "Wish I had something to clean my vest." Spoade was still watching me.

"Say," he said. "What did you hit him for? What was it he said?"

"I dont know. I dont know why I did."

"The first I knew was when you jumped up all of a sudden and said, 'Did you ever have a sister? did you?' and when he said No, you hit him. I noticed you kept on looking at him, but you didn't seem to be paying any attention to what anybody was saying until you jumped up and asked him if he had any sisters."

"Ah, he was blowing off as usual," Shreve said, "about his women. You know: like he does, before girls, so they dont know exactly what he's saying. All his damn innuendo and lying and a lot of stuff that dont make sense even. Telling us about some wench that he made a date with to meet at a dance hall in Atlantic City and stood her up and went to the hotel and went to bed and how he lay there being sorry for her waiting on the pier for him, without him there to give her what she wanted. Talking about the body's beauty and the sorry ends thereof and how tough women have it, without anything else they can do except lie on their backs. Leda lurking in the bushes, whimpering and moaning for the swan, see.[6] The son of a bitch. I'd hit him myself. Only I'd grabbed up her damn hamper of wine and done it if it had been me."

"Oh," Spoade said, "the champion of dames. Bud, you excite not only admiration, but horror." He looked at me, cold and quizzical. "Good God," he said.

"I'm sorry I hit him," I said. "Do I look too bad to go back and get it over with?"

"Apologies, hell," Shreve said. "Let them go to hell. We're going to town."

"He ought to go back so they'll know he fights like a gentleman," Spoade said. "Gets licked like one, I mean."

"Like this?" Shreve said. "With his clothes all over blood?"

"Why, all right," Spoade said. "You know best."

"He cant go around in his undershirt," Shreve said. "He's not a senior yet. Come on, let's go to town."

"You needn't come," I said. "You go on back to the picnic."

"Hell with them," Shreve said. "Come on here."

"What'll I tell them?" Spoade said. "Tell them you and Quentin had a fight too?"

"Tell them nothing," Shreve said. "Tell her her option expired at sunset. Come on, Quentin. I'll ask that woman where the nearest interurban——"

"No," I said. "I'm not going back to town."

Shreve stopped, looking at me. Turning his glasses looked like small yellow moons.

"What are you going to do?"

"I'm not going back to town yet. You go on back to the picnic. Tell them I wouldn't come back because my clothes were spoiled."

"Look here," he said. "What are you up to?"

"Nothing. I'm all right. You and Spoade go on back. I'll see you tomorrow." I went on across the yard, toward the road.

"Do you know where the station is?" Shreve said.

"I'll find it. I'll see you all tomorrow. Tell Mrs Bland I'm sorry I spoiled her party." They stood watching me. I went around the house. A rock path went down to the road. Roses grew on both sides of the path. I went through the gate, onto the road. It dropped downhill, toward the woods, and I could make out the auto beside the road. I went up the hill. The light increased as I mounted, and before I reached the top I heard a car. It sounded far away across the twilight and I stopped and

6. In Greek mythology, Zeus, while in the form of a swan, impregnates Leda, a Spartan queen.

listened to it. I couldn't make out the auto any longer, but Shreve was standing in the road before the house, looking up the hill. Behind him the yellow light lay like a wash of paint on the roof of the house. I lifted my hand and went on over the hill, listening to the car. Then the house was gone and I stopped in the green and yellow light and heard the car growing louder and louder, until just as it began to die away it ceased all together. I waited until I heard it start again. Then I went on.

As I descended the light dwindled slowly, yet at the same time without altering its quality, as if I and not light were changing, decreasing, though even when the road ran into trees you could have read a newspaper. Pretty soon I came to a lane. I turned into it. It was closer and darker than the road, but when it came out at the trolley stop — another wooden marquee — the light was still unchanged. After the lane it seemed brighter, as though I had walked through night in the lane and come out into morning again. Pretty soon the car came. I got on it, they turning to look at my eye, and found a seat on the left side.

The lights were on in the car, so while we ran between trees I couldn't see anything except my own face and a woman across the aisle with a hat sitting right on top of her head, with a broken feather in it, but when we ran out of the trees I could see the twilight again, that quality of light as if time really had stopped for a while, with the sun hanging just under the horizon, and then we passed the marquee where the old man had been eating out of the sack, and the road going on under the twilight, into twilight and the sense of water peaceful and swift beyond. Then the car went on, the draft building steadily up in the open door until it was drawing steadily through the car with the odor of summer and darkness except honeysuckle. Honeysuckle was the saddest odor of all, I think. I remember lots of them. Wistaria was one. On the rainy days when Mother wasn't feeling quite bad enough to stay away from the windows we used to play under it. When Mother stayed in bed Dilsey would put old clothes on us and let us go out in the rain because she said rain never hurt young folks. But if Mother was up we always began by playing on the porch until she said we were making too much noise, then we went out and played under the wistaria frame.

This was where I saw the river for the last time this morning, about here. I could feel water beyond the twilight, smell. When it bloomed in the spring and it rained the smell was everywhere you didn't notice it so much at other times but when it rained the smell began to come into the house at twilight either it would rain more at twilight or there was something in the light itself but it always smelled strongest then until I would lie in bed thinking when will it stop when will it stop. The draft in the door smelled of water, a damp steady breath. Sometimes I could put myself to sleep saying that over and over until after the honeysuckle got all mixed up in it the whole thing came to symbolise night and unrest I seemed to be lying neither asleep nor awake looking down a long corridor of gray halflight where all stable things had become shadowy paradoxical all I had done shadows all I had felt suffered taking visible form antic and perverse mocking without relevance inherent themselves with the denial of the significance they should have affirmed thinking I was I was not who was not was not who.

I could smell the curves of the river beyond the dusk and I saw the last light supine and tranquil upon tideflats like pieces of broken mirror, then beyond them lights began in the pale clear air, trembling a little like butterflies hovering a long way off. Benjamin the child of. How he used to sit before that mirror. Refuge unfailing in which conflict tempered silenced reconciled. Benjamin the child of mine old age held hostage into Egypt.[7] O Benjamin. Dilsey said it was because Mother was too proud for him. They come into white people's lives like that in sudden sharp black trickles that isolate white facts for an instant in unarguable truth like under a microscope; the rest of the time just voices that laugh when you see nothing to laugh at, tears when no reason for tears. They will bet on the odd or even number of mourners at a funeral. A brothel full of them in Memphis went into a religious trance ran naked into the street. It took three policemen to subdue one of them. Yes Jesus O good man Jesus O that good man.

The car stopped. I got out, with them looking at my eye. When the trolley came it was full. I stopped on the back platform.

"Seats up front," the conductor said. I looked into the car. There were no seats on the left side.

"I'm not going far," I said. "I'll just stand here."

We crossed the river. The bridge, that is, arching slow and high into space, between silence and nothingness where lights — yellow and red and green — trembled in the clear air, repeating themselves.

"Better go up front and get a seat," the conductor said.

"I get off pretty soon," I said. "A couple of blocks."

I got off before we reached the postoffice. They'd all be sitting around somewhere by now though, and then I was hearing my watch and I began to listen for the chimes and I touched Shreve's letter through my coat, the bitten shadows of the elms flowing upon my hand. And then as I turned into the quad the chimes did begin and I went on while the notes came up like ripples on a pool and passed me and went on, saying Quarter to what? All right. Quarter to what.

Our windows were dark. The entrance was empty. I walked close to the left wall when I entered, but it was empty: just the stairs curving up into shadows echoes of feet in the sad generations like light dust upon the shadows, my feet waking them like dust, lightly to settle again.

I could see the letter before I turned the light on, propped against a book on the table so I would see it. Calling him my husband. And then

7. See Genesis 42–44.

Spoade said they were going somewhere, would not be back until late, and Mrs Bland would need another cavalier. But I would have seen him and he cannot get another car for an hour because after six oclock. I took out my watch and listened to it clicking away, not knowing it couldn't even lie. Then I laid it face up on the table and took Mrs Bland's letter and tore it across and dropped the pieces into the waste basket and took off my coat, vest, collar, tie and shirt. The tie was spoiled too, but then niggers. Maybe a pattern of blood he could call that the one Christ was wearing. I found the gasoline in Shreve's room and spread the vest on the table, where it would be flat, and opened the gasoline.

the first car in town a girl Girl that's what Jason couldn't bear smell of gasoline making him sick then got madder than ever because a girl Girl had no sister but Benjamin Benjamin the child of my sorrowful[8] *if I'd just had a mother so I could say Mother Mother* It took a lot of gasoline, and then I couldn't tell if it was still the stain or just the gasoline. It had started the cut to smarting again so when I went to wash I hung the vest on a chair and lowered the light cord so that the bulb would be drying the splotch. I washed my face and hands, but even then I could smell it within the soap stinging, constricting the nostrils a little. Then I opened the bag and took the shirt and collar and tie out and put the bloody ones in and closed the bag, and dressed. While I was brushing my hair the half hour went. But there was until the three quarters anyway, except suppose *seeing on the rushing darkness only his own face no broken feather unless two of them but not two like that going to Boston the same night then my face his face for an instant across the crashing when out of darkness two lighted windows in rigid fleeing crash gone his face and mine just I see saw did I see not goodbye the marquee empty of eating the road empty in darkness in silence the bridge arching into silence darkness sleep the water peaceful and swift not goodbye*

I turned out the light and went into my bedroom, out of the gasoline but I could still smell it. I stood at the window the curtains moved slow out of the darkness touching my face like someone breathing asleep, breathing slow into the darkness again, leaving the touch. *After they had gone up stairs Mother lay back in her chair, the camphor handkerchief to her mouth. Father hasn't moved he still sat beside her holding her hand the bellowing hammering away like no place for it in silence* When I was little there was a picture in one of our books, a dark place into which a single weak ray of light came slanting upon two faces lifted out of the shadow. *You know what I'd do if I were King?* she never was a queen or a fairy she was always a king or a giant or a general *I'd break that place open and drag them out and I'd whip them good* It was torn out, jagged out. I was glad. I'd have to turn back to it until the dungeon was Mother herself she and Father upward into weak light

8. See Genesis 35.18.

holding hands and us lost somewhere below even them without even a
ray of light. Then the honeysuckle got into it. As soon as I turned off
the light and tried to go to sleep it would begin to come into the room
in waves building and building up until I would have to pant to get any
air at all out of it until I would have to get up and feel my way like when
I was a little boy *hands can see touching in the mind shaping unseen
door Door now nothing hands can see* My nose could see gasoline, the
vest on the table, the door. The corridor was still empty of all the feet in
sad generations seeking water. *yet the eyes unseeing clenched like teeth
not disbelieving doubting even the absence of pain shin ankle knee the
long invisible flowing of the stair-railing where a misstep in the darkness
filled with sleeping Mother Father Caddy Jason Maury door I am not
afraid only Mother Father Caddy Jason Maury geting so far ahead sleeping I will sleep fast when I door Door door* It was empty too, the pipes,
the porcelain, the stained quiet walls, the throne of contemplation. I
had forgotten the glass, but I could *hands can see cooling fingers invisible swan-throat where less than Moses rod*[9] *the glass touch tentative not
to drumming lean cool throat drumming cooling the metal the glass full
overfull cooling the glass the fingers flushing sleep leaving the taste of
dampened sleep in the long silence of the throat* I returned up the corridor, waking the lost feet in whispering battalions in the silence, into
the gasoline, the watch telling its furious lie on the dark table. Then the
curtains breathing out of the dark upon my face, leaving the breathing
upon my face. A quarter hour yet. And then I'll not be. The peacefullest
words. Peacefullest words. *Non fui. Sum. Fui. Non sum.*[1] Somewhere
I heard bells once. Mississippi or Massachusetts. I was. I am not. Massachusetts or Mississippi. Shreve has a bottle in his trunk. *Aren't you
even going to open it* Mr and Mrs Jason Richmond Compson announce
the *Three times. Days. Aren't you even going to open it* marriage of
their daughter Candace *that liquor teaches you to confuse the means
with the end* I am. Drink. I was not. Let us sell Benjy's pasture so that
Quentin may go to Harvard and I may knock my bones together and
together. I will be dead in. Was it one year Caddy said. Shreve has a
bottle in his trunk. Sir I will not need Shreve's I have sold Benjy's pasture and I can be dead in Harvard Caddy said in the caverns and the
grottoes of the sea tumbling peacefully to the wavering tides because
Harvard is such a fine sound forty acres is no high price for a fine sound.
A fine dead sound we will swap Benjy's pasture for a fine dead sound. It
will last him a long time because he cannot hear it unless he can smell
it *as soon as she came in the door he began to cry* I thought all the
time it was just one of those town squirts that Father was always teasing
her about until. I didn't notice him any more than any other stranger

9. See Exodus 17.6 and Numbers 20.11.
1. I was not. I am. I was. I am not.

drummer or what thought they were army shirts until all of a sudden I
knew he wasn't thinking of me at all as a potential source of harm but
was thinking of her when he looked at me was looking at me through
her like through a piece of colored glass   *why must you meddle with me
dont you know it wont do any good I thought you'd have left that for
Mother and Jason*
   did Mother set Jason to spy on you   I wouldn't have.
   *Women only use other people's codes of honor it's because she loves
Caddy*   staying downstairs even when she was sick so Father couldn't
kid Uncle Maury before Jason Father said Uncle Maury was too poor a
classicist to risk the blind immortal boy in person he should have chosen
Jason because Jason would have made only the same kind of blunder
Uncle Maury himself would have made not one to get him a black eye
the Patterson boy was smaller than Jason too they sold the kites for a
nickel a piece until the trouble over finances Jason got a new partner
still smaller one small enough anyway because T. P. said Jason still
treasurer but Father said why should Uncle Maury work if he Father
could support five or six niggers that did nothing at all but sit with their
feet in the oven he certainly could board and lodge Uncle Maury now
and then and lend him a little money who kept his Father's belief in the
celestial derivation of his own species at such a fine heat then Mother
would cry and say that Father believed his people were better than hers
that he was ridiculing Uncle Maury to teach us the same thing she
couldn't see that Father was teaching us that all men are just accumulations dolls stuffed with sawdust swept up from the trash heaps where
all previous dolls had been thrown away the sawdust flowing from what
wound in what side [2] that not for me died not. It used to be I thought of
death as a man something like Grandfather a friend of his a kind of
private and particular friend like we used to think of Grandfather's desk
not to touch it not even to talk loud in the room where it was I always
thought of them as being together somewhere all the time waiting for
old Colonel Sartoris to come down and sit with them waiting on a high
place beyond cedar trees Colonel Sartoris was on a still higher place
looking out across at something and they were waiting for him to get
done looking at it and come down Grandfather wore his uniform and
we could hear the murmur of their voices from beyond the cedars they
were always talking and Grandfather was always right
   The three quarters began. The first note sounded, measured and tranquil, serenely peremptory, emptying the unhurried silence for the next
one and that's it if people could only change one another forever that
way merge like a flame swirling up for an instant then blown cleanly out
along the cool eternal dark instead of lying there trying not to think of

2. See John 19.34. Compare with the hymn "Rock of Ages," written by Augustus Montague
Toplady.

the swing until all cedars came to have that vivid dead smell of perfume
that Benjy hated so. Just by imagining the clump it seemed to me that I
could hear whispers secret surges smell the beating of hot blood under
wild unsecret flesh watching against red eyelids the swine untethered in
pairs rushing coupled into the sea [3] and he we must just stay awake and
see evil done for a little while its not always and i it doesnt have to be
even that long for a man of courage and he do you consider that courage
and i yes sir dont you and he every man is the arbiter of his own virtues
whether or not you consider it courageous is of more importance than
the act itself than any act otherwise you could not be in earnest and i
you dont believe i am serious and he i think you are too serious to give
me any cause for alarm you wouldnt have felt driven to the expedient of
telling me you had committed incest otherwise and i i wasnt lying i
wasnt lying and he you wanted to sublimate a piece of natural human
folly into a horror and then exorcise it with truth and i it was to isolate
her out of the loud world so that it would have to flee us of necessity and
then the sound of it would be as though it had never been and he did
you try to make her do it and i i was afraid to i was afraid she might and
then it wouldnt have done any good but if i could tell you we did it
would have been so and then the others wouldnt be so and then the
world would roar away and he and now this other you are not lying now
either but you are still blind to what is in yourself to that part of general
truth the sequence of natural events and their causes which shadows
every mans brow even benjys you are not thinking of finitude you are
contemplating an apotheosis in which a temporary state of mind will
become symmetrical above the flesh and aware both of itself and of the
flesh it will not quite discard you will not even be dead and i temporary
and he you cannot bear to think that someday it will no longer hurt you
like this now were getting at it you seem to regard it merely as an experience that will whiten your hair overnight so to speak without altering
your appearance at all you wont do it under these conditions it will be a
gamble and the strange thing is that man who is conceived by accident
and whose every breath is a fresh cast with dice already loaded against
him will not face that final main which he knows before hand he has
assuredly to face without essaying expedients ranging all the way from
violence to petty chicanery that would not deceive a child until someday
in very disgust he risks everything on a single blind turn of a card no
man ever does that under the first fury of despair or remorse or bereavement he does it only when he has realised that even the despair or remorse
or bereavement is not particularly important to the dark diceman and i
temporary and he it is hard believing to think that a love or a sorrow is a
bond purchased without design and which matures willynilly and is
recalled without warning to be replaced by whatever issue the gods hap-

3. See Matthew 8.28–32; Luke 8.26–34.

pen to be floating at the time no you will not do that until you come to
believe that even she was not quite worth despair perhaps and i i will
never do that nobody knows what i know and he i think youd better go
on up to cambridge right away you might go up into maine for a month
you can afford it if you are careful it might be a good thing watching
pennies has healed more scars than jesus and i suppose i realise what
you believe i will realise up there next week or next month and he then
you will remember that for you to go to harvard has been your mothers
dream since you were born and no compson has ever disappointed a
lady and i temporary it will be better for me for all of us and he every
man is the arbiter of his own virtues but let no man prescribe for another
mans wellbeing and i temporary and he was the saddest word of all there
is nothing else in the world its not despair until time its not even time
until it was

The last note sounded. At last it stopped vibrating and the darkness
was still again. I entered the sitting room and turned on the light. I put
my vest on. The gasoline was faint now, barely noticeable, and in the
mirror the stain didn't show. Not like my eye did, anyway. I put on my
coat. Shreve's letter crackled through the cloth and I took it out and
examined the address, and put it in my side pocket. Then I carried the
watch into Shreve's room and put it in his drawer and went to my room
and got a fresh handkerchief and went to the door and put my hand on
the light switch. Then I remembered I hadn't brushed my teeth, so I
had to open the bag again. I found my toothbrush and got some of
Shreve's paste and went out and brushed my teeth. I squeezed the brush
as dry as I could and put it back in the bag and shut it, and went to the
door again. Before I snapped the light out I looked around to see if there
was anything else, then I saw that I had forgotten my hat. I'd have to go
by the postoffice and I'd be sure to meet some of them, and they'd think
I was a Harvard Square student making like he was a senior. I had forgotten to brush it too, but Shreve had a brush, so I didn't have to open
the bag any more.

April Sixth, 1928.

Once a bitch always a bitch, what I say. I says you're lucky if her playing
out of school is all that worries you. I says she ought to be down there
in that kitchen right now, instead of up there in her room, gobbing paint
on her face and waiting for six niggers that cant even stand up out of a
chair unless they've got a pan full of bread and meat to balance them,
to fix breakfast for her. And Mother says,

"But to have the school authorities think that I have no control over
her, that I cant———"

"Well," I says. "You cant can you? You never have tried to do anything with her," I says. "How do you expect to begin this late, when she's seventeen years old?"

She thought about that for a while.

"But to have them think that . . . I didn't even know she had a report card. She told me last fall that they had quit using them this year. And now for Professor Junkin to call me on the telephone and tell me if she's absent one more time, she will have to leave school. How does she do it? Where does she go? You're down town all day; you ought to see her if she stays on the streets."

"Yes," I says. "If she stayed on the streets. I dont reckon she'd be playing out of school just to do something she could do in public," I says.

"What do you mean?" she says.

"I dont mean anything," I says. "I just answered your question." Then she begun to cry again, talking about how her own flesh and blood rose up to curse her.

"You asked me," I says.

"I dont mean you," she says. "You are the only one of them that isn't a reproach to me."

"Sure," I says. "I never had time to be. I never had time to go to Harvard or drink myself into the ground. I had to work. But of course if you want me to follow her around and see what she does, I can quit the store and get a job where I can work at night. Then I can watch her during the day and you can use Ben for the night shift."

"I know I'm just a trouble and a burden to you," she says, crying on the pillow.

"I ought to know it," I says. "You've been telling me that for thirty years. Even Ben ought to know it now. Do you want me to say anything to her about it?"

"Do you think it will do any good?" she says.

"Not if you come down there interfering just when I get started," I says. "If you want me to control her, just say so and keep your hands off. Everytime I try to, you come butting in and then she gives both of us the laugh."

"Remember she's your own flesh and blood," she says.

"Sure," I says, "that's just what I'm thinking of—flesh. And a little blood too, if I had my way. When people act like niggers, no matter who they are the only thing to do is treat them like a nigger."

"I'm afraid you'll lose your temper with her," she says.

"Well," I says. "You haven't had much luck with your system. You want me to do anything about it, or not? Say one way or the other; I've got to get on to work."

"I know you have to slave your life away for us," she says. "You know if I had my way, you'd have an office of your own to go to, and hours that became a Bascomb. Because you are a Bascomb, despite your name.

I know that if your father could have foreseen——"

"Well," I says, "I reckon he's entitled to guess wrong now and then, like anybody else, even a Smith or a Jones." She begun to cry again.

"To hear you speak bitterly of your dead father," she says.

"All right," I says, "all right. Have it your way. But as I haven't got an office, I'll have to get on to what I have got. Do you want me to say anything to her?"

"I'm afraid you'll lose your temper with her," she says.

"All right," I says. "I wont say anything, then."

"But something must be done," she says. "To have people think I permit her to stay out of school and run about the streets, or that I cant prevent her doing it. . . . Jason, Jason," she says. "How could you. How could you leave me with these burdens."

"Now, now," I says. "You'll make yourself sick. Why dont you either lock her up all day too, or turn her over to me and quit worrying over her?"

"My own flesh and blood," she says, crying. So I says,

"All right. I'll tend to her. Quit crying, now."

"Dont lose your temper," she says. "She's just a child, remember."

"No," I says. "I wont." I went out, closing the door.

"Jason," she says. I didn't answer. I went down the hall. "Jason," she says beyond the door. I went on down stairs. There wasn't anybody in the diningroom, then I heard her in the kitchen. She was trying to make Dilsey let her have another cup of coffee. I went in.

"I reckon that's your school costume, is it?" I says. "Or maybe today's a holiday?"

"Just a half a cup, Dilsey," she says. "Please."

"No, suh," Dilsey says. "I aint gwine do it. You aint got no business wid mo'n one cup, a seventeen year old gal, let lone whut Miss Cahline say. You go on and git dressed for school, so you kin ride to town wid Jason. You fixin to be late again."

"No she's not," I says. "We're going to fix that right now." She looked at me, the cup in her hand. She brushed her hair back from her face, her kimono slipping off her shoulder. "You put that cup down and come in here a minute," I says.

"What for?" she says.

"Come on," I says. "Put that cup in the sink and come in here."

"What you up to now, Jason?" Dilsey says.

"You may think you can run over me like you do your grandmother and everybody else," I says. "But you'll find out different. I'll give you ten seconds to put that cup down like I told you."

She quit looking at me. She looked at Dilsey. "What time is it, Dilsey?" she says. "When it's ten seconds, you whistle. Just a half a cup. Dilsey, pl——"

I grabbed her by the arm. She dropped the cup. It broke on the floor and she jerked back, looking at me, but I held her arm. Dilsey got up from her chair.

"You, Jason," she says.

"You turn me loose," Quentin says. "I'll slap you."

"You will, will you?" I says. "You will will you?" She slapped at me. I caught that hand too and held her like a wildcat. "You will, will you?" I says. "You think you will?"

"You, Jason!" Dilsey says. I dragged her into the diningroom. Her kimono came unfastened, flapping about her, dam near naked. Dilsey came hobbling along. I turned and kicked the door shut in her face.

"You keep out of here," I says.

Quentin was leaning against the table, fastening her kimono. I looked at her.

"Now," I says. "I want to know what you mean, playing out of school and telling your grandmother lies and forging her name on your report and worrying her sick. What do you mean by it?"

She didn't say anything. She was fastening her kimono up under her chin, pulling it tight around her, looking at me. She hadn't got around to painting herself yet and her face looked like she had polished it with a gun rag. I went and grabbed her wrist. "What do you mean?" I says.

"None of your damn business," she says. "You turn me loose."

Dilsey came in the door. "You, Jason," she says.

"You get out of here, like I told you," I says, not even looking back. "I want to know where you go when you play out of school," I says. "You keep off the streets, or I'd see you. Who do you play out with? Are you hiding out in the woods with one of those dam slick-headed jelly-beans? Is that where you go?"

"You — you old goddam!" she says. She fought, but I held her. "You damn old goddam!" she says.

"I'll show you," I says. "You may can scare an old woman off, but I'll show you who's got hold of you now." I held her with one hand, then she quit fighting and watched me, her eyes getting wide and black.

"What are you going to do?" she says.

"You wait until I get this belt out and I'll show you," I says, pulling my belt out. Then Dilsey grabbed my arm.

"Jason," she says. "You, Jason! Aint you shamed of yourself."

"Dilsey," Quentin says. "Dilsey."

"I aint gwine let him," Dilsey says. "Dont you worry, honey." She held to my arm. Then the belt came out and I jerked loose and flung her away. She stumbled into the table. She was so old she couldn't do any more than move hardly. But that's all right: we need somebody in the kitchen to eat up the grub the young ones cant tote off. She came hobbling between us, trying to hold me again. "Hit me, den," she says, "ef nothin else but hittin somebody wont do you. Hit me," she says.

"You think I wont?" I says.

"I dont put no devilment beyond you," she says. Then I heard Mother on the stairs. I might have known she wasn't going to keep out of it. I let go. She stumbled back against the wall, holding her kimono shut.

"All right," I says. "We'll just put this off a while. But dont think you can run it over me. I'm not an old woman, nor an old half dead nigger, either. You dam little slut," I says.

"Dilsey," she says. "Dilsey, I want my mother."

Dilsey went to her. "Now, now," she says. "He aint gwine so much as lay his hand on you while Ise here." Mother came on down the stairs.

"Jason," she says. "Dilsey."

"Now, now," Dilsey says. "I aint gwine let him tech you." She put her hand on Quentin. She knocked it down.

"You damn old nigger," she says. She ran toward the door.

"Dilsey," Mother says on the stairs. Quentin ran up the stairs, passing her. "Quentin," Mother says. "You, Quentin." Quentin ran on. I could hear her when she reached the top, then in the hall. Then the door slammed.

Mother had stopped. Then she came on. "Dilsey," she says.

"All right," Dilsey says. "Ise comin. You go on and git dat car and wait now," she says, "so you kin cahy her to school."

"Dont you worry," I says. "I'll take her to school and I'm going to see that she stays there. I've started this thing, and I'm going through with it."

"Jason," Mother says on the stairs.

"Go on, now," Dilsey says, going toward the door. "You want to git her started too? Ise comin, Miss Cahline."

I went on out. I could hear them on the steps. "You go on back to bed now," Dilsey was saying. "Dont you know you aint feeling well enough to git up yet? Go on back, now. I'm gwine to see she gits to school in time."

I went on out the back to back the car out, then I had to go all the way round to the front before I found them.

"I thought I told you to put that tire on the back of the car," I says.

"I aint had time," Luster says. "Aint nobody to watch him till mammy git done in de kitchen."

"Yes," I says. "I feed a whole dam kitchen full of niggers to follow around after him, but if I want an automobile tire changed, I have to do it myself."

"I aint had nobody to leave him wid," he says. Then he begun moaning and slobbering.

"Take him on round to the back," I says. "What the hell makes you want to keep him around here where people can see him?" I made them go on, before he got started bellowing good. It's bad enough on Sundays, with that dam field full of people that haven't got a side show and six niggers to feed, knocking a dam oversize mothball around. He's going to keep on running up and down that fence and bellowing every time they come in sight until first thing I know they're going to begin charging me golf dues, then Mother and Dilsey'll have to get a couple of china door knobs and a walking stick and work it out, unless I play at night with a lantern. Then they'd send us all to Jackson, maybe. God knows, they'd hold Old Home week when that happened.

I went on back to the garage. There was the tire, leaning against the wall, but be damned if I was going to put it on. I backed out and turned around. She was standing by the drive. I says,

"I know you haven't got any books: I just want to ask you what you did with them, if it's any of my business. Of course I haven't got any right to ask," I says. "I'm just the one that paid $11.65 for them last September."

"Mother buys my books," she says. "There's not a cent of your money on me. I'd starve first."

"Yes?" I says. "You tell your grandmother that and see what she says. You dont look all the way naked," I says, "even if that stuff on your face does hide more of you than anything else you've got on."

"Do you think your money or hers either paid for a cent of this?" she says.

"Ask your grandmother," I says. "Ask her what became of those checks. You saw her burn one of them, as I remember." She wasn't even listening, with her face all gummed up with paint and her eyes hard as a fice dog's.

"Do you know what I'd do if I thought your money or hers either bought one cent of this?" she says, putting her hand on her dress.

"What would you do?" I says. "Wear a barrel?"

"I'd tear it right off and throw it into the street," she says. "Dont you believe me?"

"Sure you would," I says. "You do it every time."

"See if I wouldn't," she says. She grabbed the neck of her dress in both hands and made like she would tear it.

"You tear that dress," I says, "and I'll give you a whipping right here that you'll remember all your life."

"See if I dont," she says. Then I saw that she really was trying to tear it, to tear it right off of her. By the time I got the car stopped and grabbed her hands there was about a dozen people looking. It made me so mad for a minute it kind of blinded me.

"You do a thing like that again and I'll make you sorry you ever drew breath," I says.

"I'm sorry now," she says. She quit, then her eyes turned kind of funny and I says to myself if you cry here in this car, on the street, I'll whip you. I'll wear you out. Lucky for her she didn't, so I turned her wrists loose and drove on. Luckily we were near an alley, where I could turn into the back street and dodge the square. They were already putting the tent up in Beard's lot. Earl had already given me the two passes for our show windows. She sat there with her face turned away, chewing her lip. "I'm sorry now," she says. "I dont see why I was ever born."

"And I know of at least one other person that dont understand all he knows about that," I says. I stopped in front of the school house. The bell had rung, and the last of them were just going in. "You're on time for once, anyway," I says. "Are you going in there and stay there, or am I coming with you and make you?" She got out and banged the door. "Remember what I say," I says. "I mean it. Let me hear one more time that you are slipping up and down back alleys with one of those dam squirts."

She turned back at that, "I dont slip around," she says, "I dare anybody to know everything I do."

"And they all know it, too," I says. "Everybody in this town knows what you are. But I wont have it anymore, you hear? I dont care what you do, myself," I says. "But I've got a position in this town, and I'm not going to have any member of my family going on like a nigger wench. You hear me?"

"I dont care," she says. "I'm bad and I'm going to hell, and I dont care. I'd rather be in hell than anywhere where you are."

"If I hear one more time that you haven't been to school, you'll wish you were in hell," I says. She turned and ran on across the yard. "One more time, remember," I says. She didn't look back.

I went to the postoffice and got the mail and drove on to the store and parked. Earl looked at me when I came in. I gave him a chance to say something about my being late, but he just said,

"Those cultivators have come. You'd better help Uncle Job put them up."

I went on to the barn, where old Job was uncrating them, at the rate of about three bolts to the hour.

"You ought to be working for me," I says. "Every other no-count nigger in town eats in my kitchen."

'I works to suit de man whut pays me Sat'dy night," he says. "When I does dat, it dont leave me a whole lot of time to please other folks." He screwed up a nut. "Aint nobody works much in dis country cep de boll-weevil, noways," he says.

"You'd better be glad you're not a boll-weevil waiting on those cultivators," I says. "You'd work yourself to death before they'd be ready to prevent you."

"Dat's de troof," he says. "Boll-weevil got tough time. Work ev'y day in de week out in de hot sun, rain er shine. Aint got no front porch to set on en watch de wattermilyuns growin en Sat'dy dont mean nothin a-tall to him."

"Saturday wouldn't mean nothing to you, either," I says, "if it depended on me to pay you wages. Get those things out of the crates now and drag them inside."

I opened her letter first and took the check out. Just like a woman. Six days late. Yet they try to make men believe that they're capable of conducting a business. How long would a man that thought the first of the month came on the sixth last in business. And like as not, when they sent the bank statement out, she would want to know why I never deposited my salary until the sixth. Things like that never occur to a woman.

> "I had no answer to my letter about Quentin's easter dress. Did it arrive all right? I've had no answer to the last two letters I wrote her, though the check in the second one was cashed with the other check. Is she sick? Let me know at once or I'll come there and see for myself. You promised you would let me know when she needed things. I will expect to hear from you before the 10th. No you'd better wire me at once. You are opening my letters to her. I know that as well as if I were looking at you. You'd better wire me at once about her to this address."

About that time Earl started yelling at Job, so I put them away and went over to try to put some life into him. What this country needs is white labor. Let these dam trifling niggers starve for a couple of years, then they'd see what a soft thing they have.

Along toward ten oclock I went up front. There was a drummer there. It was a couple of minutes to ten, and I invited him up the street to get a dope.[1] We got to talking about crops.

"There's nothing to it," I says. "Cotton is a speculator's crop. They fill the farmer full of hot air and get him to raise a big crop for them to whipsaw[2] on the market, to trim the suckers with. Do you think the farmer gets anything out of it except a red neck and a hump in his back? You think the man that sweats to put it into the ground gets a red cent more than a bare living," I says. "Let him make a big crop and it wont be worth picking; let him make a small crop and he wont have enough to gin. And what for? so a bunch of dam eastern jews I'm not talking about men of the jewish religion," I says. "I've known some jews that were fine citizens. You might be one yourself," I says.

"No," he says. "I'm an American."

"No offense," I says. "I give every man his due, regardless of religion or anything else. I have nothing against jews as an individual," I says. "It's just the race. You'll admit that they produce nothing. They follow the pioneers into a new country and sell them clothes."

1. The first edition reads "coca-cola," for which "dope" was a slang term.
2. To win two bets at one time, as in a gambling game; here—the cotton market.

"You're thinking of Armenians," he says, "aren't you. A pioneer wouldn't have any use for new clothes."

"No offense," I says. "I dont hold a man's religion against him."

"Sure," he says. "I'm an American. My folks have some French blood, why I have a nose like this. I'm an American, all right."

"So am I," I says. "Not many of us left. What I'm talking about is the fellows that sit up there in New York and trim the sucker gamblers."

"That's right," he says. "Nothing to gambling, for a poor man. There ought to be a law against it."

"Dont you think I'm right?" I says.

"Yes," he says. "I guess you're right. The farmer catches it coming and going."

"I know I'm right," I says. "It's a sucker game, unless a man gets inside information from somebody that knows what's going on. I happen to be associated with some people who're right there on the ground. They have one of the biggest manipulators in New York for an adviser. Way I do it," I says, "I never risk much at a time. It's the fellow that thinks he knows it all and is trying to make a killing with three dollars that they're laying for. That's why they are in the business."

Then it struck ten. I went up to the telegraph office. It opened up a little, just like they said. I went into the corner and took out the telegram again, just to be sure. While I was looking at it a report came in. It was up two points. They were all buying. I could tell that from what they were saying. Getting aboard. Like they didn't know it could go but one way. Like there was a law or something against doing anything but buying. Well, I reckon those eastern jews have got to live too. But I'll be damned if it hasn't come to a pretty pass when any dam foreigner that cant make a living in the country where God put him, can come to this one and take money right out of an American's pockets. It was up two points more. Four points. But hell, they were right there and knew what was going on. And if I wasn't going to take the advice, what was I paying them ten dollars a month for. I went out, then I remembered and came back and sent the wire. "All well. Q writing today."

"Q?" the operator says.

"Yes," I says. "Q. Cant you spell Q?"

"I just asked to be sure," he says.

"You send it like I wrote it and I'll guarantee you to be sure," I says. "Send it collect."

"What you sending, Jason?" Doc Wright says, looking over my shoulder. "Is that a code message to buy?"

"That's all right about that," I says. "You boys use your own judgment. You know more about it than those New York folks do."

"Well, I ought to," Doc says. "I'd a saved money this year raising it at two cents a pound."

Another report came in. It was down a point.

"Jason's selling," Hopkins says. "Look at his face."

"That's all right about what I'm doing," I says. "You boys follow your own judgment. Those rich New York jews have got to live like everybody else," I says.

I went on back to the store. Earl was busy up front. I went on back to the desk and read Lorraine's letter. "Dear daddy wish you were here. No good parties when daddys out of town I miss my sweet daddy." I reckon she does. Last time I gave her forty dollars. Gave it to her. I never promise a woman anything nor let her know what I'm going to give her. That's the only way to manage them. Always keep them guessing. If you cant think of any other way to surprise them, give them a bust in the jaw.

I tore it up and burned it over the spittoon. I make it a rule never to keep a scrap of paper bearing a woman's hand, and I never write them at all. Lorraine is always after me to write to her but I says anything I forgot to tell you will save till I get to Memphis again but I says I dont mind you writing me now and then in a plain envelope, but if you ever try to call me up on the telephone, Memphis wont hold you I says. I says when I'm up there I'm one of the boys, but I'm not going to have any woman calling me on the telephone. Here I says, giving her the forty dollars. If you ever get drunk and take a notion to call me on the phone, just remember this and count ten before you do it.

"When'll that be?" she says.

"What?" I says.

"When you're coming back," she says.

"I'll let you know," I says. Then she tried to buy a beer, but I wouldn't let her. "Keep your money," I says. "Buy yourself a dress with it." I gave the maid a five, too. After all, like I say money has no value; it's just the way you spend it. It dont belong to anybody, so why try to hoard it. It just belongs to the man that can get it and keep it. There's a man right here in Jefferson made a lot of money selling rotten goods to niggers, lived in a room over the store about the size of a pigpen, and did his own cooking. About four or five years ago he was taken sick. Scared the hell out of him so that when he was up again he joined the church and bought himself a Chinese missionary, five thousand dollars a year. I often think how mad he'll be if he was to die and find out there's not any heaven, when he thinks about that five thousand a year. Like I say, he'd better go on and die now and save money.

When it was burned good I was just about to shove the others into my coat when all of a sudden something told me to open Quentin's before I went home, but about that time Earl started yelling for me up front, so I put them away and went and waited on the dam redneck while he spent fifteen minutes deciding whether he wanted a twenty cent hame string or a thirty-five cent one.

"You'd better take that good one," I says, "How do you fellows ever expect to get ahead, trying to work with cheap equipment?"

"If this one aint any good," he says, "why have you got it on sale?"

"I didn't say it wasn't any good," I says. "I said it's not as good as that other one."

"How do you know it's not," he says. "You ever use airy one of them?"

"Because they dont ask thirty-five cents for it," I says. "That's how I know it's not as good."

He held the twenty cent one in his hands, drawing it through his fingers. "I reckon I'll take this hyer one," he says. I offered to take it and wrap it, but he rolled it up and put it in his overalls. Then he took out a tobacco sack and finally got it untied and shook some coins out. He handed me a quarter. "That fifteen cents will buy me a snack of dinner," he says.

"All right," I says. "You're the doctor. But dont come complaining to me next year when you have to buy a new outfit."

"I aint makin next year's crop yit," he says. Finally I got rid of him, but every time I took that letter out something would come up. They were all in town for the show, coming in in droves to give their money to something that brought nothing to the town and wouldn't leave anything except what those grafters in the Mayor's office will split among themselves, and Earl chasing back and forth like a hen in a coop, saying "Yes, ma'am, Mr Compson will wait on you. Jason, show this lady a churn or a nickel's worth of screen hooks."

Well, Jason likes work. I says no I never had university advantages because at Harvard they teach you how to go for a swim at night without knowing how to swim and at Sewanee they dont even teach you what water is.[3] I says you might send me to the state University; maybe I'll learn how to stop my clock with a nose spray and then you can send Ben to the Navy I says or to the cavalry anyway, they use geldings in the cavalry. Then when she sent Quentin home for me to feed too I says I guess that's right too, instead of me having to go way up north for a job they sent the job down here to me and then Mother begun to cry and I says it's not that I have any objection to having it here; if it's any satisfaction to you I'll quit work and nurse it myself and let you and Dilsey keep the flour barrel full, or Ben. Rent him out to a sideshow; there must be folks somewhere that would pay a dime to see him, then she cried more and kept saying my poor afflicted baby and I says yes he'll be quite a help to you when he gets his growth not being more than one and a half times as high as me now and she says she'd be dead soon and then we'd all be better off and so I says all right, all right, have it your way. It's your grandchild, which is more than any other grandparents it's got can say for certain. Only I says it's only a question of time. If you believe

3. Jason's father went to the University of the South, also known as Sewanee.

she'll do what she says and not try to see it, you fool yourself because the first time that was the Mother kept on saying thank God you are not a Compson except in name, because you are all I have left now, you and Maury and I says well I could spare Uncle Maury myself and then they came and said they were ready to start. Mother stopped crying then. She pulled her veil down and we went down stairs. Uncle Maury was coming out of the diningroom, his handkerchief to his mouth. They kind of made a lane and we went out the door just in time to see Dilsey driving Ben and T. P. back around the corner. We went down the steps and got in. Uncle Maury kept saying Poor little sister, poor little sister, talking around his mouth and patting Mother's hand. Talking around whatever it was.

"Have you got your band on?" she says. "Why dont they go on, before Benjamin comes out and makes a spectacle. Poor little boy. He doesn't know. He cant even realise."

"There, there," Uncle Maury says, patting her hand, talking around his mouth. "It's better so. Let him be unaware of bereavement until he has to."

"Other women have their children to support them in times like this." Mother says.

"You have Jason and me," he says.

"It's so terrible to me," she says. "Having the two of them like this, in less than two years."

"There, there." he says. After a while he kind of sneaked his hand to his mouth and dropped them out the window. Then I knew what I had been smelling. Clove stems. [4] I reckon he thought that the least he could do at Father's or maybe the sideboard thought it was still Father and tripped him up when he passed. Like I say, if he had to sell something to send Quentin to Harvard we'd all been a dam sight better off if he'd sold that sideboard and bought himself a one-armed strait jacket with part of the money. I reckon the reason all the Compson gave out before it got to me like Mother says, is that he drank it up. At least I never heard of him offering to sell anything to send me to Harvard.

So he kept on patting her hand and saying "Poor little sister," patting her hand with one of the black gloves that we got the bill for four days later because it was the twenty-sixth because it was the same day one month that Father went up there and got it and brought it home and wouldn't tell anything about where she was or anything and Mother crying and saying "And you didn't even see him? You didn't even try to get him to make any provision for it?" and Father says "No she shall not touch his money not one cent of it" and Mother says "He can be forced to by law. He can prove nothing, unless —— Jason Compson," she says. "Were you fool enough to tell —— "

4. Cloves were often used to conceal the odor of alcohol on the breath.

"Hush, Caroline," Father says, then he sent me to help Dilsey get that old cradle out of the attic and I says,

"Well, they brought my job home tonight" because all the time we kept hoping they'd get things straightened out and he'd keep her because Mother kept saying she would at least have enough regard for the family not to jeopardise my chance after she and Quentin had had theirs.

"And whar else do she belong?" Dilsey says. "Who else gwine raise her cep me? Aint I raised ev'y one of y'all?"

"And a dam fine job you made of it," I says. "Anyway it'll give her something to sure enough worry over now." So we carried the cradle down and Dilsey started to set it up in her old room. Then Mother started sure enough.

"Hush, Miss Cahline," Dilsey says. "You gwine wake her up."

"In there?" Mother says. "To be contaminated by that atmosphere? It'll be hard enough as it is, with the heritage she already has."

"Hush," Father says. "Dont be silly."

"Why aint she gwine sleep in here," Dilsey says. "In the same room whar I put her maw to bed ev'y night of her life since she was big enough to sleep by herself."

"You dont know," Mother says. "To have my own daughter cast off by her husband. Poor little innocent baby," she says, looking at Quentin. "You will never know the suffering you've caused."

"Hush, Caroline," Father says.

"What you want to go on like that fo Jason fer?" Dilsey says.

"I've tried to protect him," Mother says. "I've always tried to protect him from it. At least I can do my best to shield her."

"How sleepin in dis room gwine hurt her, I like to know," Dilsey says.

"I cant help it," Mother says. "I know I'm just a troublesome old woman. But I know that people cannot flout God's laws with impunity."

"Nonsense," Father says. "Fix it in Miss Caroline's room then, Dilsey."

"You can say nonsense," Mother says. "But she must never know. She must never even learn that name. Dilsey, I forbid you ever to speak that name in her hearing. If she could grow up never to know that she had a mother, I would thank God."

"Dont be a fool," Father says.

"I have never interfered with the way you brought them up," Mother says. "But now I cannot stand anymore. We must decide this now, tonight. Either that name is never to be spoken in her hearing, or she must go, or I will go. Take your choice."

"Hush," Father says. "You're just upset. Fix it in here, Dilsey."

"En you's about sick too," Dilsey says. "You looks like a hant. You git in bed and I'll fix you a toddy and see kin you sleep. I bet you aint had a full night's sleep since you lef."

"No," Mother says. "Dont you know what the doctor says? Why must you encourage him to drink? That's what's the matter with him now. Look at me, I suffer too, but I'm not so weak that I must kill myself with whiskey."

"Fiddlesticks," Father says. "What do doctors know? They make their livings advising people to do whatever they are not doing at the time, which is the extent of anyone's knowledge of the degenerate ape. You'll have a minister in to hold my hand next." Then Mother cried, and he went out. Went down stairs, and then I heard the sideboard. I woke up and heard him going down again. Mother had gone to sleep or something, because the house was quiet at last. He was trying to be quiet too, because I couldn't hear him, only the bottom of his nightshirt and his bare legs in front of the sideboard.

Dilsey fixed the cradle and undressed her and put her in it. She never had waked up since he brought her in the house.

"She pretty near too big fer hit," Dilsey says. "Dar now. I gwine spread me a pallet right acrost de hall, so you wont need to git up in de night."

"I wont sleep," Mother says. "You go on home. I wont mind. I'll be happy to give the rest of my life to her, if I can just prevent—— "

"Hush, now," Dilsey says. "We gwine take keer of her. En you go on to bed too," she says to me. "You got to go to school tomorrow."

So I went out, then Mother called me back and cried on me a while.

"You are my only hope," she says. "Every night I thank God for you." While we were waiting there for them to start she says Thank God if he had to be taken too, it is you left me and not Quentin. Thank God you are not a Compson, because all I have left now is you and Maury and I says, Well I could spare Uncle Maury myself. Well, he kept on patting her hand with his black glove, talking away from her. He took them off when his turn with the shovel came. He got up near the first, where they were holding the umbrellas over them, stamping every now and then and trying to kick the mud off their feet and sticking to the shovels so they'd have to knock it off, making a hollow sound when it fell on it, and when I stepped back around the hack I could see him behind a tombstone, taking another one out of a bottle. I thought he never was going to stop because I had on my new suit too, but it happened that there wasn't much mud on the wheels yet, only Mother saw it and says I dont know when you'll ever have another one and Uncle Maury says, "Now, now. Dont you worry at all. You have me to depend on, always."

And we have. Always. The fourth letter was from him. But there wasn't any need to open it. I could have written it myself, or recited it to her from memory, adding ten dollars just to be safe. But I had a hunch about that other letter. I just felt that it was about time she was up to some of her tricks again. She got pretty wise after that first time. She found out pretty quick that I was a different breed of cat from Father. When they begun to get it filled up toward the top Mother started crying sure enough, so Uncle Maury got in with her and drove off. He says You can come in with somebody: they'll be glad to give you a lift. I'll have to take your mother on and I thought about saying, Yes you ought to brought two bottles instead of just one only I thought about where we were, so I let them go on. Little they cared how wet I got, because then Mother could have a whale of a time being afraid I was taking pneumonia.

Well, I got to thinking about that and watching them throwing dirt into it, slapping it on anyway like they were making mortar or something or building a fence, and I began to feel sort of funny and so I decided to walk around a while. I thought that if I went toward town they'd catch up and be trying to make me get in one of them, so I went on back toward the nigger graveyard. I got under some cedars, where the rain didn't come much, only dripping now and then, where I could see when they got through and went away. After a while they were all gone and I waited a minute and came out.

I had to follow the path to keep out of the wet grass so I didn't see her until I was pretty near there, standing there in a black cloak, looking at the flowers. I knew who it was right off, before she turned and looked at me and lifted up her veil.

"Hello, Jason," she says, holding out her hand. We shook hands.

"What are you doing here?" I says. "I thought you promised her you wouldn't come back here. I thought you had more sense than that."

"Yes?" she says. She looked at the flowers again. There must have been fifty dollars' worth. Somebody had put one bunch on Quentin's. "You did?" she says.

"I'm not surprised though," I says. "I wouldn't put anything past you. You dont mind anybody. You dont give a dam about anybody."

"Oh," she says, "that job." She looked at the grave. "I'm sorry about that, Jason."

"I bet you are," I says. "You'll talk mighty meek now. But you needn't have come back. There's not anything left. Ask Uncle Maury, if you dont believe me."

"I dont want anything," she says. She looked at the grave. "Why didn't they let me know?" she says. "I just happened to see it in the paper. On the back page. Just happened to."

I didn't say anything. We stood there, looking at the grave, and then I got to thinking about when we were little and one thing and another and I got to feeling funny again, kind of mad or something, thinking about now we'd have Uncle Maury around the house all the time, running things like the way he left me to come home in the rain by myself. I says,

"A fine lot you care, sneaking in here soon as he's dead. But it wont do you any good. Dont think that you can take advantage of this to come sneaking back. If you cant stay on the horse you've got, you'll have to walk," I says. "We dont even know your name at that house," I says. "Do you know that? We dont even know your name. You'd be better off if you were down there with him and Quentin," I says. "Do you know that?"

"I know it," she says. "Jason," she says, looking at the grave, "if you'll fix it so I can see her a minute I'll give you fifty dollars."

"You haven't got fifty dollars," I says.

"Will you?" she says, not looking at me.

"Let's see it," I says. "I dont believe you've got fifty dollars."

I could see where her hands were moving under her cloak, then she held her hand out. Dam if it wasn't full of money. I could see two or three yellow ones.[5]

"Does he still give you money?" I says. "How much does he send you?"

"I'll give you a hundred," she says. "Will you?"

"Just a minute," I says. "And just like I say. I wouldn't have her know it for a thousand dollars."

"Yes," she says. "Just like you say do it. Just so I see her a minute. I wont beg or do anything. I'll go right on away."

"Give me the money," I says.

"I'll give it to you afterward," she says.

"Dont you trust me?" I says.

"No," she says. "I know you. I grew up with you."

"You're a fine one to talk about trusting people," I says. "Well," I says. "I got to get on out of the rain. Goodbye." I made to go away.

"Jason," she says. I stopped.

"Yes?" I says. "Hurry up. I'm getting wet."

"All right," she says. "Here." There wasn't anybody in sight. I went back and took the money. She still held to it. "You'll do it?" she says, looking at me from under the veil. "You promise?"

"Let go," I says. "You want somebody to come along and see us?"

She let go. I put the money in my pocket. "You'll do it, Jason?" she says. "I wouldn't ask you, if there was any other way."

"You dam right there's no other way," I says. "Sure I'll do it. I said I would, didn't I? Only you'll have to do just like I say, now."

"Yes," she says. "I will." So I told her where to be, and went to the livery stable. I hurried and got there just as they were unhitching the hack. I asked if they had paid for it yet and he said No and I said Mrs Compson forgot something and wanted it again, so they let me take it. Mink was driving. I bought him a cigar, so we drove around until it begun to get dark on the back streets where they wouldn't see him. Then Mink said he'd have to take the team on back and so I said I'd buy him another cigar and so we drove into the lane and I went across the yard

5. Also called "yellow backs." Bank notes, especially gold certificates.

to the house. I stopped in the hall until I could hear Mother and Uncle Maury upstairs, then I went on back to the kitchen. She and Ben were there with Dilsey. I said Mother wanted her and I took her into the house. I found Uncle Maury's raincoat and put it around her and picked her up and went back to the lane and got in the hack. I told Mink to drive to the depot. He was afraid to pass the stable, so we had to go the back way and I saw her standing on the corner under the light and I told Mink to drive close to the walk and when I said Go on, to give the team a bat. Then I took the raincoat off of her and held her to the window and Caddy saw her and sort of jumped forward.

"Hit 'em, Mink!" I says, and Mink gave them a cut and we went past her like a fire engine. "Now get on that train like you promised," I says. I could see her running after us through the back window. "Hit 'em again," I says. "Let's get on home." When we turned the corner she was still running.

And so I counted the money again that night and put it away, and I didn't feel so bad. I says I reckon that'll show you. I reckon you'll know now that you cant beat me out of a job and get away with it. It never occurred to me she wouldn't keep her promise and take that train. But I didn't know much about them then; I didn't have any more sense than to believe what they said, because the next morning dam if she didn't walk right into the store, only she had sense enough to wear the veil and not speak to anybody. It was Saturday morning, because I was at the store, and she came right on back to the desk where I was, walking fast.

"Liar," she says. "Liar."

"Are you crazy?" I says. "What do you mean? coming in here like this?" She started in, but I shut her off. I says, "You already cost me one job; do you want me to lose this one too? If you've got anything to say to me, I'll meet you somewhere after dark. What have you got to say to me?" I says. "Didn't I do everything I said? I said see her a minute, didn't I? Well, didn't you?" She just stood there looking at me, shaking like an ague-fit, her hands clenched and kind of jerking. "I did just what I said I would," I says. "You're the one that lied. You promised to take that train. Didn't you? Didn't you promise? If you think you can get that money back, just try it," I says. "If it'd been a thousand dollars, you'd still owe me after the risk I took. And if I see or hear you're still in town after number 17 runs," I says, "I'll tell Mother and Uncle Maury. Then hold your breath until you see her again." She just stood there, looking at me, twisting her hands together.

"Damn you," she says. "Damn you."

"Sure," I says. "That's all right too. Mind what I say, now. After number 17, and I tell them."

After she was gone I felt better. I says I reckon you'll think twice before you deprive me of a job that was promised me. I was a kid then. I believed folks when they said they'd do things. I've learned better since.

Besides, like I say I guess I dont need any man's help to get along I can stand on my own feet like I always have. Then all of a sudden I thought of Dilsey and Uncle Maury. I thought how she'd get around Dilsey and that Uncle Maury would do anything for ten dollars. And there I was, couldn't even get away from the store to protect my own Mother. Like she says, if one of you had to be taken, thank God it was you left me I can depend on you and I says well I dont reckon I'll ever get far enough from the store to get out of your reach. Somebody's got to hold on to what little we have left, I reckon.

So as soon as I got home I fixed Dilsey. I told Dilsey she had leprosy and I got the bible and read where a man's flesh rotted off and I told her that if she ever looked at her or Ben or Quentin they'd catch it too. So I thought I had everything all fixed until that day when I came home and found Ben bellowing. Raising hell and nobody could quiet him. Mother said, Well, get him the slipper then. Dilsey made out she didn't hear. Mother said it again and I says I'd go I couldn't stand that dam noise. Like I say I can stand lots of things I dont expect much from them but if I have to work all day long in a dam store dam if I dont think I deserve a little peace and quiet to eat dinner in. So I says I'd go and Dilsey says quick, "Jason!"

Well, like a flash I knew what was up, but just to make sure I went and got the slipper and brought it back, and just like I thought, when he saw it you'd thought we were killing him. So I made Dilsey own up, then I told Mother. We had to take her up to bed then, and after things got quieted down a little I put the fear of God into Dilsey. As much as you can into a nigger, that is. That's the trouble with nigger servants, when they've been with you for a long time they get so full of self importance that they're not worth a dam. Think they run the whole family.

"I like to know whut's de hurt in lettin dat po chile see her own baby," Dilsey says. "If Mr Jason was still here hit ud be different."

"Only Mr Jason's not here," I says. "I know you wont pay me any mind, but I reckon you'll do what Mother says. You keep on worrying her like this until you get her into the graveyard too, then you can fill the whole house full of ragtag and bobtail. But what did you want to let that dam boy see her for?"

"You's a cold man, Jason, if man you is," she says. "I thank de Lawd I got mo heart dan dat, even ef hit is black."

"At least I'm man enough to keep that flour barrel full," I says. "And if you do that again, you wont be eating out of it either."

So the next time I told her that if she tried Dilsey again, Mother was going to fire Dilsey and send Ben to Jackson and take Quentin and go away. She looked at me for a while. There wasn't any street light close and I couldn't see her face much. But I could feel her looking at me. When we were little when she'd get mad and couldn't do anything about it her upper lip would begin to jump. Everytime it jumped it would leave a little more of her teeth showing, and all the time she'd be as still as a post, not a muscle moving except her lip jerking higher and higher up her teeth. But she didn't say anything. She just said,

"All right. How much?"

"Well, if one look through a back window was worth a hundred," I says. So after that she behaved pretty well, only one time she asked to see a statement of the bank account.

"I know they have Mother's indorsement on them," she says. "But I want to see the bank statement. I want to see myself where those checks go."

"That's in Mother's private business," I says. "If you think you have any right to pry into her private affairs I'll tell her you believe those checks are being misappropriated and you want an audit because you dont trust her."

She didn't say anything or move. I could hear her whispering Damn you oh damn you oh damn you.

"Say it out," I says. "I dont reckon it's any secret what you and I think of one another. Maybe you want the money back," I says.

"Listen, Jason," she says. "Dont lie to me now. About her. I wont ask to see anything. If that isn't enough, I'll send more each month. Just promise that she'll —— that she —— You can do that. Things for her. Be kind to her. Little things that I cant, they wont let. . . . But you wont. You never had a drop of warm blood in you. Listen," she says. "If you'll get Mother to let me have her back, I'll give you a thousand dollars."

"You haven't got a thousand dollars," I says. "I know you're lying now."

"Yes I have. I will have. I can get it."

"And I know how you'll get it," I says. "You'll get it the same way you got her. And when she gets big enough ——" Then I thought she really was going to hit at me, and then I didn't know what she was going to do. She acted for a minute like some kind of a toy that's wound up too tight and about to burst all to pieces.

"Oh, I'm crazy," she says. "I'm insane. I cant take her. Keep her. What am I thinking of. Jason," she says, grabbing my arm. Her hands were hot as fever. "You'll have to promise to take care of her, to —— She's kin to you; your own flesh and blood. Promise, Jason. You have Father's name: do you think I'd have to ask him twice? once, even?"

"That's so," I says. "He did leave me something. What do you want me to do," I says. "Buy an apron and a go-cart? I never got you into this," I says. "I run more risk than you do, because you haven't got anything at stake. So if you expect ——"

"No," she says, then she begun to laugh and to try to hold it back all at the same time. "No. I have nothing at stake," she says, making that noise, putting her hands to her mouth. "Nuh-nuh-nothing," she says.

"Here," I says. "Stop that!"

"I'm tr-trying to," she says, holding her hands over her mouth. "Oh God, oh God."

"I'm going away from here," I says. "I cant be seen here. You get on out of town now, you hear?"

"Wait," she says, catching my arm. "I've stopped. I wont again. You promise, Jason?" she says, and me feeling her eyes almost like they were touching my face. "You promise? Mother——that money——if sometimes she needs things—— If I send checks for her to you, other ones besides those, you'll give them to her? You wont tell? You'll see that she has things like other girls?"

"Sure," I says, "As long as you behave and do like I tell you."

And so when Earl came up front with his hat on he says, "I'm going to step up to Rogers' and get a snack. We wont have time to go home to dinner, I reckon."

"What's the matter we wont have time?" I says.

"With this show in town and all," he says. "They're going to give an afternoon performance too, and they'll all want to get done trading in time to go to it. So we'd better just run up to Rogers'."

"All right," I says. "It's your stomach. If you want to make a slave of yourself to your business, it's all right with me."

"I reckon you'll never be a slave to any business," he says.

"Not unless it's Jason Compson's business," I says.

So when I went back and opened it the only thing that surprised me was it was a money order not a check. Yes, sir. You cant trust a one of them. After all the risk I'd taken, risking Mother finding out about her coming down here once or twice a year sometimes, and me having to tell Mother lies about it. That's gratitude for you. And I wouldn't put it past her to try to notify the postoffice not to let anyone except her cash it. Giving a kid like that fifty dollars. Why I never saw fifty dollars until I was twenty-one years old, with all the other boys with the afternoon off and all day Saturday and me working in a store. Like I say, how can they expect anybody to control her, with her giving her money behind our backs. She has the same home you had I says, and the same raising. I reckon Mother is a better judge of what she needs than you are, that haven't even got a home. "If you want to give her money," I says, "you send it to Mother, dont be giving it to her. If I've got to run this risk every few months, you'll have to do like I say, or it's out."

And just about the time I got ready to begin on it because if Earl thought I was going to dash up the street and gobble two bits worth of indigestion on his account he was bad fooled. I may not be sitting with my feet on a mahogany desk but I am being payed for what I do inside this building and if I cant manage to live a civilised life outside of it I'll go where I can. I can stand on my own feet; I dont need any man's mahogany desk to prop me up. So just about the time I got ready to start

I'd have to drop everything and run to sell some redneck a dime's worth of nails or something, and Earl up there gobbling a sandwich and half way back already, like as not, and then I found that all the blanks were gone. I remembered then that I had aimed to get some more, but it was too late now, and then I looked up and there she came. In the back door. I heard her asking old Job if I was there. I just had time to stick them in the drawer and close it.

She came around to the desk. I looked at my watch.

"You been to dinner already?" I says. "It's just twelve; I just heard it strike. You must have flown home and back."

"I'm not going home to dinner," she says. "Did I get a letter today?"

"Were you expecting one?" I says. "Have you got a sweetie that can write?"

"From Mother," she says. "Did I get a letter from Mother?" she says, looking at me.

"Mother got one from her," I says. "I haven't opened it. You'll have to wait until she opens it. She'll let you see it, I imagine."

"Please, Jason," she says, not paying any attention. "Did I get one?"

"What's the matter?" I says. "I never knew you to be this anxious about anybody. You must expect some money from her."

"She said she——" she says. "Please, Jason," she says. "Did I?"

"You must have been to school today, after all," I says. "Somewhere where they taught you to say please. Wait a minute, while I wait on that customer."

I went and waited on him. When I turned to come back she was out of sight behind the desk. I ran. I ran around the desk and caught her as she jerked her hand out of the drawer. I took the letter away from her, beating her knuckles on the desk until she let go.

"You would, would you?" I says.

"Give it to me," she says. "You've already opened it. Give it to me. Please, Jason. It's mine. I saw the name."

"I'll take a hame string to you," I says. "That's what I'll give you. Going into my papers."

"Is there some money in it?" she says, reaching for it. "She said she would send me some money. She promised she would. Give it to me."

"What do you want with money?" I says.

"She said she would," she says. "Give it to me. Please, Jason. I wont ever ask you anything again, if you'll give it to me this time."

"I'm going to, if you'll give me time," I says. I took the letter and the money order out and gave her the letter. She reached for the money order, not hardly glancing at the letter. "You'll have to sign it first," I says.

"How much is it?" she says.

"Read the letter," I says. "I reckon it'll say."

She read it fast, in about two looks.

"It dont say," she says, looking up. She dropped the letter to the floor. "How much is it?"

"It's ten dollars," I says.

"Ten dollars?" she says, staring at me.

"And you ought to be dam glad to get that," I says. "A kid like you. What are you in such a rush for money all of a sudden for?"

"Ten dollars?" she says, like she was talking in her sleep. "Just ten dollars?" She made a grab at the money order. "You're lying," she says. "Thief!" she says. "Thief!"

"You would, would you?" I says, holding her off.

"Give it to me!" she says. "It's mine. She sent it to me. I will see it. I will."

"You will?" I says, holding her. "How're you going to do it?"

"Just let me see it, Jason," she says. "Please. I wont ask you for anything again."

"Think I'm lying, do you?" I says. "Just for that you wont see it."

"But just ten dollars," she says. "She told me she——she told me ——Jason, please please please. I've got to have some money. I've just got to. Give it to me, Jason. I'll do anything if you will."

"Tell me what you've got to have money for," I says.

"I've got to have it," she says. She was looking at me. Then all of a sudden she quit looking at me without moving her eyes at all. I knew she was going to lie. "It's some money I owe," she says. "I've got to pay it. I've got to pay it today."

"Who to?" I says. Her hands were sort of twisting. I could watch her trying to think of a lie to tell. "Have you been charging things at stores again?" I says. "You needn't bother to tell me that. If you can find anybody in this town that'll charge anything to you after what I told them, I'll eat it."

"It's a girl," she says. "It's a girl. I borrowed some money from a girl. I've got to pay it back. Jason, give it to me. Please. I'll do anything. I've got to have it. Mother will pay you. I'll write to her to pay you and that I wont ever ask her for anything again. You can see the letter. Please, Jason. I've got to have it."

"Tell me what you want with it, and I'll see about it," I says. "Tell me." She just stood there, with her hands working against her dress. "All right," I says. "If ten dollars is too little for you, I'll just take it home to Mother, and you know what'll happen to it then. Of course, if you're so rich you dont need ten dollars——"

She stood there, looking at the floor, kind of mumbling to herself. "She said she would send me some money. She said she sends money here and you say she dont send any. She said she's sent a lot of money here. She says it's for me. That it's for me to have some of it. And you say we haven't got any money."

"You know as much about that as I do," I says. "You've seen what happens to those checks."

"Yes," she says, looking at the floor. "Ten dollars," she says. "Ten dollars."

"And you'd better thank your stars it's ten dollars," I says. "Here," I says. I put the money order face down on the desk, holding my hand on it. "Sign it."

"Will you let me see it?" she says. "I just want to look at it. Whatever it says, I wont ask for but ten dollars. You can have the rest. I just want to see it."

"Not after the way you've acted," I says. "You've got to learn one thing, and that is that when I tell you to do something, you've got it to do. You sign your name on that line."

She took the pen, but instead of signing it she just stood there with her head bent and the pen shaking in her hand. Just like her mother. "Oh, God," she says, "oh, God."

"Yes," I says. "That's one thing you'll have to learn if you never learn anything else. Sign it now, and get on out of here."

She signed it. "Where's the money?" she says. I took the order and blotted it and put it in my pocket. Then I gave her the ten dollars.

"Now you go on back to school this afternoon, you hear?" I says. She didn't answer. She crumpled the bill up in her hand like it was a rag or something and went on out the front door just as Earl came in. A customer came in with him and they stopped up front. I gathered up the things and put on my hat and went up front.

"Been much busy?" Earl says.

"Not much," I says. He looked out the door.

"That your car over yonder?" he says. "Better not try to go out home to dinner. We'll likely have another rush just before the show opens. Get you a lunch at Rogers' and put a ticket in the drawer."

"Much obliged," I says. "I can still manage to feed myself, I reckon."

And right there he'd stay, watching that door like a hawk until I came through it again. Well, he'd just have to watch it for a while; I was doing the best I could. The time before I says that's the last one now; you'll have to remember to get some more right away. But who can remember anything in all this hurrah. And now this dam show had to come here the one day I'd have to hunt all over town for a blank check, besides all the other things I had to do to keep the house running, and Earl watching the door like a hawk.

I went to the printing shop and told him I wanted to play a joke on a fellow, but he didn't have anything. Then he told me to have a look in the old opera house, where somebody had stored a lot of papers and junk out of the old Merchants' and Farmers' Bank when it failed, so I dodged up a few more alleys so Earl couldn't see me and finally found old man Simmons and got the key from him and went up there and dug around. At last I found a pad on a Saint Louis bank. And of course she'd pick this one time to look at it close. Well, it would have to do. I couldn't waste any more time now.

I went back to the store. "Forgot some papers Mother wants to go to the bank," I says. I went back to the desk and fixed the check. Trying to hurry and all, I says to myself it's a good thing her eyes are giving out, with that little whore in the house, a Christian forbearing woman like Mother. I says you know just as well as I do what she's going to grow up into but I says that's your business, if you want to keep her and raise her in your house just because of Father. Then she would begin to cry and say it was her own flesh and blood so I just says All right. Have it your way. I can stand it if you can.

I fixed the letter up again and glued it back and went out.

"Try not to be gone any longer than you can help," Earl says.

"All right," I says. I went to the telegraph office. The smart boys were all there.

"Any of you boys made your million yet?" I says.

"Who can do anything, with a market like that?" Doc says.

"What's it doing?" I says. I went in and looked. It was three points under the opening. "You boys are not going to let a little thing like the cotton market beat you, are you?" I says. "I thought you were too smart for that."

"Smart, hell," Doc says. "It was down twelve points at twelve oclock. Cleaned me out."

"Twelve points?" I says. "Why the hell didn't somebody let me know? Why didn't you let me know?" I says to the operator.

"I take it as it comes in," he says. "I'm not running a bucket shop."[6]

"You're smart, aren't you?" I says. "Seems to me, with the money I spend with you, you could take time to call me up. Or maybe your dam company's in a conspiracy with those dam eastern sharks."

He didn't say anything. He made like he was busy.

"You're getting a little too big for your pants," I says. "First thing you know you'll be working for a living."

"What's the matter with you?" Doc says. "You're still three points to the good."

"Yes," I says. "If I happened to be selling. I haven't mentioned that yet, I think. You boys all cleaned out?"

"I got caught twice," Doc says. "I switched just in time."

"Well," I. O. Snopes says, "I've picked hit; I reckon taint no more than fair fer hit to pick me once in a while."

So I left them buying and selling among themselves at a nickel a point. I found a nigger and sent him for my car and stood on the corner

6. A fraudulent securities brokerage.

and waited. I couldn't see Earl looking up and down the street, with one eye on the clock, because I couldn't see the door from here. After about a week he got back with it.

"Where the hell have you been?" I says. "Riding around where the wenches could see you?"

"I come straight as I could," he says. "I had to drive clean around the square, wid all dem wagons."

I never found a nigger yet that didn't have an airtight alibi for whatever he did. But just turn one loose in a car and he's bound to show off. I got in and went on around the square. I caught a glimpse of Earl in the door across the square.

I went straight to the kitchen and told Dilsey to hurry up with dinner.

"Quentin aint come yit," she says.

"What of that?" I says. "You'll be telling me next that Luster's not quite ready to eat yet. Quentin knows when meals are served in this house. Hurry up with it, now."

Mother was in her room. I gave her the letter. She opened it and took the check out and sat holding it in her hand. I went and got the shovel from the corner and gave her a match. "Come on," I says. "Get it over with. You'll be crying in a minute."

She took the match, but she didn't strike it. She sat there, looking at the check. Just like I said it would be.

"I hate to do it," she says. "To increase your burden by adding Quentin. . . ."

"I guess we'll get along," I says. "Come on. Get it over with."

But she just sat there, holding the check.

"This one is on a different bank," she says. "They have been on an Indianapolis bank."

"Yes," I says. "Women are allowed to do that too."

"Do what?" she says.

"Keep money in two different banks," I says.

"Oh," she says. She looked at the check a while. "I'm glad to know she's so . . . she has so much. . . . God sees that I am doing right," she says.

"Come on," I says. "Finish it. Get the fun over."

"Fun?" she says. "When I think——"

"I thought you were burning this two hundred dollars a month for fun," I says. "Come on, now. Want me to strike the match?"

"I could bring myself to accept them," she says. "For my children's sake. I have no pride."

"You'd never be satisfied," I says. "You know you wouldn't. You've settled that once, let it stay settled. We can get along."

"I leave everything to you," she says. "But sometimes I become afraid that in doing this I am depriving you all of what is rightfully yours.

Perhaps I shall be punished for it. If you want me to, I will smother my pride and accept them."

"What would be the good in beginning now, when you've been destroying them for fifteen years?" I says. "If you keep on doing it, you have lost nothing, but if you'd begin to take them now, you'll have lost fifty thousand dollars. We've got along so far, haven't we?" I says. "I haven't seen you in the poorhouse yet."

"Yes," she says. "We Bascombs need nobody's charity. Certainly not that of a fallen woman."

She struck the match and lit the check and put it in the shovel, and then the envelope, and watched them burn.

"You dont know what it is," she says. "Thank God you will never know what a mother feels."

"There are lots of women in this world no better than her," I says.

"But they are not my daughters," she says. "It's not myself," she says. "I'd gladly take her back, sins and all, because she is my flesh and blood. It's for Quentin's sake."

Well, I could have said it wasn't much chance of anybody hurting Quentin much, but like I say I dont expect much but I do want to eat and sleep without a couple of women squabbling and crying in the house.

"And yours," she says. "I know how you feel toward her."

"Let her come back," I says, "far as I'm concerned."

"No," she says. "I owe that to your father's memory."

"When he was trying all the time to persuade you to let her come home when Herbert threw her out?" I says.

"You dont understand," she says. "I know you dont intend to make it more difficult for me. But it's my place to suffer for my children," she says. "I can bear it."

"Seems to me you go to a lot of unnecessary trouble doing it," I says. The paper burned out. I carried it to the grate and put it in. "It just seems a shame to me to burn up good money," I says.

"Let me never see the day when my children will have to accept that, the wages of sin," she says. "I'd rather see even you dead in your coffin first."

"Have it your way," I says. "Are we going to have dinner soon?" I says. "Because if we're not, I'll have to go on back. We're pretty busy today." She got up. "I've told her once," I says. "It seems she's waiting on Quentin or Luster or somebody. Here, I'll call her. Wait." But she went to the head of the stairs and called.

"Quentin aint come yit," Dilsey says.

"Well, I'll have to get on back," I says. "I can get a sandwich down-town. I dont want to interfere with Dilsey's arrangements," I says. Well, that got her started again, with Dilsey hobbling and mumbling back and forth, saying,

"All right, all right, Ise puttin hit on fast as I kin."

"I try to please you all," Mother says. "I try to make things as easy for you as I can."

"I'm not complaining, am I?" I says. "Have I said a word except I had to go back to work?"

"I know," she says. "I know you haven't had the chance the others had, that you've had to bury yourself in a little country store. I wanted you to get ahead. I knew your father would never realise that you were the only one who had any business sense, and then when everything else failed I believed that when she married, and Herbert . . . after his promise——"

"Well, he was probably lying too," I says. "He may not have even had a bank. And if he had, I dont reckon he'd have to come all the way to Mississippi to get a man for it."

We ate a while. I could hear Ben in the kitchen, where Luster was feeding him. Like I say, if we've got to feed another mouth and she wont take that money, why not send him down to Jackson. He'll be happier there, with people like him. I says God knows there's little enough room for pride in this family, but it dont take much pride to not like to see a thirty year old man playing around the yard with a nigger boy, running up and down the fence and lowing like a cow whenever they play golf over there. I says if they'd sent him to Jackson at first we'd all be better off today. I says, you've done your duty by him; you've done all anybody can expect of you and more than most folks would do, so why not send him there and get that much benefit out of the taxes we pay. Then she says, "I'll be gone soon. I know I'm just a burden to you" and I says "You've been saying that so long that I'm beginning to believe you" only I says you'd better be sure and not let me know you're gone because I'll sure have him on number seventeen that night and I says I think I know a place where they'll take her too and the name of it's not Milk street and Honey avenue [7] either. Then she begun to cry and I says All right all right I have as much pride about my kinfolks as anybody even if I dont always know where they come from.

We ate for a while. Mother sent Dilsey to the front to look for Quentin again.

"I keep telling you she's not coming to dinner," I says.

"She knows better than that," Mother says. "She knows I dont permit her to run about the streets and not come home at meal time. Did you look good, Dilsey?"

"Dont let her, then," I says.

"What can I do," she says. "You have all of you flouted me. Always."

"If you wouldn't come interfering, I'd make her mind," I says. "It

7. See Exodus 3.8, 17.

wouldn't take me but about one day to straighten her out."

"You'd be too brutal with her," she says. "You have your Uncle Maury's temper."

That reminded me of the letter. I took it out and handed it to her. "You wont have to open it," I says. "The bank will let you know how much it is this time."

"It's addressed to you," she says.

"Go on and open it," I says. She opened it and read it and handed it to me.

" 'My dear young nephew,' it says,

'You will be glad to learn that I am now in a position to avail myself of an opportunity regarding which, for reasons which I shall make obvious to you, I shall not go into details until I have an opportunity to divulge it to you in a more secure manner. My business experience has taught me to be chary of committing anything of a confidential nature to any more concrete medium than speech, and my extreme precaution in this instance should give you some inkling of its value. Needless to say, I have just completed a most exhaustive examination of all its phases, and I feel no hesitancy in telling you that it is that sort of golden chance that comes but once in a lifetime, and I now see clearly before me that goal toward which I have long and unflaggingly striven: i.e., the ultimate solidification of my affairs by which I may restore to its rightful position that family of which I have the honor to be the sole remaining male descendant; that family in which I have ever included your lady mother and her children.

'As it so happens, I am not quite in a position to avail myself of this opportunity to the uttermost which it warrants, but rather than go out of the family to do so, I am today drawing upon your Mother's bank for the small sum necessary to complement my own initial investment, for which I herewith enclose, as a matter of formality, my note of hand at eight percent. per annum. Needless to say, this is merely a formality, to secure your Mother in the event of that circumstance of which man is ever the plaything and sport. For naturally I shall employ this sum as though it were my own and so permit your Mother to avail herself of this opportunity which my exhaustive investigation has shown to be a bonanza — if you will permit the vulgarism — of the first water and purest ray serene.[8]

'This is in confidence, you will understand, from one business man to another; we will harvest our own vineyards, eh? And knowing your Mother's delicate health and that timorousness which such delicately nurtured Southern ladies would naturally feel regarding matters of business, and their charming proneness to divulge unwit-

8. See Thomas Gray, "Elegy Written in a Country Churchyard," line 53.

tingly such matters in conversation, I would suggest that you do not mention it to her at all. On second thought, I advise you not to do so. It might be better to simply restore this sum to the bank at some future date, say, in a lump sum with the other small sums for which I am indebted to her, and say nothing about it at all. It is our duty to shield her from the crass material world as much as possible.

'Your affectionate Uncle,
'Maury L. Bascomb.' "

"What do you want to do about it?" I says, flipping it across the table.

"I know you grudge what I give him," she says.

"It's your money," I says. "If you want to throw it to the birds even, it's your business."

"He's my own brother," Mother says. "He's the last Bascomb. When we are gone there wont be any more of them."

"That'll be hard on somebody, I guess," I says. "All right, all right," I says. "It's your money. Do as you please with it. You want me to tell the bank to pay it?"

"I know you begrudge him," she says. "I realise the burden on your shoulders. When I'm gone it will be easier on you."

"I could make it easier right now," I says. "All right, all right, I wont mention it again. Move all bedlam in here if you want to."

"He's your own brother," she says. "Even if he is afflicted."

"I'll take your bank book," I says. "I'll draw my check today."

"He kept you waiting six days," she says. "Are you sure the business is sound? It seems strange to me that a solvent business cannot pay its employees promptly."

"He's all right," I says. "Safe as a bank. I tell him not to bother about mine until we get done collecting every month. That's why it's late sometimes."

"I just couldn't bear to have you lose the little I had to invest for you," she says. "I've often thought that Earl is not a good business man. I know he doesn't take you into his confidence to the extent that your investment in the business should warrant. I'm going to speak to him."

"No, you let him alone," I says. "It's his business."

"You have a thousand dollars in it."

"You let him alone," I says. "I'm watching things. I have your power of attorney. It'll be all right."

"You dont know what a comfort you are to me," she says. "You have always been my pride and joy, but when you came to me of your own accord and insisted on banking your salary each month in my name, I thanked God it was you left me if they had to be taken."

"They were all right," I says. "They did the best they could, I reckon."

"When you talk that way I know you are thinking bitterly of your father's memory," she says. "You have a right to, I suppose. But it breaks my heart to hear you."

I got up. "If you've got any crying to do," I says, "you'll have to do it alone, because I've got to get on back. I'll get the bank book."

"I'll get it," she says.

"Keep still," I says. "I'll get it." I went up stairs and got the bank book out of her desk and went back to town. I went to the bank and deposited the check and the money order and the other ten, and stopped at the telegraph office. It was one point above the opening. I had already lost thirteen points, all because she had to come helling in there at twelve, worrying me about that letter.

"What time did that report come in?" I says.

"About an hour ago," he says.

"An hour ago?" I says. "What are we paying you for?" I says. "Weekly reports? How do you expect a man to do anything? The whole dam top could blow off and we'd not know it."

"I dont expect you to do anything," he says. "They changed that law making folks play the cotton market."

"They have?" I says. "I hadn't heard. They must have sent the news out over the Western Union."

I went back to the store. Thirteen points. Dam if I believe anybody knows anything about the dam thing except the ones that sit back in those New York offices and watch the country suckers come up and beg them to take their money. Well, a man that just calls shows he has no faith in himself, and like I say if you aren't going to take the advice, what's the use in paying money for it. Besides, these people are right up there on the ground; they know everything that's going on. I could feel the telegram in my pocket. I'd just have to prove that they were using the telegraph company to defraud. That would constitute a bucket shop. And I wouldn't hesitate that long, either. Only be damned if it doesn't look like a company as big and rich as the Western Union could get a market report out on time. Half as quick as they'll get a wire to you saying Your account closed out. But what the hell do they care about the people. They're hand in glove with that New York crowd. Anybody could see that.

When I came in Earl looked at his watch. But he didn't say anything until the customer was gone. Then he says,

"You go home to dinner?"

"I had to go to the dentist," I says because it's not any of his business where I eat but I've got to be in the store with him all the afternoon. And with his jaw running off after all I've stood. You take a little two by four country storekeeper like I say it takes a man with just five hundred dollars to worry about it fifty thousand dollars' worth.

"You might have told me," he says. "I expected you back right away."

"I'll trade you this tooth and give you ten dollars to boot, any time,"

I says. "Our agreement was an hour for dinner," I says, "and if you dont like the way I do, you know what you can do about it."

"I've known that some time," he says. "If it hadn't been for your mother I'd have done it before now, too. She's a lady I've got a lot of sympathy for, Jason. Too bad some other folks I know cant say as much."

"Then you can keep it," I says. "When we need any sympathy I'll let you know in plenty of time."

"I've protected you about that business a long time, Jason," he says.

"Yes?" I says, letting him go on. Listening to what he would say before I shut him up.

"I believe I know more about where that automobile came from than she does."

"You think so, do you?" I says. "When are you going to spread the news that I stole it from my mother?"

"I dont say anything," he says. "I know you have her power of attorney. And I know she still believes that thousand dollars is in this business."

"All right," I says. "Since you know so much, I'll tell you a little more: go to the bank and ask them whose account I've been depositing a hundred and sixty dollars on the first of every month for twelve years."

"I dont say anything," he says. "I just ask you to be a little more careful after this."

I never said anything more. It doesn't do any good. I've found that when a man gets into a rut the best thing you can do is let him stay there. And when a man gets it in his head that he's got to tell something on you for your own good, goodnight. I'm glad I haven't got the sort of conscience I've got to nurse like a sick puppy all the time. If I'd ever be as careful over anything as he is to keep his little shirt tail full of business from making him more than eight percent. I reckon he thinks they'd get him on the usury law if he netted more than eight percent. What the hell chance has a man got, tied down in a town like this and to a business like this. Why I could take his business in one year and fix him so he'd never have to work again, only he'd give it all away to the church or something. If there's one thing gets under my skin, it's a dam hypocrite. A man that thinks anything he dont understand all about must be crooked and that first chance he gets he's morally bound to tell the third party what's none of his business to tell. Like I say if I thought every time a man did something I didn't know all about he was bound to be a crook, I reckon I wouldn't have any trouble finding something back there on those books that you wouldn't see any use for running and telling somebody I thought ought to know about it, when for all I knew they might know a dam sight more about it now than I did, and if they didn't it was dam little of my business anyway and he says, "My books are open to anybody. Anybody that has any claim or believes she has any claim on this business can go back there and welcome."

"Sure, you wont tell," I says. "You couldn't square your conscience with that. You'll just take her back there and let her find it. You wont tell, yourself."

"I'm not trying to meddle in your business," he says. "I know you missed out on some things like Quentin had. But your mother has had a misfortunate life too, and if she was to come in here and ask me why you quit, I'd have to tell her. It aint that thousand dollars. You know that. It's because a man never gets anywhere if fact and his ledgers dont square. And I'm not going to lie to anybody, for myself or anybody else."

"Well, then," I says. "I reckon that conscience of yours is a more valuable clerk than I am; it dont have to go home at noon to eat. Only dont let it interfere with my appetite," I says, because how the hell can I do anything right, with that dam family and her not making any effort to control her nor any of them like that time when she happened to see one of them kissing Caddy and all next day she went around the house in a black dress and a veil and even Father couldn't get her to say a word except crying and saying her little daughter was dead and Caddy about fifteen then only in three years she'd been wearing haircloth or probably sandpaper at that rate. Do you think I can afford to have her running about the streets with every drummer that comes to town, I says, and them telling the new ones up and down the road where to pick up a hot one when they made Jefferson. I haven't got much pride, I cant afford it with a kitchen full of niggers to feed and robbing the state asylum of its star freshman. Blood, I says, governors and generals. It's a dam good thing we never had any kings and presidents; we'd all be down there at Jackson chasing butterflies. I says it'd be bad enough if it was mine; I'd at least be sure it was a bastard to begin with, and now even the Lord doesn't know that for certain probably.

So after a while I heard the band start up, and then they begun to clear out. Headed for the show, every one of them. Haggling over a twenty cent hame string to save fifteen cents, so they can give it to a bunch of Yankees that come in and pay maybe ten dollars for the privilege. I went on out to the back.

"Well," I says. "If you dont look out, that bolt will grow into your hand. And then I'm going to take an axe and chop it out. What do you reckon the boll-weevils'll eat if you dont get those cultivators in shape to raise them a crop?" I says, "sage grass?"

"Dem folks sho do play dem horns," he says. "Tell me man in dat show kin play a tune on a handsaw. Pick hit like a banjo."

"Listen," I says. "Do you know how much that show'll spend in this town? About ten dollars," I says. "The ten dollars Buck Turpin has in his pocket right now."

"Whut dey give Mr Buck ten dollars fer?" he says.

"For the privilege of showing here," I says. "You can put the balance of what they'll spend in your eye."

"You mean dey pays ten dollars jest to give dey show here?" he says.

"That's all," I says, "And how much do you reckon —— "

"Gret day," he says. "You mean to tell me dey chargin um to let um show here? I'd pay ten dollars to see dat man pick dat saw, ef I had to. I figures dat tomorrow mawnin I be still owin um nine dollars and six bits at dat rate."

And then a Yankee will talk your head off about niggers getting ahead. Get them ahead, what I say. Get them so far ahead you cant find one south of Louisville with a blood hound. Because when I told him about how they'd pick up Saturday night and carry off at least a thousand dollars out of the county, he says,

"I dont begridge um. I kin sho afford my two bits."

"Two bits hell," I says. "That dont begin it. How about the dime or fifteen cents you'll spend for a dam two cent box of candy or something. How about the time you're wasting right now, listening to that band."

"Dat's de troof," he says. "Well, ef I lives twell night hit's gwine to be two bits mo dey takin out of town, dat's sho."

"Then you're a fool," I says.

"Well," he says. "I dont spute dat neither. Ef dat uz a crime, all chain-gangs wouldn't be black."

Well, just about that time I happened to look up the alley and saw her. When I stepped back and looked at my watch I didn't notice at the time who he was because I was looking at the watch. It was just two thirty, forty-five minutes before anybody but me expected her to be out. So when I looked around the door the first thing I saw was the red tie he had on and I was thinking what the hell kind of a man would wear a red tie. But she was sneaking along the alley, watching the door, so I wasn't thinking anything about him until they had gone past. I was wondering if she'd have so little respect for me that she'd not only play out of school when I told her not to, but would walk right past the store, daring me not to see her. Only she couldn't see into the door because the sun fell straight into it and it was like trying to see through an automobile search-light, so I stood there and watched her go on past, with her face painted up like a dam clown's and her hair all gummed and twisted and a dress that if a woman had come out doors even on Gayoso or Beale[9] street when I was a young fellow with no more than that to cover her legs and behind, she'd been thrown in jail. I'll be damned if they dont dress like they were trying to make every man they passed on the street want to reach out and clap his hand on it. And so I was thinking what kind of a dam man would wear a red tie when all of a sudden I knew he was one of those show folks well as if she'd told me. Well, I can stand a lot; if I couldn't dam if I wouldn't be in a hell of a fix, so when they turned the corner I jumped down and followed. Me, without any hat, in the middle

9. Streets in Memphis.

of the afternoon, having to chase up and down back alleys because of my mother's good name. Like I say you cant do anything with a woman like that, if she's got it in her. If it's in her blood, you cant do anything with her. The only thing you can do is to get rid of her, let her go on and live with her own sort.

I went on to the street, but they were out of sight. And there I was, without any hat, looking like I was crazy too. Like a man would naturally think, one of them is crazy and another one drowned himself and the other one was turned out into the street by her husband, what's the reason the rest of them are not crazy too. All the time I could see them watching me like a hawk, waiting for a chance to say Well I'm not surprised I expected it all the time the whole family's crazy. Selling land to send him to Harvard and paying taxes to support a state University all the time that I never saw except twice at a baseball game and not letting her daughter's name be spoken on the place until after a while Father wouldn't even come down town anymore but just sat there all day with the decanter I could see the bottom of his nightshirt and his bare legs and hear the decanter clinking until finally T. P. had to pour it for him and she says You have no respect for your Father's memory and I says I dont know why not it sure is preserved well enough to last only if I'm crazy too God knows what I'll do about it just to look at water makes me sick and I'd just as soon swallow gasoline as a glass of whiskey and Lorraine telling them he may not drink but if you dont believe he's a man I can tell you how to find out she says If I catch you fooling with any of these whores you know what I'll do she says I'll whip her grabbing at her I'll whip her as long as I can find her she says and I says if I dont drink that's my business but have you ever found me short I says I'll buy you enough beer to take a bath in if you want it because I've got every respect for a good honest whore because with Mother's health and the position I try to uphold to have her with no more respect for what I try to do for her than to make her name and my name and my Mother's name a byword in the town.

She had dodged out of sight somewhere. Saw me coming and dodged into another alley, running up and down the alleys with a dam show man in a red tie that everybody would look at and think what kind of a dam man would wear a red tie. Well, the boy kept speaking to me and so I took the telegram without knowing I had taken it. I didn't realise what it was until I was signing for it, and I tore it open without even caring much what it was. I knew all the time what it would be, I reckon. That was the only thing else that could happen, especially holding it up until I had already had the check entered on the pass book.

I dont see how a city no bigger than New York can hold enough people to take the money away from us country suckers. Work like hell all day every day, send them your money and get a little piece of paper back, Your account closed at 20.62. Teasing you along, letting you pile up a little paper profit, then bang! Your account closed at 20.62. And if that wasn't enough, paying ten dollars a month to somebody to tell you how to lose it fast, that either dont know anything about it or is in cahoots with the telegraph company. Well, I'm done with them. They've sucked me in for the last time. Any fool except a fellow that hasn't got any more sense than to take a jew's word for anything could tell the market was going up all the time, with the whole dam delta about to be flooded again and the cotton washed right out of the ground like it was last year. Let it wash a man's crop out of the ground year after year, and them up there in Washington spending fifty thousand dollars a day keeping an army in Nicarauga[1] or some place. Of course it'll overflow again, and then cotton'll be worth thirty cents a pound. Well, I just want to hit them one time and get my money back. I dont want a killing; only these small town gamblers are out for that, I just want my money back that these dam jews have gotten with all their guaranteed inside dope. Then I'm through; they can kiss my foot for every other red cent of mine they get.

I went back to the store. It was half past three almost. Dam little time to do anything in, but then I am used to that. I never had to go to Harvard to learn that. The band had quit playing. Got them all inside now, and they wouldn't have to waste any more wind. Earl says,

"He found you, did he? He was in here with it a while ago. I thought you were out back somewhere."

"Yes," I says. "I got it. They couldn't keep it away from me all afternoon. The town's too small. I've got to go out home a minute," I says. "You can dock me if it'll make you feel any better."

"Go ahead," he says, "I can handle it now. No bad news, I hope."

"You'll have to go to the telegraph office and find that out," I says. "They'll have time to tell you. I haven't."

"I just asked," he says. "Your mother knows she can depend on me."

"She'll appreciate it," I says. "I wont be gone any longer than I have to."

"Take your time," he says. "I can handle it now. You go ahead."

I got the car and went home. Once this morning, twice at noon, and now again, with her and having to chase all over town and having to beg them to let me eat a little of the food I am paying for. Sometimes I think what's the use of anything. With the precedent I've been set I must be crazy to keep on. And now I reckon I'll get home just in time to take a nice long drive after a basket of tomatoes or something and then have to go back to town smelling like a camphor factory so my head wont explode right on my shoulders. I keep telling her there's not a dam thing in that aspirin except flour and water for imaginary invalids. I says you

1. Noel Polk has changed this spelling to correspond with the manuscript version, which reflects Jason's pronunciation of Nicaragua.

dont know what a headache is. I says you think I'd fool with that dam car at all if it depended on me. I says I can get along without one I've learned to get along without lots of things but if you want to risk yourself in that old wornout surrey with a halfgrown nigger boy all right because I says God looks after Ben's kind, God knows He ought to do something for him but if you think I'm going to trust a thousand dollars' worth of delicate machinery to a halfgrown nigger or a grown one either, you'd better buy him one yourself because I says you like to ride in the car and you know you do.

Dilsey said she was in the house. I went on into the hall and listened, but I didn't hear anything. I went up stairs, but just as I passed her door she called me.

"I just wanted to know who it was," she says. "I'm here alone so much that I hear every sound."

"You dont have to stay here," I says. "You could spend the whole day visiting like other women, if you wanted to." She came to the door.

"I thought maybe you were sick," she says. "Having to hurry through your dinner like you did."

"Better luck next time," I says. "What do you want?"

"Is anything wrong?" she says.

"What could be?" I says. "Cant I come home in the middle of the afternoon without upsetting the whole house?"

"Have you seen Quentin?" she says.

"She's in school," I says.

"It's after three," she says. "I heard the clock strike at least a half an hour ago. She ought to be home by now."

"Ought she?" I says. "When have you ever seen her before dark?"

"She ought to be home," she says. "When I was a girl——"

"You had somebody to make you behave yourself," I says. "She hasn't."

"I cant do anything with her," she says. "I've tried and I've tried."

"And you wont let me, for some reason," I says. "So you ought to be satisfied." I went on to my room. I turned the key easy and stood there until the knob turned. Then she says,

"Jason."

"What," I says.

"I just thought something was wrong."

"Not in here," I says. "You've come to the wrong place."

"I dont mean to worry you," she says.

"I'm glad to hear that," I says. "I wasn't sure. I thought I might have been mistaken. Do you want anything?"

After a while she says, "No. Not any thing." Then she went away. I took the box down and counted out the money and hid the box again and unlocked the door and went out. I thought about the camphor, but it would be too late now, anyway. And I'd just have one more round trip. She was at her door, waiting.

"You want anything from town?" I says.

"No," she says. "I dont mean to meddle in your affairs. But I dont know what I'd do if anything happened to you, Jason."

"I'm all right," I says. "Just a headache."

"I wish you'd take some aspirin," she says. "I know you're not going to stop using the car."

"What's the car got to do with it?" I says. "How can a car give a man a headache?"

"You know gasoline always made you sick," she says. "Ever since you were a child. I wish you'd take some aspirin."

"Keep on wishing it," I says. "It wont hurt you."

I got in the car and started back to town. I had just turned onto the street when I saw a ford coming helling toward me. All of a sudden it stopped. I could hear the wheels sliding and it slewed around and backed and whirled and just as I was thinking what the hell they were up to, I saw that red tie. Then I recognised her face looking back through the window. It whirled into the alley. I saw it turn again, but when I got to the back street it was just disappearing, running like hell.

I saw red. When I recognised that red tie, after all I had told her, I forgot about everything. I never thought about my head even until I came to the first forks and had to stop. Yet we spend money and spend money on roads and dam if it isn't like trying to drive over a sheet of corrugated iron roofing. I'd like to know how a man could be expected to keep up with even a wheelbarrow. I think too much of my car; I'm not going to hammer it to pieces like it was a ford. Chances were they had stolen it, anyway, so why should they give a dam. Like I say blood always tells. If you've got blood like that in you, you'll do anything. I says whatever claim you believe she has on you has already been discharged; I says from now on you have only yourself to blame because you know what any sensible person would do. I says if I've got to spend half my time being a dam detective, at least I'll go where I can get paid for it.

So I had to stop there at the forks. Then I remembered it. It felt like somebody was inside with a hammer, beating on it. I says I've tried to keep you from being worried by her; I says far as I'm concerned, let her go to hell as fast as she pleases and the sooner the better. I says what else do you expect except every dam drummer and cheap show that comes to town because even these town jellybeans give her the go-by now. You dont know what goes on I says, you dont hear the talk that I hear and you can just bet I shut them up too. I says my people owned slaves here when you all were running little shirt tail country stores and farming land no nigger would look at on shares.

If they ever farmed it. It's a good thing the Lord did something for this country; the folks that live on it never have. Friday afternoon, and from right here I could see three miles of land that hadn't even been broken,

and every able bodied man in the county in town at that show. I might
have been a stranger starving to death, and there wasn't a soul in sight
to ask which way to town even. And she trying to get me to take aspirin.
I says when I eat bread I'll do it at the table. I says you always talking
about how much you give up for us when you could buy ten new dresses
a year on the money you spend for those dam patent medicines. It's not
something to cure it I need it's just a even break not to have to have
them but as long as I have to work ten hours a day to support a kitchen
full of niggers in the style they're accustomed to and send them to the
show where every other nigger in the county, only he was late already.
By the time he got there it would be over.

After a while he got up to the car and when I finally got it through his
head if two people in a ford had passed him, he said yes. So I went on,
and when I came to where the wagon road turned off I could see the tire
tracks. Ab Russell was in his lot, but I didn't bother to ask him and I
hadn't got out of sight of his barn hardly when I saw the ford. They had
tried to hide it. Done about as well at it as she did at everything else she
did. Like I say it's not that I object to so much; maybe she cant help
that, it's because she hasn't even got enough consideration for her own
family to have any discretion. I'm afraid all the time I'll run into them
right in the middle of the street or under a wagon on the square, like a
couple of dogs.

I parked and got out. And now I'd have to go way around and cross a
plowed field, the only one I had seen since I left town, with every step
like somebody was walking along behind me, hitting me on the head
with a club. I kept thinking that when I got across the field at least I'd
have something level to walk on, that wouldn't jolt me every step, but
when I got into the woods it was full of underbrush and I had to twist
around through it, and then I came to a ditch full of briers. I went along
it for a while, but it got thicker and thicker, and all the time Earl probably telephoning home about where I was and getting Mother all upset
again.

When I finally got through I had had to wind around so much that I
had to stop and figure out just where the car would be. I knew they
wouldn't be far from it, just under the closest bush, so I turned and
worked back toward the road. Then I couldn't tell just how far I was, so
I'd have to stop and listen, and then with my legs not using so much
blood, it all would go into my head like it would explode any minute,
and the sun getting down just to where it could shine straight into my
eyes and my ears ringing so I couldn't hear anything. I went on, trying
to move quiet, then I heard a dog or something and I knew that when
he scented me he'd have to come helling up, then it would be all off.

I had gotten beggar lice and twigs and stuff all over me, inside my
clothes and shoes and all, and then I happened to look around and I had
my hand right on a bunch of poison oak. The only thing I couldn't

understand was why it was just poison oak and not a snake or something. So I didn't even bother to move it. I just stood there until the dog went away. Then I went on.

I didn't have any idea where the car was now. I couldn't think about anything except my head, and I'd just stand in one place and sort of wonder if I had really seen a ford even, and I didn't even care much whether I had or not. Like I say, let her lay out all day and all night with everthing in town that wears pants, what do I care. I dont owe anything to anybody that has no more consideration for me, that wouldn't be a dam bit above planting that ford there and making me spend a whole afternoon and Earl taking her back there and showing her the books just because he's too dam virtuous for this world. I says you'll have one hell of a time in heaven, without anybody's business to meddle in only dont you ever let me catch you at it I says, I close my eyes to it because of your grandmother, but just you let me catch you doing it one time on this place, where my mother lives. These dam little slick haired squirts, thinking they are raising so much hell, I'll show them something about hell I says, and you too. I'll make him think that dam red tie is the latch string to hell, if he thinks he can run the woods with my niece.

With the sun and all in my eyes and my blood going so I kept thinking every time my head would go on and burst and get it over with, with briers and things grabbing at me, then I came onto the sand ditch where they had been and I recognised the tree where the car was, and just as I got out of the ditch and started running I heard the car start. It went off fast, blowing the horn. They kept on blowing it, like it was saying Yah. Yah. Yaaahhhhhhhh, going out of sight. I got to the road just in time to see it go out of sight.

By the time I got up to where my car was, they were clean out of sight, the horn still blowing. Well, I never thought anything about it except I was saying Run. Run back to town. Run home and try to convince Mother that I never saw you in that car. Try to make her believe that I dont know who he was. Try to make her believe that I didn't miss ten feet of catching you in that ditch. Try to make her believe you were standing up, too.

It kept on saying Yahhhhh, Yahhhhh, Yaaahhhhhhhhh, getting fainter and fainter. Then it quit, and I could hear a cow lowing up at Russell's barn. And still I never thought. I went up to the door and opened it and raised my foot. I kind of thought then that the car was leaning a little more than the slant of the road would be, but I never found it out until I got in and started off.

Well, I just sat there. It was getting on toward sundown, and town was about five miles. They never even had guts enough to puncture it, to jab a hole in it. They just let the air out. I just stood there for a while, thinking about that kitchen full of niggers and not one of them had time to lift a tire onto the rack and screw up a couple of bolts. It was kind of

funny because even she couldn't have seen far enough ahead to take the
pump out on purpose, unless she thought about it while he was letting
out the air maybe. But what it probably was was somebody took it out
and gave it to Ben to play with for a squirt gun because they'd take the
whole car to pieces if he wanted it and Dilsey says, Aint nobody teched
yo car. What we want to fool with hit fer? and I says You're a nigger.
You're lucky, do you know it? I says I'll swap with you any day because
it takes a white man not to have anymore sense than to worry about what
a little slut of a girl does.

I walked up to Russell's. He had a pump. That was just an oversight
on their part, I reckon. Only I still couldn't believe she'd have had the
nerve to. I kept thinking that. I dont know why it is I cant seem to learn
that a woman'll do anything. I kept thinking, Let's forget for a while
how I feel toward you and how you feel toward me: I just wouldn't do
you this way. I wouldn't do you this way no matter what you had done
to me. Because like I say blood is blood and you cant get around it. It's
not playing a joke that any eight year old boy could have thought of, it's
letting your own uncle be laughed at by a man that would wear a red
tie. They come into town and call us all a bunch of hicks and think it's
too small to hold them. Well he doesn't know just how right he is. And
her too. If that's the way she feels about it, she'd better keep right on
going and a dam good riddance.

I stopped and returned Russell's pump and drove on to town. I went
to the drugstore and got a shot[2] and then I went to the telegraph office.
It had closed at 20.21, forty points down. Forty times five dollars; buy
something with that if you can, and she'll say, I've got to have it I've just
got to and I'll say that's too bad you'll have to try somebody else, I
haven't got any money; I've been too busy to make any.

I just looked at him.

"I'll tell you some news," I says. "You'll be astonished to learn that I
am interested in the cotton market," I says. "That never occurred to
you, did it?"

"I did my best to deliver it," he says. "I tried the store twice and called
up your house, but they didn't know where you were," he says, digging
in the drawer.

"Deliver what?" I says. He handed me a telegram. "What time did
this come?" I says.

"About half past three," he says.

"And now it's ten minutes past five," I says.

"I tried to deliver it," he says. "I couldn't find you."

"That's not my fault, is it?" I says. I opened it, just to see what kind
of a lie they'd tell me this time. They must be in one hell of a shape if

2. The first edition reads "coca-cola," for which "shot" was a slang term.

they've got to come all the way to Mississippi to steal ten dollars a month. Sell, it says. The market will be unstable, with a general downward tendency. Do not be alarmed following government report.

"How much would a message like this cost?" I says. He told me.

"They paid it," he says.

"Then I owe them that much," I says. "I already knew this. Send this collect," I says, taking a blank. Buy, I wrote, Market just on point of blowing its head off. Occasional flurries for purpose of hooking a few more country suckers who haven't got in to the telegraph office yet. Do not be alarmed. "Send that collect," I says.

He looked at the message, then he looked at the clock. "Market closed an hour ago," he says.

"Well," I says. "That's not my fault either. I didn't invent it; I just bought a little of it while under the impression that the telegraph company would keep me informed as to what it was doing."

"A report is posted whenever it comes in," he says.

"Yes," I says. "And in Memphis they have it on a blackboard every ten seconds," I says. "I was within sixty-seven miles of there once this afternoon."

He looked at the message. "You want to send this?" he says.

"I still haven't changed my mind," I says. I wrote the other one out and counted the money. "And this one too, if you're sure you can spell b-u-y."

I went back to the store. I could hear the band from down the street. Prohibition's a fine thing. Used to be they'd come in Saturday with just one pair of shoes in the family and him wearing them, and they'd go down to the express office and get his package; now they all go to the show barefooted, with the merchants in the door like a row of tigers or something in a cage, watching them pass. Earl says,

"I hope it wasn't anything serious."

"What?" I says. He looked at his watch. Then he went to the door and looked at the courthouse clock. "You ought to have a dollar watch," I says. "It wont cost you so much to believe it's lying each time."

"What?" he says.

"Nothing," I says. "Hope I haven't inconvenienced you."

"We were not busy much," he says. "They all went to the show. It's all right."

"If it's not all right," I says, "you know what you can do about it."

"I said it was all right," he says.

"I heard you," I says. "And if it's not all right, you know what you can do about it."

"Do you want to quit?" he says.

"It's not my business," I says. "My wishes dont matter. But dont get the idea that you are protecting me by keeping me."

"You'd be a good business man if you'd let yourself, Jason," he says.

"At least I can tend to my own business and let other people's alone," I says.

"I dont know why you are trying to make me fire you," he says. "You know you could quit anytime and there wouldn't be any hard feelings between us."

"Maybe that's why I dont quit," I says. "As long as I tend to my job, that's what you are paying me for." I went on to the back and got a drink of water and went on out to the back door. Job had the cultivators all set up at last. It was quiet there, and pretty soon my head got a little easier. I could hear them singing now, and then the band played again. Well, let them get every quarter and dime in the county; it was no skin off my back. I've done what I could; a man that can live as long as I have and not know when to quit is a fool. Especially as it's no business of mine. If it was my own daughter now it would be different, because she wouldn't have time to; she'd have to work some to feed a few invalids and idiots and niggers, because how could I have the face to bring anybody there. I've too much respect for anybody to do that. I'm a man, I can stand it, it's my own flesh and blood and I'd like to see the color of the man's eyes that would speak disrespectful of any woman that was my friend it's these dam good women that do it I'd like to see the good, church-going woman that's half as square as Lorraine, whore or no whore. Like I say if I was to get married you'd go up like a balloon and you know it and she says I want you to be happy to have a family of your own not to slave your life away for us. But I'll be gone soon and then you can take a wife but you'll never find a woman who is worthy of you and I says yes I could. You'd get right up out of your grave you know you would. I says no thank you I have all the women I can take care of now if I married a wife she'd probably turn out to be a hophead or something. That's all we lack in this family, I says.

The sun was down beyond the Methodist church now, and the pigeons were flying back and forth around the steeple, and when the band stopped I could hear them cooing. It hadn't been four months since Christmas, and yet they were almost as thick as ever. I reckon Parson Walthall was getting a belly full of them now. You'd have thought we were shooting people, with him making speeches and even holding onto a man's gun when they came over. Talking about peace on earth good will toward all and not a sparrow can fall to earth.[3] But what does he care how thick they get, he hasn't got anything to do: what does he care what time it is. He pays no taxes, he doesn't have to see his money going every year to have the courthouse clock cleaned to where it'll run. They had to pay a man forty-five dollars to clean it. I counted over a hundred half-hatched

3. See Matthew 10.29: "Are not two sparrows sold for a farthing? and one of them shall not fall on the ground without your Father."

pigeons on the ground. You'd think they'd have sense enough to leave town. It's a good thing I dont have anymore ties than a pigeon, I'll say that.

The band was playing again, a loud fast tune, like they were breaking up. I reckon they'd be satisfied now. Maybe they'd have enough music to entertain them while they drove fourteen or fifteen miles home and unharnessed in the dark and fed the stock and milked. All they'd have to do would be to whistle the music and tell the jokes to the live stock in the barn, and then they could count up how much they'd made by not taking the stock to the show too. They could figure that if a man had five children and seven mules, he cleared a quarter by taking his family to the show. Just like that. Earl came back with a couple of packages.

"Here's some more stuff going out," he says. "Where's Uncle Job?"

"Gone to the show, I imagine," I says. "Unless you watched him."

"He doesn't slip off," he says. "I can depend on him."

"Meaning me by that," I says.

He went to the door and looked out, listening.

"That's a good band," he says. "It's about time they were breaking up, I'd say."

"Unless they're going to spend the night there," I says. The swallows had begun, and I could hear the sparrows beginning to swarm in the trees in the courthouse yard. Every once in a while a bunch of them would come swirling around in sight above the roof, then go away. They are as big a nuisance as the pigeons, to my notion. You cant even sit in the courthouse yard for them. First thing you know, bing. Right on your hat. But it would take a millionaire to afford to shoot them at five cents a shot. If they'd just put a little poison out there in the square, they'd get rid of them in a day, because if a merchant cant keep his stock from running around the square, he'd better try to deal in something besides chickens, something that dont eat, like plows or onions. And if a man dont keep his dogs up, he either dont want it or he hasn't any business with one. Like I say if all the businesses in a town are run like country businesses, you're going to have a country town.

"It wont do you any good if they have broke up," I says. "They'll have to hitch up and take out to get home by midnight as it is."

"Well," he says. "They enjoy it. Let them spend a little money on a show now and then. A hill farmer works pretty hard and gets mighty little for it."

"There's no law making them farm in the hills," I says. "Or anywhere else."

"Where would you and me be, if it wasn't for the farmers?" he says.

"I'd be home right now," I says. "Lying down, with an ice pack on my head."

"You have these headaches too often," he says. "Why dont you have your teeth examined good? Did he go over them all this morning?"

"Did who?" I says.

"You said you went to the dentist this morning."

"Do you object to my having the headache on your time?" I says. "Is that it?" They were crossing the alley now, coming up from the show.

"There they come," he says. "I reckon I better get up front." He went on. It's a curious thing how, no matter what's wrong with you, a man'll tell you to have your teeth examined and a woman'll tell you to get married. It always takes a man that never made much at any thing to tell you how to run your business, though. Like these college professors without a whole pair of socks to his name, telling you how to make a million in ten years, and a woman that couldn't even get a husband can always tell you how to raise a family.

Old man Job came up with the wagon. After a while he got through wrapping the lines around the whip socket.

"Well," I says. "Was it a good show?"

"I aint been yit," he says. "But I kin be arrested in dat tent tonight, dough."

"Like hell you haven't," I says. "You've been away from here since three oclock. Mr Earl was just back here looking for you."

"I been tendin to my business," he says. "Mr Earl knows whar I been."

"You may can fool him," I says. "I wont tell on you."

"Den he's de onliest man here I'd try to fool," he says. "Whut I want to waste my time foolin a man whut I dont keer whether I sees him Sat'dy night er not? I wont try to fool you," he says. "You too smart fer me. Yes, suh," he says, looking busy as hell, putting five or six little packages into the wagon. "You's too smart fer me. Aint a man in dis town kin keep up wid you fer smartness. You fools a man whut so smart he cant even keep up wid hisself," he says, getting in the wagon and unwrapping the reins.

"Who's that?" I says.

"Dat's Mr Jason Compson," he says. "Git up dar, Dan!"

One of the wheels was just about to come off. I watched to see if he'd get out of the alley before it did. Just turn any vehicle over to a nigger, though. I says that old rattletrap's just an eyesore, yet you'll keep it standing there in the carriage house a hundred years just so that boy can ride to the cemetery once a week. I says he's not the first fellow that'll have to do things he doesn't want to. I'd make him ride in that car like a civilised man or stay at home. What does he know about where he goes or what he goes in, and us keeping a carriage and a horse so he can take a ride on Sunday afternoon.

A lot Job cared whether the wheel came off or not, long as he wouldn't have too far to walk back. Like I say the only place for them is in the field, where they'd have to work from sunup to sundown. They cant stand prosperity or an easy job. Let one stay around white people for a while and he's not worth killing. They get so they can outguess you about work before your very eyes, like Roskus the only mistake he ever made was he got careless one day and died. Shirking and stealing and giving you a little more lip and a little more lip until some day you have to lay them out with a scantling or something. Well, it's Earl's business. But I'd hate to have my business advertised over this town by an old doddering nigger and a wagon that you thought every time it turned a corner it would come all to pieces.

The sun was all high up in the air now, and inside it was beginning to get dark. I went up front. The square was empty. Earl was back closing the safe, and then the clock begun to strike.

"You lock the back door?" he says. I went back and locked it and came back. "I suppose you're going to the show tonight," he says. "I gave you those passes yesterday, didn't I?"

"Yes," I says. "You want them back?"

"No, no," he says. "I just forgot whether I gave them to you or not. No sense in wasting them."

He locked the door and said Goodnight and went on. The sparrows were still rattling away in the trees, but the square was empty except for a few cars. There was a ford in front of the drugstore, but I didn't even look at it. I know when I've had enough of anything. I dont mind trying to help her, but I know when I've had enough. I guess I could teach Luster to drive it, then they could chase her all day long if they wanted to, and I could stay home and play with Ben.

I went in and got a couple of cigars. Then I thought I'd have another headache shot for luck, and I stood and talked with them a while.

"Well," Mac says. "I reckon you've got your money on the Yankees this year."

"What for?" I says.

"The Pennant," he says. "Not anything in the league can beat them."

"Like hell there's not," I says. "They're shot," I says. "You think a team can be that lucky forever?"

"I dont call it luck," Mac says.

"I wouldn't bet on any team that fellow Ruth played on," I says. "Even if I knew it was going to win."

"Yes?" Mac says.

"I can name you a dozen men in either league who're more valuable than he is," I says.

"What have you got against Ruth?" Mac says.

"Nothing," I says. "I haven't got any thing against him. I dont even like to look at his picture." I went on out. The lights were coming on, and people going along the streets toward home. Sometimes the sparrows never got still until full dark. The night they turned on the new lights around the courthouse it waked them up and they were flying

around and blundering into the lights all night long. They kept it up two
or three nights, then one morning they were all gone. Then after about
two months they all came back again.

I drove on home. There were no lights in the house yet, but they'd
all be looking out the windows, and Dilsey jawing away in the kitchen
like it was her own food she was having to keep hot until I got there.
You'd think to hear her that there wasn't but one supper in the world,
and that was the one she had to keep back a few minutes on my account.
Well at least I could come home one time without finding Ben and that
nigger hanging on the gate like a bear and a monkey in the same cage.
Just let it come toward sundown and he'd head for the gate like a cow
for the barn, hanging onto it and bobbing his head and sort of moaning
to himself. That's a hog for punishment for you. If what had happened
to him for fooling with open gates had happened to me, I never would
want to see another one. I often wondered what he'd be thinking about,
down there at the gate, watching the girls going home from school,
trying to want something he couldn't even remember he didn't and
couldn't want any longer. And what he'd think when they'd be undressing him and he'd happen to take a look at himself and begin to cry like
he'd do. But like I say they never did enough of that. I says I know what
you need you need what they did to Ben then you'd behave. And if you
dont know what that was I says, ask Dilsey to tell you.

There was a light in Mother's room. I put the car up and went on into
the kitchen. Luster and Ben were there.

"Where's Dilsey?" I says. "Putting supper on?"

"She up stairs wid Miss Cahline," Luster says. "Dey been goin hit.
Ever since Miss Quentin come home. Mammy up there keepin um fum
fightin. Is dat show come, Mr Jason?"

"Yes," I says.

"I thought I heard de band," he says. "Wish I could go," he says. "I
could ef I jes had a quarter."

Dilsey came in. "You come, is you?" she says. "Whut you been up
to dis evenin? You knows how much work I got to do; whyn't you git
here on time?"

"Maybe I went to the show," I says. "Is supper ready?"

"Wish I could go," Luster says. "I could ef I jes had a quarter."

"You aint got no bisiness at no show," Dilsey says. "You go on in de
house and set down," she says. "Dont you go up stairs and git um started
again, now."

"What's the matter?" I says.

"Quentin come in a while ago and says you been follerin her around
all evenin and den Miss Cahline jumped on her. Whyn't you let her
alone? Cant you live in de same house wid yo own blood niece widout
quoilin?"

"I cant quarrel with her," I says, "because I haven't seen her since this morning. What does she say I've done now? made her go to school? That's pretty bad," I says.

"Well, you tend to yo business and let her lone," Dilsey says. "I'll take keer of her ef you'n Miss Cahline'll let me. Go on in dar now and behave yoself twell I git supper on."

"Ef I jes had a quarter," Luster says, "I could go to dat show."

"En ef you had wings you could fly to heaven," Dilsey says. "I dont want to hear another word about dat show."

"That reminds me," I says. "I've got a couple of tickets they gave me." I took them out of my coat.

"You fixin to use um?" Luster says.

"Not me," I says. "I wouldn't go to it for ten dollars."

"Gimme one of um, Mr Jason," he says.

"I'll sell you one," I says. "How about it?"

"I aint got no money," he says.

"That's too bad," I says. I made to go out.

"Gimme one of um, Mr Jason," he says. "You aint gwine need um bofe."

"Hush yo mouf," Dilsey says. "Dont you know he aint gwine give nothin away?"

"How much you want fer hit?" he says.

"Five cents," I says.

"I aint got dat much," he says.

"How much you got?" I says.

"I aint got nothin," he says.

"All right," I says. I went on.

"Mr Jason," he says.

"Whyn't you hush up?" Dilsey says, "He jes teasin you. He fixin to use dem tickets hisself. Go on, Jason, and let him lone."

"I dont want them," I says. I came back to the stove. "I came in here to burn them up. But if you want to buy one for a nickel?" I says, looking at him and opening the stove lid.

"I aint got dat much," he says.

"All right," I says. I dropped one of them in the stove.

"You, Jason," Dilsey says. "Aint you shamed?"

"Mr Jason," he says. "Please, suh. I'll fix dem tires ev'y day fer a mont."

"I need the cash," I says. "You can have it for a nickel."

"Hush, Luster," Dilsey says. She jerked him back. "Go on," she says. "Drop hit in. Go on. Git hit over with."

"You can have it for a nickel," I says.

"Go on," Dilsey says. "He aint got no nickel. Go on. Drop hit in."

"All right," I says. I dropped it in and Dilsey shut the stove.

"A big growed man like you," she says. "Git on outen my kitchen. Hush," she says to Luster. "Dont you git Benjy started. I'll git you a quarter fum Frony tonight and you kin go tomorrow night. Hush up, now."

I went on into the living room. I couldn't hear anything from upstairs. I opened the paper. After a while Ben and Luster came in. Ben went to the dark place on the wall where the mirror used to be, rubbing his hands on it and slobbering and moaning. Luster began punching at the fire.

"What're you doing?" I says. "We dont need any fire tonight."

"I tryin to keep him quiet," he says. "Hit always cold Easter," he says.

"Only this is not Easter," I says. "Let it alone."

He put the poker back and got the cushion out of Mother's chair and gave it to Ben, and he hunkered down in front of the fireplace and got quiet.

I read the paper. There hadn't been a sound from upstairs when Dilsey came in and sent Ben and Luster on to the kitchen and said supper was ready.

"All right," I says. She went out. I sat there, reading the paper. After a while I heard Dilsey looking in at the door.

"Whyn't you come on and eat?" she says.

"I'm waiting for supper," I says.

"Hit's on the table," she says. "I done told you."

"Is it?" I says. "Excuse me. I didn't hear anybody come down."

"They aint comin," she says. "You come on and eat, so I can take something up to them."

"Are they sick?" I says. "What did the doctor say it was? Not Small-pox, I hope."

"Come on here, Jason," she says. "So I kin git done."

"All right," I says, raising the paper again. "I'm waiting for supper now."

I could feel her watching me at the door. I read the paper.

"Whut you want to act like this fer?" she says. "When you knows how much bother I has anyway."

"If Mother is any sicker than she was when she came down to dinner, all right," I says. "But as long as I am buying food for people younger than I am, they'll have to come down to the table to eat it. Let me know when supper's ready," I says, reading the paper again. I heard her climbing the stairs, dragging her feet and grunting and groaning like they were straight up and three feet apart. I heard her at Mother's door, then I heard her calling Quentin, like the door was locked, then she went back to Mother's room and then Mother went and talked to Quentin. Then they came down stairs. I read the paper.

Dilsey came back to the door. "Come on," she says, "fo you kin think up some mo devilment. You just tryin yoself tonight."

I went to the diningroom. Quentin was sitting with her head bent.

She had painted her face again. Her nose looked like a porcelain insulator.

"I'm glad you feel well enough to come down," I says to Mother.

"It's little enough I can do for you, to come to the table," she says. "No matter how I feel. I realise that when a man works all day he likes to be surrounded by his family at the supper table. I want to please you. I only wish you and Quentin got along better. It would be easier for me."

"We get along all right," I says. "I dont mind her staying locked up in her room all day if she wants to. But I cant have all this whoop-de-do and sulking at mealtimes. I know that's a lot to ask her, but I'm that way in my own house. Your house, I meant to say."

"It's yours," Mother says. "You are the head of it now."

Quentin hadn't looked up. I helped the plates and she begun to eat.

"Did you get a good piece of meat?" I says. "If you didn't, I'll try to find you a better one."

She didn't say anything.

"I say, did you get a good piece of meat?" I says.

"What?" she says. "Yes. It's all right."

"Will you have some more rice?" I says.

"No," she says.

"Better let me give you some more," I says.

"I dont want any more," she says.

"Not at all," I says. "You're welcome."

"Is your headache gone?" Mother says.

"Headache?" I says.

"I was afraid you were developing one," she says. "When you came in this afternoon."

"Oh," I says. "No, it didn't show up. We stayed so busy this afternoon I forgot about it."

"Was that why you were late?" Mother says. I could see Quentin listening. I looked at her. Her knife and fork were still going, but I caught her looking at me, then she looked at her plate again. I says,

"No. I loaned my car to a fellow about three oclock and I had to wait until he got back with it." I ate for a while.

"Who was it?" Mother says.

"It was one of those show men," I says. "It seems his sister's husband was out riding with some town woman, and he was chasing them."

Quentin sat perfectly still, chewing.

"You ought not to lend your car to people like that," Mother says. "You are too generous with it. That's why I never call on you for it if I can help it."

"I was beginning to think that myself, for a while," I says. "But he got back, all right. He says he found what he was looking for."

"Who was the woman?" Mother says.

"I'll tell you later," I says. "I dont like to talk about such things before Quentin."

Quentin had quit eating. Every once in a while she'd take a drink of water, then she'd sit there crumbling a biscuit up, her face bent over her plate.

"Yes," Mother says. "I suppose women who stay shut up like I do have no idea what goes on in this town."

"Yes," I says. "They dont."

"My life has been so different from that," Mother says. "Thank God I dont know about such wickedness. I dont even want to know about it. I'm not like most people."

I didn't say any more. Quentin sat there, crumbling the biscuit until I quit eating. Then she says,

"Can I go now?" without looking at anybody.

"What?" I says. "Sure, you can go. Were you waiting on us?"

She looked at me. She had crumpled all the bread, but her hands still went on like they were crumpling it yet and her eyes looked like they were cornered or something and then she started biting her mouth like it ought to have poisoned her, with all that red lead.

"Grandmother," she says. "Grandmother——"

"Did you want something else to eat?" I says.

"Why does he treat me like this, Grandmother?" she says. "I never hurt him."

"I want you all to get along with one another," Mother says. "You are all that's left now, and I do want you all to get along better."

"It's his fault," she says. "He wont let me alone, and I have to. If he doesn't want me here, why wont he let me go back to——"

"That's enough," I says. "Not another word."

"Then why wont he let me alone?" she says. "He——he just——"

"He is the nearest thing to a father you've ever had," Mother says. "It's his bread you and I eat. It's only right that he should expect obedience from you."

"It's his fault," she says. She jumped up. "He makes me do it. If he would just——" she looked at us, her eyes cornered, kind of jerking her arms against her sides.

"If I would just what?" I says.

"Whatever I do, it's your fault," she says. "If I'm bad, it's because I had to be. You made me. I wish I was dead. I wish we were all dead." Then she ran. We heard her run up the stairs. Then a door slammed.

"That's the first sensible thing she ever said," I says.

"She didn't go to school today," Mother says.

"How do you know?" I says. "Were you down town?"

"I just know," she says. "I wish you could be kinder to her."

"If I did that I'd have to arrange to see her more than once a day," I says. "You'll have to make her come to the table every meal. Then I could give her an extra piece of meat every time."

"There are little things you could do," she says.

"Like not paying any attention when you ask me to see that she goes to school?" I says.

"She didn't go to school today," she says. "I just know she didn't. She says she went for a car ride with one of the boys this afternoon and you followed her."

"How could I," I says, "when somebody had my car all afternoon? Whether or not she was in school today is already past," I says. "If you've got to worry about it, worry about next Monday."

"I wanted you and she to get along with one another," she says. "But she has inherited all of the headstrong traits. Quentin's too. I thought at the time, with the heritage she would already have, to give her that name, too. Sometimes I think she is the judgment of both of them upon me."

"Good Lord," I says. "You've got a fine mind. No wonder you keep yourself sick all the time."

"What?" she says. "I dont understand."

"I hope not," I says. "A good woman misses a lot she's better off without knowing."

"They were both that way," she says. "They would make interest with your father against me when I tried to correct them. He was always saying they didn't need controlling, that they already knew what cleanliness and honesty were, which was all that anyone could hope to be taught. And now I hope he's satisfied."

"You've got Ben to depend on," I says. "Cheer up."

"They deliberately shut me out of their lives," she says. "It was always her and Quentin. They were always conspiring against me. Against you too, though you were too young to realise it. They always looked on you and me as outsiders, like they did your Uncle Maury. I always told your father that they were allowed too much freedom, to be together too much. When Quentin started to school we had to let her go the next year, so she could be with him. She couldn't bear for any of you to do anything she couldn't. It was vanity in her, vanity and false pride. And then when her troubles began I knew that Quentin would feel that he had to do something just as bad. But I didn't believe that he would have been so selfish as to —— I didn't dream that he —— "

"Maybe he knew it was going to be a girl," I says. "And that one more of them would be more than he could stand."

"He could have controlled her," she says. "He seemed to be the only person she had any consideration for. But that is a part of the judgment too, I suppose."

"Yes," I says. "Too bad it wasn't me instead of him. You'd be a lot better off."

"You say things like that to hurt me," she says. "I deserve it though. When they began to sell the land to send Quentin to Harvard I told your father that he must make an equal provision for you. Then when Herbert offered to take you into the bank I said, Jason is provided for now, and when all the expense began to pile up and I was forced to sell our furniture and the rest of the pasture, I wrote her at once because I said she will realise that she and Quentin have had their share and part of Jason's too and that it depends on her now to compensate him. I said she will do that out of respect for her father. I believed that, then. But I'm just a poor old woman; I was raised to believe that people would deny themselves for their own flesh and blood. It's my fault. You were right to reproach me."

"Do you think I need any man's help to stand on my feet?" I says. "Let alone a woman that cant name the father of her own child."

"Jason," she says.

"All right," I says. "I didn't mean that. Of course not."

"If I believed that were possible, after all my suffering."

"Of course it's not," I says. "I didn't mean it."

"I hope that at least is spared me," she says.

"Sure it is," I says. "She's too much like both of them to doubt that."

"I couldn't bear that," she says.

"Then quit thinking about it," I says. "Has she been worrying you any more about getting out at night?"

"No. I made her realise that it was for her own good and that she'd thank me for it some day. She takes her books with her and studies after I lock the door. I see the light on as late as eleven oclock some nights."

"How do you know she's studying?" I says.

"I dont know what else she'd do in there alone," she says. "She never did read any."

"No," I says. "You wouldn't know. And you can thank your stars for that," I says. Only what would be the use in saying it aloud. It would just have her crying on me again.

I heard her go up stairs. Then she called Quentin and Quentin says What? through the door. "Goodnight," Mother says. Then I heard the key in the lock, and Mother went back to her room.

When I finished my cigar and went up, the light was still on. I could see the empty keyhole, but I couldn't hear a sound. She studied quiet. Maybe she learned that in school. I told Mother goodnight and went on to my room and got the box out and counted it again. I could hear the Great American Gelding snoring away like a planing mill. I read some-where they'd fix men that way to give them women's voices. But maybe he didn't know what they'd done to him. I dont reckon he even knew what he had been trying to do, or why Mr Burgess knocked him out with the fence picket. And if they'd just sent him on to Jackson while he was under the ether, he'd never have known the difference. But that would have been too simple for a Compson to think of. Not half complex enough. Having to wait to do it at all until he broke out and tried to run a little girl down on the street with her own father looking at him. Well, like I say they never started soon enough with their cutting, and they quit too quick. I know at least two more that needed something like that, and one of them not over a mile away, either. But then I dont reckon even that would do any good. Like I say once a bitch always a bitch. And just let me have twenty-four hours without any dam New York jew to advise me what it's going to do. I dont want to make a killing; save that to suck in the smart gamblers with. I just want an even chance to get my money back. And once I've done that they can bring all Beale street and all bedlam in here and two of them can sleep in my bed and another one can have my place at the table too.

April Eighth, 1928.

The day dawned bleak and chill, a moving wall of gray light out of the northeast which, instead of dissolving into moisture, seemed to disintegrate into minute and venomous particles, like dust that, when Dilsey opened the door of the cabin and emerged, needled laterally into her flesh, precipitating not so much a moisture as a substance partaking of the quality of thin, not quite congealed oil. She wore a stiff black straw hat perched upon her turban, and a maroon velvet cape with a border of mangy and anonymous fur above a dress of purple silk, and she stood in the door for a while with her myriad and sunken face lifted to the weather, and one gaunt hand flac-soled as the belly of a fish, then she moved the cape aside and examined the bosom of her gown.

The gown fell gauntly from her shoulders, across her fallen breasts, then tightened upon her paunch and fell again, ballooning a little above the nether garments which she would remove layer by layer as the spring accomplished and the warm days, in color regal and moribund. She had been a big woman once but now her skeleton rose, draped loosely in unpadded skin that tightened again upon a paunch almost dropsical, as though muscle and tissue had been courage or fortitude which the days or the years had consumed until only the indomitable skeleton was left rising like a ruin or a landmark above the somnolent and impervious guts, and above that the collapsed face that gave the impression of the bones themselves being outside the flesh, lifted into the driving day with an expression at once fatalistic and of a child's astonished disappointment, until she turned and entered the house again and closed the door.

The earth immediately about the door was bare. It had a patina, as though from the soles of bare feet in generations, like old silver or the walls of Mexican houses which have been plastered by hand. Beside the house, shading it in summer, stood three mulberry trees, the fledged leaves that would later be broad and placid as the palms of hands streaming flatly undulant upon the driving air. A pair of jaybirds came up from nowhere, whirled up on the blast like gaudy scraps of cloth or paper and lodged in the mulberries, where they swung in raucous tilt and recover, screaming into the wind that ripped their harsh cries onward and away like scraps of paper or of cloth in turn. Then three more joined them and they swung and tilted in the wrung branches for a time, screaming. The door of the cabin opened and Dilsey emerged once more, this time in a man's felt hat and an army overcoat, beneath the frayed skirts of which her blue gingham dress fell in uneven balloonings, streaming too about her as she crossed the yard and mounted the steps to the kitchen door.

A moment later she emerged, carrying an open umbrella now, which she slanted ahead into the wind, and crossed to the woodpile and laid the umbrella down, still open. Immediately she caught at it and arrested it and held to it for a while, looking about her. Then she closed it and laid it down and stacked stovewood into her crooked arm, against her breast, and picked up the umbrella and got it open at last and returned to the steps and held the wood precariously balanced while she contrived to close the umbrella, which she propped in the corner just within the door. She dumped the wood into the box behind the stove. Then she removed the overcoat and hat and took a soiled apron down from the wall and put it on and built a fire in the stove. While she was doing so, rattling the grate bars and clattering the lids, Mrs Compson began to call her from the head of the stairs.

She wore a dressing gown of quilted black satin, holding it close under her chin. In the other hand she held a red rubber hot water bottle and she stood at the head of the back stairway, calling "Dilsey" at steady and inflectionless intervals into the quiet stairwell that descended into complete darkness, then opened again where a gray window fell across it. "Dilsey," she called, without inflection or emphasis or haste, as though she were not listening for a reply at all. "Dilsey."

Dilsey answered and ceased clattering the stove, but before she could cross the kitchen Mrs Compson called her again, and before she crossed the diningroom and brought her head into relief against the gray splash of the window, still again.

"All right," Dilsey said. "All right, here I is. I'll fill hit soon ez I git some hot water." She gathered up her skirts and mounted the stairs, wholly blotting the gray light. "Put hit down dar en g'awn back to bed."

"I couldn't understand what was the matter," Mrs Compson said. "I've been lying awake for an hour at least, without hearing a sound from the kitchen."

"You put hit down and g'awn back to bed," Dilsey said. She toiled painfully up the steps, shapeless, breathing heavily. "I'll have de fire gwine in a minute, en de water hot in two mo."

"I've been lying there for an hour, at least," Mrs Compson said. "I thought maybe you were waiting for me to come down and start the fire."

Dilsey reached the top of the stairs and took the water bottle. "I'll fix hit in a minute," she said. "Luster overslep dis mawnin, up half de night at dat show. I gwine build de fire myself. Go on now, so you wont wake de others twell I ready."

"If you permit Luster to do things that interfere with his work, you'll have to suffer for it yourself," Mrs Compson said. "Jason wont like this if he hears about it. You know he wont."

" 'Twusn't none of Jason's money he went on," Dilsey said. "Dat's one thing sho." She went on down the stairs. Mrs Compson returned to her room. As she got into bed again she could hear Dilsey yet descending the stairs with a sort of painful and terrific slowness that would have become maddening had it not presently ceased beyond the flapping diminishment of the pantry door.

She entered the kitchen and built up the fire and began to prepare breakfast. In the midst of this she ceased and went to the window and looked out toward her cabin, then she went to the door and opened it and shouted into the driving weather.

"Luster!" she shouted, standing to listen, tilting her face from the wind. "You, Luster!" She listened, then as she prepared to shout again Luster appeared around the corner of the kitchen.

"Ma'am?" he said innocently, so innocently that Dilsey looked down at him, for a moment motionless, with something more than mere surprise.

"Whar you at?" she said.

"Nowhere," he said. "Jes in de cellar."

"Whut you doin in de cellar?" she said. "Dont stand dar in de rain, fool," she said.

"Aint doin nothin," he said. He came up the steps.

"Dont you dare come in dis do widout a armful of wood," she said. "Here I done had to tote yo wood en build yo fire bofe. Didn't I tole you not to leave dis place last night befo dat woodbox wus full to de top?"

"I did," Luster said. "I filled hit."

"Whar hit gone to, den?"

"I dont know'm. I aint teched hit."

"Well, you git hit full up now," she said. "And git on up dar en see bout Benjy."

She shut the door. Luster went to the woodpile. The five jaybirds whirled over the house, screaming, and into the mulberries again. He watched them. He picked up a rock and threw it. "Whoo," he said. "Git on back to hell, whar you belong at. 'Taint Monday yit." [1]

He loaded himself mountainously with stove wood. He could not see over it, and he staggered to the steps and up them and blundered crashing against the door, shedding billets. Then Dilsey came and opened the door for him and he blundered across the kitchen. "You, Luster!" she shouted, but he had already hurled the wood into the box with a thunderous crash. "Hah!" he said.

"Is you tryin to wake up de whole house?" Dilsey said. She hit him on the back of his head with the flat of her hand. "Go on up dar and git Benjy dressed, now."

"Yessum," he said. He went toward the outer door.

"Whar you gwine?" Dilsey said.

"I thought I better go round de house en in by de front, so I wont wake up Miss Cahline en dem."

"You go on up dem back stairs like I tole you en git Benjy's clothes on him," Dilsey said. "Go on, now."

"Yessum," Luster said. He returned and left by the diningroom door. After a while it ceased to flap. Dilsey prepared to make biscuit. As she ground the sifter steadily above the bread board, she sang, to herself at first, something without particular tune or words, repetitive, mournful and plaintive, austere, as she ground a faint, steady snowing of flour onto the bread board. The stove had begun to heat the room and to fill it with murmurous minors of the fire, and presently she was singing louder, as if her voice too had been thawed out by the growing warmth, and then Mrs Compson called her name again from within the house. Dilsey raised her face as if her eyes could and did penetrate the walls and ceiling and saw the old woman in her quilted dressing gown at the head of the stairs, calling her name with machinelike regularity.

"Oh, Lawd," Dilsey said. She set the sifter down and swept up the hem of her apron and wiped her hands and caught up the bottle from the chair on which she had laid it and gathered her apron about the handle of the kettle which was now jetting faintly. "Jes a minute," she called. "De water jes dis minute got hot."

It was not the bottle which Mrs Compson wanted, however, and clutching it by the neck like a dead hen Dilsey went to the foot of the stairs and looked upward.

"Aint Luster up dar wid him?" she said.

"Luster hasn't been in the house. I've been lying here listening for him. I knew he would be late, but I did hope he'd come in time to keep

---

1. In folk belief, jaybirds go to hell on Friday and come out on Monday. Some say the jaybirds sold themselves to the devil for an ear of corn and are obliged to take a grain of sand to him to make his fire hot. Others regard the jaybirds as the devil's messengers, who tell him of people's sins.

Benjamin from disturbing Jason on Jason's one day in the week to sleep in the morning."

"I dont see how you expect anybody to sleep, wid you standin in de hall, holl'in at folks fum de crack of dawn," Dilsey said. She began to mount the stairs, toiling heavily. "I sont dat boy up dar half an hour ago."

Mrs Compson watched her, holding the dressing gown under her chin. "What are you going to do?" she said.

"Gwine git Benjy dressed en bring him down to de kitchen, whar he wont wake Jason en Quentin," Dilsey said.

"Haven't you started breakfast yet?"

"I'll tend to dat too," Dilsey said. "You better git back in bed twell Luster make yo fire. Hit cold dis mawnin."

"I know it," Mrs Compson said. "My feet are like ice. They were so cold they waked me up." She watched Dilsey mount the stairs. It took her a long while. "You know how it frets Jason when breakfast is late," Mrs Compson said.

"I cant do but one thing at a time," Dilsey said. "You git on back to bed, fo I has you on my hands dis mawnin too."

"If you're going to drop everything to dress Benjamin, I'd better come down and get breakfast. You know as well as I do how Jason acts when it's late."

"En who gwine eat yo messin?" Dilsey said. "Tell me dat. Go on now," she said, toiling upward. Mrs Compson stood watching her as she mounted, steadying herself against the wall with one hand, holding her skirts up with the other.

"Are you going to wake him up just to dress him?" she said.

Dilsey stopped. With her foot lifted to the next step she stood there, her hand against the wall and the gray splash of the window behind her, motionless and shapeless she loomed.

"He aint awake den?" she said.

"He wasn't when I looked in," Mrs Compson said. "But it's past his time. He never does sleep after half past seven. You know he doesn't."

Dilsey said nothing. She made no further move, but though she could not see her save as a blobby shape without depth, Mrs Compson knew that she had lowered her face a little and that she stood now like cows do in the rain, holding the empty water bottle by its neck.

"You're not the one who has to bear it," Mrs Compson said. "It's not your responsibility. You can go away. You dont have to bear the brunt of it day in and day out. You owe nothing to them, to Mr Compson's memory. I know you have never had any tenderness for Jason. You've never tried to conceal it."

Dilsey said nothing. She turned slowly and descended, lowering her body from step to step, as a small child does, her hand against the wall.

"You go on and let him alone," she said. "Dont go in dar no mo, now. I'll send Luster up soon as I find him. Let him alone, now."

She returned to the kitchen. She looked into the stove, then she drew her apron over her head and donned the overcoat and opened the outer door and looked up and down the yard. The weather drove upon her flesh, harsh and minute, but the scene was empty of all else that moved. She descended the steps, gingerly, as if for silence, and went around the corner of the kitchen. As she did so Luster emerged quickly and innocently from the cellar door.

Dilsey stopped. "Whut you up to?" she said.

"Nothin," Luster said. "Mr Jason say fer me to find out whar dat water leak in de cellar fum."

"En when wus hit he say fer you to do dat?" Dilsey said. "Last New Year's day, wasn't hit?"

"I thought I jes be lookin whiles dey sleep," Luster said. Dilsey went to the cellar door. He stood aside and she peered down into the obscurity odorous of dank earth and mold and rubber.

"Huh," Dilsey said. She looked at Luster again. He met her gaze blandly, innocent and open. "I dont know whut you up to, but you aint got no business doin hit. You jes tryin me too dis mawnin cause de others is, aint you? You git on up dar en see to Benjy, you hear?"

"Yessum," Luster said. He went on toward the kitchen steps, swiftly.

"Here," Dilsey said. "You git me another armful of wood while I got you."

"Yessum," he said. He passed her on the steps and went to the woodpile. When he blundered again at the door a moment later, again invisible and blind within and beyond his wooden avatar, Dilsey opened the door and guided him across the kitchen with a firm hand.

"Jes thow hit at dat box again," she said. "Jes thow hit."

"I got to," Luster said, panting. "I cant put hit down no other way."

"Den you stand dar en hold hit a while," Dilsey said. She unloaded him a stick at a time. "Whut got into you dis mawnin? Here I sont you fer wood en you aint never brought mo'n six sticks at a time to save yo life twell today. Whut you fixin to ax me kin you do now? Aint dat show lef town yit?"

"Yessum. Hit done gone."

She put the last stick into the box. "Now you go on up dar wid Benjy, like I tole you befo," she said. "And I dont want nobody else yellin down dem stairs at me twell I rings de bell. You hear me."

"Yessum," Luster said. He vanished through the swing door. Dilsey put some more wood in the stove and returned to the bread board. Presently she began to sing again.

The room grew warmer. Soon Dilsey's skin had taken on a rich, lustrous quality as compared with that as of a faint dusting of wood ashes which both it and Luster's had worn as she moved about the kitchen, gathering about her the raw materials of food, coordinating the meal. On the wall above a cupboard, invisible save at night, by lamp light and even then evincing an enigmatic profundity because it had but one hand, a cabinet clock ticked, then with a preliminary sound as if it had cleared its throat, struck five times.

"Eight oclock," Dilsey said. She ceased and tilted her head upward, listening. But there was no sound save the clock and the fire. She opened the oven and looked at the pan of bread, then stooping she paused while someone descended the stairs. She heard the feet cross the diningroom, then the swing door opened and Luster entered, followed by a big man who appeared to have been shaped of some substance whose particles would not or did not cohere to one another or to the frame which supported it. His skin was dead looking and hairless; dropsical too, he moved with a shambling gait like a trained bear. His hair was pale and fine. It had been brushed smoothly down upon his brow like that of children in daguerrotypes. His eyes were clear, of the pale sweet blue of cornflowers, his thick mouth hung open, drooling a little.

"Is he cold?" Dilsey said. She wiped her hands on her apron and touched his hand.

"Ef he aint, I is," Luster said. "Always cold Easter. Aint never seen hit fail. Miss Cahline say ef you aint got time to fix her hot water bottle to never mind about hit."

"Oh, Lawd," Dilsey said. She drew a chair into the corner between the woodbox and the stove. The man went obediently and sat in it. "Look in de dinin room and see whar I laid dat bottle down," Dilsey said. Luster fetched the bottle from the diningroom and Dilsey filled it and gave it to him. "Hurry up, now," she said. "See ef Jason wake now. Tell em hit's all ready."

Luster went out. Ben sat beside the stove. He sat loosely, utterly motionless save for his head, which made a continual bobbing sort of movement as he watched Dilsey with his sweet vague gaze as she moved about. Luster returned.

"He up," he said. "Miss Cahline say put hit on de table." He came to the stove and spread his hands palm down above the firebox. "He up, too," he said. "Gwine hit wid bofe feet dis mawnin."

"Whut's de matter now?" Dilsey said. "Git away fum dar. How kin I do anything wid you standin over de stove?"

"I cold," Luster said.

"You ought to thought about dat whiles you wus down dar in dat cellar," Dilsey said. "Whut de matter wid Jason?"

"Sayin me en Benjy broke dat winder in his room."

"Is dey one broke?" Dilsey said.

"Dat's whut he sayin," Luster said. "Say I broke hit."

"How could you, when he keep hit locked all day en night?"

"Say I broke hit chunkin rocks at hit," Luster said.

"En did you?"

"Nome," Luster said.

"Dont lie to me, boy," Dilsey said.

"I never done hit," Luster said. "Ask Benjy ef I did. I aint stud'in dat winder."

"Who could a broke hit, den?" Dilsey said. "He jes tryin hisself, to wake Quentin up," she said, taking the pan of biscuits out of the stove.

"Reckin so," Luster said. "Dese funny folks. Glad I aint none of em."

"Aint none of who?" Dilsey said. "Lemme tell you somethin, nigger boy, you got jes es much Compson devilment in you es any of em. Is you right sho you never broke dat window?"

"Whut I want to break hit fur?"

"Whut you do any of yo devilment fur?" Dilsey said. "Watch him now, so he cant burn his hand again twell I git de table set."

She went to the diningroom, where they heard her moving about, then she returned and set a plate at the kitchen table and set food there. Ben watched her, slobbering, making a faint, eager sound.

"All right, honey," she said. "Here yo breakfast. Bring his chair, Luster." Luster moved the chair up and Ben sat down, whimpering and slobbering. Dilsey tied a cloth about his neck and wiped his mouth with the end of it. "And see kin you keep fum messin up his clothes one time," she said, handing Luster a spoon.

Ben ceased whimpering. He watched the spoon as it rose to his mouth. It was as if even eagerness were musclebound in him too, and hunger itself inarticulate, not knowing it is hunger. Luster fed him with skill and detachment. Now and then his attention would return long enough to enable him to feint the spoon and cause Ben to close his mouth upon the empty air, but it was apparent that Luster's mind was elsewhere. His other hand lay on the back of the chair and upon that dead surface it moved tentatively, delicately, as if he were picking an inaudible tune out of the dead void, and once he even forgot to tease Ben with the spoon while his fingers teased out of the slain wood a soundless and involved arpeggio until Ben recalled him by whimpering again.

In the diningroom Dilsey moved back and forth. Presently she rang a small clear bell, then in the kitchen Luster heard Mrs Compson and Jason descending, and Jason's voice, and he rolled his eyes whitely with listening.

"Sure, I know they didn't break it," Jason said. "Sure, I know that. Maybe the change of weather broke it."

"I dont see how it could have," Mrs Compson said. "Your room stays locked all day long, just as you leave it when you go to town. None of us ever go in there except Sunday, to clean it. I dont want you to think that I would go where I'm not wanted, or that I would permit anyone else to."

"I never said you broke it, did I?" Jason said.

"I dont want to go in your room," Mrs Compson said. "I respect anybody's private affairs. I wouldn't put my foot over the threshold, even if I had a key."

"Yes," Jason said. "I know your keys wont fit. That's why I had the lock changed. What I want to know is, how that window got broken."

"Luster say he didn't do hit," Dilsey said.

"I knew that without asking him," Jason said. "Where's Quentin?" he said.

"Where she is ev'y Sunday mawnin," Dilsey said. "Whut got into you de last few days, anyhow?"

"Well, we're going to change all that," Jason said. "Go up and tell her breakfast is ready."

"You leave her alone now, Jason," Dilsey said. "She gits up fer breakfast ev'y week mawnin, en Miss Cahline lets her stay in bed ev'y Sunday. You knows dat."

"I cant keep a kitchen full of niggers to wait on her pleasure, much as I'd like to," Jason said. "Go and tell her to come down to breakfast."

"Aint nobody have to wait on her," Dilsey said. "I puts her breakfast in de warmer en she——"

"Did you hear me?" Jason said.

"I hears you," Dilsey said. "All I been hearin, when you in de house. Ef hit aint Quentin er yo maw, hit's Luster en Benjy. Whut you let him go on dat way fer, Miss Cahline?"

"You'd better do as he says," Mrs Compson said. "He's head of the house now. It's his right to require us to respect his wishes. I try to do it, and if I can, you can too."

" 'Taint no sense in him bein so bad tempered he got to make Quentin git up jes to suit him," Dilsey said. "Maybe you think she broke dat window."

"She would, if she happened to think of it," Jason said. "You go and do what I told you."

"En I wouldn't blame her none ef she did," Dilsey said, going toward the stairs. "Wid you naggin at her all de blessed time you in de house."

"Hush, Dilsey," Mrs Compson said. "It's neither your place nor mine to tell Jason what to do. Sometimes I think he is wrong, but I try to obey his wishes for you all's sakes. If I'm strong enough to come to the table, Quentin can too."

Dilsey went out. They heard her mounting the stairs. They heard her a long while on the stairs.

"You've got a prize set of servants," Jason said. He helped his mother and himself to food. "Did you ever have one that was worth killing? You must have had some before I was big enough to remember."

"I have to humor them," Mrs Compson said. "I have to depend on them so completely. It's not as if I were strong. I wish I were. I wish I could do all the house work myself. I could at least take that much off your shoulders."

"And a fine pigsty we'd live in, too," Jason said. "Hurry up, Dilsey," he shouted.

"I know you blame me," Mrs Compson said, "for letting them off to go to church today."

"Go where?" Jason said. "Hasn't that damn show left yet?"

"To church," Mrs Compson said. "The darkies are having a special Easter service. I promised Dilsey two weeks ago that they could get off."

"Which means we'll eat cold dinner," Jason said, "or none at all."

"I know it's my fault," Mrs Compson said. "I know you blame me."

"For what?" Jason said. "You never resurrected Christ, did you?"

They heard Dilsey mount the final stair, then her slow feet overhead.

"Quentin," she said. When she called the first time Jason laid his knife and fork down and he and his mother appeared to wait across the table from one another in identical attitudes; the one cold and shrewd, with close-thatched brown hair curled into two stubborn hooks, one on either side of his forehead like a bartender in caricature, and hazel eyes with black-ringed irises like marbles, the other cold and querulous, with perfectly white hair and eyes pouched and baffled and so dark as to appear to be all pupil or all iris.

"Quentin," Dilsey said. "Get up, honey. Dey waitin breakfast on you."

"I cant understand how that window got broken," Mrs Compson said. "Are you sure it was done yesterday? It could have been like that a long time, with the warm weather. The upper sash, behind the shade like that."

"I've told you for the last time that it happened yesterday," Jason said. "Dont you reckon I know the room I live in? Do you reckon I could have lived in it a week with a hole in the window you could stick your hand. . . ." his voice ceased, ebbed, left him staring at his mother with eyes that for an instant were quite empty of anything. It was as though his eyes were holding their breath, while his mother looked at him, her face flaccid and querulous, interminable, clairvoyant yet obtuse. As they sat so Dilsey said,

"Quentin. Dont play wid me, honey. Come on to breakfast, honey. Dey waitin fer you."

"I cant understand it," Mrs Compson said. "It's just as if somebody had tried to break into the house——" Jason sprang up. His chair crashed over backward. "What——" Mrs Compson said, staring at him as he ran past her and went jumping up the stairs, where he met Dilsey. His face was now in shadow, and Dilsey said,

"She sullin. Yo maw aint unlocked——" But Jason ran on past her and along the corridor to a door. He didn't call. He grasped the knob and tried it, then he stood with the knob in his hand and his head bent a little, as if he were listening to something much further away than the dimensioned room beyond the door, and which he already heard. His attitude was that of one who goes through the motions of listening in order to deceive himself as to what he already hears. Behind him Mrs Compson mounted the stairs, calling his name. Then she saw Dilsey and she quit calling him and began to call Dilsey instead.

"I told you she aint unlocked dat do yit," Dilsey said.

When she spoke he turned and ran toward her, but his voice was quiet, matter of fact. "She carry the key with her?" he said. "Has she got it now, I mean, or will she have———"

"Dilsey," Mrs Compson said on the stairs.

"Is which?" Dilsey said. "Whyn't you let———"

"The key," Jason said. "To that room. Does she carry it with her all the time. Mother." Then he saw Mrs Compson and he went down the stairs and met her. "Give me the key," he said. He fell to pawing at the pockets of the rusty black dressing sacque she wore. She resisted.

"Jason," she said. "Jason! Are you and Dilsey trying to put me to bed again?" she said, trying to fend him off. "Cant you even let me have Sunday in peace?"

"The key," Jason said, pawing at her. "Give it here." He looked back at the door, as if he expected it to fly open before he could get back to it with the key he did not yet have.

"You, Dilsey!" Mrs Compson said, clutching her sacque about her.

"Give me the key, you old fool!" Jason cried suddenly. From her pocket he tugged a huge bunch of rusted keys on an iron ring like a mediaeval jailer's and ran back up the hall with the two women behind him.

"You, Jason!" Mrs Compson said. "He will never find the right one," she said. "You know I never let anyone take my keys, Dilsey," she said. She began to wail.

"Hush," Dilsey said. "He aint gwine do nothin to her. I aint gwine let him."

"But on Sunday morning, in my own house," Mrs Compson said. "When I've tried so hard to raise them christians. Let me find the right key, Jason," she said. She put her hand on his arm. Then she began to struggle with him, but he flung her aside with a motion of his elbow and looked around at her for a moment, his eyes cold and harried, then he turned to the door again and the unwieldy keys.

"Hush," Dilsey said. "You, Jason!"

"Something terrible has happened," Mrs Compson said, wailing again. "I know it has. You, Jason," she said, grasping at him again. "He wont even let me find the key to a room in my own house!"

"Now, now," Dilsey said. "Whut kin happen? I right here. I aint gwine let him hurt her. Quentin," she said, raising her voice, "dont you be skeered, honey, I'se right here."

The door opened, swung inward. He stood in it for a moment, hiding the room, then he stepped aside. "Go in," he said in a thick, light voice. They went in. It was not a girl's room. It was not anybody's room, and the faint scent of cheap cosmetics and the few feminine objects and the other evidences of crude and hopeless efforts to feminise it but added to its anonymity, giving it that dead and stereotyped transience of rooms in assignation houses. The bed had not been disturbed. On the floor lay a soiled undergarment of cheap silk a little too pink, from a half open bureau drawer dangled a single stocking. The window was open. A pear tree grew there, close against the house. It was in bloom and the branches scraped and rasped against the house and the myriad air, driving in the window, brought into the room the forlorn scent of the blossoms.

"Dar now," Dilsey said. "Didn't I told you she all right?"

"All right?" Mrs Compson said. Dilsey followed her into the room and touched her.

"You come on and lay down, now," she said. "I find her in ten minutes."

Mrs Compson shook her off. "Find the note," she said. "Quentin left a note when he did it."

"All right," Dilsey said. "I'll find hit. You come on to yo room, now."

"I knew the minute they named her Quentin this would happen," Mrs Compson said. She went to the bureau and began to turn over the scattered objects there — scent, bottles, a box of powder, a chewed pencil, a pair of scissors with one broken blade lying upon a darned scarf dusted with powder and stained with rouge. "Find the note," she said.

"I is," Dilsey said. "You come on, now. Me and Jason'll find hit. You come on to yo room."

"Jason," Mrs Compson said. "Where is he?" She went to the door. Dilsey followed her on down the hall, to another door. It was closed. "Jason," she called through the door. There was no answer. She tried the knob, then she called him again. But there was still no answer, for he was hurling things backward out of the closet, garments, shoes, a suitcase. Then he emerged carrying a sawn section of tongue-and-groove planking and laid it down and entered the closet again and emerged with a metal box. He set it on the bed and stood looking at the broken lock while he dug a keyring from his pocket and selected a key, and for a time longer he stood with the selected key in his hand, looking at the broken lock. Then he put the keys back in his pocket and carefully tilted the contents of the box out upon the bed. Still carefully he sorted the papers, taking them up one at a time and shaking them. Then he upended the box and shook it too and slowly replaced the papers and stood again, looking at the broken lock, with the box in his hands and his head bent. Outside the window he heard some jaybirds swirl shrieking past and away, their cries whipping away along the wind, and an automobile passed somewhere and died away also. His mother spoke his name again beyond the door, but he didn't move. He heard Dilsey lead her away up the hall, and then a door closed. Then he replaced the box in the closet and flung the garments back into it and went down stairs to the telephone. While he stood there with the receiver to his ear waiting Dilsey came down the stairs. She looked at him, without stopping, and went on.

The wire opened. "This is Jason Compson," he said, his voice so harsh and thick that he had to repeat himself. "Jason Compson," he said, controlling his voice. "Have a car ready, with a deputy, if you cant go, in ten minutes. I'll be there——What? ——Robbery. My house. I know who it——Robbery, I say. Have a car read——What? Aren't you a paid law enforcement——Yes, I'll be there in five minutes. Have that car ready to leave at once. If you dont, I'll report it to the governor."

He clapped the receiver back and crossed the diningroom, where the scarce broken meal lay cold now on the table, and entered the kitchen. Dilsey was filling the hot water bottle. Ben sat, tranquil and empty. Beside him Luster looked like a fice dog, brightly watchful. He was eating something. Jason went on across the kitchen.

"Aint you going to eat no breakfast?" Dilsey said. He paid her no attention. "Go on en eat yo breakfast, Jason." He went on. The outer door banged behind him. Luster rose and went to the window and looked out.

"Whoo," he said. "Whut happenin up dar? He been beatin Miss Quentin?"

"You hush yo mouf," Dilsey said. "You git Benjy started now en I beat yo head off. You keep him quiet es you kin twell I git back, now." She screwed the cap on the bottle and went out. They heard her go up the stairs, then they heard Jason pass the house in his car. Then there was no sound in the kitchen save the simmering murmur of the kettle and the clock.

"You know whut I bet?" Luster said. "I bet he beat her. I bet he knock her in de head en now he gone fer de doctor. Dat's whut I bet." The clock tick-tocked, solemn and profound. It might have been the dry pulse of the decaying house itself, after a while it whirred and cleared its throat and struck six times. Ben looked up at it, then he looked at the bulletlike silhouette of Luster's head in the window and he begun to bob his head again, drooling. He whimpered.

"Hush up, looney," Luster said without turning. "Look like we aint gwine git to go to no church today." But Ben sat in the chair, his big soft hands dangling between his knees, moaning faintly. Suddenly he wept, a slow bellowing sound, meaningless and sustained. "Hush," Luster said. He turned and lifted his hand. "You want me to whup you?" But Ben looked at him, bellowing slowly with each expiration. Luster came and shook him. "You hush dis minute!" he shouted. "Here," he said. He hauled Ben out of the chair and dragged the chair around facing the stove and opened the door to the firebox and shoved Ben into the chair. They looked like a tug nudging at a clumsy tanker in a narrow dock. Ben sat down again facing the rosy door. He hushed. Then they heard the clock again, and Dilsey slow on the stairs. When she entered he began to whimper again. Then he lifted his voice.

"Whut you done to him?" Dilsey said. "Why cant you let him lone dis mawnin, of all times?"

"I aint doin nothin to him," Luster said. "Mr Jason skeered him, dat's whut hit is. He aint kilt Miss Quentin, is he?"

"Hush, Benjy," Dilsey said. He hushed. She went to the window and looked out. "Is it quit rainin?" she said.

"Yessum," Luster said. "Quit long time ago."

"Den y'all go out do's a while," she said. "I jes got Miss Cahline quiet now."

"Is we gwine to church?" Luster said.

"I let you know bout dat when de time come. You keep him away fum de house twell I calls you."

"Kin we go to de pastuh?" Luster said.

"All right. Only you keep him away fum de house. I done stood all I kin."

"Yessum," Luster said. "Whar Mr Jason gone, mammy?"

"Dat's some mo of yo business, aint it?" Dilsey said. She began to clear the table. "Hush, Benjy. Luster gwine take you out to play."

"Whut he done to Miss Quentin, mammy?" Luster said.

"Aint done nothin to her. You all git on outen here."

"I bet she aint here," Luster said.

Dilsey looked at him. "How you know she aint here?"

"Me and Benjy seed her clamb out de window last night. Didn't us, Benjy?"

"You did?" Dilsey said, looking at him.

"We sees her doin hit ev'y night," Luster said. "Clamb right down dat pear tree."

"Dont you lie to me, nigger boy," Dilsey said.

"I aint lyin. Ask Benjy ef I is."

"Whyn't you say somethin about it, den?"

" 'Twarn't none o my business," Luster said. "I aint gwine git mixed up in white folks' business. Come on here, Benjy, les go out do's."

They went out. Dilsey stood for a while at the table, then she went and cleared the breakfast things from the diningroom and ate her breakfast and cleaned up the kitchen. Then she removed her apron and hung it up and went to the foot of the stairs and listened for a moment. There was no sound. She donned the overcoat and the hat and went across to her cabin.

The rain had stopped. The air now drove out of the southeast, broken overhead into blue patches. Upon the crest of a hill beyond the trees and roofs and spires of town sunlight lay like a pale scrap of cloth, was blotted away. Upon the air a bell came, then as if at a signal, other bells took up the sound and repeated it.

The cabin door opened and Dilsey emerged, again in the maroon cape and the purple gown, and wearing soiled white elbow-length gloves and minus her headcloth now. She came into the yard and called Luster. She waited a while, then she went to the house and around it to the cellar door, moving close to the wall, and looked into the door. Ben sat on the steps. Before him Luster squatted on the damp floor. He held a saw in his left hand, the blade sprung a little by pressure of his hand, and he was in the act of striking the blade with the worn wooden mallet with which she had been making beaten biscuit for more than thirty years. The saw gave forth a single sluggish twang that ceased with lifeless alacrity, leaving the blade in a thin clean curve between Luster's hand and the floor. Still, inscrutable, it bellied.

"Dat's de way he done hit," Luster said. "I jes aint foun de right thing to hit it wid."

"Dat's whut you doin, is it?" Dilsey said. "Bring me dat mallet," she said.

"I aint hurt hit," Luster said.

"Bring hit here," Dilsey said. "Put dat saw whar you got hit first."

He put the saw away and brought the mallet to her. Then Ben wailed again, hopeless and prolonged. It was nothing. Just sound. It might have been all time and injustice and sorrow become vocal for an instant by a conjunction of planets.

"Listen at him," Luster said. "He been gwine on dat way ev'y since you sont us outen de house. I dont know whut got in to him dis mawnin."

"Bring him here," Dilsey said.

"Come on, Benjy," Luster said. He went back down the steps and took Ben's arm. He came obediently, wailing, that slow hoarse sound that ships make, that seems to begin before the sound itself has started, seems to cease before the sound itself has stopped.

"Run and git his cap," Dilsey said. "Dont make no noise Miss Cahline kin hear. Hurry, now. We already late."

"She gwine hear him anyhow, ef you dont stop him," Luster said.

"He stop when we git off de place," Dilsey said. "He smellin hit. Dat's whut hit is."

"Smell whut, mammy?" Luster said.

"You go git dat cap," Dilsey said. Luster went on. They stood in the cellar door, Ben one step below her. The sky was broken now into scudding patches that dragged their swift shadows up out of the shabby garden, over the broken fence and across the yard. Dilsey stroked Ben's head, slowly and steadily, smoothing the bang upon his brow. He wailed quietly, unhurriedly. "Hush," Dilsey said. "Hush, now. We be gone in a minute. Hush, now." He wailed quietly and steadily.

Luster returned, wearing a stiff new straw hat with a colored band and carrying a cloth cap. The hat seemed to isolate Luster's skull in the beholder's eye as a spotlight would, in all its individual planes and angles. So peculiarly individual was its shape that at first glance the hat appeared to be on the head of someone standing immediately behind Luster. Dilsey looked at the hat.

"Whyn't you wear yo old hat?" she said.

"Couldn't find hit," Luster said.

"I bet you couldn't. I bet you fixed hit last night so you couldn't find hit. You fixin to ruin dat un."

"Aw, mammy," Luster said. "Hit aint gwine rain."

"How you know? You go git dat old hat en put dat new un away."

"Aw, mammy."

"Den you go git de umbreller."

"Aw, mammy."

"Take yo choice," Dilsey said. "Git yo old hat, er de umbreller. I dont keer which."

Luster went to the cabin. Ben wailed quietly.

"Come on," Dilsey said. "Dey kin ketch up wid us. We gwine to hear de singin." They went around the house, toward the gate. "Hush," Dilsey said from time to time as they went down the drive. They reached the gate. Dilsey opened it. Luster was coming down the drive behind them, carrying the umbrella. A woman was with him. "Here dey come," Dilsey said. They passed out the gate. "Now, den," she said. Ben ceased. Luster and his mother overtook them. Frony wore a dress of bright blue silk and a flowered hat. She was a thin woman, with a flat, pleasant face.

"You got six weeks' work right dar on yo back," Dilsey said. "Whut you gwine do ef hit rain?"

"Git wet, I reckon," Frony said. "I aint never stopped no rain yit."

"Mammy always talkin bout hit gwine rain," Luster said.

"Ef I dont worry bout y'all, I dont know who is," Dilsey said. "Come on, we already late."

"Rev'un Shegog gwine preach today," Frony said.

"Is?" Dilsey said. "Who him?"

"He fum Saint Looey," Frony said. "Dat big preacher."

"Huh," Dilsey said. "Whut dey needs is a man kin put de fear of God into dese here triflin young niggers."

"Rev'un Shegog kin do dat," Frony said. "So dey tells."

They went on along the street. Along its quiet length white people in bright clumps moved churchward, under the windy bells, walking now and then in the random and tentative sun. The wind was gusty, out of the southeast, chill and raw after the warm days.

"I wish you wouldn't keep on bringin him to church, mammy," Frony said. "Folks talkin."

"Whut folks?" Dilsey said.

"I hears em," Frony said.

"And I knows whut kind of folks," Dilsey said. "Trash white folks. Dat's who it is. Thinks he aint good enough fer white church, but nigger church aint good enough fer him."

"Dey talks, jes de same," Frony said.

"Den you send um to me," Dilsey said. "Tell um de good Lawd dont keer whether he bright er not. Dont nobody but white trash keer dat."

A street turned off at right angles, descending, and became a dirt road. On either hand the land dropped more sharply; a broad flat dotted with small cabins whose weathered roofs were on a level with the crown of the road. They were set in small grassless plots littered with broken things, bricks, planks, crockery, things of a once utilitarian value. What growth there was consisted of rank weeds and the trees were mulberries and locusts and sycamores — trees that partook also of the foul desiccation which surrounded the houses; trees whose very burgeoning seemed to be the sad and stubborn remnant of September, as if even spring had passed them by, leaving them to feed upon the rich and unmistakable smell of negroes in which they grew.

From the doors negroes spoke to them as they passed, to Dilsey usually:

"Sis' Gibson! How you dis mawnin?"

"I'm well. Is you well?"

"I'm right well, I thank you."

They emerged from the cabins and struggled up the shaling levee to the road — men in staid, hard brown or black, with gold watch chains and now and then a stick; young men in cheap violent blues or stripes and swaggering hats; women a little stiffly sibilant, and children in garments bought second hand of white people, who looked at Ben with the covertness of nocturnal animals:

"I bet you wont go up en tech him."

"How come I wont?"

"I bet you wont. I bet you skeered to."

"He wont hurt folks. He des a looney."

"How come a looney wont hurt folks?"

"Dat un wont. I teched him."

"I bet you wont now."

"Case Miss Dilsey lookin."

"You wont no ways."

"He dont hurt folks. He des a looney."

And steadily the older people speaking to Dilsey, though, unless they were quite old, Dilsey permitted Frony to respond.

"Mammy aint feelin well dis mawnin."

"Dat's too bad. But Rev'un Shegog'll kyo dat. He'll give her de comfort en de unburdenin."

The road rose again, to a scene like a painted backdrop. Notched into a cut of red clay crowned with oaks the road appeared to stop short off, like a cut ribbon. Beside it a weathered church lifted its crazy steeple like a painted church, and the whole scene was as flat and without perspective as a painted cardboard set upon the ultimate edge of the flat earth, against the windy sunlight of space and April and a midmorning filled with bells. Toward the church they thronged with slow sabbath deliberation, the women and children went on in, the men stopped outside and talked in quiet groups until the bell ceased ringing. Then they too entered.

The church had been decorated, with sparse flowers from kitchen gardens and hedgerows, and with streamers of colored crepe paper. Above the pulpit hung a battered Christmas bell, the accordion sort that collapses. The pulpit was empty, though the choir was already in place, fanning themselves although it was not warm.

Most of the women were gathered on one side of the room. They were talking. Then the bell struck one time and they dispersed to their seats and the congregation sat for an instant, expectant. The bell struck again one time. The choir rose and began to sing and the congregation turned its head as one as six small children — four girls with tight pigtails bound with small scraps of cloth like butterflies, and two boys with close napped heads — entered and marched up the aisle, strung together in a harness of white ribbons and flowers, and followed by two men in single file. The second man was huge, of a light coffee color, imposing in a frock coat and white tie. His head was magisterial and profound, his neck rolled above his collar in rich folds. But he was familiar to them, and so the heads were still reverted when he had passed, and it was not until the choir ceased singing that they realised that the visiting clergyman had already entered, and when they saw the man who had preceded their minister enter the pulpit still ahead of him an indescribable sound went up, a sigh, a sound of astonishment and disappointment.

The visitor was undersized, in a shabby alpaca coat. He had a wizened black face like a small, aged monkey. And all the while that the choir sang again and while the six children rose and sang in thin, frightened, tuneless whispers, they watched the insignificant looking man sitting dwarfed and countrified by the minister's imposing bulk, with something like consternation. They were still looking at him with consternation and unbelief when the minister rose and introduced him in rich, rolling tones whose very unction served to increase the visitor's insignificance.

"En dey brung dat all de way fum Saint Looey," Frony whispered.

"I've knowed de Lawd to use cuiser tools dan dat," Dilsey said. "Hush, now," she said to Ben. "Dey fixin to sing again in a minute."

When the visitor rose to speak he sounded like a white man. His voice was level and cold. It sounded too big to have come from him and they listened at first through curiosity, as they would have to a monkey talking. They began to watch him as they would a man on a tight rope. They even forgot his insignificant appearance in the virtuosity with which he ran and poised and swooped upon the cold inflectionless wire of his voice, so that at last, when with a sort of swooping glide he came to rest again beside the reading desk with one arm resting upon it at shoulder height and his monkey body as reft of all motion as a mummy or an emptied vessel, the congregation sighed as if it waked from a collective dream and moved a little in its seats. Behind the pulpit the choir fanned steadily. Dilsey whispered, "Hush, now. Dey fixin to sing in a minute."

Then a voice said, "Brethren."

The preacher had not moved. His arm lay yet across the desk, and he still held that pose while the voice died in sonorous echoes between the walls. It was as different as day and dark from his former tone, with a sad, timbrous quality like an alto horn, sinking into their hearts and speaking there again when it had ceased in fading and cumulate echoes.

"Brethren and sisteren," it said again. The preacher removed his arm and he began to walk back and forth before the desk, his hands clasped behind him, a meagre figure, hunched over upon itself like that of one long immured in striving with the implacable earth, "I got the recollection and the blood of the Lamb!" He tramped steadily back and forth beneath the twisted paper and the Christmas bell, hunched, his hands clasped behind him. He was like a worn small rock whelmed by the successive waves of his voice. With his body he seemed to feed the voice that, succubus like, had fleshed its teeth in him. And the congregation seemed to watch with its own eyes while the voice consumed him, until he was nothing and they were nothing and there was not even a voice but instead their hearts were speaking to one another in chanting measures beyond the need for words, so that when he came to rest against the reading desk, his monkey face lifted and his whole attitude that of a serene, tortured crucifix that transcended its shabbiness and insignificance and made it of no moment, a long moaning expulsion of breath rose from them, and a woman's single soprano: "Yes, Jesus!"

As the scudding day passed overhead the dingy windows glowed and faded in ghostly retrograde. A car passed along the road outside, laboring in the sand, died away. Dilsey sat bolt upright, her hand on Ben's knee. Two tears slid down her fallen cheeks, in and out of the myriad coruscations of immolation and abnegation and time.

"Brethren," the minister said in a harsh whisper, without moving.

"Yes, Jesus!" the woman's voice said, hushed yet.

"Breddren en sistuhn!" His voice rang again, with the horns. He removed his arm and stood erect and raised his hands. "I got de ricklick-shun en de blood of de Lamb!" [2] They did not mark just when his into-nation, his pronunciation, became negroid, they just sat swaying a little in their seats as the voice took them into itself.

"When de long, cold——Oh, I tells you, breddren, when de long, cold. . . . I sees de light en I sees de word, [3] po sinner! Dey passed away in Egypt, de swingin chariots; de generations passed away. [4] Wus a rich man: whar he now, O breddren? Wus a po man: whar he now, O sis-tuhn? [5] Oh I tells you, ef you aint got de milk en de dew of de old salvation when de long, cold years rolls away!"

"Yes, Jesus!"

"I tells you, breddren, en I tells you, sistuhn, dey'll come a time. Po sinner sayin Let me lay down wid de Lawd, lemme lay down my load. Den whut Jesus gwine say, O breddren? O sistuhn? Is you got de rick-lickshun en de Blood of de Lamb? Case I aint gwine load down heaven!"

He fumbled in his coat and took out a handkerchief and mopped his face. A low concerted sound rose from the congregation: "Mmmmm-mmmmmmmm!" The woman's voice said, "Yes, Jesus! Jesus!"

"Breddren! Look at dem little chillen settin dar. Jesus wus like dat once. He mammy suffered de glory en de pangs. Sometime maybe she helt him at de nightfall, whilst de angels singin him to sleep; maybe she look out de do en see de Roman po-lice passin." He tramped back and forth, mopping his face. "Listen, breddren! I sees de day. Ma'y settin in de do wid Jesus on her lap, de little Jesus. Like dem chillen dar, de little Jesus. I hears de angels singin de peaceful songs en de glory; I sees de closin eyes; sees Mary jump up, sees de sojer face: We gwine to kill! We gwine to kill! We gwine to kill yo little Jesus! I hears de weepin en de lamentation of de po mammy widout de salvation en de word of God!" [6]

"Mmmmmmmmmmmmmmmmmmm! Jesus! Little Jesus!" and another voice, rising:

"I sees, O Jesus! Oh I sees!" and still another, without words, like bubbles rising in water.

"I sees hit, breddren! I sees hit! Sees de blastin, blindin sight! I sees Calvary, wid de sacred trees, sees de thief en de murderer en de least of dese; I hears de boastin en de braggin: Ef you be Jesus, lif up yo tree en walk! [7] I hears de wailin of women en de evenin lamentations; I hears de weepin en de cryin en de turnt-away face of God: dey done kilt Jesus; dey done kilt my Son!"

"Mmmmmmmmmmmmmmm. Jesus! I sees, O Jesus!"

"O blind sinner! Breddren, I tells you; sistuhn, I says to you, when de

2. See Revelation 7.14.
3. See John 1.1–4.
4. See Genesis 50.22–26.
5. See Luke 16.19–24.
6. See Matthew 2.16.
7. See Matthew 27.39–44 and Mark 2.9.

Lawd did turn His mighty face, say, Aint gwine overload heaven! I can
see de widowed God shet His do; I sees de whelmin flood roll between;
I sees de darkness en de death everlastin upon de generations. Den, lo!
Breddren! Yes, breddren! Whut I see? Whut I see, O sinner? I sees de
resurrection en de light; sees de meek Jesus sayin Dey kilt me dat ye shall
live again; I died dat dem whut sees en believes shall never die.[8] Breddren, O breddren! I sees de doom crack en de golden horns shoutin
down de glory,[9] en de arisen dead whut got de blood en de ricklickshun
of de Lamb!"

In the midst of the voices and the hands Ben sat, rapt in his sweet
blue gaze. Dilsey sat bolt upright beside, crying rigidly and quietly in
the annealment and the blood of the remembered Lamb.

As they walked through the bright noon, up the sandy road with the
dispersing congregation talking easily again group to group, she continued to weep, unmindful of the talk.

"He sho a preacher, mon! He didn't look like much at first, but hush!"

"He seed de power en de glory."

"Yes, suh. He seed hit. Face to face he seed hit."

Dilsey made no sound, her face did not quiver as the tears took their
sunken and devious courses, walking with her head up, making no effort
to dry them away even.

"Whyn't you quit dat, mammy?" Frony said. "Wid all dese people
lookin. We be passin white folks soon."

"I've seed de first en de last," Dilsey said. "Never you mind me."[1]

"First en last whut?" Frony said.

"Never you mind," Dilsey said. "I seed de beginnin, en now I sees de
endin."

Before they reached the street though she stopped and lifted her skirt
and dried her eyes on the hem of her topmost underskirt. Then they
went on. Ben shambled along beside Dilsey, watching Luster who anticked
along ahead, the umbrella in his hand and his new straw hat slanted
viciously in the sunlight, like a big foolish dog watching a small clever
one. They reached the gate and entered. Immediately Ben began to
whimper again, and for a while all of them looked up the drive at the
square, paintless house with its rotting portico.

"Whut's gwine on up dar today?" Frony said. "Somethin is."

"Nothin," Dilsey said. "You tend to yo business en let de whitefolks
tend to deir'n."

"Somethin is," Frony said. "I heard him first thing dis mawnin. 'Taint
none of my business, dough."

"En I knows whut, too," Luster said.

"You knows mo dan you got any use fer," Dilsey said. "Aint you jes

8. See John 11.25–26; Romans 5.8; I Corinthians 15.22.
9. See Revelation 8.
1. See Revelation 22.13.

heard Frony say hit aint none of yo business? You take Benjy on to de back and keep him quiet twell I put dinner on."

"I knows whar Miss Quentin is," Luster said.

"Den jes keep hit," Dilsey said. "Soon es Quentin need any of yo egvice, I'll let you know. Y'all g'awn en play in de back, now."

"You know whut gwine happen soon es dey start playin dat ball over yonder," Luster said.

"Dey wont start fer a while yit. By dat time T. P. be here to take him ridin. Here, you gimme dat new hat."

Luster gave her the hat and he and Ben went on across the back yard. Ben was still whimpering, though not loud. Dilsey and Frony went to the cabin. After a while Dilsey emerged, again in the faded calico dress, and went to the kitchen. The fire had died down. There was no sound in the house. She put on the apron and went up stairs. There was no sound anywhere. Quentin's room was as they had left it. She entered and picked up the undergarment and put the stocking back in the drawer and closed it. Mrs Compson's door was closed. Dilsey stood beside it for a moment, listening. Then she opened it and entered, entered a pervading reek of camphor. The shades were drawn, the room in halflight, and the bed, so that at first she thought Mrs Compson was asleep and was about to close the door when the other spoke.

"Well?" she said. "What is it?"

"Hit's me," Dilsey said. "You want anything?"

Mrs Compson didn't answer. After a while, without moving her head at all, she said: "Where's Jason?"

"He aint come back yit," Dilsey said. "Whut you want?"

Mrs Compson said nothing. Like so many cold, weak people, when faced at last by the incontrovertible disaster she exhumed from somewhere a sort of fortitude, strength. In her case it was an unshakable conviction regarding the yet unplumbed event. "Well," she said presently. "Did you find it?"

"Find whut? Whut you talkin about?"

"The note. At least she would have enough consideration to leave a note. Even Quentin did that."

"Whut you talkin about?" Dilsey said. "Dont you know she all right? I bet she be walkin right in dis do befo dark."

"Fiddlesticks," Mrs Compson said. "It's in the blood. Like uncle, like niece. Or mother. I dont know which would be worse. I dont seem to care."

"Whut you keep on talkin that way fur?" Dilsey said. "Whut she want to do anything like that fur?"

"I dont know. What reason did Quentin have? Under God's heaven what reason did he have? It cant be simply to flout and hurt me. Whoever God is, He would not permit that. I'm a lady. You might not believe that from my offspring, but I am."

"You des wait en see," Dilsey said. "She be here by night, right dar in her bed." Mrs Compson said nothing. The camphor soaked cloth lay upon her brow. The black robe lay across the foot of the bed. Dilsey stood with her hand on the door knob.

"Well," Mrs Compson said. "What do you want? Are you going to fix some dinner for Jason and Benjamin, or not?"

"Jason aint come yit," Dilsey said. "I gwine fix somethin. You sho you dont want nothin? Yo bottle still hot enough?"

"You might hand me my bible."

"I give hit to you dis mawnin, befo I left."

"You laid it on the edge of the bed. How long did you expect it to stay there?"

Dilsey crossed to the bed and groped among the shadows beneath the edge of it and found the bible, face down. She smoothed the bent pages and laid the book on the bed again. Mrs Compson didn't open her eyes. Her hair and the pillow were the same color, beneath the wimple of the medicated cloth she looked like an old nun praying. "Dont put it there again," she said, without opening her eyes. "That's where you put it before. Do you want me to have to get out of bed to pick it up?"

Dilsey reached the book across her and laid it on the broad side of the bed. "You cant see to read, noways," she said. "You want me to raise de shade a little?"

"No. Let them alone. Go on and fix Jason something to eat."

Dilsey went out. She closed the door and returned to the kitchen. The stove was almost cold. While she stood there the clock above the cupboard struck ten times. "One oclock," she said aloud. "Jason aint comin home. Ise seed de first en de last," she said, looking at the cold stove. "I seed de first en de last." She set out some cold food on a table. As she moved back and forth she sang, a hymn. She sang the first two lines over and over to the complete tune. She arranged the meal and went to the door and called Luster, and after a time Luster and Ben entered. Ben was still moaning a little, as to himself.

"He aint never quit," Luster said.

"Y'all come on en eat," Dilsey said. "Jason aint comin to dinner." They sat down at the table. Ben could manage solid food pretty well for himself, though even now, with cold food before him, Dilsey tied a cloth about his neck. He and Luster ate. Dilsey moved about the kitchen, singing the two lines of the hymn which she remembered. "Y'all kin g'awn en eat," she said. "Jason aint comin home."

He was twenty miles away at that time. When he left the house he drove rapidly to town, overreaching the slow sabbath groups and the peremptory bells along the broken air. He crossed the empty square and turned into a narrow street that was abruptly quieter even yet, and stopped before a frame house and went up the flower bordered walk to the porch.

Beyond the screen door people were talking. As he lifted his hand to knock he heard steps, so he withheld his hand until a big man in black broadcloth trousers and a stiff bosomed white shirt without collar opened the door. He had vigorous untidy iron-gray hair and his gray eyes were round and shiny like a little boy's. He took Jason's hand and drew him into the house, still shaking it.

"Come right in," he said. "Come right in."

"You ready to go now?" Jason said.

"Walk right in," the other said, propelling him by the elbow into a room where a man and a woman sat. "You know Myrtle's husband, dont you? Jason Compson, Vernon."

"Yes," Jason said. He did not even look at the man, and as the sheriff drew a chair across the room the man said,

"We'll go out so you can talk. Come on, Myrtle."

"No, no," the sheriff said. "You folks keep your seat. I reckon it aint that serious, Jason? Have a seat."

"I'll tell you as we go along," Jason said. "Get your hat and coat."

"We'll go out," the man said, rising.

"Keep your seat," the sheriff said. "Me and Jason will go out on the porch."

"You get your hat and coat," Jason said. "They've already got a twelve hour start." The sheriff led the way back to the porch. A man and a woman passing spoke to him. He responded with a hearty florid gesture. Bells were still ringing, from the direction of the section known as Nigger Hollow. "Get your hat, Sheriff," Jason said. The sheriff drew up two chairs.

"Have a seat and tell me what the trouble is."

"I told you over the phone," Jason said, standing. "I did that to save time. Am I going to have to go to law to compel you to do your sworn duty?"

"You sit down and tell me about it," the sheriff said. "I'll take care of you all right."

"Care, hell," Jason said. "Is this what you call taking care of me?"

"You're the one that's holding us up," the sheriff said. "You sit down and tell me about it."

Jason told him, his sense of injury and impotence feeding upon its own sound, so that after a time he forgot his haste in the violent cumulation of his self justification and his outrage. The sheriff watched him steadily with his cold shiny eyes.

"But you dont know they done it," he said. "You just think so."

"Dont know?" Jason said. "When I spent two damn days chasing her through alleys, trying to keep her away from him, after I told her what I'd do to her if I ever caught her with him, and you say I dont know that that little b——"

"Now, then," the sheriff said. "That'll do. That's enough of that." He looked out across the street, his hands in his pockets.

"And when I come to you, a commissioned officer of the law," Jason said.

"That show's in Mottson this week," the sheriff said.

"Yes," Jason said. "And if I could find a law officer that gave a solitary damn about protecting the people that elected him to office, I'd be there too by now." He repeated his story, harshly recapitulant, seeming to get an actual pleasure out of his outrage and impotence. The sheriff did not appear to be listening at all.

"Jason," he said. "What were you doing with three thousand dollars hid in the house?"

"What?" Jason said. "That's my business where I keep my money. Your business is to help me get it back."

"Did your mother know you had that much on the place?"

"Look here," Jason said. "My house has been robbed. I know who did it and I know where they are. I come to you as the commissioned officer of the law, and I ask you once more, are you going to make any effort to recover my property, or not?"

"What do you aim to do with that girl, if you catch them?"

"Nothing," Jason said. "Not anything. I wouldn't lay my hand on her. The bitch that cost me a job, the one chance I ever had to get ahead, that killed my father and is shortening my mother's life every day and made my name a laughing stock in the town. I wont do anything to her," he said. "Not anything."

"You drove that girl into running off, Jason," the sheriff said.

"How I conduct my family is no business of yours," Jason said. "Are you going to help me or not?"

"You drove her away from home," the sheriff said. "And I have some suspicions about who that money belongs to that I dont reckon I'll ever know for certain."

Jason stood, slowly wringing the brim of his hat in his hands. He said quietly: "You're not going to make any effort to catch them for me?"

"That's not any of my business, Jason. If you had any actual proof, I'd have to act. But without that I dont figger it's any of my business."

"That's your answer, is it?" Jason said. "Think well, now."

"That's it, Jason."

"All right," Jason said. He put his hat on. "You'll regret this. I wont be helpless. This is not Russia, where just because he wears a little metal badge, a man is immune to law." He went down the steps and got in his car and started the engine. The sheriff watched him drive away, turn, and rush past the house toward town.

The bells were ringing again, high in the scudding sunlight in bright disorderly tatters of sound. He stopped at a filling station and had his tires examined and the tank filled.

"Gwine on a trip, is you?" the negro asked him. He didn't answer. "Look like hit gwine fair off, after all," the negro said.

"Fair off, hell." Jason said. "It'll be raining like hell by twelve oclock."
He looked at the sky, thinking about rain, about the slick clay roads,
himself stalled somewhere miles from town. He thought about it with a
sort of triumph, of the fact that he was going to miss dinner, that by
starting now and so serving his compulsion of haste, he would be at the
greatest possible distance from both towns when noon came. It seemed
to him that in this circumstance was giving him a break, so he said to
the negro:

"What the hell are you doing? Has somebody paid you to keep this
car standing here as long as you can?"

"Dis here ti' aint got no air a-tall in hit," the negro said.

"Then get the hell away from there and let me have that tube," Jason
said.

"Hit up now," the negro said, rising. "You kin ride now."

Jason got in and started the engine and drove off. He went into second
gear, the engine spluttering and gasping, and he raced the engine, jamming the throttle down and snapping the choker in and out savagely.
"It's going to rain," he said. "Get me half way there, and rain like hell."
And he drove on out of the bells and out of town, thinking of himself
slogging through the mud, hunting a team. "And every damn one of
them will be at church." He thought of how he'd find a church at last
and take a team and of the owner coming out, shoutin' at him and of
himself striking the man down. "I'm Jason Compson. See if you can
stop me. See if you can elect a man to office that can stop me," he said,
thinking of himself entering the courthouse with a file of soldiers and
dragging the sheriff out. "Thinks he can sit with his hands folded and
see me lose my job. I'll show him about jobs." Of his niece he did not
think at all, nor of the arbitrary valuation of the money. Neither of them
had had entity or individuality for him for ten years: together they merely
symbolised the job in the bank of which he had been deprived before he
ever got it.

The air brightened, the running shadow patches were now the obverse,
and it seemed to him that the fact that the day was clearing was another
cunning stroke on the part of the foe, the fresh battle toward which he
was carrying ancient wounds. From time to time he passed churches,
unpainted frame buildings with sheet iron steeples, surrounded by teth-
ered teams and shabby motorcars, and it seemed to him that each of
them was a picketpost where the rear guards of Circumstance peeped
fleetingly back at him. "And damn You, too," he said. "See if You can
stop me," thinking of himself, his file of soldiers with the manacled
sheriff in the rear, dragging Omnipotence down from his throne, if necessary; of the embattled legions of both hell and heaven through which
he tore his way and put his hands at last on his fleeing niece.

The wind was out of the southeast. It blew steadily upon his cheek. It
seemed that he could feel the prolonged blow of it sinking through his

skull, and suddenly with an old premonition he clapped the brakes on and stopped and sat perfectly still. Then he lifted his hand to his neck and began to curse, and sat there, cursing in a harsh whisper. When it was necessary for him to drive for any length of time he fortified himself with a handkerchief soaked in camphor, which he would tie about his throat when clear of town, thus inhaling the fumes, and he got out and lifted the seat cushion on the chance that there might be a forgotten one there. He looked beneath both seats and stood again for a while, cursing, seeing himself mocked by his own triumphing. He closed his eyes, leaning on the door. He could return and get the forgotten camphor, or he could go on. In either case, his head would be splitting, but at home he could be sure of finding camphor on Sunday, while if he went on he could not be sure. But if he went back, he would be an hour and a half later in reaching Mottson. "Maybe I can drive slow," he said. "Maybe I can drive slow, thinking of something else. . . ."

He got in and started. "I'll think of something else," he said, so he thought about Lorraine. He imagined himself in bed with her, only he was just lying beside her, pleading with her to help him, then he thought of the money again, and that he had been outwitted by a woman, a girl. If he could just believe it was the man who had robbed him. But to have been robbed of that which was to have compensated him for the lost job, which he had acquired through so much effort and risk, by the very symbol of the lost job itself, and worst of all, by a bitch of a girl. He drove on, shielding his face from the steady wind with the corner of his coat.

He could see the opposed forces of his destiny and his will drawing swiftly together now, toward a junction that would be irrevocable; he became cunning. I cant make a blunder, he told himself. There would be just one right thing, without alternatives: he must do that. He believed that both of them would know him on sight, while he'd have to trust to seeing her first, unless the man still wore the red tie. And the fact that he must depend on that red tie seemed to be the sum of the impending disaster; he could almost smell it, feel it above the throbbing of his head.

He crested the final hill. Smoke lay in the valley, and roofs, a spire or two above trees. He drove down the hill and into the town, slowing, telling himself again of the need for caution, to find where the tent was located first. He could not see very well now, and he knew that it was the disaster which kept telling him to go directly and get something for his head. At a filling station they told him that the tent was not up yet, but that the show cars were on a siding at the station. He drove there.

Two gaudily painted pullman cars stood on the track. He reconnoitred them before he got out. He was trying to breathe shallowly, so that the blood would not beat so in his skull. He got out and went along the station wall, watching the cars. A few garments hung out of the windows, limp and crinkled, as though they had been recently laundered. On the earth beside the steps of one sat three canvas chairs. But he saw no sign of life at all until a man in a dirty apron came to the door and emptied a pan of dishwater with a broad gesture, the sunlight glinting on the metal belly of the pan, then entered the car again.

Now I'll have to take him by surprise, before he can warn them, he thought. It never occurred to him that they might not be there, in the car. That they should not be there, that the whole result should not hinge on whether he saw them first or they saw him first, would be opposed to all nature and contrary to the whole rhythm of events. And more than that: he must see them first, get the money back, then what they did would be of no importance to him, while otherwise the whole world would know that he, Jason Compson, had been robbed by Quentin, his niece, a bitch.

He reconnoitred again. Then he went to the car and mounted the steps, swiftly and quietly, and paused at the door. The galley was dark, rank with stale food. The man was a white blur, singing in a cracked, shaky tenor. An old man, he thought, and not as big as I am. He entered the car as the man looked up.

"Hey?" the man said, stopping his song.

"Where are they?" Jason said. "Quick, now. In the sleeping car?"

"Where's who?" the man said.

"Dont lie to me," Jason said. He blundered on in the cluttered obscurity.

"What's that?" the other said. "Who you calling a liar?" and when Jason grasped his shoulder he exclaimed, "Look out, fellow!"

"Dont lie," Jason said. "Where are they?"

"Why, you bastard," the man said. His arm was frail and thin in Jason's grasp. He tried to wrench free, then he turned and fell to scrabbling on the littered table behind him.

"Come on," Jason said. "Where are they?"

"I'll tell you where they are," the man shrieked. "Lemme find my butcher knife."

"Here," Jason said, trying to hold the other. "I'm just asking you a question."

"You bastard," the other shrieked, scrabbling at the table. Jason tried to grasp him in both arms, trying to prison the puny fury of him. The man's body felt so old, so frail, yet so fatally singlepurposed that for the first time Jason saw clear and unshadowed the disaster toward which he rushed.

"Quit it!" he said. "Here. Here! I'll get out. Give me time, and I'll get out."

"Call me a liar," the other wailed. "Lemme go. Lemme go just one minute. I'll show you."

Jason glared wildly about, holding the other. Outside it was now bright and sunny, swift and bright and empty, and he thought of the people

soon to be going quietly home to Sunday dinner, decorously festive, and
of himself trying to hold the fatal, furious little old man whom he dared
not release long enough to turn his back and run.

"Will you quit long enough for me to get out?" he said. "Will you?"
But the other still struggled, and Jason freed one hand and struck him
on the head. A clumsy, hurried blow, and not hard, but the other slumped
immediately and slid clattering among pans and buckets to the floor.
Jason stood above him, panting, listening. Then he turned and ran from
the car. At the door he restrained himself and descended more slowly
and stood there again. His breath made a hah hah hah sound and he
stood there trying to repress it, darting his gaze this way and that, when
at a scuffling sound behind him he turned in time to see the little old
man leaping awkwardly and furiously from the vestibule, a rusty hatchet
high in his hand.

He grasped at the hatchet, feeling no shock but knowing that he was
falling, thinking So this is how it'll end, and he believed that he was
about to die and when something crashed against the back of his head
he thought How did he hit me there? Only maybe he hit me a long time
ago, he thought, And I just now felt it, and he thought Hurry. Hurry.
Get it over with, and then a furious desire not to die seized him and he
struggled, hearing the old man wailing and cursing in his cracked voice.

He still struggled when they hauled him to his feet, but they held him
and he ceased.

"Am I bleeding much?" he said. "The back of my head. Am I bleeding?" He was still saying that while he felt himself being propelled rapidly away, heard the old man's thin furious voice dying away behind
him. "Look at my head," he said. "Wait, I'——"

"Wait, hell," the man who held him said. "That damn little wasp'll
kill you. Keep going. You aint hurt."

"He hit me," Jason said. "Am I bleeding?"

"Keep going," the other said. He led Jason on around the corner of
the station, to the empty platform where an express truck stood, where
grass grew rigidly in a plot bordered with rigid flowers and a sign in
electric lights: Keep your 👁 on Mottson, the gap filled by a human
eye with an electric pupil. The man released him.

"Now," he said. "You get on out of here and stay out. What were you
trying to do? commit suicide?"

"I was looking for two people," Jason said. "I just asked him where
they were."

"Who you looking for?"

"It's a girl," Jason said. "And a man. He had on a red tie in Jefferson
yesterday. With this show. They robbed me."

"Oh," the man said. "You're the one, are you. Well, they aint here."

"I reckon so," Jason said. He leaned against the wall and put his hand
to the back of his head and looked at his palm. "I thought I was bleed-

ing," he said. "I thought he hit me with that hatchet."

"You hit your head on the rail," the man said. "You better go on. They aint here."

"Yes. He said they were not here. I thought he was lying."

"Do you think I'm lying?" the man said.

"No," Jason said. "I know they're not here."

"I told him to get the hell out of there, both of them," the man said. "I wont have nothing like that in my show. I run a respectable show, with a respectable troupe."

"Yes," Jason said. "You dont know where they went?"

"No. And I dont want to know. No member of my show can pull a stunt like that. You her . . . brother?"

"No," Jason said. "It dont matter. I just wanted to see them. You sure he didn't hit me? No blood, I mean."

"There would have been blood if I hadn't got there when I did. You stay away from here, now. That little bastard'll kill you. That your car yonder?"

"Yes."

"Well, you get in it and go back to Jefferson. If you find them, it wont be in my show. I run a respectable show. You say they robbed you?"

"No," Jason said. "It dont make any difference." He went to the car and got in. What is it I must do? he thought. Then he remembered. He started the engine and drove slowly up the street until he found a drugstore. The door was locked. He stood for a while with his hand on the knob and his head bent a little. Then he turned away and when a man came along after a while he asked if there was a drugstore open anywhere, but there was not. Then he asked when the northbound train ran, and the man told him at two thirty. He crossed the pavement and got in the car again and sat there. After a while two negro lads passed. He called to them.

"Can either of you boys drive a car?"

"Yes, suh."

"What'll you charge to drive me to Jefferson right away?"

They looked at one another, murmuring.

"I'll pay a dollar," Jason said.

They murmured again. "Couldn't go fer dat," one said.

"What will you go for?"

"Kin you go?" one said.

"I cant git off," the other said. "Whyn't you drive him up dar? You aint got nothin to do."

"Yes I is."

"Whut you got to do?"

They murmured again, laughing.

"I'll give you two dollars," Jason said. "Either of you."

"I cant git away neither," the first said.

"All right," Jason said. "Go on."

He sat there for some time. He heard a clock strike the half hour, then people began to pass, in Sunday and easter clothes. Some looked at him as they passed, at the man sitting quietly behind the wheel of a small car, with his invisible life ravelled out about him like a wornout sock, and went on. After a while a negro in overalls came up.

"Is you de one wants to go to Jefferson?" he said.

"Yes," Jason said. "What'll you charge me?"

"Fo dollars."

"Give you two."

"Cant go fer no less'n fo." The man in the car sat quietly. He wasn't even looking at him. The negro said, "You want me er not?"

"All right," Jason said. "Get in."

He moved over and the negro took the wheel. Jason closed his eyes. I can get something for it at Jefferson, he told himself, easing himself to the jolting, I can get something there. They drove on, along the streets where people were turning peacefully into houses and Sunday dinners, and on out of town. He thought that. He wasn't thinking of home, where Ben and Luster were eating cold dinner at the kitchen table. Something — the absence of disaster, threat, in any constant evil — permitted him to forget Jefferson as any place which he had ever seen before, where his life must resume itself.

When Ben and Luster were done Dilsey sent them outdoors. "And see kin you let him alone twell fo oclock. T. P. be here den."

"Yessum," Luster said, They went out. Dilsey ate her dinner and cleared up the kitchen. Then she went to the foot of the stairs and listened, but there was no sound. She returned through the kitchen and out the outer door and stopped on the steps. Ben and Luster were not in sight, but while she stood there she heard another sluggish twang from the direction of the cellar door and she went to the door and looked down upon a repetition of the morning's scene.

"He done hit jes dat way," Luster said. He contemplated the motionless saw with a kind of hopeful dejection. "I aint got de right thing to hit it wid yit," he said.

"En you aint gwine find hit down here, neither," Dilsey said. "You take him on out in de sun. You bofe get pneumonia down here on dis wet flo."

She waited and watched them cross the yard toward a clump of cedar trees near the fence. Then she went on to her cabin.

"Now, dont you git started," Luster said. "I had enough trouble wid you today." There was a hammock made of barrel staves slatted into woven wires. Luster lay down in the swing, but Ben went on vaguely and purposelessly. He began to whimper again. "Hush, now," Luster said. "I fixin to whup you." He lay back in the swing. Ben had stopped moving, but Luster could hear him whimpering. "Is you gwine hush,

er aint you?" Luster said. He got up and followed and came upon Ben
squatting before a small mound of earth. At either end of it an empty
bottle of blue glass that once contained poison was fixed in the ground.
In one was a withered stalk of jimson weed. Ben squatted before it,
moaning, a slow, inarticulate sound. Still moaning he sought vaguely
about and found a twig and put it in the other bottle. "Whyn't you
hush?" Luster said. "You want me to give you somethin to sho nough
moan about? Sposin I does dis." He knelt and swept the bottle suddenly
up and behind him. Ben ceased moaning. He squatted, looking at the
small depression where the bottle had sat, then as he drew his lungs full
Luster brought the bottle back into view. "Hush!" he hissed. "Dont you
dast to beller! Dont you. Dar hit is. See? Here. You fixin to start ef you
stays here. Come on, les go see ef dey started knockin ball yit." He took
Ben's arm and drew him up and they went to the fence and stood side
by side there, peering between the matted honeysuckle not yet in bloom.
    "Dar," Luster said. "Dar come some. See um?"
    They watched the foursome play onto the green and out, and move
to the tee and drive. Ben watched, whimpering, slobbering. When the
foursome went on he followed along the fence, bobbing and moaning.
One said,
    "Here, caddie. Bring the bag."
    "Hush, Benjy," Luster said, but Ben went on at his shambling trot,
clinging to the fence, wailing in his hoarse, hopeless voice. The man
played and went on, Ben keeping pace with him until the fence turned
at right angles, and he clung to the fence, watching the people move on
and away.
    "Will you hush now?" Luster said. "Will you hush now?" He shook
Ben's arm. Ben clung to the fence, wailing steadily and hoarsely. "Aint
you gwine stop?" Luster said. "Or is you?" Ben gazed through the fence.
"All right, den," Luster said. "You want somethin to beller about?" He
looked over his shoulder, toward the house. Then he whispered: "Caddy!
Beller now. Caddy! Caddy! Caddy!"
    A moment later, in the slow intervals of Ben's voice, Luster heard
Dilsey calling. He took Ben by the arm and they crossed the yard toward
her.
    "I tole you he warn't gwine stay quiet," Luster said.
    "You vilyun!" Dilsey said. "Whut you done to him?"
    "I aint done nothin. I tole you when dem folks start playin, he git
started up."
    "You come on here," Dilsey said. "Hush, Benjy. Hush, now." But
he wouldn't hush. They crossed the yard quickly and went to the cabin
and entered. "Run git dat shoe," Dilsey said. "Dont you sturb Miss
Cahline, now. Ef she say anything, tell her I got him. Go on, now; you
kin sho do dat right, I reckon." Luster went out. Dilsey led Ben to the

bed and drew him down beside her and she held him, rocking back and forth, wiping his drooling mouth upon the hem of her skirt. "Hush, now," she said, stroking his head. "Hush. Dilsey got you." But he bellowed slowly, abjectly, without tears; the grave hopeless sound of all voiceless misery under the sun. Luster returned, carrying a white satin slipper. It was yellow now, and cracked, and soiled, and when they gave it into Ben's hand he hushed for a while. But he still whimpered, and soon he lifted his voice again.

"You reckon you kin find T. P.?" Dilsey said.

"He say yistiddy he gwine out to St John's today. Say he be back at fo."

Dilsey rocked back and forth, stroking Ben's head.

"Dis long time, O Jesus," she said. "Dis long time."

"I kin drive dat surrey, mammy," Luster said.

"You kill bofe y'all," Dilsey said. "You do hit fer devilment. I knows you got plenty sense to. But I cant trust you. Hush, now," she said. "Hush. Hush."

"Nome I wont," Luster said. "I drives wid T. P." Dilsey rocked back and forth, holding Ben. "Miss Cahline say ef you cant quiet him, she gwine git up en come down en do hit."

"Hush, honey," Dilsey said, stroking Ben's head. "Luster, honey," she said. "Will you think about yo ole mammy en drive dat surrey right?"

"Yessum," Luster said. "I drive hit jes like T. P."

Dilsey stroked Ben's head, rocking back and forth. "I does de bes I kin," she said. "Lawd knows dat. Go git it, den," she said, rising. Luster scuttled out. Ben held the slipper, crying. "Hush, now. Luster gone to git de surrey en take you to de graveyard. We aint gwine risk gittin yo cap," she said. She went to a closet contrived of a calico curtain hung across a corner of the room and got the felt hat she had worn. "We's down to worse'n dis, ef folks jes knowed," she said. "You's de Lawd's chile, anyway. En I be His'n too, fo long, praise Jesus. Here." She put the hat on his head and buttoned his coat. He wailed steadily. She took the slipper from him and put it away and they went out. Luster came up, with an ancient white horse in a battered and lopsided surrey.

"You gwine be careful, Luster?" she said.

"Yessum," Luster said. She helped Ben into the back seat. He had ceased crying, but now he began to whimper again.

"Hit's his flower," Luster said. "Wait, I'll git him one."

"You set right dar," Dilsey said. She went and took the cheekstrap. "Now, hurry en git him one." Luster ran around the house, toward the garden. He came back with a single narcissus.

"Dat un broke," Dilsey said. "Whyn't you git him a good un?"

"Hit de onliest one I could find," Luster said, "Y'all took all of um Friday to dec'rate de church. Wait, I'll fix hit." So while Dilsey held the horse Luster put a splint on the flower stalk with a twig and two bits of string and gave it to Ben. Then he mounted and took the reins. Dilsey still held the bridle.

"You knows de way now?" she said. "Up de street, round de square, to de graveyard, den straight back home."

"Yessum," Luster said. "Hum up, Queenie."

"You gwine be careful, now?"

"Yessum." Dilsey released the bridle.

"Hum up, Queenie," Luster said.

"Here," Dilsey said. "You han me dat whup."

"Aw, mammy," Luster said.

"Give hit here," Dilsey said, approaching the wheel. Luster gave it to her reluctantly.

"I wont never git Queenie started now."

"Never you mind about dat," Dilsey said. "Queenie know mo bout whar she gwine dan you does. All you got to do es set dar en hold dem reins. You knows de way, now?"

"Yessum. Same way T. P. goes ev'y Sunday."

"Den you do de same thing dis Sunday."

"Cose I is. Aint I drove fer T. P. mo'n a hund'ed times?"

"Den do hit again," Dilsey said. "G'awn, now. En ef you hurts Benjy, nigger boy, I dont know whut I do. You bound fer de chain gang, but I'll send you dar fo even chain gang ready fer you."

"Yessum," Luster said. "Hum up, Queenie."

He flapped the lines on Queenie's broad back and the surrey lurched into motion.

"You, Luster!" Dilsey said.

"Hum up, dar!" Luster said. He flapped the lines again. With subterranean rumblings Queenie jogged slowly down the drive and turned into the street, where Luster exhorted her into a gait resembling a prolonged and suspended fall in a forward direction.

Ben quit whimpering. He sat in the middle of the seat, holding the repaired flower upright in his fist, his eyes serene and ineffable. Directly before him Luster's bullet head turned backward continually until the house passed from view, then he pulled to the side of the street and while Ben watched him he descended and broke a switch from a hedge. Queenie lowered her head and fell to cropping the grass until Luster mounted and hauled her head up and harried her into motion again, then he squared his elbows and with the switch and the reins held high he assumed a swaggering attitude out of all proportion to the sedate clopping of Queenie's hooves and the organlike basso of her internal accompaniment. Motors passed them, and pedestrians; once a group of half grown negroes:

"Dar Luster. Whar you gwine, Luster? To de boneyard?"

"Hi," Luster said. "Aint de same boneyard y'all headed fer. Hum up, elefump."

They approached the square, where the Confederate soldier gazed with empty eyes beneath his marble hand in wind and weather. Luster took still another notch in himself and gave the impervious Queenie a cut with the switch, casting his glance about the square. "Dar Mr Jason car," he said, then he spied another group of negroes. "Les show dem niggers how quality does, Benjy," he said. "Whut you say?" He looked back. Ben sat, holding the flower in his fist, his gaze empty and untroubled. Luster hit Queenie again and swung her to the left at the monument.

For an instant Ben sat in an utter hiatus. Then he bellowed. Bellow on bellow, his voice mounted, with scarce interval for breath. There was more than astonishment in it, it was horror; shock; agony eyeless, tongueless; just sound, and Luster's eyes backrolling for a white instant. "Gret God," he said. "Hush! Hush! Gret God!" He whirled again and struck Queenie with the switch. It broke and he cast it away and with Ben's voice mounting toward its unbelievable crescendo Luster caught up the end of the reins and leaned forward as Jason came jumping across the square and onto the step.

With a backhanded blow he hurled Luster aside and caught the reins and sawed Queenie about and doubled the reins back and slashed her across the hips. He cut her again and again, into a plunging gallop, while Ben's hoarse agony roared about them, and swung her about to the right of the monument. Then he struck Luster over the head with his fist.

"Dont you know any better than to take him to the left?" he said. He reached back and struck Ben, breaking the flower stalk again. "Shut up!" he said. "Shut up!" He jerked Queenie back and jumped down. "Get to hell on home with him. If you ever cross that gate with him again, I'll kill you!"

"Yes, suh!" Luster said. He took the reins and hit Queenie with the end of them. "Git up! Git up, dar! Benjy, fer God's sake!"

Ben's voice roared and roared. Queenie moved again, her feet began to clop-clop steadily again, and at once Ben hushed. Luster looked quickly back over his shoulder, then he drove on. The broken flower drooped over Ben's fist and his eyes were empty and blue and serene again as cornice and façade flowed smoothly once more from left to right, post and tree, window and doorway and signboard each in its ordered place.

New York, N.Y.
October 1928

BACKGROUNDS

WILLIAM FAULKNER

Appendix
Compson
1699–1945 †

The "Compson Appendix" did not appear with the original 1929 printing of *The Sound and the Fury* and is not a part of the novel proper. Faulkner composed this piece, "Appendix/Compson, 1699–1945," in the fall of 1945 when Malcolm Cowley was preparing *The Portable Faulkner* for Viking Press. "I should have done this when I wrote the book," Faulkner wrote Cowley. "Then the whole thing would have fallen into pattern like a jigsaw puzzle when the magician's wand touched it." Later, when Random House was preparing the Modern Library edition of *The Sound and the Fury*, Faulkner recommended that the "Appendix" appear first. "When you read it," he wrote Robert N. Linscott, "you will see how it is the key to the whole book, and after reading it, the 4 sections as they stand now fall into clarity and place." In another letter to Linscott he corrected the Viking title for the appendix which read "The Compsons." He said, "It should be, simply:

COMPSON

1699–1945

Because it's really an obituary, not a segregation."

The appendix was reprinted under Faulkner's direction in two subsequent editions of *The Sound and the Fury*.

IKKEMOTUBBE. A dispossessed American king. Called "l'Homme" (and sometimes "de l'homme") by his fosterbrother, a Chevalier of France, who had he not been born too late could have been among the brightest in that glittering galaxy of knightly blackguards who were Napoleon's marshals, who thus translated the Chickasaw title meaning "The Man"; which translation Ikkemotubbe, himself a man of wit and imagination as well as a shrewd judge of character, including his own, carried one step further and anglicised it to "Doom." Who granted out of his vast lost domain a solid square mile of virgin North Mississippi dirt as truly angled as the four corners of a cardtable top (forested then because these were the old days before 1833 when the stars fell and Jefferson Mississippi was one long rambling onestorey mudchinked log building housing the Chickasaw Agent and his tradingpost store) to the grandson of a Scottish refugee who had lost his own birthright by casting his lot with a king who himself had been dispossessed. This in partial return for the right to proceed in peace, by whatever means he and his people saw fit,

† From *The Portable Faulkner*, ed. by Malcolm Cowley (New York: Random House, 1946). Copyright © 1946 by Random House, Inc., taken from the Random House publication, *The Sound and the Fury* by Willim Faulkner.

afoot or a horse provided they were Chickasaw horses, to the wild western land presently to be called Oklahoma: not knowing then about the oil.

JACKSON. A Great White Father with a sword. (An old duellist, a brawling lean fierce mangy durable imperishable old lion who set the wellbeing of the nation above the White House and the health of his new political party above either and above them all set not his wife's honor[1] but the principle that honor must be defended whether it was or not because defended it was whether or not.) Who patented sealed and countersigned the grant with his own hand in his gold tepee in Wassi Town,[2] not knowing about the oil either: so that one day the homeless descendants of the dispossessed would ride supine with drink and splendidly comatose above the dusty allotted harborage of their bones in specially built scarletpainted hearses and fire-engines.

These were Compsons:

QUENTIN MACLACHAN. Son of a Glasgow printer, orphaned and raised by his mother's people in the Perth highlands. Fled to Carolina from Culloden Moor[3] with a claymore and the tartan he wore by day and slept under by night, and little else. At eighty, having fought once against an English king and lost, he would not make that mistake twice and so fled again one night in 1779, with his infant grandson and the tartan (the claymore had vanished, along with his son, the grandson's father, from one of Tarleton's regiments on a Georgia battlefield[4] about a year ago) into Kentucky, where a neighbor named Boon or Boone had already established a settlement.

CHARLES STUART. Attainted and proscribed by name and grade in his British regiment. Left for dead in a Georgia swamp by his own retreating army and then by the advancing American one, both of which were wrong. He still had the claymore even when on his homemade wooden leg he finally overtook his father and son four years later at Harrodsburg,

1. Andrew Jackson's wife Rachel married Jackson thinking that her first husband had divorced her, but he had not. Two years after she and Jackson married, her first husband, Lewis Robards, did obtain a divorce on grounds of desertion and adultery. She and Jackson remarried, but scandal followed them, especially after Jackson's political rise. He fought several duels over the issue, including one in 1806 with Charles Dickinson, in which Dickinson was killed.
2. Washington.
3. The site of the April 16, 1746, battle in northwest Scotland, in which British forces under the Duke of Cumberland defeated Highland Jacobite forces under Prince Charles Edward, thus ending the last armed outbreak of the Stuart cause. The battle is notorious for the slaughter of Highland wounded after the battle.
4. Banastre Tarleton (1754–1833) was a British officer during the American Revolution who led a bloody campaign through the South. The major battles were in the Carolinas, where in the Battle of Cowpens he fought against Colonel Beal's Georgians.

Kentucky, just in time to bury the father and enter upon a long period of being a split personality while still trying to be the schoolteacher which he believed he wanted to be, until he gave up at last and became the gambler he actually was and which no Compson seemed to realize they all were provided the gambit was desperate and the odds long enough. Succeeded at last in risking not only his neck but the security of his family and the very integrity of the name he would leave behind him, by joining the confederation headed by an acquaintance named Wilkinson[5] (a man of considerable talent and influence and intellect and power) in a plot to secede the whole Mississippi Valley from the United States and join it to Spain. Fled in his turn when the bubble burst (as anyone except a Compson schoolteacher should have known it would), himself unique in being the only one of the plotters who had to flee the country: this not from the vengeance and retribution of the government which he had attempted to dismember, but from the furious revulsion of his late confederates now frantic for their own safety. He was not expelled from the United States, he talked himself countryless, his expulsion due not to the treason but to his having been so vocal and vociferant in the conduct of it, burning each bridge vocally behind him before he had even reached the place to build the next one: so that it was no provost marshal nor even a civic agency but his late coplotters themselves who put afoot the movement to evict him from Kentucky and the United States and, if they had caught him, probably from the world too. Fled by night, running true to family tradition, with his son and the old claymore and the tartan.

JASON LYCURGUS. Who, driven perhaps by the compulsion of the flamboyant name given him by the sardonic embittered woodenlegged indomitable father who perhaps still believed with his heart that what he wanted to be was a classicist schoolteacher, rode up the Natchez Trace one day in 1811 with a pair of fine pistols and one meagre saddlebag on a small lightwaisted but stronghocked mare which could do the first two furlongs in definitely under the halfminute and the next two in not appreciably more, though that was all. But it was enough: who reached the Chickasaw Agency at Okatoba (which in 1860 was still called Old Jefferson) and went no further. Who within six months was the Agent's clerk and within twelve his partner, officially still the clerk though actually halfowner of what was now a considerable store stocked with the mare's winnings in races against the horses of Ikkemotubbe's young men which he, Compson, was always careful to limit to a quarter or at most three furlongs; and in the next year it was Ikkemotubbe who owned the little mare and Compson owned the solid square mile of land which someday would be almost in the center of the town of Jefferson, forested then and

5. James Wilkinson (1757–1825): Brigadier General who represented the U.S. in the Louisiana Purchase (1803); he was tried for his part in the Aaron Burr conspiracy but was acquitted.

still forested twenty years later though rather a park than a forest by that
time, with its slavequarters and stables and kitchengardens and the formal lawns and promenades and pavilions laid out by the same architect
who built the columned porticoed house furnished by steamboat from
France and New Orleans, and still the square intact mile in 1840 (with
not only the little white village called Jefferson beginning to enclose it
but an entire white county about to surround it because in a few years
now Ikkemotubbe's descendants and people would be gone, those
remaining living not as warriors and hunters but as white men—as shiftless farmers or, here and there, the masters of what they too called plan-
tations and the owners of shiftless slaves, a little dirtier than the white
man, a little lazier, a little crueller—until at last even the wild blood
itself would have vanished, to be seen only occasionally in the noseshape
of a Negro on a cottonwagon or a white sawmill hand or trapper or
locomotive fireman), known as the Compson Domain then, since now
it was fit to breed princes, statesmen and generals and bishops, to avenge
the dispossessed Compsons from Culloden and Carolina and Kentucky,
then known as the Governor's house because sure enough in time it did
produce or at least spawn a governor—Quentin MacLachan again, after
the Culloden grandfather—and still known as the Old Governor's even
after it had spawned (1861) a general—(called so by predetermined accord
and agreement by the whole town and county, as though they knew even
then and beforehand that the old governor was the last Compson who
would not fail at everything he touched save longevity or suicide)—the
Brigadier Jason Lycurgus II who failed at Shiloh in '62 and failed again
though not so badly at Resaca in '64, who put the first mortgage on the
still intact square mile to a New England carpetbagger in '66, after the
old town had been burned by the Federal General Smith and the new
little town, in time to be populated mainly by the descendants not of
Compsons but of Snopeses,[6] had begun to encroach and then nibble at
and into it as the failed brigadier spent the next forty years selling fragments of it off to keep up the mortgage on the remainder: until one day
in 1900 he died quietly on an army cot in the hunting and fishing camp
in the Tallahatchie River bottom where he passed most of the end of his
days.

   And even the old governor was forgotten now; what was left of the old
square mile was now known merely as the Compson place—the weed-
choked traces of the old ruined lawns and promenades, the house which
had needed painting too long already, the scaling columns of the portico
where Jason III (bred for a lawyer and indeed he kept an office upstairs
above the Square, where entombed in dusty filingcases some of the old-
est names in the county—Holston and Sutpen, Grenier and Beauchamp

6. The Snopes clan play prominent roles in Faulkner's fiction, but particularly in *The Hamlet*,
The Town, and *The Mansion*.

and Coldfield—faded year by year among the bottomless labyrinths of chancery: and who knows what dream in the perennial heart of his father, now completing the third of his three avatars—the one as son of a brilliant and gallant statesman, the second as battleleader of brave and gallant men, the third as a sort of privileged pseudo–Daniel Boone–Robinson Crusoe, who had not returned to juvenility because actually he had never left it—that that lawyer's office might again be the anteroom to the governor's mansion and the old splendor) sat all day long with a decanter of whiskey and a litter of dogeared Horaces and Livys and Catulluses,[7] composing (it was said) caustic and satiric eulogies on both his dead and his living fellowtownsmen, who sold the last of the property, except that fragment containing the house and the kitchengarden and the collapsing stables and one servant's cabin in which Dilsey's family lived, to a golfclub for the ready money with which his daughter Candace could have her fine wedding in April and his son Quentin could finish one year at Harvard and commit suicide in the following June of 1910; already known as the Old Compson place even while Compsons were still living in it on that spring dusk in 1928 when the old governor's doomed lost nameless seventeen-year-old greatgreat-granddaughter robbed her last remaining sane male relative (her uncle Jason IV) of his secret hoard of money and climbed down a rainpipe and ran off with a pitchman in a travelling streetshow, and still known as the Old Compson place long after all traces of Compsons were gone from it: after the widowed mother died and Jason IV, no longer needing to fear Dilsey now, committed his idiot brother, Benjamin, to the State Asylum in Jackson and sold the house to a countryman who operated it as a boarding house for juries and horse- and muletraders, and still known as the Old Compson place even after the boardinghouse (and presently the golfcourse too) had vanished and the old square mile was even intact again in row after row of small crowded jerrybuilt individuallyowned demiurban bungalows.

And these:

QUENTIN III. Who loved not his sister's body but some concept of Compson honor precariously and (he knew well) only temporarily supported by the minute fragile membrane of her maidenhead as a miniature replica of all the whole vast globy earth may be poised on the nose of a trained seal. Who loved not the idea of the incest which he would not commit, but some presbyterian concept of its eternal punishment: he, not God, could by that means cast himself and his sister both into

---

7. Horace (Quintus Horatius Flaccus), 65–8 B.C., a Roman poet; Livy (Titus Livius), 59 B.C.–A.D. 17, a Roman historian; Catullus (Gaius Valerius Catullus), c.84–c.54 B.C., a Roman poet and epigrammatist.

hell, where he could guard her forever and keep her forevermore intact amid the eternal fires. But who loved death above all, who loved only death, loved and lived in a deliberate and almost perverted anticipation of death as a lover loves and deliberately refrains from the waiting willing friendly tender incredible body of his beloved, until he can no longer bear not the refraining but the restraint and so flings, hurls himself, relinquishing, drowning. Committed suicide in Cambridge Massachusetts, June 1910, two months after his sister's wedding, waiting first to complete the current academic year and so get the full value of his paid-in-advance tuition, not because he had his old Culloden and Carolina and Kentucky grandfathers in him but because the remaining piece of the old Compson mile which had been sold to pay for his sister's wedding and his year at Harvard had been the one thing, excepting that same sister and the sight of an open fire, which his youngest brother, born an idiot, had loved.

CANDACE (CADDY). Doomed and knew it, accepted the doom without either seeking or fleeing it. Loved her brother despite him, loved not only him but loved in him that bitter prophet and inflexible corruptless judge of what he considered the family's honor and its doom, as he thought he loved but really hated in her what he considered the frail doomed vessel of its pride and the foul instrument of its disgrace; not only this, she loved him not only in spite of but because of the fact that he himself was incapable of love, accepting the fact that he must value above all not her but the virginity of which she was custodian and on which she placed no value whatever: the frail physical stricture which to her was no more than a hangnail would have been. Knew the brother loved death best of all and was not jealous, would (and perhaps in the calculation and deliberation of her marriage did) have handed him the hypothetical hemlock. Was two months pregnant with another man's child which regardless of what its sex would be she had already named Quentin after the brother whom they both (she and her brother) knew was already the same as dead, when she married (1910) an extremely eligible young Indianian she and her mother had met while vacationing at French Lick the summer before. Divorced by him 1911. Married 1920 to a minor movingpicture magnate, Hollywood California. Divorced by mutual agreement, Mexico 1925. Vanished in Paris with the German occupation, 1940, still beautiful and probably still wealthy too since she did not look within fifteen years of her actual fortyeight, and was not heard of again. Except there was a woman in Jefferson, the county librarian, a mousesized and -colored woman who had never married, who had passed through the city schools in the same class with Candace Compson and then spent the rest of her life trying to keep *Forever Amber* in its orderly overlapping avatars and *Jurgen* and *Tom Jones*[8] out of the

8. *Forever Amber*, a novel by Kathleen Winsor, published in 1944 and banned in Boston as

hands of the highschool juniors and seniors who could reach them down
without even having to tip-toe from the back shelves where she herself
would have to stand on a box to hide them. One day in 1943, after a
week of a distraction bordering on disintegration almost, during which
those entering the library would find her always in the act of hurriedly
closing her desk drawer and turning the key in it (so that the matrons,
wives of the bankers and doctors and lawyers, some of whom had also
been in that old highschool class, who came and went in the afternoons
with the copies of the *Forever Ambers* and the volumes of Thorne Smith[9]
carefully wrapped from view in sheets of Memphis and Jackson newspapers, believed she was on the verge of illness or perhaps even loss of
mind) she closed and locked the library in the middle of the afternoon
and with her handbag clasped tightly under her arm and two feverish
spots of determination in her ordinarily colorless cheeks, she entered the
farmers' supply store where Jason IV had started as a clerk and where he
now owned his own business as a buyer of and dealer in cotton, striding
on through that gloomy cavern which only men ever entered—a cavern
cluttered and walled and stalagmitehung with plows and discs and loops
of tracechain and singletrees and mulecollars and sidemeat and cheap
shoes and horselinament and flour and molasses, gloomy because the
goods it contained were not shown but hidden rather since those who
supplied Mississippi farmers or at least Negro Mississippi farmers for a
share of the crop did not wish, until that crop was made and its value
approximately computable, to show them what they could learn to want
but only to supply them on specific demand with what they could not
help but need—and strode on back to Jason's particular domain in the
rear: a railed enclosure cluttered with shelves and pigeonholes bearing
spiked dust-and-lintgathering gin receipts and ledgers and cottonsamples
and rank with the blended smell of cheese and kerosene and harnessoil
and the tremendous iron stove against which chewed tobacco had been
spat for almost a hundred years, and up to the long high sloping counter
behind which Jason stood and, not looking again at the overalled men
who had quietly stopped talking and even chewing when she entered,
with a kind of fainting desperation she opened the handbag and fumbled
something out of it and laid it open on the counter and stood trembling
and breathing rapidly while Jason looked down at it—a picture, a photograph in color clipped obviously from a slick magazine—a picture filled
with luxury and money and sunlight—a Cannebière[1] backdrop of
mountains and palms and cypresses and the sea, an open powerful
expensive chromiumtrimmed sports car, the woman's face hatless between
a rich scarf and a seal coat, ageless and beautiful, cold serene and damned;

obscene; *Jurgen,* a sensational novel by James Branch Cabell, published in 1919; *Tom Jones, a
Foundling,* by Henry Fielding, published in 1749—all novels which she regarded as scandalous.
9. Thorne Smith, a humorous writer, 1893–1934.
1. Main street in Marseilles, France.

beside her a handsome lean man of middleage in the ribbons and tabs
of a German staffgeneral—and the mousesized mousecolored spinster
trembling and aghast at her own temerity, staring across it at the childless bachelor in whom ended that long line of men who had had something in them of decency and pride even after they had begun to fail at
the integrity and the pride had become mostly vanity and selfpity: from
the expatriate who had to flee his native land with little else except his
life yet who still refused to accept defeat, through the man who gambled
his life and his good name twice and lost twice and declined to accept
that either, and the one who with only a clever small quarterhorse for
tool avenged his dispossessed father and grandfather and gained a prin-
cipality, and the brilliant and gallant governor and the general who though
he failed at leading in battle brave and gallant men at least risked his
own life too in the failing, to the cultured dipsomaniac who sold the last
of his patrimony not to buy drink but to give one of his descendants at
least the best chance in life he could think of.

'It's Caddy!' the librarian whispered. 'We must save her!'

'It's Cad, all right,' Jason said. Then he began to laugh. He stood
there laughing above the picture, above the cold beautiful face now
creased and dogeared from its week's sojourn in the desk drawer and the
handbag. And the librarian knew why he was laughing, who had not
called him anything but Mr Compson for thirty-two years now, ever
since the day in 1911 when Candace, cast off by her husband, had
brought her infant daughter home and left the child and departed by the
next train, to return no more, and not only the Negro cook, Dilsey, but
the librarian too divined by simple instinct that Jason was somehow using
the child's life and its illegitimacy both to blackmail the mother not only
into staying away from Jefferson for the rest of her life but into appoint-
ing him sole unchallengeable trustee of the money she would send for
the child's maintenance, and had refused to speak to him at all since
that day in 1928 when the daughter climbed down the rainpipe and ran
away with the pitchman.

'Jason!' she cried. 'We must save her! Jason! Jason!'—and still crying
it even when he took up the picture between thumb and finger and
threw it back across the counter toward her.

'That Candace?' he said. 'Dont make me laugh. This bitch aint thirty
yet. The other one's fifty now.'

And the library was still locked all the next day too when at three
oclock in the afternoon, footsore and spent yet still unflagging and still
clasping the handbag tightly under her arm, she turned into a neat small
yard in the Negro residence section of Memphis and mounted the steps
of the neat small house and rang the bell and the door opened and a
black woman of about her own age looked quietly out at her. 'It's Frony,
isn't it?' the librarian said. 'Dont you remember me—Melissa Meek,
from Jefferson—'

'Yes,' the Negress said. 'Come in. You want to see Mama.' And she entered the room, the neat yet cluttered bedroom of an old Negro, rank with the smell of old people, old women, old Negroes, where the old woman herself sat in a rocker beside the hearth where even though it was June a fire smoldered—a big woman once, in faded clean calico and an immaculate turban wound round her head above the bleared and now apparently almost sightless eyes—and put the dogeared clipping into the black hands which, like the women of her race, were still as supple and delicately shaped as they had been when she was thirty or twenty or even seventeen.

'It's Caddy!' the librarian said. 'It is! Dilsey! Dilsey!'

'What did he say?' the old Negress said. And the librarian knew whom she meant by 'he', nor did the librarian marvel, not only that the old Negress would know that she (the librarian) would know whom she meant by the 'he', but that the old Negress would know at once that she had already shown the picture to Jason.

'Dont you know what he said?' she cried. 'When he realised she was in danger, he said it was her, even if I hadn't even had a picture to show him. But as soon as he realised that somebody, anybody, even just me, wanted to save her, would try to save her, he said it wasn't. But it is! Look at it!'

'Look at my eyes,' the old Negress said. 'How can I see that picture?'

'Call Frony!' the librarian cried. 'She will know her!' But already the old Negress was folding the clipping carefully back into its old creases, handing it back.

'My eyes aint any good anymore,' she said. 'I cant see it.'

And that was all. At six oclock she fought her way through the crowded bus terminal, the bag clutched under one arm and the return half of her roundtrip ticket in the other hand, and was swept out onto the roaring platform on the diurnal tide of a few middleaged civilians but mostly soldiers and sailors enroute either to leave or to death and the homeless young women, their companions, who for two years now had lived from day to day in pullmans and hotels when they were lucky and in day-coaches and busses and stations and lobbies and public restrooms when not, pausing only long enough to drop their foals in charity wards or policestations and then move on again, and fought her way into the bus, smaller than any other there so that her feet touched the floor only occasionally until a shape (a man in khaki; she couldn't see him at all because she was already crying) rose and picked her up bodily and set her into a seat next the window, where still crying quietly she could look out upon the fleeing city as it streaked past and then was behind and presently now she would be home again, safe in Jefferson where life lived too with all its incomprehensible passion and turmoil and grief and fury and despair, but here at six oclock you could close the covers on it and even the weightless hand of a child could put it back among its unfeatured kindred on the quiet eternal shelves and turn the key upon it for the whole and dreamless night. *Yes* she thought, crying quietly *that was it she didn't want to see it know whether it was Caddy or not because she knows Caddy doesn't want to be saved hasn't anything anymore worth being saved for nothing worth being lost that she can lose*

JASON IV.   The first sane Compson since before Culloden and (a childless bachelor) hence the last. Logical rational contained and even a philosopher in the old stoic tradition: thinking nothing whatever of God one way or the other and simply considering the police and so fearing and respecting only the Negro woman, his sworn enemy since his birth and his mortal one since that day in 1911 when she too divined by simple clairvoyance that he was somehow using his infant niece's illegitimacy to blackmail its mother, who cooked the food he ate. Who not only fended off and held his own with Compsons but competed and held his own with the Snopeses who took over the little town following the turn of the century as the Compsons and Sartorises and their ilk faded from it (no Snopes, but Jason Compson himself who as soon as his mother died—the niece had already climbed down the rainpipe and vanished so Dilsey no longer had either of these clubs to hold over him—committed his idiot younger brother to the state and vacated the old house, first chopping up the vast oncesplendid rooms into what he called apartments and selling the whole thing to a countryman who opened a boardinghouse in it), though this was not difficult since to him all the rest of the town and the world and the human race too except himself were Compsons, inexplicable yet quite predictable in that they were in no sense whatever to be trusted. Who, all the money from the sale of the pasture having gone for his sister's wedding and his brother's course at Harvard, used his own niggard savings out of his meagre wages as a storeclerk to send himself to a Memphis school where he learned to class and grade cotton, and so established his own business with which, following his dipsomaniac father's death, he assumed the entire burden of the rotting family in the rotting house, supporting his idiot brother because of their mother, sacrificing what pleasures might have been the right and just due and even the necessity of a thirty-year-old bachelor, so that his mother's life might continue as nearly as possible to what it had been; this not because he loved her but (a sane man always) simply because he was afraid of the Negro cook whom he could not even force to leave, even when he tried to stop paying her weekly wages; and who despite all this, still managed to save almost three thousand dollars ($2840.50) as he reported it on the night his niece stole it; in niggard and agonised dimes and quarters and halfdollars, which hoard he kept in no bank because to him a banker too was just one more Compson, but hid in a locked bureau drawer in his bedroom whose bed he made and changed himself since he kept the bedroom door locked all the time save when he was passing through it. Who, following a fumbling abortive attempt by his idiot brother on a passing female child, had himself appointed the idiot's guardian without letting their mother know and so was able to have the creature castrated before the mother even knew it was out of the house, and who following the mother's death in 1933 was able to free himself forever not only from the idiot brother and the house but from the Negro woman too, moving into a pair of offices up a flight of stairs above the supplystore containing his cotton ledgers and samples, which he had converted into a bedroom-kitchen-bath, in and out of which on weekends there would be seen a big plain friendly brazen-haired pleasantfaced woman no longer very young, in round picture hats and (in its season) an imitation fur coat, the two of them, the middleaged cottonbuyer and the woman whom the town called, simply, his friend from Memphis, seen at the local picture show on Saturday night and on Sunday morning mounting the apartment stairs with paper bags from the grocer's containing loaves and eggs and oranges and cans of soup, domestic, uxorious, connubial, until the late afternoon bus carried her back to Memphis. He was emancipated now. He was free. 'In 1865,' he would say, 'Abe Lincoln freed the niggers from the Compsons. In 1933, Jason Compson freed the Compsons from the niggers.'

BENJAMIN. Born Maury, after his mother's only brother: a handsome flashing swaggering workless bachelor who borrowed money from almost anyone, even Dilsey although she was a Negro, explaining to her as he withdrew his hand from his pocket that she was not only in his eyes the same as a member of his sister's family, she would be considered a born lady anywhere in any eyes. Who, when at last even his mother realised what he was and insisted weeping that his name must be changed, was rechristened Benjamin by his brother Quentin (Benjamin, our lastborn, sold into Egypt). Who loved three things: the pasture which was sold to pay for Candace's wedding and to send Quentin to Harvard, his sister Candace, firelight. Who lost none of them because he could not remember his sister but only the loss of her, and firelight was the same bright shape as going to sleep, and the pasture was even better sold than before because now he and TP could not only follow timeless along the fence the motions which it did not even matter to him were humanbe-ings swinging golfsticks, TP could lead them to clumps of grass or weeds where there would appear suddenly in TP's hand small white spherules which competed with and even conquered what he did not even know was gravity and all the immutable laws when released from the hand toward plank floor or smokehouse wall or concrete sidewalk. Gelded 1913. Committed to the State Asylum, Jackson 1933. Lost nothing then either because, as with his sister, he remembered not the pasture but only its loss, and firelight was still the same bright shape of sleep.

QUENTIN. The last. Candace's daughter. Fatherless nine months before her birth, nameless at birth and already doomed to be unwed from the instant the dividing egg determined its sex. Who at seventeen, on the one thousand eight hundred ninetyfifth anniversary of the day before the resurrection of Our Lord, swung herself by a rainpipe from the window of the room in which her uncle had locked her at noon, to the locked window of his own locked and empty bedroom and broke a pane and entered the window and with the uncle's firepoker burst open the locked bureau drawer and took the money (it was not $2840.50 either, it was almost seven thousand dollars and this was Jason's rage, the red unbearable fury which on that night and at intervals recurring with little or no diminishment for the next five years, made him seriously believe would at some unwarned instant destroy him, kill him as instantaneously dead as a bullet or a lightningbolt: that although he had been robbed not of a mere petty three thousand dollars but of almost seven thousand he couldn't even tell anybody; because he had been robbed of seven thousand dollars instead of just three he could not only never receive justification—he did not want sympathy—from other men unlucky enough to have one bitch for a sister and another for a niece, he couldn't even go to the police; because he had lost four thousand dollars which did not belong to him he couldn't even recover the three thousand which did since those first four thousand dollars were not only the legal property of his niece as a part of the money supplied for her support and maintenance by her mother over the last sixteen years, they did not exist at all, having been officially recorded as expended and consumed in the annual reports he submitted to the district Chancellor, as required of him as guardian and trustee by his bondsmen: so that he had been robbed not only of his thievings but his savings too, and by his own victim; he had been robbed not only of the four thousand dollars which he had risked jail to acquire but of the three thousand which he had hoarded at the price of sacrifice and denial, almost a nickel and a dime at a time, over a period of almost twenty years: and this not only by his own victim but by a child who did it at one blow, without premeditation or plan, not even knowing or even caring how much she would find when she broke the drawer open; and now he couldn't even go to the police for help: he who had considered the police always, never given them any trouble, had paid the taxes for years which supported them in parasitic and sadistic idleness; not only that, he didn't dare pursue the girl himself because he might catch her and she would talk, so that his only recourse was a vain dream which kept him tossing and sweating on nights two and three and even four years after the event, when he should have forgotten about it: of catching her without warning, springing on her out of the dark, before she had spent all the money, and murder her before she had time to open her mouth) and climbed down the same rainpipe in the dusk and ran away with the pitchman who was already under sentence for bigamy. And so vanished; whatever occupation overtook her would have arrived in no chromium Mercedes; whatever snapshot would have contained no general of staff.

And that was all. These others were not Compsons. They were black:

TP. Who wore on Memphis's Beale Street the fine bright cheap intransigent clothes manufactured specifically for him by the owners of Chicago and New York sweatshops.

FRONY. Who married a pullman porter and went to St Louis to live and later moved back to Memphis to make a home for her mother since Dilsey refused to go further than that.

LUSTER. A man, aged 14. Who was not only capable of the complete care and security of an idiot twice his age and three times his size, but could keep him entertained.

DILSEY.
They endured.

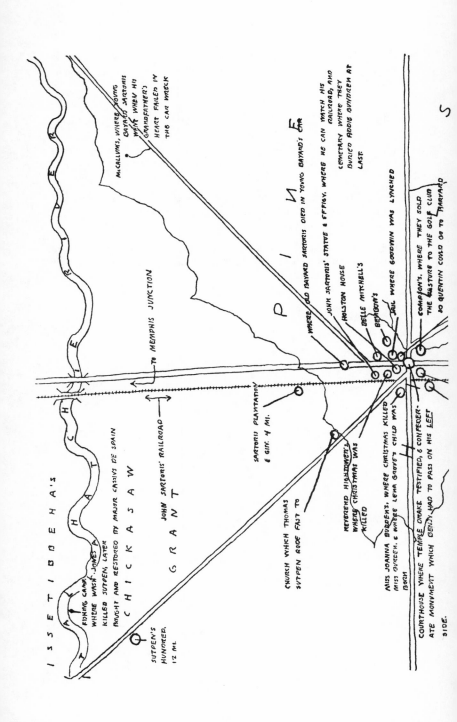

ISSETIBBEHA'S

FISHING CAMP,
WHERE WASH JONES
KILLED SUTPEN, LATER
BOUGHT AND RESTORED BY MAJOR CASSIUS DE SPAIN

C H I C K A S A W   G R A N T

JOHN SARTORIS' RAILROAD

SUTPEN'S
HUNDRED,
12 MI.

CHURCH WHICH THOMAS
SUTPEN RODE FAST TO

MISS JOANNA BURDEN'S, WHERE CHRISTMAS KILLED
MISS BURDEN, & WHERE LENA GROVE'S CHILD WAS
BORN

REVEREND HIGHTOWER'S,
WHERE CHRISTMAS WAS
KILLED

COURTHOUSE WHERE TEMPLE DRAKE TESTIFIED, & CONFEDER-
ATE MONUMENT WHICH BENBY HAD TO PASS ON HIS LEFT
SIDE.

SARTORIS PLANTATION
& GIN, 4 MI.

TO MEMPHIS JUNCTION

McCALLUM'S, WHERE YOUNG
BAYARD SARTORIS
WENT WHEN HIS
GRANDFATHER'S
HEART FAILED IN
THE CAR WRECK

CEMETARY WHERE THEY
BURIED ADDIE BUNDREN AT
LAST

JOHN SARTORIS' STATUE & EFFIGY, WHERE HE CAN WATCH HIS
RAILROAD, AND

WHERE OLD BAYARD SARTORIS DIED IN YOUNG BAYARD'S CAR

HOLSTON HOUSE

BELLE MITCHELL'S

BENBOW'S

JAIL, WHERE GOODWIN WAS LYNCHED

COMPSON'S, WHERE THEY SOLD
THE PASTURE TO THE GOLF CLUB
SO QUENTIN COULD GO TO HARVARD

P I N E

S

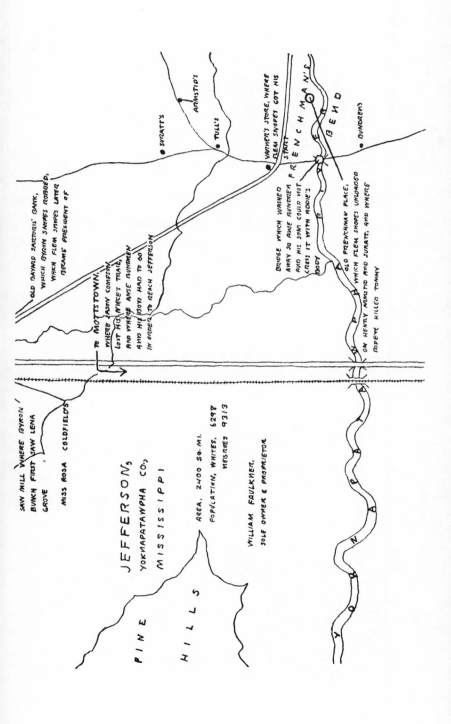

SAW MILL WHERE BYRON
BUNCH FIRST SAW LENA
GROVE

MISS ROSA COLDFIELD'S

JEFFERSON,
YOKNAPATAWPHA CO,
MISSISSIPPI

AREA, 2400 SQ. MI.
POPULATION, WHITES, 6298
NEGROES 9313

WILLIAM FAULKNER,
SOLE OWNER & PROPRIETOR

PINE HILLS

OLD BAYARD SARTORIS' BANK,
WHICH BYRON SNOPES ROBBED,
WHICH FLEM SNOPES LATER
BECAME PRESIDENT OF

TO MOTTSTOWN,
WHERE JASON COMPSON
LOST HIS NIECE'S TRAIL,
AND WHERE ANSE BUNDREN
AND HIS BOYS HAD TO GO
IN ORDER TO REACH JEFFERSON

SURATT'S

TULL'S

ARMSTID'S

VARNER'S STORE, WHERE
FLEM SNOPES GOT HIS
START

FRENCHMAN'S BEND

BRIDGE WHICH WASHED
AWAY SO ANSE BUNDREN
AND HIS SONS COULD NOT
CROSS IT WITH ADDIE'S
BODY

OLD FRENCHMAN PLACE,
WHICH FLEM SNOPES UNLOADED
ON HENRY ARMSTID AND SURATT, AND WHERE
POPEYE KILLED TOMMY

SNOPES'

BUNDREN'S

YOKNAPATAWPHA

WILLIAM FAULKNER

Selected Letters †

To Mrs. Walter B. McLean, Memphis

Wednesday [late Sept. 1927] [Oxford]

Dear Aunt Bama—

. . . .

Grandest weathers. I finished the book today.[1] Will get it off tomorrow, and next time I come up, I'll bring it to you. I dont know when that'll be, as I have a job of work I'll be doing this month. Painting signs.

Much love
William

To Horace Liveright, New York

sunday,—october [16 Oct. 1927] oxford miss

Dear Mr Liveright—

At last and certainly, * * * I have written THE book, of which those other things were but foals.[2] I believe it is the damdest best book you'll look at this year, and any other publisher. It goes forward to you by mail Monday.

. . . .

I am enclosing a few suggestions for the printer: will you look over them and, if possible, smooth the printer's fur, cajole him, some way. He's been punctuating my stuff to death; giving me gratis quotation marks and premiums of commas that I dont need.

I dont think that even the bird who named 'Soldiers' Pay' can improve on my title.

Best regards to everyone.

William Faulkner

† From *Selected Letters of William Faulkner*, ed. Joseph Blotner (New York: Random House, 1977). Copyright © 1977 by Random House, Inc. Reprinted by permission. The exact locations of the manuscripts and typescripts of Faulkner's letters are indicated in Blotner's edition.

1. Faulkner dated the last page of the typescript of *Flags in the Dust* "29 September 1927." The fact that this date fell on a Thursday creates a discrepancy with the dating of "Wednesday" as shown above. The letter is placed here, however, because the only other possibility would be *Mosquitoes*, the last typescript page of which is dated "Pascagoula, Miss/1 Sept 1926." This date did fall on a Wednesday, but the references in the letter above to possible visits to Memphis and to imminent painting jobs suggest Oxford, and therefore *Flags in the Dust*, rather than Pascagoula and *Mosquitoes*.

2. Compare T. E. Lawrence, *Revolt in the Desert* (New York, 1927), p. 288: "At Um el Surab the Handley stood majestic on the grass, with the Bristols like tiny fledglings beneath its spread of wings. Round it admired the Arabs, saying, 'Indeed and at last they have sent us THE aeroplane, of which these things were foals.' "

I also have an idea for a jacket. I will paint it and send it up for your approval soon.

To Horace Liveright, New York

30 november [1927]   Oxford, Miss

Dear Mr Liveright—

It's too bad you dont like Flags in the Dust. Unless you are holding it against that $200.00 you advanced me in the summer, I'd like for you to fire it on back to me, as I shall try it on someone else. I still believe it is the book which will make my name for me as a writer.

I am working spasmodically on a book which will take three or four years to do; also I have started another which I shall finish by spring, I believe. And so if you are not holding the mss against that super-advance, send her on back, and I'll get to work on the other one. Anyway, will you let me know as soon as possible your intentions?

Regards to everyone.

                                                    William Faulkner

---

Flags in the Dust, *retitled* Sartoris, *was accepted by Harcourt, Brace and Company in a contract dated 20 September 1928, with delivery of the novel specified for 7 October 1928. It was probably late September when Faulkner went to New York. There his last ties with Liveright were severed.*

To Mrs. Walter B. McLean, Memphis

Wednesday [probably Oct. 1928]   New York City
                                                      c/o Ben Wasson [3]
                                                      146 MacDougal St.

Dear Aunt Bama—

* * * Harcourt Brace & Co bought me from Liveright. Much, much nicer there. Book will be out in Feb. Also another one, the damndest book I ever read. [4] I dont believe anyone will publish it for 10 years. Harcourt swear they will, but I dont believe it.

Having a rotten time, as usual. I hate this place.

Love to Uncle Walter, and to you as ever.

                                                    William Faulkner

3. A friend from the University of Mississippi, Wasson was acting as Faulkner's literary agent.
4. *The Sound and the Fury.*

To Alfred Harcourt, New York

18 Feb. 1929　　　　　　　　　　　　　　　　　Oxford, Miss.

Dear Mr Harcourt—

My copies of SARTORIS came promptly. I like the appearance of the book very much indeed. Will you let me take this opportunity to thank the office, as well as yourself? I had intended writing my thanks sooner, but I have got involved in another novel, and I have been behind in correspondence since.

About the Sound & Fury ms. That is all right. I did not believe that anyone would publish it; I had no definite plan to submit it to anyone. I told Hal about it once and he dared me to bring it to him. And so it really was to him that I submitted it, more as a curiosity than aught else. I am sorry it did not go over with you all, but I will not say I did not expect that result. Thank you for delivering it to him.[5]

Spring has come here—a false one, of course; just enough to catch fruit trees and flowers with their pants down about next month. It's nice while it lasts, though.

Sincerely,
[s] William Faulkner
[t] Wm Faulkner.

On 20 June 1929, Faulkner married Estelle Oldham Franklin. While they were honeymooning in Pascagoula, Mississippi, he received the proofs of The Sound and the Fury, *which Wasson had partially edited.*

To Ben Wasson, New York

[early summer, 1929]　　　　　　　　　　　　　Pascagoula, Miss.

Dear Ben—

Thank you for the letter.

I received the proof. It seemed pretty tough to me, so I corrected it as written, adding a few more italics where the original seemed obscure on second reading. Your reason for the change, i.e., that with italics only 2 different dates were indicated I do not think sound for 2 reasons. First, I do not see that the use of breaks clarifies it any more; second, there are more than 4 dates involved. The ones I recall off-hand are: Damuddy dies. Benjy is 3. (2) His name is changed. He is 5. (3) Caddy's wedding. He is 14. (4) He tries to rape a young girl and is castrated. 15. (5) Quentin's death. (6) His father's death. (7) A visit to the cemetery at 18. (7)

---

5. Harrison Smith ["Hal"] was leaving Harcourt, Brace to become a partner in the firm of Jonathan Cape and Harrison Smith, which would publish *The Sound and the Fury* on 7 Oct. 1929.

[sic] The day of the anecdote, he is 33. These are just a few I recall. So your reason explodes itself.

But the main reason is, a break indicates an objective change in tempo, while the objective picture here should be a continuous whole, since the thought transference is subjective; i.e., in Ben's mind and not in the reader's eye. I think italics are necessary to establish for the reader Benjy's confusion; that unbroken-surfaced confusion of an idiot which is outwardly a dynamic and logical coherence. To gain this, by using breaks it will be necessary to write an induction for each transference. I wish publishing was advanced enough to use colored ink for such, as I argued with you and Hal in the speak-easy that day. But the form in which you now have it is pretty tough. It presents a most dull and poorly articulated picture to my eye. If something must be done, it were better to re-write this whole section objectively, like the 4th section. I think it is rotten, as is. But if you wont have it so, I'll just have to save the idea until publishing grows up to it. Anyway, change all the italics. You overlooked one of them. Also, the parts written in italics will all have to be punctuated again. You'd better see to that, since you're all for coherence. And dont make any more additions to the script, bud. I know you mean well, but so do I. I effaced the 2 or 3 you made.

We have a very pleasant place on the beach here. I swim and fish and row a little. Estelle sends love.

I hope you will think better of this. Your reason above disproves itself. I purposely used italics for both actual scenes and remembered scenes for the reason, not to indicate the different dates of happenings, but merely to permit the reader to anticipate a thought-transference, letting the recollection postulate its own date. Surely you see this.

                                                            Bill

---

The following fragment comes from one of the letters Faulkner subsequently sent to Wasson in the process of revision.

To Ben Wasson, New York

[early summer, 1929]   [Oxford]

Italics here indicate a speech by one person within a speech by another, so as not to use quotes within quotes, my use of italics has been too without definite plan, I suppose i.e., they do not always indicate a thought transference as in this case, but the only other manner of doing this paragraph seems clumsy still to me, since it breaks the questions interminably of Mrs Compson's drivelling talk if set like the below:

'. . . You must think, Mother said.

'Hold still now, Versh said. He put etc.

'Some day I'll be gone etc., Mother said.
'Now stop, Versh said.
'Come here and kiss . . . Mother said.

. . . .
Galley 6
Set first three lines of new scene in italics. Transference indicated
then. I should have done this, but missed it. Sorry.
. . . .
Excuse recent letter. Didnt mean to be stubborn and inconsiderate.
Believe I am right, tho. And I was not blaming you with it. I just went
to you with it because I think you are more interested in the book than
anyone there, and I know that us both think alike about it, as we already
argued this very point last fall. Excuse it anyway. Estelle sends regards.

Love to all.
Bill

BEN WASSON

[Publishing *The Sound and the Fury*] †

The morning after I completed my work,[1] and after a night of mild
celebration, Bill came to my room as usual, though this time somewhat
earlier than had become his custom. He didn't greet me with his softly
spoken "good morning" but merely tossed a large obviously filled envelope on the bed. "Read this one, Bud," he said. "It's a real son of a
bitch."

I removed the manuscript and read the title on the first page: *The
Sound and the Fury*.

"This one's the greatest I'll ever write. Just read it," he said, and abruptly
left.

The next morning he again arrived. I had stayed up late, enthralled
with his magnificent new manuscript. It left me emotionally stirred for
many hours. After telling him so, I said that the sheer technical outra-
geousness and freshness of the Benjy section made it hard to follow. He
said he knew that it was demanding.

"If I could only get it printed the way it ought to be with different
color types for the different times in Benjy's section recording the flow

---

† From *Count No 'Count: Flashbacks to Faulkner* (Jackson: University Press of Mississippi, 1983),
84–97. Copyright © 1983 by the University Press of Mississippi. Reprinted by permission.
1. Wasson had been working on the manuscript of *Flags in the Dust*, which Harcourt published
January 31, 1929, as *Sartoris*. The full text as Faulkner wrote it was not published with his original
title until 1973 by Random House.

of events for him, it would make it simpler, probably. I don't reckon, though, it'll ever be printed that way, and this'll have to be the best, with the italics indicating the changes of events."

He was planning to leave the next day for Oxford. He asked me to take the manuscript to Hal Smith, since he was afraid to leave it in his or my place. He asked that Hal give him a quick decision. And he also requested that I take some watercolor sketches he had painted for possible use on the jacket of *Sartoris*, the name either he, Hal, or I had suggested as the title to replace *Flags in the Dust*. The sketches showed different versions of a black plowing with a mule, the earth being turned over, and, overhead, a blue-washed sky. It was a rather colorful job, but Harcourt, much to Bill's regret, did not accept it. When I delivered the manuscript of *Sound*, Hal ordered that it be placed in a safe.

On what was supposedly Bill's last night in New York during that visit, a few of us celebrated again. We were always celebrating something or other: an arrival, a departure, a completed picture, a just-finished book or story, or the sale of a poem or manuscript.

On this night, I noticed Bill's body had become less slim and he was wearing his moustache thicker than usual. Throughout the years, he kept his hair about the same length, but from time to time he altered the style of his moustache and occasionally grew a beard.

I left the celebration earlier than the others, either because I wanted to do some polishing on my own manuscript or because I had imbibed too much white wine. In the morning, I was awakened by a faint tapping on the door. I opened it and Bill came in, his expression woebegone.

"I got my pocket picked or lost my pocketbook," he said, and turned his back to me. "Kick me." He turned to me again. "Anyhow, it's vanished. I wonder if you'd go with me to see Hal and try to get him to let me have money enough to get back to Mississippi?"

Hal was amused by the story. Lyle Saxon and Bill Spratling felt that Bill should have an extra amount of money for his train ride south, and they scrounged around and fattened his new wallet.

As I bade him good-bye at the station, he thanked me and said: "Let me know about *The Sound and the Fury*. I'm counting on that one."

Now to squeeze together as closely as I can—and without too much verbosity—events that took place before Bill and I were together again. These events had a great bearing on our relationship and the future of his career as a writer.

Just before Christmas, 1928, Hal Smith broke away from Harcourt, Brace, and, with the English publisher, Jonathan Cape, formed a new firm, Cape and Smith. The departure of Smith from Harcourt was not pleasant. It left ripples of discord and enmity in its wake. Harcourt was particularly incensed at the departure of Louise Bonino, who was to become a mainstay of the new firm.

*   *   *

One of Hal's first talks with me was about the manuscript of *The Sound and the Fury*. "If it's as marvelous as you say it is, I want it for our first list," he said. So I went to Harcourt, Brace, where it was released to me because they had decided it was too poor a publishing risk.

*   *   *

Hal placed the manuscript of *The Sound and the Fury* in the capable hands of Robert Ballou, technical manager, who, as soon as possible, sent it to a printer. The printer returned galley proofs, and Hal grew more excited about the novel. Lenore Marshall, who was in the editorial department, thought it an extraordinary piece of writing and fell in with the small group of admirers.

Then I had a new idea. Evelyn Scott, a distinguished though unconventional lady from Tennessee, whose novels are now sadly neglected and mostly forgotten, was a blue ribbon author on the first list of Cape and Smith. Her big novel about the Civil War, *The Wave*, led the list, and Hal persuaded the prestigious Literary Guild to announce it as one of its choices. The guild's imprimatur added great distinction to any book, fiction or nonfiction. I suggested to Hal that he have Miss Scott read the galley proof and give us her opinion. My hunch was that she would like it. Hal readily agreed, so after telephoning, I took it to her.

*   *   *

"I'll read it right away and write you what I think of it," she told me as our interview ended.

In a few days, a messenger brought me a package containing the *Sound* galleys. When I extracted them and read her enclosed letter, I rushed downstairs to Hal's office with it. Her enthusiastic and understanding remarks also excited Hal. He rubbed his nose and squinted his eyes at me: "Go see her again and thank her for this fine letter. See if she won't write more in detail about the second part of the manuscript. She seems to skimp over it."

"That'll be a lot of trouble for Miss Scott," I said.

"If her additional comments are as penetrating, tell her we'll make all of it into a handsome pamphlet, of course featuring her as its author, and we'll distribute it with the compliments of Cape and Smith to critics and book dealers and send it out with our salesmen. Go telephone her now. We'll talk money later."

That's what I did and what Evelyn Scott did and what Hal Smith did, and it all added up to a fine publicity brochure, tastefully designed by Arthur Hawkins and disseminated as Hal suggested.

*   *   *

I read the galley proofs of *Sound* before forwarding them to Bill. I was reading mostly for typographical errors and misspellings. In reading the Benjy section I arrogantly and heedlessly and, yes, ignorantly, decided I could improve the method of telling and do something about the italics. I don't recall what I did, but when Bill received the proofs he wrote me an angry letter, asking that the section be set in type as he had indicated and written it, with no more tampering on my part. Obviously and plainly he was indignant with me. Later he wrote a less harsh letter about the matter, but this was the first time I had been on the receiving end of his lightening bolts of wrath.

I wasn't stupid enough to try to defend what I had done, and when Bill wrote me that he knew I meant well, he couldn't have put it more scathingly. It was, though, the only unpleasantness between us, and neither of us, in the years that followed, ever referred to it.

*   *   *

WILLIAM FAULKNER

An Introduction for *The Sound and the Fury* †

No version of Faulkner's introduction to *The Sound and the Fury* was published during his lifetime, but two have since been published, both edited by James B. Meriwether. Although there is some overlap between them, there are also differences, and both are valuable *[Editor]*.

For a new edition of *The Sound and the Fury* which was announced in 1933 but was never published, William Faulkner wrote an introduction that for years was supposed to have survived only in an incomplete four-page typescript which he preserved among his papers. The recent discovery of the missing first page makes possible the publication here, for the first time, of a Faulkner document of unique critical and biographical significance.

*   *   *

I wrote this book and learned to read. I had learned a little about writing from Soldiers' Pay—how to approach language, words: not with seriousness so much, as an essayist does, but with a kind of alert respect,

† From "An Introduction for *The Sound and the Fury,*" ed. James B. Meriwether, *The Southern Review* 8 (N.S., 1972): 705–10. Copyright © 1972 by the Estate of William Faulkner. Reprinted by permission of James B. Meriwether. As printed here, Faulkner's typescript has been reproduced exactly, except for the correction of five obvious typing errors: 708.27 withoyt] without; 708.32 agao] ago; 709.10 begn] began; 709.19 give] given; 710.11 withoyt] without

as you approach dynamite; even with joy, as you approach women: perhaps with the same secretly unscrupulous intentions. But when I finished The Sound and the Fury I discovered that there is actually something to which the shabby term Art not only can, but must, be applied. I discovered then that I had gone through all that I had ever read, from Henry James through Henty to newspaper murders, without making any distinction or digesting any of it, as a moth or a goat might. After The Sound and The Fury and without heeding to open another book and in a series of delayed repercussions like summer thunder, I discovered the Flauberts and Dostoievskys and Conrads whose books I had read ten years ago. With The Sound and the Fury I learned to read and quit reading, since I have read nothing since.

Nor do I seem to have learned anything since. While writing Sanctuary, the next novel to The Sound and the Fury, that part of me which learned as I wrote, which perhaps is the very force which drives a writer to the travail of invention and the drudgery of putting seventy-five or a hundred thousand words on paper, was absent because I was still reading by repercussion the books which I had swallowed whole ten years and more ago. I learned only from the writing of Sanctuary that there was something missing; something which The Sound and the Fury gave me and Sanctuary did not. When I began As I Lay Dying I had discovered what it was and knew that it would be also missing in this case because this would be a deliberate book. I set out deliberately to write a tour-de-force. Before I ever put pen to paper and set down the first word, I knew what the last word would be and almost where the last period would fall. Before I began I said, I am going to write a book by which, at a pinch, I can stand or fall if I never touch ink again. So when I finished it the cold satisfaction was there, as I had expected, but as I had also expected the other quality which The Sound and the Fury had given me was absent: that emotion definite and physical and yet nebulous to describe: that ecstasy, that eager and joyous faith and anticipation of surprise which the yet unmarred sheet beneath my hand held inviolate and unfailing, waiting for release. It was not there in As I Lay Dying. I said, It is because I knew too much about this book before I began to write it. I said, More than likely I shall never again have to know this much about a book before I begin to write it, and next time it will return. I waited almost two years, then I began Light in August, knowing no more about it than a young woman, pregnant, walking along a strange country road. I thought, I will recapture it now, since I know no more about this book than I did about The Sound and the Fury when I sat down before the first blank page.

It did not return. The written pages grew in number. The story was going pretty well: I would sit down to it each morning without reluctance yet still without that anticipation and that joy which alone ever made writing pleasure to me. The book was almost finished before I acquiesced to the fact that it would not recur, since I was now aware before each word was written down just what the people would do, since now I was deliberately choosing among possibilities and probabilities of behavior and weighing and measuring each choice by the scale of the Jameses and Conrads and Balzacs. I knew that I had read too much, that I had reached that stage which all young writers must pass through, in which he believes that he has learned too much about his trade. I received a copy of the printed book and I found that I didn't even want to see what kind of jacket Smith had put on it. I seemed to have a vision of it and the other ones subsequent to The Sound and The Fury ranked in order upon a shelf while I looked at the titled backs of them with a flagging attention which was almost distaste, and upon which each succeeding title registered less and less, until at last Attention itself seemed to say, Thank God I shall never need to open any one of them again. I believed that I knew then why I had not recaptured that first ecstasy, and that I should never again recapture it; that whatever novels I should write in the future would be written without reluctance, but also without anticipation or joy: that in the Sound and The Fury I had already put perhaps the only thing in literature which would ever move me very much: Caddy climbing the pear tree [1] to look in the window at her grandmother's funeral while Quentin and Jason and Benjy and the negroes looked up at the muddy seat of her drawers.

This is the only one of the seven novels which I wrote without any accompanying feeling of drive or effort, or any following feeling of exhaustion or relief or distaste. When I began it I had no plan at all. I wasn't even writing a book. I was thinking of books, publication, only in the reverse, in saying to myself, I wont have to worry about publishers liking or not liking this at all. Four years before I had written Soldiers' Pay. It didn't take long to write and it got published quickly and made me about five hundred dollars. I said, Writing novels is easy. You dont make much doing it, but it is easy. I wrote Mosquitoes. It wasn't quite so easy to write and it didn't get published quite as quickly and it made me about four hundred dollars. I said, Apparently there is more to writing novels, being a novelist, than I thought. I wrote Sartoris. It took much longer, and the publisher refused it at once. But I continued to shop it about for three years with a stubborn and fading hope, perhaps to justify the time which I had spent writing it. This hope died slowly, though it didn't hurt at all. One day I seemed to shut a door between me and all publishers' addresses and book lists. I said to myself, Now I can write. Now I can make myself a vase like that which the old Roman kept at his bedside and wore the rim slowly away with kissing it. [2] So I,

---

1. See *The Sound and the Fury*, p. 24. Faulkner referred to the tree in different ways at different times.
2. Faulkner alludes to a scene in the first chapter of Henryk Sienkiewicz's historical novel *Quo Vadis* (1895).

who had never had a sister and was fated to lose my daughter in infancy,
set out to make myself a beautiful and tragic little girl.

WILLIAM FAULKNER

An Introduction to *The Sound and the Fury* †

For a new edition of *The Sound and the Fury* that was to be published by
Random House, Faulkner wrote, during the summer of 1933, an introduction that survives in several partial and complete manuscript and typescript
drafts. One of them, apparently the last, was published in the SOUTHERN
REVIEW, 8 (N.S., *Autumn 1972*), 705–710. *The following longer and quite
different version also merits publication in its own right, and it is at least
possible that it was written later, rather than earlier, than the one that has
been published.*

*   *   *

Art is no part of southern life. In the North it seems to be different. It
is the hardest minor stone in Manhattan's foundation. It is a part of the
glitter or shabbiness of the streets. The arrowing buildings rise out of it
and because of it, to be torn down and arrow again. There will be people
leading small bourgeois lives (those countless and almost invisible bones
of its articulation, lacking any one of which the whole skeleton might
collapse) whose bread will derive from it—polyglot boys and girls progressing from tenement schools to editorial rooms and art galleries; men
with grey hair and paunches who run linotype machines and take up
tickets at concerts and then go sedately home to Brooklyn and suburban
stations where children and grandchildren await them—long after the
descendants of Irish politicians and Neapolitan racketeers are as forgotten as the wild Indians and the pigeon.

And of Chicago too: of that rhythm not always with harmony or tune;
lusty, loudvoiced, always changing and always young; drawing from a
river basin which is almost a continent young men and women into its
living unrest and then spewing them forth again to write Chicago in
New England and Virginia and Europe. But in the South art, to become
visible at all, must become a ceremony, a spectacle; something between
a gypsy encampment and a church bazaar given by a handful of alien
mummers who must waste themselves in protest and active self-defense
until there is nothing left with which to speak—a single week, say, of
furious endeavor for a show to be held on Friday night and then struck
and vanished, leaving only a paint-stiffened smock or a worn out type-

† From William Faulkner, "An Introduction to *The Sound and the Fury*," *Mississippi Quarterly*
26 (Summer 1973): 410–415. Copyright © 1973 by Mrs. Jill Faulkner Summers, Executrix for
the Estate of William Faulkner.

writer ribbon in the corner and perhaps a small bill for cheesecloth or
bunting in the hands of an astonished and bewildered tradesman.

Perhaps this is because the South (I speak in the sense of the indigenous dream of any given collection of men having something in common, be it only geography and climate, which shape their economic
and spiritual aspirations into cities, into a pattern of houses or behavior)
is old since dead. New York, whatever it may believe of itself, is young
since alive; it is still a logical and unbroken progression from the Dutch.
And Chicago even boasts of being young. But the South, as Chicago is
the Middlewest and New York the East, is dead, killed by the Civil War.
There is a thing known whimsically as the New South to be sure, but it
is not the south. It is a land of Immigrants who are rebuilding the towns
and cities into replicas of towns and cities in Kansas and Iowa and Illinois, with skyscrapers and striped canvas awnings instead of wooden bal-
conies, and teaching the young men who sell the gasoline and the
waitresses in the restaurants to say O yeah? and to speak with hard r's,
and hanging over the intersections of quiet and shaded streets where no
one save Northern tourists in Cadillacs and Lincolns ever pass at a gait
faster than a horse trots, changing red-and-green lights and savage and
peremptory bells.

Yet this art, which has no place in southern life, is almost the sum
total of the Southern artist. It is his breath, blood, flesh, all. Not so
much that it is forced back upon him or that he is forced bodily into it
by the circumstance; forced to choose, lady and tiger fashion, between
being an artist and being a man. He does it deliberately; he wishes it so.
This has always been true of him and of him alone. Only Southerners
have taken horsewhips and pistols to editors about the treatment or mal-
treatment of their manuscript. This—the actual pistols—was in the old
days, of course, we no longer succumb to the impulse. But it is still
there, still within us.

Because it is himself that the Southerner is writing about, not about
his environment: who has, figuratively speaking, taken the artist in him
in one hand and his milieu in the other and thrust the one into the other
like a clawing and spitting cat into a croker sack. And he writes. We
have never got and probably will never get, anywhere with music or the
plastic forms. We need to talk, to tell, since oratory is our heritage. We
seem to try in the simple furious breathing (or writing) span of the individual to draw a savage indictment of the contemporary scene or to escape
from it into a makebelieve region of swords and magnolias and mock-
ingbirds which perhaps never existed anywhere. Both of the courses are
rooted in sentiment; perhaps the ones who write savagely and bitterly of
the incest in clayfloored cabins are the most sentimental. Anyway, each
course is a matter of violent partizanship, in which the writer unconsciously writes into every line and phrase his violent despairs and rages
and frustrations or his violent prophesies of still more violent hopes.

That cold intellect which can write with calm and complete detachment and gusto of its contemporary scene is not among us; I do not believe there lives the Southern writer who can say without lying that writing is any fun to him. Perhaps we do not want it to be.

I seem to have tried both of the courses. I have tried to escape and I have tried to indict. After five years I look back at *The Sound and The Fury* and see that that was the turning point: in this book I did both at one time. When I began the book, I had no plan at all. I wasn't even writing a book. Previous to it I had written three novels, with progressively decreasing ease and pleasure, and reward or emolument. The third one was shopped about for three years during which I sent it from publisher to publisher with a kind of stubborn and fading hope of at least justifying the paper I had used and the time I had spent writing it. This hope must have died at last, because one day it suddenly seemed as if a door had clapped silently and forever to between me and all publishers' addresses and booklists and I said to myself, Now I can write. Now I can just write. Whereupon I, who had three brothers and no sisters and was destined to lose my first daughter in infancy, began to write about a little girl.

I did not realise then that I was trying to manufacture the sister which I did not have and the daughter which I was to lose, though the former might have been apparent from the fact that Caddy had three brothers almost before I wrote her name on paper. I just began to write about a brother and a sister splashing one another in the brook and the sister fell and wet her clothing and the smallest brother cried, thinking that the sister was conquered or perhaps hurt. Or perhaps he knew that he was the baby and that she would quit whatever water battles to comfort him. When she did so, when she quit the water fight and stooped in her wet garments above him, the entire story, which is all told by that same little brother in the first section, seemed to explode on the paper before me.

I saw that peaceful glinting of that branch was to become the dark, harsh flowing of time sweeping her to where she could not return to comfort him, but that just separation, division, would not be enough, not far enough. It must sweep her into dishonor and shame too. And that Benjy must never grow beyond this moment; that for him all knowing must begin and end with that fierce, panting, paused and stooping wet figure which smelled like trees. That he must never grow up to where the grief of bereavement could be leavened with understanding and hence the alleviation of rage as in the case of Jason, and of oblivion as in the case of Quentin.

I saw that they had been sent to the pasture to spend the afternoon to get them away from the house during the grandmother's funeral in order that the three brothers and the nigger children could look up at the muddy seat of Caddy's drawers as she climbed the tree to look in the window at the funeral, without then realising the symbology of the soiled drawers, for here again hers was the courage which was to face later with honor the sha ie which she was to engender, which Quentin and Jason could not face: the one taking refuge in suicide, the other in vindictive rage which drove him to rob his bastard niece of the meagre sums which Caddy could send her. For I had already gone on to night and the bedroom and Dilsey with the mudstained drawers scrubbing the naked backside of that doomed little girl—trying to cleanse with the sorry byblow of its soiling that body, flesh, whose shame they symbolised and prophesied, as though she already saw the dark future and the part she was to play in it trying to hold that crumbling household together.

Then the story was complete, finished. There was Dilsey to be the future, to stand above the fallen ruins of the family like a ruined chimney, gaunt, patient and indomitable; and Benjy to be the past. He had to be an idiot so that, like Dilsey, he could be impervious to the future, though unlike her by refusing to accept it at all. Without thought or comprehension; shapeless, neuter, like something eyeless and voiceless which might have lived, existed merely because of its ability to suffer, in the beginning of life; half fluid, groping: a pallid and helpless mass of all mindless agony under sun, in time yet not of it save that he could nightly carry with him that fierce, courageous being who was to him but a touch and a sound that may be heard on any golf links and a smell like trees, into the slow bright shapes of sleep.

The story is all there, in the first section as Benjy told it. I did not try deliberately to make it obscure; when I realised that the story might be printed, I took three more sections, all longer than Benjy's, to try to clarify it. But when I wrote Benjy's section, I was not writing it to be printed. If I were to do it over now I would do it differently, because the writing of it as it now stands taught me both how to write and how to read, and even more: It taught me what I had already read, because on completing it I discovered, in a series of repercussions like summer thunder, the Flauberts and Conrads and Turgenievs which as much as ten years before I had consumed whole and without assimilating at all, as a moth or a goat might. I have read nothing since; I have not had to. And I have learned but one thing since about writing. That is, that the emotion definite and physical and yet nebulous to describe which the writing of Benjy's section of *The Sound and The Fury* gave me—that ecstasy, that eager and joyous faith and anticipation of surprise which the yet unmarred sheets beneath my hand held inviolate and unfailing— will not return. The unreluctance to begin, the cold satisfaction in work well and arduously done, is there and will continue to be there as long as I can do it well. But that other will not return. I shall never know it again.

So I wrote Quentin's and Jason's sections, trying to clarify Benjy's. But I saw that I was merely temporising; That I should have to get completely out of the book. I realised that there would be compensations, that in a sense I could then give a final turn to the screw and extract some ultimate distillation. Yet it took me better than a month to take pen and write *The day dawned bleak and chill* before I did so. There is a story somewhere about an old Roman who kept at his bedside a Tyrrhenian vase which he loved and the rim of which he wore slowly away with kissing it.[1] I had made myself a vase, but I suppose I knew all the time that I could not live forever inside of it, that perhaps to have it so that I too could lie in bed and look at it would be better; surely so when that day should come when not only the ecstasy of writing would be gone, but the unreluctance and the something worth saying too. It's fine to think that you will leave something behind you when you die, but it's better to have made something you can die with. Much better the muddy bottom of a little doomed girl climbing a blooming pear tree in April to look in the window at the funeral.

Oxford.

19 August, 1933.

WILLIAM FAULKNER

Interview with
Jean Stein vanden Heuvel †

*   *   *

FAULKNER: * * * Since none of my work has met my own standards, I must judge it on the basis of that one which caused me the most grief and anguish, as the mother loves the child who became the thief or murderer more than the one who became the priest.

Q: What work is that?

FAULKNER: *The Sound and the Fury.* I wrote it five separate times trying to tell the story, to rid myself of the dream which would continue to anguish me until I did. It's a tragedy of two lost women: Caddy and her daughter. Dilsey is one of my own favorite characters because she is brave, courageous, generous, gentle and honest. She's much more brave and honest and generous than me.

Q: How did *The Sound and the Fury* begin?

1. Faulkner alludes to a scene in the first chapter of Henryk Sienkiewicz's historical novel *Quo Vadis* (1895).

† Reprinted from *Lion in the Garden: Interviews with William Faulkner*, 1926–1962, ed. James B. Meriwether and Michael Millgate (New York: Random House, 1968), 244–46. By permission of the University of Nebraska Press. Copyright © 1968 by James B. Meriwether and Michael Millgate. With Michael Millgate's compliments. Most of this interview took place in New York early in 1956. It was first published as the twelfth in the series "The Art of Fiction" in *The Paris Review*, Spring 1956.

FAULKNER: It began with a mental picture. I didn't realize at the time it was symbolical. The picture was of the muddy seat of a little girl's drawers in a pear tree where she could see through a window where her grandmother's funeral was taking place and report what was happening to her brothers on the ground below. By the time I explained who they were and what they were doing and how her pants got muddy, I realized it would be impossible to get all of it into a short story and that it would have to be a book. And then I realized the symbolism of the soiled pants, and that image was replaced by the one of the fatherless and motherless girl climbing down the rainpipe to escape from the only home she had, where she had never been offered love or affection or understanding. I had already begun to tell it through the eyes of the idiot child since I felt that it would be more effective as told by someone capable only of knowing what happened, but not why. I saw that I had not told the story that time. I tried to tell it again, the same story through the eyes of another brother. That was still not it. I told it for the third time through the eyes of the third brother. That was still not it. I tried to gather the pieces together and fill in the gaps by making myself the spokesman. It was still not complete, not until 15 years after the book was published when I wrote as an appendix to another book the final effort to get the story told and off my mind, so that I myself could have some peace from it. It's the book I feel tenderest towards. I couldn't leave it alone, and I never could tell it right, though I tried hard and would like to try again, though I'd probably fail again.

Q: What emotion does Benjy arouse in you?

FAULKNER: The only emotion I can have for Benjy is grief and pity for all mankind. You can't feel anything for Benjy because he doesn't feel anything. The only thing I can feel about him personally is concern as to whether he is believable as I created him. He was a prologue like the gravedigger in the Elizabethan dramas. He serves his purpose and is gone. Benjy is incapable of good and evil because he had no knowledge of good and evil.

Q: Could Benjy feel love?

FAULKNER: Benjy wasn't rational enough even to be selfish. He was an animal. He recognized tenderness and love though he could not have named them, and it was the threat to tenderness and love that caused him to bellow when he felt the change in Caddy. He no longer had Caddy; being an idiot he was not even aware that Caddy was missing. He knew only that something was wrong, which left a vacuum in which he grieved. He tried to fill that vacuum. The only thing was he had one of Caddy's discarded slippers. The slipper was his tenderness and love which he could not have named, but he knew only that it was missing. He was dirty because he couldn't coordinate and because dirt meant nothing to him. He could no more distinguish between

dirt and cleanliness than between good and evil. The slipper gave him
comfort even though he no longer remembered the person to whom
it had once belonged, any more than he could remember why he
grieved. If Caddy had reappeared he probably would not have known
her.

Q: Does the narcissus given to Benjy have some significance?

FAULKNER: The narcissus was given to Benjy to distract his attention.
It was simply a flower which happened to be handy that 5th of April.[1]
It was not deliberate.

WILLIAM FAULKNER

Class Conferences at the University of Virginia †

From February to June of 1957 and 1958, William Faulkner was Writer-in-
Residence at the University of Virginia under a grant from the Emily Clark
Balch Fund for American Literature. The following interviews are excerpted
from the texts of thirty-seven group conferences in which Faulkner partici-
pated. The tapes of these discussions are now housed in the Alderman Library
of the University of Virginia.

February 15, 1957

Session One

Graduate Course in American Fiction

. . .

Q: Mr. Faulkner, in *The Sound and the Fury* the first three sections of
that book are narrated by one of the four Compson children, and in
view of the fact that Caddy figures so prominently, is there any particular reason why you didn't have a section with—giving her views or
impressions of what went on?

A: That's a good question. That—the explanation of that whole book
is in that. It began with the picture of the little girl's muddy drawers,
climbing that tree to look in the parlor window with her brothers that
didn't have the courage to climb the tree waiting to see what she saw.
And I tried first to tell it with one brother, and that wasn't enough.
That was Section One. I tried with another brother, and that wasn't

---

1. The fourth section of *The Sound and the Fury* is actually dated April 8.
† Reprinted with permission from *Faulkner in the University: Class Conferences at the University
of Virginia, 1957–1958*, ed. Frederick L. Gwynn and Joseph Blotner (New York: Vintage Books,
Random House, 1965; University Press of Virginia, 1959; reprinted 1977), 1–3, 6, 17–19, 31–
32, 61–65, 68, 76–77, 84–87, 94–95, 132, 147–148, 197, 204–205, 261–263, 274.

enough. That was Section Two. I tried the third brother, because Caddy was still to me too beautiful and too moving to reduce her to telling what was going on, that it would be more passionate to see her through somebody else's eyes, I thought. And that failed and I tried myself—the fourth section—to tell what happened, and I still failed.

. . .

Q: Speaking of Caddy, is there any way of getting her back from the clutches of the Nazis, where she ends up in the Appendix?

A: I think that that would be a betrayal of Caddy, that it is best to leave her where she is. If she were resurrected there'd be something a little shabby, a little anti-climactic about it, about this. Her tragedy to me is the best I could do with it—unless, as I said, I could start over and write the book again and that can't be.

. . .

Q: Mr. Faulkner, I am interested in the symbolism in *The Sound and the Fury*, and I wasn't able to figure exactly the significance of the shadow symbol in Quentin. It's referred to over and over again: he steps in the shadow, shadow is before him, the shadow is often after him. Well then, what is the significance of this shadow?

A. That wasn't a deliberate symbolism. I would say that that shadow that stayed on his mind so much was foreknowledge of his own death, that he was—Death is here, shall I step into it, or shall I step away from it a little longer? I won't escape it, but shall I accept it now or shall I put it off until next Friday? I think that if it had any reason that must have been it.

* * *

Q: Mr. Faulkner, I'd like to ask you about Quentin and his relationship with his father. I think many readers get the impression that Quentin is the way he is to a large extent because of his father's lack of values, or the fact that he doesn't seem to pass down to his son many values that will sustain him. Do you think that Quentin winds up the way he does primarily because of that, or are we meant to see, would you say, that the action that comes primarily from what he is, abetted by what he gets from his father?

A: The action as portrayed by Quentin was transmitted to him through his father. There was a basic failure before that. The grandfather had been a failed brigadier twice in the Civil War. It was the—the basic failure Quentin inherited through his father, or beyond his father. It was a—something had happened somewhere between the first Compson and Quentin. The first Compson was a bold ruthless man who came into Mississippi as a free forester to grasp where and when he could and wanted to, and established what should have been a princely line, and that princely line decayed.

*   *   *

Q: Mr. Faulkner, I've been very much interested in what it seems to
me you did—maybe you didn't—in *The Sound and the Fury*, in the
character of Caddy. To me she is a very sympathetic character, perhaps the most sympathetic white woman in the book, and yet we get
pictures of her only through someone else's comments and most of
these comments are quite [?] and wouldn't lead you to admire her on
the surface, and yet I do. Did you mean for us to have this feeling for
Caddy, and if so, how did you go about reducing her to the negative
picture we get of her?

A: To me she was the beautiful one, she was my heart's darling. That's
what I wrote the book about and I used the tools which seemed to me
the proper tools to try to tell, try to draw the picture of Caddy.

*   *   *

March 13, 1957
Session Eight

Undergraduate Course in Contemporary Literature

Q: What is your purpose in writing into the first section of *The Sound
and the Fury* passages that seem disjointed in themselves if the idea is
not connected with one another?

A: That was part of the failure. It seemed to me that the book approached
nearer the dream if the groundwork of it was laid by the idiot, who
was incapable of relevancy. That's—I agree with you too, that's a bad
method, but to me it seemed the best way to do it, that I shifted those
sections back and forth to see where they went best, but my final
decision was that though that was not right, that was the best to do it,
that was simply the groundwork for that story, as that idiot child saw
it. He himself didn't know what he was seeing. That the only thing
that held him into any sort of reality, into the world at all, was the
trust that he had for his sister, that he knew that she loved him and
would defend him, and so she was the whole world to him, and these
things were flashes that were reflected on her as in a mirror. He didn't
know what they meant.

*   *   *

April 15, 1957

Session Ten

Visitors from Virginia Colleges

*   *   *

Q: In that connection, did you write it in the order in which it was published?

A: Yes. . . . I wrote the Benjy part first. That wasn't good enough so I wrote the Quentin part. That still wasn't good enough. I let Jason try it. That still wasn't enough. I let Faulkner try it and that still wasn't enough, and so about twenty years afterward I wrote an appendix still trying to make that book what—match the dream.

*   *   *

Q: Then may I ask if all of these characters in *The Sound and the Fury*—that you would call them "good people"?

A: I would call them tragic people. The good people, Dilsey, the Negro woman, she was a good human being. That she held that family together for not the hope of reward but just because it was the decent and proper thing to do.

*   *   *

CULTURAL AND
HISTORICAL CONTEXTS

C. VANN WOODWARD

The Irony of Southern History †

In a time when nationalism sweeps everything else before it, as it does at present, the regional historian is likely to be oppressed by a sense of his unimportance. America is the all-important subject, and national ideas, national institutions, and national policies are the themes that compel attention. Foreign peoples, eager to know what this New World colossus means to them and their immediate future, are impatient with details of regional variations, and Americans, intent on the need for national unity, tend to minimize their importance. New England, the West, and other regions are occasionally permitted to speak for the nation. But the South is thought to be hedged about with peculiarities that set it apart as unique. As a standpoint from which to write American history it is regarded as eccentric and, as a background for an historian, something of a handicap to be overcome.

Of the eccentric position of the South in the nation there are admittedly many remaining indications. I do not think, however, that this eccentricity need be regarded as entirely a handicap. In fact, I think that it could possibly be turned to advantage by the Southern historian, both in understanding American history and in interpreting it to non-Americans. For from a broader point of view it is not the South but America that is unique among the peoples of the world. This peculiarity arises out of the American legend of success and victory, a legend that is not shared by any other people of the civilized world. The collective will of this country has simply never known what it means to be confronted by complete frustration. Whether by luck, by abundant resources, by ingenuity, by technology, by organizing cleverness, or by sheer force of arms America has been able to overcome every major historic crisis—economic, political, or foreign—with which it has had to cope. This remarkable record has naturally left a deep imprint upon the American mind. It explains in large part the national faith in unlimited progress, in the efficacy of material means, in the importance of mass and speed, the worship of success, and the belief in the invincibility of American arms.

The legend has been supported by an unbroken succession of victorious wars. Battles have been lost, and whole campaigns—but not wars. In the course of their national history Americans, who have been called a bellicose though unmartial people, have fought eight wars, and so far

† Reprinted by permission of Louisiana State University Press from *The Burden of Southern History*, 167–91. Copyright © 1960 and 1968 by Louisiana State University Press. Copyright © 1988 by C. Vann Woodward.

without so much as one South African fiasco such as England encountered in the heyday of her power. This unique good fortune has isolated America, I think rather dangerously, from the common experience of the rest of mankind, all the great peoples of which have without exception known the bitter taste of defeat and humiliation. It has fostered the tacit conviction that American ideals, values, and principles inevitably prevail in the end. That conviction has never received a name, nor even so much explicit formulation as the old concept of Manifest Destiny. It is assumed, not discussed. And the assumption exposes us to the temptation of believing that we are somehow immune from the forces of history.

The country that has come nearest to approximating the American legend of success and victory is England. The nearness of continental rivals and the precariousness of the balance of power, however, bred in the English an historical sophistication that prevented the legend from flourishing as luxuriantly as it has in the American climate. Only briefly toward the end of the Victorian period did the legend threaten to get out of hand in England. Arnold J. Toynbee has recalled those piping days in a reminiscent passage. "I remember watching the Diamond Jubilee[1] procession myself as a small boy," he writes. "I remember the atmosphere. It was: well, here we are on the top of the world, and we have arrived at this peak to stay there—forever! There is, of course, a thing called history, but history is something unpleasant that happens to other people. We are comfortably outside all that. I am sure, if I had been a small boy in New York in 1897 I should have felt the same. Of course, if I had been a small boy in 1897 in the Southern part of the United States, I should not have felt the same; I should then have known from my parents that history had happened to my people in my part of the world."

The South has had its full share of illusions, fantasies, and pretensions, and it has continued to cling to some of them with an astonishing tenacity that defies explanation. But the illusion that "history is something unpleasant that happens to other people" is certainly not one of them—not in the face of accumulated evidence and memory to the contrary. It is true that there have been many Southern converts to the gospel of progress and success, and there was even a period following Reconstruction when it seemed possible that these converts might carry a reluctant region with them. But the conversion was never anywhere near complete. Full participation in the legend of irresistible progress, success, and victory could, after all, only be vicarious at best. For the inescapable facts of history were that the South had repeatedly met with frustration and failure. It had learned what it was to be faced with eco-

---

1. Queen Victoria's Diamond Jubilee, 1896, celebrating the sixtieth anniversary of her ascent to the throne.

nomic, social, and political problems that refused to yield to all the ingenuity, patience, and intelligence that a people could bring to bear upon them. It had learned to accommodate itself to conditions that it swore it would never accept, and it had learned the taste left in the mouth by the swallowing of one's own words. It had learned to live for long decades in quite un-American poverty, and it had learned the equally un-American lesson of submission. For the South had undergone an experience that it could share with no other part of America—though it is shared by nearly all the peoples of Europe and Asia—the experience of military defeat, occupation, and reconstruction. Nothing about this history was conducive to the theory that the South was the darling of divine providence.

ROBERT PENN WARREN

Faulkner: Past and Future †

*   *   *

Let us look back to the place and time when Faulkner began to write.

In a profound way Faulkner resembles Robert Frost, and his relation to the South resembles that of Robert Frost to New England. Both men seem so deeply demanded by their moment in history, at the very end of their respective cultures, that, forgetting the matter of genius, one is tempted to say that the moment is the man, and the man a role created by the moment. Both Faulkner and Frost were firmly and intransigently rooted in Old America, the America which was liquidated by the First World War, and both were even more firmly and intransigently rooted in a particular locality and in the history of a locality. Both made a characteristic drama out of the locality and the history, and both—most importantly of all—created a role, a *persona*, a mask that defined a relation to the locality and the world beyond, and the mask gave the voice. Both, that is, knowing the shape and feel of life in a particular place and time, felt the story of man-in-nature and of man-in-community, and could, therefore, take the particular locality as a vantage point from which to criticize modernity for its defective view of man-in-nature and man-in-community. Last of all, in a paradoxical way, the appeal that both Faulkner and Frost have for the world of modernity stems from the fact that they represent something strange and lost—something that the modern

† From Robert Penn Warren, ed., "Introduction: Faulkner: Past and Future." *Faulkner: A Collection of Critical Essays*, (Englewood Cliffs, N.J.: Prentice-Hall, 1966), 1–22. Used by permission of the publisher, Prentice-Hall, a division of Simon & Schuster, Englewood Cliffs, N.J.

world is deeply ambivalent about and therefore cannot quite ignore, no matter how much it would like to ignore it.

* * *

The South which Faulkner had grown up in—particularly the rural South—was cut-off, inward-turning, backward-looking. It was a culture frozen in its virtues and vices, and even for the generation that grew up after World War I, that South offered an image of massive immobility in all ways, an image, if one was romantic, of the unchangeableness of the human condition, beautiful, sad, painful, tragic—sunlight slanting over a mellow autumn field, a field the more precious for the fact that its yield had been meagre.

Even if one had read enough history to know that things *do* change, that even the romantic image in the head was the result of prior changes, that the image of an elegiac autumn implied the prior image of a summer of violent energies, the image still persisted, as though the process of history had led to this stubbornly, and preciously, held vision of non-history.

Strangely, this elegiac vision in which energy was sublimated into poetry was coupled with another vision, a sort of antithetical vision, in which violence irrationally erupted through the autumn serenity to create the characteristic "Southern" drama. And in another way the vision of the South was paradoxical. The South, with its immobility, seemed the true challenge to youthful energy that always demands change, and at the same time it was, as I have indicated, the place where history *had* been, had already fulfilled itself, had died—and could be contemplated.

But this vision of non-history is only half the matter. The First World War had brought America into a shocking cultural collision with Europe. For the South, the shock in the period was even greater than for the North. The South, withdrawn and somnolent, came into collision not only with Europe but with the North and the new order there. It is true that in some ways the effects of World War I seemed more obvious in the North; for instance, the great Northern industrial and financial establishment was now out of debt and dominant in the world, with all the consequences which this entailed. But such changes in the North were changes, not so much of kind, as of degree. In the South, on the other hand, the changes, even if often concealed, were often more radical and dramatic; there were profound tensions, deep inner divisions of loyalties, new ambitions set against old pieties, new opportunities, new despairs, new moral problems, or rather, old problems which had never been articulated and confronted—all the things that stir a man, or a society, to utterance. The South, then, offered the classic situation of a world stung and stirred, by cultural shock, to create an art, in order to objectify and grasp the nature of its own inner drama.

The very style of this new utterance in the South is instructive. There was, of course, a strain of realism in the South, best exemplified in that period by Ellen Glasgow and T. S. Stribling, but this strain was not dominant. A variant of symbolism was often characteristic, as might be expected from the nearly irreconcilable tensions and the deep inwardness of the drama with which it dealt. Furthermore, as a fact to be associated with the tendency toward symbolism, Southern writing was often radical in method—more radical, by and large, than the writing in other parts of the country. Its radicalism often had a European orientation, its ancestors in Dostoevsky, Conrad, Baudelaire, Proust, Joyce, and Yeats; and the Americans it found most compelling were usually those with a European bias—James, Eliot, Pound, Hart Crane. If in the moment of cultural shock Southern writers were impelled to explore the traditional basis of their world, the language and techniques which many of them used for that exploration were antitraditional. This fact, in itself, implies the very spiritual tensions in the work; for a language and a technique are not mere instruments, they are gauges of attitude, instruments of evaluation and modes of discovery, and even against a man's will may modify what he makes of his own world. At the same time, as another point of tension, in contrast to the sophistication of technique, the folk tradition, especially folk humor, was very much alive for many Southern writers. We must recall, as the most obvious example, that Faulkner is a great humorist, in the line of Mark Twain, as well as a great technical virtuoso.

As a technician, Faulkner, except for his peers, Melville and James, is the most profound experimenter in the novel that America has produced. But the experiments were developed out of—that is, were not merely applied to—an anguishing research into the Southern past and the continuing implications of that past. We may remark, for instance, that the period when Faulkner developed his experiments is the period when his fundamental insights were achieved, when he pierced the crust of his traditional material, when he most deeply dramatized the key moral issues of Southern life. In that strange interfusion which seems to be characteristic of such a situation of cultural shock, the complexity of issues demanded the technique, but at the same time, the issues would not have been available, been visible in fact, without the technique. The cultural shock and the technical development go hand in hand.

The great period of Faulkner's achievement—from *The Sound and the Fury* to *The Hamlet*—overlaps, too, with the Depression and the time of the premonitory shadows of World War II, with another time, that is, of deep cultural shock. The tension and changes in this time were acute. This is not to say that Faulkner specifically took the Depression as a subject, but it is to say that the Depression accentuated the issues of time and change which Faulkner had already located as seminal for him. The sense of unchangeableness of the human condition which had characterized the life of the rural South even after World

War I, was now, suddenly, with the Depression, changed. Conversation turned to the question of what could be done to "change" things, even if for some people the desired change was, paradoxically enough, to change things back to their old unchangeableness; to escape, to phrase it another way, from *history-as-lived* back to *history-as-contemplated*; from *history-as-action* to *history-as-ritual*. But even to change back to unchangeableness would be a kind of change. There was, then, no way to avoid the notion of change; you had to take a bite, willy-nilly, of the apple from the mysterious tree that had sprung up in the Confederate garden.

We can, in fact, think of the poles of Faulkner's work as *history-as-action* and *history-as-ritual*. We may even see this polarity as related to another which he was so fond of—and so indefinite in the formulation of—the polarity of fact and truth. We may see it, too, in the drama of his outraged Platonism—outraged by the world and the flesh.

*   *   *

RICHARD H. KING

A Southern Renaissance †

In 1975 the leading historian of the South in the post-World War II era, C. Vann Woodward, sought to define the Southern Renaissance and to specify the conditions of its emergence.[1] "Why the Southern Renaissance?" was characteristically Woodwardian in its lack of dogmatism, its lucid summations and deft criticisms, and its tendency toward equivocation. Locating the origins of the Renaissance in 1929, the year that saw the publication of Thomas Wolfe's *Look Homeward, Angel* and William Faulkner's *The Sound and the Fury*, Woodward characterized it as a flowering of the "literary arts—poetry, fiction and drama."[2] Although Woodward suggested no point at which the literary well ran dry, one might conveniently locate the end of the main phase of the Renaissance somewhere around 1955. After that year the South was preoccupied with "other voices, other rooms."

This is not to say that Southerners stopped writing or that nothing of worth appeared after the mid-1950s. Far from it. But by this point the figures dealt with in my study were either dead or past their creative

† From A *Southern Renaissance: The Cultural Awakening of the American South, 1930–1955* (New York: Oxford University Press, 1980), 3–38. Copyright © 1980 by Oxford University Press. Reprinted by permission.
1. C. Vann Woodward, "Why the Southern Renaissance?" *Virginia Quarterly Review 51*, No. 2 (Spring 1975), 222–39.
2. *Ibid.*, p. 222.

peaks. * * * The apogee had been reached; the Renaissance had become a tradition.

Woodward went on to survey the various explanations that had been advanced for the Renaissance. He rejected as absurd the "sociological" explanations that saw the cultural flowering as the issue of Southern prosperity or industrialization, a newly discovered liberal spirit, or the infusion of new blood from the outside. He then proceeded to dismiss the "defensive" theory, which he attributed to W. J. Cash. In this account the Renaissance was the attempt of Southern writers to justify themselves and their society in the face of a hostile American society. Finally, however, Woodward gave a qualified nod of approval to Allen Tate's "backward glance" thesis: the Renaissance was the product of the creative tension between the Southern past and the pressures of the modern world.

But the Tate thesis did not entirely satisfy Woodward either. First, it failed to explain why the Renaissance happened precisely when it did; and, second, it failed to account for the literary productivity of Southern writers after World War II. Thus the backward glance notion provided the "necessary conditions" but not any sort of final explanation. To add specificity to Tate's thesis, Woodward drew upon Cleanth Brooks, a critic who had been closely associated with the Agrarians at Vanderbilt University in the 1920s and their hostile view of modern culture. According to Brooks, the Southern experience had been marked by a feeling for the concrete and specific, a familiarity with conflict, a sense of community and religious wholeness, a belief that the mystery of human nature defied rational explanation or manipulation, and a sense of the tragic. This was the fertile ground in which the South's artistic and intellectual promptings took root and flourished.

Woodward was properly skeptical that any determinate relationship between historical causes and cultural results could be drawn; but he was also perhaps overly defensive. Indeed it is difficult to imagine what a scientific (in the sense of "natural" scientific) explanation of the Southern Renaissance would loook like. Besides this knotty theoretical issue, however, Woodward's essay suggested other matters that called for further analysis.

*   *   *

Finally, though there is no gainsaying some of the regional characteristics that Woodward draws from Brooks, it should be noted that they are generally conservative traits or tend to be most eagerly embraced by the party of the past. But the Renaissance was by no means the exclusive property of the conservative spirit and those who protested the appearance of the modern world. Second, some of these alleged characteristics of the Southern experience are questionable. It is difficult to see, for instance, how one can speak of the Southern fear of abstraction when the section has been addled over the years by all sorts of chimerical

causes and collective delusions. Nor does the Southern claim on the
tragic sense appear very strong if one assumes that the tragic sense requires
insight into the circumstances which have led to grief. The South has
rarely shown much of that insight. More generally, Woodward might
have placed greater emphasis upon what is implied in the Tate thesis:
the *dissolution* of the social and cultural context that nurtured these
characteristics made way for the literary and intellectual resurgence in
the South circa 1930.

If Woodward's essay represents the conventional account of the origins
of the Southern Renaissance, there are other accounts which bid for
attention. Writing in what might be called the neo-Catholic tradition of
the Tate wing of the Vanderbilt Agrarians, Lewis Simpson claims that
the Renaissance was most centrally about "memory and history." Though
the restoration of an agrarian order was ostensibly its goal, the Renaissance sought "to assert the redemptive meaning of the classical-Christian
past in its bearing on the present."[3] Thus, according to Simpson, the
Renaissance was less literary than religious; it was "a search for images
of existence which will express the truth that man's essential nature lies
in his possession of the moral community of memory and history."[4]
What the Renaissance resisted was the corrosive pessimism of modernity
and the utopian faith that knowledge can change "the very constitution
of being" and that history can be abolished.[5]

Simpson's interpretive account of the Renaissance is both more interesting and less pertinent than Woodward's. Surely history and memory,
loss and absence, were central preoccupations in much Southern writing
in the years after 1930 (as they were in much writing before those years).
But Simpson's claim that Faulkner and his contemporaries were essentially religious writers is debatable, to put it mildly. Nor does Simpson
give any examples of powerful utopian impulses at work in the South in
these years. Whatever else may be said about Southern liberals and
reformers, they were hardly wild-eyed radicals or soft-headed dreamers.
Finally, Simpson's account fails to ground the Renaissance in its specific
(Southern) historical setting. Instead, he sees it as a counterattack against
the spirit of modernity and the gnostic strain in Western political thought
articulated first by Joachim of Floris in the twelfth century. His was
intellectual history with a vengeance.

What then was the Southern Renaissance? Put briefly: the writers and
intellectuals of the South after the late 1920s were engaged in an attempt
to come to terms not only with the inherited values of the Southern
tradition but also with a certain way of perceiving and dealing with the
past, what Nietzsche called "monumental" historical consciousness. It

---

3. Lewis Simpson, "The Southern Recovery of Memory and History," *Sewanee Review* 82 (1974),
p. 5.
4. *Ibid.*, p. 9.
5. *Ibid.*, p. 13.

was vitally important for them to decide whether the past was of any use at all in the present; and, if so, in what ways? Put another way, the relationship between present and past which the Renaissance writers explored was fraught with ambivalence and ambiguity. The "object" of their historical consciousness was a tradition whose essential figures were the father and the grandfather and whose essential structure was the literal and symbolic family. In sum, the Renaissance writers sought to come to terms with what I call the "Southern family romance."

*   *   *

The Southern Family Romance

"Every culture lives inside its own dream," Lewis Mumford once observed;[6] and the Southern family romance was the South's dream. Though related to the "plantation legend" of ante-bellum popular fiction and similar expressions in post-Reconstruction popular fiction, the Southern family romance was never expressed in any consistent theoretical or literary way.[7] One must find it "between the lines," as it were, of Southern literature and life, for it was the collective fantasy which made up the "structure of feeling" of that culture. It constituted the values, attitudes, and beliefs that white Southerners expressed in their attitudes toward the region itself, the family, the relationship between the races and sexes, and between the elite and the masses.

But why "family romance"? The South was historically an agrarian society which lacked strong extra-familial institutions. The plantation itself was conceived of as structured like a family. It was relatively homogeneous and resolutely patriarchal in fact and in self-conception. It was not uncommon, as W. J. Cash noted in his *The Mind of the South*, for a rural Southern county to be dominated by a very few families and its populace, both black and white, to bear a small number of surnames and certain striking physical resemblances. Moreover, intermarriage among close kin was not at all uncommon and had a certain economic rationale among upper-class whites.[8] Beyond this there was a strong strain

---

6. Quoted in Richard Hoggart, *The Uses of Literacy* (New York: Oxford University Press, 1957; Beacon Press, 1961), p. 133.

7. Besides William R. Taylor, *Cavalier and Yankee* (New York: George Braziller, 1961; Anchor, 1963), and Rollin Osterweiss, *Romanticism and Nationalism in the Old South* (New Haven: Yale University Press, 1949), see Paul Buck, *The Road to Reunion: 1865–1900* (Boston: Little, Brown, 1937); Francis Pendleton Gaines, *The Southern Plantation: A Study in the Development and Accuracy of a Tradition* (New York: Columbia University Press, 1924; Peter Smith, 1962); and Lawrence J. Friedman, *The White Savage* (Englewood Cliffs, N.J: Prentice-Hall, 1970), chapter 4.

8. Besides W. J. Cash, *The Mind of the South* (1941; New York: Vintage Books, 1960), and Eugene Genovese, *The World the Slaveholders Made* (New York: Pantheon, 1969), see Bertram Wyatt-Brown, "The Ideal Typology and Ante-Bellum Southern History: A Testing of a New Approach," *Societas* 5, No. 1 (Winter 1975), 1–29; and Paul Conner, "Patriarchy: Old World and New," *American Quarterly* 17, No. 1 (Spring 1965), 48–62.

in Southern thought which saw society as the family writ large. For thinkers such as George Fitzhugh, the society-as-family was the ideal toward which Southern society should strive. Individual and regional identity, self-worth, and status were determined by family relationships. The actual family was destiny; and the region was conceived of as a vast metaphorical family, hierarchically organized and organically linked by (pseudo-) ties of blood.

Further, the term "family romance" has a specific meaning within psychoanalytic thought. In a brief introduction to Otto Rank's *The Myth of the Birth of the Hero*, Freud used "family romance" to describe the situation in which a child begins to view realistically the parents he had originally idealized and taken to be the sum of all human virtue. In reaction to his disappointment and what is often displacement from the center of attention, his "royal highness," the child, may imagine that he is adopted or a stepchild whose "real" (imaginary) parents are of noble lineage or powerful station. At the core of the young child's reaction Freud saw resentment at having been abandoned and a fantasized denial of abandonment.[9]

The notion of the family romance was elaborated further in Rank's essay. According to Rank, myths were the "dreams of the masses of people."[1] In the presence of an actual hero, a group will draw upon its own childhood fantasies, most centrally the family romance, which is a variation of the Oedipus story, to explain the hero's origins and his fate. By idealizing the cultural hero, the members of the group can justify their own revolt (in reality or fantasy) against their parents.

Rank went on to elaborate upon and explain the pattern which he had found in the stories of mythical figures. For instance, in the life of the hero the desire to be rid of the parents is reversed; it is the parents who wish to be rid of the young man. In the collective myth and in the family romance, the parents are generally split into "real" and "foster" and sometimes into "good" and "bad." Sometimes the foster parents are of lowly origin or are even animals. The myth of the hero culminates when the son returns to displace the father and, in the case of Oedipus, to marry the mother. Thereby he assumes the high or noble station which is rightly his.[2]

It was in the context of thoroughgoing social change after 1830 that an early version of the Southern family romance first surfaced—"the plantation legend." Writers in both sections of the country, particularly

9. Sigmund Freud, "Family Romances," *The Sexual Enlightenment of Children*, ed. by Philip Rieff (New York: Collier Books, 1974), pp. 41–45.
1. Otto Rank, *The Myth of the Birth of the Hero*, ed. by Philip Freund (New York: Vintage, 1959), p. 9.
2. In her *The Ego and the Mechanisms of Defense* (London: Hogarth Press, 1976) Anna Freud gives examples from case histories in which animals serve as stand-ins for the father and reverse the negative perceptions of him: they become friendly and helpful. Slaying the dragon or frightening the beast is a variation on this theme in fairy tales.

popular novelists, found much that troubled them in the restless, acquisitive society of those times. To these writers and their readers, the Rev-
olutionary era seemed the age of heroes, one marked by public-spirited
heroism and cultural achievement. By contrast, American society in the
age of Jackson seemed hopelessly materialistic and a cultural wasteland.
Decline had set in.

By way of cultural compensation, popular fiction pictured Southern
society as essentially different from the rest of the country. It was more
stable and settled than the chaotic West, less acquisitive and venal than
the commercial Northeast. At the center of this popular image of the
South was the plantation legend, which expressed a yearning for "intellectual distinction, genteel taste, private and public decorum."[3] But the
legend was also shadowed by the fear of the family's dissolution. Its hero,
the Southern Cavalier, had to "kneel down before the altar of femininity
and familial benevolence."[4] It was felt that if somehow Yankee energy
and Southern grace could be united, ultimately, America's future would
be right.

Besides the idealization of the planter, the celebration of the feminine, and the lip service paid to the family, the plantation legend also
existed to justify slavery or at least minimize its malevolence. The slave
was pictured in "his dependence and helplessness" and "unquenchable
happiness"; in more tense moments his "animality" was emphasized.[5]
The process of sentimentalization was reflected in both the image of the
woman and the slave. All were made part of the family. Not surprisingly, Southerners rejected the notion that they were peculiarly cruel or
unjust. Rather, slave-holding became emblematic of a higher concern
for a helpless and uncivilized race whom the Southern "fathers" and
"mothers" gently but firmly disciplined.

If the prewar plantation legend emphasized the differences between
the sections, the popular literature of the post-Reconstruction period
served as a means of sectional reconciliation. Even more than the prewar plantation literature, this fiction was suffused with nostalgia for a
way of life which had "gone with the wind." Once again the cultural
distinctiveness of the Old South was emphasized. While the rest of the
nation was becoming increasingly heterogeneous, the South prided itself
on its aristocratic origins and bemoaned the destruction of the aristocratic way of life. Indeed, as late as the 1930s (and some will remember
more recently), sociologist Hortense Powdermaker observed that middle-
class white Southerners were obsessed with establishing their aristocratic
credentials. Those who denied or disdained such connections were rare.[6]
Another central theme in the fiction of writers such as Thomas Nelson

3. Taylor, *Cavalier and Yankee*, p. 124.
4. *Ibid.*, p. 126.
5. *Ibid.*, p. 283.
6. Hortense Powdermaker, *After Freedom* (New York: Atheneum, 1968).

Page and Thomas Dixon, author of *The Clansman*, from which the film *The Birth of a Nation* was made, was the way in which the good white folk of both sections united against those who insisted upon black equality, now that slavery had been destroyed. "The devoted slave" was contrasted with "the confused freedman."[7] Though few favored the restoration of the peculiar institution, the justification for racial segregation and black subordination stood at the center of this popular fiction.

This post-Reconstruction popular fiction was the imaginative expression of the "New South Creed," a vision advanced by Southern intellectuals and publicists. The New South Creed emphasized the need for industrial development, diversified agriculture, sectional reconciliation, and racial comity, with blacks placed in a subordinate position. Though the New South Creed was a "modernizing" ideology, it also paid homage to the Old South and the Lost Cause. In this sense it was the post-Reconstruction expression of the Southern attempt to square the cultural circle, to combine the best of the Old South with the spirit of modern industrial capitalism.

*   *   *

At this point, it would be well to draw back and flesh out more fully the notion of the family romance, Southern style, as it stood at the beginning of World War I. At the center of the family romance, in its patriarchal expression, was the father. Powerful though the Southern woman might be in fact, she was distinctly subordinate in the romance to the powerful and heroic father. As the romance emerged in the post-Civil War years less emphasis was placed upon the Cavalier per se. The "father" came to be the gracious, courteous, but tough planter of the pre-War years who had led the heroic and collective struggle against the Yankees. He was the "presiding presence" in the romance; and, as he faded from the scene, the grandsons in the early years of the century idealized the great hero of the romance even more. Measured against the heroic generation of the grandfathers, the fathers seemed rather unheroic and prosaic to their sons. The family romance thus pitted son against father and often joined grandson and grandfather. Further, though many Southerners embraced the gospel of progress in the post-Reconstruction years, this optimistic stance was shadowed by the strong suspicion that the age of heroes lay in the past. Decline was an integral part of the Southern family romance.[8]

7. Paul Buck, *The Road to Renunion: 1865–1900* (Boston: Little, Brown, 1937), p. 213.
8. The grandson-grandfather alliance is implicit in the family romance. As Ernest Jones notes in "The Significance of the Grandfather for the Fate of the Individual" and "The Phantasy of the Reversal of Generations," *Papers on Psycho-analysis* (London: Ballière, Tindall, and Cox, 1918), pp. 652–57, 658–63, the grandfather can serve as the heroic substitute for the demoted father. In his "Reflections on American Identity" in *Childhood and Society*, 2nd rev. ed. (New York: W. W. Norton, 1963), Erik Erikson observes how American mothers often hold up their fathers to their sons as figures of power and integrity while subtly rejecting their husbands (pp. 312–14).

If the Southern family romance placed the father-son relationship at its center, the white woman was expected to play the role of the mother. As mistress of the plantation she was the lady bountiful, caring for the wants and needs of her family, both white and black. A prime, though late, example of this characterization is Ellen O'Hara, Scarlett's mother in *Gone With the Wind*. The Southern woman was caught in a social double-bind: toward men she was to be submissive, meek and gentle; with the children and slaves and in the management of the household, she was supposed to display competence, initiative, and energy. But she remained a shadowy figure, always there and ever necessary, but rarely emerging in full force. She was "queen of the home."[9]

Another way of understanding the role of the mother in the Southern family romance is to observe that sexuality or erotic appeal was denied her. In extreme form she was stripped of any emotional, nurturing attributes at all. Eventually, she came to assume a quasi-Virgin Mary role as the aesexual mother of the Southern male hero. It is of course difficult to know what the relationship between this cultural role and the reality of Southern life was. Lillian Smith was to observe that her mother's generation (that of the late nineteenth century) shied away from anything having to do with sexuality or the body. It became an object of disgust, a matter of shame. And though Anne Firor Scott has challenged Smith's indictment of Southern women's coldness and antisensuality, the accepted values of the culture, reinforced by Victorian morality, surely had a profound effect.[1]

One can only speculate that the cultural denial of sexuality or nurturing warmth to the white woman must have something to do with the lack of strongly sexed women in much of the literature of the Southern Renaissance. One thinks here of Tate's *The Fathers*, which opens with the funeral of Lacy Buchan's mother, of Faulkner's series of neurasthenic women, castrating bitches, spiky but asexual older aunts and grandmothers, and the absence of the mother in "The Bear" or her shadowy role in *Absalom, Absalom!*; of Will Percy's neglect of his mother in his autobiography; of Carson McCullers's *A Member of the Wedding*, and indeed all her stories in which a mother scarcely appears; and of Lillian Smith's *Strange Fruit* and *Killers of the Dream*. In the case of Faulkner, it was not, as we shall see, that his mother played a minor role—far from it. But Southern women remained neglected figures in the cultural articulations and literary renderings of the family romance.

Thus to break the hold of the family romance it was not the father alone, but the grandfather as well, who had to be demystified.

9. This phrase comes from Anne F. Scott, *The Southern Lady: From Pedestal to Politics, 1830–1930* (Chicago: University of Chicago Press, 1970). See also Carrol Smith-Rosenberg, "The Hysterical Woman: Sex Roles and Role Conflict in 19th Century America," *Social Research* 39 (Winter 1972), 652–78; and Barbara Welter, "The Cult of True Womanhood: 1820–60," *American Quarterly* 18 (Summer 1966), 151–74.

1. Scott, *The Southern Lady*, p. 218.

If (in the family romance) the white father and mother assumed dominant positions, blacks occupied the role of permanently delegitimized and often literally illegitimate children. Yet there was a central contradiction at the core of the notion of the South as a "family." On the one hand racial ideology dictated that blacks could not be acknowledged as literal members of the family. * * * To recognize blacks would be to soil the purity of the racial-social lineage, the infrastructure of the tradition. On the other hand the family romance also claimed that blacks were "childlike" and thus permanent members of the metaphorical Southern family. To take the family romance literally would be to negate it; and this is what happened in the writings of Faulkner and Lillian Smith.

Emotional ambivalence and role reversals can readily be seen in the actual and fantasized roles of black men and women in the romance. The black male was ideally a loyal figure of childlike wisdom and Christian charity, a wise and forgiving grandfather or naïve, childlike retainer. Yet he might also be the "bad Nigger," the rapist and the insurrectionist, bent on exacting his blood lust from whites. D. W. Griffith's *The Birth of a Nation*, based on Thomas Dixon's *The Clansman*, and again *Gone With the Wind* present both of these aspects quite clearly.

Similar contradictions existed in the role of the black woman. In his analysis, Rank observed that the foster "mothering agent" of the mythological hero was usually someone of low or peasant origin or even, as in the Romulus and Remus legend, an animal. With this in mind, the ambiguities inherent in the role of the black "mammy" became clearer. Because of her skin color, she was an illegitimate sibling, childlike though not without force of will. Yet the romance, and sometimes reality, contradicted this image by presenting her as the loving foster mother to whom the Southern hero owed all. In this role, as the legendary "kind animal," she was a cultural rebuke to the stereotypically cold and distant white mother. In Lillian Smith's work she becomes the "real" mother; that is, the one who nurtures and truly mothers. And yet the black woman was also regarded as sexually ardent and animal-like in passion. Thus she was a sultry temptress and nurturing mammy, inferior sibling and true parent, incestuous object and idealized mother. What linked these rather contradictory roles was the fact that to the black woman were attributed the emotional impulses denied to the white woman.

Thus, in the reality and cultural fantasy of the South, the roles of parent and child attributed to white and black respectively were affirmed, denied, and inverted. Emotional acknowledgment was often accompanied by social denial. The burdens of this psycho-cultural romance fell most heavily on the black male and the white female. The white woman was denied sexual and nurturing attributes, which were displaced onto the black woman. Analogously, the black man suffered the worst of both worlds: as symbolic phallus he was particularly open to violent retaliation, most horribly in the castration rituals that accompanied lynching, while as wise "uncle" he was denied authentic manhood. The actual black family was most vulnerable in its paternal role, for the black father lacked control over the actual or symbolic systems of survival, while the white family was weakest in its maternal position. To the former was denied power; to the latter, sexuality. Hence, as we shall see, the ultimate challenge to the family romance was the sexual relationship of black men and white women, a violation of the incest and the miscegenation taboos.

This then was the Southern family romance, the central fantasy structure of Southern culture, as the 1920s gave way to the Depression decade. As we have seen, the family romance was riven with contradictions, particularly in its vision of blacks and its ambiguous assessment of the claims of the past measured against the vision of the future. With social and economic stability disappearing, the tradition of the family romance came under intense scrutiny. This was the assignment and the burden of the generation of the 1930s.

CAROLYN PORTER

Faulkner's America †

The antebellum South's self-made man driven by entrepreneurial aspirations has been obscured, largely by two opposed historical interpretations, neither of which is congruent with Faulkner's. The first and less formidable of the two is that of the prewar South as a land of yeoman farmers, a vision first projected during the Roosevelt era by Frank Owsley and the Agrarians at Vanderbilt. Using census records, Owsley and his students found a significant majority of small farmers, and argued that they constituted the backbone of a Southern democracy; this argument called into question the traditional view of a plantation aristocracy dominating the Old South from behind white porticos and fragrant magnolias. Critics soon discredited many of Owsley's statistical methods, and subsequent research has considerably muddied the waters first stirred up by Owsley's insistence upon the hegemony of Plain Folk. Yet the literary wing of the Vanderbilt movement has continued to exercise its influence, especially over our view of Southern writers, and therefore it is worth clarifying the differences between Faulkner's social vision and Owsley's.

There is no doubt, of course, about Faulkner's recognition of, and respect for, the small farmers of the South, nor about his view of the

†From *Seeing and Being: The Plight of the Participant Observer in Emerson, James, Adams, and Faulkner* (Middletown: Wesleyan University Press, 1981), 222–30.

South as populated largely by them. He once pointed out at the University of Virginia that "the elegance of the colonial plantation didn't exist" in his country, which was still frontier, a place where people "lived from day to day with a bluff and crude hardiness, but with a certain simplicity." Faulkner's fiction depicts many small farmers from the hills, usually with genuine sympathy for their straitened circumstances. But Faulkner's vision of the prewar South's class structure, as he described it to Malcolm Cowley, while acknowledging "a middle class fixed upon the land," does not finally accord with Owsley's vision, essentially because for Faulkner that class harbors men with aspirations to rise. Responding to the questions of why no significant literature was produced in the South in this period, Faulkner told Cowley:

> There was no literate middle class to produce a literature. In a pastoral cityless land they lived remote and at economic war with both slave and slaveholder. When they emerged, gradually, son by infrequent son, like Old Sutpen, it was not to establish themselves as a middle class but to make themselves barons, too.

It would appear that Faulkner's view has much to recommend it over Owsley's. For one thing, the political behavior of the small farmers in Mississippi suggests that they had their ambitions as well as their resentments. While their support for the Confederacy was not always wholehearted, we cannot infer from this that they were all free of the desire to emulate the Cotton Snobs. How, for example, are we to interpret the debate that occurred in the Mississippi legislature in 1852 over a bill to prohibit the importation of slaves? The small farmers opposed the bill on the grounds that the rich planters would be able to get around the restriction (as they indeed had done before), and acquire more slaves, while the small farmers would not, and thus their capacity to extend and develop their property would be seriously hindered. At the time there was a labor shortage, a problem which affected the large planters much less than the small. A small planter who had succeeded in expanding his landholdings might be unable to realize a profit for lack of a labor force to cultivate his cotton. Many of these farmers were doubtless fighting a defensive battle rather than an aggressive one; as in the Northeast, rising and declining men were often fighting concentrated wealth for different motives. But clearly, given the economic as well as the social value of slaves, the debate over their importation suggests that there was built into the small farmers' bitter conflict with the Cotton Snobs of the Delta an aspiration among some at least to close the economic distance between the two. Faulkner's vision of the antebellum farmer acknowledges, as Owsley's cannot, the dynamic quality of the social structure, reflected in the aspirations of some farmers to emerge from the ranks of the yeomanry. More important, Faulkner's view encompasses what Owsley's struggles to exclude; Owsley's thesis produces its benign and comforting picture of a Southern democracy made up of common men only by excluding as exceptions those common men who happen to be black and enslaved by those other exceptions who are white slaveowners. Such exceptions do not prove any rule; on the contrary, they constitute one. Faulkner, by contrast, clearly regards the farmer's "economic war with both slave and slaveholder" as a central feature of his social position. But whether Faulkner's historical vision is superior to Owsley's—as I think it certainly is—is less important than the fact of its difference. The difference ultimately derives from the fact that Faulkner, unlike the Agrarians of the 1930s and 1940s, did not view the Old South as a world uncontaminated by the spirit of capitalism. Given the essential continuity of both his great-grandfather's career—from Whig lawyer with landed property to railroad entrepreneur—and his grandfather's—from law partner of a Lamar protégé to banker and owner of a variety of businesses to be handed on to his sons—Faulkner could hardly have failed to recognize the longstanding presence of the entrepreneurial drive in his "country." [1]

More decisive by far than Owsley's thesis in obscuring the entrepreneurial designs of the South's rising men has been their use of slave labor and the futile and twisted defenses they were constrained to make of it. Louis Hartz put their dilemma most effectively in a classic description of John Taylor's frustrated response to it:

In the time of Jefferson the agony of the South had been complex. Not only had John Taylor been embarrassed by slavery because of liberalism, but he had been embarrassed by liberalism because even then he had nourished a Disraelian streak. Now, in the age of Fitzhugh, when both of these problems would seem to have been solved, Taylor discovered that he could not be a real Disraeli even if given a chance to be one. He was a plantation capitalist, and in the Southwest, for all of its stratified social life, he was a very new, very raw, very fierce plantation capitalist. And so the sweat that had to go into making the South medieval was even greater than the sweat that had gone into making it modern.

In recent years, new sweat has gone into making the Old South a paternalistic society based on a slave economy rather than a capitalist one. While Faulkner's vision of the antebellum South has a good deal more in common with Eugene Genovese's than with Owsley's, it nonetheless conflicts decisively with Genovese's view of the South as a paternalistic society which rightly thought of itself as fundamentally distinct from, and opposed to, the North's competitive capitalist system. Once again,

1. Frederick L. Gwynn and Joseph L. Blotner, eds., *Faulkner in the University* (New York: Vintage, 1965), 131; Faulkner, "To Malcolm Cowley," January 1946, in Joseph L. Blotner, ed., *Selected Letters of William Faulkner* (New York: Random House, 1977), 216; Paul W. Gates, *The Farmer's Age: Agriculture, 1815–1860* (New York: Holt, Rinehart, 1960) 151; and Frank L. Owsley, *Plain Folks of the Old South* (Baton Rouge: LSU Press, 1950).

the point of deepest conflict lies in the issue of the parvenu, the rising man of the period whose aristocratic pretensions Genovese reads as evidence of a distinctive paternalist ideology dominating the South. His classic statement of this position comes in his attack on Wilbur Cash in *The World the Slaveholders Made*, where Genovese argues that such pretensions ought to be taken seriously as indications of the difference between the social vision inspiring Southerners and that inspiring Northerners, rather than merely as a thin veneer covering a raw Southern parvenu. "The questions," Genovese says, "come to these: Did the rising planters of the Southwest during the 1830's have before them, as an ideal future for themselves and their children, Virginia or Massachusetts? the Cavalier or the financier? Were they, in their economy and social relations, going down a bourgeois or an aristocratic road?" Lest there be any doubt about how distinct these roads are in Genovese's mind, it is worth quoting another passage, this one from *The Political Economy of Slavery*:

> At their best, Southern ideals constituted a rejection of the crass, vulgar, inhumane elements of capitalist society. The slaveholders simply could not accept the idea that the cash nexus offered a permissible basis for human relations. Even the vulgar parvenu of the Southwest embraced the plantation myth and refused to make a virtue of necessity by glorifying the competitive side of slavery as civilization's highest achievement. The slaveholders generally, and the planters in particular, did identify their own ideals with the essence of civilization, and given their sense of honor, were prepared to defend them at any cost.

It is worth remarking, of course, that "at their best," Northern ideals also constituted a rejection of the evils of capitalist society; the South in the antebellum period was by no means alone in staunchly rejecting the cash nexus as a "permissible basis for human relations." But presumably, Genovese would not dispute this point, since his primary aim is to underscore the extent to which the plantation myth provided a social and cultural vehicle for such ideals which was decisively different from any the North could offer, and this because for Genovese, the paternalist ideology fits a slave economy, not a capitalist one.[2]

This claim has a good deal to recommend it on logical grounds, and in traversing those grounds over the years, Genovese has shown how deeply paternalism saturated the consciousness of the Old South. Faulkner's approach to the antebellum South in *Absalom, Absalom!* relies heavily upon a similar apprehension of paternalism's hegemony, but for Faulkner, paternalism is rooted in American, not merely Southern, his-

2. Louis Hartz, *The Liberal Tradition in America* (New York: Harcourt, Brace, 1955), 149; Eugene Genovese, *The World the Slaveholders Made* (New York: Vintage, 1971), 139; and Eugene Genovese, *The Political Economy of Slavery* (New York: Vintage, 1961), 30.

tory and the conflicts—both theoretical and historical—into which it led the South had their origin not in an opposition between two economic systems at war with one another, but rather in a set of contradictions inherent in American capitalist development. Again, I think Faulkner's view has much to recommend it over Genovese's, but I do not wish to argue that point so much as to call attention to the difference between the two. The ideological dominance of paternalism in the South need not be disputed in order to realize that both the plantation myth and the paternalism inscribed in it were themselves the product of capitalist expansion.

Even a brief review of the plantation legend's history reveals why the rising planter of the Southwest never faced the choice Genovese implies he made in refusing to glorify "the competitive side of slavery." As William O. Taylor has shown, it was not really until the 1830s that the plantation legend as we have come to know it first developed. Previously, the South had been regarded, at least by most cultivated Northerners, as a land of barbaric "Tuckahoes." Only with *Swallow Barn*, published in 1832, did the plantation begin to assume those trappings of pastoral grace and refinement for which it has since become famous. John Pendleton Kennedy started out in *Swallow Barn* making fun of Tidewater Virginia and ended up sentimentalizing and finally eulogizing it as an image of an ideal America. Why did this happen? Kennedy himself was no planter; he was the son of a Baltimore merchant whose country home was not in the Tidewater, but in the Cumberland district of Virginia. Taylor explores this question at length, and in the process reveals just how deeply rooted was the plantation myth in a capitalist America. For one thing, the plantation ideal would serve as the repository of traditional rural values; thus *Swallow Barn* met a widespread need to "sentimentalize country life" felt by urban dwellers who had left the provinces to make their way in the cities, where lay both the opportunities for rising, and the corruptions attendant upon them.[3]

In addition to projecting a pastoral retreat from city life, the plantation legend had other compensatory attractions to offer as well. It incorporated, for example, one of the major, if not *the* major, nineteenth-century strategies for protecting human relations from the contamination of the cash nexus—the cult of domesticity promulgated most notably by Sarah Hale in *Godey's Lady's Book*. Sarah Hale set out to combat the opportunism and corruption of the marketplace by sanctifying the home and elevating the role of wife-and-mother to the position of the mainstay of social cohesion and the fountainhead of moral influence. The ideological value of the home was itself tied to an expanding capitalism, of course. As the nineteenth century unfolded, women's position was

---

3. William O. Taylor, *Cavalier and Yankee* (Garden City, N. Y.: Doubleday, 1963) 156–72, 165.

increasingly undermined; no longer called upon to produce what they could now purchase, women moved into the only role in the marketplace available to them, that of consumer. Insofar as they remained producers, they produced words, sentiment, and influence, all in an effort to stem the tide of social atomization by an appeal to the home as the bulwark of idealism. The plantation legend served as a perfect vehicle for the values of home and hearth, as Harriet Beecher Stowe understood, with well-known consequences. In *Uncle Tom's Cabin*, she appealed to the values of the home against those of the marketplace, focusing her harshest criticism not on the South, whose paternalistic ideals she shared, but on the bourgeois rapacity of slave traders and overseers, and on the hypocrisy of Northern clergymen. Stowe did not speak for the North as against the South; she spoke for the values of the family against those of the businessman, an opposition in fact far more visible in Northern society than in Southern, where the business was cotton and the businessman a planter. As Taylor remarks, the plantation myth "was not the South's image concocted to propagandize the North, nor was it the woman's or the man's; it was the nineteenth century's. Thackeray's plantation was scarcely different." Nor did the century's more acute ciritcal observers fail to see the actual motives being at once served and obscured by the myth. Balzac's Jacques Collin (alias M. Vautrin, alias Cheat-Death) makes those motives clear in the middle of his stunning address to Eugène Rastignat in *Père Goriot*:

> You see I have a fancy. My notion is to go and live the patriarchal life on a great estate, say a hundred thousand acres, in the United States of America, in the deep South. I intend to be a planter, to have slaves, earn a few nice little millions selling my cattle, my tobacco, my timber, living like a monarch, doing as I like, leading a life unimaginable by people here where we live crouched in a burro made of stone and plaster.

The words "patriarchal life," of course, have a special irony in a novel demonstrating just what happens to fathers in a society increasingly dominated by the cash nexus. To a man with Balzac's knoweldge of and attachment to a genuine aristocracy, the plantation myth was just as vulnerable a screen for entrepreneurial designs as the rhetoric of the "technological sublime" has proved to be. Perhaps it is partly due to a long-standing confusion in the minds of Americans over the difference between capitalist and aristocrat that they have never really been able to resist altogether the plantation myth's attractions. In any case, they have hardly ever succeeded at seeing the myth in such a critical light as Balzac sheds on it. [4]

One reason for the myth's long and virulent career, one suspects, is

4. Taylor, *Cavalier and Yankee*, 92–99, 287–94, 143; Honoré de Balzac, *Old Goriot*, trans. Marian Ayton Crawford (London: Penguin, 1951), 131.

that it is deeply bound up with American aspirations. At least it originated with these aspirations. As Taylor notes, the creation of the impet-
uous Southern Cavalier and the nostalgic portrayal of plantation life
were themselves, in the first instance, the work of the "New Men" of
the postrevolutionary era, "aspiring men" whose appeal to traditional
rural and familial values was made in response to wrenching internal
anxieties about the implications and consequences of their own aspirations to rise. A disaffected Northern Whig like John Kirke Paulding, for
example, having made his way up in society, was increasingly disturbed
by the very social dynamism which had made that rise possible, as well
as by the machine-run future it presented for America. In his efforts to
devise an ideal American identity, modeled after a George Washington
who embodied the virtues of the natural aristocrat and the transcendent
Yankee, Paulding blended the virtues of Southerner, Northerner, and
Westerner, trying to preserve a noble and manly independence without
sacrificing the aspirations of the self-made man. Born in the vexed minds
of the aspiring men of the 1830s, the plantation legend was revived in
the 1880s and 1890s, in the service of another group of rising men—this
time in the South. The Redeemers having wrested control of their states
from the forces of Reconstruction—and this through the collusion of
men like L. Q. C. Lamar with Northern Republicans—the aspiring men
of the late nineteenth century reinvented the "Old South" while pouring
their energies into building the new. The paradox is dramatized by
Faulkner's own grandfather, J. W. T. Falkner, who sported the classic
white suit and panama hat of the Southern Colonel while accumulating
land and businesses galore from his seat in his Oxford bank. In short,
the restoration of the Old South was enacted in the interests of those
who were most actively engaged in exploiting the New South's resources,
as C. Vann Woodward has demonstrated with implacable logic. As
Woodward puts it, "this archaic romanticism, this idealizing of the past,
proceeded from the mouths of the most active propagandists of the New
Order. And this with no apparent sense of inconsistency, certainly none
of duplicity." In neither phase of its history did acceptance of the plantation legend apparently imply an opposition to entrepreneurial designs.
In both its inception and its revival, in both North and South, and both
before and after the war, the plantation legend served the interests of
aspiring men.[5]

5. Taylor, *Cavalier and Yankee*, 179–81, 46, 204–39; C. Vann Woodward, *Origins of the New South, 1877–1913* (Baton Rouge: LSU Press, 1971), 157.

CRITICISM

JEAN-PAUL SARTRE

On *The Sound and the Fury:*
Time in the Work of Faulkner †

The first thing that strikes one in reading *The Sound and the Fury* is its
technical oddity. Why has Faulkner broken up the time of his story and
scrambled the pieces? Why is the first window that opens out on this
fictional world the consciousness of an idiot? The reader is tempted to
look for guide-marks and to re-establish the chronology for himself:

> Jason and Caroline Compson have had three sons and a daugh-
> ter. The daughter, Caddy, has given herself to Dalton Ames and
> become pregnant by him. Forced to get hold of a husband quickly
> . . .

Here the reader stops, for he realizes he is telling another story. Faulkner did not first conceive this orderly plot so as to shuffle it afterwards
like a pack of cards; he could not tell it in any other way. In the classical
novel, action involves a central complication; for example, the murder
of old Karamazov or the meeting of Edouard and Bernard in *The Coiners.*
But we look in vain for such a complication in *The Sound and the Fury.*
Is it the castration of Benjy or Caddy's wretched amorous adventure or
Quentin's suicide or Jason's hatred of his niece? As soon as we begin to
look at any episode, it opens up to reveal behind it other episodes, all
the other episodes. Nothing happens; the story does not unfold; we discover it under each word, like an obscene and obstructing presence,
more or less condensed, depending upon the particular case. It would
be a mistake to regard these irregularities as gratuitous exercises in virtuosity. A fictional technique always relates back to the novelist's metaphysics. The critic's task is to define the latter before evaluating the former.
Now, it is immediately obvious that Faulkner's metaphysics is a metaphysics of time.

Man's misfortune lies in his being time-bound.

> . . . a man is the sum of his misfortunes. One day you'd think
> misfortune would get tired, but then time is your misfortune . . .

Such is the real subject of the book. And if the technique Faulkner
has adopted seems at first a negation of temporality, the reason is that
we confuse temporality with chronology. It was man who invented dates
and clocks.

† From *Literary and Philosophical Essays,* trans. Annette Michelson (London: Rider, 1955), 79–
87. Reprinted by permission of Rosica Colin, Ltd., London. © Editions Gallimard 1947, 1975.

> Constant speculation regarding the position of mechanical hands on an arbitrary dial which is a symptom of mind-function. Excrement Father said like sweating.

In order to arrive at real time, we must abandon this invented measure which is not a measure of anything.

> . . . time is dead as long as it is being clicked off by little wheels; only when the clock stops does time come to life.

Thus, Quentin's gesture of breaking his watch has a symbolic value; it gives us access to a time without clocks. The time of Benjy, the idiot, who does not know how to tell time, is also clockless.

What is thereupon revealed to us is the present, and not the ideal limit whose place is neatly marked out between past and future. Faulkner's present is essentially catastrophic. It is the event which creeps up on us like a thief, huge, unthinkable—which creeps up on us and then disappears. Beyond this present time there is nothing, since the future does not exist. The present rises up from sources unknown to us and drives away another present; it is forever beginning anew. "And . . . and . . . and then." Like Dos Passos, but much more discreetly, Faulkner makes an accretion of his narrative. The actions themselves, even when seen by those who perform them, burst and scatter on entering the present.

> I went to the dresser and took up the watch with the face still down. I tapped the crystal on the dresser and caught the fragments of glass in my hand and put them into the ashtray and twisted the hands off and put them in the tray. The watch ticked on.

The other aspect of this present is what I shall call a sinking in. I use this expression, for want of a better one, to indicate a kind of motionless movement of this formless monster. In Faulkner's work, there is never any progression, never anything which comes from the future. The present has not first been a future possibility, and when my friend, after having been *he for whom I am waiting*, finally appears. No, to be present means to appear without any reason and to sink in. This sinking in is not an abstract view. It is within things themselves that Faulkner perceives it and tries to make it felt.

> The train swung around the curve, the engine puffing with short, heavy blasts, and they passed smoothly from sight that way, with that quality of shabby and timeless patience, of static serenity . . .

And again,

> Beneath the sag of the buggy the hooves neatly rapid like motions of a lady doing embroidery, *diminishing without progress*[1] like a figure on a treadmill being drawn rapidly off-stage.

1. The author's [Faulkner's] *italics*.

It seems as though Faulkner has laid hold of a frozen speed at the very heart of things; he is grazed by congealed spurts that wane and dwindle without moving.

This fleeting and unimaginable immobility can, however, be arrested and pondered. Quentin can say, "I broke my watch," but when he says it, his gesture is *past*. The past is named and related; it can, to a certain extent, be fixed by concepts or recognized by the heart. We pointed out earlier, in connection with *Sartoris*, that Faulkner always showed events when they were already over. In *The Sound and the Fury* everything has already happened. It is this that enables us to understand that strange remark by one of the heroes, "*Fui. Non sum.*"[2] In this sense, too, Faulkner is able to make man a sum total without a future: "The sum of his climactic experiences," "The sum of his misfortunes," "The sum of what have you." At every moment, one draws a line, since the present is nothing but a chaotic din, a future that is past. Faulkner's vision of the world can be compared to that of a man sitting in an open car and looking backwards. At every moment, formless shadows, flickerings, faint tremblings and patches of light rise up on either side of him, and only afterwards, when he has a little perspective, do they become trees and men and cars.

The past takes on a sort of super-reality; its contours are hard and clear, unchangeable. The present, nameless and fleeting, is helpless before it. It is full of gaps, and, through these gaps, things of the past, fixed, motionless and silent as judges or glances, come to invade it. Faulkner's monologues remind one of aeroplane trips full of air-pockets. At each pocket, the hero's consciousness "sinks back into the past" and rises only to sink back again. The present is not; it becomes. Everything *was*. In *Sartoris*, the past was called "the stories" because it was a matter of family memories that had been constructed, because Faulkner had not yet found his technique.

In *The Sound and the Fury* he is more individual and more undecided. But it is so strong an obsession that he is sometimes apt to disguise the present, and the present moves along in the shadow, like an underground river, and reappears only when it itself is past. When Quentin insults Bland,[3] he is not even aware of doing so; he is reliving his dispute with Dalton Ames. And when Bland punches his nose, this brawl is covered over and hidden by Quentin's past brawl with Ames. Later on, Shreve relates how Bland hit Quentin; he relates this scene because it has become a story, but while it was unfolding in the present, it was only a furtive movement, covered over by veils. Someone once told me about an old monitor who had grown senile. His memory had stopped like a broken watch; it had been arrested at his fortieth year. He was sixty, but

2. "I was. I am not" [*Editor*].
3. Compare the dialogue with Bland inserted into the middle of the dialogue with Ames: "Did you ever have a sister?" etc., and the inextricable confusion of the two fights.

didn't know it. His last memory was that of a schoolyard and his daily walk around it. Thus, he interpreted his present in terms of his past and walked about his table, convinced that he was watching students during recreation.

Faulkner's characters are like that, only worse, for their past, which is in order, does not assume chronological order. It is, in actual fact, a matter of emotional constellations. Around a few central themes (Caddy's pregnancy, Benjy's castration, Quentin's suicide) gravitate innumerable silent masses. Whence the absurdity of the chronology of "the assertive and contradictory assurance" of the clock. The order of the past is the order of the heart. It would be wrong to think that when the present is past it becomes our closest memory. Its metamorphosis can cause it to sink to the bottom of our memory, just as it can leave it floating on the surface. Only its own density and the dramatic meaning of our life can determine at what level it will remain.

Such is the nature of Faulkner's time. Isn't there something familiar about it? This unspeakable present, leaking at every seam, these sudden invasions of the past, this emotional order, the opposite of the voluntary and intellectual order that is chronological but lacking in reality, these memories, these monstrous and discontinuous obsessions, these intermittences of the heart—are not these reminiscent of the lost and recaptured time of Marcel Proust? I am not unaware of the differences between the two; I know, for instance, that for Proust salvation lies in time itself, in the full reappearance of the past. For Faulkner, on the contrary, the past is never lost, unfortunately; it is always there, it is an obsession. One escapes from the temporal world only through mystic ecstasies. A mystic is always a man who wishes to forget something, his self or, more often, language or objective representations. For Faulkner, time must be forgotten.

'Quentin, I give you the mausoleum of all hope and desire; it's rather excruciatingly apt that you will use it to gain the reductio ad absurdum of all human experience which can fit your individual needs no better than it fitted his or his father's. I give it to you not that you may remember time, *but that you might forget it now and then for a moment* and not spend all your breath trying to conquer it. Because no battle is ever won he said. They are not even fought. The field only reveals to man his own folly and despair, and victory is an illusion of philosophers and fools.'

It is because he has forgotten time that the hunted negro in *Light in August* suddenly achieves his strange and horrible happiness.

It's not when you realize that nothing can help you—religion, pride, anything—it's when you realize that you don't need any aid.

But for Faulkner, as for Proust, time is, above all, *that which sepa-rates*. One recalls the astonishment of the Proustian heroes who can no longer enter into their past loves, of those lovers depicted in *Les Plaisirs et Les Jours*,[4] clutching their passions, afraid they will pass and knowing they will. We find the same anguish in Faulkner.

> . . . people cannot do anything very dreadful at all, they cannot even remember tomorrow what seemed dreadful today . . .

and

> . . . a love or a sorrow is a bond purchased without design and which matures willynilly and is recalled without warning to be replaced by whatever issue the gods happen to be floating at the time . . .

To tell the truth, Proust's fictional technique *should have been* Faulkner's. It was the logical conclusion of his metaphysics. But Faulkner is a lost man, and it is because he feels lost that he takes risks and pursues his thought to its uttermost consequences. Proust is a Frenchman and a classicist. The French lose themselves only a little at a time and always manage to find themselves again. Eloquence, intellectuality and a liking for clear ideas were responsible for Proust's retaining at least the sem-blance of chronology.

The basic reason for this relationship is to be found in a very general literary phenomenon. Most of the great contemporary authors, Proust, Joyce, Dos Passos, Faulkner, Gide, and Virginia Woolf, have tried, each in his own way, to distort time. Some of them have deprived it of its past and future in order to reduce it to the pure intuition of the instant; others, like Dos Passos, have made of it a dead and closed memory. Proust and Faulkner have simply decapitated it. They have deprived it of its future, that is, its dimension of deeds and freedom. Proust's heroes never undertake anything. They do, of course, make plans, but their plans remain stuck to them and cannot be projected like a bridge beyond the present. They are day-dreams that are put to flight by reality. The Albertine[5] who appears is not the one we were expecting, and the expec-tation was merely a slight, inconsequential hesitation, limited to the moment only. As to Faulkner's heroes, they never look ahead. They face backwards as the car carries them along. The coming suicide which casts its shadow over Quentin's last day is not a human possibility; not for a second does Quentin envisage the possibility of *not* killing himself. This suicide is an immobile wall, a *thing* which he approaches back-wards, and which he neither wants to nor can conceive.

4. A novel by Marcel Proust, c. 1924 [*Editor*].
5. In *A la recherche du temps perdu* (*A Remembrance of Things Past*) by Proust, Albertine is a lesbian attracted by and to the narrator.

. . . you seem to regard it merely as an experience that will whiten your hair overnight so to speak without altering your appearance at all . . .

It is not an *undertaking*, but a fatality. In losing its element of possibility it ceases to exist in the future. It is already present, and Faulkner's entire art aims at suggesting to us that Quentin's monologues and his last walk *are already* his suicide. This, I think, explains the following curious paradox: Quentin thinks of his last day in the past, like someone who is remembering. But in that case, since the hero's last thoughts coincide approximately with the bursting of his memory and its annihilation, who is remembering? The inevitable reply is that the novelist's skill consists in the choice of the present moment from which he narrates the past. And Faulkner, like Salacrou in *L'Inconnu d'Arras*,[6] has chosen the infinitesimal instant of death. Thus, when Quentin's memory begins to unravel its recollections ("Through the wall I heard Shreve's bed-springs and then his slippers on the floor hishing. I got up . . .") *he is already dead*. All this artistry and, to speak frankly, all this illusion are meant, then, merely as substitutions for the intuition of the future lacking in the author himself. This explains everything, particularly the irrationality of time; since the present is the unexpected, the formless can be determined only by an excess of memories. We now also understand why duration is "man's characteristic misfortune." If the future has reality, time withdraws us from the past and brings us nearer to the future; but if you do away with the future, time is no longer that which separates, that which cuts the present off from itself. "You cannot bear to think that someday it will no longer hurt you like this." Man spends his life struggling against time, and time, like an acid, eats away at man, eats him away from himself and prevents him from fulfilling his human character. Everything is absurd. "Life is a tale told by an idiot, full of sound and fury, signifying nothing."

But is man's time without a future? I can understand that the nail's time, or the clod's or the atom's, is a perpetual present. But is man a thinking nail? If you begin by plunging him into universal time, the time of planets and nebulae, of tertiary flexures' and animal species, as into a bath of sulphuric acid, then the question is settled. However, a consciousness buffeted so from one instant to another ought, *first of all*, to be a consciousness and then, *afterwards*, to be temporal; does anyone believe that time can come to it from the outside? Consciousness can "exist within time" only on condition that it becomes time as a result of the very movement by which it becomes consciousness. It must become "temporalized," as Heidegger says. We can no longer arrest man at each present and define him as "the sum of what he has." The nature of

---

6. Armand Salacrou, a contemporary French dramatist (born 1899), who wrote *L'Inconnu d'Arras*, *(The Unknown Woman from Arras)*, in which a man learns of his wife's infidelity and kills himself.

consciousness implies, on the contrary, that it project itself into the future. We can understand what it is only through what it will be. It is determined in its present being by its own possibilities. This is what Heidegger calls "the silent force of the possible." You will not recognize within yourself Faulkner's man, a creature bereft of possibilities and explicable only in terms of what he has been. Try to pin down your consciousness and probe it. You will see that it is hollow. In it you will find only the future.

I do not even speak of your plans and expectations. But the very gesture that you catch in passing has meaning for you only if you project its fulfilment out of it, out of yourself, into the not-yet. This very cup, with its bottom that you do not see—that you might see, that is, at the end of a movement you have not yet made—this white sheet of paper, whose underside is hidden (but you could turn over the sheet) and all the stable and bulky objects that surround us display their most immediate and densest qualities in the future. Man is not the sum of what he has, but the totality of what he does not yet have, of what he might have. And if we steep ourselves thus in the future, is not the formless brutality of the present thereby attenuated? The single event does not spring on us like a thief, since it is, by nature, a Having-been-future. And if a historian wishes to explain the past, must he not first seek out its future? I am afraid that the absurdity that Faulkner finds in a human life is one that he himself has put there. Not that life is not absurd, but there is another kind of absurdity.

Why have Faulkner and so many other writers chosen this particular absurdity which is so un-novelistic and so untrue? I think we should have to look for the reasons in the social conditions of our present life. Faulkner's despair seems to me to precede his metaphysics. For him, as for all of us, the future is closed. Everything we see and experience impels us to say, "This can't last." And yet change is not even conceivable, except in the form of a cataclysm. We are living in a time of impossible revolutions, and Faulkner uses his extraordinary art to describe our suffocation and a world dying of old age. I like his art, but I do not believe in his metaphysics. A closed future is still a future. "Even if human reality has nothing more 'before' it, even if 'its account is closed,' its being is still determined by this 'self-anticipation.' The loss of all hope, for example, does not deprive human reality of its possibilities; it is simply a way of *being* toward these same possibilities."[7]

7. Heidegger, *Sein und Zeit.*

IRVING HOWE

Faulkner and the Negroes †

All of the tensions in Faulkner's work reach an extreme in his present-
ment of Negro life and character. Problems of value, which in his novels
emerge as problems of perception, become magnified and exacerbated
when he writes about Negroes. In saying this, I would stress that my
concern is not with Faulkner's explicit views about the "racial question,"
or at least that my concern with those views extends no further than the
way they condition the novels. In their own right, Faulkner's opinions
are usually the least interesting aspect of his work: they matter only when
absorbed into his art, there to undergo transformations of a kind that
justify our speaking of literature as a mode of creation.

Complex and ambiguous responses to the Negroes are predictable,
almost conventional among sensitive Southern writers; they stem partly
from an inheritance of guilt and uncertainty, partly from a ripening of
heart. But in Faulkner's fiction, beneath its worried surface of attitude
and idea, there is also a remarkable steadiness of feeling toward the Negro.
His opinions change, his early assurance melts away, his sympathies
visibly enlarge; but always there is a return to one central image, an
image of memory and longing.

*   *   *

In *The Sound and the Fury* the only happy memories the Compsons
retain are memories of scenes in which white and Negro children play
together. In *Absalom, Absalom!* there are no glimpses of friendship
between boys of the two races, but the pioneer innocence of young Sutpen is defined as a freedom from both racial feeling and economic
acquisitiveness. In "The Bear" the boy, Isaac McCaslin, unconsciously—and then with considered assent—claims as his spiritual parent the old Negro, Sam Fathers; and a similar claim determines the
relationship between Chick Mallison and Lucas Beauchamp in *Intruder
in the Dust*. In the story "Go Down, Moses" an old white woman, Miss
Worsham, explains her wish to help an old Negro woman, Mollie Beauchamp, by invoking a childhood friendship of decades ago: "Mollie and
I were born in the same month. We grew up together as sisters would."
By contrast, Joe Christmas in *Light in August* seems the most deprived
of Faulkner's characters precisely because he has no childhood memories to fall back on.

The most dramatic rendering of this theme occurs in the story "The

† From *William Faulkner: A Critical Study*, 3rd ed. (1951; Chicago: University of Chicago Press,
1975), 116–34. Copyright © 1975 by the The University of Chicago Press. Reprinted by permission.

Fire and the Hearth." For the white man Roth Edmonds, Mollie Beauchamp is "the only mother he ever knew, who had not only delivered him on that night of rain and flood . . . but moved into the very house, bringing her own child, the white child and the black one sleeping in the same room with her so that she could suckle them both." As a boy, Roth feels that his home and the home of his Negro friend Henry Beauchamp have "become interchangeable: himself and his foster-brother sleeping on the same pallet in the white man's house or in the same bed in the negro's and eating of the same food at the table in either, actually preferring the negro house. . . ." And then the moment of pride: Roth refuses to share his bed with Henry and lies alone "in a rigid fury of the grief he could not explain, the shame he would not admit." Later he knew "it was grief and was ready to admit it was shame also, wanted to admit it only it was too late then, forever and forever." Forever and forever—the terribleness of this estrangement recurs in Faulkner's work, not simply as a theme, but as a cry of loss and bafflement.

Beneath the white man's racial uneasiness there often beats an impatience with the devices by which men keep themselves apart. Ultimately the whole apparatus of separation must seem too wearisome in its constant call to alertness, too costly in its tax on the emotions, and simply tedious as a brake on spontaneous life. The white man is repeatedly tempted by a memory playing on the rim of his consciousness: a memory of boyhood, when he could live as a brother with his Ringo or Henry Beauchamp—his Nigger Jim or Queequeg—and not yet wince under the needle of self-consciousness. The memory—or a longing in the guise of memory—can be downed by the will and blunted by convention, but it is too lovely and in some final sense too real to be discarded entirely. Beneath the pretense to superiority, the white man reaches for what is true: the time when he could compare bits of knowledge about locomotives with Ringo, share food with Henry Beauchamp, not in equality or out of it—for the mere knowledge of either is a poison—but in a chaste companionship. This is what the white man has lost, forever and forever; and the Negro need not remind him of it, he need only walk past him on the street.

It is a memory fed by guilt. As a confession of failure within society, it shows that status has brought not satisfaction but grief and shame. By questioning the entirety of adult relations, it reveals a hidden weight of despair. Because it glances at the possibilities of life beyond society, the writer can imagine it only in a setting of pastoral simplicity or childhood affection. It is a plea to be forgiven for what is and perhaps—but here Faulkner is uncertain—must be. And it is a yearning to find release, to fall away from the burden of one's whiteness.

Touching as this vision of lost fraternity is, it involves an outrageous naïveté. As Leslie Fielder has remarked, the white man "dreams of his acceptance at the breast he has most utterly offended. It is a dream so sentimental, so outrageous, so desperate that it redeems our concept of boyhood from nostalgia to tragedy." Miss Worsham says of Mollie Beauchamp, "We grew up together as sisters would"—but how many decades of distance have intervened she does not add. It is as though she and Roth Edmonds and all the other whites unconsciously hoped they need but turn again to their childhood companions to find in undiminished purity the love destroyed by caste. How the Negroes themselves might look upon this violated dream they do not think—perhaps they do not dare—to ask.

This image of the white man's longing is not, of course, unique to Faulkner; it appears with astonishing frequency in American writing, and often together with that pastoral impulse so strong among our novelists and poets. Faulkner has rendered it with a particular urgency and sadness, in a setting where at best the races live in quiet rancor. That he has repeatedly turned to this image may be considered a triumph of instinct, but the shape and weight he had given it are a triumph of art.

No such singleness or steadiness can be found in Faulkner's more conscious depiction of the Negro. One finds, instead, a progression from Southern stereotype to personal vision, interrupted by occasional retreats to inherited phobias and to an ideology that is morally inadequate to the vision. These shifting attitudes may be broken into three stages, each symbolized by a major Negro character: Dilsey, Joe Christmas and Lucas Beauchamp.

*   *   *

A gifted artist can salvage significant images of life from the most familiar notions: witness Dilsey in *The Sound and the Fury*. Dilsey is a figure remarkable for her poise, her hard realism, her ability to maintain her selfhood under humiliating conditions. Yet the conception behind Dilsey does not seriously clash with the view of the Negro that could be held by a white man vaguely committed to a benevolent racial superiority. Accepting her inferior status and surviving as a human being despite that acceptance, Dilsey is the last of Faulkner's major Negro characters who can still feel that the South is a "natural" community to which they entirely belong. No sensitive reader would care to deny her strength and moral beauty, but I should like to register a dissent from the effort of certain critics to apotheosize her as the embodiment of Christian resignation and endurance. The terms in which Dilsey is conceived are thoroughly historical, and by their nature become increasingly unavailable to us: a fact which if it does not lessen our admiration for her as a figure in a novel, does limit our capacity to regard her as a moral archetype or model. [1]

1. But is not Don Quixote, surely a moral archetype, also conceived in historical terms unavailable to us? Yes, he is. Don Quixote, however, survives as a figure "beyond" history, we no longer care about his historical genesis or purpose; while Dilsey, we cannot but remember, is a woman

In *The Sound and the Fury* there is an important modulation of attitude toward the Negro. While Dilsey's strength and goodness may be acceptable to traditional paternalism, she gradually assumes a role not quite traditional for the Southern Negro; she becomes, toward the end of the book, an articulate moral critic, the observer with whom the action of the novel is registered and through whom its meanings are amplified. She is not merely the old darky in the kitchen clamping at the absurd and evil ways of the folks up front; at the climax of the novel she rises beyond that role, to a concern with universal problems of justice. This is not to suggest that Dilsey is in any way a rebel against the old order of Southern life. She regards most of the Compsons with contempt not because they are white or representative of the ruling social group but because they do not fulfill the obligations that have accrued to their status. Judging the whites in terms of their own proclaimed values, she criticizes not their exploitation of Negroes but their moral mistreatment of each other. This judgment, held with force and purity, leads Dilsey to a principled respect for the human person as such. When the name of the idiot Compson child is changed from Maury to Benjy, she snaps: "He *ain't wore out the name he was born with yet, is he.*" When her daughter whines that "people talk" because Dilsey brings Benjy to the Negro church, the old woman replies: "Tell um the good Lawd don't keer whether he smart or not. Dont nobody but poor white trash keer dat." This sense of honor toward every person in her orbit, this absolute security in her own judgment, is Dilsey's most admirable trait, and a sign, as well, of the more complex treatment of Negroes that is to appear in Faulkner's books.

*   *   *

RALPH ELLISON

Twentieth-Century Fiction and the Black Mask of Humanity †

When this essay was published in 1953, it was prefaced with the following note:

> "When I started rewriting this essay it occurred to me that its value might be somewhat increased if it remained very much as I wrote it

caught up in the recent historical condition of the Southern Negro. Whether time will do for Dilsey what it has done for Don Quixote, no one can say.

† From *Shadow and Act* (New York: Random House, 1953, 1964), 24–44. Written in 1946. Published in *Confluence*, December 1953. Copyright © 1953 by Random House, Inc. Reprinted by permission of Random House, Inc.

during 1946. For in that form it is what a young member of a minority felt about much of our writing. Thus I've left in much of the bias and short-sightedness, for it says perhaps as much about me as a member of a minority as it does about literature. I hope you still find the essay useful, and I'd like to see an editorial note stating that this is an unpublished piece written not long after the Second World War."

* * *

The major difference between nineteenth- and twentieth-century writers is not in the latter's lack of personal rituals—a property of all fiction worthy of being termed literature—but in the social effect aroused within their respective readers. Melville's ritual (and his rhetoric) was based upon materials that were more easily available, say, than Hemingway's. They represented a blending of his personal myth with universal myths as traditional as any used by Shakespeare or the Bible, while until *For Whom the Bell Tolls* Hemingway's was weighted on the personal side. The difference in terms of perspective of belief is that Melville's belief could still find a public object. Whatever else his works were "about" they also managed to be about democracy. But by our day the democratic dream had become too shaky a structure to support the furious pressures of the artist's doubt. And as always when the belief which nurtures a great social myth declines, large sections of society become prey to superstition. For man without myth is Othello with Desdemona gone: chaos descends, faith vanishes and superstitions prowl in the mind.

Hard-boiled writing is said to appeal through its presentation of sheer fact, rather than through rhetoric. The writer puts nothing down but what he pragmatically "knows." But actually one "fact" itself—which in literature must be presented simultaneously as image and as event— became a rhetorical unit. And the symbolic ritual which has set off the "fact"—that is, the fact unorganized by vital social myths (which might incorporate the findings of science and still contain elements of mystery)—is the rite of superstition. The superstitious individual responds to the capricious event, the fact that seems to explode in his face through blind fatality. For it is the creative function of myth to protect the individual from the irrational, and since it is here in the realm of the irrational that, impervious to science, the stereotype grows, we see that the Negro stereotype is really an image of the unorganized, irrational forces of American life, forces through which, by projecting them in forms of images of an easily dominated minority, the white individual seeks to be at home in the vast unknown world of America. Perhaps the object of the stereotype is not so much to crush the Negro as to console the white man.

Certainly there is justification for this view when we consider the work of William Faulkner. In Faulkner most of the relationships * * * between the Negro and contemporary writing come to focus: the social and the personal, the moral and the technical, the nineteenth-century emphasis upon morality and the modern accent upon the personal myth. And on the strictly literary level he is prolific and complex enough to speak for those Southern writers who are aggressively anti-Negro and for those younger writers who appear most sincerely interested in depicting the Negro as a rounded human being. What is more, he is the greatest artist the South has produced. While too complex to be given more than a glance in these notes, even a glance is more revealing of what lies back of the distortion of the Negro in modern writing than any attempt at a group survey might be.

Faulkner's attitude is mixed. Taking his cue from the Southern mentality in which the Negro is often dissociated into a malignant stereotype (the bad nigger) on the one hand and a benign stereotype (the good nigger) on the other, most often Faulkner presents characters embodying both. The dual function of this dissociation seems to be that of avoiding moral pain and thus to justify the South's racial code. But since such a social order harms whites no less than blacks, the sensitive Southerner, the artist, is apt to feel its effects acutely—and within the deepest levels of his personality. For not only is the social division forced upon the Negro by the ritualized ethic of discrimination, but upon the white man by the strictly enforced set of anti-Negro taboos. The conflict is always with him. Indeed, so rigidly has the recognition of Negro humanity been tabooed that the white Southerner is apt to associate any form of personal rebellion with the Negro. So that for the Southern artist the Negro becomes a symbol of his personal rebellion, his guilt and his repression of it. The Negro is thus a compelling object of fascination, and this we see very clearly in Faulkner.

Sometimes in Faulkner the Negro is simply a villain, but by an unconsciously ironic transvaluation his villainy consists, as with Loosh in *The Unvanquished*, of desiring his freedom. Or again the Negro appears benign, as with Ringo, of the same novel, who uses his talent not to seek personal freedom but to remain the loyal and resourceful retainer. Not that I criticize loyalty in itself, but that loyalty given where one's humanity is unrecognized seems a bit obscene. And yet in Faulkner's story "The Bear," he brings us as close to the moral implication of the Negro as Twain or Melville. In the famous "difficult" fourth section, which Malcolm Cowley advises us to skip very much as Hemingway would have us skip the end of *Huckleberry Finn*, we find an argument in progress in which one voice (that of a Southern abolitionist) seeks to define Negro humanity against the other's enumeration of those stereotypes which many Southerners believe to be the Negro's basic traits. Significantly the mentor of the young hero of this story, a man of great moral stature, is socially a Negro.

Indeed, through his many novels and short stories, Faulkner fights out the moral problem which was repressed after the nineteenth century, and it was shocking for some to discover that for all his concern with the South, Faulkner was actually seeking out the nature of man. Thus we must turn to him for that continuity of moral purpose which made for the greatness of our classics. As for the Negro minority, he has been more willing perhaps than any other artist to start with the stereotype, accept it as true, and then seek out the human truth which it hides. Perhaps his is the example for our writers to follow, for in his work technique has been put once more to the task of creating value.

Which leaves these final things to be said. First, that this is meant as no plea for white writers to define Negro humanity, but to recognize the broader aspects of their own. Secondly, Negro writers and those of the other minorities have their own task of contributing to the total image of the American by depicting the experience of their own groups. Certainly theirs is the task of defining Negro humanity, as this can no more be accomplished by others than freedom, which must be won again and again each day, can be conferred upon another. A people must define itself, and minorities have the responsibility of having their ideals and images recognized as part of the composite image which is that of the still forming American people.

The other thing to be said is that while it is unlikely that American writing will ever retrace the way to the nineteenth century, it might be worth while to point out that for all its technical experimentation it is nevertheless an ethical instrument, and as such it might well exercise some choice in the kind of ethic it prefers to support. The artist is no freer than the society in which he lives, and in the United States the writers who stereotype or ignore the Negro and other minorities in the final analysis stereotype and distort their own humanity. Mark Twain knew that in *his* America humanity masked its face with blackness.

OLGA W. VICKERY

The Sound and the Fury: A Study in Perspective †

The Sound and the Fury was the first of Faulkner's novels to make the question of form and technique an unavoidable critical issue. In any discussion of its structure the controlling assumption should be that there are plausible reasons for the particular arrangement of the four sections and for the use of the stream of consciousness technique in the first three and not in the fourth. Jean-Paul Sartre's comment that the moment the

† Reprinted by permission of Louisiana State University Press from *The Novels of William Faulkner: A Critical Interpretation.* Copyright © 1959, 1964 by Louisiana State University Press. Copyright © 1987, 1992 by John B. Vickery. Page references in brackets are to this Norton Critical Edition.

reader attempts to isolate the plot content "he notices that he is telling another story"[1] indicates the need for such an assumption, not only for any light that may be thrown on *The Sound and the Fury* but for any insight that may emerge concerning Faulkner's method and achievement.

In connection with the interdependence of the sections it has been pointed out that the water-splashing episode "presents all the main characters in situations which foreshadow the main action."[2] Equally important is the fact that the structure of the novel is paralleled by the events of the entire evening of which the water-splashing is only a part. These events reveal the typical gestures and reactions of the four children to each other and to the mysterious advent of death. They chart the range and kind of each of their responses to a new experience. In this way the evening partakes of the dual nature of the novel: primarily it is an objective, dramatic scene revealing the relations and tensions which exist among the children, but at the same time it is a study in perspective. Between the fact of Damuddy's death and the reader stands not only the primitive mind of the narrator, Benjy, but the diverse attitudes of the other children and the deliberate uncommunicativeness of the adults. The result is not needless complexity or confusion but rather, in Henry James's words, "a certain fullness of truth—truth diffused, distributed and, as it were, atmospheric."[3]

Within the novel as a whole it is Caddy's surrender to Dalton Ames which serves both as the source of dramatic tension and as the focal point for the various perspectives. This is evident in the fact that the sequence of events is not caused by her act—which could be responded to in very different ways—but by the significance which each of her brothers actually attributes to it. As a result, the four sections appear quite unrelated even though they repeat certain incidents and are concerned with the same problem, namely, Caddy and her loss of virginity. Although there is a progressive revelation or rather clarification of the plot, each of the sections is itself static. The consciousness of a character becomes the actual agent illuminating and being illuminated by the central situation. Everything is immobilized in this pattern; there is no development of either character or plot in the traditional manner. This impression is reinforced not only by the shortness of time directly involved in each section but by the absence of any shifts in style of the kind that,

1. "Time in Faulkner: 'The Sound and the Fury'," *La Nouvelle Revue française*, 52 (June 1939) and 53 (July 1939), translated and reprinted in *William Faulkner: Two Decades of Criticism*, ed. F. J. Hoffman and O. W. Vickery (East Lansing, 1951), 180.
2. Lawrence E. Bowling, "The Technique of 'The Sound and the Fury'," *Kenyon Rev.*, 10 (Autumn 1948), reprinted in *Two Decades*, p. 177. At this point I should like to acknowledge my general indebtedness to Bowling's article. Rather than duplicate his points, I have assumed them to be established beyond the need for further elaboration. Hence my analysis largely deals with elements which he has not considered.
3. *The Art of the Novel: Critical Prefaces*, ed. R. P. Blackmur (New York, 1934), 154.

for example, accompany the growing maturity of Cash Bundren in *As I Lay Dying*.

By fixing the structure while leaving the central situation ambiguous, Faulkner forces the reader to reconstruct the story and to apprehend its significance for himself. Consequently, the reader recovers the story at the same time as he grasps the relation of Benjy, Quentin, and Jason to it. This, in turn, is dependent on his comprehension of the relation between the present and the past events with which each of the first three sections deals. As he proceeds from one section to the next, there is a gradual clarification of events, a rounding out of the fragments of scenes and conversations which Benjy reports. Thus, with respect to the plot the four sections are inextricably connected, but with respect to the central situation they are quite distinct and self-sufficient. As related to the central focus, each of the first three sections presents a version of the same facts which is at once the truth and a complete distortion of the truth. It would appear, then, that the theme of *The Sound and the Fury*, as revealed by the structure, is the relation between the act and man's apprehension of the act, between the event and the interpretation. This relation is by no means a rigid or inelastic thing but is a matter of shifting perspective, for, in a sense, each man creates his own truth. This does not mean that truth does not exist or that it is fragmentary or that it is unknowable; it only insists that truth is a matter of the heart's response as well as the mind's logic.

In keeping with this theme each of the first three sections presents a well demarcated and quite isolated world built around one of these splinters of truth. The fact that Benjy is dumb is symbolic of the closed nature of these worlds; communication is impossible when Caddy who is central to all three means something different to each. For Benjy she is the smell of trees; for Quentin, honor; and for Jason, money or at least the means of obtaining it. Yet these intense private dramas are taking place in a public world primarily concerned with observable behavior. Accordingly, in the fourth section we are shown what an interested but unimplicated observer would see of the Compsons. For the first time we realize that Benjy has blue eyes, that Mrs. Compson habitually wears black dressing gowns and that Jason looks somewhat like a caricature of a bartender. Moreover, since we are prevented from sharing in the consciousness and memories of the characters, Caddy is no longer an immediate center. Nevertheless, through the conflict between Jason and Miss Quentin the final repercussions of her affair penetrate into the life of Jefferson and even Mottson. And out of the Compson house, itself a symbol of isolation, one person, Dilsey, emerges to grasp the truth which must be felt as well as stated.

Out of the relation that Benjy, Quentin and Jason bear to Caddy yet another pattern emerges: a gradual progression from the completely closed and private world of the first section to the completely public world of the fourth. * * * Moreover, each of these shifts from the private to the public world is accompanied by a corresponding shift in the form of apprehension. With Benjy we are restricted entirely to sensation which cannot be communicated; quite appropriately therefore Benjy is unable to speak. * * * Quentin's world is almost as isolated and inflexible as Benjy's, but its order is based on abstractions rather than sensations. Thus, his section is filled with echoes, both literary and Biblical, phrases, names quoted out of context but falling neatly into the pattern of his thought. These echoes assume the quality of a ritual by which he attempts to conjure experience into conformity with his wishes. * * * The third section shows a greater degree of clarity though not of objectivity. The reason for this is that Jason operates in terms of a logic which forms the basis of social communication. We may not approve the direction in which his logic takes him, but that his actions are the result of clear, orderly thinking in terms of cause and effect cannot be disputed. * * * It is part of the general satiric intent of this section that Jason's obvious distortion of Caddy should be associated with logic and reason, for it throws a new perspective not only on the actions of the Compsons but on Jason, the representative of the "rational" man.

The objective nature of the fourth section precludes the use of any single level of apprehension, yet it provokes the most complex response. Dilsey * * * becomes through her actions alone the embodiment of the truth of the heart which is synonymous with morality. The acceptance of whatever time brings, the absence of questioning and petty protests, enables her to create order out of circumstance rather than in defiance of it, and in so doing she gains both dignity and significance for her life. In a sense, Dilsey represents a final perspective directed toward the past and the Compsons, but it is also the reader's perspective for which Dilsey merely provides the vantage point. This fact suggests another reason for the objective narration in this section: to use Dilsey as a point of view character would be to destroy her efficacy as the ethical norm, for that would give us but one more splinter of the truth confined and conditioned by the mind which grasped it.

Our first impression of the Benjy section is that it presents a state of utter chaos for which the only possible justification is the fact that Benjy is an idiot and therefore has a right to be confused. But out of this disorder two patterns emerge: the one, completely independent of public perspective, constitutes Benjy's world, the other serves as the author's guide for enabling the reader to grasp the fragments as a comprehensible order. With respect to the latter, Lawrence Bowling has pointed out both Faulkner's use of italics to indicate shifts in time and the fact that the reasons for such shifts occurring are easily recognizable. An object, a sound, an incident may propel the mind toward some point in the past where a similar experience took place.

Equally important is the fact that there are actually very few scenes involved despite the length of time covered. The events of 7 April 1928 are easily identified because of the prominence given to Luster in them. * * * Otherwise, there are but three extended episodes: one taking place some time in 1898, the day Damuddy died; the second occurring on the evening Benjy received his new name; and the last consisting of the scene of Caddy's wedding. * * *

With consummate skill the repetitions and identifying sensations which are used to guide the reader are also used as the basis of Benjy's own ordering of experience. Benjy's mind works not by association which is dependent, to some extent, on an ability to discriminate as well as compare but by mechanical identification. Thus, being caught on the fence while walking with Luster does not recall an associated feeling or fact but the exact replica of the incident. More important is the fact that the three deaths in the family, which Benjy senses are repetitions of each other, provoke an identical response. What he reacts to is the fact of death, or the fact of being caught on the fence. To differentiate in terms of time and circumstance is a logical matter and therefore beyond Benjy's range of apprehension.

* * *

Benjy's world is made up not only of sensations but of sensations to which he attributes an independent existence. This is further emphasized by his inflexible identification of one word with one object. Very seldom, for example, is the name of a speaker replaced by a pronoun in his section. Each person is freed from the multiplicity of descriptive relations which make him at once man and brother, father, Negro or white. For Benjy, he is forever fixed as simply Jason, Quentin or Luster. In the one scene where Benjy is brought into contact with Luster's friends, parts of the dialogue are consistently attributed to Luster, but the answers appear to come out of the air. Benjy does not know the names of these strangers and to give then an identity in terms of description is beyond his power. His literalism finds its sharpest illustration in the scene where the cries of the golfers are heard. "Caddy" can mean only one thing and elicit only one response.

Benjy both orders and evaluates his experience with this same rigidity. The objects he has learned to recognize constitute an inflexible pattern which he defends against novelty or change with every bellow in his overgrown body. At what time or under what circumstances the small mound of earth which Dilsey calls his graveyard was formed and marked with two empty bottles of blue glass holding withered stalks of jimson weed is unimportant. But that this arrangement, once established, should remain unchanged in the slightest detail is of the utmost importance. When Luster removes one of the bottles, Benjy is momentarily shocked into a silence which is immediately succeeded by the roar of protest. It is not that the bottle has any intrinsic value for Benjy, but merely that it forms part of the pattern which must not be disturbed. The fixed route to the graveyard is also sacred; Benjy is overwhelmed with horror and agony when Luster takes the wrong turn only to subside the minute the mistake is corrected.

Within this rigid world Caddy is at once the focus of order and the instrument of its destruction. The pasture, the fire and sleep, the three things Benjy loves most, are associated with her, as is illustrated by the recurrent phrase "Caddy smelled like trees," his refusal to go to sleep without her and his memory of her during the rainy evening. On that evening, for a brief moment, everything in his world was in its proper place. Caddy both realizes and respects his fear of change: while playing at the Branch she is quick to reassure him that she is not really going to run away; later, she washes off her perfume and gives the rest of it to Dilsey in order to reassure him. Even when she has accepted the inevitability of change for herself and is preparing to marry Herbert, she tries to bind Quentin to a promise of seeing that Benjy's life is not further disordered by his being committed to a mental institution. Yet what Benjy most expects of Caddy is the one thing she cannot give him, for his expectation is based on his complete indifference to or rather ignorance of time. As long as Caddy is in time, she cannot free either herself or his world from change. His dependence on her physical presence, her scent of trees, is subject to constant threats which he fends off to the best of his ability. Sin and perfume are equally resented as intrusions of change into his arbitrary and absolute pattern. Thus, Caddy, as in the Quentin section, is at once identified with the rigid order of Benjy's private world and with the disorder of actual experience. Depending on which of the two is dominant at the moment, Benjy moans or smiles serenely.

*   *   *

Quentin too has constructed for himself a private world to which Caddy is essential, a world which is threatened and finally destroyed by her involvement in circumstance. His hopeless and endless brooding is but Benjy's moan become articulate though not rational. However, his order is based on emotions rather than sensations, on concepts rather than physical objects. And whereas Benjy is saved by being outside time, Quentin is destroyed by his excessive awareness of it. For the former, both the pattern and its disordering are eternally present as his alternation between moaning and smiling demonstrates; for the latter, the pattern has become a part of the past which cannot be recaptured and contentment has been replaced by despair. Quentin can neither accept nor reconcile himself to that change or to the possibility that a further change may make even his despair a thing of the past, and so he chooses death as a means of escaping the situation.

The structure of the section with its two sets of events, one past and the other present, reflects Quentin's problem. Throughout the day he can proceed quite mechanically with such chores as getting dressed, packing, writing letters and generally tidying up the loose ends of his life at Harvard. To a large extent he can even make the appropriate gestures and speak the proper words expected of him by others. Meanwhile, his mind is occupied with echoes of the past which make themselves felt with increasing intensity until they threaten to prevent even a mechanical attention to the details of living through that final day. Quentin cannot escape either his memories of the past or his involvement in the present.

*   *   *

The order which Quentin had once built around Caddy is as rigid and inflexible as Benjy's and it shares Benjy's fear of change and his expectation that all experience should conform to his pattern. The cause of his ineffectuality and his ultimate destruction is the fact that his system antecedes his experience and eventually is held in defiance of experience. His is an ethical order based on words, on "fine, dead sounds," the meaning of which he has yet to learn. Insofar as virginity is a concept, associated with virtue and honor, it becomes the center of Quentin's world, and since it is also physically present in Caddy, it forms a precarious link between his world and that of experience. Mr. Compson remarks that virginity is merely a transient physical state which has been given its ethical significance by men. What they have chosen to make it mean is something which is a defiance of nature, an artificial isolation of the woman. * * * Since his emotional responses center on these concepts, Quentin is quite incapable of love for any human being, even Caddy. Despite his feverish preoccupation with ethics, he is unable to perform any ethical actions himself; even his death is not so much a protest as it is simply a withdrawal. Thus, it is not the time that is out of joint but Quentin's relation to time.

*   *   *

The symbols and recurrent phrases that run through Quentin's section both intensify the emotional impact and reinforce the meaning. Such names as Jesus, St. Francis, Moses, Washington, and Byron not only add a richness of historical and literary allusion but convey the nature of Quentin's world. Into that world Benjy is admitted as "Benjamin the child of mine old age held hostage into Egypt" and Caddy as Eve or Little Sister Death. Mr. Compson forces an entry not as father or friend but as a voice which can juggle words and ideas while insisting on their emptiness. As for Quentin, he sees himself as the hero of the family drama, "the bitter prophet and inflexible corruptless judge." Part of his outrage and frustration in connection with Caddy is that neither her husband nor her lover seems worthy, in his eyes, of assuming a role in his world: Herbert is obviously despicable and Ames refuses to act in terms of Quentin's preconceptions.

The heavy, choking fragrance of honeysuckle dramatizes the conflict between his order and the blind forces of nature which constantly threaten to destroy it. Honeysuckle is the rife animality of sex, the incomprehensible and hateful world for which Caddy has abandoned his paradise, and hence it is also the symbol of his defeat. Yet honeysuckle is only a sensation, just as Caddy's affair with Ames is simply a natural event. It is Quentin who makes of the one a symbol of "night and unrest" and of the other the unforgivable sin. The references to roses have a similar function in that they too are associated with sex, but they are identified with a single scene, that of Caddy's wedding. Therefore, they are at once the symbol of the world he fears and of his irrevocable betrayal by that world.

*   *   *

The constant references to the shadows and the mirror emphasize the barrier between Quentin and reality. It is not only Benjy but also Quentin who sees Caddy's wedding reflected in the mirror. Caddy, however, cannot be confined to its surface; she runs not only out of the mirror but out of his and Benjy's world. Similarly, Quentin sees her and Ames not as people but as silhouettes distorted against the sky. He is lost amid these shadows, feeling that they falsify the objects they pretend to reflect, yet unable to reach out beyond them. It is significant that he sees only those aspects of Caddy as shadows which he cannot incorporate into his world: it is her love affair and her marriage which he finds perverse, mocking, denying the significance they should have affirmed. The same feeling of mockery is present in his insistence that he has tricked his shadow. A man who is dead needs no shadow, but still his accompanies him throughout the day as if it were mirroring reality when in truth it is but aping another illusion.

The number of times that the shadow images are fused with images of water indicates that death by water is Quentin's way of reconciling his two worlds, of merging shadow and reality and tempering their conflict. Whatever suggestion of purification may be present, water is primarily a symbol of oblivion for Quentin. Narcissa Benbow[4] can act as if a little water would clear her of her deed, but as Dilsey's determined scouring of Caddy's bottom shows, the stains of one's experience are not that easily removed. Both Quentin and Caddy run to the Branch to surrender themselves to its hypnotic rhythm which, like sleep, soothes the mind into unconsciousness, blurring thought and emotion, eliminating the necessity for acting. It is in the hope of making this peace eternal that Quentin surrenders his body to the water where the hard knots of cir-

4. Narcissa Benbow figures prominently in *Sartoris, Flags in the Dust,* and *Sanctuary [Editor].*

cumstance will be untangled and the roof of wind will stand forever
between him and the loud world.

With Jason's section we enter into a world far different from Benjy's
or Quentin's, yet related to theirs through Caddy. It represents a third
possible way of reacting to experience, as distorted yet as "true" as the
former two. Since Jason reacts logically rather than emotionally, his
section offers no barriers to comprehension. His particular method of
ordering and explaining his actions in terms of cause and effect, profit
and loss, is all too familiar. Yet logic, presumably the basis of human
communication and hence of society, isolates Jason as effectively as the
moral abstractions of Quentin or the complete dependence on sensations of Benjy. In the midst of Jefferson or even his family, he is by
necessity as well as by choice alone. And instead of being concerned, he
glories in his self-sufficiency. * * *

One of Jason's dominant characteristics, and the main source of humor,
is his pride that he has no illusions about his family or himself. The
humor, however, arises not from the situation but from the way in which
Jason talks about it. * * * The conviction that he alone has a firm grasp
on reality results in a literalism untouched by any hint of qualification
in Jason's thinking. Through it we get a new and welcome perspective
on the Compsons, but it is just a perspective and not the final word that
Jason makes it out to be. It is his very insistence on facing facts that
causes his distorted view of Caddy, his family and the whole human
race. He cannot imagine that there might be other facts, other aspects
of the situation, than the ones that directly affect him; as a result, he
sees certain things so clearly that all others escape him. In the process
logic replaces truth, and law, justice. * * * He is not concerned with
either Caddy or her daughter except as they enter into the pattern of loss
and recompense and finally loss again. In short, his is a world reduced
to calculation in which no subjective claims are tolerated and no margin
for error allowed.

This calculating approach to experience pervades his every act, no
matter how trivial. * * * It is his method of assuming control over experience by preventing himself from becoming involved in circumstances
he has not foreseen. His control over the Compson house reveals the
same tendency to think in terms of contracts.

Jason's concern with forms of action rather than with the actions
themselves is reflected in his legalistic view of society and especially of
ethics. It is on this view that the double irony of Miss Quentin's theft of
his thievings hinges. He has retrieved his losses, suffered because of Caddy,
at the expense of Caddy's daughter without actually breaking any law.
* * * However, with her one unpremeditated act Miss Quentin destroys
the work of years; more important, she is as safe from prosecution despite
her heedlessness as Jason was because of all his care. Legally, she has

only stolen what already belonged to her. When Jason demands an endorsement of his just indignation from the sheriff, the latter refuses to help on the basis of the very letter of the law Jason had so carefully observed. * * * During his frantic pursuit of Miss Quentin the nature of the conflict in which Jason is involved becomes explicit. He realizes that his enemy is not his niece or even the man with the red tie; rather it is "the sequence of natural events and their causes which shadows every mans [sic] brow." From the first he had distrusted everything which he could not himself control. Unlike Quentin for whom reality lay in ethical concepts, Jason had learned to believe in whatever he could hold in his hands or keep in his pocket. That alone could be protected from chance and change. * * * Yet even that is vulnerable to circumstance, to the accidental juxtaposition in place and time of a girl's whim and a man's red tie. Hence his outrage that Miss Quentin should have taken the money more or less on impulse; had her act been deliberate, calculated, he could have foreseen it and so guarded against it. The red tie becomes for him the symbol of the irrational, the antithesis of his own careful logic.

*   *   *

In the last section we finally emerge from the closed world of the Compson Mile into the public world as represented by Jefferson [and] * * * Dilsey emerges not only as a Negro servant in the Compson household but as a human being. With nothing to judge but her actions, with no prolonged ethical or religious polemics, her very presence enables the reader to achieve a final perspective on the lives of the Compsons. Mrs. Compson's nagging self-pity, Jason's carping exactions, Miss Quentin's thoughtlessness gain a dramatic actuality lacking while they were being filtered through an individual consciousness. Various contrasts between Dilsey and the others are delineated with striking clarity. The contrast becomes actual conflict where Dilsey and Jason are concerned. It is not only that Dilsey "survives," because, for that matter, so does Jason, but that her endurance has strength to suffer without rancor as well as to resist, to accept as well as to protest. She is the only one who challenges his word in the household, who defends the absent Caddy, Miss Quentin, Benjy and even Luster from his anger. But more important, she challenges the validity and efficacy of his world by a passive and irrational resistance to which he has no counter. That someone should work without pay is so foreign to his system that he is helpless in the face of it.

There is no doubt but that Dilsey is meant to represent the ethical norm, the realizing and acting out of one's humanity; it is from this that the Compsons have deviated, each into his separate world. The mother and [Quentin and Jason] have abandoned their humanity for the sake of pride or vanity or self-pity. Both Benjy and Caddy are tests of the family's humanity, he simply because he is not fully human and she because her conduct creates a socio-moral hiatus between the family and Jefferson. Benjy's behavior is a constant trial to the family and to this extent counterpoints Caddy's lone disgracing act. Both challenge the family's capacity for understanding and forgiveness and the family fails both. Quite appropriately, the Compson Mile exists in an atmosphere not only of disintegration but of constriction. The property shrinks as the town begins "to encroach and then nibble at and into it" (p. 7) [206]. The only room which seems to be lived in is Dilsey's kitchen; the others are so many private mausoleums. While each of the Compsons to some extent attempts to coerce experience and to deny his involvement in the sequence of natural events and their causes, Dilsey accepts whatever time brings. She alone never suffers that moment of rejection which is equated with death.

By working with circumstance instead of against it she creates order out of disorder; by accommodating herself to change she manages to keep the Compson household in some semblance of decency. While occupied with getting breakfast, she is yet able to start the fire in Luster's inexplicable absence, provide a hot water bottle for Mrs. Compson, see to Benjy's needs and soothe various ruffled tempers. All this despite the constant interruptions of Luster's perverseness, Benjy's moaning, Mrs. Compson's complaints, and even Jason's maniacal fury. Nor is Dilsey's attitude of acceptance confined to the minor disorders of daily tasks. The same calmness is evident with regard to Caddy's affair, Quentin's suicide and the arrival of Caddy's baby. As she herself states: she has brought up Caddy and can do the same for Miss Quentin. And if it so happens that their conduct mocks all her care and love, then it is time to find another order in the subsequent confusion. Dilsey's attitude, as she lives it, is formed by her instinctive feeling that whatever happens must be met with courage and dignity in which there is no room for passivity or pessimism.

Her ability to stand steadfast without faltering "before the hopeless juggernaut of circumstance" finds further expression in her patient preoccupation with the present, which is the only possible way of living with time. This does not imply that Dilsey is cut off from the past but only that she deals with it as it is caught up in the present without attempting to perpetuate a part of it as Quentin does, or to circumvent it as Jason tries to do. In a sense, she is a living record of all that has happened to the Compsons made significant by her own strength and courage. It is a record of pain and suffering and change but also of endurance and permanence in change.

In describing Dilsey as an ethical norm it should be stressed that she propounds no system, no code of behavior or belief, and this despite the emphasis on the Easter service which she attends. Neither in her attitude nor in the service itself is there any reference to sin and punishment but

only to suffering and its surcease. At no time does Dilsey judge any of
the Compsons, not even Jason, though she does object at one point to
those who frown on Benjy's presence in a Negro church. But her presence enables the reader to judge not systems but actions and hence to
grasp the truth instinctively: "They [Negroes] come into white people's
lives like that in sudden sharp black trickles that isolate white facts for an
instant in unarguable truth like under a microscope" (p. 189) [108]. And
though she does not judge, Dilsey is never deceived; her comprehension
of the relations between Caddy and the rest of the family is unerring.

Dilsey's participation in the Easter service is the one meaningful ritual
in the book. As she proceeds sedately from house to church, acknowledging greetings with proper reserve and dignity, she is still conscious of
being, in some sense, a member of the Compson household with a
certain prestige and obligations. With each member of the congregation
similarly conscious of his own distinctive position in society, the Reverend Shegog begins using the magic of his voice. When he concludes,
communication has been replaced by communion in which each member loses his identity but finds his humanity and the knowledge that all
men are equal and brothers in their suffering.

Out of Dilsey's actions and her participation in the Easter service arise
once more the simple verities of human life, "the old universal truths
lacking which any story is ephemeral and doomed—love and honor and
pity and pride and compassion and sacrifice."[5] It is these truths which
throw the final illumination not only on Caddy and the whole sequence
of events that started with her affair but also on what each of the Compsons believed her to be. The splinters of truth presented in the first three
sections reverberate with the sound and the fury signifying nothing. But
out of those same events, the same disorder and confusion, come Dilsey's triumph and her peace, lending significance not only to her own
life but to the book as a whole.

CLEANTH BROOKS

Man, Time, and Eternity †

The salient technical feature of *The Sound and the Fury* is the use of
four different points of view in the presentation of the breakup of the
Compson family. * * * The story is told through one obsessed consciousness after another, as we pass from Benjy's near-mindlessness to

5. The Stockholm Address. [Faulkner's speech of acceptance upon the award of the Nobel Prize
for Literature—*Editor*.]
† From *William Faulkner: The Yoknapatawpha Country* (New Haven and London: Yale University Press, 1963), 325–48. Copyright © 1963 by Yale University Press. Reprinted by permission.
Page references in brackets are to this Norton Critical Edition.

the obsessed mind of Quentin and then to the very differently obsessed mind of Jason. * * * The reader's movement through the book is a progression from murkiness to increasing enlightenment, and this is natural, since we start with the mind of an idiot, go on next through the memories and reveries of the Hamlet-like Quentin, and come finally to the observations of the brittle, would-be rationalist Jason. Part of the sense of enlightenment comes simply from the fact that we are traversing the same territory in circling movements, and the cumulative effect of names and characterizations begins to dramatize for us with compelling urgency a situation we have come to accept almost as our own. * * * We * * * learn what it is like to live in such a family through being forced to share the minds of the three brothers in their special kinds of obsession. The sense of frustration and "entrapment" is overpowering. * * * There is, therefore, as we move toward the end of the book, the sense of coming out into an objective world, a world in which objects take on firmness of outline and density and weight, in which objective truth, and not mere obsessional impressions, exists. Though the fourth section is not passed through Dilsey's mind, it is dominated by Dilsey; and the world in which Dilsey moves is an objective world, not simply the projection of a distempered spirit.

The states of consciousness of the three brothers provide three quite different modes of interpretation. Consider them, for a moment, under the rubric of poetry. Benjy's section is filled with a kind of primitive poetry, a poetry of the senses, rendered with great immediacy, in which the world—for Benjy a kind of confused, blooming buzz—registers with great sensory impact but with minimal intelligibility. Quentin's section is filled with poetry too, though his is essentially decadent: sensitive but neurotic and hopeless, as it rings sadly through a series of dying falls. Entering Jason's section, we have no poetry at all, since Jason, the "sane" man, has consciously purged his mind of every trace of this perilous and impractical stuff. * * * With the last section we again encounter poetry, but of a more usual kind, especially in those passages which reveal Dilsey's reaction to the Easter service; and here it is neither primitive nor decadent, but whole, complex, and mature.

We can look at the four sections in quite another way, noticing what different conceptions of love they imply. Benjy represents love in its most simple and childlike form. His love for Caddy is intense and unreflective. * * * Quentin's love for Caddy is self-conscious, formal, even abstract, * * * but Quentin is not really in love with his sister's body, only in love with a notion of virginity that he associates with her. * * * In contrast with this incestuously Platonic lover, Jason has no love for Caddy at all, and no love for anyone else. His notion of the proper amatory relationship is to provide himself with a "good honest whore." The relationship he desires is a commercial one: * * * Jason, if he could, would reduce all relationships to commercial transactions.

Another way in which to contrast the first three sections is to observe the different notions of time held by the Compson brothers. * * * Jean-Paul Sartre has argued * * * that Faulkner's characters, because they are committed to the past, are helpless. The Faulknerian character's point of view, as Sartre described it in a graphic metaphor, is that of a passenger looking backward from a speeding car, who sees, flowing away from him, the landscape he is traversing. For him the future is not in view, the present is too blurred to make out, and he can see clearly only the past as it streams away before his obsessed and backward-looking gaze.[1] Sartre's account of the matter does apply in good measure to Quentin, but it does not apply to many of Faulkner's characters and it is certainly not to be attributed to Faulkner himself. Perhaps a more accurate way of stating the truth that inheres in Sartre's view is to say: man's very freedom is bound up with his sense of having some kind of future. Unless he can look ahead to the future, he is not free. The relation that the three Compson brothers bear to the future and to time in general has everything to do, therefore, with their status as human beings.

Benjy * * * is locked almost completely into a timeless present. He has not much more sense of time than an animal has, and therefore he possesses not much more freedom than an animal does. * * * Quentin's obsession with the past is in fact a repudiation of the future. * * * Caddy's betrayal of her honor and the fact that she is cut off forever from Quentin mean that he possesses no future he is willing to contemplate. * * * Jason, by insisting on seeing time only with regard to something to be done, is incapable of any real living. * * * Jason is so committed to preparation for the future that he is almost as enslaved as are his brothers.

* * * To Dilsey neither the past nor the future nor the present is oppressive, because to her they are all aspects of eternity, and her ultimate commitment is to eternity. It may be useful therefore to notice how the plight of each of the brothers constitutes a false interpretation of eternity. Benjy lives in a specious eternity: his present does not include all in timelessness—past, present, and future gathered together in a total pattern—but is a purely negative eternity, since it contains no past and no future. Quentin, we may say, wants to take eternity by storm—to reach it by a sort of shortcut, which in effect means freezing into permanence one fleeting moment of the past. Eternity is thus for Quentin not something which fulfills and enfolds all time, but simply a particular segment of time, like one note of music infinitely sustained. Jason is committed neither to a timeless present nor to a frozen past but to a making ready for the truly happy state. Jason's eternity is the empty mirage

---

1. "A Propos de *Le Bruit et la fureur*," *La Nouvelle Revue française*, 52 (1939); Eng. trans. in *William Faulkner: Three Decades of Criticism*, Frederick J. Hoffman and Olga W. Vickery, eds. (Michigan State University Press, 1960), 225–32.

of an oasis toward which he is constantly flogging his tired camel and his tired self.

Though these patternings do emerge from a contemplation of the first three sections, and though they are important for an understanding of the novel, they do not show on the surface. The reader's impression of *The Sound and the Fury* is not of an elaborately formal abstract structure but quite the reverse. Rarely has a novel appeared so completely disordered and unconnected and accidental in its concreteness. Benjy's section has notoriously seemed a clutter of facts and memories, hard particularities and irrational concretions, a cluster that illustrates nothing and points nowhere. Quentin's section is only less difficult than Benjy's, though certainly quite as rich in conveying the sounds, smells, and shapes of a particular world. It is the apparent formlessness of so much of the book that has tempted the commentators to insist upon the underlying patterns. The patterns are there, but the knowledge that they are there is bought too dearly if it results in turning the three brothers into abstractions, mere stages in a dialectic. Quentin, for example, is a human being who, in spite of his anguished speculations upon the nature of time, is related to a culture; he is not a monstrous abstraction but a young man who has received a grievous psychic wound.

A way of seeing Quentin in a different, and perhaps a fuller, perspective is to note that he is another of Faulkner's many Puritans. * * * Quentin reveals his Puritanism most obviously in his alarm at the breakdown of sexual morality. When the standards of sexual morals are challenged, a common reaction and one quite natural to Puritanism is to try to define some point beyond which surely no one would venture to transgress—to find at least one act so horrible that everyone would be repelled by it.

*   *   *

Whatever the special causes of Quentin's spiritual malaise, the general conditioning cause is quite evident. The curse upon Quentin and the rest of the Compsons is the presence of their hypochondriac, whining mother. Again and again on his last day of life he says to himself, "If I only had a mother," and he remembers associating his mother with a scene pictured in one of the books in the family library. There was portrayed "a dark place into which a single weak ray of light came slanting upon two faces lifted out of the shadow." In Quentin's troubled memory the pictured faces become those of his mother and father. He remembers that he would feel a compulsion to turn back to the picture until "the dungeon was Mother herself she and Father upward into weak light holding hands and us lost somewhere below even them without even a ray of light." Remembering his mother on the day of his death, Quentin says to himself: "Done in Mother's mind though. Finished. Finished. Then we were all poisoned."

The Sound and the Fury has on occasion been read as another Faulknerian document describing the fall of the Old South. Perhaps it is, but what it most clearly records is the downfall of a particular family, and the case seems rather special. The basic cause of the breakup of the Compson family * * * is the cold and self-centered mother who is sensitive about the social status of her own family, the Bascombs, who feels the birth of an idiot son as a kind of personal affront, who spoils and corrupts her favorite son, and who withholds any real love and affection from her other children and her husband. Caroline Compson is not so much an actively wicked and evil person as a cold weight of negativity which paralyzes the normal family relationships. She is certainly at the root of Quentin's lack of confidence in himself and his inverted pride.

*   *   *

Quentin was apparently very close to his father and the influence of his father on him was obviously very powerful. The whole of the Quentin section is saturated with what "Father said" and with references to comparisons that Father used and observations about life that Father made. Though his father seems to have counseled acquiescence in the meaninglessness of existence, it is plain that it was from him that Quentin derived his high notion of the claims of honor. Quentin has not the slightest doubt as to what he ought to do: he ought to drive Caddy's seducer out of town, and if the seducer refuses to go, he ought to shoot him. But Quentin is not up to the heroic role. He tries, but he cannot even hurt Ames, much less kill him. Caddy sees Quentin as simply meddling in her affairs, the quixotic little brother who is to be pitied but not feared or respected.

*   *   *

The third brother, Jason, has repudiated the code of honor. He has adopted for himself a purely practical formula for conduct. Money is what counts. He wants none of Quentin's nonsense nor of the other kinds of nonsense in which people believe—or in which they pretend to believe. But though Jason's ostensible code is purely practical, reducing every action to its cash value, his conduct has in fact its nonpractical aspect. For Jason harbors a great deal of nonpractical and irrational bitterness, even sadism. When, in order to see the disappointment upon Luster's face, Jason deliberately drops the passes to the minstrel show into the fire, he is satisfying his perverted emotion even though he pretends to be merely throwing away what cannot be sold. His stealing systematically the money that Caddy is sending for the benefit of her daughter answers to his mercantilism, but Jason is not content to steal Quentin's allowance. He also wants the enjoyment of teasing and hurting the girl. * * * Jason does not love even his mother, Faulkner tells us, for he is "a sane man always," and love always involves a contradiction of such sanity. Benjy's idiocy and Quentin's quixotic madness are finally less inhuman than Jason's sanity. * * *

The section devoted to Jason has in it some of the most brilliant writing that Faulkner ever did. Jason is a brutal and cold-hearted man, but he does have a certain wit and a brittle logic which allows him to cap any remark made to him by his defiant niece or his ailing mother or one of his business associates. Jason is rarely at a loss, and he is so self-righteous in his bitterness that many of his comments carry a kind of nasty conviction.

* * *

For some eighty pages, in a coldly furious monologue, Jason pitilessly exposes himself * * * as one of the half-dozen of Faulkner's most accomplished villains. * * * Even so, in this company of prime villains * * * Jason's treatment of his sister, his idiot brother, and his niece shows studied cruelty that is unmatched by any of Faulkner's other villains.

A common trait in Faulkner's villains is the lack of any capacity for love. Their lack of love shows itself in two ways, two ways that come eventually to the same thing: their attitudes toward nature and toward women. They do not respond to nature—they may very well violate nature. In quite the same way, they have no interest in women, or use them as means to their own ends. * * *

The disintegration that took place in the Compson family after Jason became its head is revealed most clearly and terribly in the character of Candace's daughter, Quentin. * * * Reared in a loveless home, lacking even what her mother had had in the way of family companionship, she shows the effect of the pressures that have been exerted upon her all her life. In a way the girl senses what has misshaped her. At one point she appeals, in her desperation, to Mrs. Compson, saying: "Why does [Jason] treat me like this, Grandmother? I never hurt him" (p. 276) [162]. And when her grandmother tells her that Jason "is the nearest thing to a father you've ever had. It's his bread you and I eat. It's only right that he should expect obedience from you," the girl jumps up and says to Jason: "Whatever I do, it's your fault. If I'm bad, it's because I had to be. You made me. I wish I was dead. I wish we were all dead" (p. 277) [162].

* * * Faulkner, to be sure, does not sentimentalize Quentin. He does not minimize her shortcomings or imply that she was the mere victim of her environment, but his bitterest judgment upon Jason and what Jason's cruelty entailed is in his presentation of what Jason has caused Caddy's baby to become.

The downfall of the house of Compson is the kind of degeneration which can occur, and has occurred, anywhere at any time. William Butler Yeats' play *Purgatory* is a moving dramatization of the end of a great house in Ireland. The play ends with the last member of the family, a murderous-minded old tinker, standing outside the ruins of the

ancestral house; but the burning of that house and the decay of the
family have no special connection with the troubles of Ireland. According to the author, the disaster resulted from a bad marriage! The real
significance of the Southern setting in *The Sound and the Fury* resides,
as so often elsewhere in Faulkner, in the fact that the breakdown
of a family can be exhibited more poignantly and significantly in a
society which is old-fashioned and in which the family is still at the
center. * * *

The decay of the Compsons can be viewed, however, not merely with
reference to the Southern past but to the contemporary American scene.
It is tempting to read it as a parable of the disintegration of modern man.
Individuals no longer sustained by familial and cultural unity are alienated and lost in private worlds. One thinks here not merely of Caddy,
homeless, the sexual adventuress adrift in the world, or of Quentin, out
of touch with reality and moving inevitably to his death, but also and
even primarily of Jason, for whom the breakup of the family means an
active rejection of claims and responsibilities, and with it, a sense of
liberation. Jason resolves to be himself and to be self-sufficient. He says:
"Besides, like I say I guess I dont need any man's help to get along I can
stand on my own feet like I always have" (p. 224) [130]. Jason prides
himself in managing matters by himself and—since this is the other
side of the same coin—refuses to heed the claims of anyone but
himself. * * *

The one member of the Compson household who represents a unify-
ing and sustaining force is the Negro servant Dilsey. She tries to take
care of Benjy and to give the girl Quentin the mothering she needs. In
contrast to Mrs. Compson's vanity and whining self-pity, Dilsey exhibits
charity and rugged good sense. * * * We are told that she had once been
a big woman, but now the unpadded skin is loosely draped upon "the
indomitable skeleton" which is left "rising like a ruin or a landmark
above the somnolent and impervious guts, and above that the collapsed
face that gave the impression of the bones themselves being outside the
flesh, lifted into the driving day with an expression at once fatalistic and
of a child's astonished disappointment" (p. 282) [165]. What the expression means is best interpreted by what she says and does in the novel,
but the description clearly points to something other than mindless
cheeriness. Dilsey's essential hopefulness has not been obliterated; she
is not an embittered woman, but her optimism has been chastened by
hurt and disappointment.

*   *   *

Dilsey's poverty and her status as a member of a deprived race do not
* * * assure her nobility, but they may have had something to do with
her remaining close to a concrete world of values so that she is less
perverted by abstraction and more honest than are most white people in

recognizing what is essential and basic. In general, Faulkner's Negro characters show less false pride, less false idealism, and more seasoned discipline in human relationships. Dilsey's race has also had something to do with keeping her close to a world still informed by religion. These matters are important: just how important they are is revealed by the emphasis Faulkner gives to the Easter service that Dilsey attends.

The Compson family—whatever may be true of the white community at large in the Jefferson of 1910—has lost its religion. Quentin's sad reveries are filled with references to Jesus and Saint Francis, but it is plain that he has retreated into some kind of Stoicism, a version which is reflected in his father's advice to him: "We must just stay awake and see evil done for a little." Quentin's reply is that "it doesn't have to be even that long for a man of courage" (p. 195) [112], and the act of courage in the Roman style takes Quentin into the river. Mrs. Compson, when she finds that the girl Quentin has eloped, asks Dilsey to bring her the Bible, but obviously Mrs. Compson knows nothing about either sin or redemption. Her deepest concern is with gentility and social position. And Jason, as we have seen, worships only the almighty dollar.

The first three sections of the book do little to carry forward the story of what happened at the Compsons' on the Easter weekend. * * * Easter Sunday breaks bleak and chill and gray. It begins appropriately with Mrs. Compson's complaining and Dilsey's getting the fire started and the household tasks going, but once it is discovered that Quentin is not in her room, events accelerate. All of Jason's frenetic activity comes to a head when he makes the horrified discovery that his victim has found out where he has hidden the money that he has stolen from her and has escaped with it. But we do not immediately follow Jason on his frantic pursuit of his niece. Instead, once Jason is out of the house on his way to the sheriff's, we follow Dilsey and Benjy to church for the Easter service, and this service, in which Dilsey finds her exaltation, is counterpointed against Jason's attempt to find his niece and retrieve the money.

The eloquent sermon to which Dilsey listens sitting "bolt upright" and with tears sliding "down her fallen cheeks" (p. 311) [183] describes Mary's sorrow and the crucifixion of Jesus, but ends with the promise of resurrection and of ultimate glory in which all the arisen dead "whut got de blood en de ricklickshun of de Lamb" (p. 313) [185] shall participate. It is a vision of eternity which gives meaning to time and will wipe away all tears in a final vindication of goodness and in a full consolation of those who mourn. Beside Dilsey, Benjy sits, "rapt in his sweet blue gaze," as if he, too, understood. As Dilsey continues to weep on her way home, her daughter Frony tries to make her stop crying, pointing out that people are looking and that they will be passing white folks soon. But Dilsey does not care what people think and, caught up in her own vision, says to Frony: "I've seed de first en de last." And when Frony asks "First en last whut?" Dilsey tells her: "Never you mind. I seed de beginnin, en now I sees de endin" (p. 313) [185]. With the girl Quentin's departure, the sad story of the Compson family is now at an end. All are dead or departed except the whining hypochondriac Mrs. Compson, the cold and sterile bachelor Jason, and the uncomprehending Benjy.

Easter morning brings to Dilsey a vision that gives meaning to human events, but the Mrs. Compson to whom she returns is still full of uncomprehending reproaches. Mrs. Compson cannot understand why this latest disaster has befallen her. "It cant be simply to hurt and flout me. Whoever God is, He would not permit that. I'm a lady. You might not believe that from my offspring, but I am" (p. 315) [186]. In the meantime, Jason is off on his vain pursuit.

                              *   *   *

MICHAEL MILLGATE

The Sound and the Fury: [Story and Novel] †

Perhaps the single most arresting fact about the manuscript of *The Sound and the Fury* is that the first page bears the undeleted title "Twilight."[1] Clearly the title was no more than tentative: it may, indeed, have been the title of the original short story from which the novel grew, and it is worth noting in this respect its closeness to "That Evening Sun Go Down," the quotation from W. C. Handy's "St. Louis Blues" used as the title of another story of the Compson children on its first publication. But it is interesting to speculate whether the title was intended to apply to the one section or to the work as a whole and on its possible breadth of reference in either case. As a title for the first section alone, "Twilight" would presumably refer to the half-world of Benjy himself, held in a state of timeless suspension between the light and the dark, comprehension and incomprehension, between the human and the animal. As a title for the whole book, the word immediately suggests the decay of the Compson family caught at the moment when the dimmed glory of its eminent past is about to fade into ultimate extinction.

In Quentin's section, in particular, twilight, as a condition of light and a moment in time, takes on very considerable importance. In his most agonizing recollections of Caddy, he sees her at twilight, sitting in

† From *The Achievement of William Faulkner* (New York: Random House, 1966), 94–111. Reprinted by permission of the Peters Fraser & Dunlop Group Ltd.
1. Alderman Library, University of Virginia.

the cleansing waters of the branch and surrounded by the scent of honeysuckle, and these three elements of the scene—the twilight, the water, and the honeysuckle—take on an obsessive significance for Quentin himself and operate as recurrent symbols throughout this section of the novel. As water is associated with cleansing, redemption, peace, and death, and the honeysuckle with warm Southern nights and Caddy's passionate sexuality, so twilight, "that quality of light as if time really had stopped for a while" (pp. 209–10) [107],[2] becomes inextricably confused in Quentin's mind with the scents of water and of honeysuckle until "the whole thing came to symbolise night and unrest" (p. 211) [107]. Quentin continues:

> I seemed to be lying neither asleep nor awake looking down a long corridor of grey halflight where all stable things had become shadowy paradoxical all I had done shadows all I had felt suffered taking visible form antic and perverse mocking without relevance inherent themselves with the denial of the significance they should have affirmed thinking I was I was not who was not was not who. (p. 211) [107–8]

This passage would seem to be central to the meaning both of the particular section and of the book as a whole. There has just been a momentary anticipation of Quentin's carefully planned final release through death by water—traveling back into Cambridge he becomes aware of "the road going on under the twilight, into twilight and the sense of water peaceful and swift beyond" (p. 210) [107] and we realize that Quentin himself is at this moment not merely midway between sanity and madness but precisely poised between waking and sleeping, between life and death.[3] His world has become in fact "shadowy paradoxical"—we have just seen his actual fight with Gerald Bland overlaid in his consciousness by his remembered fight with Dalton Ames—and, for all the apparent orderliness of his actions, he has finally lost his sense of personal identity ("thinking I was I was not who was not was not who"). The passage, in this respect, seems also to relate directly to the passage in *Macbeth* from which Faulkner took his final title for the book, and specifically to its descriptions of life as "a walking shadow," a tale "signifying nothing."

The phrase about "all stable things" becoming "shadowy paradoxical" aptly defines the hallucinatory world of the Quentin section, but it is also relevant to the treatment of "fact," of "truth," throughout the novel. Like *Absalom, Absalom!*, *The Sound and the Fury* is in part concerned with the elusiveness, the multivalence, of truth, or at least with man's persistent and perhaps necessary tendency to make of truth a personal thing: each man, apprehending some fragment of the truth, seizes upon

2. All page references are to the first edition (New York, Jonathan Cape and Harrison Smith, 1929). Page references in brackets are to this Norton Critical Edition.
3. See *A Green Bough*, Poem X, entitled "Twilight" on its first publication in *Contempo*, 1 (February 1, 1932): 1.

that fragment as though it were the whole truth and elaborates it into a total vision of the world, rigidly exclusive and hence utterly fallacious. This forms an essential part of the conception which Faulkner dramatized through the interior monologues of the first three sections of *The Sound and the Fury*, and the novel might thus be considered as in some sense a development, much richer than anything of which Anderson himself was capable, of the "theory of the grotesque" propounded at the beginning of *Winesburg, Ohio*:

> The old man has listed hundreds of the truths in his book. . . . There was the truth of virginity and the truth of passion, the truth of wealth and of poverty, of thrift and of profligacy, of carelessness and abandon. Hundreds and hundreds were the truths and they were all beautiful.
> And then the people came along. Each as he appeared snatched up one of the truths and some who were quite strong snatched up a dozen of them.
> It was the truths that made the people grotesques. The old man had quite an elaborate theory concerning the matter. It was his notion that the moment one of the people took one of the truths to himself, called it his truth, and tried to live his life by it, he became a grotesque and the truth he embraced became a falsehood.[4]

Faulkner admired *Winesburg, Ohio*, and there is a discernible similarity between Anderson's conception of Winesburg and Faulkner's creation of Jefferson, the town which he had begun somewhat painstakingly to lay out in *Sartoris* and which in *The Sound and the Fury* is for the first time integrated into the structure and action of the novel. In 1925 Faulkner especially praised *Winesburg, Ohio* for its "ground of fecund earth and corn in the green spring and the slow, full hot summer and the rigorous masculine winter that hurts it not, but makes it stronger";[5] he praised it, that is to say, for just that recurrent evocation of the land and the moving seasons which he himself achieved in *Soldiers' Pay* and *Sartoris* and which is also present, though less persistently and much less obviously, in *The Sound and the Fury*. Some of the time-levels in the Benjy section can be identified by their allusions to the cold, the rain, and so on, while Quentin, in his section, is intensely aware, with the heightened sensitivity of a man about to die, of the countryside through which he walks:

> In the orchard the bees sounded like a wind getting up, a sound caught by a spell just under crescendo and sustained. The lane went along the wall, arched over, shattered with bloom, dissolving

4. Sherwood Anderson, *Winesburg, Ohio* (New York, 1919), 4–5.
5. Faulkner's *Dallas Morning News* article on Anderson, in *Princeton University Library Chronicle*, 18 (Spring 1957): 90.

into trees. Sunlight slanted into it, sparse and eager. Yellow butterflies flickered along the shade like flecks of sun. (p. 151) [77]

. . . It was at the Nagano Seminar in 1955 that Faulkner gave his
fullest account of how *The Sound and the Fury* came to be written.[6] A
number of points here demand discussion. In the first place, there is a
good deal of evidence to support Faulkner's statement that the novel
began as a short story. Maurice Coindreau recalls Faulkner telling him:

> "Ce roman, à l'origine, ne devait être qu'une nouvelle, me dit, un
> jour, William Faulkner. J'avais songé qu'il serait intéressant d'ima-
> giner les pensées d'un groupe d'enfants, le jour de l'enterrement de
> leur grand'mère dont on leur a caché la mort, leur curiosité devant
> l'agitation de la maison, leurs efforts pour percer le mystère, les
> suppositions qui leur viennent à l'esprit."
> ["Originally this novel was to be only a story," William Faulkner
> told me one day. "I thought it would be interesting to imagine the
> thoughts of a group of children on the day of the burial of their
> grandmother whose death had been concealed from them, their
> curiosity about the excitement in the house, their efforts to pene-
> trate the mystery, the ideas which came to their minds."][7]

It was to be a story, therefore, similar in conception to "That Evening
Sun," in which the Compson children are again placed in a situation
whose adult significance they do not fully comprehend; Faulkner published the story in March 1931, and he had written it at the very latest
by October 1930.[8] With this in mind we can quite readily disentangle
from the opening section of *The Sound and the Fury*, where they occur
in chronological and logical sequence, the sometimes quite widely separated fragments of a short story, "without plot," describing the experiences of the Compson children on the night of their grandmother's funeral;
it is in the course of this material, moreover, that we first meet the image
of Caddy's muddy drawers—seen from below as she clambers up the tree
outside the Compson house in order to see what is happening inside—
which, on other occasions, Faulkner spoke of as the basic image from
which the whole book originated.

The pattern established by Faulkner's disposition of the novel's four
sections can be viewed in a number of different ways, and they have
been seen, for example, as exemplifying different levels of consciousness, different modes of apprehension or cognition, contrasted states of
innocence and experience; M. Coindreau speaks of them as four movements of a symphony.[9] All these elements are present, and there is an

6. Robert A. Jelliffe, ed., *Faulkner at Nagano* (Tokyo: Kenkyusha, 1962), 103–5.
7. Maurice Coindreau, Preface to *Le bruit et la fureur* (Paris, 1949), 7.
8. James B. Meriwether, *The Literary Career of William Faulkner: A Bibliographical Study*
(Princeton, 1961), 175.
9. Coindreau, *op. cit.*, pp. 9–12.

over-all movement outward from Benjy's intensely private world to the fully public and social world of the fourth section. The pattern, however, is not solely progressive: despite the superficial affinities between the first and second sections on the one hand and the third and fourth sections on the other, the most fundamental relationships would seem to be those between the first and last sections, which offer a high degree of objectivity, and between the second and third, which are both intensely subjective. Benjy is a first-person narrator, as are Quentin and Jason, but his observations do not pass through an intelligence which is capable of ordering, and hence distorting, them; he reports the events of which he is a spectator, and even those in which he is himself a participator, with camera-like fidelity. His view of Caddy, it is true, is highly personal, but we infer this view from the scenes which his camera-mind records; Benjy does not himself interpret this or other situations and events; still less does he attempt to impose a distorted interpretation upon the reader, as, in effect, do Quentin and Jason. Nor does he himself judge people, although he becomes the instrument by which the other characters are judged, their behavior toward him serving as a touchstone of their humanity.

Faulkner seems to have worked gradually toward the convention of pure objectivity which he follows in the Benjy section, and it is interesting to see the trend of his revisions, between manuscript and published work, to the well known scene in which Benjy burns his hand. The incident begins in the manuscript as follows:

> "Ow, mammy," Luster said. "Ow, mammy." I put my hand out to the firedoor.
> "Dont let him!" Dilsey said, "Catch him back." My hand jerked back and I put it in my mouth, and Dilsey caught me. I could still hear the clock between the times when my voice was going. Dilsey reached back and hit Luster on the head.
> "Git that soda," she said. She took my hand out of my mouth. My voice went louder then. I tried to put it back, but Dilsey held it. She sprinkled soda on it. "Look in the pantry . . ." [1]

The published text reads as follows:

> "Ow, mammy." Luster said. "Ow, mammy."
> I put my hand out to where the fire had been.
> "Catch him." Dilsey said. "Catch him back."
> My hand jerked back and I put it in my mouth and Dilsey caught me. I could still hear the clock between my voice. Dilsey reached back and hit Luster on the head. My voice was going loud every time.
> "Get that soda." Dilsey said. She took my hand out of my mouth.

---

1. Manuscript, Alderman Library, p. 26.

> My voice went louder then and my hand tried to go back to my
> mouth, but Dilsey held it. My voice went loud. She sprinkled soda
> on my hand.
>   "Look in the pantry . . ." (p. 72) [38]

. . . Some of the revisions are more substantial . . . and it will be useful
to look more closely at the changes made between the manuscript of the
novel and the bound carbon typescript, both now in the Alderman Library.
Several of the discrepancies between these two versions reveal Faulkner
working toward what was to prove at once an elaboration and a simplification of his technique in the opening section of the book. Thus the
first page of the manuscript lacks all the references to Luster's hunting
in the grass for his lost quarter and to the fact that the day is Benjy's
birthday which appear in the typescript and on pages 1 and 2 of the
published text, and in the manuscript version as a whole there is an
almost total absence of material relating to Luster's search for the quarter,
to his desire to go to the show, to Benjy's birthday, or to Benjy's age.
Faulkner presumably realized before or during the process of reworking
the first section that the allusions to Benjy's birthday and, still more, to
Luster's search for the missing quarter could be made to serve as a kind
of motif or signal of present time in the section and thus assist the reader
in keeping his bearings among the shifting and merging time-planes. . . .
    In both manuscript and typescript Faulkner had indicated by means
of underlining that he wished the breaks in time sequence within the
Benjy section to be suggested by changes back and forth between roman
and italic type: it seems not to have been his intention that all such
breaks should be accompanied by a type change, but rather that occasional italicization should alert the reader to the kind of process going
on in Benjy's mind. In his admirable article on the textual history of the
novel, James B. Meriwether has shown that when Faulkner received the
galley proofs from Cape and Smith he found that considerable editorial
changes had been made in the first section, apparently by his friend and
literary agent, Ben Wasson, whom Cape and Smith had recently appointed
as an assistant editor. In particular, the device of italicization had been
abandoned and replaced by the insertion of breaks in the text (i.e., wider
spaces between lines) at points where breaks in the time sequence
occurred.[2] Wasson had presumably defended his action on the grounds
that italicization permitted the differentiation of only two dates, whereas
at least four distinct times were actually involved. Faulkner replied,
rejecting these arguments and explaining why he had restored the italics
as they had appeared in his typescript and even added a few more in
order to avoid obscurity; his letter, forcefully phrased, reveals beyond all

2. James B. Meriwether, "Notes on the Textual History of *The Sound and the Fury*," *Papers of
the Bibliographical Society of America*, 56 (1962): 294–99.

question the absolute self-confidence and intellectual clarity with which he regarded the finished novel and the technical experimentation which it embodied.[3]

. . . In reworking the manuscript version of the second section Faulkner made for more extensive additions and revisions than in the preceding section. This becomes immediately clear from a comparison between the opening paragraph of the manuscript and the corresponding passage in the published book. The manuscript reads:

> The shadow of the sash fell across the curtains between 7 and 8 oclock, and then I was hearing the watch. again, But I didn't and I lay there looking at the sinister bar across the rosy and motionless curtains, listening to the watch. Hearing it, that is. I dont suppose anybody deliberately listens to a watch or a clock. You dont have to. You can be oblivious to the sound for a long while, then in a second of ticking it can create in the mind unbroken the long diminishing parade of time you did not hear. Where up the long and lonely arrowing of light rays you might see Jesus walking, like. The true Son of Man: he had no sister. Nazarene and Roman and Virginian, they had no sister one minute she was
> Beyond the wall Shreve's bedsprings complained thinly,. . .[4]

Here for comparison are the opening paragraphs of section two in the published book:

> When the shadow of the sash appeared on the curtains it was between seven and eight oclock and then I was in time again, hearing the watch. It was Grandfather's and when Father gave it to me he said, Quentin, I give you the mausoleum of all hope and desire; it's rather excrutiating-ly apt that you will use it to gain the reducto absurdum of all human experience which can fit your individual needs no better than it fitted his or his father's. I give it to you not that you may remember time, but that you might forget it now and then for a moment and not spend all your breath trying to conquer it. Because no battle is ever won he said. They are not even fought. The field only reveals to man his own folly and despair, and victory is an illusion of philosophers and fools.
>
> It was propped against the collar box and I lay listening to it. Hearing it, that is. I dont suppose anybody ever deliberately listens to a watch or a clock. You dont have to. You can be oblivious to the sound for a long while, then in a second of ticking it can create in the mind unbroken the long diminishing parade of time you didn't hear. Like Father said down the long and lonely light-rays

3. A.l.s., Faulkner to Wasson, n.d., in Massey Collection, Alderman Library. [See letter to Ben Wasson (early summer, 1929), reprinted above, pp. 220–21—Editor.]
4. Manuscript, Alderman Library, p. 34 (reproduced as Fig. 10 of *The Literary Career of William Faulkner*).

you might see Jesus walking, like. And the good Saint Francis that said Little Sister Death, that never had a sister.

Through the wall I heard Shreve's bed-springs . . . (pp. 93–94) [49]

Faulkner's alterations achieve certain improvements in phrasing and elaborate the insistence on time, but perhaps the most interesting of the new elements are the references to Mr. Compson. Throughout the section, as revised in the carbon typescript and the published book, Quentin's mind runs on his father almost as much as it does on Caddy. Quentin is, of course, very much like his father in many ways, and in his obsession with family tradition and honor it is understandable that he should refer to his father, the head of the family, as a transmitter of that tradition and as a source of authority and advice. The irony of this situation, however, and a major cause of Quentin's tragedy, is that just as his mother has failed him as a source of love so his father fails him utterly in all his roles of progenitor, confessor, and counselor. He has become, indeed, Quentin's principal enemy, his cold and even cynical logic persistently undermining the very basis of all those idealistic concepts to which Quentin so passionately holds. Throughout the section there is a battle in progress between Quentin's romantic idealism and Mr. Compson's somewhat cynical realism, a battle which is not finally resolved in *The Sound and the Fury* and which is resumed on an even larger scale in *Absalom, Absalom!* Indeed, if we are to understand that the discussion between Quentin and his father at the end of the section is purely a figment of Quentin's imagination and never actually took place, then it has to be said that in *The Sound and the Fury* the battle is never properly joined—as, according to Mr. Compson himself, no battle ever is—and that it is, rather, a series of skirmishes in which Quentin suffers a progressive erosion of his position and a steady depletion of his reserves. Father and son are, in any case, too much alike in their fondness for words, for abstractions, and in choosing to evade life—the one in drink, the other in suicide—rather than actively confront it.

Whenever Quentin acts, his concern is for the act's significance as a gesture rather than for its practical efficacy. He seeks pertinaciously for occasions to fight in defence of his sister's honor, knowing in advance that he will be beaten, and concerned in retrospect only that he has performed the act in its ritualistic and symbolic aspects. It is the fight with Gerald Bland which reveals most clearly the degree to which Quentin's obsessions have divorced him from actuality since throughout the struggle it is the remembered fight with Dalton Ames which remains for Quentin the superior reality. Throughout a whole day of quite extraordinary incidents—with two fights, an arrest, a court hearing, much movement, and many encounters—Quentin's mind remains preoccupied with the past. It is almost as though Faulkner were playing on the idea that a drowning man sees his whole life pass before him, and we come to realize that this last day of Quentin's is a kind of suspended moment before death.

Quentin's own obsession with time derives primarily from his recognition of it as the dimension in which change occurs and in which Caddy's actions have efficacy and significance. His search is for a means of arresting time at a moment of achieved perfection, a moment when he and Caddy could be eternally together in the simplicity of their childhood relationship; his idea of announcing that he and Caddy had committed incest was, paradoxically, a scheme for regaining lost innocence:

> it was to isolate her out of the loud world so that it would have to flee us of necessity and then the sound of it would be as though it had never been . . . if I could tell you we did it would have been so and then the others wouldnt be so and then the world would roar away . . . (p. 220) [112]

The similarity between this conception and the image of motion in stasis which haunted Faulkner throughout his life, especially as embodied in Keats' "Ode to a Grecian Urn," suggests—as do the echoes of Joyce— that Quentin is in some measure a version of the artist, or at least the aesthete, as hero. But Quentin's conception is artificial, rigid, life-denying: as Mr. Compson observes, "Purity is a negative state and therefore contrary to nature. It's nature is hurting you not Caddy . . ." (p. 143) [74]. The inadequacy of Quentin's position is exposed in terms of Caddy and her vitality and humanity. In the Benjy section we recognize Caddy as the principal sustainer of such family unity as survives: we glimpse her as the liveliest spirit among the children and their natural leader, as the protector and comforter of Benjy, and even as the pacifier of her mother, and it is highly significant for us as well as for Benjy that she is persistently associated with such elemental things as the fire, the pasture, the smell of trees, and sleep. . . .

Caddy finds an outlet from family repression in sexual activity, but she is also both a principle and a symbol of social disruption. Her assertion of individuality is much less positive and urgent than that of such a character as Ursula Brangwen in D. H. Lawrence's *The Rainbow;* even so, she is brought, like Ursula, to break with traditional patterns and, in so doing, to demonstrate just how moribund those patterns have become, how irrelevant both to modern conditions and to the needs of the human psyche. It is possible to feel, however, that although Caddy is the core of the book she is not herself a wholly successful creation. Faulkner often spoke of Caddy, outside the novel, with an intensely passionate devotion: "To me she was the beautiful one," he said at the University of Virginia, "she was my heart's darling. That's what I wrote the book about and I used the tools which seemed to me the proper tools to try to tell, try to draw the picture of Caddy."[5] The original image of the little girl with the muddy drawers grew into the rich and complex conception of Caddy, beautiful and tragic both as child and as woman, but although this conception is already present in the first section of the novel it is evoked, necessarily, in somewhat fragmentary fashion, as we glimpse Caddy in various family situations, as we sense how much she means to Benjy, as we come to associate her, through Benjy, with images of brightness, comfort, and loss. In the second section Caddy is more clearly visible, and there are passages of remembered dialogue as revealing of Caddy's character as of Quentin's, but the world of Quentin's section is so unstable, so hallucinatory, that the figure of Caddy, like so much else, is enveloped in uncertainty. In Jason's section Caddy's agony is most movingly evoked, but only briefly so, while in the final section of the book she is no more than a memory.

It was an essential element in Faulkner's over-all conception of the novel that Caddy never be seen directly but only through the eyes of her three brothers, each with his own self-centered demands to make upon her, each with his own limitations and obsessions. Asked at Virginia why he did not give a section to Caddy herself, Faulkner replied that it seemed more "passionate" to do it through her brothers, and one is reminded of his remarks at Nagano about the beauty of description by understatement and indirection: "Remember, all Tolstoy said about Anna Karenina was that she was beautiful and could see in the dark like a cat. That's all he ever said to describe her. And every man has a different idea of what's beautiful. And it's best to take the gesture, the shadow of the branch, and let the mind create the tree."[6] It certainly seems likely that to have made Caddy a "voice" in the novel would have diminished her importance as a central, focal figure. As the book stands, however, Caddy emerges incompletely from the first two sections, and in the last two attention shifts progressively from her to her daughter, Quentin. The different limitation in the viewpoints of Benjy, Quentin, and Jason makes unavoidable the shadowiness, the imprecision, of Caddy's presentation: because the mind of each is so closed upon its own obsessions it is scarcely true to speak of their interior monologues as throwing light upon Caddy from a variety of angles; it is rather as though a series of photographs in differing focus were superimposed one upon the other, blurring all clarity of outline or detail. The novel revolves upon Caddy, but Caddy herself escapes satisfactory definition, and her daughter's tragedy, simply because it is more directly presented, is in some ways more moving.

It is characteristic that Jason should be the only member of the Compson family who is able to cope with the practical and social implications of Caddy's defection. Where Mrs. Compson can only moistly complain,

5. Frederick L. Gwynn and Joseph L. Blotner, eds., *Faulkner in the University: Class Conferences at the University of Virginia 1957–1958* (Charlottesville, 1959), 6.
6. *Faulkner at Nagano*, p. 72.

Benjy bellow his incomprehending grief, Quentin commit suicide, Jason can adjust himself to the situation and turn it to his own advantage and profit. Jason—the one Compson who was capable of meeting Snopes on his own ground, as Faulkner wrote to Malcolm Cowley[7]—becomes in this way the representative of the new commercial South, and his section strikes a specifically contemporary note in its evocation of the petty businessman, with Jason himself appearing, in this role, as a typical figure, sharing the fundamental characteristics of a legion of other small businessmen in North and South alike. It is perhaps for this reason that Jason's seems much the least "Southern" of the sections. If it also seems the most readily detachable section—it was the one which Faulkner first suggested for inclusion in *The Portable Faulkner*[8]—that is a measure of the degree to which Jason's singleminded and ruthless pursuit of material self-interest serves to isolate him not only from his family but from the community as a whole. . . . His contempt for the town is only exceeded by his contempt for his own family, its history, and its pretensions:

> Blood, I says, governors and generals. It's a damn good thing we never had any kings and presidents; we'd all be down there at Jackson chasing butterflies. (p. 286) [144]

Since Jason's instincts are commercial and materialistic, they are also antirural and antitraditional: his is a willed deracination from the community in which he continues to live. As we have seen, however, it is this very materialism and deracination which makes Jason the one male Compson with any practical competence.

The progression from Benjy's section through Quentin's to Jason's is accompanied by an increasing sense of social reality: Benjy is remote in his idiocy and innocence, Quentin moves from the isolation of his half-mad idealism into the total withdrawal of suicide, but Jason is wholly in the world, acutely sensitive to social values, swimming with the contemporary commercial current. The action of the novel is thus presented increasingly in terms of social, economic, and political perspectives; it is Jason who first refers, however ironically, to the family's more distinguished past, and it is not until the last section of the novel that we are first given an image of the Compson house in all its decrepitude. To interpret *The Sound and the Fury* simply as a socio-economic study of the decline of a Southern family is obviously inadequate; what can be said is that this is one of the novel's many aspects, and one which becomes increasingly important as the book proceeds. It seems possible that Faulkner felt that he had created the social context of the action in insufficient detail, that the book did not clearly evoke the patterns of manners and customs within which his characters moved: the Compson

7. T.l.s., Faulkner to Cowley, n.d., Yale University Library.
8. *Ibid.*

"Appendix" he wrote for *The Portable Faulkner* is devoted partly to clarifying the meaning of the novel at certain points but primarily to the
elaboration of the Compsons' family history and to the further definition
of their place in the social and economic life of Jefferson. It is in the
Appendix, too, that we find the abundantly particularized description of
the farmers' supply store which Jason now owns and which Miss Melissa
Meek valiantly enters,

> striding on through that gloomy cavern which only men ever
> entered—a cavern cluttered and walled and stalagmite-hung with
> plows and discs and loops of tracechain and singletrees and mule
> collars and sidemeat and cheap shoes and horse linament and flour
> and molasses . . .[9]

It must be admitted that each of the first three sections of *The Sound
and the Fury* has about it some suggestion of the *tour de force*: the Quentin section seems a deliberate exercise in the Joycean mode, while the
Jason section raises to the level of art the self-revelatory interior monologue of the unimaginative man which Sinclair Lewis had developed in
Babbitt and *The Man Who Knew Coolidge*, published in 1922 and 1928
respectively. The Benjy section seems to have been more exclusively
Faulkner's invention, a deliberate attempt to extend the boundaries of
the novel beyond the point to which Joyce had already pushed them.
Yet Faulkner never regarded the book as a *tour de force*; unlike *As I Lay
Dying*, *The Sound and the Fury* was a book which took him a long time
and much agony to write, and his adoption in the final section of the
point of view of the omniscient author seems to have been forced upon
him not by the demands of a deliberate design but by the more immediate pressures stemming from an urgent need for self-expression.

In various accounts of the writing of *The Sound and the Fury* Faulkner says that having failed in three attempts to tell the story, to rid himself of the "dream," he had tried in the final section to pull the whole
novel together, retelling the central story more directly and clearly. In
fact, the section contributes relatively little to our understanding of the
narrative events touched upon in earlier sections. * * * Simply by giving
us for the first time detailed physical descriptions of Dilsey, Benjy, Jason,
and Mrs. Compson, Faulkner—playing on some of the most fundamental of human responses to storytelling—effectively modifies our feelings
toward them. Simply by recreating in such detail the routine of Dilsey's
day, evoking the qualities demanded in performing such duties in a
household such as that of the Compsons', Faulkner allows her to emerge
for the first time both as a fully drawn character and as a powerful positive presence. When the action shifts to Jason and his vain pursuit of
Quentin we notice that many of his experiences have something in common with Quentin's experiences during the last day of his life—there

9. Malcolm Cowley, ed., *The Portable Faulkner* (New York, 1946), 745–46.

are, for example, the journeyings back and forth, the moments of violence, the unsatisfactory brushes with the representatives of the law—and we come finally to recognize that, for all the differences between them, both brothers display a similar obsessiveness and fundamental irrationality. . . .

It is . . . tempting, in the final section, to see in the immensely positive figure of Dilsey, and the importance given to her, a certain over-all reassurance and even serenity; but although the section does contain positives which to some extent offset the negations of the previous sections, it would be too much to say that the novel closes on a note of unqualified affirmation. Dilsey "endures," but her endurance is tested not in acts of spectacular heroism but in her submission to the tedious, trivial . . . and wilfully inconsiderate demands made upon her by the Compson family. . . . The Easter Sunday service in the Negro church is immensely moving, an apotheosis of simplicity, innocence, and love, with Dilsey and Benjy as the central figures:

> In the midst of the voices and the hands Ben sat, rapt in his sweet blue gaze. Dilsey sat bolt upright beside, crying rigidly and quietly in the annealment and the blood of the remembered Lamb. (pp. 370–71) [185]

But the moment passes; the sense of human communion rapidly dissolves as they move into the world of "white folks" (p. 371) [185] and return to the Compson house, described now for the first time and seen as a symbol of decay:

> They reached the gate and entered. Immediately Ben began to whimper again, and for a while all of them looked up the drive at the square, paintless house with its rotting portico. (p. 372) [185]

It is clear, however, that Faulkner does not intend any simple moral division between the Negroes and their white employers. Luster in particular has been less impressed by the service than by the performance on the musical saw he had witnessed the previous night, and in his treatment of Benjy he displays a streak of mischievous cruelty. Dilsey tries to comfort Ben, but she is forced to rely upon the treacherous Luster to take him to the cemetery and it is with a note of pathetic resignation that she says, "I does de bes I kin" (p. 396) [197]. On the final pages of the novel it is pride, the sin which has been the downfall of the Compson family, which induces Luster to drive to the left at the monument instead of to the right, and if the final restoration of Benjy's sense of order seems at first to offer a positive conclusion to the novel we must also remember that the order thus invoked is one purely of habit, entirely lacking in inherent justification, and that it is restored by Jason, whose concern is not with humanity or morality or justice but only with social appearances. As so often in this novel, such meaning as at first sight the incidents appear to possess proves on closer inspection to dissolve into uncertainty and paradox.

In Shakespeare's play, Macbeth's "sound and fury" soliloquy is spoken as death approaches, and by the end of Faulkner's novel the doom of the Compson family seems about to be finally accomplished. In *Macbeth* the forces of good, embodied in Malcolm and Macduff, are gathering strength and it is perhaps characteristic of the desperate mood of *The Sound and the Fury* that the forces of good are not so readily identifiable, nor seen as ultimately triumphant. Yet in *Macbeth* the forces of good are external to Macbeth and Lady Macbeth, whereas in *The Sound and the Fury* some of the elements making for life do appear within the Compson family group, most notably in Dilsey but also in Caddy and her daughter. It is Quentin who gives Luster the quarter he so desires, it is Quentin who struggles in the last section to maintain at least some semblance of family harmony and order but who finally breaks down under Jason's verbal torture, and it is perhaps to be taken as a sign of hope—especially in view of the resurrection images which some critics have perceived in the description of her empty room—that Quentin finally makes good her escape and that, unlike her mother, she leaves no hostage behind. In the Compson genealogy Faulkner speaks of Quentin in pessimistic terms, yet the suggestion that Faulkner wanted to write a novel about Quentin after her departure from Jefferson[1] at least indicates that he felt the Compsons were not yet finished with, that there was more to be said—or perhaps only more to be suffered.

JOHN T. IRWIN

[Doubling and Incest in *The Sound and the Fury*] †

*   *   *

Quentin's love of death incorporates his incestuous love for his sister precisely because his sister, as a substitute for Quentin's mother, is synonymous with death. On the morning of the day he dies, Quentin thinks, "I dont suppose anybody ever deliberately listens to a watch or a clock. You dont have to. You can be oblivious to the sound for a long while,

1. Robert Linscott, "Faulkner Without Fanfare," *Esquire*, 60 (July 1963): 38.
† From *Doubling and Incest/Repetition and Revenge: A Speculative Reading of Faulkner* (Baltimore and London: Johns Hopkins University Press, 1975), 153–72. Copyright © 1975 by The Johns Hopkins University Press. Reprinted by permission of The Johns Hopkins University Press. Page references in brackets are to this Norton Critical Edition.

then in a second of ticking it can create in the mind unbroken the long diminishing parade of time you didn't hear. Like Father said down the long and lonely lightrays you might see Jesus walking, like. And the good Saint Francis that said Little Sister Death, that never had a sister. . . . That Christ was not crucified: he was worn away by a minute clicking of little wheels. That had no sister" (pp. 95–96) [49]. Christ had no sister, but he had a mother with whom he becomes progressively identified, so that, for example, when he is taken down from sacrificing his life on the phallic tree, he is laid in his mother's lap, and the iconography of the Pietà becomes that of the Madonna and Child. As a further link between Quentin's suicide and Christ's sacrifice, we should note that the principle of sacrifice is the same as that of self-castration— the giving up of a part to save the whole, and in both sacrifice and self-castration the part is given up to save the whole from the wrath of the father. But in Christ's sacrifice and Quentin's suicide, the *son* is the part that is given up, and self-castration is death. In his discussion of the sacrifices of Isaac and Jesus, Rosolato points out that for the psychotic the notion of sacrifice becomes the fantasy of murder or suicide. The psychotic concept of sacrifice is located in the realm of an Idealized Father whose image blends the images of the Father and the Mother: "in reality, one can intervene for the other; they are interchangeable in a single ambivalence." In this situation, sacrifice "is a manner of extricating oneself from all genealogy and merging oneself with that megalomaniac and punctiform image." Rosolato adds that "to this situation central for psychosis, always in quest of an impossible sacrifice in which the subject would be himself the agent or the victim, corresponds, in myth, the connecting point of the Passion and the Sacrifice." [1] The essence of Christ's sacrifice and Quentin's suicide is that in each the subject is both the agent and the victim, at once active and passive, a conjunction of masculine and feminine.

If the Biblical context of Candace's name [2] suggests that Quentin is his sister's eunuch, then it is worth noting that in the Gospels Christ recommends that his disciples make themselves eunuchs for the kingdom of heaven: "For there are some eunuchs, which were so born from *their* mother's womb: and there are some eunuchs, which were made eunuchs of men: and there be eunuchs, which have made themselves eunuchs for the kingdom of heaven's sake. He that is able to receive *it*, let him receive *it*" (Matthew, 19:12). In Quentin's distorted version of Christ's sacrifice, what is transmitted beyond death is not the phallic power but the interruption of that power. A few months after Quentin's suicide, Candace's daughter is born, and she is named Quentin after her dead uncle. The female Quentin is an embodiment of that interruption

1. Guy Rosolato, *Essais sur le symbolique* (Paris: Gallimard, 1969), 63 *[Editor]*.
2. See Acts, 8:26–31, where Candace, Queen of the Ethiopians, is associated with a eunuch of great authority whom she has put in charge of all her treasures *[Editor]*.

of genealogy effected by her uncle's death, for as Faulkner says, she is "fatherless nine months before her birth, nameless at birth and already doomed to be unwed from the instant the dividing egg determined its sex" (p. 19) [214]. There is as well in this transmission of interrupted genealogy an element of revenge, a reversal inflicted on a substitute, for as the male Quentin's death is put in the context of Christ's death and resurrection, so the female Quentin, on the day before Easter in 1928, escapes from the womb of the Compson home, stealing in the process the money that her Uncle Jason had withheld from her allowance—a theft that is presented as a symbolic castration of Jason (who is his father's namesake and who had his younger brother Benjy gelded) by the dead Quentin's namesake. Faulkner says of Jason, "Of his niece he did not think at all, nor the arbitrary valuation of the money. Neither of them had had entity or individuality for him for ten years; together they merely symbolized the job in the bank of which he had been deprived before he ever got it. . . . 'I'll think of something else,' he said, so he thought about Lorraine. He imagined himself in bed with her, only he was just lying beside her, pleading with her to help him, then he thought of the money again, and that he had been outwitted by a woman, a girl. If he could just believe it was the man who had robbed him. But to have been robbed of that which was to have compensated him for the lost job, which he had acquired through so much effort and risk, by the very symbol of the lost job itself, and worst of all, by a bitch of a girl" (pp. 321, 323) [191, 192]. Since Jason's friend Lorraine is a prostitute, the theft of Jason's money is a castration of his power to buy sex, and since the money that was stolen was in part money that Jason had stolen from his niece, Jason is rendered impotent, he is powerless to gain any legal redress. Jason dies a childless bachelor.

* * *

As a counterpoint to the transmission of interrupted physical genealogy that we find in the English runner [in A *Fable*] and the female Quentin, the two youngest male descendants of the Sutpen and Compson families, the black Jim Bond and the white Benjy Compson, are both congenital idiots whose physical condition, in this final instance of black-white doubling, evokes the traditional biological punishment of that incest from which all doubling springs. But of course, no real physical incest occurs in the Sutpen or Compson families as far as we know, so that the condition of Jim Bond and Benjy Compson is a symbol of that psychological incest that pervades both families and that makes the families in turn symbolic of a place and a time.

One could continue indefinitely multiplying examples of doubling between the stories of the Sutpen and Compson families and finding in other Faulkner novels incidents in which these doublings are doubled again, but by now we have established the outlines and the importance of a structure that is central to Faulkner's work. In this structure, the struggle between the father and the son in the incest complex is played out again and again in a series of spatial and temporal repetitions, a series of substitutive doublings and reversals in which generation in time becomes a self-perpetuating cycle of revenge on a substitute, the passing on from father to son of a fated repetition as a positive or a negative inheritance. Religion as "the longing for the father," to use Freud's phrase, attempts, successfully or not, to release man from this spirit of revenge through the mechanism of sacrifice and the alliance of the father and the son. In sacrifice, the impulses of the father against the son and those of the son against the father are simultaneously acted out on a symbolic, mediatory third term, so that the contrary impulses momentarily cancel each other out in a single act with a double psychological significance. Yet obviously, religious sacrifice as an institutionalized substitute for those impulses is also a conscious, communal preserver and transmitter of those impulses, capable at any moment of reconverting the symbolic death struggle between father and son into the real death struggle.

This structure, as I have tried to present it in all its complexity, exists in no single Faulkner novel nor in the sum total of those novels; it exists, rather, in that imaginative space that the novels create *in between* themselves by their interaction. The analysis of one novel will not reveal it, nor will it be revealed by an analysis of all the novels in a process of simple addition, for since the structure is created by means of an interplay between texts, it must be approached through a critical process that, like the solving of a simultaneous equation, oscillates between two or more texts at once. The key to the critical oscillation that I have attempted between *Absalom, Absalom!* and *The Sound and the Fury* is, of course, the figure of Quentin Compson—Quentin, whose own oscillation constantly transforms action into narration and narration into action.

It is tempting to see in Quentin a surrogate of Faulkner, a double who is fated to retell and reenact the same story throughout his life just as Faulkner seemed fated to retell in different ways the same story again and again and, insofar as narration is action, to reenact that story as well. And just as Quentin's retellings and reenactments are experienced as failures that compel him to further repetitions that will correct those failures but that are themselves experienced as failures in turn, so Faulkner's comments on his own writing express his sense of the failures of his narratives, failures that compel him to retell the story again and again. In one of his conferences at the University of Virginia, Faulkner said of the composition of *The Sound and the Fury:* "It was, I thought, a short story, something that could be done in about two pages, a thousand words, I found out it couldn't. I finished it the first time, and it wasn't right, so I wrote it again, and that was Quentin, that wasn't right. I wrote it again, that was Jason, that wasn't right, then I tried to let Faulkner do it, that still was wrong."

It is as if, in the character of Quentin, Faulkner embodied, and perhaps tried to exorcise, certain elements present in himself and in his need to be a writer. Certainly, Quentin evokes that father-son struggle that a man inevitably has with his own literary progenitors when he attempts to become an "author." He evokes as well Faulkner's apparent sense of the act of writing as a progressive dismemberment of the self in which parts of the living subject are cut off to become objectified in language, to become (from the writer's point of view) detached and deadened, drained, in that specific embodiment, of their obsessive emotional content. In this process of piecemeal self-destruction, the author, the living subject, is gradually transformed into the detached object—his books. And this process of literary self-dismemberment is the author's response to the threat of death; it is a using up, a consuming of the self in the act of writing in order to escape from that annihilation of the self that is the inevitable outcome of physical generation, to escape by means of an ablative process of artistic creation in which the self is worn away to leave only a disembodied voice on the page to survive the writer's death, a voice that represents the interruption of a physical generative power and the transmission, through the author's books, of the phallic generative power of the creative imagination. This act of writing is sacrificial and mediatory, a gradual sacrificing of the self in an attempt to attain immortality through the mediation of language. It is as well an active willing of the author's passivity in the grip of time, for since time inevitably wears away the self to nothing, that actively willed wearing away of the self in the ablative process of creation is an attempt to transform necessity into a virtue, *ananke* into *virtù*, a fate into a power. Clearly, for Faulkner, writing is a kind of doubling in which the author's self is reconstituted within the realm of language as the Other, a narcissistic mirroring of the self to which the author's reaction is at once a fascinated self-love and an equally fascinated self-hatred. In one of the conferences at Virginia, Faulkner said that *Absalom* was in part "the story of Quentin Compson's hatred of the bad qualities in the country he loves." There is a sense in which that ambivalence, that "hatred of the bad qualities in the country he loves," defines as well Faulkner's novelistic effort, his relationship to a geographic and an artistic, an outer and an inner, "fatherland." The structure that we have found in the interplay between *Absalom, Absalom!* and *The Sound and the Fury* is central to Faulkner's novels precisely because it is, for Faulkner, central to the art of writing novels.

*   *   *

In 1933 Faulkner wrote an introduction for a new edition of *The Sound and the Fury*, an introduction that he decided not to publish and that remained unpublished for almost forty years. In it he describes the genesis of the novel:

. . . one day it suddenly seemed as if a door had clapped silently and forever to between me and all publishers' addresses and booklists and I said to myself, Now I can write. Now I can just write. Whereupon I, who had three brothers and no sisters and was destined to lose my first daughter in infancy, began to write about a little girl.

I did not realise then that I was trying to manufacture the sister which I did not have and the daughter which I was to lose, though the former might have been apparent from the fact that Caddy had three brothers almost before I wrote her name on paper.[3]

Later in the introduction he says that since writing *The Sound and the Fury* he learned that "the emotion definite and physical and yet nebulous to describe which the writing of Benjy's section of *The Sound and the Fury* gave me—that ecstasy, that eager and joyous faith and anticipation of surprise which the yet unmarred sheets beneath my hand held inviolate and unfailing—will not return. The unreluctance to begin, the cold satisfaction in work well and arduously done, is there and will continue to be there as long as I can do it well. But that other will not return. I shall never know it again" (pp. 160–61) [231]. What Faulkner describes here is the author's sense of the loss of the original virgin space ("that ecstasy, that eager and joyous faith and anticipation of surprise which the yet unmarred sheets beneath my hand held inviolate and unfailing") and his mature acceptance of repetition ("The unreluctance to begin, the cold satisfaction in work well and arduously done, is there and will continue to be there as long as I can do it well").

The introduction ends:

> There is a story somewhere about an old Roman who kept at his bedside a Tyrrhenian vase which he loved and the rim of which he wore slowly away with kissing it. I had made myself a vase, but I suppose I knew all the time that I could not live forever inside of it, that perhaps to have it so that I too could lie in bed and look at it would be better; surely so when that day should come when not only the ecstasy of writing would be gone, but the unreluctance and the something worth saying too. It's fine to think that you will leave something behind you when you die, but it's better to have made something you can die with. Much better the muddy bottom of a little doomed girl climbing a blooming pear tree in April to look in the window at the funeral.   (p. 161) [231]

Faulkner revised the introduction several times. In its final version, in which Faulkner doubles Quentin's own words in the novel, the ending fuses a series of images that are separated in earlier versions:

3. William Faulkner, "An Introduction to *The Sound and the Fury*," in *A Faulkner Miscellany*, ed. James B. Meriwether (Jackson: University of Mississippi Press, 1974), 158–59 [229–30]. Unless otherwise noted, subsequent quotations from the introduction are taken from this edition.

> One day I seemed to shut a door between me and all publishers'
> addresses and book lists. I said to myself, Now I can write. Now I
> can make myself a vase like that which the old Roman kept at his
> bedside and wore the rim slowly away with kissing it. So I, who had
> never had a sister and was fated to lose my daughter in infancy, set
> out to make myself a beautiful and tragic little girl.[4]

Faulkner realized that it is precisely because the novelist stands outside the dark door, wanting to enter the dark room but unable to, that
he *is* a novelist, that he must imagine what takes place beyond the door.
Indeed, it is just that tension toward the dark room that he cannot enter
that makes that room the source of all his imaginings—the womb of art.
He understood that a writer's relation to his material and to the work of
art is always a loss, a separation, a cutting off, a self-castration that transforms the masculine artist into the feminine-masculine vase of the work.
He knew that in this act of progressive self-destruction "the author's actual
self is the one that goes down," that the writer ends up identifying himself not with what remains but with what is lost, the detached object that
is the work. It is precisely by a loss, by a cutting off or separation that
the artist's self and his other self, the work, mutually constitute one
another—loss is the very condition of their existence. Discussing the
image of Candace in the stream, that "beautiful and tragic little girl"
that stands for the artist's lost, other self, Faulkner said,

> I saw that peaceful glinting of that branch was to become the dark,
> harsh flowing of time sweeping her to where she could not return
> to comfort him, but that just separation, division, would not be
> enough, not far enough. It must sweep her into dishonor and shame
> too. And that Benjy must never grow beyond this moment; that for
> him all knowing must begin and end with that fierce, panting, paused
> and stooping wet figure which smelled like trees. That he must
> never grow up to where the grief of bereavement could be leavened
> with understanding and hence the alleviation of rage as in the case
> of Jason, and of oblivion as in the case of Quentin.   (p. 159)
>   [230]

4. William Faulkner, "An Introduction for *The Sound and the Fury*," ed. James B. Meriwether,
The Southern Review, n.s., 8, 4 (Autumn 1972): 710 [227].

MYRA JEHLEN

[Faulkner's Fiction and Southern Society] †

The land's living symbol—a formal group of ritual almost mystic significance identical and monotonous as milestones tying the county's ultimate rim as milestones would: the beast the plow and the man integrated in one foundationed into the frozen wave of their furrow tremendous with effort yet at the same time vacant of progress, ponderable immovable and immobile like groups of wrestling statuary set against the land's immensity.[1]

The pastoral backwaters of Mississippi seem not to have afforded Faulkner much peace. The stories and novels of the Yoknapatawpha saga are tense with extreme, unresolvable contradictions which led one critic to suggest that the works indeed constitute a "quest for failure."[2] A major contention of this essay is that the tensions and dissonances in Faulkner's writing were neither temperamental nor linguistic in origin[3] but expressed the author's profoundly discordant view of Southern life.[4]

The passage cited above captures the paradoxically violent paralysis pervading Yoknapatawpha, and the farming image is altogether appro-

† From *Class and Character in Faulkner's South* (New York: Columbia University Press, 1976), 19–46. Copyright © 1976 Columbia University Press. Reprinted with the permission of the publisher. Page references in brackets are to this Norton Critical Edition.
1. William Faulkner, *Intruder in the Dust* (New York, 1948), 147.
2. Walter J. Slatoff, *Quest for Failure* (Ithaca, N.Y., 1960). Slatoff notes the preponderance of oxymorons in Faulkner's style and suggests that these express the author's reluctance to resolve fictional conflicts.
3. Slatoff attributes Faulkner's preference for irresolution to his "temperament." See "The Edge of Order: The Pattern of Faulkner's Rhetoric," reprinted in *William Faulkner: Three Decades of Criticism*, ed. Frederick J. Hoffman and Olga W. Vickery (East Lansing, Mich., 1960), 197–98. The linguistic origin has been proposed by James L. Guetti in his book *Limits of Metaphor: A Study of Melville, Conrad and Faulkner* (Ithaca, N.Y., 1967). Guetti argues that for Melville, Conrad, and Faulkner "the problem of order" is "linguistic" rather than "ideological" (p. 11). The "narrative difficulty" for these writers "is that of using language in such a way as to prevent one's recognition of the arbitrariness and exclusiveness of composed linguistic systems" (p. 4). But while this interpretation is highly resonant for us, concerned as we are with both the validity and viability of language, it does not seem to me applicable to Melville or Faulkner, whose efforts are rather focused on the tensions not "within language" but "between language and a non-linguistic reality" (p. 4).
4. Cleanth Brooks, in an important study, *The Yoknapatawpha Country* (New Haven, Conn., 1963), has as a central thesis a view of the South and of Faulkner's perception of it which is directly opposed to the one I develop here. Brooks sums it up this way: "Most of all, [the Yoknapatawpha] society is bound together by unspoken assumptions—that is to say, it is a true community" (p. 368). As is already evident, I do not think this society or its real-life model is much united, nor do I think that Faulkner thought it was, at least while he was writing his most important works. There Yoknapatawpha and the South appear deeply rent by moral and ideological antagonisms rooted in a discordant class structure. I can see little evidence for Brooks's hopeful conclusion that "even lack of purpose and value take on special meaning when brought into Faulkner's world, for its very disorders are eloquent of the possibilities of order. . . ." (p. 368). Faulkner's seems to me on the contrary one of the most troubled and unresolved visions in America's troubled and unresolved literature.

priate because the agrarian issue was the central one in Faulkner's indecision. For in defining his ideal of rural life, he was torn between two
forms of agrarianism, both native to his region, but so opposed in their
values and social implications that their partisans were joined in warfare
long before the Civil War. Although the legendary cavalier has represented the South nationally, the region always had many more farmers
than leisured planters. The struggle between these two agrarian groups
roughly constitutes Southern political history, until the year 1939 anyway, and therefore through Faulkner's most impressionable and produc-
tive years. Each group rightly viewed the other as a threat to its survival.
Sensitized by their dread of slave insurrections, the planters at times
feared a redneck revolution. Of course the rednecks did seek a revolution
of sorts or, at any rate, redistribution of the land and an equal share in
political power.

The myths in which the antagonists embodied their aspirations became
essential weapons in their fight.[5] The farmers cast themselves as Jeffersonian yeomen, upright tillers of the soil, the salt of the American earth.[6]
The planters invoked classical ideas of order to legitimize their feudal
system and argued that only a leisure class could attain the esthetic and
ethical excellence to forward the course of civilization.[7] The common
folk replied that their righteous labor fed the spirit as well as the body.
They were translating into the Southern vernacular the words of Hector
St. John de Crèvecoeur who had written over a century earlier that "the
salubrious effluvia of the earth animate our spirits, and serve to inspire
us."[8] Most of Faulkner's contemporaries in the South seem to have
aligned themselves with one or the other side. The majority of those
involved in the Southern renascence of the twenties and thirties[9] agreed
with Stark Young of Mississippi that "in talking about Southern characteristics we are talking largely of a certain life in the Old South, a life
founded on land and the ownership of slaves." They defined agriculture
as "a form of labor that is pursued with intelligence and leisure."[1] On
the other hand, there were those like Ben Robertson who proudly claimed
that his North Carolina ancestors were "plain people, . . . hickory-nut
homespun Southerners." "Like Jefferson," he explained, "we believe in

5. In *Origins of the New South, 1877–1913, A History of the South*, Vol. IX (Louisiana State
Univ. Press and the Little Field Fund for Southern History of the Univ. of Texas, 1951), C. Vann
Woodward describes the way the Populists appealed to the Jeffersonian myth to validate their
efforts and concludes that the myth was crucial to their success.
6. The figure of the American yeoman has been analyzed in a number of works, chief of which
is Henry Nash Smith's *Virgin Land, The American West as Symbol and Myth* (New York, 1961).
7. The Southern cavalier and his values are exhaustively described in William R. Taylor, *Cavalier and Yankee: The Old South and the National Character* (Garden City, N.Y., 1963).
8. J. Hector St. John de Crèvecoeur, *Letters from an American Farmer* (New York, 1957), 12.
The *Letters* first appeared in 1782.
9. I refer, for example, to many of the group who cooperated in writing *I'll Take My Stand: The
South and the Agrarian Tradition* (New York, 1962): Donald Davidson, Lyle H. Lanier, Stark
Young, Allen Tate, Andrew Nelson Lytle, F. L. Owsley, and John Crowe Ransom. The book, a
collection of essays, appeared in 1930.
1. *I'll Take My Stand*, p. xxix.

a country of small farms, with every family independent. . . . We believe in hard day labor. . . . All that eat should sweat."[2] Faulkner was heir to both of these viewpoints and unable fully to approve either one.

Since this ambivalence is a central theme of the essay, I should state at the outset that, far from regretting or condemning it, I consider it the source of Faulkner's literary greatness. In fact one might speculate that some such ambivalence is the source of all artistic achievement. Resolution and clarity may yield theory, but the practice of literature seems to require another inspiration altogether. The well-known story of Faulkner's ranking of contemporary writers, giving first place to those who attempted the most and proved it by not succeeding, may well express his sense that the resolution of problems can be paradoxically fatal to the work, while the unceasing drive to resolve them is the very dynamic of creation. Something like this, at any rate, inspired Faulkner, whose own ambivalence was surely one of the most creative any writer ever suffered from.

In principle he seems to have endorsed Jeffersonian values. Yet it is clear from the preponderance in his major fiction of lords over peasants that he felt the lords were the crux of the matter, the ones upon whom everything depended and foundered. This deference to a class whose way of life he considered ethically unwholesome, and the inverse, his inability to identify with the farmers, who, however abjectly, wore the yeoman's mantle, largely inspired the author's tragic vision of the South.[3] He did attempt a more hopeful vision focused on such modified aristocrats as Gavin Stevens and his nephew Charles Mallison. The scion of an old plantation family and himself committed to an abstract agrarianism which reveres the land however it is used, Stevens is the county's impartial district attorney, thus, it would seem, escaping the limitations in Faulkner's mind of either agrarian party. Gavin even makes gestures toward reconciling the lords and the peasants in regard to such matters as educational and linguistic differences, for, unspoiled by the most enviable credentials,[4] he loves nothing better than long laconic afternoons on the porch of the general store, savoring a colloquial "chaw" with the locals. But whether King's English or vernacular, all Stevens can finally offer are words, an urbane commentary which views the passing of the Old South as one of life's cosmic ironies. Faulkner himself seems to have been less disposed to be philosophical about it; his sorrow is more rebellious than Gavin's and becomes at times a frantic search

2. Ben Robertson, *Red Hills and Cotton: An Upcountry Memory* (New York, 1942), 98.
3. Especially after his speech of acceptance for the Nobel Prize Faulkner himself and his critics tended to stress his affirmations and optimism. But these take the form mostly of abstract pieties while his "nays" are concretely realized in his best works such as *The Sound and the Fury* and *Absalom, Absalom!*
4. Stevens holds degrees from Harvard and Heidelberg universities. By "critical independence" I mean a stance resembling that of Georg Lukacs' definition of the critical realist writer, in *Studies in European Realism* and *Realism in Our Time.*

for an explanation—which, however, when it emerged in his work proved unacceptable because it implied that the major guilt was the planters'.

His emotional, perhaps "esthetic," bias in favor of aristocrats not only kept Faulkner in turmoil over the meaning of the Southern rural tradition, but also caused him some literary difficulties. These appear especially in the very uneven Snopes trilogy, *The Hamlet, The Town,* and *The Mansion,* written relatively late in Faulkner's career and thus coinciding with a slight but artistically significant drift to the political right. By this I refer, of course, not to a declared shift from left to right—the very small distance he moved would be of scant interest to a practical politician—but to something more subtle having to do with the way he interpreted his material and with the degree of critical independence he maintained toward his subject. In discussing Faulkner's political thinking, I mean simply his social judgment—most significantly, the social categories in which he grouped individuals and by which their uniqueness was, for him, more or less attenuated. This aspect of his political views is especially important because it contributed to the definition of his characters. Faulkner's class bias was thus directly involved in the formal, most purely "artistic" aspects of his writing. The aristocrat Bayard Sartoris and the redneck Flem Snopes, for example, originate as characters in a political viewpoint which is in this respect indistinguishable from literary vision. And the fact that Sartoris is in formal terms a three-dimensional character and Flem Snopes an allegorical cipher is not so much a matter of artistic choice as of social judgment. Indeed, that Faulkner regarded the upper class less critically toward the end of his career is here first of literary and only secondly of biographical or political interest.

At any rate, during the years 1925 to 1940, when his major works appeared *(Sartoris, The Sound and the Fury, Light in August, Absalom, Absalom!,* most of the stories in *Go Down, Moses,* and much of *The Hamlet),* Faulkner's attitude toward Southern society remained essentially constant, defined uneasily by the indecision described earlier. Under its influence he began with *Sartoris* (1929) an exploration of plantation history which reached an artistic and intellectual culmination in *Absalom, Absalom!* (1936).

Sartoris, Absalom, Absalom! and the other major cavalier novel, *The Sound and the Fury,* share a central plot, the story of a young man who wishes he could look toward the future but who is self-destructively driven to recall a fatal past. In *Sartoris,* Bayard tries to reconstruct the death of his brother while wondering all the time whether he himself has not also been killed, "trying to remember, feel, a bullet going into his own body that might have slain him at the same instant."[5] Quentin Compson

5. William Faulkner, *Sartoris* (New York, 1961), 272.

recalls the past in *The Sound and the Fury* while in the process of committing suicide, simultaneously succeeding in both. In *Absalom, Absalom!* Quentin dies vicariously. The development of this "recalling plot"
through the Yoknapatawpha plantation novels charts the general progress of Faulkner's early literary thinking.

*   *   *

The Sound and the Fury * * * demythologized the young aristocrat.
Where Bayard Sartoris was for the most part only another version of the
legendary cavalier, Quentin Compson is a more modern character trying
merely to make moral sense out of the doom which has overtaken his
family. If he attaches undue symbolic value to his sister's virginity, it is
less for the sake of cavalier values than out of a need for a point of moral
reference amid the increasing anomie of his surroundings. But, as if
coming closer to the reality of the cavalier's inadequacy had triggered a
general skepticism in Faulkner, *The Sound and the Fury* is at once tentatively historical and uncertain about the significance of history. Even
more radically, it implicitly questions the validity of literary statements
and the value of language. (Later Faulkner would explain the four separate sections of the novel as successive failures to tell a single story.)[6]
   This skepticism marks an acute phase in Faulkner's tensely uncertain
attitude toward the South and therefore toward his writing about it. But
ironically, the novels of this period, *The Sound and the Fury* and *As I
Lay Dying*, have been taken to represent the essential Faulkner who
emerges as a prophet of the modern angst beset by doubts about the
meaning of meaning and the uncertainties of linguistic communication.
Thus a critic has recently written that "the basic emphasis in . . . Faulkner is not upon some ultimate ideal of truth or reality, or even upon
some standard ideological dichotomy or paradox, but upon the unreality
of imaginative structure of any sort and upon the radical linguistic nature—
as opposed to ideological nature—of the problem of order."[7]

   The dichotomy of ideology and language is a familiar one, especially
in the several kinds of formalism where it functions to exclude ideological questions. Made to choose, what critic would declare himself
unconcerned with the literary values of his text? But actually, if the
dichotomy is ever valid, it certainly isn't for Faulkner, whose formal,
linguistic problems in defining the Yoknapatawpha universe are (as I will
try to show in subsequent chapters) inextricably ideological as well. In
The Sound and the Fury with respect to the aristocratic South and, in a
parallel way, in the redneck *As I Lay Dying*, Faulkner explores the limits

6. *Faulkner in the University* (Class Conferences at the University of Virginia, 1957–58), ed.
Frederick L. Gwynn and Joseph L. Blotner (New York, 1965), i.
7. James Guetti, *The Limits of Metaphor: A Study of Melville, Conrad, and Faulkner* (Ithaca,
New York: Cornell University Press, 1967), 11.

of perception and language precisely because like Melville's Ahab he is driven to pierce false masks, the myths which he is coming more and more to realize have distorted Southern reality. In other words, Faulkner cares so much about perception in these novels because there is something he wants to see clearly but can't. His examinations of personal visions are thus directed outward to a public landscape. Bayard Sartoris, Quentin Compson, and Addie Bundren all try to penetrate the surrounding gloom, to communicate with reality not for the sake of communication but in order to know. Indeed they might even have found some comfort in the idea that there was no truth behind the one they created themselves, but Faulkner refuses to yield them (and himself) that comparative safety. Their terrified urgency expresses instead their reluctant recognition that the resistant, mysterious world about them is also inescapably real.

It is true that these characters also try to escape that recognition by projecting worlds outside history such as the inchoate universe of the idiot Benjy and the timeless realm of his brother Quentin. Quentin does argue that time is merely a "mechanical progression" without inherent significance. He refers to objectively measured time and to the concept of causality as masks concealing reality. There is a clock time and there is a real time existing within each individual mind: "clocks slay time; only when the clock stops does time come to life."[8] He therefore breaks his watch and withdraws into his own mind where events and sensations exist statically suspended until they suddenly cease to exist at all.

Quentin is here making a Bergsonian distinction between duration and externally flowing, measurable time. Bergson defines duration as an internally experienced time measured not by clocks or other external standards, but according to one's internal consciousness. Since this personal time measures only an individual's awareness of an event or experience, it is not, as clock time is, a medium of constant flux and process, but rather a static, if extended, single moment. In Bergson's words, "duration is essentially the continuation of that which no longer exists into that which exists now."[9] Thus duration actually negates the passage of time; Quentin's argument, that the only real time is duration, transforms history into mere illusion, a period of daydreaming. And because ordering reality according to duration rather than external time is necessarily a completely individual act, it tends to make social relationships as well as historical situations merely accidental poses of no necessary relevance to an individual's inner self. But *The Sound and the Fury* also makes it clear that there is no way out of history and time but in death;

8. William Faulkner, *The Sound and the Fury* (New York, 1959), 71 [54].
9. Henri Bergson, *Durée et simultanéité, à propos de la théorie d'Einstein* (Paris, 1931), 62. The original text reads: "la durée est essentiellement une continuation de ce qui n'est plus dans ce qui est."

Quentin breaks his watch and dies. The novel clearly warns us against adopting his views.

But it cannot itself transcend those views, and so, caught on behalf of its characters between a deadly history and personal annihilation, it becomes hopelessly paralyzed and can only repeat itself over and over. (The famous Dilsey episode, something of a Hallelujah chorus, is really no more redemptive than any other section. Perhaps Faulkner realized that no degree of endurance by a nigger mammy could reverse the disintegration of the aristocratic South.) The first version of the Compson story is narrated by its last male descendant, a mental incompetent castrated for the sake of public security. The second section depicts Quentin's total recall at the last moment of a life doomed at birth, and the third is told by * * * Jason, the only functional Compson and Faulkner's most despicable character anywhere in the Yoknapatawpha saga.

The "irrational brutality" of the Compsons' life has been attributed by Jean-Paul Sartre to "the author's lack of any intuitive knowledge of the future."[1] For Sartre the meaning of events lies above all in their potential development; but without disputing the general validity of this view, one must question its relevance to Faulkner, whose cavalier theme is necessarily about the past. What generates the hopelessness of *The Sound and the Fury* is, on the contrary, the author's failure to visualize the past in other than the conventional terms which we have already seen contain no answers to his questions. Quentin is driven to madness finally by the apparent arbitrariness, the mechanical entropy, with which the catastrophic present has succeeded a respectable, even a proud past. Once the Compson lands and honor were intact, men were men and life was good; now even those who have retained their wealth only parody the old values. The Kentuckians Gerald Bland and his mother shrilly portray the new-money vulgarity which has incomprehensibly risen to power. Mrs. Bland loves to tell anecdotes illustrating her son's princely temperament. "I remember the one," Quentin muses suicidally, "how Gerald throws his nigger downstairs and how the nigger pled to be allowed to matriculate in the divinity school to be near marster marse Gerald and how he ran all the way to the station beside the carriage with tears in his eyes when marse Gerald rid away. . . ."[2] The Blands are repugnant, of course, but what makes them so? Quentin's objection to the little vignette of marse Gerald and the nigger seems to be mainly a matter of taste. Unwilling or unable to ask whether they have debased his heritage or only exposed it, he thus sticks at the execrable manners by which the Blands destroy the civilized facade he has leaned on. At this point there is not much difference between Quentin's attachment to the conven-

1. Jean-Paul Sartre, "Time in Faulkner: *The Sound and the Fury*," reprinted in *William Faulkner: Three Decades of Criticism*, p. 231.
2. *The Sound and the Fury*, p. 85 [68].

tions of cavalier culture and Benjy's blind insistence on any pattern that has become familiar. As the chilling close of the novel warns, such arbitrary orders threaten imminently to dissolve into chaos. Benjy has been accustomed to his rides into town to follow a particular route counterclockwise around the square. This time his driver goes around it clockwise. Horrified by this violation of his sense of order and propriety, Benjy howls piercingly until the course of the carriage is reversed and "cornice and facade flowed smoothly once more from left to right; post and tree, window and doorway, and signboard, each in its ordered place."[3] The novel's last words, "each in its ordered place," imply radical disbelief in the meaningfulness of all orders, including necessarily the ordering vision of fiction. At this nadir of Faulkner's struggle with his own ambivalence toward the South, he seems almost ready to identify with Quentin Compson who, when he determined that life was meaningless, simply stopped.

DONALD M. KARTIGANER

[The Meaning of Form in] *The Sound and the Fury* †

I

When Random House decided in 1946 to combine *The Sound and the Fury* and *As I Lay Dying* in a single Modern Library volume, the motive presumably had little to do with any formal or thematic relationship between the two novels. Faulkner did not care for the idea: " 'I had never thought of TSAF and AS I LAY DYING in the same breath.' " He preferred that *The Sound and the Fury* be paired with "Wild Palms," the story from the novel by that title; " 'the part of it about the doctor who performed the abortion on his own sweetheart.' "[1]

And yet the joining of Faulkner's first major novels was perfectly appropriate, and not only because, as he once said, "both of them happened to have a sister in a roaring gang of menfolks."[2] Each novel revolves around a single, sorely tried family. *The Sound and the Fury* portrays family tribulation as a decline from greatness: idiocy, madness, alcoholism, promiscuity, and theft as symptoms of a tragic Fall of Southern Princes. The Bundrens, however, with their own representatives of mental

---

3. *The Sound and the Fury*, p. 224 [199].
† From *The Fragile Thread: The Meaning of Form in Faulkner's Novels* (Amherst: University of Massachusetts Press, 1979), 3–22. Copyright © 1979 by The University of Massachusetts Press. Page references in brackets are to this Norton Critical Edition.
1. Joseph Blotner, *Faulkner: A Biography*, 2 vols. (New York: Random House, 1974), 2: 1208. For an early interpretation see Carvel Collins, "The Pairing of *The Sound and the Fury* and *As I Lay Dying*," *Princeton University Library Chronicle* 18 (Spring 1957): 114–23.
2. Frederick L. Gwynn and Joseph Blotner, eds., *Faulkner in the University, Class Conferences at the University of Virginia 1957–1958* (Charlottesville: University of Virginia Press, 1959), 207.

disorder, illicit sex, and double-dealing, have nowhere to go but up. Instead of family decay, *As I Lay Dying* tells a comic tale of perseverance at a price. Unburdened with governors and generals (a sure sign of degeneracy, says Jason Compson), the Bundrens need only haul Addie's moldering body to Jefferson and put her third son, Darl, on a train to Jackson in order to persuade us that they will survive. Their only war is the Great War, and rather than bullet holes in the dining-room table their souvenir is a French spyglass with "a woman and a pig with two backs and no face."

Most of the major characters of *The Sound and the Fury* are reborn in *As I Lay Dying*, in guises suited to their new social status. The tragic Caddy, whose pregnancy drives her father further into dipsomania, one brother to suicide and another to thievery, becomes the naive though equally fertile Dewey Dell. Quentin, the sensitive artist figure transforming his sister's sex life into a Byronic tale of mortal sin, becomes the articulate and impotent visionary Darl. Jason's pretense to efficiency reappears in the more attractive Cash, himself cooly competent, although as helpless as Jason in the face of extremity. And finally Benjy, childlike at thirty-three, becomes the real child Vardaman. By no means an idiot, Vardaman yet owns a child's perception that enables him to identify his dead mother and a fish—as remarkable in its own way as Benjy's ability to smell his grandmother's death or the feeling of guilt in his sister. The Compsons' black servants, of course, are missing in *As I Lay Dying*. There is no Dilsey to cook, raise the children, nurse the sick, or "endure"; for these things the Bundrens need no one but themselves.

The telling of these two novels also suggests a repetition with variation. Both *The Sound and the Fury* and *As I Lay Dying* come to us as a succession of stream-of-consciousness monologues, each novel a version of Faulkner's usual reversed picaresque structure: not a sequence of bizarre incidents happening to a single hero, but a sequence of bizarre heroes happening to a single incident. But here as well the two novels diverge, becoming parodies of each other. In *The Sound and the Fury* individual consciousness assumes an extreme freedom, nearly unbounded by the pressure of plot. The Easter weekend which is the novel's present, whether from the point of view of its Christian implications or its secular events such as Benjy's birthday or Jason's habitual chasing of his niece, scarcely amounts to a controlling structure. The tale each of the four narrators is trying to tell, the history and meaning of four children growing up in the South and in the first quarter of this century, is the tale that fails to come clear. This is the point Faulkner made in his account of the writing of the novel.

> And that's how that book grew. That is, I wrote that same story four times. None of them were right, but I had anguished so much that I could not throw any of it away and start over, so I printed it in the

four sections. That was not a deliberate *tour de force* at all, the book just grew that way. That I was still trying to tell one story which moved me very much and each time I failed, but I had put so much anguish into it that I couldn't throw it away, like the mother that had four bad children, that she would have been better off if they all had been eliminated, but she couldn't relinquish any of them. And that's the reason I have the most tenderness for that book, because it failed four times.[3]

In *As I Lay Dying* the rambling interior monologues become short staccato bursts, as if consciousness, faced with the obstacles of fire and flood, can spare only moments for sensibility. Moreover, a complete *action* takes place, and with a clarity rather startling for a Faulkner novel: a death and a movement from one place to another, curbing the isolated minds and motives into a service of that action. There is nothing in *The Sound and the Fury* like the journey to Jefferson, an easily paraphrased plot that begins with Addie Bundren's request to be buried with her people and concludes with a fitting tranquillity of bananas, graphophones, and the appearance of an odd little woman introduced as Mrs. Bundren. Action, in other words, becomes a form of control, urging the Bundrens—as voices and as actors—toward the completion of a tale and a quest. This external pressure on consciousness is also the source of the novel's absurd comedy.

Faulkner's comments on the writing of *As I Lay Dying* are as instructive as those on *The Sound and the Fury*. The two novels eventually came to represent for him two kinds of writing, one in which a book "grows," as if possessing a life of its own, another in which a book is more deliberately composed, everything in it predetermined. He called *As I Lay Dying* tour de force, which he insisted the earlier novel was not. "Sometimes," Faulkner said, "technique charges in and takes command of the dream before the writer himself can get his hands on it. That is *tour de force* and the finished work is simply a matter of fitting bricks neatly together, since the writer knows probably every single word right to the end before he puts the first one down. This happened with *As I Lay Dying*."[4] *A Fable*, a much bigger and more ambitious book,

3. James B. Meriwether and Michael Millgate, eds., *Lion in the Garden, Interviews with William Faulkner 1926–1962* (New York: Random House, 1968), 147. Faulkner repeated this account on several occasions: in a 1955 interview with Cynthia Grenier; a 1956 interview with Jean Stein (both reprinted in *Lion in the Garden*); in *Faulkner in the University*, pp. 1, 31–32; in Joseph L. Fant and Robert Ashley, eds., *Faulkner at West Point* (New York: Random House, 1964), 109–11; and in two recently printed drafts of an intended introduction to the novel, written in 1933: James B. Meriwether, "An Introduction for *The Sound and the Fury*," *Southern Review*, n.s. 8 (October 1972): 705–10, and James B. Meriwether, "An Introduction to *The Sound and the Fury*," *Mississippi Quarterly* 26 (Summer 1973): 410–15.
4. Meriwether and Millgate, *Lion in the Garden*, p. 244. Blotner's accounts of the writing of both novels indicate that Faulkner, while exaggerating a bit the ease with which he wrote *As I Lay Dying*, was fairly accurate in his comments. See *Faulkner: A Biography* 1:566–79, 587–90, 633–42. The manuscript of *As I Lay Dying* seems to have been completed in forty-seven days, the typescript a month later. Faulkner's attitudes toward the relative merits of these novels were

was also tour de force because "I knew exactly what I wanted to do, but it took me nine years to find how to do it. But I knew what I wanted to do." "I simply used a formula," he said, "a proven formula in our western culture to tell something which I wanted to tell."[5]

The formula that assisted the writing of As I Lay Dying and A Fable is comparable to, if not identical with, the pressure of plot that organizes these novels, whether in the form of the journey or the life and death of Christ. The Sound and the Fury, for the most part, is without such pressure; it is the book that struggles, with all the signs of its struggles showing, toward wholeness.

Yet both novels, despite the differences, are about failures of telling, about what Michael Millgate calls "the problem of the elusiveness of truth."[6] They are like tragic and comic masks of a single meditation on the mysteries of absence: the departed sister, the dead mother, both of whom bring to life the imaginations of bereft families. It is as if the vacant space in which Caddy or Addie since stood is now the dark silence of significant speech, an absence waiting to be filled with meaning.

The Sound and the Fury is more obviously this kind of novel, for its sorrow is rooted in the failure of each of its four voices to summon up, singly or collectively, a persuasive account of what it is that has happened to the Compsons. "When I began it," Faulkner wrote, "I had no plan at all. I wasn't even writing a book";[7] and the novel suggests nothing so much as its own effort to discover the plan implicit to itself, the book it might become were language eloquent enough, were the telling of stories free enough of bias and imposition, were the human mind capable of imagining the truth.

As I Lay Dying keeps its secret better hidden. After all, the journey is completed, the body has been placed in the ground where it belongs; a story has been enacted and told. But the story and the journey may comprise an empty form, for the motives of each of the Bundrens (with the exception of Jewel) vary so greatly from the alleged motives of that journey that the design is at least partially detached from the consciousnesses that give it life, from the people who implement it through their actions. More important, the most incisive vision in the novel—that of Darl—has nothing whatever to do with the controlling action. The clearcut structure of As I Lay Dying, in other words, becomes a symbol of rigidity, of the imagination imprisoned in an action remote from its own

---

not always the same. In a 1932 interview with Henry Nash Smith he thought As I Lay Dying his best work (Lion in the Garden, p. 32); by the time of his 1955 interviews in Japan he thought it was his worst, or the one he "like(d) the least" (Lion in the Garden, p. 180).
5. Ibid, pp. 226, 99.
6. Michael Millgate, The Achievement of William Faulkner (New York: Random House, 1966), 106. See also André Bleikasten, The Most Splendid Failure: Faulkner's "The Sound and the Fury" (Bloomington: Indiana University Press, 1976), 51–66. This is a major study of the novel, valuable not only for its interpretation but for its collation of the criticism.
7. Faulkner, "An Introduction for The Sound and the Fury," p. 710.

deepest motives. The quest has been carried out, but what has been won?

In the two novels we find a radical questioning both of the possibilities of effective human effort and the possibilities of fiction: whether the novel of consciousness, of process, can complete itself in some kind of coherent whole, or whether the novel of action, of product, can be the culmination rather than the violation of consciousness.

II

The Sound and the Fury is the four-times-told tale that opens with a date and the disorder of an idiot's mind and concludes with "post and tree, window and doorway, and signboard, each in its ordered place." But this final order is one that has meaning only for the idiot: a sequence of objects that, when viewed from one perspective rather than another, can calm Benjy into a serene silence. The reader remains in a welter of contradictory visions.

None of the four tales speaks to another, each imagined order cancels out the one that precedes it. Truth is the meaningless sum of four items that seem to have no business being added: Benjy plus Quentin plus Jason plus the "narrator." " 'You bring them together,' " as Faulkner wrote in *Absalom, Absalom!*, " '. . . and . . . nothing happens.' " This atomized Southern family, caught in the conflicts of ancient honor, modern commercialism, self-pity, cynicism, diseased love, becomes Faulkner's impassioned metaphor for the modern crisis of meaning. And *The Sound and the Fury* becomes, paradoxically, a vital expression of the failure of imagination, an approximation of what, for Frank Kermode, is no novel at all: "a discontinuous unorganized middle" that lacks the beginning and end of novel-time.[8]

Neither in the figure of Caddy, for some an organizing center of the novel, nor in the well-wrought fourth narrative do we find an adequate basis of unity in the work. The former possibility has been encouraged in several places by Faulkner himself, who claimed that the story began with the image of Caddy in the tree, and that she is its center, "what I wrote the book about."[9] But rather than a means of binding the fragments together, the image is itself complicated by the fragmentation. It moves into that isolation within the memory, eternal and not quite relevant, that all the major images of the novel possess. Millgate reveals a common uneasiness about this problem: "The novel revolves upon Caddy, but Caddy herself escapes satisfactory definition."[1] The accumulation of monologues results in neither a unity of vision nor a unity of envisioners.

8. Frank Kermode, *The Sense of an Ending* (New York: Oxford University Press, 1967), 140.
9. Gwynn and Blotner, *Faulkner in the University*, p. 6.
1. Millgate, *The Achievement of William Faulkner*, p. 98.

The Benjy section represents extreme objectivity, a condition impossible to the ordinary mind and far in excess of even the most naturalistic fiction. In their sections Quentin and Jason are extremely subjective, each imposing a distorted view on experience, in exact contrast to Benjy, who can abstract no order at all. The fourth section is the voice of the traditional novelist, combining in moderation the qualities of the first three sections: objective in that it seems to tell us faithfully and credibly what happens (our faith in Quentin and Jason is, of course, minimal), and at the same time interpretive but without obvious distortion. Following upon the total immersion in experience or self of the three brothers, the last section is told entirely from without, and establishes the kind of comprehensive but still fixed clarity we expect to find in fiction. And yet for those very qualities, which for many are its strengths, it does not—even as the others do not—tell us what we most need to know. [2]

The Benjy section comes first in the novel for the simple reason that Benjy, of all the narrators, cannot lie, which is to say he cannot create. Being an idiot, Benjy is perception prior to consciousness, prior to the human need to abstract from events an intelligible order. His monologue is a series of frozen pictures, offered without bias: "Through the fence; between the curling flower spaces, I could see them hitting"; " 'What do you want.' Jason said. He had his hands in his pockets and a pencil behind his ear"; "[Father] drank and set the glass down and went and put his hand on Mother's shoulder." His metaphors have the status of fact: "Caddy smelled like trees." [3]

The quality of Benjy's memory is the chief indicator of his non-human perception, for he does not recollect the past: he relives it.

"Wait a minute." Luster said. "You snagged on that nail again. Cant you never crawl through here without snagging on that nail."

Caddy uncaught me and we crawled through. Uncle Maury said to not let anybody see us, so we better stoop over, Caddy said. Stoop over, Benjy. Like this, see. We stooped over and crossed the garden, where the flowers rasped and rattled against us. The ground was hard. We climbed the fence, where the pigs were grunting and snuffing. I expect they're sorry because one of them got killed today, Caddy said. The ground was hard, churned and knotted.

2. My position here should not be confused with that of Walter Slatoff, "The Edge of Order: The Pattern of Faulkner's Rhetoric," in *William Faulkner: Three Decades of Criticism*, and *Quest for Failure: A Study of William Faulkner* (Ithaca: Cornell University Press, 1960), who has argued that Faulkner deliberately fails to resolve *any* of his novels, "that every one of Faulkner's experiments with form and style . . . is a movement away from order and coherence." The quest in Faulkner is not for failure but for form, to move *toward* coherence but only in ways acceptable to the modern writer. The attack on conceptual art, the need to create an illusion of process in fiction, to create persuasive yet not static forms—these are the motives of the great twentieth-century writers, who refuse only the kinds of resolution Slatoff is insisting on, not resolution itself.
3. William Faulkner, *The Sound and the Fury* (New York: Random House, Vintage Books, 1954), reproduced photographically from a copy of the first printing, 1929, pp. 1, 12, 53, 51. Subsequent page references within this chapter will be to this edition. [Bracketed page references are to this Norton Critical Edition—*Editor.*]

> *Keep your hands in your pockets, Caddy said. Or they'll get froze.*
> *You don't want your hands froze on Christmas, do you.*
> "It's too cold out there." Versh said. "You dont want to go out
> doors." (p. 3) [3–4]

The sequence begins in the present, April 7, 1928, with Benjy and
Luster crawling through a fence to get to the branch, where Luster hopes
to find a golf ball. It shifts to a winter day of Benjy's childhood, when
he and Caddy are also crawling through a fence on their way to deliver
a note from Uncle Maury to Mrs. Patterson. The scene shifts again to
earlier the same day, before Caddy has come home from school.

These shifts are triggered by a nail, a fence, the coldness—some object
or quality that abruptly springs Benjy into a different time zone, each
one of which is as alive and real for Benjy as the present. Strictly speaking he "remembers" nothing. As Faulkner said of Benjy in 1955, "To
that idiot, time was not a continuation, it was an instant, there was no
yesterday and no tomorrow, it all is this moment, it all is [now] to him.
He cannot distinguish between what was last year and what will be
tomorrow, he doesn't know whether he dreamed it, or saw it."[4]

Time as duration—Bergsonian time—is what Faulkner is alluding to
here; and it is this sense of time that Benjy, by virtue of his idiocy, has
abandoned. Memory does not serve him as it serves the normal mind,
becoming part of the mind and integral to the stream of constantly created perception that makes it up: the past which, as Bergson put it, "gnaws
into the future and which swells as it advances."[5] Benjy does not recall,
and therefore cannot interpret, the past from the perspective of the present; nor does the past help to determine that perspective. Instead of past
and present being a continuum, each influencing the meaning of the
other, they have no temporal dimension at all. They are isolated, auton-
omous moments that do not come "before" or "after."

This freedom from time makes Benjy a unique narrator indeed. He
does not perceive reality but is at one with it; he does not need to create
his life but rather possesses it with a striking immediacy. There is a
timelessness in the scenes Benjy relives, but it is not the timelessness of
art, abstracting time into meaning. It is the absence of the need for art.

Benjy's monologue, then, does not constitute an interpretation at all;
what he tells us is life, not text. Emerging as if from the vantage point
of eternal stasis, where each moment lived (whether for the first or fif-
tieth time) is the original moment and the only moment, unaffected by
any of the others, this telling is an affront to the existence of narration
or of novels. As Bleikasten says, it "is the very negation of narrative."[6]

---

4. Meriwether and Millgate, *Lion in the Garden*, pp. 147–48.
5. Henri Bergson, *Creative Evolution*, trans. Arthur Mitchell (New York: Random House, Modern Library, 1944), 7. For a discussion of Bergson and a note on Faulkner's knowledge of his
work, see Part Four.
6. Bleikasten, *The Most Splendid Failure*, p. 86.

This is one of the reasons why the Benjy section has such a hold on us, why we attribute to it an authority we never think of granting the others, especially the narratives of his two brothers. Spoken with the awareness that time is always present, and thus missing that sense of consecutiveness necessary to our quick understanding, Benjy's monologue is difficult; yet the cause of that difficulty persuades us that this is truth, not art.

The irony, however, and the reason why the novel does not simply end with this section, is that while Benjy is not himself formulating an interpretation, his succession of lived images passes over into *our* interpretation, becomes a temporal fiction of Compson history that is so clear it is unbelievable. Benjy's scenes, despite fractured chronology and abrupt transitions, meld into a set of clear and consistent character portraits— two-dimensional figures with the sharpness of allegorical signposts that elicit from us simplistic evaluations empty of deep moral insight. "But for the very reason for their simplicity," one critic has written, "Benjy's responses function as a quick moral index to events."[7] This is indeed the effect of Benjy's monologue and its danger.

The following passage, taken from the end of Benjy's monologue, is typical. This is the night of Damuddy's death, when Quentin, Caddy, Jason, and Benjy (between the ages of three and eight) are being put to bed:

> There were two beds. Quentin got in the other one. He turned his face to the wall. Dilsey put Jason in with him. Caddy took her dress off.
> "Just look at your drawers." Dilsey said. "You better be glad your ma aint seen you."
> "I already told on her." Jason said.
> "I bound you would." Dilsey said.
> "And see what you got by it." Caddy said. "Tattletale."
> "What did I get by it." Jason said.
> "Whyn't you get your nightie on." Dilsey said. She went and helped Caddy take off her bodice and drawers. "Just look at you." Dilsey said. She wadded the drawers and scrubbed Caddy behind with them. "It done soaked clean through onto you." she said. "But you wont get no bath this night. Here." She put Caddy's nightie on her and Caddy climbed into the bed and Dilsey went to the door and stood with her hand on the light. "You all be quiet now, you hear." she said.
> "All right." Caddy said. "Mother's not coming in tonight." she said. "So we still have to mind me."
> "Yes." Dilsey said. "Go to sleep now."
> "Mother's sick." Caddy said. "She and Damuddy are both sick."

7. John W. Hunt, *William Faulkner: Art in Theological Tension* (Syracuse: Syracuse University Press, 1965), 89.

"Hush." Dilsey said. "You go to sleep."

The room went black, except the door. Then the door went black. Caddy said, "Hush, Maury," putting her hand on me. So I stayed hushed. We could hear us. We could hear the dark.

It went away, and Father looked at us. He looked at Quentin and Jason, then he came and kissed Caddy and put his hand on my head.

"Is Mother very sick." Caddy said.

"No." Father said. "Are you going to take good care of Maury."

"Yes." Caddy said. (pp. 91–92) [47–48]

Within the space of a single, short scene, each member of the Compson household is definitively characterized. Quentin is the figure of impotence, the one who turns his face to the wall, expressing his futile outrage at all that has gone on that day. Jason, meanness personified, has already told on Caddy—without particular benefit, although he does not realize this. Dilsey is the loyal retainer, the embodiment of responsible affection, who undresses and cleans up Caddy, and sees to it that all the children are in bed. Mother's lack of responsibility is defined by her absence: she is "sick." Father makes his appearance, to look at Jason and Quentin, and to kiss Caddy and touch Benjy (still named Maury): *almost* the responsible parent but playing his favorites and, in his last words, delegating responsibility for Benjy to Caddy. Caddy herself is love, the one who can quiet Benjy down with the touch of her hand. She is also the boldness of youth as both her dirty underwear and confident assumption of the mother's role indicate.

What is so striking about this scene is not only that the meaning of each character can be summarized in an abstract word or two, but that, although the scene comes at the end of Benjy's monologue, the characters are the same as they were in the beginning. They exhibit little change or development; nor can Benjy develop significantly his understanding of them. Each character must be himself over and over again, bearing, like a gift of birth, his inescapable moral worth.

Life—for the scenes Benjy witnesses are at one level the most authentic in the novel—retains the power of its rawness, its freedom from structure; yet simultaneously it passes into the order of our interpretation: a coherent fiction implying all-too-clear moral attitudes. And the demands of our own reader's role are such that it is impossible for us to reverse the process, to return this charged but implausible text to its state of pure presence in the mind of the nonnarrator where it originates.

The most difficult task in reading *The Sound and the Fury* is to get beyond this opening section, for finally Benjy is demonstrating poverty of the pure witness of what is unquestionably there. Benjy's monologue is never less, or more, than truth. We must pass on to the next three sections in which this truth confronts deliberate distortion: vested interests organizing, plotting—consciously or unconsciously, violently or subtly. And with these distortions the cautionary fable we have gleaned from Benjy's images collapses into new complexities: Caddy's promises succumb to need, Jason's ruthlessness turns over into psychotic paranoia, Quentin's futility rages in dreams of murder and incest.

Yet the collapse is not total, as much of the criticism of the novel attests. Not the least irony of *The Sound and the Fury* is that we are tempted most by an absolutism that the whole structure of the novel teaches us to dismiss: not because it is not true but because it is not the truth of what it means to be human in that world which, so this novel asserts, is the one that exists.

III

Following Benjy's freedom from time and interpretation comes the time-possessed Quentin, who wants nothing more than to *replace* life with interpretation. Reality for Quentin is primarily change—in particular the change implicit to the sexual identity of his sister Caddy—and interpretation, metaphor, is the created ground of permanence in which change is eliminated. Caddy's development from child to adolescent and her subsequent loss of virginity epitomizes that change which, in Quentin's mind, is the essence of confusion.

> until after the honeysuckle got all mixed up in it the whole thing came to symbolise night and unrest I seemed to be lying neither asleep nor awake looking down a long corridor of grey halflight where all stable things had become shadowy paradoxical all I had done shadows all I had felt suffered taking visible form antic and perverse mocking without relevance inherent themselves with the denial of the significance they should have affirmed thinking I was I was not who was not was not who. (p. 211) [107–8]

Against this vision of formlessness Quentin props a Byronic fable of incest between himself and Caddy, thus gilding what Father calls her "natural human folly" (p. 220) [112] into a horrific one. Through metaphor he informs his confusion with the clarity of hell: "*the pointing and the horror walled by the clean flame*" (p. 144) [74]. But what is most important is that this hell, and the incest that enables Quentin and Caddy to deserve it, is purely imaginary. In the crucial interview that brings Quentin's monologue to a close, Father asks him: "did you try to make her do it and i i was afraid to i was afraid she might and then it wouldnt have done any good but if i could tell you we did it would have been so and then the others wouldnt be so and then the world would roar away" (p. 220) [112].

"if i could tell you we did it would have been so. . . ." It is not an actual hell reserved for actual sinners that Quentin wants, but his invented one whose unreality frees it from a confusing and disappointing world.

Purity for Quentin lies in a fiction, *known* as a fiction and priding itself on its indifference to reality. He is trying to transform life from within its midst, to convert dull promiscuity to sin, his dreary frustrations into a hell of rich and well-defined despair. It is a hell necessarily unreal: actual incest with Caddy "wouldnt have done any good."

Confronted everywhere with his impotence, Quentin is desperate to believe in the power of words alone: to substitute for what-is the names of what-is-not. He wants to convince Caddy of the reality of his fantasy, not that they have literally made love but that words have a substance more real than bodies.

> . . . *I'll tell you how it was it was a crime we did a terrible crime it*
> *cannot be hid you think it can but wait   Poor Quentin youve*
> *never done that have you   and I'll tell you how it was I'll tell*
> *Father then itll have to be because you love Father then we'll have*
> *to go away amid the pointing and the horror the clean flame I'll*
> *make you say we did I'm stronger than you I'll make you know we*
> *did you thought it was them but it was me listen I fooled you all the*
> *time it was me* (p. 185) [94]

Quentin tries to get Caddy to accede to this fantasy, to see words as the originator rather than the imitator of deeds. This is Quentin's willful decadence, a version of his subsequent suicide in that it puts the world away, using metaphor as a wedge between language and life. As Mr. Compson says, Quentin is trying to make "a temporary state of mind . . . symmetrical above the flesh" (p. 220) [112]. In this sense he is like the three young boys in Cambridge talking about what they might do with the prize money for a fish they neither have caught nor have any hope of catching: "They all talked at once, their voices insistent and contradictory and impatient, making of unreality a possibility, then a probability, then an incontrovertible fact, as people will when their desires become words" (p. 145) [75].

Quentin's need to alter an unbearable reality through language owes much to the teachings of his father. On the first page of Quentin's monologue we read: "Because no battle is ever won he said. They are not even fought. The field only reveals to man his own folly and despair, and victory is an illusion of philosophers and fools" (p. 93) [48]. And shortly before the end: "Father was teaching us that all men are just accumulations dolls stuffed with sawdust swept up from the trash heaps where all previous dolls had been thrown away" (p. 218) [111]. Mr. Compson's theme has been the futility of human action.

Anxious to believe his father is wrong, Quentin clings to the moral codes of Southern antebellum myth: if a woman has been deflowered it can only be because "he made you do it let him he was stronger than you," and a loyal brother will avenge her: "tomorrow Ill kill him I swear I will" (p. 187) [95]. But finally this melodramatic interpretation of events will not do, and so Quentin escapes the cynicism of his father by embracing fully the idea of impotence: the pure fantasy of incest that signals the abandonment of time and his entrance into a world of words.

Quentin's behavior on June 2, 1910, parallels his quest for an irrelevant language. He moves toward a stylization of his life by separating his deeds from his purposes, the conduct of his last day from the impact of its destination. Cutting his thumb on his broken watch crystal, Quentin administers iodine in order to prevent infection; he attends to the matters of packing his belongings, writing farewell notes, stacking books, like someone going on vacation or moving to another town. At the end he carefully removes a blood stain from his vest, washes, cleans his teeth, and brushes his hat, before leaving his room to drown himself.

Both forms of metaphor, verbal and behavioral, move toward suicide. Driving words further and further from facts, style from purpose, art from meaning, Quentin is inside his death—the place without life—for much of his monologue. And yet, since the pride of his fiction-making is its admitted distance from the real, Quentin cannot help but acknowledge the agony of what is: that he has not committed incest with Caddy, that she has had several lovers, that she is pregnant with one man's child and is married to another, a "blackguard." There is in all this an affront that Quentin's artistry cannot conceal or bear. His only triumph is that he has proved his father wrong at least about one thing: "no man ever does that [commits suicide] under the first fury of despair or remorse or bereavement" (p. 221) [112].

The deliberate flight from fact that dominates Quentin's monologue reverses the effect of Benjy's monologue that precedes it. Benjy has made us aware of the distortions of the *literal*; his language is exact, free of bias. It is truth, not metaphor. Yet this exaggerated objectivism results in the most simplistic of moral designs. Quentin, on the other hand, has plunged into metaphor; but in doing so he reduces subjectivism to an art of decadence: "symmetrical above the flesh."

IV

"The first sane Compson since before Culloden," Faulkner said of Jason in the Appendix to *The Sound and the Fury* written sixteen years after the novel. This is a view that has been adopted wholly or in part by many readers of the novel, although one wonders how anyone, especially Faulkner, could have considered Jason sane or rational.[8] Surely

8. See, for example, Olga Vickery, *The Novels of William Faulkner* (Baton Rouge: Louisiana State University Press, 1964): "that [Jason's] actions are the results of clear, orderly thinking in terms of cause and effect cannot be disputed" (p. 31); and Floyd Watkins, "The Word and the Deed in Faulkner's First Great Novels," in *William Faulkner: Four Decades of Criticism*, ed. Linda Welshimer Wagner (East Lansing: Michigan State University Press, 1973): "Jason, however, is too sane and rational ever to make associations which are illogical and poetic" (p. 228). For a contrasting view see Edmond Volpe, *A Reader's Guide to William Faulkner* (New York: Farrar, Straus and Giroux, The Noonday Press, 1964), 119–24.

Jason is as removed from what we generally consider sanity as any character in *The Sound and the Fury*. He is in fact far less aware of what is actually real than his brother Quentin. Such is our quickness in the twentieth century to polarize rationality and emotion, intellectual and intuitive responses, that critical interpretation of *The Sound and the Fury* has found it easy to set Jason up as its rational villain, the opposite number of the high-minded, intuitive Sartorises and Compsons, and probably, with white-trash Snopeses and invading Yankees, the secret of the fall of man in the Faulkner world. Such a thesis is hardly adequate for the kind of complexity Faulkner offers us here and elsewhere in his fiction. Faulkner may indeed be on the side of intuition, particularly as Bergson described it, but in his best work he does not demonstrate that preference by neat categories of the kind in which Jason has been pigeonholed.

A man who says, "I wouldn't bet on any team that fellow Ruth played on. . . . Even if I knew it was going to win" (p. 314) [157]—to pick out only one example—is hardly the epitome of cold-hearted business-like behavior. And that he could ever have "competed with and held his own with the Snopeses" (p. 420) [212], as Faulkner writes in the Appendix, is incredible. No man who is fooled and humiliated so many times in one day by everyone from Miss Quentin to Old Man Job is going to be a match for Flem Snopes, whose coldly analytic inhumanity has so often been wrongly identified with Jason. The latter's insistence that he would not bet on a sure winner is not only irrational, it is even the mark of a curious idealism. It is also a significant, usually ignored, side of this pathetic man who spends his Good Friday crucifying himself on the crosses he alone provides.

A psychotic, some wit once said, is a man who honestly believes that two plus two equals five; a neurotic knows very well that two plus two equals four—but it bothers him. Let this be our hint as to the difference between Jason and Quentin, for Quentin deliberately composes an incest fable in order to deal with a reality he cannot face. That it *is* a fable is something he himself insists on. Jason, however, confuses the real and the illusory, and is quite unaware of the way he arranges his own punishment. Standing between him and reality is his need to hold on to two opposing views of himself: one is that he is completely sufficient, the other is that he is the scapegoat of the world. On one hand Jason considers himself an effective operator, family head, market speculator, brainy swindler of Caddy and her daughter, a man of keen business sense. On the other hand he nurtures the dream of his victimization, his suffering at the hands of the Compsons, the Gibsons, his boss Earl, even the telegraph company.

Jason's entire monologue wanders through a maze of contradiction that cannot be reduced to mere hypocrisy or rationalization. With $7,000 stashed away, the accumulation of fifteen years of theft, Jason thinks "money has no value; it's just the way you spend it. It dont belong to anybody, so why try to hoard it" (p. 241) [122]. Regretting that he must be a detective (p. 297) [149], he yet makes the pursuit of his niece Quentin a major project. Insisting only that she show "discretion," fearing that someday he'll find her "under a wagon on the square" (p. 299) [150], he nevertheless chases her far out into the country on a day when nearly everyone else is at the traveling show in town, when there is no one to see her but himself. He scoffs at Compson pride in blood (p. 286) [144], yet later it is his and his mother's name that Quentin is making "a byword in the town" (p. 291) [146]. He firmly believes that it is Caddy who has deceived *him*, who has broken her promises to him, and that Quentin, in letting the air out of his tires, has given back far more than she has received: "I just wouldn't do you this way. I wouldn't do you this way no matter what you had done to me" (p. 303) [152]. And in the midst of all this double-dealing and plain fraud, Jason can sincerely say, "If there's one thing gets under my skin, it's a damn hypocrite" (p. 285) [143].

Within this web of opposed purposes—is it comfort or suffering that he seeks?—Jason seems absent of any objective awareness of those realities most relevant to him. He is confusion incarnate, guilty of all he seems to hate, hating his own image in others, the least sane and the most perversely imaginative of all the Compsons. When the world threatens him with satisfaction, when his niece heeds his insistence on discretion by driving with her man friend into an abandoned countryside, Jason chases after her, contradicting his own wishes so that his pain can be adequate to his unintelligible need. Quentin creates in order to avoid suffering, Jason, to experience it.

Surely we cannot match criteria of sanity or cold logic with what goes on in Jason's mind on April 6, 1928. For Bergson, the analytic mind is capable of the "ingenious arrangement of immobilities."[9] It is the kind of perception that orders reality rather than entering into sympathetic union with it. But Jason's organization of things is so confused and contradictory that we can hardly observe in him the sense of conscious control that Bergson identifies with the analytic mind. Jason's most obvious quality, visible in all his pratfalls, is his inability to *utilize* reality, to make it integral to a specific design. To compare him with Faulkner's master of analytic reasoning, Flem Snopes, is to see how absurdly distant he is from Flem.

The meanness with which Jason confronts the world is the cover that scarcely conceals his lack of self-knowledge. His agony is real, but he cannot begin to explain its source or its meaning. The only language he can risk is the stream of impotent insult he inflicts on everything around

9. Henri Bergson, *A Study in Metaphysics: The Creative Mind*, trans. Mabelle L. Andison (Totawa, New Jersey: Littlefield, Adams & Co., 1970), 127.

him. The result, after the pathos of Benjy and the occasionally burden-some rhetorical self-indulgence of Quentin, is some uproarious invec-tive: "I haven't got much pride, I can't afford it with a kitchen full of niggers to feed and robbing the state asylum of its star freshman. Blood, I says, governors and generals. It's a damn good thing we never had any kings and presidents; we'd all be down there at Jackson chasing butter-flies" (p. 286) [144]. Following Benjy and Quentin, this sort of thing comes as bracing, if low, comedy. And it reminds us, even in this grim study of family disintegration, of the variety of Faulkner's voices and his daring willingness to use them.

Thus Faulkner adds still one more piece to his exploration of the possibilities of vision. Still subjective, as opposed to the more objective first and fourth sections, but substantially different from Quentin's, Jason's is the mind that seems to have dissolved the boundaries of fact and invention, not as they might be dissolved in the collaboration within a supreme fiction, but as in the furthest stages of paranoia. The great irony of the section is that Jason is the one Compson who creates the appear-ance of ordinary social existence: he holds a job, wears a hat, visits a whorehouse regularly, and manages to fool his mother into burning what she believes are Caddy's checks. But his existence is actually a chaos of confused motion, utter disorder within the mind. Quentin, preparing methodically for suicide, is a study in contrast.

V

With "April Eighth 1928" the novel moves outward, away from the sealed monologues of Benjy, Quentin, and Jason. The telling of the Compson history from within passes to the telling from without. It is the last possibility Faulkner must exhaust in order to make his wasteland of sensibility complete: the traditional fictional method of the removed nar-rator describing objectively the characters and the events and, without a sense of excessive intrusion, interpreting them for us.

For the first time in the book we get novelistic description: weather, place, persons, the appearance of things as from the eye of a detached but interested spectator: "The day dawned bleak and chill, a moving wall of grey light out of the northeast which, instead of dissolving into mois-ture, seemed to disintegrate into minute and venomous particles, like dust that, when Dilsey opened the door of the cabin and emerged, needled laterally into her flesh, precipitating not so much a moisture as a sub-stance partaking of the quality of thin, not quite congealed oil" (p. 330) [165]. And with this description a new voice enters the novel: "She had been a big woman once but now her skeleton rose, draped loosely in unpadded skin that tightened again upon a paunch almost dropsical, as though muscle and tissue had been courage or fortitude which the days or the years had consumed until only the indomitable skeleton was left rising like a ruin or a landmark above the somnolent and impervious guts . . ." (p. 331) [165]. It is a rhetorical voice, set apart from the chaos and the distortion we have already seen. And from its secure perch, intimate with the events yet aloof from the pain of being a Compson, this voice seeks to tell us the meaning of what has come before.

Benjy, so brilliantly rendered in his own voice in the first section, is now described from the outside.

> Luster entered, followed by a big man who appeared to have been shaped of some substance whose particles would not or did not cohere to one another or to the frame which supported it. His skin was dead looking and hairless; dropsical too, he moved with a shambling gait like a trained bear. His hair was pale and fine. It had been brushed smoothly down upon his brow like that of children in daguerrotypes. His eyes were clear, of the pale sweet blue of cornflowers, his thick mouth hung open, drooling a little. (p. 342) [171]

One is almost shocked by the description—is this Benjy? Having wrestled with the processes of his mind, we find this external view like the portrait of someone else, another idiot from another novel. Not only described, he is also interpreted: "Then Ben wailed again, hopeless and prolonged. It was nothing. Just sound. It might have been all time and injustice and sorrow become vocal for an instant by a conjunction of planets" (p. 359) [179].

Jason, once again in pursuit of Quentin, this time for the $7,000 she has taken from his room, is also described, "with close-thatched brown hair curled into two stubborn hooks, one on either side of his forehead like a bartender in caricature" (p. 348) [174], and his meaning is wrested from the confusion of his own monologue. The narrator focuses chiefly on the bank job promised Jason years ago, which he never received because of Caddy's divorce from Herbert. It is supposedly neither Quentin nor the money that he is really chasing: "they merely symbolized the job in the bank of which he had been deprived before he ever got it" (p. 382) [190]. What has been stolen from him this time is simply "that which was to have compensated him for the lost job, which he had acquired through so much effort and risk, by the very symbol of the lost job itself" (pp. 383–84) [191].

With both Benjy and Jason a great deal has been lost in the abstraction of meaning from movement. From the total immersion of the private monologue we move to the detached external view; from confused and confusing versions of reality we get an orderly, consistent portrait of the Compson family. And yet this clarity does not explain; these interpretations of Jason and Benjy seem pale and inadequate beside their respective monologues. Can Jason's terrible confusion, for example, really be embraced by the motive attributed to him in this section? There is a

curious irrelevancy here, as if in this achieved meaning one were reading about different characters entirely. And yet in the earlier monologues we have already seen the inadequacies of personal distortion and
the two-dimensional clarity of pure perception.

My point here is not simply a determined refusal to admit the com-
prehensiveness of what I am reading. It is rather to recognize that in this
fourth attempt to tell the Compson story we are still faced with the problems of the first three, namely, a failure of the creation of a sufficient
form. And this failure becomes itself the form, and therefore the meaning, of *The Sound and the Fury.* The four fragments, each a fully achieved
expression of voice operating within the severest limitations, remain separate and incoherent.[1]

The fourth section is, of course, the easiest to read. It is divided into
four parts: the scene in the house Easter morning, showing Dilsey at
work and the discovery of the stolen money; the Easter service at church;
Jason's pursuit of Quentin; and the short scene in which Luster tries to
take Benjy to the graveyard through town. The polarities of Dilsey's and
the Compson's existence are emphatic, especially in the juxtaposition of
the Easter service, in its celebration of God's time, and Jason's mad
chase, his striving in the context of human time. Dilsey, understanding
the broken clock in the kitchen or the "beginning and the ending" in
church, has a sure grasp of both.

Dilsey has been pointed to as the one source of value in the novel,
supported by the comment in what seems to me an invariably mislead-
ing appendix, and it is clear that she embodies much that the Compsons
lack, especially a sense of duty to her position as servant and her total
faith in God.[2] It is also clear that her service to the family has not been

1. Some of Faulkner's most important critics have seen greater resolution in the fourth section
than I think is actually there. Concentrating on Dilsey, Olga Vickery writes that "her very presence enables the reader to achieve a final perspective on the lives of the Compsons" (*The Novels
of William Faulkner,* p. 47). Hyatt Waggoner notes: "[the fourth section's] implicit perspective is
based on judgments which we ourselves have been brought to the point of making" (*William
Faulkner: From Jefferson to the World* [Lexington: University of Kentucky Press, 1959], 58). And
Peter Swiggart writes: "The language of Dilsey's section suggests the point of view of a reader who
has struggled long and arduously with *The Sound and the Fury,* and who now recognizes beneath
the 'cluttered obscurity' an extraordinary clarity of action and theme" (*The Art of Faulkner's Novels*
[Austin: University of Texas Press, 1962], 107). Margaret Blanchard, in "The Rhetoric of Communion: Voice in *The Sound and the Fury,*" *American Literature* 41 (January 1970), argues that
the final section of the novel "provides no summing-up, no final interpretation," (555), yet asserts
that the reader, because of the altered narrative perspective, can now "adopt . . . the narrator's
tone, no matter how demanding its implications" (563). My own view is that this tone and interpretation of events must remain unacceptable to the reader, precisely because he has read the first
three sections. Closer to me in interpretation is Beverly Gross, "Form and Fulfillment in *The
Sound and the Fury,*" *Modern Language Quarterly* 29 (December 1968), who argues that the
fragmentation of the novel insures against a traditional conclusion that "convert[s] order out of
disorder, equilibrium out of tensions, meaning out of mystery." Rather, the book concludes with
the abiding effect of Benjy's last howls, "the novel's most intense depiction of sound and fury"
(444).
2. For an exception to this common view see John V. Hagopian, "Nihilism in Faulkner's *The
Sound and the Fury,*" *Modern Fiction Studies* 13 (Spring 1967): 45–55, who argues that the
novel's nihilistic close explicitly denies Dilsey's Christian perspective. See also his bibliographical
note on previous interpretations of Dilsey.

enough to save it, and that even her own children disobey her often, in certain instances emulating the Compson sin of pride. Her religious faith is remote as far as the Compsons are concerned. If the Christian myth is being put forth here as a source of order in the world, it clearly has only ironic reference to them.

> "I know you blame me," Mrs. Compson said, "for letting them off to go to church today."
> "Go where?" Jason said. "Hasn't that damn show left yet?" (p. 348) [174]

But Dilsey is irrelevant not only to the Compsons but to those assumptions of the nature of reality basic to the novel. Unlike the other members of the Compson household, and unlike the perspective implicit to this fragmented novel, Dilsey possesses a "mythic" view of the world, the assurance of an enduring order that presides over human existence, organizing it into an intelligible history. It is an order she has not invented but inherited, a traditional Christianity providing meaning and direction to her life. Outside the dissonance and distortion of the first three narratives, the grotesque visions we can never dismiss or corroborate, Dilsey's orthodoxy is a controlled and clear point of view—yet it is remote from that complexity of existence by which the novel lives.

Dilsey transcends chaos by her vision of Christian order.

> "I've seed de first en de last," Dilsey said. "Never you mind me."
> "First en last whut?" Frony said.
> "Never you mind," Dilsey said. "I seed de beginnin, en now sees de endin." (p. 371) [185]

This is what Quentin wishes he could do: see in the midst of action the direction of action, understand the living moment because it is part of a history that has already, and always, ended. Dilsey has this gift because she is a Christian. She exists not as one whose life unfolds in surprise, each moment a new and frightening Now, but as one who knows every step of the way because there is in fact only one history. The traditional narrative form of this section of *The Sound and the Fury* rests on similar assumptions. Its externally placed perspective, its clear plotting, its coherent analysis of what the behavior of Benjy and Jason means—all of these are basic to a fiction that believes in endings and their power to press into service, and thus make intelligible, each single moment. Dilsey is the center of "April Eighth 1928" because she is the spiritual embodiment of the fictional tradition in which it is told.

Dilsey has what Frank Kermode calls a sense of an ending. For her, the deterioration of the Compsons only confirms the demise of the godless and prideful, and brings still nearer the moment toward which all history moves. Yet the whole of *The Sound and the Fury* does not subscribe to the implications of ending, in terms of either the resolution of action into meaning or the reconciliation of fragments into a controlling system. Dilsey's special understanding, as Frony's question makes clear— " 'First en last whut?' "—is unavailable to any of the major characters in the novel. Nor is it available to the reader unless he ignores three-fourths of that novel, which flatly juxtaposes the last section against the three others that are inconsistent with it, and even confronts Dilsey (and the Easter service that articulates her mode of belief) with the spectacle of Jason's frantic chase after Quentin.[3]

Challenging Dilsey's religious vision is the same sense of time in motion, of a reality intractable to any mental construct, that lays bare the distortions of Quentin and Jason and transforms Benjy's timeless perspective, free of distortion, into a frozen imitation of experience. Neither in the Dilsey section, whatever the power of her characterization or sheer attractiveness as a human being, nor anywhere else in the novel do we see demonstrated the ability of the human imagination to render persuasively the order of things. Instead there is the sense of motion without meaning, of voices in separate rooms talking to no one: the sound and fury that fails to signify.

The Sound and the Fury reads like an anthology of fictional forms, each one of which Faulkner tests and finds wanting. The novel insists on the poverty of created meaning, although in doing so it possesses, like "The Waste Land," a power that for many readers the later works cannot equal. There is Benjy's unmediated vision of pure presence, that makes of art a kind of impertinence. There are the grotesque orderings of Quentin and Jason—one an effete escapism that seeks a reality dictated by the word, the other subjectivism crippled by paranoia. Both are parodies of the possibility that art might illuminate, not merely distort, the real. And there is the conventional nineteenth-century fiction: the orderly telling of a tale that retreats from all those suspicions of language, concept, external point of view, imposed order, that made the modern possible and necessary.

The achievement of the novel is the honesty of its experiment; we take its "failure" seriously because the attempt seems so genuine and desperate. The basic structure of a compilation of voices or discrete stories is one Faulkner returned to again and again, but never with such a candid admission of the limitations of art. Behind the novel is some as yet vague conception of what literature in the twentieth-century might be. Acknowledging, insisting on decreation, making real the time prior to prearrangement, The Sound and the Fury yet strives for wholeness, an articulation of design: the form not imposed like a myth from the past, but the form that is the consequence of contingent being.

3. See Bleikasten, The Most Splendid Failure, p. 184.

Nearly two decades later, Wallace Stevens expressed the hope of an age.

> To discover an order as of
> A season, to discover summer and know it,
>
> To discover winter and know it well, to find,
> Not to impose, not to have reasoned at all,
> Out of nothing to have come on major weather,
>
> It is possible, possible, possible. It must
> Be possible. It must be that in time
> The real will from its crude compoundings come [4]

The impressiveness of *The Sound and the Fury* is that it accepts nothing it cannot earn. It will have only "major weather." And so the novel sits like a stillborn colossus, always on the verge of beginning.

DAVID MINTER

Faulkner, Childhood, and the Making of
The Sound and the Fury [†]

Early in 1928, while he was still trying to recover from Horace Liveright's rejection of *Flags in the Dust*, William Faulkner began writing stories about four children named Compson. A few months earlier, his spirits had been high. Confident that he had just finished the best book any publisher would see that year, he had begun designing a dust jacket for his third novel. His first book, *The Marble Faun*, had sold few copies, and neither of his previous novels, *Soldiers' Pay* and *Mosquitoes*, had done very well. But *Flags in the Dust* had given him a sense of great discovery, and he was counting on it to make his name for him as a writer. Following Liveright's letter, which described the novel as "diffuse and non-integral," lacking "plot, dimension and projection," Faulkner's mood became not only bitter but morbid. For several weeks he moved back and forth between threats to give up writing and take a job, and efforts to revise his manuscript or even re-write the whole thing. Yet nothing seemed to help—neither the threats, which he probably knew to be empty, nor the efforts, which left him feeling confused and even

4. "Notes Toward a Supreme Fiction," in *The Collected Poems of Wallace Stevens* (New York: Alfred Knopf, 1954), 403–4.
† From *American Literature* (Durham, N.C.: Duke University Press, 1979), 51 (3): 376–93.

hopeless. Finally, he decided to re-type his manuscript and send it to Ben Wasson, a friend who had agreed to act as his agent.[1]

The disappointment Faulkner experienced in the aftermath of Liveright's blunt rejection was intensified by the solitude it imposed. He had enjoyed sharing the modest success of his earlier books, particularly with his mother, with old friends like Phil Stone, and with his childhood sweetheart, Estelle Oldham Franklin. But he found it impossible to share failure. "Don't Complain—Don't Explain" was the motto his mother had hung in the family kitchen and imprinted on the minds of her sons.[2] To her eldest son the experience of failure proved not only more painful but more solitary than any anticipation of it. Soon he also found himself immersed in a deep personal crisis, the contours of which remain a mystery. Several years later he spoke to Maurice Coindreau of a severe strain imposed by "difficulties of an intimate kind" ("des difficultes d'order intime").[3] To no one was he more specific. In a letter to his favorite aunt, he refers to a charming, shallow woman, "Like a lovely vase." "Thank God I've no money," he added, "or I'd marry her."[4] But what if anything his intimate difficulties had to do with his new love, we do not know. What we know is that the difficulties touched much. "You know, after all," he said to an acquaintance, "they put you in a pine box and in a few days the worms have you. Someone might cry for a day or two and after that they've forgotten all about you."[5]

As his depression deepened, Faulkner began reviewing his commitment to his vocation. Unable to throw it over, he determined to alter his attitude toward it—specifically by relinquishing hope of great recognition and reward. For several years, he had written in order to publish. After *Soldiers' Pay* that had meant writing with Horace Liveright before him. Yet, as his work had become more satisfying to him, it had become less acceptable to Liveright. Refusing to go back to writing things he now thought "youngly glamorous," like *Soldiers' Pay*, or "trashily smart," like *Mosquitoes*, he decided to go on even if it meant relinquishing his dream of success.[6]

His hope faded slowly, he recalled, but fade it did. "One day I seemed to shut a door between me and all publishers' addresses and book lists. I said to myself, Now I can write"—by which he meant that he could

1. See Faulkner to Liveright, Sunday,—October [16 Oct. 1927]; 30 November [1927]; and [mid or late Feb. 1928] in Joseph Blotner, ed., *Selected Letters of William Faulkner* (New York: Random House, 1977), 38–39. For Liveright's letter of rejection, see Joseph Blotner, *Faulkner: A Biography* (New York: Random House, 1974), 559–560.
2. Murry C. Falkner, *The Falkners of Mississippi: A Memoir* (Baton Rouge: Louisiana State University Press, 1967), 9–10.
3. Maurice Coindreau, Introduction, *Le bruit et la fureur* (Paris: Gallimard, 1938), 14. See also James B. Meriwether, "Notes on the Textual History of *The Sound and the Fury*," *Papers of the Bibliographical Society of America*, 56 (1962): 228.
4. See Faulkner to Mrs. Walter B. McLean, quoted in Blotner, *Faulkner*, pp. 562–563.
5. J. W. Harmon in *William Faulkner of Oxford*, ed. James W. Webb and A. Wigfall Green (Baton Rouge: Louisiana State University Press, 1965), 93–94.
6. Faulkner to Liveright [mid or late Feb. 1928], *Selected Letters*, pp. 39–40.

write for himself alone. Almost immediately he felt free. Writing "without any accompanying feeling of drive or effort, or any following feeling of exhaustion or relief or distaste," he began with no plan at all. He did not even think of his manuscript as a book. "I was thinking of books, publication, only in . . . reverse, in saying to myself, I wont have to worry about publishers liking or not liking this at all."[7]

More immediately, however, what going on and feeling free to write for himself meant was going back—not only to stories about children but to experiences from his own childhood and to characters he associated with himself and his brothers. Taking a line from "St. Louis Blues," which he had heard W. C. Handy play years before, he called the first Compson story "That Evening Sun Go Down." The second he called "A Justice." In both stories children face dark, foreboding experiences without adequate support. At the end of "A Justice" they move through a "strange, faintly sinister suspension of twilight"—an image which provided the title for another story, which Faulkner began in early spring.

Called "Twilight," the third of the Compson stories engaged him for several months, and became *The Sound and the Fury*, his first great novel. Through the earlier stories he had come to see the Compson children poised at the end of childhood and the beginning of awareness, facing scenes that lie beyond their powers of understanding and feeling emotions that lie beyond their powers of expression. In the second story, as twilight descends and their world begins to fade, loss, consternation, and bafflement become almost all they know.

This moment, which the stories discovered and the novel explores, possessed particular poignancy for Faulkner—a fact confirmed by scattered comments as well as by the deep resonance of the novel and the story of its making. "Art reminds us of our youth," Fairchild says in *Mosquitoes*, "of that age when life don't need to have her face lifted every so often for you to consider her beautiful."[8] "It's over very soon," Faulkner remarked as he observed his daughter nearing the end of her youth. "This is the end of it. She'll grow into a woman."[9] During the creation of the Compson children, he became not merely private but secretive. Even the people to whom he had talked and written most freely while working on *Flags in the Dust*—his mother and aunt, Phil Stone and Estelle Franklin—knew nothing about his new work until it was finished.[1] Although he was capable, as he once remarked, of saying almost anything in an interview, and on some subjects enjoyed contradicting himself, his comments on *The Sound and the Fury* remained

7. See both versions of Faulkner's Introduction to *The Sound and the Fury*, one in *The Southern Review*, 13 (Autumn 1972): 705–710; and one in *The Mississippi Quarterly*, 26 (Summer 1973): 410–415 [225–32; page references in brackets are to this Norton Critical Edition].
8. *Mosquitoes* (New York: Boni and Liveright, 1927), 319.
9. See Faulkner as quoted in Blotner, *Faulkner*, p. 1169.
1. See both versions of the Introduction to *The Sound and the Fury* cited in note 7 above; and Blotner, *Faulkner*, pp. 570–571 and 578–580.

basically consistent for more than thirty years. Even when the emotion
they express is muted and the information they convey is limited, they
show that the novel occupied a special place in his experience and in
his memory. The brooding nostalgia which informs the novel also survived it: it entered interviews for years to come, and it dominated the
"introduction" he wrote to *The Sound and the Fury* in the early thirties,
both as emotion recalled and as emotion shared. Looking back on the
painful yet splendid months of crisis during which he wrote *The Sound
and the Fury*, Faulkner was able to discover emotions similar to those
which that crisis enabled him to discover in childhood.

Like *Flags in the Dust*, *The Sound and the Fury* is set in Jefferson and
recalls family history. The Compson family, like the Sartoris family,
mirrors Faulkner's deepest sense of his family's story as a story of declen-
sion. But *The Sound and the Fury* is more bleak and more compelling.
It is also more personal, primarily because the third or parental generation, which in *Flags in the Dust* is virtually deleted as having no story,
plays a major role in *The Sound and the Fury*.[2] Despite its pathos, *Flags*
remains almost exuberant; and despite its use of family legends, it remains
open, accessible. Faulkner's changed mood, his new attitude and needs,
altered not only his way of working but his way of writing. A moving
story of four children and their inadequate parents, *The Sound and the
Fury* is thematically regressive, stylistically and formally innovative. If
being free to write for himself implied freedom to recover more personal
materials, being free of concern about publishers' addresses implied freedom to become more experimental. The novel thus represented a move
back toward home, family, childhood, and a move toward the interior;
but it also represented an astonishing breakthrough.[3] Furthermore, both
of its fundamental principles, the regressive and the innovative, possessed several corollaries. Its regressive principle we see, first, in the presence of the three Compson brothers, who recall Faulkner's own family
configuration, and second, in the use of memory and repetition as formal principles.[4] Faulkner possessed the three Compson brothers, as he
later put it, almost before he put pen to paper. He took a central event
and several germinating images from the death of the grandmother he
and his brothers called Damuddy, after whose lingering illness and funeral
they were sent from home so that it could be fumigated. For Faulkner,
as for Gertrude Stein, memory is always repetition, being and living

2. See Faulkner's explanation of his deletion of the parental generation from *Flags in the Dust* in
Faulkner in the University, ed. Frederick L. Gwynn and Joseph Blotner (Charlottesville, Va.:
University Press of Virginia, 1959), 251.
3. See Conrad Aiken, "William Faulkner: The Novel as Form," in *Faulkner: A Collection of
Critical Essays*, ed. R. P. Warren (Englewood Cliffs, N.J.: Prentice-Hall, 1966), 51.
4. Faulkner had three brothers, of course, but during the crucial years to which his memory
turned in *The Sound and the Fury*, he had only two. Leila Dean Swift, the grandmother whom
the first three Falkner boys called Damuddy, died on June 1, 1907. The youngest of the four
Falkner boys, Dean Swift Falkner, was born August 15, 1907. Also see Faulkner as quoted in the
statement cited in note 1 [on p. 351].

never repetition. *The Sound and the Fury*, he was fond of remarking, was a single story several times told. But memory was never for him simple repetition. He used the remembered as he used the actual: less to denominate lived events, relationships, and configurations, with their attendant attributes and emotions, than to objectify them and so be free to analyze and play with them. To place the past under the aspect of the present, the present under the aspect of the past, was to start from the regressive toward the innovative. Like the novel's regressive principle, its innovative principle possessed several corollaries, as we see, for example, in its gradual evocation of Caddy, the sister he added to memory, and in its slow progression from private toward more public worlds.[5]

The parental generation, which exists in *Flags in the Dust* only for the sake of family continuity, is crucial in *The Sound and the Fury*. Jason is aggressive in expressing the contempt he feels for his mother and especially his father. Although Benjy shares neither Jason's contempt nor the preoccupations it inspires, he does feel the vacancies his parents' inadequacies have created in his life. Although Quentin disguises his resentment, it surfaces. Like Benjy's and Quentin's obsessive attachments to Caddy, Jason's animosity toward her originates in wounds inflicted by Mr. and Mrs. Compson. In short, it is in Caddy that each brother's discontent finds its focus, as we see in their various evocations of her.

To the end of his life, Faulkner spoke of Caddy with deep devotion. She was, he suggested, both the sister of his imagination and "the daughter of his mind."[6] Born of his own discontent, she was for him "the beautiful one," his "heart's darling."[7] It was Caddy, or more precisely, Faulkner's feeling for the emerging Caddy, that turned a story called "Twilight" into a novel called *The Sound and the Fury*: "I loved her so much," he said, that "I couldn't decide to give her life just for the duration of a short story. She deserved more than that. So my novel was created, almost in spite of myself."[8]

In the same statements in which Faulkner stressed the quality of his love for Caddy, he emphasized the extent to which his novel grew as he worked on it. One source of that growth derived from Faulkner's discovery of repetition as a technical principle. Having presented Benjy's experience, he found that it was so "incomprehensible, even I could not have told what was going on then, so I had to write another chapter." The second section accordingly became both a clarification and a counter-

5. See Aiken as cited in note 3 on p. 346.
6. See the discussions of Caddy in the Introduction cited in note 7 on p. 345; *Mosquitoes*, p. 339; and "Books and Things: Joseph Hergesheimer," in *William Faulkner: Early Prose and Poetry*, ed. Carvel Collins (Boston: Little, Brown, 1962), 101–103. The quoted phrase is a translation of an Italian phrase quoted in the last of these pieces, p. 102.
7. *Faulkner in the University*, p. 6.
8. See Faulkner as quoted in the translation of Maurice Coindreau's Introduction to *The Sound and the Fury*, in *The Mississippi Quarterly*, 19 (Summer 1966): 109.

point to the first, just as the third became both of these to the second.[9]
The story moves from the remote and strange world of Benjy's idiocy
and innocence, where sensations and basic responses are all we have;
through the intensely subjective as well as private world of Quentin's
bizarre idealism, where thought shapes sensation and feeling into a kind
of decadent poetic prose full of idiosyncratic allusions and patterns; to
the more familiar, even commonsensical meanness of Jason's materialism, where rage and self-pity find expression in colloquialisms and clichés.
Because it is more conventional, Jason's section is more accessible, even
more public. Yet it too describes a circle of its own.[1] Wanting to move
from three peculiar and private worlds toward a more public and social
one, Faulkner adopted a more detached voice. The fourth section comes
to us as though from "an outsider." The story, as it finally emerged, tells
not only of four children and their family, but of a larger world, itself at
twilight. "And that's how that book grew. That is, I wrote that same
story four times. . . . That was not a deliberate *tour de force* at all, the
book just grew that way. . . . I was still trying to tell one story which
moved me very much and each time I failed. . . ."[2]

Given the novel's technical brilliance, it is easy to forget how simple
and how moving its basic story is. In it we observe four children come
of age amid the decay and dissolution of their family. It began, Faulkner
recalled, with "a brother and a sister splashing one another in the brook"
where they had been sent to play during the funeral of a grandmother
they called Damuddy. From the play in the brook came what Faulkner
several times referred to as the central image in the novel—Caddy's muddy
drawers. As she clambers up a tree outside the Compson home to observe
the funeral inside, we and her brothers see them from below. From
these episodes, Faulkner got several things: his sense of the branch as
"the dark, harsh flowing of time" which was sweeping Caddy away from
her brothers; his sense that the girl who had the courage to climb the
tree would also find the courage to face change and loss; and his sense
that the brothers who waited below would respond very differently—that
Benjy would feel but never understand his loss; that Quentin would seek
oblivion rather than face his; and that Jason would meet his with vindictive rage and terrible ambition.[3] The novel thus focuses not only on
three brothers Faulkner possessed when he began, but also on Caddy,
the figure he added to memory—which is to say, on the child whose
story he never directly told as well as on those whose stories he directly
tells. His decision to approach Caddy only by indirection, through the
needs and demands of her brothers, was in part technical, as he repeat-

9. Robert A. Jelliffe, ed., *Faulkner at Nagano* (Tokyo: Kenkyusha, 1956), 104.
1. See F. H. Bradley, *Appearance and Reality* (New York: Macmillan, 1908), 346; and T. S.
Eliot's note to line 142 of *The Waste Land*.
2. *Faulkner at Nagano*, pp. 103–105.
3. See both versions of Faulkner's Introduction, cited in note 7 on p. 345; and compare *Faulkner
in the University*, pp. 31–32.

edly insisted. By the time he came to the fourth telling, he wanted a more detached, public voice. In addition, he thought indirection more "passionate." It was, he said, more moving to present "the shadow of the branch, and let the [reader's] mind create the tree."[4]

But in fact Caddy grew as she is presented, by indirection—in response to needs shared by Faulkner and his characters. Having discovered Benjy, in whose idiocy he saw "the blind, self-centeredness of innocence, typified by children," he "became interested in the relationship of the idiot to the world that he was in but would never be able to cope with. . . ." What particularly agitated him was where such a one as Benjy could find "the tenderness, the help, to shield him. . . ."[5] The answer he hit upon had nothing to do with Mr. and Mrs. Compson, and only a little to do with Dilsey. Mr. Compson is a weak, nihilistic alcoholic who toys with the emotions and needs of his children. Even when he feels sympathy and compassion, he fails to show it effectively. Mrs.Compson is a cold, self-involved woman who expends her energies worrying about her ailments, complaining about her life, and clinging to her notions of respectability. "If I could say Mother. Mother," Quentin says to himself. Dilsey, who distinctly recalls Mammy Caroline Barr, to whom Faulkner later dedicated Go Down, Moses, epitomizes the kind of Christian Faulkner most deeply admired. She is saved by a minimum of theology. Though her understanding is small, her wisdom and love are large. Living in the world of the Compsons, she commits herself to the immediate; she "does de bes' " she can to fill the vacancies left in the lives of the children around her by their loveless and faithless parents. Since by virtue of her love and faith she is part of a larger world, she is able not only to help the children but "to stand above the fallen ruins of the family. . . ."[6] She has seen, she says, the first and the last. But Dilsey's life combines a measure of effective action with a measure of pathetic resignation. Most of Benjy's needs for tenderness and comfort, if not help and protection, he takes to his sister. And it was thus, Faulkner said, that "the character of his sister began to emerge. . . ."[7] Like Benjy, Quentin and Jason also turn toward Caddy, seeking to find in her some way of meeting needs ignored or thwarted by their parents. Treasuring some concept of family honor his parents seem to him to have forfeited, Quentin seeks to turn his fair and beautiful sister into a fair, unravished, and unravishable maiden. Lusting after an inheritance, and believing

---

4. Faulkner at Nagano, p. 72. Compare this statement with Mallarmé's assertion: "Nommer un objet, c'est supprimer les trois-quarts de la jouissance du poème. . . ." ["To name an object is to suppress three-fourths of the pleasure of the poem. . . ."] See also A. G. Lehmann, The Symbolist Aesthetic in France, 1885–1895 (Oxford: Blackwell, 1950), particularly chapters 1, 2, and 6.
5. James B. Meriwether and Michael Millgate, eds., Lion in the Garden: Interviews with William Faulkner, 1926–1962 (New York: Random House, 1968), 146.
6. See p. 414 [230] of the second version of Faulkner's Introduction to The Sound and the Fury, cited in note 7, p. 345.
7. See Lion in the Garden, pp. 146–147.

his parents to have sold his birthright, Jason tries to make Caddy the instrument of a substitute fortune.

The parental generation, which exists in *Flags in the Dust* only for the sake of continuity, thus plays a crucial if destructive role in *The Sound and the Fury*. Several readers have felt that Faulkner's sympathies as a fictionist lay more with men than with women.[8] But his fathers, at least, rarely fare better than his mothers, the decisive direction of his sympathy being toward children, as we see most clearly in *The Sound and the Fury*, but clearly too in works that followed it. Jewel Bundren must live without a visible father, while Darl discovers that in some fundamental sense he "never had a mother." Thomas Sutpen's children live and die without an adequate father. Rosa Coldfield lives a long life only to discover that she had lost childhood before she possessed it. Yet, even as they resemble the deprived and often deserted or orphaned children of Charles Dickens, Faulkner's children also resemble Hawthorne's Pyncheons. Held without gentleness, they are still held fast. Suffering from a malady that resembles claustrophobia no less than from fear of desertion, they find repetition easy, independence and innovation almost impossible.

Although he is aggressive in expressing the hostility he feels for his parents, Jason is never able satisfactorily to avenge himself on them. Accordingly, he takes his victims where he finds them, his preference being for those who are most helpless, like Benjy and Luster, or most desperate, like Caddy. Enlarged, the contempt he feels for his family enables him to reject the past and embrace the New South, which he does without recognizing in himself vulgar versions of the materialism and self-pity that we associate with his mother. Left without sufficient tenderness and love, Quentin, Caddy, and Benjy turn toward Dilsey and each other. Without becoming aggressive, Benjy feels the vacancies his parents create in his life. All instinctively, he tries to hold fast to those moments in which Caddy meets his need for tenderness. In Quentin, we observe a very different desire: he wants to possess moments only as he would have them. Like the hero of Pound's *Cantos*, Quentin lives wondering whether any sight can be worth the beauty of his thought. His dis-ease with the immediate, which becomes a desire to escape time itself, accounts for the strange convolutions of his mind and the strange transformations of his emotions. In the end it leads him to a still harbor, where he fastidiously completes the logic of his father's life. Unlike her brothers, Caddy establishes her independence and achieves freedom. But her flight severs ties, making it impossible for her to help Quentin, comfort Benjy, or protect her daughter. Finally, freedom sweeps "her

8. See Albert J. Guerard, *The Triumph of the Novel* (New York: Oxford University Press, 1976), 109–135.

into dishonor and shame. . . ."[9] Deserted by her mother, Miss Quentin is left no one with whom to learn love, and so repeats her mother's dishonor and flight without ever knowing her tenderness. If in the story of Jason we observe the near-triumph of all that is repugnant, in the stories of Caddy and Miss Quentin we observe the degradation of all that is beautiful. No modern story has done more than theirs to explore Yeats's terrible vision of modernity in "The Second Coming," where the "best lack all conviction," while the "worst are full of passionate intensity."

Faulkner thus seems to have discovered Caddy as he presents her—through the felt needs of her brothers. Only later did he realize that he had also been trying to meet needs of his own: that in Caddy he had created the sister he had wanted but never had and the daughter he was fated to lose, "though the former might have been apparent," he added, "from the fact that Caddy had three brothers almost before I wrote her name on paper."[1] Taken together, the Compson brothers body forth needs Faulkner expressed through his creation of Caddy. In Benjy's need for tenderness we see something of the emotional confluence which precipitated the writing of *The Sound and the Fury*. The ecstasy and relief Faulkner associated with the writing of the novel as a whole, he associated particularly with the writing of Benjy's section.[2] In Jason's preoccupation with making a fortune, we see a vulgar version of the hope Faulkner was trying to relinquish. In Quentin's Manichaean revulsion toward all things material and physical, we see both a version of the imagination Allen Tate called "angelic" and a version of the moral sensibility that Faulkner associated with the fastidious aesthete.[3] It is more than an accident of imagery that Quentin, another of Faulkner's poets *manqués*, seeks refuge, first, in the frail "vessel" he calls Caddy, and then, in something very like the "still harbor" in which Faulkner had earlier imagined Joseph Hergesheimer submerging himself—"where the age cannot hurt him and where rumor of the world reaches him only as a far faint sound of rain."[4]

In one of his more elaborate as well as more suggestive descriptions of what the creation of Caddy meant to him, Faulkner associated her with one of his favorite images.

> I said to myself, Now I can write. Now I can make myself a vase like that which the old Roman kept at his bedside and wore the rim slowly away with kissing it. So I, who had never had a sister and

9. See p. 413 [227] of the second version of Faulkner's Introduction to *The Sound and the Fury*, cited in note 7, p. 345.
1. Ibid.
2. Ibid., p. 414.
3. See Allen Tate, "The Angelic Imagination," *The Man of Letters in the Modern World* (New York: Noonday Press, 1955), 113–131; and Robert M. Slabey, "The 'Romanticism' of *The Sound and the Fury*," *The Mississippi Quarterly*, 16 (Summer 1963): 152–157.
4. "Books and Things: Joseph Hergesheimer," *Early Prose and Poetry*, p. 102.

was fated to lose my daughter in infancy, set out to make myself a beautiful and tragic little girl.[5]

The image of the urn or vase had turned up earlier in a review of Hergesheimer's fiction; in Faulkner's unpublished novel about Elmer Hodge; in *Mosquitoes*; and in *Flags in the Dust*. It had made a recent appearance in the letter to Aunt Bama describing his new love, and it would make several later appearances. It was an image, we may fairly assume, which possessed special force for Faulkner, and several connotations, at least three of which are of crucial significance.

The simplest of these, stressing desire for shelter or escape, Faulkner first associated with Hergesheimer's "still harbor" and later with "the classic and serene vase" which shelters Gail Hightower "from the harsh gale of living."[6] In *The Sound and the Fury* Benjy comes to us as a wholly dependent creature seeking shelter. Sentenced to stillness and silence—"like something eyeless and voiceless which . . . existed merely because of its ability to suffer"[7]—he is all need and all helplessness. What loss of Caddy means to him is a life of unrelieved, and for him meaningless, suffering. For Quentin, on the other hand, it means despair. In him the desire for relief and shelter becomes desire for escape. In one of the New Orleans sketches, Faulkner introduces a girl who presents herself to her lover as "Little sister Death." In an allegory written in 1926 for Helen Baird, who was busy rejecting his love, he reintroduces the figure called Little sister Death, this time in the company of a courtly knight and lover—which is, of course, one of the roles Quentin seeks to play.[8] At first all of Quentin's desire seems to focus on Caddy as the maiden of his dreams. But as his desire becomes associated with "night and unrest," Caddy begins to merge with "Little sister Death"—that is, with an incestuous love forbidden on threat of death. Rendered impotent by that threat, Quentin comes to love, not the body of his sister, nor even some concept of Compson honor, but death itself. In the end, he ceremoniously gives himself, not to Caddy, but to the river. "The saddest thing about love," says a character in *Soldiers' Pay*, "is that not only the love cannot last forever, but even the heartbreak is soon forgotten." Quentin kills himself in part as punishment for his forbidden desires;

5. See p. 710 [227] of the first version of Faulkner's Introduction to *The Sound and the Fury*, cited in note 7, p. 345.
6. See the works cited in note 6, p. 347; compare *Light in August* (New York: Harrison Smith and Robert Haas, 1932), 453.
7. See p. 414 [230–31] of the second version of Faulkner's Introduction to *The Sound and the Fury*, cited in note 7, p. 345.
8. See "The Kid Learns," in *William Faulkner: New Orleans Sketches*, ed. Carvel Collins (New York: Random House, 1958), 91. See also "Mayday," the allegory Faulkner wrote for Helen Baird, as discussed by Blotner, *Faulkner*, pp. 510-511; by Cleanth Brooks, "The Image of Helen Baird in Faulkner's Early Poetry and Fiction," *The Sewanee Review*, 85 (Spring 1977): 220–222; and by Cleanth Brooks, *William Faulkner, Toward Yoknapatawpha and Beyond* (New Haven, Conn.: Yale University Press, 1978), 47–52. A facsimile of *Mayday* edited by Carvel Collins has recently been published by the University of Notre Dame Press (1977). See also Collins, Introduction, *New Orleans Sketches*, pp. xxiv-xxv.

in part because Caddy proves corruptible; in part, perhaps, because he decides "that even she was not quite worth despair." But he also kills himself because he fears his own inconstancy. What he discovers in himself is deep psychological impotence. He is unable to play either of the heroic roles—as seducer or as avenger—that he deems appropriate to his fiction of himself as a gallant, chivalric lover. What he fears is that he will ultimately fail, too, in the role of the despairing lover. What he cannot abide is the prospect of a moment when Caddy's corruption no longer matters to him.[9]

Never before had Faulkner expressed anxiety so deep and diverse. In Quentin it is not only immediate failure that we observe; it is the prospect of ultimate failure. Later, Faulkner associated the writing of *The Sound and the Fury* specifically with anxiety about a moment "when not only the ecstasy of writing would be gone, but the unreluctance and the something worth saying too."[1] Coming and going throughout his life, that anxiety came finally to haunt him. But as early as his creation of Quentin he saw clearly the destructive potential of the desire to escape it. If he wrote *The Sound and the Fury* in part to find shelter, he also wrote it knowing that he would have to emerge from it. "I had made myself a vase," he said, though "I suppose I knew all the time that I could not live forever inside of it. . . ."[2] Having finished *The Sound and the Fury*, he in fact found emergence traumatic. Still, it is probably fair to say that he knew all along what awaited him. Certainly his novel possessed other possibilities than shelter and escape for him, just as the image through which he sought to convey his sense of it possessed other connotations, including one that is clearly erotic and one that is clearly aesthetic.

The place to begin untangling the erotic is the relation between the old Roman who kept the vase at his bedside so that he could kiss it and "the withered cuckold husband that took the Decameron to bed with him every night. . . ."[3] These two figures are not only committed to a kind of substitution; they practice a kind of auto-eroticism. The old Roman is superior only if we assume that he is the maker of his vase—in which case he resembles Horace Benbow, who in *Flags in the Dust* makes an "almost perfect vase" which he keeps by his bedside and calls by his sister's name. With Horace and his vase, we might seem to have come full circle, back to Faulkner and his "heart's darling."[4] In *The Sound*

9. See *Soldiers' Pay* (New York: Boni and Liveright, 1926), 318. Compare Faulkner's statement, years later, to Meta Carpenter: "What is valuable is what you have lost, since then you never had the chance to wear out and so lose it shabbily. . . ." Quoted in Meta Carpenter Wilde and Orin Borsten, *A Loving Gentleman* (New York: Simon and Schuster, 1976), 317.
1. See p. 415 of the second version of Faulkner's Introduction to *The Sound and the Fury*, cited in note 7, p. 345.
2. Ibid.
3. *Mosquitoes*, p. 210.
4. Compare *Flags in the Dust* (New York: Random House, 1973), 153–154, 162; and *Faulkner in the University*, p. 6.

and the Fury affection of brother for sister and sister for brother becomes
the archetype of love; and with Caddy and Quentin, the incestuous
potential of that love clearly surfaces—as it had in *Elmer, Mosquitoes,*
and *Flags in the Dust,* and as it would in *Absalom, Absalom!.*

The circle, however, is less perfect than it might at first appear, since
at least one difference between Horace Benbow and William Faulkner
is both obvious and crucial. Whereas Horace's amber vase is a substitute
for a sister he has but is forbidden and fears to possess, Faulkner's is a
substitute for the sister he never had. In this regard Horace Benbow is
closer to Elmer Hodge, Faulkner to the sculptor named Gordon in *Mosquitoes.* Elmer is in fact a more timid as well as an earlier version of
Horace. Working with his paints—"thick-bodied and female and at the
same time phallic: hermaphroditic"—Elmer creates figures he associates
with something "that he dreaded yet longed for." The thing he both
seeks and shuns is a "vague shape" he holds in his mind; its origins are
his mother and a sister named Jo-Addie. Like Horace's, Elmer's art is
devoted to imaginative possession of figures he is forbidden and fears
sexually to possess.[5] When Horace calls his amber vase by his sister's
name, he articulates what Elmer merely feels. Like Elmer, however,
Horace makes indirect or imaginative possession a means of avoiding
the fate Quentin enacts. Through their art, Elmer and Horace are able
to achieve satisfaction that soothes one kind of despair without arousing
guilt that might lead to another.[6]

In *Mosquitoes,* the origins of Gordon's "feminine ideal" remain obscure,
though his art is quite clearly devoted to creation and possession of her.
For Gordon as for Elmer and Horace, the erotic and the aesthetic are
inseparable. A man is always writing, Dawson Fairchild remarks, for
"some woman"; if she is not "a flesh and blood creature," she is at least
"the symbol of a desire," and "she is feminine."[7] In their art Elmer and
Horace work toward a figure that is actual, making art a substitute for
love of a real woman. Gordon, on the other hand, associates art with an
ideal whose identity remains vague. We know of it two things—that it is
feminine and that it represents what Henry James called the beautiful
circuit and subterfuge of thought and desire. Whereas Horace expresses
his love for a real woman through his art, Gordon expresses his devotion
to his sculpted ideal by pursuing, temporarily, a woman named Patricia
who interests him only because she happens to resemble "the virginal
breastless torso of a girl" he has already sculpted.[8] Whereas Horace is a

---

5. The *Elmer* manuscripts are in the William Faulkner Collections, University of Virginia Library.
For a valuable discussion of them, see Thomas L. McHaney, "The Elmer Papers: Faulkner's
Comic Portraits of the Artist," *The Mississippi Quarterly,* 26 (Summer 1973): 281–311.
6. See the manuscripts cited in note 5, above, and compare *Flags in the Dust,* pp. 153–154,
162.
7. *Mosquitoes,* p. 250.
8. See John Irwin, *Doubling & Incest, Repetition & Revenge* (Baltimore: Johns Hopkins University Press, 1975), 160–161; and *Mosquitoes,* pp. 11, 24, 28, 47–48.

failed, inconstant artist, Gordon is a consecrated one, the difference being that Gordon devotes his life as well as his art to pursuing the figure which exists perfectly only in thought and imagination.

On a voyage to Europe, shortly after finishing *Soldiers' Pay* and before beginning *Elmer* and *Mosquitoes*, Faulkner told William Spratling that he thought love and death the "only two basic compulsions on earth. . . ."[9] What engaged his imagination as much as either of these compulsions, however, was his sense of the relation of each to the other and of both to art. The amber vase Horace calls Narcissa, he also addresses "as Thou still unravished bride of quietude."[1] "There is a story somewhere," Faulkner said,

> about an old Roman who kept at his bedside a Tyrrhenian vase which he loved and the rim of which he wore slowly away with kissing it. I had made myself a vase, but I suppose I knew all the time that I could not live forever inside of it, that perhaps to have it so that I too could lie in bed and look at it would be better; surely so when that day should come when not only the ecstasy of writing would be gone, but the unreluctance and the something worth saying too. It's fine to think that you will leave something behind you when you die, but it's better to have made something you can die with.[2]

In this brief statement, the vase becomes both Caddy and *The Sound and the Fury*; both "the beautiful one" for whom he created the novel as a commodious space, and the novel in which she found protection, even privacy, as well as expression. Through its basic doubleness, the vase becomes many things: a haven or shelter into which the artist may retreat; a feminine ideal to which he gives his devotion; a work of art which he can leave behind when he is dead; and a burial urn which will contain one expression of his self as artist. If it is a mouth he may freely kiss, it is also a world in which he may find shelter; if it is a womb he may enter, it is also a space in which his troubled spirit may find both temporary rest and lasting expression.[3]

Of all his novels, it was for *The Sound and the Fury* that Faulkner felt "the most tenderness."[4] Writing it not only renewed his sense of purpose and hope;[5] it also gave him an "emotion definite and physical and yet nebulous to describe. . . ." Caught up in it, he experienced a kind of ecstasy, particularly in the "eager and joyous faith and anticipation of surprise which the yet unmarred sheets beneath my hand held inviolate

---

9. William Spratling, "Chronicle of a Friendship: William Faulkner in New Orleans," *The Texas Quarterly,* 9 (Spring 1966): 38.
1. See the works cited in note 6, above.
2. See p. 415 [231] of the second version of Faulkner's Introduction to *The Sound and the Fury,* cited in note 7, p. 345.
3. See Irwin, *Doubling & Incest,* pp. 162–163.
4. *Lion in the Garden,* p. 147.
5. See *Faulkner in the University,* p. 67.

and unfailing. . . ."[6] Such language may at first glance seem surprising. For *The Sound and the Fury* is, as Faulkner once noted, a "dark story of madness and hatred," and it clearly cost him dearly.[7] Having finished it, he moved to New York, where he continued revising it. "I worked so hard at that book," he said later, "that I doubt if there's anything in it that didn't belong there."[8] As he neared the end for which he had labored hard, he drew back, dreading completion as though it meant "cutting off the supply, destroying the source. . . ." Perhaps like Rilke and Proust, he associated "the completed" with silence.[9] Having finished his revisions, he contrived for himself an interface of silence and pain. Happening by his flat one evening, Jim Devine and Leon Scales found him alone, unconscious, huddled on the floor, empty bottles scattered around him.[1]

What *The Sound and the Fury* represented to him, however, he had anticipated in *Mosquitoes:* a work "in which the hackneyed accidents which make up this world—love and life and death and sex and sorrow—brought together by chance in perfect proportions, take on a kind of splendid and timeless beauty."[2] In the years to come, he would think of his fourth novel as a grand failure. Imperfect success would always be his ideal. To continue his effort to match his "dream of perfection," he needed dissatisfaction as well as hope. If failure might drive him to despair, success might deprive him of purpose: "it takes only one book to do it. It's not the sum of a lot of scribbling, it's one perfect book, you see. It's one single urn or shape that you want. . . ."[3]

Faulkner wanted, he once wrote Malcolm Cowley, "to be, as a private individual, abolished and voided from history." It was his aim to make his books the sole remaining sign of his life. Informing such statements is a definite need for privacy. But informing them, too, is a tacit conception of his relation to his art: that his authentic self was the self variously and nebulously yet definitely bodied forth by his fictions.[4] It is in this deeper rather than in the usual sense that his fiction is autobiographical. It is of his self expressive, which is to say, creative. "I have never known anyone," a brother wrote,

6. See p. 414 [231] of the second version of Faulkner's Introduction to *The Sound and the Fury*, cited in note 7, p. 345.
7. Quoted by Coindreau, Introduction to *The Sound and the Fury*, *The Mississippi Quarterly*, 19 (Summer 1966): 109.
8. Quoted in Blotner, *Faulkner*, pp. 589–590.
9. See W. H. Auden, Sonnet XXIII, in "In Time of War," in W. H. Auden and Christopher Isherwood, *Journey to a War* (New York: Random House, 1938). Compare Auden, Sonnet XIX in "Sonnets from China," *Collected Shorter Poems, 1927–1957* (New York: Random House, 1966). See also *Absalom, Absalom!* (New York: Random House, 1936), 373–374.
1. See Blotner, *Faulkner*, pp. 590–591.
2. *Mosquitoes*, p. 339.
3. *Faulkner in the University*, p. 65. Compare *Soldiers' Pay*, p. 283.
4. To Malcolm Cowley, Friday [February 11, 1949], in *The Faulkner-Cowley File* (New York: Viking Press, 1966), 126. See Irwin, *Doubling & Incest*, pp. 171–172.

who identified himself with his writings more than Bill did. . . .

Sometimes it was hard to tell which was which, which one Bill was, himself or the one in the story. And yet you knew somehow that the two of them were the same, they were one and inseparable.[5]

Faulkner knew that characters, "those shady but ingenious shapes," were a way of exploring, projecting, reaffirming both the life he lived and the tacit, secret life underlying it. At least once he was moved to wonder if he "had invented the world" of his fiction "or if it had invented me. . . ."[6]

Like indirect knowing, however, imperfect success, which implies partial completion, carries several connotations. Both the decision to approach Caddy only by indirection and the need to describe the novel as a series of imperfect acts partially completed ally it with the complex. They are in part a tribute to epistemological problems and in part a sign that beauty is difficult—that those things most worth seeing, knowing, and saying can never be directly seen, known, and said. But indirection and incompletion are also useful strategies for approaching forbidden scenes, uttering forbidden words, committing dangerous acts. For Elmer Hodge, both his sister Jo-Addie and behind her "the dark woman. The dark mother," are associated with a "vague shape [s]omewhere back in his mind"—the core for him of everything he dreads and desires. Since attainment, the only satisfying act, is not only dangerous but forbidden, and therefore both can't and must be his aim, Elmer's life and art become crude strategies of approximation. The opposite of crude, the art of *The Sound and the Fury* is nonetheless an art of concealment as well as disclosure—of delay, avoidance, evasion—particularly where Caddy is concerned. Beyond Faulkner's sense that indirection was more passionate lay his awareness that it was also less dangerous. For him both desire and hesitancy touched almost everything, making his imagination as illusive as it is allusive, and his art preeminently an art of surmise and conjecture.

In *Flags in the Dust* he had taken ingenious possession of a heritage which he proceeded both to dismember and reconstruct. In *The Sound and the Fury* he took possession of the pain and muted love of his childhood—its dislocations and vacancies, its forbidden needs and desires. The loss we observe in *The Sound and the Fury* is associated with parental weakness and inadequacy—with parental frigidity, judgment, and rejection. In the figure of Dilsey Faulkner re-created the haven of love he had found in Mammy Callie; in the figure of Caddy, he created one he knew only through longing. If the first of these figures is all maternal,

---

5. John Faulkner, *My Brother Bill* (New York: Trident Press, 1963), 275.
6. This quote is from a manuscript fragment in the Beinecke Library, Yale University. It is quoted in Blotner, *Faulkner*, p. 584.

the second is curiously mixed. In the figure of the sister he never had, we see not only a sister but a mother (the role she most clearly plays for Benjy) and a lover (the possibility most clearly forbidden). Like the emotion Faulkner experienced in writing it, the novel's central figure comes to us as one "definite and physical yet nebulous. . . ." Needing to conceal even as he disclosed her, Faulkner created in Caddy Compson a heroine who perfectly corresponds to her world: like it, she was born of regression and evasion, and like it, she transcends them.

WARWICK WADLINGTON

The Sound and the Fury: A Logic of Tragedy†

In the same year that Joseph Wood Krutch made his famous claim that tragedy was contrary to the modern temper, William Faulkner published a paradoxical refutation. Krutch sought to define and decry his age by appealing to a traditional standard. *The Sound and the Fury* shows that the standard of tragedy contains the logic of its own failure. Yet critics have typically discussed the novel as if it could be described by some comparatively stable model, apart from the debate over the possibility of tragedy.[1]

In the post-Enlightenment, pathos has become the term of contradistinction to tragedy. According to the most widespread view, tragedy involves suffering that results mainly from the protagonist's action, which is usually persistent, decisive—heroic. The mode of pathos, by contrast, is said to involve a relatively passive suffering, not springing from action

†From *American Literature* 53(4): 409–23. Copyright Duke University Press, 1981. Reprinted with permission of the publisher.

1. Evelyn Scott apparently made the connection immediately between Krutch's *The Modern Temper* and Faulkner's novel in *On William Faulkner's "The Sound and the Fury"* (New York: Cape and Smith, 1929), pp. 6–7.

Two likely sources for Faulkner's probable familiarity with the debate over modern tragedy were his affiliation with the knowledgeable *Double Dealer* circle in New Orleans, and Ludwig Lewisohn's *A Modern Book of Criticism*, which he owned dating from this period. See especially Julius Weis Friend, "Joseph Conrad: An Appreciation," *Double Dealer*, 7 (1924), 3–5; and Joseph T. Shipley, "The Growth of Tragedy," 7 (1925), 191–94. For an attack on traditional critical narrowness, and particularly on the New Humanists in the Lewisohn anthology, see Lewisohn's "Introduction," his "A Note on Tragedy," and Johannes Volkelt's "The Philosophical Implications of Tragedy."

For Faulkner's ambivalence at the limits put on great art by the modern situation and audience, see "On Criticism" (originally published in *Double Dealer*, 1925) in *William Faulkner: Early Prose and Poetry*, ed. Carvel Collins (Boston: Little, Brown, 1962). For his numerous explicit and implicit claims that his works were tragic, consult *Faulkner in the University*, ed. Frederick L. Gwynn and Joseph L. Blotner (Charlottesville: Univ. Press of Virginia, 1977), pp. 41–42 and passim; and *Lion in the Garden*, ed. James B. Meriwether and Michael Millgate (New York: Random House, 1968), p. 14 and passim. Representative views of Faulkner's tragedy in realtion to modernism are Cleanth Brooks, *William Faulkner; The Yoknapatawpha Country* (New Haven, Conn.: Yale Univ. Press, 1963), pp. 295–324; and John L. Longley, *The Tragic Mask: A Study of Faulkner's Heroes* (Chapel Hill: Univ. of North Carolina Press, 1963).

but inflicted by circumstances. In terms of the linked root meanings of pathos (passion, suffering), tragedy is held to be pathos resulting from heroic action.

The stress on action, legitimized by Aristotle's poetics and ethics, was part of the general cultural defense of responsible human endeavor from the philosophy of mechanistic determinism. For many, the horror of a universe of mere physical motion could be summed up as an oppressive passivity in which, as Matthew Arnold wrote, "there is everything to be endured, nothing to be done."[2] The emphasis on the difference between tragedy and pathos—that is, between action and passivity—was thus fundamentally polemic in nature if not always in tone. By the beginning of Faulkner's career, tragedy had become *the* prestigious literary genre. Pathos had largely lost its neutral, descriptive connotation and was increasingly a term of denigration, especially in the form "pathetic." Influential theorists like the New Humanists upheld a conservative position by accentuating this difference. "Tragic" had become a weapon useful for excoriating the naturalists, the "Freudians," and "the school of cruelty." Yet important writers since at least Dostoevski had reflected the modern idea of passive man while also seeking to reformulate the possibilities of human action. Sometimes these possibilities were found at the very center of apparent passivity, where pathos is describable by its etymological kin, pathology.[3]

But action is not the only usual discriminator of tragedy. In Aristotle's account, the mimesis of action arouses in the audience certain passions and subjects them to catharsis. A catastrophe is instrumental in effecting this tragic relief. In pathos, by contrast, there is no final crisis, no resolution and emotional disburdening. Passion is the inconclusive fate.

The traditional conception (or kind) of tragedy we consider here focuses typically on the drastic either/or to which life may be reduced, in a tightening spiral of narrowing options. *Antigone, Hamlet, Moby-Dick,* and *The Mayor of Casterbridge,* for example, follow this pattern, as does the *Oresteia* until the last-moment reversal. Hegel's theory speaks powerfully to such cases by treating tragedy as the collision of contradictory views. In Hegel's Absolute, variances are merely *differences,* but when concretized in human action they become contradictory *oppositions* liable to tragic conflict.

---

2. Preface to the 1853 edition of poems, in *The Portable Matthew Arnold,* ed. Lionel Trilling (New York: Viking, 1966), p. 187. Arnold is explaining why he has eliminated, as not truly tragic, his "Empedocles on Etna" from this edition. For the problem of passivity in modern fiction, including *Light in August,* see Harold J. Kaplan, *The Passive Voice* (Athens; Ohio Univ. Press, 1966).

3. A. C. Bradley was probably the most influential contemporary proponent of action as the distinctive mark of tragedy (e.g., *Shakespearean Tragedy,* 1904). Cf. T. S. Eliot's view (c. 1919) that Hamlet's passivity and excessive emotion made "a subject of study for pathologists"—"Hamlet and His Problems," *Selected Essays* (New York: Harcourt, 1950), p. 126.

Although the tragedy/pathos distinction is commonplace, the latter mode is rarely examined; one such discussion is my "Pathos and Dreiser," *Southern Review,* 7, N.S. (1971), 411–29, which in a somewhat different form extends my present comments.

Hegel aside for the moment, the idea of contradictory opposition itself points to connections between pairs of concepts that seem simply opposed—the modern temper and the heroic, and tragedy and pathos. In *The Heroic Temper*, Bernard Knox authoritatively defines the hall-mark of Sophocles' tragic heroes: "Their watchword is: 'he who is not with me is against me.' "[4] Sophoclean tragedy dramatizes the usually unavailing attempts of advisors to persuade the intransigent heroes—Ajax, Antigone, Electra, Oedipus, Philoctetes—to abandon the self-destructive polarization of their outraged self-esteem against the world.[5] The Sophoclean heroic outlook is the relatively rare consequence of a severe threat to personal worth that arouses the exceptional person to this uncompromisingly dichotomous attitude. Let us imagine a case, however, in which the essential binary quality of this temper became widespread. Such would be the result if dichotomy were the usual struc-ture of consciousness. The protagonist then would be surrounded by those who, at bottom, experience life in no less starkly divisive terms than he or she does on the tragic occasion. Rather than being a moni-tory, awe-inspiring anomaly as in Sophocles, polarization would be a constant daily potential. The result would be strikingly different from Sophoclean tragedy, though bearing the prototype's mark. The ironic product is the odd suspension of heroic temper and "unheroism" in tone and mood of *The Sound and the Fury*.

In a traditional conception like Hegel's, tragedy advances through the revelation of oppositions to their resolution. Faulkner's novel, however, probes to an inchoate, divisive logic of tragedy operating throughout thought and experience. *The Sound and the Fury* relocates the schism of tragedy in a basically dichotomous worldview. And in so doing, it discloses the potential of tragedy to become continuous with its antitype, pathos. Insofar as tragedy conventionally entails resolution, the very ubiquity of tragic schism ironically produces the repetitious, inconclu-sive situation of tragedy's opposite. Instead of catastrophe, there is repeated disaster.[6]

The Compsons' schismatic, incipiently tragic mental habits are strik-ingly—though perversely—like a two-value logic. This ordinary formal logic depends upon the Aristotelian law of identity according to which an entity can only be what it is: A is A. Given the assumption of uniform entities, to say that a thing is simultaneously something else violates the law of noncontradiction. This is the logic of arithmetic (which Mr. Compson's language of "sum" and "problem" reflects) in which an answer

4. Bernard M. W. Knox, *The Heroic Temper: Studies in Sophoclean Tragedy* (Berkeley: Univ. of California Press, 1964), p. 21.
5. Knox, pp. 1–44.
6. For other attempts to define the special tragic status of the novel, see Lawrance Thompson, *William Faulkner: An Introduction and Interpretation*, 2nd ed. (New York: Holt, Rinehart and Winston, 1967), pp. 167–69; and James M. Mellard, "The Sound and the Fury: Quentin Comp-son and Faulkner's 'Tragedy of Passion,' " *Studies in the Novel*, 2 (1970), 61–75.

is always either right or wrong. A characteristic form is the mathematical proof that depends on showing contradiction—the *reductio ad absurdum*. As formal logic, this binary ordering is unexceptionable. As the foundation for a wholesale system of dichotomy taken as the sole orientation to reality, such a logic becomes disastrous. Matters that call for the recognition of compound entities, gradations, and probabilities are continually reduced to the Yes or No of tragic dilemma.[7]

When polarized options are habitual, crisis becomes attrition, and passion a banal repetition. Christ was not crucified, Mr. Compson tells Quentin, but worn away by the minute clicking of time's little wheels. "If things just finished themselves," Quentin thinks at one point. "Again," he concludes, is the "Saddest [word] of all."[8] He yearns for decisive calamity, some unburdening conclusiveness, however terrible. He yearns, that is, for a kind of tragedy that is not his. Not surprisingly, Quentin has been the primary focus for discussing the novel's tragic dimensions. He will provide our focus as well.

The absence of tragic closure in the novel, then, does not stem from a view that there can be no momentous catastrophe in a modern "everyday" world for reasons unrelated to the tragic process. Such an extrinsic view underlies the opinions of those like Krutch and George Steiner who have analyzed the death of tragedy. Rather, in Faulkner, the binary logic that produces in the first instance the tragic heroic crisis must also eventuate in devastating *everydayness:* tomorrow and tomorrow. . . . Faulkner's title echoes the most famous protest against a life without climax. But Macbeth, by finding his resolving action, diverts his drama from the idiotic tomorrows signifying nothing. The period of Faulkner's great modern tragedies begins with a statement of the disqualification of such tragedy by its own logic. Put concisely, in the words of Quentin's false comforter: "tragedy is second-hand" (p. 143) [74].

I

Quentin's first memory upon waking is of his father giving him Grandfather's watch with the observation that it is "the mausoleum of all hope and desire; it's rather excrutiating-ly apt that you will use it to gain the reducto absurdum of all human experience which can fit your individual needs no better than it fitted his or his father's. I give it to you not that you may remember time, but that you might forget it now and then for a moment and not spend all your breath trying to conquer it" (p. 93) [48]. Time and time-consciousness contradict human experience, as the

7. As Walter J. Ong notes, in a totally binary orientation, the proper distinction disappears between a two-*value* system (true versus false) and the two-*place* order of dichotomy. *Ramus, Method, and the Decay of Dialogue* (Cambridge, Mass.: Harvard Univ. Press, 1958), p. 210.
8. *The Sound and the Fury* (New York: Modern Library, 1967), pp. 97, 118 [50, 61]. Subsequent references will appear in the text. Page references in brackets are to this Norton Critical Edition.

reference to *reductio ad absurdum* indicates. It is, in Mr. Compson's phrase, excruciatingly apt that Quentin's interior monologue begin with this appeal to contradiction, which obsesses Quentin as much as time does. In fact, one obsession is implicit in the other. The association is made overt again when he sees watches in a store window as displaying "a dozen different hours and each with the same assertive and contradictory assurance that mine had, without any hands at all. Contradicting one another" (p. 104) [54].

What strikes Quentin about the boys quarreling at the bridge is that their voices are "insistent and contradictory and impatient" (p. 145) [75]. He has assimilated his father's habit of thinking in terms of conflicts between assertive irreconcilable opposites, as in Mr. Compson's arithmetical definition of man as the "sum of his climactic experiences. . . . Man the sum of what have you. A problem in impure properties carried tediously to an unvarying nil: stalemate of dust and desire" (p. 153) [78]. Again two things—dust and desire—contradict one another in conflict, leaving a "nil." Similarly, to prove to Quentin that Caddy's virginity was always an illusion, Mr. Compson reasons by contradiction: "Women are never virgins. Purity is a negative state and therefore contrary to nature" (p. 143) [73–74].

Quentin and his father tend to experience difference as contradiction, multiplicity as a stalemated war between "impure properties." The whole novel traces the fault lines of this mental set. A universe of antagonisms is formed, all divided and subdivided, as awareness focuses on each, into further bifurcations of "A and not-A."

This universe appears in the blanket social distinction between the "quality" and the nonquality. The first category is further divided by Mrs. Compson's obsession with the status of Compsons versus that of Bascombs, and the latter heading divided into her ne'er-do-well brother Maury and her son Jason, her "salvation" and a true Bascomb. The binary set informs her belief that "there is no halfway ground that a woman is either a lady or not" (p. 127) [66], as well as Jason's identical idea that "Once a bitch always a bitch" (p. 223) [113]. It structures Jason's efforts to apply his commercial scheme of credits and debits to all areas of human relationship. It is resplendent in the moment when he believes his life will reach a heroic climax: "He could see the opposed forces of his destiny and his will drawing swiftly together now, toward a junction that would be irrevocable. . . . There would be just one right thing, without alternatives: he must do that" (p. 384) [191]. In this binary universe, as in Hegel's idea of tragic collison, all *distinctions* become *divisions*. Subtly or overtly, the daily craving is Jason's lust for clearly opposed forces, the one right thing to do.

To be immersed into Benjy's perspective, which reduces everything to an unqualified opposition (Caddy and not-Caddy), is our proper introduction to the Compson experience of life. As in the novel's first scene, the mental landscape is without middle ground or nuance—there is only this side of the fence or that side of the fence. Yet Faulkner consistently evokes a luxuriant polysemous wealth. Aside from Benjy's lack of normal organic development, his mental processes differ from those of the rest of the family only in degree, not in kind of simplification. In a sense his schematic is larger than life, but it shows what is in the life.

There can be strength in such a view, for it licenses an exhilarating call to arms, literal or figurative, of friends unified against a monolithic enemy. This ethos in general both attracted Faulkner and aroused his intense suspicion. Benjy's daily existence, however, most incisively illustrates that strength must be followed by impotence as the "enemy" increases and meaning becomes fragile.

Life's myriad variety through time is only experienced under a single undiscriminating rubric of the false (inferior, detrimental, unreal) opposing repeatedly that which is alone true and valuable. In other words, if all differences are opposites, then the opposition will grow very numerous. In compensation for this, as time passes the categories are made ever more rigid and uncompromising. Thus more of life's possibilities are excluded only to reappear as an increased repetition of the negative more insistently battering at one's citadel. In proportion as the impending collapse is suspected, a sound and fury arises in protest and defense. This is the moribund stage of the process, the "loud world" (p. 220) [112] on which the novel concentrates. Benjy's bellow and Mrs. Compson's wail echo Quentin's outraged cry as he attacks the shadowy company of Caddy's seducers in the person of Gerald Bland.

Benjy's scream upon being driven to the left rather than to the right of the Confederate soldier statue is the novel's final instance of the fragility of meaning resulting from dichotomy, "each in its ordered place" (p. 401) [199]. To offend against any item is to offend against all, the whole category of right. Living on such terms means being haunted by the vulnerability of the self erected upon this system, and consequently being preoccupied with security. This apprehension flares up startlingly in Quentin's fantasy of his father rushing to deal with Benjy's interruption of Caddy's wedding: "Father had a V-shaped silver cuirass on his running chest" (p. 100) [52]. The one kind of heroic invulnerability, which brought the dashing Compson forebears to their power, is archaic, grotesquely helpless to deal with what follows from it, as son from father. As time discloses, the impotent pathos is an inherent potential of its seeming contrary of vigorous action. It is not just around the Confederate monument, but in it.

The Compsons' isolation, frequently noted, is more than a historically accurate representation of the separatism of a caste society, as are all the images of enclosure and boundaries—fences, gates, streams, doors, locked rooms, prisons. The continual bickering, vengefulness, and whining manifest the nervous strain of the besieged. Quentin's desperate fantasy of incest is in its own way a rigorous extension of the inbreeding attitude of a household that feels itself surrounded by relative nonentities.

All this is why the frequent critical comment that Quentin is not heroic is both correct and not to the main point, as are discussions that begin and end with his pathology. But to see the heroic etiology of Quentin's, and his family's, unheroic condition is to begin to see what kind of work one is reading.

Walter J. Slatoff makes an explicit distinction in Faulkner's works between pathology and tragedy.[9] Often, however, there is a more subtle, implicit tendency among Faulkner's commentators to ignore or downplay the pathological element when discussing the tragic, or vice versa. The other tendency is to use both ideas but fail to confront their problematic relationship, so that the generic term becomes a rather flaccid compliment. One of the best critics of the novel, André Bleikasten, writes at length of "Quentin's tragedy of inheritance," yet "tragedy" seems undeservedly honorific because for Bleikasten "there is of course nothing heroic about Quentin," whose "story can be read as an ironic inversion of the familiar journey of the Romantic ego."[1] Bleikasten's discussion, seasoned with the words "tragic" and "tragedy," considers pathology alone. He attempts to relate Quentin's weakness to the daunting consciousness of a dominating ancestral figure which prevents Mr. Compson and Quentin from fulfilling their generational roles—both become mere impotent sons of the dead Father. Yet this is a needless reading of the historical dimension of *Absalom, Absalom!* back into *The Sound and the Fury.* There are valuable Freudian insights in Bleikasten's analysis, as in the similar approach of John Irwin.[2] However, in *this* novel we are not presented the debilitating awareness of an ancestral father but a structure of consciousness itself inherited all too faithfully from him and his like, with the decay of the family line intrinsic in it.

In his own way, Mr. Compson tries to counter his family's fixation upon victory or defeat: "Because no battle is ever won. . . . They are not even fought. The field only reveals to man his own folly and despair, and victory is an illusion of philosophers and fools." But this view still manifests an embattled life, in the form of a deadlock paralyzing action. Life is a cold war.

The factuality and calculations we associated not with the heroic but the modern age in reality reflect this cold war of the latter days of heroic

9. *Quest for Failure: A Study of William Faulkner* (Ithaca, N.Y.: Cornell Univ. Press, 1960), pp. 152, 193. This stimulating treatment of contradiction partly misrepresents its subject by overlooking its tragic thematic implications.
1. *The Most Splendid Failure: Faulkner's "The Sound and the Fury"* (Bloomington: Indiana Univ. Press, 1976), p. 142.
2. Cf. also the latter's stress on Quentin's active willing of passivity, associated with Faulkner's art—John T. Irwin, *Doubling and Incest / Repetition and Revenge: A Speculative Reading of Faulkner* (Baltimore: John Hopkins Univ. Press, 1975), p. 164 and passim.

action. The fatal dichotomies of value are cut from the same cloth as the binary reduction of value to arithmetic. Quentin's later recollections of the "reducto absurdum" statement show clearly that his father's admonition concerns more than the time-consciousness that critics have stressed. Sardonically, Quentin computes his suicide: "The displacement of water is equal to the something of something. Reducto absurdum of all human experience, and two six-pound flat-irons weigh more than one tailor's goose" (p. 111) [57].[3] In this framework, personal experience is simply another item to be counted; it is, indeed, not *personal*, but a public objective fact. Mr. Compson "understands" the deadly effect on personal hope and desire of a consciousness ruled by number and the hateful siege of contraries. But fittingly, his language contradicts him. The personal human experience he sees imperiled is denatured by his own formula, "sum of climatic experiences."

II

The Compson children seek to escape from the passivity of their suffering, a condition ironically produced by the binary worldview traditionally suited to heroic action. The central, insidious cause of their debility is that this same orientation threatens to alienate them from their own experience. The attempt to reclaim the personal dimension of their lives, consequently, is a deeply purposeful act, a nascent counter to passivity. For Quentin, the crucial issue is his passion.[4]

The implications of a two-value system for passion are considerable. The one-or-nothing of dichotomy is reflected in the heroic gambler heritage of staking all "on a single blind turn of a card" (p. 221) [112], as all do in their conflicting ways. Applied to relationships, this orientation can make for the single-minded loyalty Faulkner esteems highly. The tragic defect of this virtue is the narrow emotional exclusiveness that plagues the Compsons.

For Mrs. Compson the one-and-only who commands her devotion is Jason. Quentin is partly influenced by his maternal abandonment, which he feels acutely, to intensify his attachment to Caddy into fixation. To stake one's emotional life on the turn of one card is to become liable to suffering. But the Compson ethos goes farther in associating emotion with pain. For all the Compson children the emotions have been given the unhealthy tinge of an ordeal or affliction, so that for them we are justified in speaking of passions in the double sense of feeling and suffering. The mother's donning black when Caddy is first kissed can stand for the whole joyless association.

Quentin's nearly stupefied "temporary" punctuates his father's well-

3. See also p. 105.
4. For a fine discussion of emotion as structuring theme, see Carey Wall, "*The Sound and the Fury*: The Emotional Center," *Midwest Quarterly*, 2 (1970), 371–87.

meaning argument that time will remove all pain. If Quentin cannot have his exclusive One, Caddy, then he desires a permanent grief over the loss, for at least grief preserves feeling. He has had to learn that feeling is suffering, but then to be faced with the loss of suffering too is unthinkable.

As we saw, there is an inherent tendency in a two-value classification to treat varied negative features of life as an undifferentiated set, as if they constituted the same evil repeated through time. To Benjy, a single agony of loss recurs daily in many guises. In Quentin's more complex version, a broken leg in childhood provides him an index-pain recurring as a gasping "ah ah ah." So too from a broader standpoint the father reassures Quentin that the dishonor of sisters recurs in life, that "tragedy is second-hand." Again the father implicitly devalues Quentin's passion by denying that it is distinctive, individual, no matter how many it analogues. Instead of being his, it is threatened with being unredeemably anonymous, not only derivative but lacking even the distinctive archetype of the Passion: "Father was teaching us that all men are just accumulations dolls stuffed with sawdust swept up from the trash heaps where all previous dolls had been thrown away the sawdust flowing from what wound in what side that not for me died not" (p. 218) [111]. For the father, passion is passive: "a love or a sorrow is a bond purchased without design and . . . matures willynilly and is recalled without warning to be replaced by whatever issue the gods happen to be floating at the time" (p. 221) [112]. The father's kind of individualism honors the personal quality of experience only in a passionless integrity: "whether or not you consider [an act] courageous is of more importance than the act itself than any act" (p. 219) [112].

Similar in their experience of time, father and son diverge in their view of emotions. Mr. Compson advocates that the rational person disavow his own passion as time's minion, a weakness and "impure property." His alcoholism is his suicidal tribute to—and Faulkner's comment on—this Stoic aim. The philosophy the father offers ends not by diminishing Quentin's pain but by threatening its significance.[5]

Quentin is faced, then, with the "reducto absurdum" of the objective absolutist approach to life and its mirror image, temporal nihilism. From these perspectives, human experience becomes mere fact as its personal quality is erased: *my* hope, *my* desire, *your* love, and *your* loss become meaningless. The schema that began by making a decisive cut between what was on my side and what was not concludes by enfeebling the very idea of *mine*. Each character is threatened with a radical dispossession. Benjy and Quentin in particular experience even their own body processes, thoughts, and actions as alienated. The Compson world frus-

5. For the contrary view that Quentin completely shares his father's Stoic philosophy, see Brooks, p. 344, and John W. Hunt, *William Faulkner: Art in Theological Tension* (Syracuse, N.Y.: Syracuse Univ. Press, 1965), p. 50.

trates the individualism it espouses by a binary orientation that in effect denies basic self-esteem. Despite their aversion to anomaly, the Compsons live this fundamental contradiction. Yet they neither subside into numbness nor yield their stubborn hold on personal value. They continue to grasp both individualism and a self-defeating way of founding it. Although tragedy within their world is "second-hand," we as readers can see in such persistence a necessary element of tragedy.

Among the brothers Compson, this tragic persistence in vindicating the personal includes a tendency to cloistered subjectivism, a habit of self-justification, and a reaction against whatever diminishes uniqueness. Here we find also the cause of their possessiveness. Each brother clutches at something exclusively his, to supply from the public world what is lacking in the private. If *my* experience is alienated, I try to reclaim something I believe mine and wrongly taken from me. This is the truth underlying Jason's rationalization that his greed and thievery are excused by "getting back his own." And Benjy and Quentin each deploys the similar fable of "his" Caddy and her symbolic substitutes as objects of passion. To adopt Faulkner's later comment, such efforts reveal the most basic meaning of "aveng[ing] the dispossessed Compsons" (Appendix, p. 408) [206].

Caddy, too, for all her rebellion against the family, still dramatizes its orientation when she incites Quentin to think himself her possessor, able to dispose of her as he will, in their scenes by the branch. Indeed, her development recapitulates the family's progression along the continuum from active to passive. The young Caddy who demands that brothers and servants obey her during the period of Damuddy's death, who pushes Natalie down the ladder, fights with Quentin, and dreams of being a general, giant, or king, is the same Caddy who later lies passive under the phallic knife Quentin holds to her throat and acts out a surrender to her imagined sexual "opponent": "yes I hate him I would die for him"; "yes Ill do anything you want me to anything yes . . . she lifted her face then I saw she wasn't even looking at me at all I could see [her eyes'] white rim" (pp. 188, 194) [95, 99]. At the same time, however, she performs what a psychologist would call a passive aggression, for she controls and "owns" Quentin by her sexual display, especially when he realizes at its climax that she imagines herself in someone else's arms.

According to the Compsons' orientation, the chosen One must be uniform, without the "impure property" represented by the young Caddy's muddy drawers. Further, her many anonymous suitors undermine the idea of possessing her exclusively, distinctively. Thus Quentin is both fascinated and nauseated by sexuality, which subverts instead of supporting his dualism. When he imagines anonymous intercourse, vital boundaries dissolve between an impure "imperious" inner realm and a vulnerable outer: "Then know that some man that all those mysterious and imperious concealed. . . . Liquid putrefaction like drowned things floating like pale rubber flabbily filled getting the odour of honeysuckle all mixed up" (p. 159) [81].

Symbolizing Caddy, twilight above all stands for the mixed, liminal, shadowy phenomena that are ill sorted by binary consciousness. Twilight evokes for Quentin a vision that his doing and suffering are taunted by inadmissible paradox:

> I seemed to be lying neither asleep nor awake looking down a long corridor of grey halflight where all stable things had become shadowy paradoxical all I had done shadows all I had felt suffered taking visible form antic and perverse mocking without relevance inherent themselves with the denial of the significance they should have affirmed thinking I was I was not who was not was not who. (p. 211) [107–8]

The doubtful self is enervated by the dichotomy that is not so much thought as uncomfortably inhabited, as in the long corridor between the polarized realms of the House of Compson. Made intimate guests there, we can experience, if not assent to, Quentin's conviction: better a suicide that promises, however fantastically, to transform all this.

III

We have distinguished two phases in the novel's tragic process: the decline of action into passivity, and the attempt at reversal. In the first, Quentin's pathos, both pathological and nonpathological, derives from a logic of tragedy that Faulkner has read back into daily life. In the second, Quentin's effort to reclaim the personal by commitment to his passion creates the passion necessary to tragedy. Passion itself becomes purposeful action and transcends the condition of simple passivity.

Yet this necessary condition of traditional tragedy is not a sufficient condition. Not only is catastrophe lacking, but there is no direct recognition of suffering such as sometimes, in effect, substitues for catastrophe (*Prometheus Bound*) or augments it. In the *Philoctetes*, for example, there is an "audience" within the play, Neoptolemus, whose final acknowledgment, rather than exploitation, of the hero's suffering is the crux of the play, releasing our emotions. But Quentin's personal experience has no standing in the public factual world. The impassive eyes staring at him everywhere on his last day represent the objective "ordered certitude" that "sees injustice done" (p. 155) [79], like the "cruel unwinking minds" in his memory of school-children who know the correct facts (p. 108) [55]. Quentin's pain cannot be tragic in this view because, as George Eliot says of Dorothea's tragedy in *Middlemarch*, "we do not expect people to be deeply moved by what is not unusual."[6]

6. (Boston: Houghton Mifflin, 1965), p. 144.

It is made maddeningly plain to Quentin that his trouble at a sister's maturity and "dishonor" is too familiarly recurrent in life to be considered unusual. The very aberration—the really unusual form and degree—of his response is exacerbated by his desperation to break out of a vicious circle of the usual. The repetition-bound binary outlook that fosters his pathos also prevents others from certifying that his pain is significant.

Catharsis is thus carefully displaced from Quentin to Dilsey. And Dilsey is not so much an agent whose own suffering is witnessed as she is the novel's central sympathizing—yet in a key sense alienated—witness, audience. Reverend Shegog's Easter sermon, with its contagious refrain "I sees," evokes the one Passion that has sufficient public standing to release the congregation's passions, otherwise "banal" and inexpressible. The communally validated Passion, shut off from Quentin in Dilsey's world, combines with his own thoughts of Christ and his Passion to indicate that Quentin's death is a bid for tragic recognition. Quentin, in short, improvises his own passion, a suicidal "autogethsemane."[7] Its intended public impact is confirmed by his vision of himself and Caddy in hell: "*the two of us amid the pointing and the horror beyond the clean flame. . . . Only you and me then amid the pointing and the horror walled by the clean flame*" (p. 144) [74]. If others cannot sympathize, then their impassivity will be stripped away. In this embattled conclusive suffering, a victory could be claimed for the defiant heroic temper as its passion is witnessed with antipathy.

Quentin's suicide, an act both momentous and his exclusively, is meant as an adequate public sign of his personal experience. But his signal is taken by others as yet another repetiton of Compson disaster, their "curse." Within the novel's setting, this symbol lacks empathetic reading. That we will supply this crucial lack is Faulkner's own gamble on creating tragedy in defiance of its instability. For we can view the passion displayed within the book in a way that the characters cannot, and yet the difficulty of the internal monologues necessary for this intimacy challenges our ability to witness. If by now readers can surmount this barrier, another has remained: the common two-value assumption of an unbridgeable division between tragedy and pathos.

IV

In keeping with the key role that the ideal of tragedy has played in the controversy over modernist writers like Faulkner, George Marion O'Donnell defended him as a "traditional moralist" who, like Quentin, was always "*striving toward* the condition of tragedy. He is the Quentin Compson . . . of modern fiction."

Since O'Donnell's landmark 1939 essay, a dominant tendency in

7. *Mosquitoes* (New York: Liveright, 1927), p. 48.

Faulkner criticism, represented by the invaluable work of Cowley, Warren, and Brooks, has emphasized "the conflict between traditionalism
and the anti-traditional modern world in which it is immersed."[8] The
conflict is real. In arguing for the dialectical continuity between tragedy
and pathos in *The Sound and the Fury*, however, in effect I have argued
that here—and I believe in Faulkner generally—the continuity between
these worlds is as true and important as the change from one to the other
and their conflict. Such a view accords with Faulkner's repeated assertion that certain basic human traits, types, and life-patterns continue
throughout history, though constantly in new forms. There is, in fact, a
continuity *of* conflict for the inheritors of the heroic temper and its fate-
ful logic.

JOHN T. MATTHEWS

The Discovery of Loss in *The Sound and the Fury* †

Some of Faulkner's most provocative comments about language and fiction occur in the recent published typescripts of a preface for a printing
of *The Sound and the Fury* contemplated for 1933.[1] Matched with some
of Faulkner's less familiar public remarks about his writing, the preface
elaborates the cluster of ideas I have been discussing and forecasts the
major concerns of my readings in later chapters. In conversation Faulkner's statements about his craft are often cryptic, obvious, or cheerfully
false. He always encouraged questioners to read him (rather than to talk
to him), and the preface represents the deliberation of a written text: " 'I
have worked on it a good deal, like on a poem almost, and I think that
it is all right now.' "[2] Looking at *The Sound and the Fury* after several
years, Faulkner recalls that his fourth novel gave him new freedom as a
writer; disappointed with *Sartoris*' repeated rejection, Faulkner "seemed
to shut a door between me and all publishers' addresses and book lists. I
said to myself, Now I can write."[3] *The Sound and the Fury* figures decisively in Faulkner's career for many reasons, one of which is its liberat-
ing recognition of the properties of fictional language. According to the

8. "Faulkner's Mythology," *Kenyon Review*, 1 (1939), 299, 285.

† From *The Play of Faulkner's Language* (Ithaca and London: Cornell University Press, 1982),
17–23, 91–114. Copyright © 1982 by Cornell University Press. Used by permission of the publisher. Page references in brackets are to this Norton Critical Edition.
1. William Faulkner, "An Introduction for *The Sound and the Fury*," ed. James B. Meriwether,
Southern Review, 8 (October 1972): 705–710. I shall refer to this draft as Introduction (*SR*). The
second draft appeared as "An Introduction to *The Sound and the Fury*," ed. James B. Meriwether,
Mississippi Quarterly, 26 (Winter 1973): 410–415; I shall refer to it as Introduction (*MQ*).
2. William Faulkner, letter to Ben Wasson, quoted in headnote to Introduction (*SR*) by James
Meriwether from the original in the Alderman Library, p. 707.
3. Introduction (*SR*), p. 710.

preface, the apprenticeship for *The Sound and the Fury* suitably had concentrated on the nature of language: "I had learned a little about writing from Soldiers' Pay—how to approach language, words."[4] In their various approaches to language Faulkner's early works explore how the writer embodies himself in his art, how objects of representation acquire presence through the mediation of language, how writing implicates the writer in an economy of losses (the loss of the original idea or of completed meaning, for example), and how the truth of a story emerges from the play of its language.

One remark in the preface—perhaps its most famous—may misleadingly conduct us back into the presence of the author. Faulkner concludes the preface to the story of the Compson brothers' loss of their sister by wondering if he was not trying to "manufacture the sister which I did not have and the daughter which I was to lose,"[5] as if novels simply compensate their authors for frustrations or losses suffered in life. André Bleikasten, in his thorough reading of the novel, adduces this statement to confirm that *The Sound and the Fury* seeks to fill a "lack and a loss" and that the preface presents a theory of art as a "transnarcissistic" object of compensation.[6] Such a formulation assumes a prior state of grief in the author's life that may be soothed by an aesthetic substitution, and Bleikasten accordingly laments our insufficient knowledge about Faulkner's rumored personal disappointments at the time he was writing *The Sound and the Fury*. But Faulkner's account is more complicated: his writing *precedes* any sense of loss, and actually precedes the fact of loss in the case of his daughter. "When I began it I had no plan at all. I wasn't even writing a book."[7] I did not realise then that I was trying to manufacture the sister. . . . I just began to write."[8] However fine a distinction this may seem to be, the consequences are considerable. To begin to write, to mark the page, *produces* the mood of bereavement, as if the use of language creates the atmosphere of mourning. Writing does not respond to loss, it initiates it; writing itself is as much a kind of loss as it is a kind of compensation. The double action—of making and losing—is figured in the preface's image of the writer as vase maker: "Now I can make myself a vase like that which the old Roman kept at his bedside and wore the rim slowly away with kissing it."[9]

In what respects does the activity of writing involve loss? How is "making" the novel like wearing it away? As he looks back on the composition of *The Sound and the Fury*, Faulkner realizes that the "ecstasy" of writing is produced by the very process that destroys it. Like the pleasure of

4. Ibid., p. 708.
5. Introduction *(MQ)*, p. 413.
6. André Bleikasten, *The Most Splendid Failure: Faulkner's "The Sound and the Fury"* (Bloomington, Ind., 1976), p. 46.
7. Introduction *(SR)*, p. 710.
8. Introduction *(MQ)*, p. 413.
9. Introduction *(SR)*, p. 710.

sexual climax, the pleasure of writing is "release[d]" as it simultaneously fulfills and exhausts itself. Writing *The Sound and the Fury* gave Faulkner "that ecstasy, that eager and joyous faith and anticipation of surprise which the yet unmarred sheet beneath my hand held inviolate and unfailing, waiting for release."[1] The young writer senses the fullness of his self-presence, of his readiness to author; yet, paradoxically, the writer consummates himself only by losing that (perhaps illusory) fullness. The writer both takes the virginity of the page ("the yet unmarred sheet . . . inviolate") and surrenders his own to that "emotion definite and physical," that ecstasy. In Faulkner's approach to *The Sound and the Fury*, conducted in earlier works, he "learned a little about . . . how to approach language . . . with joy, as you approach women: perhaps with the same secretly unscrupulous intentions."[2] Having seduced and been seduced by his words, the writer is surprised that the first ecstasy may never be repeated: "whatever novels I should write in the future would be written without reluctance, but also without anticipation or joy."[3] Thus the achievement of ecstasy is also its loss, and Faulkner foresees the remainder of his career to be barren of bliss, offering merely "cold satisfaction."

Faulkner's very way of putting this sense that the ecstasy of writing is not to return emphasizes that language can name only what is absent. The more mature author, already 'married' to his career, knows his earlier innocence only in having lost it in the ecstasy of writing. Even the adjectives Faulkner uses to describe the text's initial virginity already declare impending deflowerment—unmarred, inviolate, unfailing. And, in turn, the ecstasy of writing *The Sound and the Fury* is apprehended only when it is named in its absence; "I learned from the writing of Sanctuary [his next novel] that there was something missing; something which The Sound and the Fury gave me and Sanctuary did not."[4] The thing that is missing comes to be named ecstasy.

To become a writer was, for Faulkner, to negotiate an economy of losses: ecstasy replaces innocence, cold repetition deadens ecstasy. This economy also includes the way in which the writer transacts his 'original' idea into the written text, for such a conversion is always a kind of loss. *The Sound and the Fury* began with the picture of "Caddy climbing the pear tree to look in the window at her grandmother's funeral" while her brothers watch below.[5] Having "put" that image into the book, Faulkner simultaneously realizes and loses "the only thing in literature which would ever move me very much." Subsequent novels may never bring him the ecstasy he felt in writing *The Sound and the Fury* because what that novel has made, it has also lost; what it has represented, it has

1. Ibid., p. 709.
2. Ibid., p. 708.
3. Ibid., p. 710.
4. Ibid., p. 709.
5. Ibid., p. 710.

marred; the vase it has fashioned, it wears away. Surely Caddy—the "little girl" "manufactured" by the text—never achieves the presence or substance of a 'real' character; she is memorable precisely because she inhabits the memories of her brothers and the novel, and memory for Faulkner never transcends the sense of loss. Like the vase, the novel is a cold, bedside shape that at best parodies a living body. Faulkner confirms the idea of writing as a destruction or loss of original presence on several occasions. Earlier in the preface, of course, he says that the "approach to language" is like the approach to "dynamite" and "women"; language as readily triggers explosion as ecstasy. Or perhaps it triggers them simultaneously. When asked to describe his "ideal woman," Faulkner replies that "I couldn't describe her by color of hair, color of eyes, because once she is described, then somehow she vanishes."[6] Faulkner extends this idea of writing as loss in his comments about the relationship between the germ of a story and its embodiment. As if generalizing from the example of *The Sound and the Fury*'s seminal image, Faulkner remarks:

> There's always a moment in experience—a thought—an incident—that's there. Then all I do is work up to that moment. I figure what must have happened before to lead people to that particular moment, and I work away from it, finding out how people act after that moment.[7]

If we compare this account even superficially with some of the famous incidents 'in' Faulkner's novels, we might argue that, like the ideal woman, the kernel of the story is precisely what vanishes into the words that describe it. Caddy's tree climbing, in fact, appears only fragmentedly in Benjy's section and hardly at all thereafter, as if the novel advances by losing the initial image in its own writing. Quentin's suicide, the murders of Charles Bon and Joanna Burden, Temple Drake's rape—all central moments in their narratives—function more as absences in the stories that surround them. As he outlines in the passage above, Faulkner does construct the narrative as leading up to and away from these incidents, but the events or thoughts themselves do not appear in the text. The moment of the story's origin is lost into the novel.[8] Perhaps Faulkner's remark that *The Sound and the Fury* is a novel about "the lost Caddy" carries a more ambiguous pathos than we have generally allowed.[9]

Faulkner refers to the paradox of fiction's loss-as-gain in his favorite

6. James B. Meriwether and Michael Millgate, eds., *Lion in the Garden: Interviews with William Faulkner, 1926–1962* (New York, 1968), p. 127.
7. Ibid., p. 220.
8. I first noticed this idea in Faulkner's preface after a graduate student at Boston University, Stuart H. Johnson, made a similar argument about the relationship between the prefaces of Henry James and the plots of the novels in an essay written for me.
9. Frederick L. Gwynn and Joseph L. Blotner, eds., *Faulkner in the University: Class Conferences at the University of Virginia, 1957–1958* (New York, 1959), p. 31.

description of *The Sound and the Fury* as his "best failure."[1] Each section tries to get the story "right," and each fails; the novel advances by admitting its own impossibility, accumulates authority by impugning it, succeeds by failing. *The Sound and the Fury* embodies this aspect of Faulkner's mature aesthetic; his paradoxical descriptions are not pointless riddles but rather terse formulae to describe the subversion of resolved meaning, closed form, and full representation by the language that aspires to those very achievements.

Just as the described objects of language "somehow vanish," so the writer must confront his own disappearance into his words. We are used to thinking of the kinds of presence that authors retain as they convert themselves into texts that survive them, but Faulkner also notices the distance and deathliness of written selfhood. A narrator's voice is one way for an author to *be* in a text, yet in *The Sound and the Fury* Faulkner is so far 'in' the opening three sections that he seems to disappear. By assuming the modes of perception—the visual rhetoric, we might call it—of each of the Compson brothers, Faulkner suppresses the distinctive qualities of the Faulknerian voice. When that more conventional voice finally appears in the last section of the novel, Faulkner surprisingly emphasizes its difference from the author's proper voice, which seems paradoxically to inhabit more fully the idiosyncrasies of the earlier sections. "I should have to get completely out of the book,"[2] Faulkner recalls about conceiving the last section. In such a view, the novel frames the absences of both its subject and its author: "It's fine to think that you will leave something behind you when you die, *but it's better to have made something you can die with*. Much better the muddy bottom of a little doomed girl climbing a blooming pear tree in April to look in the window at the funeral."[3] Caught in Faulkner's mind as she climbs out of the book, Caddy is the figure that the novel is written to *lose*, and to whom the writer may lose himself.

* * *

The toxic bitterness of Jason's voice in section 3 assaults us by ridiculing the highly unnatural sympathies that the novel has earlier asked us to cultivate. In Jason's "sane"[4] eyes, Benjy ought to be merely the asylum's star freshman, Quentin tried to go swimming without knowing how, Mr. Compson needed nothing so much as a one-armed straitjacket, and Caddy is—once and always—"a bitch." The willful, sullen child who trips through Benjy's section repeatedly rejects and is rejected by his siblings and father, and his mother can manage no more than a formal acknowledgment of her preference for him. Jason fosters his pure

1. Ibid., p. 61.
2. Introduction (*MQ*), p. 415.
3. Ibid.; emphasis added.
4. *The Sound and the Fury* (New York, 1929; Vintage edition), "Appendix," p. 421 [212].

defection from the core of the family by fighting with Caddy, by jeal-
ously destroying Benjy's toys, or by tattling on Caddy and Quentin. Such
behavior naturally deepens into the isolation of Jason's adulthood, an
isolation sealed by paranoia and festering with masochism. Though he
believes himself excepted from the demented attachments of his brothers
and though he prides himself in upholding the responsibility, respectability, and routine of a "civilised life," Jason has not solved the Compson crisis. He has only silenced it. Like his brothers, Jason articulates a
response to loss and deprivation. But unlike them, he chooses a kind of
speech—money—that pretends no referential ties. The pursuit of money,
whether it is playing the stock market, earning a salary, or robbing his
niece's piggybank, seems like a pure attempt to restore the family's depleted
wealth. Finance, however, is not the nonsense language Jason thinks it
is; it inadvertently reveals precisely what its speaker has failed to confront: the need for intimacy with his sister. [5]

Jason's economic rites prove to be a writing of his unconscious grief.
The language of finance, like any language, is linked arbitrarily, rather
than intrinsically, to what it stands for. For the reader of Jason's writing,
its dislocated center is Caddy, who was never more than an absence in
Jason's discourse. Jason's economy seeks, on the one hand, to establish
an order for his life that differs from the disorder Caddy causes in Quentin's. Yet seeming to ignore her, on the other hand, Jason's writing also
pursues—all the while deferring—a representation of Caddy in his life.
Jason's language covertly manufactures the sister he never had.

Even to her favorite son, Mrs. Compson can offer no sustained warmth
or security. Driven like his brothers to supplement her insufficiency,
Jason finds Quentin in Caddy's arms and Benjy in her bed. As a result,
he comes to depend on his grandmother for the attention he has been
refused elsewhere. The connection is not one that attracts much of the
novel's attention because it serves chiefly to establish a more extreme
version of the crisis of "filling the vacuum." For Jason's Damuddy dies
at the very instant her most natural replacement, Caddy, also 'dies.' This
is an excessive eruption of spacing and death at the origin, and it determines the third Compson brother's recoil from the obligations of creative supplementation.

Jason reacts violently to the loss of Damuddy:

> After a while even Jason was through eating, and he began to cry.
> "Now you got to tune up." Dilsey said.
> "He does it every night since Damuddy was sick and he cant
> sleep with her." Caddy said. (31) [17]

5. I want to go beyond the view that Jason uses his niece as a surrogate to displace his repressed
incestuous desire for Caddy. John L. Longley, Jr. (*The Tragic Mask: A Study of Faulkner's Heroes*
[Chapel Hill, N.C., 1957]), suggests that Jason's "hatred is transference of his deeply repressed
incestuous attraction toward Quentin" and, through her, toward Caddy (p. 147). But I see Quentin as only one denomination in Jason's elaborate financial articulation of sexual frustration.

> "Do you think buzzards are going to undress Damuddy." Caddy said. "You're crazy."
> "You're a skizzard." Jason said. He began to cry.
> "You're a knobnot." Caddy said. Jason cried. His hands were in his pockets.
> "Jason going to be rich man." Versh said. "He holding his money all the time."
> Jason cried. (42–43 [23]

Jason never manages to replace the supplemental presence of Damuddy with another. Her absence condemns him to a perpetual sense of exclusion, diminishment, and impoverishment. For example, Mrs. Compson reminds him that " 'It was always her and Quentin. They were always conspiring against me. Against you too. . . . They always looked on you and me as outsiders' " (326) [163]. Over his father's grave he reflects about "when we were little and one thing and another and I got to feeling funny again, kind of mad or something, thinking about now we'd have Uncle Maury around the house all the time, running things like the way he left me to come home in the rain by myself" (252) [127]. Even the Compson name, which Jason equates strictly with the family fortune, is dead to Jason. "I reckon the reason all the Compson gave out before it got to me like Mother says, is that he [Mr. Compson] drank it up. At least I never heard of him offering to sell anything to send me to Harvard" (245) [124].

To be angry with Mr. Compson for drowning himself in liquor because such irresponsibility exhausts Jason's rightful patrimony might seem implausibly literal-minded—even for Jason—if it were not that he invariably interprets loss as financial setback. Caddy's pregnancy merely means the expense of a wedding; her divorce costs him the promised job in Herbert Head's bank; Quentin's suicide wastes the tuition money gained from the sale of Benjy's pasture. Jason's need for impersonal, collectible, hoardable money springs from his inability to speak his grief. Versh's joke, like so much else in Benjy's section, accurately forecasts the intimate connection between crying and pocket filling, between grief and reimbursement.

Jason recognizes that he can never afford the extravagance of suicide or cynicism: " 'I never had time to go to Harvard like Quentin or drink myself into the ground like Father. I had to work' " (224) [114]. At the same time that he resents his impoverishment, however, he also sees his "slavery" as a salvation from the intolerable self-indulgence he so scorns in the rest of his family:

> Well, Jason likes work. I says no I never had university advantages because at Harvard they teach you how to go for a swim at night without knowing how to swim and at Sewanee they dont even teach you what water is. I says you might send me to the state University; maybe I'll learn how to stop my clock with a nose spray. (243) [123]

Work unambiguously established the value of time; each minute has a negotiable worth in tangible money. Surely one source of the strength of Jason's commitment to his work is that it protests against suicide's announcement that time is worth nothing. I shall discuss similar unspoken assertions of Jason's moneymaking shortly, but we should first notice that the realm of petty finance appeals to Jason precisely because it seems devoid of anything except intrinsic significance. Time, decay, desire, incest, and sexuality seem to have no place in the financial devotions of the one Compson who refuses to be mastered by the metaphysical.

> After all, like I say money has no value; it's just the way you spend it. It dont belong to anybody, so why try to hoard it. It just belongs to the man that can get it and keep it. (241) [122]

Jason acts on the fatherly advice that Quentin refuses; money can displace grief, frustration, deprivation: "watching pennies has healed more scars than jesus" (221) [113]. And Job, after seeing Jason speed from check forging at lunch to stock jockeying to hardware huckstering, senses that Jason wants to leave something behind: " 'You fools a man whut so smart he cant even keep up wid hisself. . . . Dat's Mr. Jason Compson . . .' " (312) [156]. Jason insists that his most profound disappointment in life is nothing more than the loss of his best financial opportunity, the promised clerkship in Herbert Head's St. Louis bank. He and Mrs. Compson are sure that at least Caddy would "have enough regard for the family not to jeopardize my chance after she and Quentin had had theirs" (246) [125]. Jason's entire "chance" for a future had rested on the missed job.

Jason's pronouncement of the neutrality of money fails to convince even as he says it, of course. But what needs to be examined more fully is the extent to which Jason's financial behavior thoroughly but mutely tries to fill the vacuum of loss. The very status of Herbert Head's desperately sought job conforms to the paradigm of loss in the Compson family. Just as Mrs. Compson is the mother whose children lose her before she ever allows them to possess her, so the clerkship is "the job in the bank of which he had been deprived before he ever got it" (382) [190]. Each is an illusory presence that can be known only in its loss, a dispossession at the origin.

At Damuddy's death, Caddy, too, becomes the object that is lost before it can ever be possessed. The problem for Jason is not how to preserve moments of intimacy with Caddy in his memory (as it is for Benjy and Quentin), but how to deal with her premature death to him. He does so by accepting the apparently dead substitute of money. Jason readily exchanges Caddy's absence for the opportunity to make money; accordingly, Herbert Head must be both the one who takes Caddy away and the one who reimburses her brothers for their loss. (Quentin, of course, repudiates so offensive a compensation: "To hell with your money. . . .

you'd better stick to Jason he'd suit you better than I would" [136, 134] [70, 69].)

If Jason's decision were as uncomplicated as substituting cold cash for a cold sister, he would scarcely be inconsolable about the bungled clerkship. What Jason scarcely realizes is that the desire for money, rather than putting Caddy safely to rest, keeps the sense of her loss alive; and his irrational obsession with the single missed chance, with his doomed stock playing, and with his niece's purse strings unwittingly betrays an absolute absorption by his frustrated desire for Caddy. Quentin understands that Head's money offers more than mere compensation or diversion; to Quentin, it represents the brother-in-law's sexual potency and privilege. Even if Mrs. Compson had not virtually auctioned Caddy, Head's money would have symbolized sexual power. When he offers Quentin "a loan," he indirectly reminds him of his purchased right to intimacy with Caddy:

> No no come on I belong to the family now see I know how it is with a young fellow he has lots of private affairs it's always pretty hard to get the old man to stump up for I know havent I been there and not so long ago either but now I'm getting married and all specially up there come on dont be a fool listen when we get a chance for a real talk I want to tell you about a little widow over in town
>   I've heard about that too keep your damned money (136) [70]

Quentin won't allow his sexual threat to Caddy to be bought off so easily, but Jason will because he can never muster a claim on her. The prospect of Jason's clerking in Head's bank is the very image of a brother's subordinate respect for the husband's purchase of his sister. Precisely such a job would have enabled Jason to enact the only incest available to him as outsider, that which Mr. Compson calls "the pure and perfect incest: the brother . . . taking that virginity in the person of the brother-in-law" (*Absalom*, 96). Jason's outrage at the loss of Head's job is hardly just the pique at bad business it might seem at first. It bemoans a failure to deaden passion into greed.

Money and sexual potency are associated throughout *The Sound and the Fury*. The opening scene of the novel presents a search for three things: Benjy hunts for Caddy and Luster looks for his missing quarter and stray golf balls. Luster's search comments antically on Benjy's, for the missing quarter reminds us both that Caddy's 'loss' in the branch leads to the sale of the pasture (now the golf course) and that the loss of money is related to the loss of "balls." Luster smirks to one of the wash women:

> "You all found any balls yet."
>   . . .

"Aint you talking biggity. I bet you better not let your grandmammy hear you talking like that." (17) [10]

Benjy's castration constitutes the serious background of this banter; he
has lost his manhood to his love for Caddy, and figuratively, he has no
resources for recovery. (When Luster does manage to turn up a ball in
the branch, a golfer tricks him into giving it up.)

As Quentin refuses the potency of Head's money, so he dramatizes
his impotence in other financial transactions. He repeatedly gives away
small sums of money in mimicry of his virginal consecration to the dead
sister. On his way to the jeweler's, Quentin gives a nickel and a cigar to
two bootblacks. He looks back and notices that "the one with the cigar
was trying to sell it to the other for the nickel" (102) [53]. The prominent
association of cigars with Herbert Head's phallicism ("Thanks I dont
smoke" and "Keep your hands off of me you'd better get that cigar off
the mantel" [132, 136] [69, 70]) might also suggest that the boot-blacks
play out the kind of deal Quentin refuses. Later, Quentin ironically
purchases the little girl's companionship with his money; the moment
poignantly travesties the forbidden intimacy.

By subtly renegotiating the terms of internal crises into capital quo-
tients, Jason unwittingly invests all of his financial activities with expressive content. For example, instead of letting his mother's investment in
the hardware store mature toward a partnership for him, he secretly
withdraws the money to buy a car. The decision has nothing to do with
business acumen; the automobile gives him constant headaches (a
reminder of his inescapable victimization); acquiring it protests the
unnatural survival of his mother's authority over the family; and T. P.
irrepressibly shows off for the town girls with it, perhaps signaling Jason's
attraction to a disguised erotic flamboyance.

Jason's entanglement in the stock market similarly displaces without
eradicating fundamental sources of anxiety and frustration. Despite perpetual setbacks, Jason persists with futile schemes. The more he loses,
of course, the more deeply he is committed, since "I just want to hit
them one time and get my money back. I don't want a killing . . . I just
want my money back . . ." (292) [147]. Jason furiously believes
that for every loss there will be an equal and opposite compensation. In
fact, to the extent that the stock market both impoverishes and enriches,
it is an analogue for Caddy, who first deprives Jason and then returns a
kind of wealth to his embezzling hands. Stock transactions impersonal-
ize for Jason the cycles of gain and loss that trouble each of the Compson
brothers. And yet they also embody the very forces that have dispossessed
Jason originally. Throughout his warfare with Wall Street, Jason is at
two disadvantages: he is excluded from the center of power ("These
damn jews . . . with all their guaranteed inside dope" [292] [147]) and
he must endure comic lapses of time before he receives vital information

(" 'What are we paying you for'? I says, 'Weekly reports?' " [282] [142]).
To suffer setbacks because he is an outsider and because he is behind
time is unwittingly to reproduce the circumstances of his loss of
Caddy. Perhaps a suggestion of his namesake's behavior can be
found in one of Mr. Compson's tirelessly supplied metaphors: "it is hard
believing to think that a love or a sorrow is a bond purchased without
design and which matures willynilly and is recalled without warning to
be replaced by whatever issue the gods happen to be floating at the time"
(221) [112–13].

Jason's blind devotion to finance seems on the surface to provide a
refuge from the problems of lost love and sorrow that destroy his brothers. By reducing the stakes and by evading the expressive significance of
his gestures, Jason constructs his own "reducto [sic] ad absurdum" as an
alternative to suicide. Just as he trivializes Quentin's obsession with time
through his incessant attention to being "on time" and never getting
"enough time," so Jason shrinks the agony of loss to the annoyance of
financial reverses. The most curious and revelatory commodity in Jason's
complex economy, however, is neither his salary nor his stocks, but his
niece.

The instant that Quentin Head enters the Compson household, Jason
identifies her as the coin of an exchange: " 'Well,' " he says, realizing
that Head will withdraw the clerkship when he returns his counterfeit
wife and child, " 'they brought my job home tonight' " (246) [125].
Shortly after, he initiates his commercial custody by renting her to her
mother for $100:

> And so I counted the money again that night and put it away,
> and I didn't feel so bad. I says I reckon that'll show you. I reckon
> you'll know now that you cant beat me out of a job and get away
> with it. (255) [129].

Realizing a profit is always the kind of revenge that eases Jason. And
surely his use of his niece and his willingness to keep her reflect her
sheer monetary worth; so long as Jason possesses her, he can continue
to deflect Caddy's checks into his private coffers. His swelling cache may
literally replace the patrimony that Caddy's wedding and Quentin's suicide wasted, and Jason may enjoy the bonus of avenging his own disin-
heritance by stealing from the next generation. But like Jason's other
economies, his manipulation of Quentin is an attempt to restore emotional wealth, too.

Quentin is not a faceless chip; she is a coin that bears the imprint of
her maker. Although Jason refuses to deal with all of the ramifications
of the fact, Quentin becomes the tangible token of her mother in Caddy's absence. "Just like her mother" (265) [135], Jason fumes as he recognizes the willful eroticism of his sister in his niece. Quentin represents
the only aspect of Caddy's passion that Jason could see as an outsider:

her sexual appetite. And as Caddy's insatiability finally 'killed' her, Jason
determines to oversee her delegate. All of Jason's unadmitted outrage at
Caddy's infidelities (as she both nurtured his brothers and satisfied her
lovers) focuses on Quentin's behavior. Frustrated because he seems to
be the only male to whom Caddy has not been a whore in one way or
another, Jason deplores her daughter's careless and alluring attire while
noticing every effect ("Her kimono came unfastened, flapping about her,
damned near naked" [228] [116]). Later he hints that he needs to restrain
himself in her presence: "I'll be damned if they dont dress like they were
trying to make every man they passed on the street want to reach out
and clap his hand on it" (289) [145]. When she threatens to rip her dress
off, he stops her, as if reenacting the fatal moment of Caddy's disrobing;
and later, when he chases Quentin and the stolen money, his role is
mistaken for that of a cheated husband passing himself off as a brother.
In these respects Jason treats Quentin like the seventeen-year-old sister
he never had.

Jason's frustrated desire for Caddy also indirectly accounts for the violent zeal with which he 'fathers' Quentin. So far as his mother allows,
Jason assumes the paternal responsibilities of the family once Jason
Compson III has died. Mrs. Compson reminds Quentin that Jason "is
the nearest thing to a father you've ever had" (324) [162]. And he regularly thinks of Quentin as something like a daughter: "If it was my own
daughter now it would be different . . ." (307) [154] and "I say it'd be
bad enough if it was mine; I'd at least be sure it was a bastard to begin
with, and now even the Lord doesn't know that for certain probably"
(286–287) [144]. By playing a strong father to his niece, Jason secretly
yearns to correct his own father's silent encouragement of Caddy's and
Quentin's unnatural closeness, a closeness that steadfastly excluded him;
Jason prides himself on being "a different breed of cat from Father" (250)
[126].

To the extent that he performs as Quentin's father, Jason serves as
Caddy's remote, surrogate husband. The two quarrel about Quentin's
money, clothes, schooling, and friends in a bizarre travesty of marriage.
And yet Jason's frustration nearly brings his need for so implausible a
relationship to the surface. When he speaks of Quentin as a bastard in
the passage I quoted above, he implies that Quentin's paternity would
be certain only if *he* had fathered her—on his own sister. This bitter
suggestion of incest arises from one of Jason's darkest suspicions: that
Quentin is the offspring of his brother Quentin and Caddy. Twice in
conversations with the incomprehending Caroline Compson, Jason tor-
ments himself with the idea that he is looking at the very incarnation of
his siblings' incest:

> "Sometimes I think she is the judgment of Caddy and Quentin
> upon me."

"Good Lord," I says, "You've got a fine mind. No wonder you kept yourself sick all the time."

"What?" she says. "I dont understand."

"I hope not," I says. "A good woman misses a lot she's better off without knowing." (325) [163]

"Do you think I need any man's help to stand on my feet?" I says, "Let alone a woman that cant name the father of her own child."

"Jason," she says.

"All right," I says. "I didn't mean that. Of course not."

"If I believed that were possible, after all my suffering."

"Of course it's not," I says. "I didn't mean it."

"I hope that at least is spared me," she says.

"Sure it is," I says, "She's too much like both of them to doubt that." (327) [164]

Mrs. Compson probably accepts Jason's last statement in the spirit of her earlier one, that Quentin displays the characteristic Compson shortcomings evident in her two most Compson-like children. But Jason toys rather with the thought that Quentin's personality may be more readily explained by biology than by metaphor. By being the "nearest thing to a father" to Quentin, Jason insinuates himself into a heavily disguised, disfigured intimacy with Caddy. His transactions with her enable him to maintain perverse contact with her; and on one occasion he even experiences a flicker of what it must have been like to know Caddy: " 'Wait,' she says, catching my arm. 'I've stopped [her hysterical sobbing]. I wont again. You promise, Jason [to show her Quentin]?' she says, and me feeling her eyes almost like they were touching my face . . ." (261) [132].

Virtually all of Jason's attitudes toward money reflect his central, unspoken interest in Caddy. Even incidental annoyances correspond to deeper concerns. We might surmise that he disapproves of paying money to the outsiders in the circus (the country folks "coming in in droves to give their money to something that brought nothing to the town and wouldn't leave anything" [243] [123]) because they echo the menagerie of suitors who eventually carry Caddy away from home. (Quentin literally steals off with one of the show people.) And Jason is so preoccupied with what has been taken from him that he sees thievery all around: ". . . any damn foreigner that cant make a living in the country where God put him, can come to this one and take money right out of an American's pockets" (239) [121]. " 'When are you going to spread the news that I stole it from my mother?' " (284) [143] he asks Earl, referring to his automobile.

The one market into which Jason has never been able to buy, of course, is the one that deals Caddy. His frustration at her unavailability forces him to think of her as a kind of prostitute, who refuses herself to him because he somehow has the wrong currency. Discussing her offer of cash to buy back Quentin, Jason says, "And I know how you'll get it. . . . You'll get it the same way you got her" (260) [131]. As if to counter his exclusion from the favors of such a "whore" (as even Quentin calls her [197] [101]),[6] Jason purchases "a good honest whore" (291) [146].

Acquiring Lorraine epitomizes Jason's furious confidence in the power of money to substitute. So far as Jason can understand his need for her, Lorraine offers the pleasures of sexual intimacy ("if you dont believe he's a man I can tell you how to find out she says" [291] [146]) without the danger of emotional engagement ("I never promise a woman anything nor let her know what I'm going to give her. That's the only way to manage them" [240] [122]). She embodies the power of money to neutralize love and to preclude the sorrow of loss: "Here I says, giving her the forty dollars. If you ever get drunk and take a notion to call me on the phone, just remember this and count ten before you do it" (241) [122]. Lorraine can be repeatedly bought and lost; it is as if Jason wants to buy the power to possess and recover. What Jason may not recognize about his bought woman is that she fills all of the natural roles that Caddy's loss has disrupted. For example, Jason will never marry because he has become his mother's surrogate husband: "Like I say if I was to get married you'd go up like a balloon and you know it" (307) [154]. Such voluntary bachelordom at times suggests a kind of aversion to sexuality, and the one time we see Jason with Lorraine she seems more a protective mother than a lover: "He imagined himself in bed with her, only he was just lying beside her, pleading with her to help him, then he thought of the money again" (383) [191] Perhaps Jason's unresolved desire for Caddy threatens him with the epithet he designed for Benjy: "The Great American Gelding." Almost antically, moreover, Lorraine becomes a daughter whose good behavior and fidelity may be purchased:

> I went on back to the desk and read Lorraine's letter. "Dear daddy wish you were here. No good parties when daddys out of town I miss my sweet daddy." I reckon she does. Last time I gave her forty dollars. Gave it to her. (240) [122]

By attending strictly to finance, by maniacally interpreting and evaluating every event in terms of its monetary significance, Jason seeks to cleanse his world of the effects of Caddy's loss. Although his economies may seem self-enclosed systems, however, they articulate a deep analogue to his central deprivation. Rather than agonize over the deathly difference of the representation from the 'original,' however, as Benjy and Quentin do, Jason wants to escape through those very gaps. Money at first looks like the kind of supplement that could frankly deny its supplementarity and affirm its pure difference, resigning the original pres-

6. Jason calls Quentin "that little whore" (p. 269) [136].

ence to dead irrelevance. Surely Jason renounces actual words because they dangerously carry the aura of absent love: "I make it a rule never to keep a scrap of paper bearing a woman's hand, and I never write them at all. Lorraine is always after me to write to her but I says anything I forgot to tell you will save till I get to Memphis again" (240) [122]. If I am right, however, Jason fails colossally to deaden himself completely after the breaking of immediacy. And his failure suggests that Faulkner seeks in *The Sound and the Fury* to confront both the absolute *différance* of articulation and also the necessary illusion that there is an originary presence or locus of full meaning with which writing plays.

Jason's divorce from the word affects the nature of his monologue's performance. Although his first-person narrative closes the distance between speaker and perspective that we noticed in Benjy's section, and although the oral rhetoric of the style creates the impression of a told story (as Quentin's did not), nevertheless Jason's narrative is no public performance. As readers we may sense that we are Jason's audience, but more often than not his furious soliloquy seems never to escape the theater of his own mind. Jason performs the story for himself. It is the largest of his closed economies. We might get a sense of this privacy near the end of his monologue. At one point he reproduces an exchange between him and his mother that, we eventually learn, has been 'said' only in his mind:

> "I don't know what else she'd do in there alone," she says. "She never did read any."
> "No," I says, "You wouldn't know. And you can thank your stars for that," I says. Only what would be the use in saying it aloud. It would just have her crying on me again. (328) [164].

When Jason recounts his miseries, he speaks to himself: "He repeated his story, harshly recapitulant, seeming to get an actual pleasure out of his outrage and impotence. The sheriff did not appear to be listening at all" (378) [189].

Jason will not see that his desperate economy supplements Caddy in her absence. His urgent denial of loss and frustration deprives him of the opportunity to grieve well, to mourn imaginatively. In fact, Jason steadily flees the responsibilities of creative articulation. About his stock market misfortunes he can shrug: " 'That's not my fault either. I didn't invent it; I just bought a little of it' " (305) [153].

> So I wrote Quentin's and Jason's sections, trying to clarify Benjy's. But I saw that I was merely temporising; that I should have to get completely out of the book. I realised that there would be compensations, that in a sense I could then give a final turn to the screw and extract some ultimate distillation. Yet it took me better than a month to take pen and write *The day dawned bleak and chill* before I did so. . . . I knew that it was not anywhere near finished and

then I had to write another section from the outside with an outsider, which was the writer, to tell what had happened.[7]

The Sound and the Fury is a novel that comes to yearn for an ending. None of the first three sections presents its protagonist as having defined a dilemma and acted to resolve it; none of the three brothers even arrives at a full understanding of his situation—that is, no section describes the career of a process of intellection, as in a James novel, for example. Nor does the work conduct the reader through a progressive initiation into the workings of three profoundly idiosyncratic minds; rather, each section fiercely clenches the sympathetic reader and seems to present everything all at once—with incessant repetition. The conclusion of each section insists on irresolution. The twilight of Benjy's suspended time will not fade so long as his relics retain the glow of Caddy's touch. Quentin's "temporary" state of mind has been arrested in a permanent "apotheosis" by the refusal of the narrative to follow his body into the Charles River. The suicide is the great unspoken fact of his monologue—a finality important only because it eternalizes the present by 'unthinking' the future. And as Jason bitterly throws out his closing words, he imagines someday getting that "even chance to get my money back. And once I've done that they can bring all Beale Street and all bedlam in here" (329) [165]. Jason, too, however, remains leaning against the future; the repetitiveness of his routine and rhetoric dooms him to a life that will endlessly unravel "like a wornout sock" (391) [195]. Quentin voices the common lament: "Finished. If things just finished themselves" (97) [50].

In a novel so interested in the nature of articulation, the consequences of making an end to the fiction naturally come under selfconscious scrutiny. In the passage I quoted above Faulkner recalls both the urgent appeal of being able to tighten and secure *The Sound and the Fury*'s meaning and effects and the reluctance to begin the ending. The ambivalence informs many of Faulkner's other statements about the last section of the novel; for example:

> I finished it the first time, and it wasn't right, so I wrote it again, and that was Quentin, that wasn't right. I wrote it again, that was Jason, that wasn't right, then I tried to let Faulkner do it, that still was wrong.[8]

The virtual oxymoron of finished repeatedly captures the dilemma. To finish is to get it right; to continue is to admit insufficiencies. But if the novel stops, must the story have reached its conclusive resolution? Faulkner suggests that it need not—that, in fact, it must not—for a variety of reasons. One is that the very integrity of writing depends on preserving the discourse's *différance* even at the conclusion. In the highly personal

7. James B. Meriwether, ed., "An Introduction to *The Sound and the Fury*," *Mississippi Quarterly*, 26 (1973), 415.
8. Gwynn and Blotner, eds., *Faulkner in the University*, p. 32.

regions of *The Sound and the Fury* for Faulkner as writer ("and now I can write"), each telling seeks to present a sheerly different account. Section 4 resigns itself to an ending that does not arrive at the truth of the matter, does not enjoy special authority, deliberately defers perfect coherence and intelligibility. As a result, the novel reinvests the earlier tellings with equal merit. The joy of the discourse is its pain: there may always be another way to put the story as the novel takes pleasure in its differing and deferment. In addition, the achievement of fully resolved meaning and conclusiveness in the last stages of the novel would belie Faulkner's sense of time. Diminishment, deprivation, and loss—which comprise the site of articulation—may be dispelled or transformed temporarily (as we shall see in *Absalom*), but Faulkner's conclusions consistently revisit scenes of division, fraudulent order, and incomprehension. Time inexorably disfigures all that is shaped to protest or forget it.

Frank Kermode helps us to see that ordinarily the simple fact of an approaching end may enliven incident, gesture, tone; the conclusion necessarily completes the shape of the fiction's form and so retrospectively orders what precedes: "Ends are ends only when they are not negative but frankly transfigure the events in which they were immanent" (or, we might add, events in which the end is now seen *to have been* immanent).[9]

> No novel can avoid being in some sense what Aristotle calls 'a completed action.' This being so, all novels imitate a world of potentiality, even if this implies a philosophy disclaimed by their authors. They have a fixation on the eidetic imagery of beginning, middle, and end, potency and cause.[1]

> Time cannot be faced as coarse and actual, as a repository of the contingent; one humanizes it by fiction of orderly succession and end.[2]

The last section of *The Sound and the Fury*—"Faulkner's"—presents versions of completed actions, of fictions of orderly succession and end. Yet simultaneously it disturbs and complicates those closing procedures, accomplishing what Kermode calls the "difficult concords" of modern fiction, rich with "paradox and contradiction."[3] Dilsey's vision of "de beginnin" and "de endin" seems to promise an authorized context within which to resolve the Compson crisis. Similarly, the new authority of an 'omniscient' narrator marks the invocation of more customary narrative techniques. However, as Dilsey embraces her orthodox Christianity, and as the narrative quietly creates a sense of resolving intelligibility by rely-

9. Frank Kermode, *The Sense of an Ending: Studies in the Theory of Fiction* (London, 1966), 175.
1. Ibid., p. 138.
2. Ibid., p. 160.
3. Ibid., pp. 176, 164.

ing on 'orthodox' aesthetics, the last section also puzzles over its own inability to get it "right."

Certainly the mood of closure permeates the last section. For Dilsey, the painful passage of the body through time will culminate in the resurrection of the spirit into eternity. Sainthood will reward martyrdom; blissful death will end "dis long time": " 'En I be His'n too, fo long, praise Jesus' " (396) [197]. Shegog's sermon, as we all know, draws her tears of future release down the "myriad coruscations of immolation and abnegation and time" (368) [183]. Faith converts the passage of time from a process of attrition to one of accretion. Accordingly, Dilsey has allowed none of the Compson animosity toward time to infect her; she soberly attends to the rites of burial for the household, quietly hymning the disappearance of Quentin, the money, and Jason. And she adds her corrective voice to the words of the mangled Compson clock, expecting—even hastening—the day of the Lord: "a cabinet clock ticked, then with a preliminary sound as if it had cleared its throat, struck five times. 'Eight o clock,' Dilsey said" (341–342) [171].

Jason and Caroline Compson juxtapose private senses of ending to Dilsey's eschatology. Jason "for the first time . . . saw clear and unshadowed the disaster toward which he rushed" (386) [192]: "So this is how it'll end, and he believed that he was about to die" (387) [193]. Mrs. Compson rallies fraily: "when faced at last by the incontrovertible disaster she exhumed from somewhere a sort of fortitude, strength" (373) [186]. All of the survivors seem to live under the sentence of sovereign chronology: "The clock tick-tocked solemn and profound. It might have been the dry pulse of the decaying house itself" (355) [177].

Despite a creeping apocalypse, however, life persists. The events of the last section conjure the prospect of "de endin," of an "incontrovertible disaster," only to dispel it. Jason retrieves himself from death as he wrestles with "the fatal, furious little old man." "Give me time, and I'll get out" (386) [193], he pleads, recommitting himself to his clock-ruled world. And Dilsey's very capacity for endurance immediately enfeebles her glimpse of the transcendent, for she lapses into protecting her vision with silence. " 'Never you mind,' " she replies to Frony's effort to get her to elaborate a little on what she has seen (371) [185],[4] as if eternal truth cannot be translated into a mundane idiom. Dilsey's Christian order is predicated on a denial of the inexplicable and the contingent. Faith in a beginning and an ending seems ultimately a faith in the necessary invention of closure and coherence. In the 1946 Appendix to *The Sound and the Fury*, Dilsey refuses to imperil her fiction of an ending by acknowledging that Caddy Compson's life might have continued. The librarian seeks confirmation that her photograph is of Caddy, but

4. Dilsey's fiercely protected privacy makes her Christian vision irrelevant, according to Donald M. Kartiganer, *"The Sound and the Fury,* and Faulkner's Quest for Form," *ELH,* 37 (December 1970), 638.

Dilsey has learned from the librarian's question that Jason will join her conspiracy of silence against the past. She does not see what she will not: " 'My eyes aint any good anymore,' she said, 'I cant see it' " (418) [211]. Dilsey "humanizes" the coarseness of time by lifting a shape out of perpetual change.

Surely the theological aspects of Dilsey's Christianity have received adequate discussion, but the vision that renews its vitality for her is the result of a performance that has literary implications as well.[5] Reverend Shegog complexly figures the role of the author in his work as he strives to deliver the word that will interpret experience truly and establish the communion of speaker and hearer. Shegog's sermon creates a moment of transfigured vision for Dilsey; we might presume not only that she sees the beginning and ending of all human time in the example of Christ's death and resurrection, but also that she has fitted the rise and fall of her particular Compson family into the inevitable cycles of human history. She has accepted the end of the family. I suggest that her vision has been stimulated by the uncanny similarities between Shegog's inspired imagery and the Compson situation, and that such a transfiguration of the Compson story embodies one of the ambitions of the novel's concluding section.

A miracle of the St. Louis preacher's sermon is that it answers so much of what Dilsey calls the "Compson devilment" (344) [172]. Against Dilsey's sad sense of the house's decay, Shegog proclaims that only the "ricklickshun en de Blood of de Lamb" matters, for heaven is the only home and God's the only family worth thinking about. Though Benjamin may be "our lastborn, sold into Egypt" (Appendix, 423) [213], yet the promised land redeemed the bondage of those who " 'passed away in Egypt, de singin chariots; de generations passed away' " (368) [184]. Though Jason is the wealthy pauper, yet in heaven " 'Wus a rich man: whar he now . . . Wus a po man: whar he now . . .?' " (368–369) [184]. Even the mournful, trying self-pity of Caroline Compson appears in " 'de weepin en de lamentation of de po mammy widout de salvation en de word of God' " (369) [184].

Shegog's conjuring of the crucifixion scene touches remarkably on the death-plagued Compson past.

> "I sees hit, breddren! I sees hit! Sees de blastin, blindin sight! I sees Calvary, wid de sacred trees, sees de thief en de murderer en de least of dese; I hears de boastin and de braggin: Ef you be Jesus, lif up yo tree en walk! I hears de wailin of women en de evenin

5. Bleikasten suggests that Shegog's triumph is Faulkner's, since the preacher is the "double" of the novelist (*Most Splendid Failure*, p. 201). Bleikasten contends that the novel coalesces and reaches a kind of authoritative version in the last section, just as Shegog's voice authorizes his sermon for Dilsey. But Shegog's sermon, as I shall argue, succeeds only because Dilsey hears (or reads) it correctly. It is a private and temporary manifestation of meaning.

lamentations; I hears de weepin en de cryin en de turnt-away face
of God: dey done kilt Jesus; dey done kilt my Son!" (370) [184]

Christ's death on the sacred tree may recall the fatal trees in which Caddy
loses her innocence, dies to Benjy and Quentin, and provokes the eldest
son's self-sacrifice. Caddy climbs the tree to see death, lies down among
trees to surrender her virginity, and cloaks herself in their fragrance as
her stigma. Calvary's tree is sacred, however, because it replaces Eden's
tree of death; the second Adam redeems the site of the Fall. But Caddy's
brothers have failed to resurrect her in their separate acts of "ricklickshun." Shegog inadvertently ironizes the contrast between the two deaths
by confusing his scripture. He dramatizes the incomprehending taunts
of those who challenge the dying Christ to prove his divinity: " 'Ef you
be Jesus, lif up your tree en walk.' " Christ chooses to die before he can
triumph over death, but Caddy remains simply powerless to deny crucifying, but natural, time. In the Gospels, the crowd never asks Jesus to
lift up the tree and walk, but to "come down from the tree, if Thou art
the Christ." The phrase Shegog is thinking of comes from an episode in
Christ's earlier ministry, in which he challenges the faith of one infirm:
"Take up thy bed and walk."[6] The lapse could be Faulkner's, of course
(to the mortification of his grandfather, who made the Faulkner children
recite their memory verses at the breakfast table); but if it is not, it neatly
substitutes tree for bed, an ironic tailoring of the statement for Caddy,
for whom trees have been a bed. The miracle of neither resurrection nor
healing will save Caddy from her fatal infection by time ("*Sick how are
you sick I'm just sick*," she tells Quentin [138] [71]).

Shegog's sermon figures the self-slain Quentin, too. We might recognize both Quentin's fantasy of punished incest and Mr. Compson's
last grief in the picture of " 'de turnt-away face of God . . . dey done kilt
my Son!' " The ecstatic word of one congregation member, "like bubbles rising in water," ironically recalls Quentin's water-stilled voice, as
"de whelmin flood" that rolls between the generations evokes both the
branch and the Charles River.

The achievement of Shegog's sermon stands at the very center of a
novel's customary aspiration for its conclusion. The transfiguration of
earlier events in which the end is immanent—that process Kermode
locates in all legitimate ends—occurs for Dilsey as a result of Shegog's
performance. She can see the pattern and has discovered a fiction of
orderly succession and end. The moment epitomizes a climax of sense
with which *The Sound and the Fury* might have ended, but does not.
Shegog's sermon succeeds, moreover, because it rescues conclusiveness
from irresolution. Shegog's first sermon casts a magnificent but distant
spell on the congregation. The sheer "virtuosity" of the "cold inflectionless wire of his voice" creates the congregation's "collective dream" (366)

6. See, for example, Matthew, 27:39–40 and Matthew, 9:5–7.

[183], but it does not erect an interpretive structure, as the second does. Dilsey prepares to leave when she senses the end of Shegog's first address: " 'Hush, now. Dey fixin to sing in a minute' " (367) [183]. Knowing that his sermon has not struck, however, Reverend Shegog dramatically modulates into his listeners' dialect. The sermon succeeds because it is willing to say, and then say again; it indulges its personal voice and then accommodates its audience. The result is spectacular. Speaker and hearers experience an "immolation" of the voice, "until he was nothing and they were nothing and there was not even a voice but instead their hearts were speaking to one another in chanting measures beyond the need for words" (367) [183]. The novel, like the sermon, might have striven for the revelation of comprehensive meaning; it might have attempted, like the passage from the first to the second performance, to resolve the pauses at the end of the opening three sections into a full cadence in the last. The idiosyncratic strangeness of the monologues' voices might have yielded utterly to the accommodating familiarity of the final section. Instead, the novel prefers a difficult concord, one that denies the possibility of absolute disclosure, that beclouds the prospect of the beginning and the ending, that signals the continuation of difference and deferment.

The last section of *The Sound and the Fury* explores the resources of conventional narrative discourse only to learn that they can compose no more authoritative telling of the story than the inside accounts that have gone before. The style, for example, bears much greater resemblance to traditional ones than the styles of the monologues.[7] We welcome syntactic regularity, descriptive passages, sequential action, dialogue, and so on. But if we examine the opening sentence closely—the sentence that reminds one critic of the confident voice of many Victorian novels[8]— we may notice as well a kind of laboring:

> The day dawned bleak and chill, a moving wall of grey light out of the northeast which, instead of dissolving into moisture, seemed to disintegrate into minute and venomous particles, like dust that, when Dilsey opened the door of the cabin and emerged, needled laterally into her flesh, precipitating not so much a moisture as a substance partaking of the quality of thin, not quite congealed oil. (330) [165]

The extended syntax of this sentence suggests an impatience to refine and qualify in the very midst of the first saying, as if no simple statement can be trusted not to falsify the complexity of things. There are, for example, an immediate apposition ("a moving wall"), two restrictive modifying clauses ("which . . . seemed to disintegrate" and "that . . . needled"), two participial clauses, and a subordinate modifying clause.

7. Kartiganer sees this moment as a forecast of Faulkner's mature views of language (pp. 638–639).
8. Ibid., p. 634.

The elaborate artifice dramatizes the difficulty of saying. Action occurs, but at once qualification interrupts. The phrases "instead of dissolving" and "not so much moisture as" attempt to specify by a kind of negative circumscription. Faulkner's mature style remains attached to the idea that a thing may be described only between what it is and what it is not. * * * But these are also elements from which Faulkner takes pleasure. The need to qualify, to appose, to test all of the ways to say something, without the belief that any can succeed alone, coincides with the supplementarity of writing. The significance that writing produces 'begins' only in the movement of pure difference, and transparent meaning must remain deferred. We might also notice that Faulkner seeks strenuously to tap all of the resources for play in the language: casual assonance and consonance appear in "day"/"grey" and in "chill"/"wall"; but a more profound alliteration ties "Dilsey" to "day," "dawned," "dissolving," "disintegrate," "dust," and "door," which surely prepares for this Sunday of promised judgment, salvation, and resolution.

Like the style, other features of this "outside" narrator's discourse are concerned with presenting a more 'objective' account than the preceding monologues. The symbolism of this section tries to make itself explicit and to represent universal abstractions, but it proves as stiffly falsifying as Benjy's signs or Quentin's obsessive imagery.[9] For example, Benjy's howl "might have been all time and injustice and sorrow become vocal for an instant" (359) [179], the "sound of all voiceless misery under the sun" (395) [197]; and, to Jason, Quentin is "the very symbol of the lost job itself" (383–384) [191]. When Quentin's treachery dawns on Jason, he paws at Mrs. Compson's "rusted keys on an iron ring like a mediaeval jailer's"; Jason's impotent imprisonment in the Compson house could be no more explicitly pictured. Similarly, one of the ruling puns of Benjy's section is flushed to the surface now:

> "Here, caddie. Bring the bag."
> . . . Ben went on at his shambling trot, clinging to the fence . . .
> "All right, den" Luster said, "You want somethin to beller about?"
> ". . .Caddy! Beller now. Caddy! Caddy!" (394) [196]

In the hope of getting the story right by virtue of the author's authority, the novel forswears reticence. Instead of the deeply submerged but mercilessly coherent systems presented in the three monologues, the last section offers broader contexts but shallower understanding. For example, we may be shocked to learn, after our intimacy with Quentin Compson's mind, that his mother has no idea why he committed suicide. Though her granddaughter would appear to have no motive either, she too may have taken her life as her uncle had: and " 'what reason did Quentin have' " (374) [186]. Throughout the last section, the narrator's attention to explicit statement threatens to reduce the reader's search for

9. Ibid., p. 635.

meaning to a version of Mrs. Compson's hunt for "the note." We want
the novel to divulge its meaning by its own hand, but Faulkner avoids
both the note and the death at the ending. The last section has a status
like Dilsey's church, framed but flat: "a weathered church lifted its crazy
steeple like a painted church, and the whole scene was flat and without
perspective as a painted cardboard set upon the ultimate edge of the flat
earth" (364) [182]. *The Sound and the Fury*, in its first three sections,
has already shown the need for more than the conventional, picture-
making narrative. The fourth telling of the story sacrifices as much as it
gains by its objectivity and detachment. Indirectly, it extends one of the
abiding interests of *The Sound and the Fury*: a justification of its own
radical innovativeness. The reader's customary demand for a conventional novel is mimicked by Benjy's concluding demand for the regular
left-to-right flow of signboards past his eyes, like print on the page. The
novel arrays itself against a too simple order by feigning conclusiveness
and a conclusion. The structure of the story reflects this evasiveness.

The narrative, having apparently adopted the convention of linear
chronology in section 4, avoids an ending even as it suggests the possibility of one. The sequence of Dilsey's morning climaxes in the vision
of the beginning and the end, but the novel continues. The overall
temporal restlessness of *The Sound and the Fury* (moving from Saturday
to Friday to Sunday, from 1928 to 1910 and back again) erupts in a
looping of chronology in section 4. Jason's morning starts after Dilsey's
has ended: "He was twenty miles away at that time. When he left the
house he drove rapidly to town, overreaching the slow sabbath groups"
(376) [187]. For linear time to hold in the plot, the second sentence of
this narrative sequence should begin with a past perfect tense—to bring
us up to the narrative present: when he *had left* the house. Instead, the
day's chronology begins over at a new location. The plot displays a seam
that prepares for the centrifugal closing of *The Sound and the Fury*. The
narrative preserves the momenta of several plot lines: first, there is Dilsey's expectation of the imminent, "incontrovertible disaster," her curious sense that Jason and Quentin will not be back and that a genuinely
transfigurative "endin" looms. There are also Benjamin's dizzyingly
repetitive rituals, which figure a desperate recoil from the unresolved.
Both closures reflect an aspect of the novelist's desire to establish clarity
and stability. But the plot also withholds resolution; Jason returns home
delayed but not defeated, and his niece remains at large—the embodiment of the elusive future, her very name the sign of the past's devious
capacity to persist.

The Sound and the Fury ceases while still faithful to the recognition
that the act of articulation cannot successfully reappropriate what has
been lost. The pain of grief, the folly of denying it, the hopelessness of
recovery, the uneasy bliss of repetition and substitution, and the recognition of their failure all nourish the exceptional tensions of Faulkner's

first unquestionably major novel. We might take Luster's saw playing as the closing figure of the artist's activity: like him, the author must try to recreate on his cruder implements the enchantingly, endlessly elusive music of last night's carnival.

THADIOUS M. DAVIS

[Faulkner's "Negro" in *The Sound and the Fury*] †

Faulkner recognizes the value of the Negro in grounding *Soldiers' Pay* in a practical realism, but his Negro is a type still closely linked to a personal sense of cultural actuality and dependent upon literary treatments by other writers. The result is a stereotyped rendering of a mode of existence. Blacks remain in the background of both plot and structure, even though they emerge in the conclusion as a major thematic idea. Faulkner has not yet fully grasped the artistic importance of either his heritage as a white Mississippian or the Negro in his culture.

His third novel, *Flags in the Dust*, accepted by Harcourt, Brace under the condition that it be condensed, marks a departure from his overt concerns in *Soldiers' Pay* and *Mosquitoes* (1927) with the post–World War I malaise of veterans and artists. Completed during the fall of 1927, but not published as *Sartoris* until January, 1929, this novel initiates Faulkner's immersion in the milieu he knew best—the racially divided, parochial world of the Deep South. Written after his return to Oxford early in 1927, *Flags in the Dust* begins Faulkner's serious attempt to understand characters and motivations within the context of a particular physical environment and against the protracted background of familial heritage. Though no less intrigued by psychological responses to modern conditions, he seems more familiar with his characters, black and white, and more comfortable with their emotions and actions. As a result, Faulkner plausibly develops the people and situations introducing Yoknapatawpha County. However, his unsuccessful struggle to integrate vision and technique shows in his unwieldy narrative.

In *Flags in the Dust* Faulkner extends his treatment and conception of the Negro as contrapuntal to his primary thematic concerns. He establishes the singing of the yellow Negro cook, Elnora, as accompaniment to her housework and the activities within the Sartoris household. ("Elnora's endless minor ebbed and flowed. . . . '*Sinner riz fum de moaner's bench, / Sinner jump to de penance bench*'"; "Elnora's voice

† From *Faulkner's "Negro": Art and the Southern Context* (Baton Rouge: Louisiana State University Press, 1983), 65–73. Copyright © 1983 by Louisiana State University Press. Reprinted by permission of Louisiana State University Press.

welled in mellow falling suspense. *All folks talkin' 'bout heaven aint gwine dere.*") Her voice, a serious undercurrent heard mainly during the early chapters, is a reminder that a constant faith exists simultaneously with the despair experienced by her white employers.

Despite his sketching of Elnora, Faulkner relies heavily upon the comic value of blacks as relief from the central tensions of white life. Simon Strother, Elnora's father, and Isom, her son, are creations suggestive of plantation fiction.

* * *

Nonetheless, *Flags in the Dust* is a germinal, transitional work because in it Faulkner conceives the artistic use of the Negro which becomes central as his career progresses. In shifting the location of the despair and longing of white characters from isolated postwar experiences to southern history and familial inheritance, Faulkner discovers that the Negro is a viable means of relating his major concerns to the past, of supplying an additional perspective upon the meaning of that past, and of increasing dramatic tensions between the past and present. He places a family of black servants within the household of his major protagonists. These blacks provide access to added information about the private and public lives of the protagonists. * * * Because the Strothers are still unindividualized types from earlier literary traditions, they exist amicably as extensions of the white family, rather than as distinct people who, by virtue of their differences, can illuminate the dominant white society. Although, in connecting the Strothers to the Sartorises, Faulkner has not yet found an effective method of integrating his conception of blacks with his primary ideas about whites, he has come to an understanding of a basic contribution the black family can make to his vision.

* * *

Faulkner achieves a synthesis of the Negro with the primary concerns of his art in *The Sound and the Fury*. The process of developing the Negro as an integral part of his artistic vision leads Faulkner to a technical breakthrough in his fourth novel. Although he accents the social actuality of the Negro's place and role in the white southerner's world, he does so innovatively and respectfully. He escapes the tyranny of stereotypes by acknowledging, as no earlier novelist had, the humanity of individual black people within the family and the church—the major institutions affecting their lives. *The Sound and the Fury* clearly indicates that Faulkner's interest is in the external manifestations of the Negro's inner resources, of which he apparently was firmly convinced. While his literal understanding of blacks is largely shaped by his particular heritage and place in the white world, his artistic development of their presence in plot, structure, themes, and symbols transcends the limitations of his personal perspective.

In *The Sound and the Fury* Faulkner divides the southern world into black and white. He uses the black world, as he perceives it from the outside, in order to characterize the weaknesses or, more rarely, the strengths of the white world and its inhabitants. He draws extensively upon a family of black servants, the Gibsons, who are in close contact with the white Compson family. His tragedy, however, depends upon the blacks and whites maintaining different attitudes and values. His blacks (primarily, but not exclusively, the Gibsons) contribute to the contrapuntal design of the novel, because their voices and actions create a meaningful contrast to the disintegrating Compsons and add greater dimension to the symbolism, themes, and narrative form.

Roskus and Dilsey Gibson are patriarch and matriarch of the black family in *The Sound and the Fury*. Their children, Versh, Frony, and T. P., and grandson, Luster, progress with the younger Compsons over the pages of the novel and history. The Gibsons take care of the Compson place and family. They play strong, supportive roles and frequently dominate the action (particularly in the first and fourth sections, in which Luster and Dilsey are central figures in the narrative present). The Gibsons function to foreshadow events, as well as to reiterate motifs. They are integral to Faulkner's formal ordering principles, and they are touchstones by which those principles become familiar to the reader.

Representing opposition to the sterility and decay evidenced by the white family, the Gibsons project a vital creativity, an inventiveness in looking at life and a spiritedness in confronting it all. Frony, for example, wears her new clothes on the climactic Easter morning even if it means getting wet, because as she states, " 'I aint never stopped no rain yit.' "[1] Like the rest of the family, she accepts the natural course of things, but does not relinquish her individual will. Frony's older brother Versh also has a level-headed approach to himself and to life. He tells Benjy, the retarded Compson son: " 'You aint had to be out in the rain like I is. You's born lucky and dont know it' " (85) [45]. In other words, Benjy is born white in a region where those of his race have all the advantages. Versh quite simply places Benjy within a frame of reference that, while realistic, may be overlooked because of Benjy's idiocy. As Versh suggests, even the life of a retarded white man seems easier than that of a normal black man, because in their world blacks are circumscribed by racial restrictions to lives of hard, unrewarding work. Juxtaposed to the various kinds of lunacy demonstrated by the Compsons are the Gibsons—practical, "common-sense variety" blacks whose individual and collective voices create an eloquent contrast to the white world and form, on a level of emotion and reason, a more viable approach to life.

In the Gibson family Faulkner succeeds in capturing the symbolic

1. William Faulkner, *The Sound and the Fury* (New York: Jonathan Cape and Harrison Smith, 1929), 361 [180; page references in brackets are to this Norton Critical Edition].

and spiritual significance of a whole generation of southern blacks as they are understood by the white South. He explores the artistic possibilities inherent in traditional black life, thought, and expression. His treatment of black community suggests that the simple bonds of faith and love embodied in that community's daily relationships are ignored by the modern southerner in his search for meaning in a changing, complex society. For example, Roskus, Versh, T. P., and Luster, depicted as interchangeable elements, are present to insure the smooth operation of the place (tending the stock, driving the carriage, and caring for Benjy), but their presence also creates a sense of fused generations in a closely knit family, and of the flux of individuality bending to a stable historical community. In their closeness they represent a continuity of family that is vital to a traditional society. Dilsey at one point in Benjy's narrative remarks to the aging, arthritic Roskus, " 'T. P. getting big enough to take your place' " (34) [19]. The son's carrying on for the father, assuming his responsibilities and position, is what no Compson son is able to do, and the white family is the weaker for it.

By means of the Gibsons, Faulkner examines the experience of traditional black characters and their major institutions—the family and the church—for what that experience can reveal about interpreting life and mediating the forces of time and history. Frony, for instance, as a child interacting in family relationships (with both Compsons and Gibsons) and as an adult attending Easter services is a younger version of her mother in applying a black-centered experience to the larger white world and in instinctively recognizing the shortcomings of both. In his use of the black family and church, Faulkner realizes the significance of the Negro as the South's indigenous symbol, and he treats that symbol creatively and seriously as one pervasive influence on the imaginative life of the southern artist.

Not enough critical attention has been paid to the significance of the Gibsons as a family group adding another dimension to the contrapuntal design by framing the disintegration of a white southern family with the survival of a black family. Roskus, his sons and daughter, and even Luster have all been overshadowed by the figure of Dilsey, whose gaunt, silent presence dominates the fourth section. Dilsey is the major focus, but even on that Easter Sunday three generations of the black family make the pilgrimage together to attend the climactic Easter service. Moreover, both parents and all the children have meaningful places in the memories and action of section one and in Quentin's mind in section two. Quentin, for instance, on the train heading back south from Cambridge, suddenly realizes that he has missed "Roskus and Dilsey and them" (106) [55]. He misses not only Dilsey but the whole family. And in Benjy's section, Dilsey admonishes Roskus: " 'Your bad luck talk got them Memphis notions into Versh. That ought to satisfy you' " (37) [20]. She voices her displeasure not so much with her husband's talk of bad luck on the Compsons' place, but with such talk as being responsible for dividing her family.

Structurally the pattern of development in which "Roskus and Dilsey and them" act as counterpoint to the Compsons is a reflection of the social order of two southern classes. The interaction between the Gibsons and the Compsons is a ritual of survival enacted by the black servant class and the southern white gentility: service and loyalty in exchange for material goods and protection. The two groups, Compsons and Gibsons, occupy the same physical space, the old Compson place, yet are of two different worlds—each one impelled by its own values and priorities. Each group retains an orientation to life that, though familiar to its own peers, is private and inaccessible to the outside group. * * *

WESLEY MORRIS WITH BARBARA ALVERSON MORRIS

A Writing Lesson: The Recovery of Antigone †

Even though *The Sound and the Fury* extended Faulkner's newly begun Yoknapatawpha project into the realm of modernist experiments in narrative form, Faulkner considered the novel a failure precisely because of its modernist aesthetics. The critical tradition, correctly, has been far less willing to acknowledge that he failed to tell the story he wanted to tell, and perhaps this response reflects an understanding that the move from *Flags in the Dust* to *The Sound and the Fury* was a necessary step in the mastery of his narrative technique. Moreover, from the modernist / formalist perspective, *The Sound and the Fury* is a spectacular success. The monologic form of the first three sections; the focus of narrative time in the present and away from the past; the integration of an oedipal symbolic structure into the narrative; and the exposition of the existentialist theme of the loss of the self all recapitulate dominant modernist modes of composition and themes. Remarkably, only the setting of the narrative in the present, a strategy which emphasizes memory and the extraordinary psychosocial pressure of memory on the present, continued to serve Faulkner's emerging narrative of the South in later novels. The rest of the experimental modernist techniques of *The Sound and the Fury* are ultimately rejected, even within the novel itself. The failure of *The Sound and the Fury* arises from the subjectivism of the monologic style of modernist stream-of-consciousness technique, and from the antinarrative effects of its oedipal symbolism. Yet it is a most interesting

† From *Reading Faulkner* (Madison: University of Wisconsin Press, 1989), 133–42. Reprinted by permission.

novel simply because it contains a struggle against its own experimental limits; the composition of *The Sound and the Fury* initiated a gradual swerve away from modernist formalism.

The focus of this struggle resides in the relationship among the first three sections of the novel. The second, Quentin Compson's monologue, was written, Faulkner claimed, as the result of his realization that the story he began to tell through Benjy might ultimately be published. The shift from Benjy to Quentin is telling. Benjy's section is purely narrative while Quentin's departs from narrative; Quentin's section is more self-consciously "literary" and, ultimately, lyrical. The shift is not merely one of point of view, a change from the limited consciousness of Benjy to the mature, although neurotic, mind of Quentin. The move from Benjy to Quentin identifies a typical Faulknerian theme: the transition from childhood to adulthood, from innocence to experience. In addition, it represents a decline from authenticity. The composition of Quentin's monologue pivots on a theory of writing embedded in modernist aesthetics, on a dichotomy between an inviolable subjectivity at the core of creative expression and the destructive forces of public dissemination. The reader is reminded of Said's theory of "molestation,"[1] for the intrusion of the outside on the inside is central to *The Sound and the Fury* both as a commonplace psychoanalytic theme and as a career event. Quentin's monologue expresses the modernist anxiety of the loss of subjectivity; his obsessive talking is a case history of resistance to the intrusion of the world on his personal, private self. The section is appropriate in every way to Faulkner's own reluctant step toward publication of a story he had wished to keep private.

Quentin's section also represents a retreat into fashionable oedipal symbolism, a transition which accounts for the fact that it has become the interpretive epicenter of the novel. Benjy's section represents the experience of a loss of innocence. The hero is Benjy himself, whose innocence is violated by desire, not his but Caddy's. Benjy's consciousness is invaded by time, loss, and aloneness, although in a nonsymbolic mode, a repetitive experience linked to a rudimentary memory of a state of plentitude. Quentin's monologue expresses the utopianism of a wish to recapture such a lost innocence, a wish that grows naturally in the soil of the modernist anxiety of belatedness. Benjy, unlike his brother, Quentin, takes aggressive action against those who threaten the expression of his desire for Caddy, and as Faulkner describes Benjy's responses to Caddy's meeting with one of her lovers, we read through a consciousness, diametrically opposed to Quentin's, that has yet to be acculturated by Oedipus.

> "Benjy." Caddy said. "It's just Charlie. Dont you know Charlie."

1. Edward Said, *Beginnings: Intention and Method* (New York, 1975), 83–84.

"Where's his nigger." Charlie said. "What do they let him run around loose for."

"Hush, Benjy." Caddy said. "Go away, Charlie. He doesn't like you." Charlie went away and I hushed. I pulled at Caddy's dress.

"Why, Benjy." Caddy said. "Aren't you going to let me stay here and talk to Charlie awhile."

"Call that nigger." Charlie said. He came back. I cried louder and pulled at Caddy's dress.

"Go away, Charlie." Caddy said. Charlie came and put his hands on Caddy and I cried more. I cried loud.

"No, no." Caddy said. "No. No."

"He cant talk." Charlie said. "Caddy."

"Are you crazy." Caddy said. She began to breathe fast. "He can see. Dont. Dont." Caddy fought. They both breathed fast. "Please. Please." Caddy whispered.

"Send him away." Charlie said.

"I will." Caddy said. "Let me go."

"Will you send him away." Charlie said.

"Yes." Caddy said. "Let me go." Charlie went away. "Hush." Caddy said. "He's gone." I hushed. I could hear and feel her chest going.

"I'll have to take him to the house." she said. She took my hand. "I'm coming." she whispered.

"Wait." Charlie said. "Call the nigger."

"No." Caddy said. "I'll come back. come on, Benjy."

"Caddy." Charlie whispered, loud. We went on. "You better come back. Are you coming back." Caddy and I were running. "Caddy." Charlie said. We ran out into the moonlight, toward the kitchen.

"Caddy." Charlie said.

Caddy and I ran. We ran up the kitchen steps, onto the porch, and Caddy knelt down in the dark and held me. I could hear her and feel her chest. "I wont." she said. "I wont anymore, ever. Benjy. Benjy." Then she was crying, and I cried, and we held each other. "Hush " she said. "Hush. I wont anymore." So I hushed and Caddy got up and we went into the kitchen and turned the light on and Caddy took the kitchen soap and washed her mouth at the sink, hard. Caddy smelled like trees.[2]

This passage hinges on the contrast between Benjy's lack of language and the repetition of the word "said." Everyone else can talk. Benjy's world is not verbal but sensual, a complex of sights, sounds, and smells. The dominant sensation is visual, reinforced by repetitive references throughout the first section to Benjy's fascination with mirrors. The paradigm is neo-Freudian, Lacanian; Benjy's pre-oedipal desire for Caddy

2. William Faulkner, *The Sound and the Fury* (New York, 1929), 56–58. Hereafter cited in text as *SF*. Page references in brackets are to this Norton Critical Edition [pp. 30–31].

is set against the realm of the oedipal symbolic that names, describes, and directs cultural behavior. Language is associated with lacking ("He cant talk"), lies (Caddy does not "come back" to Charlie that night just as she does not keep her promise to Benjy: "I wont anymore, ever"), and absence (the magic name "Caddy" ceases magically to present the object of Benjy's desire). Language, in this passage and throughout Benjy's section, is associated with naming, with the identity of the speaker in verbal exchanges, and above all with narrative convention, the indication of the direction of speech, the place of the speaker in relation to the hearer.

Moreover, we read in this passage a distinction between Benjys' desire and Charlie's. While Charlie's desire is strictly gonadal, Benjy's desire is specifically not that. As a result, Benjy's desire remains inaccessible to us because it is also mysterious for the characters in the novel, and he cannot articulate it for us; it is, therefore, subject to interpretation, to the imposition from without of that language which Benjy lacks. For one who cannot express his desires, all desires in the oedipal symbolic become one. Benjy is castrated because he frightened some schoolgirls walking by his house.

> They came on. I opened the gate and they stopped, turning. I was trying to say, and I caught her, trying to say, and she screamed and I was trying to say and trying and the bright shapes began to stop and I tried to get out.
>
> (*SF*, p. 64) [34]

Benjy is victimized by oedipal language throughout his narrative; surrounded by words he cannot use, he is used by words. Deprived of his uncle Maury's name, he is verbally banished from the family. Because he cannot speak, others speak for him; an interior monologue, Benjy's narrative nonetheless is predominantly the voices of others he hears and transmits to us without a trace of distortion. He is confused by the supplemental play of language which distinguishes between "Caddy" and "caddie" because he cannot displace signifieds from signifiers. He exists consciously in a world with which he cannot communicate, repeatedly violated by that world in words he cannot utter.

What is curious is the absence of Quentin's voice in Benjy's consciousness, although our curiosity arises only as an afterthought to reading Quentin's monologue. Quentin seems, in effect, to be recreating in his mind a consciousness of time-innocence modeled on Benjy's imprisonment in the continuous present, but Quentin is far more than a mere repetition of Benjy in a different psychic register. The shift from pre-oedipal to oedipal consciousness changes everything. While Benjy's desire is sensual, bodily, for warmth, touch, and a kind of nurture, Quentin's desire is an aesthetics of disinterested interest. Quentin's desire is schizophrenic, an incestuous desire for the other of himself, Caddy, the

completion of the self to the end of eliminating desire, hence, a death
wish.

  I held the point of the knife at her throat it wont take but a second
just a second then I can do mine I can do mine then
    all right can you do yours by yourself
    yes the blades long enough Benjys in bed by now
    yes
    it wont take but a second Ill try not to hurt
    all right
    will you close your eyes
    no like this youll have to push harder
    touch your hand to it
    but she didnt move her eyes were wide open looking past my
head at the sky
    Caddy do you remember how Dilsey fussed at you because your
drawers were muddy
    dont cry
    Im not crying Caddy
    push it are you going to
    do you want me to
    yes push it
    touch your hand to it
    dont cry poor Quentin
    but I couldnt stop she held my head against her damp hard breast
I could hear her heart going firm and slow now not hammering
and the water gurgling among the willows in the dark and waves of
honeysuckle coming up the air my arm and shoulder were twisted
under me
    what is it what are you doing
    her muscles gathered I sat up
    its my knife I dropped it
    she sat up
    what time it it
    I dont know. . . .

    I got in front of her again
    Caddy
    stop it
    I held her
    Im stronger than you
    she was motionless hard and unyielding but still
    I wont fight stop you better stop
    Caddy dont Caddy
    it wont do any good dont you know it wont let me go
    the honeysuckle drizzled and drizzled I could hear the crickets

watching us in a circle she moved back went around me on towards
the trees
    you go on back to the house you neednt come
    I went on
    why dont you go on back to the house. . . .

                                              (SF, pp. 188–191) [96–97]

The parallels between this scene and the one where Benjy draws Caddy
away from her lover are obvious. Yet Faulkner here uses a different
language, a too obviously Freudian one with its doubled phallic symbol
in the knife that is both the object and the instrument of castration. It is
a powerful scene emotionally, concentrating with lyric economy themes
of incest, suicide, castration, and the intrusion of time, yet as this "literary" style breaks through we read seemingly beyond Quentin's voice,
hearing in his fantasy or remembrance a coldness in Caddy's responses
to him. Caddy seems to taunt Quentin, daring him to murder or rape
her. Her "poor Quentin" is without emotion, and she teases him about
his virginity before sending him home like a small boy. This is hardly
the partner for a romantic union of souls, and it contrasts directly with
the genuine sympathy Caddy exhibits for Benjy. Caddy's sexuality, which
is not at issue in Benjy's consciousness, is, for Quentin, "hard" and
"unyielding"; Faulkner's peculiar ideal of the little girl with muddy drawers
has long since been lost.

    If we read Quentin's section back on Benjy's we link Benjy's castration
with Caddy's sexuality; after all, it is Caddy's lie to Benjy that seems to
explain his seeking for young schoogirls as supplements for her absence.
If we read forward from Quentin's monologue, we discover that Jason
Compson as well is obsessed with Caddy, although she is present to him
in the figure of her young daughter, Quentin. Caddy serves Faulkner as
the link between all the Compson brothers, and that link would provide
a formal structure of containment for the novel. The effect is that Caddy
becomes a signifier for incestuous desires, and both Jason and Quentin
suffer a symbolic castration, a linguistic repetition of Benjy's very real
castration, as a consequence of their illicit transgressions. Thus the
authority of Quentin's oedipal symbolism is affirmed. This forgets, however, the pre-oedipal sentiment of Benjy's section, an innocence arising
from Benjy's victimization by oedipal violence. For Benjy, Caddy is no
empty signifier. Yet the idea of going into print, the writing of Quentin's
section, seemed to spark in Faulkner a retreat into convention, the abandonment of Benjy's insistent dwelling in Caddy's presence and a reworking of her into a metaphor that would provide unity for his novel.

    In recognition of the impossibility of this task, however, Faulkner
passed through monologue, and the transformation of Caddy into a free-
floating signifier, to the final section of his narrative which is initially
focused on Dilsey; there he abandoned first-person narration in favor of
authorial omniscience. The change in point of view, nevertheless, reflects

a move toward just another type of ruling metaphor, one designed to encompass extremes rather than signify original, forbidden desire. This metaphor is Dilsey. Dilsey is not a Compson, although she has served the family for many generations. Dilsey inevitably compels the narrative away from the Compsons into the symbolism of an Easter Sunday at an all black Protestant church. The subject of Reverend Shegog's Easter sermon is resurrection, but here in particular the symbolism simply does not work. Faulkner's narrative balances precariously between the Compsons and the black worshipers who rapturously listen to Shegog, between an end to the Compson family and the promise of salvation for those still repressed by the same paternal myth Quentin Compson longed to resurrect. This contrast finds a parallel in Shegog's sermon, in his *voice* which modulates from one which "sounded like a white man" to another voice that "consumed him, until he was nothing and they were nothing and there was not even a voice but instead their hearts were speaking to one another in chanting measures beyond the need for words . . ." (*SF*, pp. 366 and 367) [183].

Shegog's voice, the reader recognizes, hovers between individuality and stereotype. Yet it also suggests, perhaps inadequately, a context beyond the Compsons, one that does not merely observe and interpret the Compson world. It is no more than a moment of the otherness of an outside in this novel, for the narrative returns, in search of a conclusion, to Jason, "the first sane Compson since before Culloden and (a childless bachelor) hence the last" (*SF*, p. 420) [212]. But Jason reprised is not so much a conclusion as a stopping point. The symbolism has not contained the narrative; Benjy remains outside Oedipus, the one wholly sympathetic Compson who finally has more in common with Dilsey and the black congregation listening to Shegog's sermon than with his brothers. The story that Faulkner wants to tell cannot be contained within the monologic points of view of the three brothers or even within the Compson family itself. It cannot be symbolized in a ruling metaphor. In writing *The Sound and the Fury* Faulkner learned that monologue and oedipal symbolism were not adequate for his narrative project to write about the South.

* * *

Faulkner measured himself in the public sphere in images; he was constantly about recreating himself, and in the process he seemed to stumble upon an insight that fascinated and frightened him. Writing, as it displaces the merely private, drives toward dispersal, toward the breaking down of authority, priority, even the grand genealogical dichotomies of First Ancestors and Descendants. It is this latter breakdown that is crucial, for the genealogical order of patriarchy formed both the private (familial) and the historical discursive contexts out of which and against which Faulkner composed a printed self. Faulkner consciously adopted the role of the rebellious child, of a minor breaking open a space in the continuous order of discourse so that he might speak. He revises as a minority; perhaps it was the only position he could take as a modern southern writer. * * * Quentin evolves throughout Faulkner's career, evolves in reverse, "progresses" from the isolated figure of interior monologue in *The Sound and the Fury* to the revised figure of a discursive "commonwealth" in *Absalom, Absalom!* The transition from the earlier to the later work jars us; we read against career chronology, forward from *The Sound and the Fury* to discover in *Absalom, Absalom!* Quentin's public voice as it was prior to his private monologue in *The Sound and the Fury*. Here Faulkner transgresses modernist limits, making a bold move out of the private world of the aesthetic displacement of the real and into the public domain of social, historical discourse, from monologue to dialogue.

* * *

[For Faulkner this process] began as the opening of a narrative space for the voices of children, especially for the male Descendants of First Ancestors. Yet soon it came to embrace other minorities repressed in the paternal fiction: blacks, and, admittedly, all too infrequently, women. The question in reading Faulkner is not so much whether a mature white male southern writer can speak for others, can give a legitimate voice to children, blacks, and women, for Faulkner found this task always beyond him. The question is whether he wanted to undertake the task at all, and this he most certainly did. In transgressing the boundaries of his personal paternal fiction he discovered its social and political pervasiveness. The insight was frightening, for Faulkner's effort to represent the voice of the other, the dispersing, deconstructive voices within the paternal model of meaning, led him to venture into strange languages, those Jardine rightly notes he would have considered "mad, unconscious, improper, unclean, . . . profane."[3] Yet he did raise these voices more often than one would expect, and the inaugural event of this venture was *The Sound and the Fury* or, more precisely, the "failure" of that novel.

* * *

3. Alice A. Jardine, *Gynesis: Configurations of Woman and Modernity* (Ithaca, 1985), 73.

MINROSE C. GWIN

Hearing Caddy's Voice †

Caddy, as we have already seen, is first and foremost an image; she exists only in the minds and memories of her brothers. . . . She is in fact what woman has always been in man's imagination: the figure par excellence of the Other, a blank screen onto which he projects both his desires and his fears, his love and his hate. And insofar as this Other is a myth and a mirage, a mere fantasy of the Self, it is bound to be a perpetual deceit and an endless source of disappointment.

André Bleikasten,
*The Most Splendid Failure: Faulkner's
"The Sound and the Fury"*

But what if the object began to speak?

Luce Irigaray,
Speculum of the Other Woman

I must begin by saying that I do not believe in Caddy Compson's silence. For if I believed in it, there would be no point in beginning at all. I will admit also that, although I do not believe that Caddy is silent, I do not understand fully what she is saying. And so I am seeking Caddy Compson, * * * straining to hear untranslatable snatches of sounds. * * * [We] listen for that of which we can hear the sense but not the substance, that which is always escaping language's appropriative gesture. Certainly this tentativeness is not an accustomed posture for those of us trained in the staid uprightness of the "objective" stance. Yet, as Jane Gallop points out in her reading of Lacan, such a (non)position as ours, vulnerable and unsettling as it is, not only allows a different relationship to the many contradictory voices of a text, but calls into question "the phallic illusions of authority" and therefore is, and must be, "profoundly feminist." Our willingness to relinquish mastery, to admit that we do not know, frees us to seek out what it *is* we do not know, to become as [Roland] Barthes would have us—rereaders rather than consumers of texts.

And so when I say I am listening for Caddy's voice as it will, I believe, float up to us muted but articulate out of the feminine space of *The Sound and the Fury*, I am saying that we are listening for what we know not and for much more than we know. Just as the inscription of woman decenters and challenges the phallocentrism of Western culture and metaphysics and its "structuring of man as the central reference point of thought, and of the phallus as the symbol of sociocultural authority,"

† From *The Feminine and Faulkner: Reading (Beyond) Sexual Difference* (Knoxville: University of Tennessee Press, 1990), 34–47. Copyright © 1990 by The University of Tennessee Press. Reprinted by permission of The University of Tennessee Press.

Caddy as female subject becomes * * * the discursiveness of that space
which she *is* but which she also speaks out of. This is a space which
expands and contracts with the force of its own motion. I do not see it
as a "blank counter" or an "empty center," a "cold weight of negativity,"
or a "still point." [1] Indeed, by relinquishing our (imagined) mastery over
it, our attempts to *fix* it, we may find ourselves being engulfed by it
(much, I think, as Faulkner allowed himself to be) and losing ourselves
in it and to it. We may believe ourselves in danger.

But it is then, I believe, that we may begin to hear the whisper of
Caddy's voice from within the folds of Faulkner's text and from within
our own willingness to be absorbed into the concentric and bisexual
spaces *between* the "manifest text" of Faulkner's male creative consciousness and the "unconscious discourse" of its own feminine subjectivity. [2] * * * As Faulkner disappears into the rhetoric of the text, Caddy
emerges with her own language of desires, loss, subversion, and, of course,
creativity.

At this point our dilemma becomes linguistic: how to converse with
space, motion, force. * * * And how to listen to the language Caddy
speaks, to that voice we hear between and beyond the contours of narrative—to the space which speaks both from and toward the half-light of
the unconscious. In our yearning to hear that voice as it *is* (and not as
we would render it through the alembic of consciousness and Being) and
in our frustration at being able to catch only snatches and whispers of it,
we are tempted to become like Melissa Meek, the frantic librarian, who
seizes the frozen photographic image that will *place* Caddy somewhere
and who cries, "It's Caddy! We must save her!" Burdened by the weight
of consciousness and afraid we will not catch what it is we are meant to
hear, we might hasten to fix Caddy in history and culture, in myth, as
Other, as anima, as double, as nothing, as everything—and hence to
erect some safe, recognizable boundaries around the feminine space of
the text. Yet most of us would agree, I think, that Caddy *as character*
flows beyond our ability to read her. She is *something more* than we can
say, yet her presence is crucial to the deployment of language. [3]

We are like Benjy "trying to say" Caddy, but we, like Faulkner himself, always fail. Faulkner's feeling of failure (as well as his sense of the
splendor of it), I believe, derives from his frustrations at "trying to say"
Caddy, trying to write the female subject through a male consciousness

1. See André Bleikasten, *The Most Splendid Failure: Faulkner's "The Sound and the Fury"*
(Bloomington: Indiana University Press, 1976), pp. 58, 51; Cleanth Brooks, *William Faulkner:
The Yoknapatawpha Country* (New Haven: Yale University Press, 1963), p. 334; and Eric Sundquist, *Faulkner: The House Divided* (Baltimore: Johns Hopkins University Press) p. 10. Page references in the text are to the *The Sound and the Fury* (New York: Random House, 1929). Page
references in brackets are to this Norton Critical Edition *[Editor]*.
2. See Robert Con Davis, ed., *Lacan and Narration: The Psychoanalytic Difference in Narrative
Theory* (Baltimore: Johns Hopkins University Press, 1983), 857.
3. See Julia Kristeva, *Desire in Language: A Semiotic Approach to Literature and Art*, ed. Leon
S. Roudiez (New York: Columbia University Press, 1980), 120 *[Editor]*.

and always failing—but *in the failure* creating the enormous bisexual tensions which play themselves out so powerfully within *The Sound and the Fury*, which in fact are essential to its subversion of the whole idea of a unified subject. We know Faulkner's passion (Bleikasten uses the term "tenderness") for Caddy, his "beautiful one," his "heart's darling." Yet we also are aware that Eric Sundquist is right in saying, "There is probably no major character in literature about whom we know so little in proportion to the amount of attention she receives."[4] I would suggest another way of seeking the mystery that is Caddy, but one which I admit will not allow us to "find" her. The inevitability of our failure, though, does not mean we should not look and listen; for in seeking Caddy as feminine space and female subject-in-process we will be tracing the elusive shape of Faulkner's bisexual artistic (un)consciousness and * * * employing * * * a radical strategy of reading.

What we seek in seeking Caddy Compson is not only the language and force and mystery of woman within Faulkner's text and consciousness. This is also an inquiry into the nature of female subjectivity within a male text and the relationship of that subjectivity to what language can and cannot say. * * * Caddy's ability to speak to us as she traverses the space between presence and absence, text and nontext, the conscious and the unconscious, stretches our sense of the urgency of these questions. Simultaneously, her ability to play creatively within the bounded text of male discourse expands our sense of female energy and power, of its pressure upon the productivity of that text. Often we feel that Caddy isn't where we think she is, that her space is *somewhere else*. She is continually arising from and fading into her brothers' discourse, always in the process of emerging and disappearing in the male text. Her subjectivity, as the "punctuation" of the male discourse which bounds it, is always on the brink of *aphanisis*, fading and being lost. It thus speaks out of the play of presence and absence, moving up and down the pear tree, in and out of that hazy area between the conscious and the unconscious. * * * Benjy's final musings are indeed so strangely moving, I suggest, because they allow us to feel almost simultaneously *both* the epiphany within the maternal space created between himself and Caddy *and* its *aphanisis*:

> Father went to the door and looked at us again. Then the dark came back, and he stood black in the door, and then the door turned black again. Caddy held me and I could hear us all, and the darkness, and something I could smell. And then I could see the windows, where the trees were buzzing. Then the dark began to go in smooth, bright shapes, like it always does, even when Caddy says that I have been asleep. (*SF* 92) [48]

4. See Bleikasten and Sundquist as cited in note 1 above *[Editor]*.

And yet the paradox is that Caddy *won't* fade completely; her voice and
her presence emerge and reemerge throughout the narrative. She will
not leave us; she rushes out of the mirror of male discourse, smelling
like rain, offering Benjy's box of stars, speaking to us the language of
creative play, of *différance*, of endless deconstruction and generation.
Or grieving in a black raincoat, she appears suddenly out of nowhere on
the periphery of the text, saying . . . what?

                              *   *   *

> "Why, Benjy." she said. She looked at me and I went and she put
> her arms around me. "Did you find Caddy again." she said. "Did
> you think Caddy had run away."

Caddy's voice speaks in rhythms most of us understand, for she speaks
what Kristeva has called "maternal language" out of the maternal space
created in Benjy's discourse. The flatness and homogeneity of her speech
evoked by punctuation and syntax have the paradoxical effect of inten-
sifying the rhythms of mediation between self and other. * * * Hearing
Caddy through the flatness of Benjy's mind, we may be reminded of the
peculiar effect of hearing poetry read with a purposeful lack of expression
designed to permit the language of the text to speak itself *as language*.
Matthews has pointed to the fact that Benjy in his "fallen world of loss,
memory, time, and grief" converts time into space.[5] I would take this
idea further by suggesting that feminine space *overlays* time in the novel.
* * *
Within such a space Caddy the child becomes Caddy the mother.
Benjy the man is Benjy the child. Linear time is decentered and displaced by maternal space. Language is constitutive: Caddy's "saying"
makes it so. Within one conversation, she makes words into exchange
commodities traded for a jar of lightning bugs for Benjy and remakes
grief into pleasure:

> "If I say you and T.P. can come too, will you let him hold it."
> Caddy said.
> "Aint nobody said me and T.P. got to mind you." Frony said.
> "If I say you dont have to, will you let him hold it." Caddy said.
> "All right." Frony said. "Let him hold it, T.P. We going to watch
> them moaning."
> "They aint moaning." Caddy said. "I tell you it's a party. Are
> they moaning, Versh." (*SF* 44) [24]

Linda W. Wagner writes persuasively of Caddy's attempts to "bring [Benjy]
to speech" and of Caddy's roles as "creator and conveyor of language,"

---

5. John T. Matthews, *The Play of Faulkner's Language* (Ithaca: Cornell University Press, 1982),
65 [*Editor*].

a language of love and interconnection which is inevitably replaced by
meaningless sound and fury. Matthews thinks of these initial attempts at
definition and articulation as prefiguring an infinite play of meanings
which suggest the inability of language to "reappropriate presence and
the recognition that such a limitation opens the possibility of the endless
pleasures of writing." Although Caddy's generative maternal language is
eventually replaced, it is not lost. * * * Benjy has lost Caddy but he
remains within her maternal discourse, for her voice has imprinted both
itself and *himself* upon the receptacle of his memory. We can envision
him at the state mental hospital, still hearing her speak his name and
still recognizing the sound of her name within language—a maternal
language which traverses the chasm between her subjectivity and his.
We may look at the movement of Benjy's reality within this section as
illustration. At the beginning he has lost Caddy and is bellowing at the
sound "caddie" and yet by the end, the maternal space of Caddy * * *
has enclosed his mind with the "smooth, bright shapes" of that hazy
entry to the womb-like darkness of maternal interconnection through
which the boundaries between self and other are blurred. By its ability
to name what is not, or what seems to be absent (Benjy's subjectivity),
Caddy's maternal voice dissolves the boundary between presence and
absence and thereby creates the semiotic matrix of the novel, the unconscious discourse that will go on to speak the reciprocal rhythms between
the conscious and the unconscious in Quentin's tortured thoughts.

Although she is a girl and although she speaks as a girl, her voice
carries this referential weight because she speaks from the *position* of the
mother, whose very acts of giving birth, of gestation and nurturance,
dissolve the otherness of the other. In many of the scenes created in
Benjy's memory, Caddy encloses him within this maternal space which
transcends the teleologies of time and loss. What Caddy's voice says out
of the maternal space created for it in Benjy's mind is precisely *opposite*
to what Benjy's narrative as a whole seems to be saying, i.e., that originary plenitude can never be regained, that creativity and play have given
way to despair, rigidity, meaningless order—sound and fury signifying
nothing.[6]

The maternal Caddy deconstructs such a message. Her voice tells
another story—the creative play of *différance* within the bounded text of
Benjy's mind. With her words and touch she dissolves the boundaries
between herself and Benjy. His snatches of memories often end with
Caddy reaffirming the maternal space that connects them. For example,
Benjy remembers her persuading their mother to let her take him out in
the cold, instructing the relieved Versh not to come, and then embracing him:

---

6. More optimistically, Matthews, in *The Play of Faulkner's Language*, finds that loss opens the
way to "the fun of writing" and its continual deferment, its "play of failures."

He went on and we stopped in the hall and Caddy knelt and put her arms around me and her cold bright face against mine. She smelled like trees.

"You're not a poor baby. Are you. You've got your Caddy. Haven't you got your Caddy." (SF 8) [6]

Caddy plays creatively within the bounds of coldness and rigidity. She speaks warmth to Benjy, even as they are being used by Maury to deliver his letter: "Keep your hands in your pockets, Caddy said. Or they'll get froze. You don't want your hands froze on Christmas, do you" (3) [4]. She connects her self to Benjy's other, even to the point of becoming other to herself, speaking of herself in the third person, connecting her desires to Benjy's, pretending, "We dont like perfume ourselves" (51) [27]. * * *

Yet just as she herself fades * * * the maternal space she creates for Benjy gives way to other more disturbing spaces, and what empowerment she receives as female subject from taking the place of the mother is punctuated by depletion and darkness. As her space constricts, we begin to see her frantic response to the necessity of remaining creative within the narrow margins allowed her own desires as a subject-in-process propelled by the motion of their force. She continues to play, but her text becomes more and more bounded. She is encircled in the concentric spaces of her own maternity created within male discourse, but also of the sexuality which transgresses that maternal space, and finally and inevitably of the patriarchal world she finds herself living within as a female subject-object. She is a subject always in the process of becoming; yet movement becomes less free and eventually, in Jason's economy, impossible.

One of the scenes most often repeated in the novel and certainly among its most central is the one in which a silenced Caddy, no longer a virgin, stands in the door, first in Benjy's and then in Quentin's memories, her eyes speaking terror and despair. Cornered by Benjy's bellowing, she is completely entrapped by male discourse, by both Benjy's inarticulate and Quentin's articulate texts of woman as other. This is a scene which Benjy recalls and then immediately repeats, and it is one which erupts again and again in Quentin's tortured thoughts. Caddy has broken the Law of the Father, that which "requires that woman maintain in her own body the material substratum of the object of desire, but that she herslf never have access to desire."[7] * * * Here she is voiceless; she becomes merely a function of the discourse of others—frozen as image, as silence. Benjy recalls the same scene in two flashes. First he recalls:

Caddy came to the door and stood there, looking at Father and Mother. Her eyes flew at me, and away. I began to cry. It went

7. See Luce Irigaray, *This Sex Which Is Not One*, trans. Catherine Porter and Carolyn Burke (Ithaca: Cornell University Press, 1985), 188.

loud and I got up. Caddy came in and stood with her back to the
wall, looking at me. I went toward her, crying, and she shrank
against the wall and I saw her eyes and I cried louder and pulled at
her dress. She put her hands out but I pulled at her dress. Her eyes
ran. (SF 84) [44]

And then again:

We were in the hall. Caddy was still looking at me. Her hand
was against her mouth and I saw her eyes and I cried. We went up
the stairs. She stopped again, against the wall, looking at me and I
cried and she went on and I came on, crying, and she shrank against
the wall, looking at me. She opened the door to her room, but I
pulled at her dress and we went to the bathroom and she stood
against the door, looking at me. Then she put her arm across her
face and I pushed at her, crying. (SF 85) [44]

This is the image of Caddy silenced. She cannot remake herself in
language for Benjy. She cannot wash off or throw away her desire. This
is the moment of her entrapment, a crucial moment of the novel and
one which Quentin re-creates obsessively. If Caddy in the pear tree is
an image of her creativity and courage, of her ability to negotiate the
economies of death (that which is in the window) and life (that which is
below her, those whom she loves), then Caddy's standing in the door
with eyes, "like cornered rats" as Quentin will say of a similar scene, is
surely the opposite image. Caddy speaks out of the pear tree: she speaks
life to death and death to life. She becomes, as Bleikasten shows us, a
mediator between the two.[8] Yet she is completely entrapped before Benjy's
bellowing; more devastating, she is rendered voiceless. It is significant
and strangely disturbing that these two images of Caddy, weeping after
she has entered into her first sexual relationship, are connected in Benjy's
mind by Versh's eerie tale of maternity's disastrous effects, that of the
woman's "bluegum chillen" who eat a man: "*Possum hunters found him
in the woods, et clean*" (SF 85) [44]. Versh's story is about a woman who
has, it is implied, "*about a dozen them bluegum chillen running around
the place*" (84–85) [44]. This is the maternal space expanded to monstrous proportions, becoming enormously threatening and destructive to
the male, just as Caddy's maternal space now threatens Benjy because it
has become also the space of female sexuality. * * *
    Yet I have said that I do not believe in Caddy Compson's silence. As
female subject, she is indeed silenced at this point. But as woman-in-
effect in male discourse, as the feminine space in Faulkner's narrative,
she becomes what Irigaray calls the "*disruptive excess*" that is guilty of
"jamming the theoretical machinery itself, of suspending its pretension
to the production of a truth and of a meaning that are excessively uni-

8. Bleikasten, *The Most Splendid Failure*, p. 54.

vocal."[9] She is the text which speaks multiplicity, maternity, sexuality, and as such she retains not just one voice but many. They make Benjy bellow and Quentin despair. They drive Jason to hatred. Their power is mammoth because they are "not one." Within the constricted space of Quentin's tortured psyche, we will hear them, like the Caddy of Benjy's maternal *chora*, fading in and out. To hear Caddy within the margins of Quentin's text will require listening to a language which transgresses the bounds of consciousness, a language which must be listened to in much the same way that Caddy listened to Benjy—beyond sound and syntax, between the lines.

*   *   *

ANDRÉ BLEIKASTEN

The Quest for Eurydice †

Regarder Eurydice, sans souci du chant, dans l'impatience et l'imprud-
ence du désir qui oublie la loi, c'est cela même, *l'inspiration*.
Maurice Blanchot

A pregnant emptiness. Object-loss, world-loss, is the precondition for
all creation. Creation is in or out of the voice; *ex nihilo*.
Norman O. Brown

"The Most Splendid Failure"

With *The Sound and the Fury* something happened to Faulkner that had never happened before and would never happen again. For us, his readers, this novel is the first of his major works, a quantum leap in achievement; for the writer, however, it was much more than a book: a sudden release of creative energies, a turning point in his career, a unique experience in his life. On what the experience meant to him we are fortunate to have his own retrospective comment in the two versions of the introduction he wrote during the summer of 1933 for a new edition of the novel that was to be published by Random House.[1] Of his many statements on *The Sound and the Fury*, none provides fuller insight into

9. Irigaray, *This Sex Which Is Not One*, p. 78.
† From *The Ink of Melancholy: Faulkner's Novels from "The Sound and the Fury" to "Light in August"* (Bloomington and Indianapolis: Indiana University Press, 1990), 41–55.
1. Faulkner's introduction survives in several partial and complete manuscript and typescript drafts. Two of them have been published: "William Faulkner: An Introduction for *The Sound and the Fury*," *Southern Review*, N.S., 8 (October 1972), 705–10; "An Introduction to *The Sound and the Fury*," *Mississippi Quarterly*, 26 (Summer 1973), 410–15. Both versions were edited by James B. Meriwether.

the book's genesis, and, what is more, none gives us as sharp a sense of the emotional climate in which it was conceived and written.

> I wrote this book and learned to read. I had learned a little about writing from Soldiers' Pay—how much to approach language, words: not with seriousness so much, as an essayist does, but with a kind of alert respect, as you approach dynamite; even with joy, as you approach women: perhaps with the same secretly unscrupulous intentions. But when I finished The Sound and The Fury I discovered that there is actually something to which the shabby term Art not only can, but must be applied. I discovered then that I had gone through all that I had ever read, from Henry James through Henty to newspaper murders, without making any distinction or digesting any of it, as a moth or a goat might. After The Sound and The Fury and without heeding to open another book and in a series of delayed repercussions like summer thunder, I discovered the Flauberts and Dostoievskys and Conrads whose books I had read ten years ago. With The Sound and The fury I learned to read and quit reading, since I have read nothing since. [2]

It is with these startling reflections that Faulkner's introduction begins. If *The Sound and the Fury* was a revelation, it was first of all the revelation of Literature, through the sudden (re)discovery of all the major novelists with whom Faulkner had just joined company. True, he had read them before, but if we are to believe his testimony, his first reading had been nothing but consumption without "digestion." His second reading, on the contrary, was a process of assimilation carried to its furthest limits, that is, to the point where reading becomes writing. What Faulkner implicitly acknowledges here is that the relationship between reading and writing is one of reversibility: reading is always a virtual writing, and writing always a way of reading. In working on his fourth novel, he rediscovers the texts of his predecessors in the production of his own and becomes aware of how they interact in the chemistry of his own writing. Not that his novel simply derives from others: the process at work is one of radical transformation, a way of displacing and, eventually, replacing its models. *The Sound and the Fury*, then, may be considered a rereading of Flaubert, Dostoevsky, and Conrad—a reading at once attentive and forgetful, fascinated and treacherous, and, by virtue of its very infidelity, creative. The gesture of appropriation is also a gesture of dismissal. From now on, Faulkner can dispense with reading others. It will be enough for him to be his own reader.

The Sound and the Fury marks Faulkner's decisive encounter with Literature, his final entry into its infinite text, a space in which novels are endlessly born out of novels. With *Flags in the Dust* he had discovered that his experience as a southerner could be used for literary pur-

---

2. "An Introduction for *The Sound and the Fury*," 708 [p. 225 in this Norton Critical Edition].

poses; with *The Sound and the Fury* he came to realize that, far from being the mere expression or reflection of prior experience, writing could be in itself an experience in the fullest sense.

What Faulkner then experienced was the pure *adventure* of writing, free of any preestablished design. "When I began it," he notes, "I had no plan at all. I wasn't even writing a book."[3] And he felt free too from any external pressure or constraint; he did not even care about getting published. The commercial failure of his previous books became an encouragement to disregard the demands of the publishers as well as the expectations of his potential public. *The Sound and the Fury* would be a strictly private affair: "One day I seemed to shut a door between me and all publishers' addresses and book lists. I said to myself, Now I can write."[4]

Having cleared the ground, Faulkner discovered in himself the heretofore unsuspected power to write freely—not just for superficial "fun" but for his deepest pleasure: "Now," the text goes on, "I can make myself a vase like that which the old Roman kept at his bedside and wore the rim slowly away with kissing it."[5] *The Sound and the Fury* thus became the occasion for a doubly significant experience: through the reversal from "reading" into writing, Faulkner was at last able to appropriate his literary legacy and to transmute it into a creation irreducibly his own; yet this breakthrough to mastery was not simply a matter of artistic maturation, and it would not have been possible, perhaps, without the onrush of emotion he experienced during the composition of the novel. What made the writing of *The Sound and the Fury* such an extraordinary experience was probably more than anything else its being quickened by the dark energies of desire.

The work of art has been defined in psychoanalytic terms as a *transnarcissistic* object, meant to establish a connection between the narcissism of its producer and that of its consumer.[6] But with *The Sound and the Fury* the creative impulse, at least in its earlier phase, seems to have been rather *intranarcissistic*. The object to be shaped was to serve no other purpose than self-gratification. Giver and receiver were to be identical. As to the object itself, its narcissistic nature and function are emphasized through the image of the Tyrrhenian vase kept by the old Roman at his bedside and whose rim is slowly worn away by his kisses. Another reminder of the urn of Keats' ode, the vase is of course a para-

---

3. Ibid., 710.

4. Ibid.

5. Ibid. No one, to my knowledge, has noticed how much the anecdote about the old Roman recalls the story of Pygmalion in Ovid's *Metamorphoses*: Pygmalion falls in love with a beautiful ivory statue he has created, bedecks it with jewels, fondles its curves, and takes it to bed, praying to Venus that his wife be (or be like) his "ivory girl." The "Pygmalion comnplex" is of course common among artists, and the transformation of the manufactured woman into a living female body is probably every male novelist's dream.

6. See André Green, *Un Oeil en trop : Le Complexe d'Oedipe dans la tragédie* (Paris: Editions de Minuit, 1969), pp. 35–40.

digm of the beautiful and potentially timeless artifacts produced by art. But the point here is that the aesthetic is made one with the erotic.[7] The kissed vase is clearly a libidinal object, a fetish, standing *instead* of something else, the mark and mask of an absence. It functions as a surrogate or supplement—an assumption fully confirmed by the last sentence of Faulkner's text: "So I, who had never had a sister and was fated to lose my daughter in infancy, set out to make myself a beautiful and tragic little girl."[8]

Through the detour of a fiction, Faulkner thus attempted to make up for a lack. And the impatience and impetus of his desire were such that he felt irresistibly carried away, propelled beyond himself by what he was to call an "ecstasy":

> that other quality which The Sound and The Fury had given me
> . . . : that emotion definite and physical and yet nebulous to describe:
> that ecstasy, that eager and joyous faith and anticipation of surprise
> which the yet unmarred sheet beneath my hand held inviolate and
> unfailing, waiting for release.[9]

According to Faulkner's account of his creative experience, none of his novels sprang up more miraculously. *The Sound and the Fury*, it would seem, was an unexpected grace, a gift of the gods, and this mediumlike sense of being written through, of calling something into being he did not know he contained, was never to return. When he wrote his next book, *Sanctuary*, "there was something missing; something which The Sound and The Fury gave me and Sanctuary did not."[1] When he began *As I Lay Dying*, he knew "that it would be also missing in this case because this would be a deliberate book."[2] And with *Light in August* it had become clear to him that this "something" would elude him forever and that "whatever novels [he would] write in the future would be written without reluctance, but also without anticipation or joy."[3]

This quasi-trancelike condition was radically different from "the cold satisfaction"[4] he would derive from his later works; nor can it be compared to the lighthearted ludic approach associated with his earlier novels. Are we to assume, therefore, that this experience was unmitigated creative euphoria, sweet surrender to afflatus, and that *The Sound and the Fury* was written under the spell of an irrepressible and infallible inspiration? In his introduction of 1933 Faulkner emphasizes that "this

7. Estelle Oldham, one of the models for Caddy, is compared to "a lovely vase" in one of Faulkner's letters. See Joseph L. Blotner, *Faulkner: A Biography* (New York: Random House, 1974), p. 563. On the symbolism of the urn/vase image, see David Minter, *William Faulkner: His Life and Work* (Baltimore: Johns Hopkins University Press, 1980), p. 102.
8. "An Introduction for *The Sound and the Fury*," *Southern Review*, 710.
9. Ibid., 709.
1. Ibid.
2. Ibid.
3. Ibid., 710.
4. Ibid., 709

is the only one of the seven novels [he] wrote without any accompanying feelings of drive or effort, or any following feelings of exhaustion or relief or distaste."[5] This assertion is flatly contradicted, however, by some of his later statements on the novel. Thus, in one of the class conferences he held at the University of Virginia in 1957, he declared: "It was the one that I anguished the most over, that I worked the hardest at, that even when I knew I couldn't bring it off, I still worked at it."[6] To wonder when Faulkner told the truth is not the right question to ask, for the whole truth lies precisely in the contradiction: *The Sound and the Fury* was the child of care as well as of inspiration, of agony as well as of ecstasy.

Something of the same seeming contradiction may be detected in Faulkner's evaluation of the novel. In October 1928, after typing its final version, he proudly told his friend and literary agent Ben Wasson: "Read this, Bud. It's a real sonofabitch."[7] Yet whenever he was questioned about *The Sound and the Fury*, he referred to it in terms of "failure."[8] True, he considered it "the most gallant, the most magnificent failure,"[9] but a failure it was all the same. There had been others before; with this book, however, Faulkner met failure in a deeper, more inescapable sense—failure as the very destiny of all artistic endeavor. What then became evident to him was the sobering truth that, as Samuel Beckett put it, "to be an artist is to fail, as no other dare fail," and that "failure is his world and the shrink from it desertion."[1] Had Faulkner remained a writer of talent only, he would never have reached that awareness. Less paradoxically than it might seem, it was when the powers of language appeared to be within his grasp as never before that he came to recognize the *necessity* of failure.

Faulkner's description of the novel's genesis reads like a record of abortive attempts:

> That began as a short story, it was a story without plot, of some children being sent away from the house during the grandmother's funeral. They were too young to be told what was going on and they saw things only incidentally to the childish games they were playing, which was the lugubrious matter of removing the corpse from the house, etc., and then the idea struck me to see how much more I could have got out of the idea of the blind self-centeredness

5. Ibid., 710.
6. *Faulkner in the University*, Frederick L. Gwynn and Joseph L. Blotner, eds. (Charlottesville: University Press of Virginia, 1959), p. 61. See also *Lion in the Garden: Interviews with William Faulkner, 1926–1962*, James B. Meriwether and Michael Millgate, eds. (New York: Random House, 1968), p. 146.
7. Quoted in James B. Meriwether, "Notes on the Textual History of *The Sound and the Fury*," *Papers of the Bibliographical Society of America*, 56 (Third Quarter, 1962), 289.
8. See *FU*, pp. 61, 77; *LG*, pp. 92, 146, 180.
9. *FU*, p. 61.
1. Samuel Beckett, *Proust and Three Dialogues with Georges Duthuit* (London: John Calder, 1965), p. 125.

of innocence typified by children if one of those children had been truly innocent, that is, an idiot. So the idiot was born and then I became interested in the relationship of the idiot to the world that he was in but would never be able to cope with and just where could he get the tenderness, the help, to shield him in his innocence. I mean "innocence" in the sense that God had stricken him blind at birth, that is, mindless at birth, there was nothing he could ever do about it. And so the character of his sister began to emerge, then the brother, who, that Jason (who to me represented complete evil. He's the most vicious character in my opinion I ever thought of), then he appeared. Then it needs the protagonist, someone to tell the story, so Quentin appeared. By that time I found out I couldn't possibly tell that in a short story. And so I told the idiot's experience of that day, and that was incomprehensible, even I could not have told what was going on then, so I had to write another chapter. Then I decided to let Quentin tell his version of that same day, or that same occasion, so he told it. Then there had to be the counterpoint, which was the other brother, Jason. By that time it was completely confusing. I knew that it was not anywhere near finished and then I had to write another section from the outside with an outsider, which was the writer, to tell what had happened on that particular day. And that's how that book grew. That is, I wrote that same story four times. None of them were right, but I had anguished so much that I could not throw any of it away and start over, so I printed it in the four sections. That was not a deliberate *tour de force* at all, the book just grew that way. That I was still trying to tell one story which moved me very much and each time I failed, but I had put so much anguish into it that I couldn't throw it away, like the mother that had four bad children, that she would have been better off if they had all been eliminated, but she culdn't relinquish any of them. And that's the reason I have the most tenderness for that book, because it failed four times.[2]

Like many great modern novels—*Ulysses* and *The Magic Mountain* come at once to mind—*The Sound and the Fury* began by taking the form of a short story in the mind of its creator.[3] The novel form was almost resorted to as a *pis aller*, and the entire book may thus be seen as the outgrowth of an initial failure: Faulkner's incapacity to complete the narrative within the limits of the short story, which he considered "the most demanding form after poetry."[4] What is more, failure informs the very pattern of the novel, since its four sections represent so many vain

2. *LG*, pp. 146–47. See also p. 222.
3. The working title of the short story was "Twilight." See Blotner, *Faulkner*, p. 566. Faulkner had already written two stories about the Compson children: "That Evening Sun Go Down" (published in March 1931) and "A Justice" (both are included in William Faulkner, *These Thirteen* [New York: Jonathan Cape and Harrison Smith, 1931], and William Faulkner, *Collected Stories* [New York: Random House, 1950]).
4. *LG*, p. 238.

attempts at getting the story told. Most readers will of course dismiss this confession of impotence as an excess of modesty. Yet Faulkner's insistence on his failure was no pose. Experience had already taught him that "being a writer is having the worst vocation . . . a lonely frustrating work which is never as good as you want it to be."[5]

The Sound and the Fury had first been the sudden opening up of a boundless field of possibilities, the happy vertigo of a creation still unaware of its limitations, whose movement bore Faulkner along in quick elation, as if he were the entranced beholder of his own inventions. But once the wonder of this privileged first moment was dispelled and the book was no longer the bright mirage of desire but a work in progress, doubt and anxiety took over. And when Faulkner looked back on what he had accomplished, he knew that his work was "still not finished,"[6] that the story he so wanted to tell, the only one really worth the telling, was still to be told.

The Sound and the Fury was Faulkner's first great creative adventure. It assured him at once a major place in what has been, since Hawthorne, Poe, and Melville, the great tradition of failure in American literature. Like his American ancestors and like other modern writers from Flaubert and Mallarmé through Joyce, Kafka, Musil, and Beckett, it led him to the experience of the impossible. According to Faulkner himself, failure was the common fate of all writers of his generation: "All of us failed to match our dream of perfection."[7] Whether the blame falls on the artist or on his medium, language, everything happens as though writing could only be the gauging of a lack. Creation then ceases to be a triumphant gesture of assertion; it resigns itself to be the record of its errors, trials, and defeats, the chronicle of its successive miscarriages, the inscription of the very impossibility from which it springs.

Hence novels tend to turn into extended metaphors for the hazardous game of their writing. Novelists no longer seek to give life a semblance of order by relying on well-rounded characters and well-made plots. Instead of following a logical sequential pattern, events are subordinated to the process of the fictitious discourse itself as it takes shape or fails to do so— unfolding, infolding, progressing, regressing, turning in on itself in a never-completed quest for form and meaning.[8] What is told then is not

5. *LG*, pp. 220–21.
6. *LG*, p. 180. Significant too is Faulkner's offer to provide an appendix to the novel for the Viking *Portable Faulkner*, which Malcolm Cowley was editing in 1945. The many additions he made there to the original account of the Compson family (a number of which, incidentally, are inconsistent with the novel) are tangible testimony to his feeling that the story was "still not finished." First published in the *Portable Faulkner* in 1946, the "Appendix: Compson 1699–1945" was republished in a slightly different version in the Modern Library double volume of *The Sound and the Fury* and *As I Lay Dying* (1946) and the Random House edition of 1966. Hereafter referred to as "Appendix."
7. *LG*, p. 238.
8. On the processlike quality of the novel, see Donald M. Kartiganer, *The Fragile Thread: The Meaning of Form in Faulkner's Novels* (Amherst: University of Massachusetts Press, 1979), pp. 3–22.

only a story but the venture of its telling: the novel tends to become the narrative of an impossible narrative. Commenting upon *The Man without Qualities*, Musil once observed that "what the story of this novel amounts to is that the story which it should tell is not told."[9] Faulkner might have said as much of *The Sound and the Fury*. The fragments of his narrative flout our expectations of continuity, order, and significance, and we have to accept them as such, in all their random brokenness and final provisionality. Faulkner's text is as much the locus as the product of its gestation.

Desire at Work

The Sound and the Fury grows out of and refers back to an empty center, which one might paradoxically call eccentric or define—to borrow a phrase from Wallace Stevens—as a "center on the horizon,"[1] insofar as it represents at once the novel's origin and its *télos*, its generating principle and the ever-receding object of its quest. Which is to say again that the novel arises out of the emptiness of desire in much the same way dreams do. Like dreams, it aims at a fictive wish fulfillment, as can be seen clearly from Faulkner's own statements. Indeed, the processes at work in the writing of *The Sound and the Fury* in many ways invite comparison with the metonymic and metaphoric procedures of dream-work. Yet it is perhaps even more enlightening to relate them to what Freud termed *Trauerarbeit*, the "the work of mourning" whereby the psyche seeks to detach itself from a lost love-object. Writing, as André Green argues,

> presupposes a wound, a loss, a bereavement, which the written work will transform to the point of producing its own fictitious positivity. No creation goes without effort, without a painful labor over which it carries a pseudo-victory. It can only be a pseudo-victory because it is short-lived, because it is always contested by the author himself who feels the tireless urge to start again, and hence to negate his previous achievements, or at least to reject the idea that the result, no matter how satisfactory it may have seemed, is his last word. . . . Reading and writing are a ceaseless work of mourning. If there is a pleasure to be found in the text, we always know that this pleasure is a surrogate for a lost gratification, which we are trying to recover through other means.[2]

That literature functions as a substitute is an assumption verified by Faulkner's own testimony: "the beautiful and tragic little girl" whom he set out to create through the power of words was manifestly intended to

9. Robert Musil, *Der Mann Ohne Eigenschaften* (Hamburg: Rowohlt, 1952), p. 1640. My translation.
1. "A Primitive Like an Orb," *Collected Poems* (New York: Alfred A. Knopf, 1951), p. 443.
2. "Le Double et l'absent," *Critique*, 29 (May 1973), 403–4.

fill a vacancy. His introduction refers to absence ("I, who had never had a sister") as well as to mourning ("fated to lose my daughter in infancy"), equating in retrospect the imaginary *lack* with an actual *loss*. And interestingly, the seminal image of the novel is focused on the grandmother's death, and Faulkner's initial concern was with the Compson children's reactions to this event:

> It struck me that it would be interesting to imagine the thoughts of a group of children who were sent away from the house the day of their grandmother's funeral, their curiosity about the activity in the house, their efforts to find out what was going on, and the notions that would come into their minds.[3]

As I Lay Dying, whose composition is chronologically close to that of *The Sound and the Fury*, similarly revolves around a mother's death, and mourning, the coming to terms with loss (or the failujre to do so), figures prominently in much of Faulkner's later fiction. Mourning, then, is not only a possible key to the process of Faulkner's creation but also a motif readily traced in the novels themselves. One would like to know what its emergence at this point means in psychobiographical terms; yet, apart from the hints one can find in Faulkner's comments and above all in his fiction, there is little to gratify our curiosity. *The Sound and the Fury*, Faulkner told Maurice-Edgar Coindreau, his French translator, was written at a time when he "was beset with personal problems."[4] What these "personal problems" actually were must remain a matter of speculation.

It is fairly obvious, however, that the novels written during those years, especially *The Sound and the Fury* and *As I Lay Dying*, are novels *about* lack and loss, in which desire is always intimately bound up with grief and death. And it is clear too that they have sprung *out of* a deep sense of lack and loss—texts spun around a primal gap.

In *The Sound and the Fury* this gap is reduplicated and represented in the pathetic and intriguing figure of Caddy Compson, the lost sister. Even when the novel was still a vague project in the author's mind, "the beautiful and tragic little girl" was already there, and we find her again in the basic image which was to inform the whole book:

> perhaps the only thing in literature which would ever move me very much: Caddy climbing the pear tree to look in the window at her grandmother's funeral while Quentin and Jason and Benjy and the negroes looked up at the muddy seat of her drawers.[5]

3. Reported by M. E. Coindreau in "Preface to *The Sound and the Fury*," *The Time of William Faulkner* (Columbia: University of South Carolina Press, 1971), p. 41. The autobiographical source of the Damuddy episode is presumably the funeral of Faulkner's grandmother Lelia Swift Butler in 1907. Faulkner was then ten years old—approximately the same age as Quentin at the time of Damuddy's death in the novel.
4. Coindreau, *The Time of William Faulkner*, p. 49.
5. "An Introduction for *The Sound and the Fury*," 710 [pp. 226–27 in this Norton Critical Edition].

Out of this emotion-packed image the novel grew. In retrospect, one is tempted to read it as the latter's prefiguration, or at least as a foreshadowing of its dominant themes: an image of innocence confronted with what eludes and threatens it; an image of childhood caught on the brink of forbidden knowledge—evil, sex, death. To Faulkner it must have presented itself as an inigma to be questioned, a secret to be deciphered, and in this respect one should note the emphasis given in the little tableau to the act of seeing and watching: the three brothers looking up at Caddy's muddy drawers; Caddy looking in the window at the funeral preparations. Curiosity about sex and dying prompts their common desire to see. Yet while the boys' curiosity comes close to sexual voyeurism, their reckless sister is fascinated by the mystery of death. Caddy is the only one to climb the three of knoweldge; her brothers stay timidly below and are content with staring at the stain on her drawers. Caddy occupies in fact an intermediary position, suspended as she is between her brothers and the intriguing scene of death—a reminder, perhaps, of the mythic mediating function of woman through whom, for man, passes all knowledge about the origins, all knowledge about the twin enigmas of life and death.

One could carry the investigation further and point out the striking parallels between this scene and the "primal fantasies" postulated by psychoanalysis. The symbolic significance of the scene lies first of all in its insistence on perplexed watching. Hinging upon the question of origins, as all *ur*-fantasies do, it relates a desire to *know* back to the primitive, infantile wish to *see*. As to the ultimate objects of the children's curiosity, they are clearly designated as death and sex, but the point is that in the spatial pattern of the scene the brothers are to Caddy as Caddy is to the window, thus suggesting a virtual equation of sex (the muddy drawers) with death (Damuddy's funeral).[6] Equally noteworthy in this connection is the fact that the boys are peering at a little girl's drawers—that which both conceals and betrays her sexual identity. According to Freud, "probably no male human being is spared the terrifying shock of threatened castration at the sight of the female genitals."[7] True, there is no such shock in Faulkner's evocation of the scene; yet, curiously enough, when Freud accounts for the nature of certain fetishes by "the circumstance that the inquisitive boy used to peer up the woman's legs towards her genitals,"[8] he seems to be describing the very position of the Compson brothers in relation to Caddy. Moreover, even though castration is not referred to explicitly, it is suggested by the intersection of sex and death. Castration—the equivalent of death in the language of the unconscious—provides a further link between the two themes.

6. Note also the phonic kinship of *muddy* and *Damuddy*.
7. Freud, "Fetishism," *Standard Edition of the Complete Psychological Works of Sigmund Freud*, ed. and trans. James Strachey (London: Hogarth Press, 1964), vol. 21, p. 154.
8. Ibid., p. 155.

The whole scene may thus be read as the emblem of a dual revelation: the simultaneous discovery of sexual difference and of death. The working out of the episode of Damuddy's death in the first section of the novel definitely bears out such a reading. Revelation (etymologically the removal of the *velum*, the veil) becomes there quite literally a denudation, a laying bare: on the day when their grandmother dies, Caddy undresses at the branch—an act to which Quentin responds with violence by slapping her (20–21) [12]—and the scene is strangely echoed by Caddy's later allusions to the "undressing" of the dead mare, Nancy, by the buzzards (38) [22] and to the possibility of an identical fate for Damuddy's corpse (40) [23].[9] Once again, sex and death are brought into resonance through a common motif.

While pointing forward to what is at stake in the novel, the seminal scene also sheds light on the author's deeper motivations, for in a sense these curious children, confronted with the mysteries of sex and death, are the fictive delegates of that supreme voyeur who is none other than the novelist. He too wants to see and know. Just as we, his readers, do.

"The Beautiful One"

At the heart of the enigma: Caddy, a turbulent little Eve, rash and defiant, perched on a pear tree,[1] and already significantly associated with the Edenic innocence of trees and with mud, symbol of guilt and sin. It is her story—and that of her daughter Quentin, Caddy's debased copy—that Faulkner wanted to tell in *The Sound and the Fury*: "a tragedy of two lost women."[2] And the privileged place this book held in his affection is inseparable from his abiding tenderness for Caddy: "To me she was the beautiful one, she was my heart's darling. That's what I wrote the book about and I used the tools which seemed to me the proper tools to try to tell, try to draw the picture of Caddy."[3]

It is hardly surprising that Faulkner should have spoken of Caddy with the accents of love.[4] Wasn't she from the outset a creation of desire?

9. William Faulkner, *The Sound and the Fury* (New York: Jonathan Cape and Harrison Smith, 1929; Vintage, 1987). Page references in brackets are to this Norton Critical Edition.
1. Revealingly, in one of his later interviews Faulkner confused Caddy's pear tree with an apple tree (see *FU*, p. 31). With regard to the Edenic connotations of the scene, note that before Caddy climbs the tree "a snake [crawls] out from under the house" (*SF*, 42) [24], and a few moments later Dilsey says to her, "You Satan. . . . Come down from there" (51) [29].
2. *LG*, p. 244.
3. *FU*, p. 6.
4. Consider also what Faulkner told M. E. Coindreau: "the same thing happened to me that happens to many writers—I fell in love with one of my characters, Caddy. I loved her so much I couldnt' decide to give her life just for the duration of a short story. She deserved more than that" (*The Time of William Faulkner*, p. 41). Among the figures anticipating Caddy one might mention Juliet Bunden in "Adolescence," a story written in 1922; Frankie, in an untitled story seemingly written in 1924; Jo-Addie in "Elmer," the uncompleted novel begun in 1925; the nameless girl who turns out to be "Little sister Death" in "The Kid Learns" (1925); and Dulcie, the little heroine of *The Wishing Tree* (1927). Most of the young female characters in Faulkner's first three novels are also related to Caddy in some way or other, Patricia Robyn (*Mosquitoes*) being the one who bears the closest resemblance to her. The heroine of *The Sound and the Fury* is of course much

Before becoming the "real" sister of Benjy, Quentin, and Jason in the novel, Caddy had been Faulkner's imaginary one, invented to make up for a lack. Yet fiction here does not play the customary game of illusion; it does not work out as a consoling substitute. For Caddy is exposed as a fiction within the fiction, her presence in the novel being rendered in such a way as to make her appear throughout as a pure and poignant figure of *absence*. Caddy, "the beautiful one," is no sooner found than she is lost again. *The Sound and the Fury* does not celebrate the (imaginary) triumph of desire but reduplicates its necessary defeat. This novel is Faulkner's first descent into Hell, and Caddy remains his ever-elusive Eurydice.

That is why Caddy, the novelist's secret muse and the very soul of the novel, cannot be considered the heroine of the book in any traditional sense. A chimera to the author, she never ceases to be a chimera in the novel. To lament that she escapes satisfactory definition is hardly relevant, for she is both more and less than a "character": she is at once the focal and the vanishing point, the bewitching *image* around which everything revolves. From the writer's mind she has slipped into the narrators'; from being Faulkner's private fantasy she becomes the obsessive memory of the Compson brothers, without ever really assuming shape and substance in the space of fiction.

One might even argue that Caddy is little more than a blank counter, an empty signifier, a name in itself devoid of meaning and thus apt to receive any meaning. Her function within the novel's semantic structure could be compared to that of a joker in a game of cards; the word *Caddy* assumes meaning only in relation to the contextual network within which it occurs, and since, from one section to another, it is drawn into different verbal environments, woven into different textures, it is invested with ever-renewed significances. *Caddy* is a sign, with all the arbitrariness of the sign, and Faulkner's keen awareness of the chancy and shifting relationships between word and thing, language and meaning, is attested on the very first page of the novel by his deliberate punning on *caddie* and *Caddy*.[5] The homophony is confusing to Benjy, who mis-

more complex than any of these figures, and Faulkner's involvement with her has deep autobiographical sources. In creating her, he drew more than ever before on memories of his own childhood and adolescence. It seems safe to assume that Estelle Oldham, whom he had come to know as a little boy and with whom he fell in love as a teenager, served as a model for Caddy. But so did Sallie Murry, the tomboyish cousin to whom, as Blotner points out, Faulkner "had been almost as close as a sister" (*Faulkner*, p. 568). And one might do well to remember that Estelle also served as a model for the devastating portrait of Cecily Saunders in *Soldiers Pay*. Which is to say that Caddy, even though she rose out of the depths of Faulkner's private experience, is above all a literary creation.

5. Further name confusions are induced by the presence of two Quentins (uncle and niece) and two Jasons (father and son) and by the change of the idiot's name from Maury to Benjamin. While pointing to inbreeding and degeneracy in the Compson family, these confusions refer more generally to the precious status of the self. Name confusion leads to identity confusion. Although Faulkner's characters preserve recognizable features, the device tends to blur the boundaries between them. What is at stake here is the very concept of *character* and its function in the novel.

takes *caddie* for the name of his beloved sister, and also, ironically, to
the reader, who at this point realizes that the setting is a golf course but
is not yet in a position to understand what *caddie* evokes in Benjy's mind
or why it makes him moan with grief. Like most openings in fiction, the
golf course scene establishes the rules of the game to be played by the
readers. By exploiting from the outset the polysemy of words, Faulkner
disorients the reader, frustrates his expectations, and alerts him to the
trickeries and duplicities of language, as if to warn him that the world
he is about to enter is not *his* world. The words used in Benjy's monologue may be simple, but their familiar surfaces soon turn out to be
extremely deceptive. We must learn the alphabet and grammar of his
idiolect before we can begin to discover what his fumbling speech is all
about.

Words are an inexhaustible source of ambiguities and confusions, so
that the communication they permit is always liable to misapprehen-
sions. Words are signs everyone assembles in transitory patterns and fills
with private significances that often make sense for him alone. What
caddie means for the golfers differs from what it means for Benjy; what
it means for Benjy differs from what it means for us. Yet in its active
emptiness and extreme plasticity, language possesses formidable powers,
and the random utterance of two syllables is enough to arouse Benjy's
anguish and grief.

Caddy is just a name, or the deceptive echo of a name. On the day
when the novel begins—April 7, 1928—the person to whom it refers has
been missing from the Compson family for many years. Benjy's moaning points at once to an absence, which the perception of anything however remotely related to his lost sister instantly quickens and thickens in
his vacant mind. To Benjy, Caddy is the nearest of absences. His memory has no memories. He cannot remember, nor can he forget. For him
it is as though Caddy had only departed a few seconds ago: her trace is
forever fresh, and the merest sensation lends her absence agonizing
immediacy. In surprisingly similar ways, Caddy also haunts her brother
Quentin, holding him in her spell, leaving him no rest and no escape
except in death. And even to Jason, for all his declared indifference and
contempt, she will be a festering wound.

Yet at the same time—precisely because she is nothing but a haunting
memory—Caddy remains to the end an elusive figure, not unlike Proust's
"creatures of flight." She is the presence of what is not there, the imperious call of absence, and it is from her tantalizing remoteness that she
holds her uncanny power over those she has left.

All the scenes of the past that come to beset memory bring her closer
and remove her further away. Of Caddy nothing remains but a series of
snapshots, vivid and unreal, in which her fleeting image is forever
fixed:

Only she was running already when I heard it. In the mirror she was
running before I knew what it was. That quick, her train caught up
over her arm she ran out of the mirror like a cloud, her veil swirling
in long glints her heels brittle and fast clutching her dress onto her
shoulder with the other hand, running out of the mirror. . . .(92)
[52]

Barely glimpsed, Caddy the (no longer "unravish'd") bride at once vanishes, and all that a glance could grasp was a silent rush reflected in a
mirror. What lingers in the memory is at best the reflection of a reflection.

Or consider this other obsessive image of the lost sister, likewise linked
to an event that Quentin cannot forget, the loss of her virginity: Caddy
no longer caught running away, but immobilized in the silent sudden-
ness of her appearance: *"One minute she was standing in the door"* (91)
[51].[6] Whether Caddy's silhouette is fleetingly reflected in a mirror or
emerges unexpectedly in the doorway, there is each time the same disturbing oscillation between absence and presence, the same paradoxical
sense of receding proximity or close remoteness.

Caddy is associated time and again with the immaterial and the
impalpable: reflections (74, 87, 92, 171) [31, 44, 52, 94], shadows
(92, 178) [51–52, 98], moonlight (92) [51], a cloud (92) [51], a breath
(171) [94], "a long veil like shining wind" (45) [25]. Caddy's evanescence
in space constantly parallels her inaccessibility in time. Not that she is
ever etherealized into a conventionally "poetic" creature. But insofar as
she must remain the evasive object of desire and memory, she can be
approached and apprehended only in oblique ways. Caddy cannot be
described; she can only be *circumscribed*, conjured up through the
suggestive powers of tropes. A realistic rendering of the character is out
of the question. Only the ruses and indirections of poetic discourse can
do justice to the burning absence which Caddy "embodies" in the novel.

Literally nowhere, Caddy is metaphorically everywhere. Her presence / absence becomes diffused all over the world, pointing, like so many
feminine figures of Faulkner's earlier and later work, to an elemental
complicity between Woman and the immemorial Earth. Her swiftness
and lightness relate her to the wind; her vital warmth to "the bright,
smooth shapes" of fire (65) [37]; her muddy drawers and treelike odor[7]
to the fecundity and foulness of the land. Yet above all Caddy is the

6. The importance of this image and of the scene it heralds is confirmed by the manuscript.
Originally section 2 started thus: "One minute she was standing there. The next Benjy was yelling
and pulling at her. They went down the hall to the bathroom and stopped there, Caddy backed
against the door. . . ." This page of the manuscript is reproduced in James B. Meriwether, *The
Literary Career of William Faulkner: A Bibliographical Study* (Princeton, N.J.: Princeton University Library, 1961), illustration II.
7. The reversible girl = tree metaphor can be traced back to Faulkner's earliest work: in *The Marble Faun* poplars are compared to "slender girls"; girls are likened to trees in *The Marionettes* as
well as in *Soldiers' Pay* and *Mosquitoes*.

most enticing and most pathetic of Faulkner's nymphs. In the entire novel there is scarcely a scene in which Caddy does not appear in close conjunction with *water*. It is in the creek branch near the Compson house that she wets her dress and drawers on the day of Damuddy's death (19–21) [11–12]; it is in the same branch that Quentin and Caddy wash off the stinking mud of the pig trough after the Natalie incident (158) [85]; and it is there again that Quentin finds his sister, sitting in the water, one summer evening, after the family has discovered her affair with Dalton Ames (171) [93]. Lastly, in the third section, Jason remembers her standing over her father's grave in a drenching rain (232) [127]. Throughout the novel, water is Caddy's element, and like Caddy herself it is drawn into an extremely ambiguous symbolic pattern. In the branch scenes it is primarily the lustral water of purification rituals, and it would be easy to supply further illustrations of its cleansing function: Caddy, at fourteen, washing off the perfume to quiet Benjy (48) [27]; Caddy, washing her mouth after kissing Charlie in the swing (55) [31]; and, finally, Benjy pulling at his sister's dress, dragging her into the bathroom after the loss of her virginity (78–79) [44]. After these ritual ablutions, Caddy "smells like trees" again, except in the last scene where Benjy keeps on crying even after Caddy has bathed herself.

Water, however, is not only a symbol of purity. If it possesses a restorative power, at least in the eyes of the novels' characters, and if Faulkner at times suggests its function in Christian baptism (it rains on the night Benjy's name is changed), there are also many intimations of its erotic quality. Bathing, in particular, seems to prompt a kind of soft, sensuous, almost sensual intimacy between water and flesh, and to prurient eyes the spectable of this tender complicity may become both a scandal and a temptation. In the insidious caress of water, in the way it reveals the body in its embrace, there is something all but immodest which, even in the early childhood scene at the branch, disturbs and alarms young Quentin. For him, who then begins to act as a guardian of Caddy's "honor," the sight of the drenched dress clinging to his sister's body is no longer an innocent spectacle. And when he slaps her for having undressed, he introduces by this very gesture the first suspicion of evil into a hitherto intact childhood world.

In Quentin's reminiscences and reveries, flesh and sex are repeatedly linked to suggestions of dampness and fluidity, and as the hour of his death draws nearer, it almost seems as if the waters were slowly rising, submerging his mind and memory, bringing him ever closer to the instant of his drowning. Thus, in the long breathless memory sequence in which he relives his poignant encounter with Caddy at the branch and his subsequent meeting with Dalton Ames near the bridge (171–87) [94–104], water saturates the whole atmosphere with a silent drizzle. Quentin inhales the smell of the rain, breathes in the scene of honeysuckle wafted on the humid warmth of twilight. And out of all this mugginess emerges the body of his nymph-sister—water made flesh:

> I ran down the hill in that vacuum of crickets like a breath travel-ling across a mirror she was lying in the water her head on the sand spit the water flowing about her hips there was a little more light in the water her skirt half saturated flopped along her flanks to the waters motion in heavy ripples going nowhere renewed themselves of their own movement I stood on the bank I could smell the honeysuckle on the water gap the air seemed to drizzle with honey-suckle and with the rasping of crickets a substance you could feel on the flesh. (171–72) [94]

Once more woman's body—"her hips," "her flanks"—is associated with running water, and as Quentin watches his sister lying there, he cannot help thinking back to the day long past when she had soiled her dress and drawers: "do you remember the day damuddy died when you sat down in the water in your drawers" (174) [96]. Quentin himself is aware of the symbolic relationship between the two scenes; in retrospect the childhood episode acquires a premonitory meaning, Caddy's muddy drawers becoming an emblem of her defilement, of what Quentin con-siders to be an indelible stain on her honor: her fall from sexual inno-cence. This irremediable loss is the focal point of Quentin's obsession, an obsession eagerly feeding on every sense impression: the sight of flow-ing water, the smell of rain and honeysuckle, the chirp of crickets, shad-ows, warmth, moisture, everything melts into "a substance you could feel on the flesh." Quentin's obsession, as described here, is by no means the abstract mania for which it has been all too often mistaken by critics. Experienced at first in the sultry profusion of immedite sensations, the traumatic shock is relived by Quentin's memory with hallucinatory intensity.

There is no Proustian reunion, for Faulkner's hero. Caddy risen out of the past through the sortileges of memory is not Caddy recaptured. Memory only serves to exacerbate a sense of loss. The past is recollected in fever and pain, not in tranquillity, and the camera obscura of memory turns out to be a torture chamber. It is never a shelter; happy memories have no place in it. As far back as it can reach, Quentin's memory encounters a Caddy *already* lost: as if she had resented her brother's jealous vigilance from the outset and were impatient to flee from the prison of innocence in which he would forever keep her, she is always seen rebelling against his demands, always on the point of running away. In this respect, the scene of the muddy drawers—one of the earliest among the childhood incidents recalled in his monologue—is equally prophetic: it marks the beginning of the ineluctable movement that is to separate him from his sister. From this childhood scene to Caddy's wedding, nearly all the fragments of the past that erupt in Quentin's mind are related to Caddy's "betrayal," and each of his painful memories reenacts one moment in the process of her desertion.

Presence in absence, nearness in distance, nothing perhaps better sums up the paradox of Quentin's haunted memory than *odor*. A subtle emanation from things and beings, odor, as Sartre writes, is "a disembodied body, vaporized, remaining entire in itself, yet turned into volatile essence."[8] Like memory, it is a diffuse presence, a felt absence, a tantalizing intimation. Like symbols, it acts by indirection; to the extent that it always has the power to evoke something other than itself, to point an absence, one might consider it a "natural" metaphor. Small wonder, then, that the fragrance of *honeysuckle* is the most pregnant and most poignant symbol in the Quentin section.

Quentin associates Caddy with the odor of honeysuckle, just as Benjy associated with her with the smell of trees. But whereas in the first section "smelled like trees" functions as an index of Caddy's sexual innocence and vanishes as soon as the latter is compromised (see, for example, the perfume incident, 48–49) [27], the meaning of honeysuckle in Quentin's monologue changes as Caddy changes, and its scent is irremediably corrupted when it comes to reek in his nostrils as the smell of her sex and sin. It is noteworthy that "honeysuckle," which occurs about thirty times in section 2, is nowhere as frequent as in the scene immediately following Quentin's discovery of his sister's loss of virginity (171–87) [94–104]: the scent of honeysuckle then becomes the pivot in a shifting complex of sense impressions. After blending into the uncertain grayness of twilight (108) [53], it combines with the humidity of the atmosphere (172) [95], "coming up in damp waves" (177) [98] or drizzling like the rain (177) [98]. Through the cross-play of synesthesia, honeysuckle is made to encompass and condense the entire field of sensory experience: something at once smelled, seen, and felt, it suffuses the whole scene. Yet, while metamorphosing and expanding across space, the smell also seems to flow back to Caddy as to its source, and Quentin refers to it as though it were a carnal secretion on the surface of her skin: "the smell of honeysuckle upon her face and throat" (169) [93]; "it was on her face and throat like paint" (173) [95]. Quentin comes to resent the cloying odor as a rank indiscretion, an almost obscene exuding of the innermost secrets of the flesh. Associated with Caddy's lovemaking in the swing by the cedars and eventually equated with Caddy herself, it stands in his mind for "the bittersweet mystery of sisterly sex"[9] as well as the unbearable scandal of its violation. Quickening his obsession, it becomes the very emblem of his anguish and torment: "after the honeysuckle got all mixed up in it the whole thing came to symbolize night

8. Jean-Paul Sartre, *Baudelaire* (Paris: Gallimard, 1947), p. 201. My translation.
9. The phrase is from Harry M. Campbell and Ruel E. Foster, *William Faulkner: A Critical Appraisal* (Norman: University of Oklahoma Press, 1951), p. 54.

and unrest" (194) [107]. In his confrontation with Caddy about Dalton
Ames, his sister reminds him that he once liked the smell (176) [98];
now he hates it, cursing "that damn honeysuckle" (171) [94]. So hateful
has it become to him that it even oppresses him physically, making him
gasp for breath: "I had to pant to get any air at all out of that thick grey
honeysuckle" (173) [95]. The sweet "honey" of sisterhood, which Quentin so avidly "suckled" in his childish greed, has thickened into a suffocating substance and now has the bitter taste of loss.

Trees, water, twilight, honeysuckle—all the nature imagery related to
Caddy, so far from calling attention to itself as symbolic, seems to grow
out of the soil of subjective experience while being at the same time
inextricably bound up with the sensible world. It never hardens into the
fixed patterns of allegory; its manifold symbolism originates in the dynamic
exchanges between a self and its environment. If some of these images
run through several sections, they can never be separated from the sin-
gular voice in whose discourse they occur: reflecting both transient moods
and abiding obsessions, they belong to the shifting landscapes of individual minds.

Yet the focal ambiguity to which all these images invariably refer is
that of Caddy herself. For Caddy exists only in the memories of her
brothers, and if we come to know what she represents for and means to
Benjy, Quentin, and Jason, we never discover what she actually is. Hence
her contradictory faces: in turn sister and mother, virgin and whore,
angel and demon, she at once embodies fecundity and foulness, the
nostalgia for innocence and the call to corruption, the promise of life
and the vertigo of death. She is what woman has always been for men:
the figure par excellence of the Other, a blank screen onto which to
project their desires and their fears, their love and their hate. And insofar
as this Other is a myth and a mirage, a mere fantasy of the self, it is
bound to be a perpetual deceit and an endless source of disappointment.
Caddy, to borrow a phrase from Paul Claudel, is "the promise that cannot be kept, and her grace consists in nothing else." [1]

Even so, she is more than the sum of these fantasy images. Faulkner's
triumph in creating Caddy is that her figure eventually transcends the
abstract categories and rigid patterns in which her brothers attempt to
imprison her, just as she escapes any facile sentimentalizing or demon-
izing on the author's part. Not that the reader is enabled to infer a "true"
picture of Caddy from the information he is given in the novel. There
is little doubt, of course, that she possesses the vitality, the courage, the
capacity for love and compassion which her self-centered brothers and
parents so sadly lack. [2] It is quite obvious, too, that she is both the tragic

1. Paul Claudel, *La Ville*, 2d ed. (Paris: Mercure de France, 1920), p. 307.
2. For a discussion of Caddy in psychological and moral terms, see Catherine B. Baum, " 'The
Beautiful One': Caddy Compson as Heroine of *The Sound and the Fury*," *Modern Fiction Studies*, 13 (Spring 1967), 33–44; Eileen Gregory, "Caddy Compson's World," *Merrill Studies in The*

victim of her family and the unwitting agent of its doom. But to focus exclusively on Caddy's assumed psychology or to dwell at length on her moral significance is to miss the point. Caddy was elusive to her creator; so she is to her brothers in the novel, and so she must remain to the reader. She cannot be assessed according to the same criteria as the other characters, for she belongs in the last resort to another space, to what might be called the novel's utopia. "The true life is absent," Rimbaud wrote. Caddy is a pathetic emblem of that desired other life, while her fate poignantly confirms its impossibility in a world of alienation and disease.

Henry James thought that "a story-teller who aims at anything more than a fleeting success has no right to tell an ugly story unless he knows its beautiful counterpart."[3] The story of the Compsons is indeed "an ugly story"; Caddy, the daughter and sister of the imagination, the figure projected by "the heart's desire," is "its beautiful counterpart." Let us remember, however, that from the very beginning she was conceived of as a beautiful *and* tragic little girl. Caddy is a dream of beauty wasted and destroyed. Her presence / absence at the center and periphery of the novel signals the unfulfillment of the writer's desire as well as the inescapable incompletion of his work. Caddy's beauty is the beauty of failure.

PHILIP M. WEINSTEIN

"If I Could Say Mother": Construing the Unsayable About Faulknerian Maternity†

My title sounds insistently psychoanalytic, promising to uncover the covered-up, to find the key that will unlock the mystery and reveal its hitherto concealed treasure. This game of penetrating / mastering is itself distinctly phallic; there must be a better way to pursue the mother. I concede at the outset that I cannot say the Unsayable about Faulknerian maternity, that my argument bears most directly on the brilliantly disturbed novels between *Flags in the Dust* and *Light in August*, and that the text I shall examine at length—the source of the quotation in the title—is *The Sound and the Fury*. Faulkner's rendering of Mrs. Compson is, within the representational economy of that novel, uniquely punitive. I intend to identify the discursive model that underlies that

Sound and the Fury, compiled by James B. Meriwether (Columbus, Ohio: Charles E. Merrill, 1970), pp. 89–101.
3. Henry James, *Notes and Reviews* (Cambridge, Mass.: Dunster House, 1921), p. 226.
† From *Faulkner's Subject: A Cosmos No One Owns* (Cambridge and New York: Cambridge University Press, 1992), 29–41.

rendering, then to reconceive the model, drawing on some contemporary feminist criticism, and finally return to Mrs. Compson. At the end I shall suggest ways in which Faulkner's texts of this troubled period are trying to say Mother and how they are succeeding.[1]

"If I could say Mother" recurs twice in Quentin's section of *The Sound and the Fury*, and in each case the phrase arises out of the memory of an April 1910 conversation between Herbert Head and Mrs. Compson:

> What a pity you had no brother or sister *No sister no sister had no sister*. Dont ask Quentin he and Mr Compson both feel a little insulted when I am strong enough to come down to the table I am going on nerve now I'll pay for it after it's all over and you have taken my little daughter away from me *My little sister had no. If I could say Mother. Mother*
>
> Unless I do what I am tempted to and take you instead I don't think Mr Compson could overtake the car.
>
> Ah Herbert Candace do you hear that *She wouldn't look at me soft stubborn jaw-angle not back-looking* You needn't be jealous though it's just an old woman he's flattering a grown married daughter I cant believe it.
>
> Nonsense you look like a girl you are lots younger than Candace color in your cheeks like a girl *A face reproachful tearful an odor of camphor and of tears a voice weeping steadily and softly beyond the twilit door the twilight-colored smell of honeysuckle.*[2]

In the second passage, near the end of Quentin's section, the smell of gasoline on his shirt reevokes this same scene of Herbert and the car, and it concludes with "*if I'd just had a mother so I could say Mother Mother*" (197) [109].

Quentin's arresting phrase of abandonment is embedded, both times, in the context of Mrs. Compson's own fantasy return of adolescence. As she flirts with Herbert, drawing on the social model she used to know, that of the Southern belle, her son registers her maternal absence from his life. "Color in your cheeks like a girl *A face reproachful tearful an odor of camphor and of tears*": these are the only roles Mrs. Compson can play—premarital coquetry or postmaternal grief. Her abandonment of her children emerges here as saturated in the rituals and assumptions of her own virginal past. Between her childless adolescence and her child-complicated middle age no other viable script has become available to her. Between virginal flirtation and postmaternal complaint Mrs. Compson literally has nothing else to say.

As though to emphasize the alienation of her married state, the text

1. I want to express here a general indebtedness to my colleague Abbe Blum, who made my path through contemporary feminist criticism more manageable.
2. *The Sound and the Fury: The Corrected Text* (New York: Random House, 1987), 108 [60–61]. All page references in the text are to this edition. Those in brackets are to this Norton Critical Edition [*Editor*].

rarely pairs her with her husband. Faulkner often has Benjy's first memories of Mrs. Compson join her instead with Uncle Maury. The novel
signals recurrently that the man most on her mind, the man she uses as
a shield between herself and her husband, is Uncle Maury. In this textual sense he vies with Mr. Compson for the position of husband. (One
might argue that her textual husband is her son Jason, with whom she
maintains a peculiarly intense relationship. In this regard they echo Gerald Bland and his mother, also an oddly incestuous pairing in which the
titular husband has been conveniently removed.)[3] In either case Mr.
Compson himself is arguably the third male in his wife's life. Appearing
most saliently in Quentin's chapter, he registers textually more as his
son's father than as his wife's husband.

Her brother Maury seems to serve as her way of remaining a Bascomb, of refusing to consummate her entry into Compsonhood. (My
discovery at the Faulkner and Yoknapatawpha Conference in 1986 that
Faulkner's family pronounces Maury as Murry, the name of Faulkner's
father, may strengthen this fantasy conflation of the mother's brother
with the mother's husband.)[4] Incestuous pairings thus suggest themselves at the parental level as well, and Mrs. Compson's preference for
her brother leads with compelling logic to Quentin's preference for his
sister. Refusing to be a wife, Caroline Bascomb refuses to be a mother,
and Caddy must therefore—and fatally—play that role for her brothers.

The picture of Mrs. Compson that emerges is of a woman whose life
ceased to be narratable after her entry into marriage and its sexual consequences. She has no stories to tell that can accommodate in a positive
way even a grain of her postconsummation experience. Her entry into
mature sexuality is swiftly followed by her exit. Having delivered her
children, she takes to her bed—the childbed, not the marriage bed—
acting like a child, exacting from her children the sustenance she should
be offering them.[5]

She speaks obsessively of the rules she learned before marriage, and
of her refusal to learn anything different since:

> "Yes," Mother says. "I suppose women who stay shut up like I
> do have no idea what goes on in this town."
> "Yes," I [Jason] says, "They don't."
> "My life has been so different from that." Mother says. "Thank
> God I dont know about such wickedness. I dont even want to know
> about it. I'm not like most people." (299) [162]

3. André Bleikasten, *The Most Splendid Failure: Faulkner's "The Sound and the Fury"* (Bloomington: Indiana University Press, 1976), briefly notes this point.
4. I am indebted to conversations with James Hinkle for this information.
5. See Catherine Clément and Helene Cixous, *The Newly Born Woman*, trans. Betsy Wing
(Minneapolis: University of Minnesota Press, 1986), 39, for a portrait of the hysteric that captures
succinctly the economy of desire transformed into suffering that characterizes Mrs. Compson's
behavior: "The hysteric . . . tries to signify eros through all the possible forms of anesthesia. . . .
A witch in reverse, turned back within herself, she has put all her eroticizing into internal pain."

I am still a virgin, her camphor and tears keep saying: I don't know anything about checks, about report cards, about business deals, about what girls do on the street or within their own bedrooms. Weeping and mourning, ritually heading for the cemetery throughout the novel, she registers her marital and maternal experience as a curse that makes a mockery of all her training: "when I was a girl I was unfortunate I was only a Bascomb I was taught that there is no halfway ground that a woman is either a lady or not" (118) [66].

This rigid either-or posture indicates that it is Mrs. Compson, not her husband, who is possessed by the binarisms of the Symbolic order—but possessed by them as only someone locked into Imaginary identifications and repudiations can be. Despite John Irwin and other critics who fault Mr. Compson for not upholding paternal authority, his considerable appeal resides in his shrewd perception that a Symbolic order based upon traditional notions of morality and virginity is bankrupt, that it is an invented script. He relates to this order as a produced structure, not an inalterable essence, whereas his wife would live it as the Real itself. She thus incarnates what Roland Barthes terms the cultural code, the already known: "If we collect all such knowledge, all such vulgarisms, we create a monster, and this monster is ideology," Barthes writes. Mrs. Compson is such an ideological monster.[6]

We touch here upon the source of her failure as a mother. Deformed by her social training—a training shaped by class and race to the requirements of virginity—she abandons her own flesh and blood upon the loss of that virginity. She has outlived her image of herself. Simultaneously rushing forward to death and backward to childhood, she repeats herself and takes to black. The novel's attack upon her seems to be this: mothers are meant to nourish their young; their trucking with (male-authored) ideological scripts can only lead to overlectured and undernurtured off-spring.[7]

This paradigm of ideological insistences perverting maternal function may shed light on that strange scene in which Jason wrestles with his mother over the key to Quentin's room. Noel Polk has pointed to the repression wrought into this image of the key-laden woman but there is a sexual dimension to the assault as well. Faulkner takes a full page to show us Jason all over his mother, "pawing" at her skirt, while she resists

6. Roland Barthes, S/Z, trans. Richard Miller (New York: Hill and Wang, 1974), 97. John Irwin develops this reading of Mr. Compson throughout *Doubling and Incest/Repetition and Revenge: A Speculative Reading of Faulkner* (Baltimore: John Hopkins University Press, 1975); see especially 67, 75, 110–13, and 120–22. Bleikasten, *The Most Splendid Failure*, p. 113, also reads the father in terms of his failure as a lawgiver.
7. This is one of the reasons that Lena Grove (not to mention Dewey Dell or Eula Varner) can be rendered with such affection: she does not meddle in the Symbolic order. Her unflappable comments about a family needing to be together "when a chap comes" (*Light in August* 18) are tonally the reverse of Mrs. Compson's outraged protestations of the flouted system. On Noel Polk cited below, see "The Dungeon Was Mother Herself: William Faulkner: 1927–1931," in Doreen Fowler and Ann J. Abadie, eds, *New Directions in Faulkner Studies: Faulkner and Yoknapataw-pha, 1983* (Jackson: University Press of Mississippi,1984), 61–93.

the attack. Finally, " 'Give me the key, you old fool!' Jason cried suddenly. From her pocket he tugged a huge bunch of rusted keys on an
iron ring like a mediaeval jailer's" (325) [175]. Pawed at, pressed, her
invaded pocket reveals its cache of hideous keys like a grotesque parody
of the children who should instead have come forth from her womb.
And indeed her womb is terrifying—a space imaged here as rusted, iron,
a jailor's fortress, as was also earlier implied by Quentin's image of the
dark place in which he was imprisoned: "The dungeon was Mother herself" (198) [109].

No child escapes from this dungeon, and insofar as the dungeon is a
womb, no child gets fully born. In place of nourishment she feeds her
children repressive ideology, and they sicken on it. From Mrs. Compson's failure to mother we move through her daughter Caddy's failure to
mother and finally, reductively, into *her* daughter Quentin's refusal to
conceive. "Agnes Mabel Becky," the phrase spoken by the man in the
red tie upon seeing that shiny container connected with Quentin, is the
term used half a century ago in the South for a three-pack of condoms.[8]
Mrs. Compson's inability to nourish here literalizes into her granddaughter's well-earned decision to seal off the reproductive functions of
her womb.

Noel Polk helps us to generalize the model that Mrs. Compson fails
abysmally to uphold. He writes of Faulkner's mothers of this period as
"almost invariably, horrible people," failing to meet "even minimal
standards of human decency, much less . . . the ideal of mother love as
the epitome of selfless, unwavering care and concern." "Selfless, unwavering care and concern": this is exactly what these mothers lack. It is
also what they are posited by the culture as *supposed to possess*, and what
they are excoriated for not possessing. Freud writes in his study of Leon-
ardo: "A mother's love for the infant she suckles and cares for is something far more profound than her later affection for the growing child.
It is in the nature of a completely satisfying love-relation." Freud assumes,
as does Faulkner, that, unlike fathers (unlike all other human beings),
mothers enjoy "a completely satisfying love-relation." They *naturally*
fulfill their identity in this bond with the infant. Mothers are defined as
just those creatures whose subjective needs are supremely realized through
the act of nurturing their own offspring.

Freed from ideology themselves, reservoirs of milk and loving kind-
ness, mothers are meant to be sacred servants. *The Sound and the Fury*
hammers this point home in the fourth chapter through the massive
comparison, move for move, of Mrs. Compson with Dilsey, the latter a
perfect instance of how mothers should care for offspring. And what is

8. Paul Gaston, professor of history at the University of Virginia, supplied me with this enlightening bit of information.

Dilsey's model if not the Virgin Mary herself, celebrated in the Reverend Shegog's sermon as Jesus' inexhaustibly loving "mammy [who] suffered de glory en de pangs," who "helt him at de nightfall, whilst de angels singing him to sleep," and who filled heaven with "de weepin en de lamentation" (342) [184] at his death? This model of what a mother is supposed to do resonates throughout not just *The Sound and the Fury* but countless narratives in Western culture.

Such a model assumes that the Word—the realm of spirit, of the Symbolic—is articulated through a male voice, announcing the Kingdom of Heaven. Mary serves as the bodily carrier of the spirit. Her function is to nurse her infant son and to bemoan his tragic death. She emerges thus—in her role as the suffering mother, the ubiquitous Pietà of Western art—as a register for the emotional loss suffered through Christ's crucifixion. She herself has no new word to utter, but her natural care for her child is the precondition for his divine utterance in which he reveals his kinship with his father.

If we secularize this text, we arrive at something like the following. The domain of the father is the domain of the Spirit, of all Symbolic activities that make up culture and that achieve articulation in the medium of language. This domain takes the inherently binary form of language, an endless series of constructed oppositions that constitute the (male) paradigm of meaning itself. The domain of the mother, on the other hand, is the domain of the unfissured, prelinguistic body. Her function is so to nourish the child that he (the model for the child is implicitly male) becomes somatically prepared for the vertigo and alienation that accompany entry into the Symbolic order of the father. In other words, the time of bonding exists as a prelinguistic, prelogical plenitude in which mother and child are each other, in which self and world, self and other, interpenetrate. If successful, this quasi-magical bonding bequeathes to the child somatic sufficiency—bodily grounding—that enables him to sustain his later and lifelong encounter with the world outside himself, and eventually to deliver his word within that world.

The gender distinctions essential to this paradigm are common to the discourses of both Christianity and psychoanalysis. The mother is simultaneously sacred and subservient, the enabler but not the speaker of the word. If we return to Faulkner with this script in mind, we can better place the anger toward the mother that suffuses the early novels. In those novels the mother fails at her sacred bodily task. Charged with preoedipal responsibilities, she not only neglects these but barges into the terrain of the law, often in its most outdated and repressive forms. The unnourished child therefore emerges into the world too soon. He has no somatic grounding that might hold the imprint of the culture's proliferating codes, consequently no basis for stabilizing the "*maelstrom of unbearable real-*

ity."[9] Thus we get Benjy, Quentin, Darl, Vardaman, and Joe Christmas: boy children unsure of the integrity of their own bodies, dizzyingly vulnerable to sensory overload, unable to maintain their identity within boundaries that might stabilize the relations between past and present, there and here, self and other, male and female, child and parent, brother and sister, white and black.

French and American feminists seem to agree that this male-scripted model of the nonspeaking mother is disabling rather than empowering. In "Stabat Mater" Julia Kristeva critically explores the myth of the Virgin Mary. Focusing on the iconography of breast, ears, and tears, Kristeva reads the Virgin as a figure of speechless succor. One of Kristeva's commentators, Mary Jacobus, writes:

> The function of the Virgin Mother in Western symbolic economy (according to Kristeva) is to provide an anchor for the nonverbal and for modes of signification closer to primary processes. In the face of the fascinated fear of the powerlessness of language which sustains all belief, the Mother is a necessary pendant to the Word in Christian theology—just as the fantasized preverbal mother is a means of attempting to heal the split in language, providing an image of individual signs, plenitude, and imaginary fulness.[1]

This subtext of the ideal mother as sanctuary, as preverbal plenitude, as pendant to the word and yet also a preserve against its possible emptiness, exerts a powerful punitive influence upon the representation of women in secular texts, including (as we have seen) Faulkner's texts. Kristeva, for her part, is in the difficult position of seeking to maintain the centrality of the pre-oedipal bonding without fetishizing it or making it immune to stress. Jacobus goes on to say that "for Kristeva, division is the condition of all signifying processes. No preoedipal language, no maternal discourse, can be free of this split." Kristeva enacts this split in her essay by inserting another discourse (this one fragmented, impulsive, lyrically focused on childbirth, breastfeeding, and body parts—what she calls the "semiotic") within the surrounding "Symbolic" portion of her text.[2]

9. William Faulkner, "*Absalom, Absalom!*": *The Corrected Text* (New York: Random House, 1986), 186.
1. Mary Jacobus, "Dora and the Pregnant Madonna," in *Reading Women: Essays in Feminist Criticism* (New York: Columbia University Press, 1986), 137–93.
2. Kristeva describes the mother's extraordinary experience of one-in-two / two-in-one in terms that illuminate Faulkner's fear of and fascination with this figure: "For a mother . . . the arbitrariness that is the other (the child) goes without saying. For her the impossible is like this: it becomes one with the implacable. The other is inevitable, she seems to say, make a God of him if you like; he won't be any less natural if you do, for this other still comes from me, which is in any case not me but an endless flux of germinations. . . . This maternal quietude, more stubborn even than philosophical doubt . . . eats away at the omnipotence of the symbolic. . . . Such an attitude can be frightening if one stops to think that it may destroy everything that is specific and irreducible in the other, the child; this form of maternal love can become a straitjacket, stifling any deviant individuality. But it can also serve the speaking subject as a refuge when his symbolic carapace shatters to reveal that jagged crest where biology transpierces speech: I am thinking of moments of illness, of sexual–intellectual–physical passion, death" ("Mater" 117–18).

The entry of the "semiotic" into the discourse of maternity would both restore the place of the maternal body within language itself and announce that the mother's desire is, like all desire, conflicted and tension-filled, rather than speechlessly satisfied through the suckling of her son. Thus Kristeva would revise the male-coded scripting of maternal desire—what she punningly calls "pèreversion." These feminist revisions (in their insistence that women's desire exceeds malescripts for maternity, that women's desire must find a way into language, that maternity must be demythologized and approached from the perspective of the mother herself) allow us to see how gender biases in that previous script polarize Faulkner's representational strategies.

Let us now return to Mrs. Compson. What we see is a portrait of maternity crazily arrested in the "virginal" phase of the Virgin Mary model. Of the three divine components—succor, silence, and virginity—she has betrayed the two that Faulkner values and retained the one that he deconstructs. The ideal silent nourisher has degenerated into a nonnourishing nonstop talker. More, the language that pours out of her is wholly male-scripted; she speaks the defective Symbolic order at its most repressive.

Her white middle-class culture insists not merely that her desire be contained within mothering purposes. Rather, given the American South of the early twentieth century with its array of racial phobias and its constraining model of white womanhood, her desire is virtually taboo.[3] Enjoined to marry and procreate, Mrs. Compson is also enjoined to abhor her status as an incarnate creature replete with sexual organs. She may now appear to us more clearly what she is—a socially constructed figure—taught by her culture in such a way as to be unable to survive her own sexual initiation. The only story she has learned is a virginal one, and on this she dwells, within this she hides from the unbearable facts of her own parturition: a son whose idiocy indicts the very fertilization of egg by sperm; a daughter whose burgeoning sexuality promises, at best, the same disaster she has undergone; another son whose needs she did not (could not) assuage, and who punished her for it by committing suicide; and a third son whose fantasy name of Bascomb assures her that he is hers alone: no Compson seed in him, she is still a virgin.

Why has her adoption of the virginal script kept her from also participating in the nurturance script? Why does the tension (always latent)

---

3. Joel Kovel's *White Racism: A Psychohistory* (New York: Random House, 1970) attempts to chart psychoanalytically this intersection of latent racial phobias and overt gender models, as these operate within American black-white relations. Winthrop Jordan's authoritatve *White over Black: American Attitudes Toward the Negro, 1550–1812* (Chapel Hill: University of North Carolina Press, 1968) attends as well to the fantasy structures subtending American racism, while James Snead's *Figures of Division: William Faulkner's Major Novels* (New York: Methuen, 1986) usefully places the issue of racial polarization within the larger problematic of Western philosophy's falsely polarizing yet inescapable binarisms.

between these two "stories" become so inflamed in Faulkner's narratives? To answer this, we might look at Faulkner's representation of the female body in *The Sound and the Fury*. In so doing we discover that the other story for Mrs. Compson, the nurturance story, is simply intolerable in its fetishistic focus on the body and its linkage of fecundity with filth. The polarization of these two narratives reveals the suffocating binarism of the culture's texts of female maturation:

> Because women so delicate so mysterious Father said. Delicate equilibrium of periodical filth between two moons balanced. Moons he said full and yellow as harvest moons her hips thighs. Outside outside of them always but. Yellow. Feet soles with walking like. Then know that some man that all those mysterious and imperious concealed. With all that inside of them shapes an outward suavity waiting for a touch to. Liquid putrefaction like drowned things floating like pale rubber flabbily filled getting the odor of honeysuckle all mixed up. (*SF* 147) [81]

If the virginal story presupposes a blank body (a body, as Luce Irigaray puts it, that is "pure exchange value . . . nothing but the possibility, the place, the sign of relations between men," the body that Quentin fantasizes here is unbearably full, though no less constructed through a male lens.[4] (How telling that Mr. rather than Mrs. Compson speaks to Quentin of menstruation.) This "delicate" body is more urgently imagined as huge, moonlike (moons that sway the blood tides, moons that are her hips and thighs), filled with liquid rot, spaces that you desire to enter and in which you drown. This is a disaster site. It is also a female womb. A place of periodical filth, this womb is obsessively scripted within an economy of decay: what could grow here? The mother's threat seems most to inhere in her leaky and fluctuating wetness, a female wetness that menaces all projects of male enclosure and mastery.

Luce Irigaray has written suggestively of the male hostility to fluidity ("La mécanique des fluides," in *Ce Sexe qui n'en pas un*), and Jane Gallop discusses her argument as follows: "Fluidity has its own properties. It is not an inadequacy in relation to solidity. In phallic fantasy, the solid-closed-virginal body is opened with violence; and blood flows. The fluid here signifies defloration, wound as proof of penetration, breaking and entering, property damage. . . . [But] menstrual blood is not a wound in the closure of the body; the menstrual flow ignores the distinction virgin/deflowered." Most of Faulkner's males recoil in horror from this female economy of the blood. *Sanctuary* and *Light in August* are concerned with male-induced penetrations of the body. The blood their male protagonists focus on is the blood they can make flow, the blood whose flowing signals male mastery of the object. Or it is the symbolic

4. Luce Irigaray, *Ce Sexe qui n'en est pas un* (Paris: Editions de Minuit, 1977), 181. Translation mine.

"blood" of patriarchal lineage or racial difference, not the material blood that simultaneously—and so troublingly to the male mind—carries growth and decay.[5]

A "dry" virginal script that denies desire and repudiates intercourse, a "wet" adulterate script that concedes desire and equates the fertile womb with rot and drowning: there are not other alternatives in *The Sound and the Fury*'s lexicon for constructing maternity. "I was taught that there was no halfway ground that a woman is either a lady or not" (118) [66]. In Mrs. Compson's desiccated Symbolic world, ladies and sex organs are incompatible notions. This polarization means that, here and elsewhere, Faulkner's narrative treatment of white maternity takes a schizoid form.

On one side there is the "wet" drama—always illicit, always for not-ladies—of a sexed and rebellious younger woman heading toward unsanctioned labor (Caddy, Dewey Dell, Lena, to a certain extent Temple, Charlotte, and Eula). This drama, suffused with narrative empathy, focuses intimately upon the scandal of the penetrated and / or swelling body itself. Faulkner seems mesmerized by the image of the female body escaping the propriety of its male proprietor, usually the husband / father / brother who would confine its activity within the scripts of the Symbolic order. Because that order is (and needs to be shown as) without grounding, this drama is usually narrated with understanding. But the mothers-to-be in this drama are mute; they are mainly subsumed within their own bodies. When, later (as with Temple and Eula), Faulkner does endow them with speech, they have become defenders—often tragic defenders—of the Symbolic. It seems that they cannot simultaneously break the law and speak.

On the other side, there is the "dry" retrospective drama within which are imprisoned the proper wives, the repressed older women heading toward menopause and death. Mrs. Compson, Joanna Burden in her final phase, and of course Addie Bundren—a case unto herself—come to mind.[6] In general Faulkner cannot keep his narrative eye on the *same* woman moving through all the stages of the female life cycle. (Addie and Joanna cross into and out of sexual activity at the expense, so to speak, of their lives.) Maternity is thus a sort of narrative Waterloo: an incoherent zone his fiction can lead up to and away from but which

5. Adequate consideration of this point would take more space than I can allow here. For further discussion, see chapters 2 and 4 of *Faulkner's Subject: A Cosmos No One Owns*. See also Luce Irigaray, *The Sex Which is Not One*, trans Catherine Porter and Carolyn Burke (Ithaca: Cornell University Press, 1982), esp. 83 and 93; Roland Barthes, *Roland Barthes by Roland Barthes* (New York: Farrar, Straus, and Giroux, 1977), 69; and Teresa de Lauretis, *Alice Doesn't: Feminism, Semiotics, Cinema* (Bloomington: Indiana University Press, 1984) *[Editor]*.
6. Addie Bundren is the exception to my schema, the closest Faulkner ever comes to narrating an unco-opted female's move from virginity through intercourse and maternity and child nurturing into adulthood. This move in *As I Lay Dying*, however, is rendered as anything but continuous. Addie's remarkable awareness of body and presence of mind are premised upon the spatially and temporally unplaceable scene of her protracted dying.

none of his women can traverse and still remain themselves. Is it too much to say that once his pregnant women *deliver*, they cease to be figures of empathy or desire, for he has then entered the fantasy role of their infant needing succor? In any case, the representation of maternity ruptures on this incoherence.

With these constricting representational scripts in mind, I conclude by returning to Mrs. Compson's plight. As the quotation in my title indicates, we see her—Faulkner sees her—only through the freighted and damaged lenses of her offspring. (Indeed, psychoanalytic discourse itself, and a fortiori its commentary on the mother, has centered until recently upon the [male] child in need. What treatment the mother has received has tended to come very sharply angled.) This narrative deprivation of sympathy is decisive. Yet Mrs. Compson's gestures, when attended to against the grain of the text itself, have their pathos. Her refusal to accede to the name of Compson, for example, is heavily marked as vanity or regression, though we might also see it as a desperate attempt to preserve a shred of her own identity from the marital exchange that alters her name from that of one male to that of another. (If she were a male being exchanged, if she were Joe Christmas or Charles Etienne de St. Valery Bon, we would be invited so to read her.) Behind her tyranny within the house—she who changes others' names as though in revenge for the unwanted alteration of her own—we can espy a woman with no other moves to make.

"It is our duty to shield her [your lady mother] from the crass material world as much as possible" (258) [141], Uncle Maury writes Jason: shield her while we men invest her money in the real world of business affairs. Jason, for his part, plays the check-burning ritual upon her once a month. Men know better, they are permitted to discard when necessary the unreal rhetoric of honor (the no longer valid terms of the Symbolic). Mrs. Compson may also, at rare moments, know better—"If you want me to, I will smother my pride and accept them [the checks from Caddy]" (252) [138]—but she remains imprisoned within her learned rhetoric, forced to believe she is repudiating her daughter's money. Born and brought up within defective male Symbolic scripts, she spends each day dying within those same scripts. "The dungeon was Mother herself," Quentin thinks; his mother is the jailor. Yes, she is the jailor, but she is also the jail and inmate. Alienated from the powers of her own body, deprived by male scripts of any language of access to her bodily desires, she is the prisoner of her own womb. The dungeon is not mother but motherhood.[7]

7. Mrs. Compson's body that is not her own illustrates with uncanny aptness Foucault's claim that the body, rather than being one's private sanctuary, "is the inscribed surface of events (traced by language and dissolved by ideas), the locus of a dissociated Self (adopting the illusion of a substantial unity), and a volume in perpetual disintegration. See Michel Foucault, "Nietzsche, Genealogy, and History," in *Language, Counter-Memory, Practice: Selected Essays and Inter-*

I have sought to indicate the ways in which Faulkner's representational strategies cannot say mother. Let me finish by suggesting that the fiction of this troubled period is nevertheless engaged, paradoxically, in "trying to say" Mother. "I was trying to say," Benjy tells us, and Faulkner invents an extraordinary rhetoric to convey to us the tangled torment of Benjy's "say." What American writer has refused more forcefully the blandishments of the "already said"? Although Faulkner never spoke of it as the Symbolic order, although he never thought of language as decisively marked by gender, although he would certainly have cringed at neologisms like phallogocentrism, in a certain sense he knew. He knew that language is the Symbolic, that it comes to us alienated from our speechless feeling, and that if words are to do more than be a shape to fill a lack, they must be tortuously reinvented, recombined, such that the "self" they articulate may appear in its incarnate, decentered, and insecurely gendered pathos. And he would have agreed with poststructuralists that, even in his most ambitious undertakings, he failed to make the words * * * ever cling to the earth.

What he created in his most experimental early work seems to me analogous to Kristeva's "semiotic": a use of language that gets behind the crisp and repressed male structures of the Symbolic, and that is seeking (in its gaps and incoherences) to make its way back to the mother. Radically nonjudgmental, open to the confusions of past and present, self and other, Faulkner's experimental rhetoric enacts so often (within the character, within the reader) an experience of immediate, undemarcated identification. "The process of coming unalone is terrible," thinks Dewey Dell in *As I Lay Dying*. Faulkner in his early masterpieces frees language from its conventional forms of thinking and feeling in just such a way as to articulate this terrifying collapse of ego boundaries that is common to psychosis, to discovery, and to motherhood. The regressive urge of Faulkner's work of this period—its focus on assault, on overwhelming, on the unchosen—testifies to his desire to find words for the subject's inexpressible vulnerability, its boundary-riddled plight.[8]

Identification is itself primoridally rooted in the infantile relation with the mother; perhaps this is why Freud was so wary of its capacity to erode ego boundaries.[9] One of his recent critics writes that for Freud, "Maturity (that is, *masculine* maturity) means being well-defended against one's past, which amounts to the same thing as having a strong capacity for resisting identification. . . . In effect, Freud's picture of maturity is of a

views of Michel Foucault, trans. Donald E. Bouchard and Sherry Simon (Ithaca: Cornell University Press, 1977), 113–38.
8. See *"As I Lay Dying": The Corrected Text* (New York: Random House, 1987), 56; cf. p. 160. Put too summarily, I want to argue the following: as Faulkner freed himself from his fascination with the "semiotic," as his narratorial voice took on coherence and cultural alignment, his rhetoric became increasingly predictable and his work began to lose its capacity for outrage.
9. Bleikasten has written of the relevance of Freud's "Mourning and Melancholia" to Quentin's inability to sever his "narcissistic identification with the lost object" (*Splendid* 116). In both of these accounts identification is seen as a regressive and self-damaging move.

man driven to outrun . . . identification with the body of his mother, the original unity of mother and infant."[1]

This description sounds as much like Thomas Sutpen as it sounds unlike William Faulkner. Penetrated through and through by the history of his region and his family, Faulkner outran none of it, and he invented a rhetoric unequaled in its capacity to express penetrability, the phenomenon of being wounded. The biography and the representations in the fiction give us reason to construe him as damaged by his own mother, expelled too soon, not nourished enough.[2] But if this is so, the hunger it generated was for "chanting measures beyond the need for words" (*SF* 340) [183], and the activity it inspired was an attempt to use words to get past the Symbolic itself, "to retrieve the plenitude of the origins," as Bleikasten puts it, "by remembring the . . . body of the lost, forgotten, and unforgettable mother."[3]

"There is at least one spot in every dream at which it is unplumbable," Freud writes in *The Interpretation of Dreams*, "a navel, as it were, that is its point of contact with the unknown."[4] Freud's project of male autonomy makes him insist upon mystery here, but it is possible to know what that navel connects us with. In his early dream novels, where the experiments with language are greatest and the psychic wounds least concealed, where the mother is punished representationally and yet sought after rhetorically, Faulkner made that unsettling connection.

1. Jim Swan, "Mater and Nannies: Freud's Two Mothers and the Discovery of the Oedipus Complex," *American Imago* 31 (1974): 9–10.
2. For biographical information / speculation, see David Minter, *William Faulkner: His Life and Work* (Baltimore: Johns Hopkins University Press, 1980), 1–23; and Jay Martin, " 'The Whole Burden of Man's History of His Impossible Heart's Desire': The Early Life of William Faulkner," *American Literature* 53 (1982): 607–29.
3. André Bleikasten, "In Praise of Helen," in Doreen Fowler and Ann J. Abadie, eds., *Faulkner and Women: Faulkner and Yoknapatawpha 1985* (Jackson: University Press of Mississippi, 1986), 140.
4. Sigmund Freud, "The Interpretation of Dreams," in the *Standard Edition of the Complete Psychological Works of Sigmund Freud*, ed. and trans. James Strachey, vols. 4–5 (London: Hogarth Press, 1953–1974), 4: iii.

Selected Bibliography

LETTERS

Cowley, Malcolm, ed. *The Faulkner-Cowley File: Letters and Memories, 1944–62*. New York: Viking Press, 1966.

INTERVIEWS, ESSAYS, AND SPEECHES

Meriwether, James B. *Essays, Speeches, and Public Letters*. New York: Random House, 1965.
Fant, Joseph L., and Robert Ashley, eds. *Faulkner at West Point*. New York: Random House, 1964.

CHECKLISTS AND SURVEYS OF CRITICISM

Bassett, John. *William Faulkner: An Annotated Checklist of Criticism*. New York: David Lewis, 1972.
McHaney, Thomas L. *William Faulkner: A Reference Guide*. Boston: G. K. Hall, 1976.
Meriwether, James B. "William Faulkner." In *Fifteen Modern American Authors*, edited by Jackson R. Bryer, 175–210. Durham, N.C.: Duke University Press, 1969.

SCHOLARLY AND CRITICAL STUDIES

Adams, Richard P. *Faulkner: Myth and Motion*. Princeton, N.J.: Princeton University Press, 1968.
Aiken, Conrad. "William Faulkner: The Novel as Form." *Atlantic Monthly* 164 (November 1939): 650–54. Included in *A Reviewer's ABC*, New York: Meridian Books, 1958.
Aswell, Duncan. "The Recollection and the Blood: Jason's Role in *The Sound and the Fury*," *Mississippi Quarterly* 21 (Summer, 1968): 211–18.
Backman, Melvin. *Faulkner: The Major Years. A Critical Study*. Bloomington: Indiana University Press, 1966.
Baum, Catherine B. " 'The Beautiful One': Caddy Compson as Heroine of *The Sound and the Fury*." *Modern Fiction Studies* 13 (Spring 1967): 33–44.
Blanchard, Margaret. "The Rhetoric of Communion: Voice in *The Sound and the Fury*." *American Literature* 41 (January 1970): 555–65.
Bleikasten, André. *The Most Splendid Failure: Faulkner's "The Sound and the Fury."* Bloomington: Indiana University Press, 1976.
Blöcker, Günter. "William Faulkner." In *Die Neuen Wirklichkeiten*, Berlin: Argon Verlag, 1957. Partly translated by Jacqueline Merriam in *Faulkner: A Collection of Critical Essays*, edited by Robert Penn Warren, 122–26. Englewood Cliffs, N.J.: Prentice-Hall, 1966.
Blotner, Joseph. *Faulkner: A Biography*. 2 vols. New York: Random House, 1974.
Bowling, Lawrence E. "Faulkner: Technique of *The Sound and the Fury*." *Kenyon Review* 10 (Autumn 1948): 552–66.
———. "Faulkner: The Theme of Pride in *The Sound and the Fury*." *Modern Fiction Studies* 11 (Summer 1965): 129–39.
Brodhead, Richard. "Introduction: Faulkner and the Logic of Remaking." In *Faulkner: New Perspectives*, edited by Richard H. Brodhead, 1–19. Englewood Cliffs, N.J., Prentice-Hall, 1983.
Brooks, Cleanth. "Primitivism in *The Sound and the Fury*." In *English Institute Essays 1952*, edited by Alan S. Downer, 5–28. New York: Columbia University Press, 1954.
———. "Faulkner's Vision of Good and Evil." *Massachusetts Review* 3 (Summer 1962): 692–712.

444 BIBLIOGRAPHY

Broughton, Panthea Reid. *William Faulkner: The Abstract and the Actual*. Baton Rouge: Louisiana State University Press, 1974.

Brown, Calvin. *A Glossary of Faulkner's South*. New Haven: Yale University Press, 1976.

Chase, Richard. *The American Novel and Its Tradition*. Garden City, N.Y.: Doubleday, 1956.

Coindreau, Maurice-Edgar. "Preface to *The Sound and the Fury*." Trans. George M. Reeves. *Mississippi Quarterly* 19 (Summer 1966): 107–15 (originally published in French in 1938).

Collins, Carvel. "The Interior Monologues of *The Sound and the Fury*." In *English Institute Essays*, edited by Alan S. Downer, 29–55. New York: Columbia University Press, 1954.

Cowan, Michael H., ed. *Twentieth Century Interpretations of "The Sound and the Fury."* Englewood Cliffs, N.J.: Prentice-Hall, 1968.

Duvall, John. "Faulkner's Critics and Women: The Voice of the Community." In *Faulkner and Women: Faulkner and Yoknapatawpha 1985*, edited by Doreen Fowler and Ann J. Abadie, 41–57. Jackson: University Press of Mississippi, 1986.

Faber, M. D. "Faulkner's *The Sound and the Fury*: Object Relations and Narrative Structure." *American Imago* 34 (1977): 327–50.

Gray, Richard J. *The Literature of Memory: Modern Writers of the American South*. Baltimore: Johns Hopkins University Press, 1976.

Gresset, Michel. "Psychological Aspects of Evil in *The Sound and the Fury*." *Mississippi Quarterly* 14 (Summer 1966): 143–53.

Grimwood, Michael, *Heart in Conflict: Faulkner's Struggles with Vocation*. Athens: Georgia University Press, 1987.

Gross, Beverly. "Form and Fulfillment in *The Sound and the Fury*." *Modern Language Quarterly* 24 (December 1968): 439–49.

Guerard, Albert J. *The Triumph of the Novel: Dickens, Dostovevsky, Faulkner*. New York: Oxford University Press, 1976.

Hoffman, Frederick J. *William Faulkner*. New York: Twayne, 1961.

Hoffman, Frederick, and Olga Vickery, eds. *William Faulkner: Two Decades of Criticism*. East Lansing: Michigan State University Press, 1951.

Hoffman, Frederick, and Olga Vickery, eds. *William Faulkner: Three Decades of Criticism*, East Lansing: Michigan State University Press, 1960.

Iser, Wolfgang. "Perception, Temporality, and Action as Modes of Subjectivity. William Faulkner: *The Sound and the Fury*." In *The Implied Reader: Patterns of Communication in Prose Fiction from Bunyan to Beckett*, 136–52. Baltimore and London: Johns Hopkins University Press, 1974.

Jenkins, Lee. *Faulkner and Black-White Relations: A Psychoanalytic Approach*. New York: Columbia University Press, 1981.

Kartiganer, Donald M. "Quentin Compson and Faulkner's Drama of the Generations." In *Critical Essays on William Faulkner: The Compson Family*, edited by Arthur F. Kinney. Boston: G. K. Hall, 1982.

Kaufmann, Linda S. *Discourses of Desire: Gender, Genre, and Epistolary Fictions*. Ithaca: Cornell University Press, 1986.

Kawin, Bruce F. *Faulkner and Film*. New York: Frederick Ungar, 1977.

Kenner, Hugh, "The Last Novelist." In *A Homemade World: The American Modernist Writers*, 194–221. New York: Alfred A. Knopf, 1975.

Kinney, Arthur F. *Faulkner's Narrative Poetics: Style as Vision*. Amherst: University of Massachusetts Press, 1978.

Kort, Wesley A. "Social Time in Faulkner's Fiction." *Arizona Quarterly* 37 (1981): 101–15.

Le Breton, Maurice. "Technique et Psychologie chez William Faulkner." *Etudes Anglaises* 1 (September 1937): 418–38.

Litz, Walton. "William Faulkner's Moral Vision." *Southwest Review* 37 (Summer 1952): 200–9.

Longley, John L. *The Tragic Mask: A Study of Faulkner's Heroes*. Chapel Hill: University of North Carolina Press, 1963.

Lowrey, Perrin H. "Concepts of Time in *The Sound and the Fury*." In *English Institute Essays, 1952*, edited by Alan S. Downer, 57–82. New York: Columbia University Press, 1954.

Magny, Claude-Edmonde. "Faulkner ou l'Inversion Theologique." In *L'Âge de Roman américain*. Paris: Editions du Seuil, 1948.

Malin, Irving. *William Faulkner: An Interpretation*. Stanford, Calif.: Stanford University Press, 1957.

McHaney, Thomas L. "Robinson Jeffers' 'Tamar' and *The Sound and the Fury*." *Mississippi Quarterly* 22 (Summer 1969): 261–63.

Mellard, James M. "Caliban as Prospero: Benjy and *The Sound and the Fury*." *Novel* 3 (Spring 1970): 233–48.

———. "*The Sound and the Fury*: Quentin Compson and Faulkner's 'Tragedy of Passion.' " *Studies in the Novel* 2 (1970): 61–75.

———. "Type and Archetype: Jason Compson as 'Satirist.' " *Genre* 4 (June 1971): 173–88.

Meriwether, James B. comp. *Merrill Studies in The Sound and the Fury*. Columbus, Ohio: Charles E. Merrill, 1970.

Millgate, Jane. "Quentin Compson as Poor Player: Verbal and Social Clichés in *The Sound and the Fury*." *Revue des Langues Vivantes* (Bruxelles), 34 (1968): 40–49.

Minter, David. *William Faulkner: His Life and Work*. Baltimore: Johns Hopkins University Press, 1980.

Morris, Wesley. *Friday's Footprint: Structuralism and the Articulated Text*. Columbus: Ohio State University Press, 1979.

Mortimer, Gail L. *Faulkner's Rhetoric of Loss*. Austin: University of Texas Press, 1983.

O'Connor, William Van. *The Tangled Fire of William Faulkner*. Minneapolis: University of Minnesota Press, 1954.

Page, Sally R. *Faulkner's Women: Characterization and Meaning*. De Land, Fla.: Everett / Edwards, 1972.

Parker, Robert Dale. *Faulkner and the Novelistic Imagination*. Urbana and Chicago: University of Illinois Press, 1985.

Pitavy, François. "Quentin Compson, ou le regard du poete." *Sud* (Marseille), n 14/15 (1975): 62–80.

Polk, Noel. "The Dungeon Was Mother Herself: William Faulkner: 1927–1931." In *New Directions in Faulkner Studies: Faulkner and Yoknapatawpha 1983*, edited by Doreen Fowler and Ann J. Abadie, 61–93. Jackson: University Press of Mississippi, 1984.

———. *An Editorial Handbook for William Faulkner's "The Sound and the Fury."* New York: Garland, 1985.

Pouillon, Jean. "Temp et Destineé chez Faulkner." In *Temp et Roman*, 238–60. Paris: Gallimard, 1946.

Reed, Joseph, Jr. *Faulkner's Narrative*. New Haven and London: Yale University Press, 1973.

Rosenberg, Bruce A. "The Oral Quality of Reverend Shegog's Sermon in William Faulkner's *The Sound and the Fury*." *Literatur in Wissenschaft und Unterricht* 2 (1969): 73–88.

Ross, Stephen M. *Fiction's Inexhaustible Voice: Speech and Writing in Faulkner*. Athens: University of Georgia Press, 1989.

———. "The Loud World of Quentin Compson." *Studies in the Novel* 7 (1975): 245–57.

Scott, Evelyn, "On William Faulkner's *The Sound and the Fury*." New York: Jonathan Cape and Harrison Smith, 1929.

Sensibar, Judith L. *The Origins of Faulkner's Art*. Austin: University of Texas Press, 1984.

Slatoff, Walter J. *Quest for Failure: A Study of William Faulkner*. Ithaca, N.Y.: Cornell University Press, 1960.

Spilka, Mark. "Quentin Compson's Universal Grief." *Contemporary Literature* 11 (Autumn 1970): 451–69.

Stonum, Gary Lee. *Faulkner's Literary Career: An Internal Literary History*. Ithaca: Cornell University Press, 1979.

Strandberg, Victor. "Faulkner's Poor Parson and the Technique of Inversion." *Sewanee Review* 73 (Spring 1965): 181–90.

Straumann, Heinrich. *Faulkner*. Frankfurt am Main, Bonn: Athenaum Verlag, 1968.

Sundquist, Eric J. *Faulkner: The House Divided*. Baltimore and London: Johns Hopkins University Press, 1983.

Swiggart, Peter. "Moral and Temporal Order in *The Sound and the Fury*." *Sewanee Review* 61 (Spring 1953): 221–37.

———. *The Art of Faulkner's Novels*. Austin: University of Texas Press, 1962.

Taylor, Walter. *Faulkner's Search for a South*. Urbana: University of Illinois Press, 1983.

Thompson, Lawrence R. "Mirror Analogues in *The Sound and the Fury*." In *English Institute Essays, 1952*, edited by Alan S. Downer, 83–106. New York: Columbia University Press, 1954.

———. *William Faulkner: An Introduction and Interpretation*. New York: Barnes and Noble, 1963.

Volpe, Edmond L. *A Reader's Guide to William Faulkner*. New York: Farrar, Straus, 1964.

Wadlington, Warwick. *Reading Faulknerian Tragedy*. Ithaca: Cornell University Press, 1987.

Waggoner, Hyatt H. *William Faulkner: From Jefferson to the World*. Lexington: University of Kentucky Press, 1959.

Wagner, Linda W., ed. *Faulkner: Four Decades of Criticism*. East Lansing: Michigan State University Press, 1973.

———. "Language and Act: Caddy Compson." *Southern Literary Journal* 14 (1982): 49–61.

Warren, Robert Penn. "William Faulkner." In *Selected Essays*, 59–79. New York: Random House, 1958.

Welty, Eudora. "In Yoknapatawpha." *Hudson Review* 1 (Winter, 1949): 596–98.

Wittenberg, Judith Bryant. *Faulkner: The Transfiguration of Biography*. Lincoln: University of Nebraska Press, 1979.

————. "William Faulkner: A Feminist Consideration." In *American Novelists Revisited: Essays in Feminist Criticism*, edited by Fritz Fleischmann. Boston: G. K. Hall, 1982. Reprinted in *Modern Critical Views: William Faulkner*, edited by Harold Bloom, 233–46. New York: Chelsea House, 1986.

Wolfe, George H., ed. *Faulkner: Fifty Years After the Marble Faun*. Tuscaloosa: University of Alabama Press, 1976.

Wyatt, David M. *Prodigal Sons: A Study in Authorship and Authority*. Balitmore: Johns Hopkins University Press, 1979.

Zender, Karl. "Faulkner and the Power of Sound." *PMLA* 99 (1984): 89–108.